THE DESIGN OF PRODUCTION SYSTEMS

Van Nostrand Reinhold Industrial Engineering and Management Sciences Series

Consulting Editor: Professor Robert N. Lehrer
School of Industrial Engineering
Georgia Institute of Technology

The Design of Production Systems, *by Salah E. Elmaghraby*
Introduction to Digital Computer Applications, *by Andrew G. Favret*
The Management of Improvement: Concepts, Organization, and Strategy, *by Robert N. Lehrer*
Project Management with CPM and PERT, *by Joseph J. Moder and Cecil R. Phillips*
Analytical Models for Managerial and Engineering Economics, *by Herbert E. Schweyer*
Hospital Industrial Engineering, *by Harold E. Smalley and John R. Freeman*

CONSULTING EDITOR'S STATEMENT

Dr. Elmaghraby's book is a welcomed addition to the Van Nostrand Reinhold Series in Industrial Engineering and Management Science and a much needed contribution to the literature of the field.

The methodology of systems engineering has matured rapidly in the past decade, and its impact upon the analysis and design of production systems has been substantial. Concepts and principles which have originated in electrical, mechanical, and the other more usual systems engineering contexts have direct applicability to the analysis and design of manufacturing, managerial, and service systems—particularly when complemented by developments associated with operations research, management sciences and industrial engineering. Dr. Elmaghraby has effected this consolidation in a very pleasing and useful manner, taking full advantage of his extensive professional experience in dealing with such problems in business and industry, and as a teacher and researcher. His approach is a convincing one, drawing upon appropriate mathematical tools to assist in analysis and design, and by presentation of realistic illustrative examples. Several of these examples are threaded throughout the book to illustrate the consequence of alternative approaches to problem formulation and solution technique. Each chapter is supplemented by suggested selected references, and problem exercises. The book has been tested, with excellent results, in both college and industrial instruction. It is a unique and useful contribution which should be enthusiastically received by the academic and industrial communities.

R. N. Lehrer
Atlanta, Georgia
March 31, 1966

THE DESIGN OF
PRODUCTION SYSTEMS

SALAH E. ELMAGHRABY
Department of Industrial Administration
Yale University
New Haven, Connecticut

VAN NOSTRAND REINHOLD COMPANY
NEW YORK CINCINNATI TORONTO LONDON MELBOURNE

Van Nostrand Reinhold Company Regional Offices:
New York   Cincinnati   Chicago   Millbrae   Dallas

Van Nostrand Reinhold Company Foreign Offices:
London   Toronto   Melbourne

Copyright © 1966 by Reinhold Publishing Corporation

Library of Congress Catalog Card Number: 66-22412

Manufactured in the United States of America

Published by Van Nostrand Reinhold Company
450 West 33rd Street, New York, N.Y. 10001

15 14 13 12 11 10 9 8 7 6 5 4 3 2

**To
My Parents**

Preface

Over the past two decades there have evolved new concepts and methodologies in the areas of operations research, industrial engineering and management science as well as in the general theories of control, systems engineering and information processing, which seem to hold the promise for a profound and far reaching revolution in the design and operation of production systems.

Briefly, modern theories of optimization of constrained and unconstrained systems (of the stationary or dynamic types), have been continuously sharpened to the point where representative models of large scale systems can be constructed and manipulated to yield meaningful results. Such theories, combined with the nascent computer technology, have already transformed the strategic and tactical concepts in the military field and, if all indications are not totally misleading, will have similar, if not larger, effect on the industrial nonmilitary fields.

This book deals with the application of some of these concepts to the analysis and synthesis, i.e., the *design*, of production systems. Our point of departure is the operational system itself: its construction, the dynamic interaction of its components, its constraints, objectives, and the various approaches that can be fruitfully utilized in the conduct of the quantitative study of its performance.

In the process of defining the determinants of design, i.e., the factors that determine the final structure of the operational system, it was sometimes necessary to develop the mathematical tool and sometimes, when the tool can be safely assumed known to the reader, it was necessary to illustrate the design concept with some operational examples.

Since one of our purposes is to stimulate the reader's imagination and help him discover the relevance of these new concepts and mathematical theories, so that he may be able to use them intelligently, we attempted to reach the results in a heuristic fashion, always appealing to the reader's intuition and common sense. This is the manner in which these ideas were developed by the pioneer researchers in the first place. And this is the only manner in which new concepts and methodologies will be generated in the future.

This may, in part, explain the organization of the book. There are seven chapters. Chapter 1 discusses, in general terms, the concepts of models, objectives, and criteria for decision. It can safely be said that progress in science is progress in modeling of physical and social phenomena. Consequently, the designer should be aware of the model he is constructing of the real-life system, of the value system he is adopting, and of the criterion (or criteria) against which he is measuring the performance of his solution.

Chapter 2 deals with the graphic representation of systems. Engineers have always used graphic techniques to represent the *structure* of their designs, and systems of concern to us here are no exception. This chapter discusses three techniques: block diagramming, signal flow graphs, and activity networks. In the final analysis, all these techniques are *network* models. But they differ among themselves, and they differ from the network models discussed in Chapters 4 and 5.

The major part of Chapter 2 is devoted to activity networks, i.e., networks of PERT-CPM variety. This reflects the increasing importance of the approach and its widespread use, which necessitate a more detailed understanding of the model's scope and limitations.

Chapter 3 discusses the concept of component interaction. Basically, there are two modes of component interaction: *stationary* and *dynamic.* These two names are chosen advisedly to denote the absence of considerations of *time* in the stationary mode and the existence of time considerations in the dynamic mode. This dichotomy seems to possess some pedagogical value, especially in the critical evaluation of models of dynamic systems.

Chapters 4 and 5 may be regarded as continuations of Chapter 1, since both chapters deal with the discussion of models by focusing attention on network models and discussing these in great detail. Chapter 4 is concerned with deterministic networks of flow, which is a general model that found application in a variety of fields and is illustrated by problems in transportation, machine scheduling, sequencing, assembly line balancing, and others. Chapter 5 deals with networks of stochastic flow, i.e., networks of queues. It is easy to see the importance of these models in many operational systems in which the demand for services, or the supply of such services, or both, is stochastic.

Chapter 6 discusses the concepts of feedback control. It is inconceivable to talk about production control systems without considering, at some point, the fundamental role that feedback plays in the design of such systems. In fact, one can safely say that a well-controlled but suboptimized system is invariably preferred to a poorly controlled but highly optimized one. Yet, except for electrical engineers, engineering disciplines remain largely in the dark as far as feedback control theory is concerned.

Finally, Chapter 7 discusses the role of computers in production systems. When one recognizes the forceful impact computers and computer technology have had, and will continue to have, on our modern society, it comes as no surprise to realize that they must have a profound effect on the design and operation of production systems. Basically, the computer enters the picture in one of three roles: (a) as a data processor, (b) as an aid in design, (c) as an integral part of the production system itself. Obviously, a data processor *is* an aid to design. What is meant here by the distinction between (a) and (b) is a distinction in the *use* of the computer. For example, in (b) one finds discussions of simulation, automated design and heuristic design, which are undoubtedly "aids" of a different caliber from those in (a).

This book is the outgrowth of lecture notes to students at the senior undergraduate level and the first two years at the graduate level, as well as to groups of practicing engineers and managers. The book is intended to serve as a textbook for intermediate and advanced courses in production systems in schools of industrial engineering and administration, as well as in the more quantitatively oriented graduate business schools.

I have not attempted to cover this material in one semester; two semesters seem to be the optimal duration for relaxed and intensive coverage. It is, however, possible to present the highlights of each chapter and cover the material in one semester.

The book is also directed to practicing engineers involved in the design of production systems: industrial engineers, project and system engineers, and to managers of such systems as well as to staff personnel assisting them in the conduct of their work.

The question of assumed background is intimately related to the level of presentation. The discussion throughout the book is mostly quantitative in nature, and the reader will find the level uneven. This is simply because where I could assume prior preparation, or at least the existence of some excellent introductory books on the required background, I felt that I could build directly on that assumed foundation. On the other hand, assuming nothing beyond sophomore-level mathematics, or the absence of lucid non-specialized introductory texts on the subject requires starting "from scratch." The reader with an introductory course in operations research in his background will find he is capable of reading the book with relative ease. The more advanced sections, as well as topics which are not necessary for following the main stream of discussion, are starred and may be omitted on first reading.

The exercises at the end of each chapter are to be considered as an integral part of the text since, in the majority of cases, they serve as extensions of the concepts in the text as well as further illustrations of these concepts.

It is my pleasure to acknowledge my indebtedness to the several individuals whose assistance rendered this book possible. I am grateful to Dr. R. N. Lehrer for his encouragement, continuous support, and for his many valuable suggestions. My thanks are also due to Professors J. J. Moder of Georgia Tech, and W. T. Morris of the Ohio State University, for their constructive criticism of various chapters of the book. I owe a debt of thanks to four of my students: Owen Black, Robert Stafford, John Terry, and Julius Liff who, at one time or another, discovered various errors or indicated possible improvements. I am particularly grateful to Julius Liff for his painstaking proof-reading of the final version of the manuscript. To the two young ladies who suffered through the torturous mathematical symbols scattered throughout the book, I wish to express my deep appreciation: Mrs. Barbara de Felice and Mrs. Anne Carpenter. The editorial staff of Reinhold was most helpful throughout. In particular, I am grateful to Miss Margaret McGarr, who did the initial copy editing, and Miss Barbara-Jo Feldman, who took over the editorial task at a critical and difficult moment, but who rendered assistance cheerfully and most expertly. To my wife, who remained a "book widow" for too long, is my sincere gratitude.

The sections dealing with graph theory and network models relied heavily on the results of our continuing research in the theory of networks as applied to management control systems. This research is partially supported by NSF Grant GP-2279.

Finally, I wish to acknowledge the kind permission of the editors of Biometrika, John Wiley and Sons, Science and Technology, and the Harvard Business Review to quote from their publications.

SALAH E. ELMAGHRABY
New Haven, Connecticut
March, 1966

Contents

CHAPTER 1 / The Study of Production Systems

§1. INTRODUCTION AND HISTORICAL BACKGROUND

What Is a Production System?

The term *production* as used here should be understood in its general sense of "increasing the utility of an object or a service." Although we automatically connect the *manufacture* of an object like a car or radio with "production," almost all activities—except perhaps acts of destruction like war and genocide—can be called "production." For example, *transportation*, which is carried out in two realms—space and time—is production. (Transportation in space is the conveyance of material from one place to another; transportation in time is *inventory*, i.e., the retention of goods or services from one period to another. Electric energy stored in a battery can be cited as an example of both types of transportation: in space, when the battery is moved, and in time, since the battery is used after being charged.) Indeed, we can group under the heading "production" such diverse activities as the dissemination of news, the staging of a play, the writing of a book, and the transmission of electricity.

A *system* is any collection of *interacting* elements that operate to achieve a common goal. The definition indicates that what may be defined as a system in one context may be only a component in another. For example, to the automotive designer the automobile is a mechanical system composed of a crankshaft, connecting rods, cylinder block, pistons, piston rings, and so forth. But to the civil engineer designing a highway system, the automobile is one component of a system which includes trucks, buses, trailers and other vehicles. By further extension, a highway system, in the eyes of a government body responsible for transportation during states of emergency, is only one component of a larger system which includes air, rail, and marine transportation.

The analysis and synthesis of systems has recently been called "systems engineering," but it is not a new activity. As with other branches of science and engineering, a few decades had to pass before the activity gained sufficient stature to demand a discipline of its own.

The distinctive feature of systems engineering is its approach. The military, for example, has ceased to develop merely individual new weapons; instead it develops weapons *systems*. It is no longer feasible to construct a weapon without considering its effect on the overall fire-power capability or without developing the logistical and tactical support it requires. The same reasoning applies to industry, where the philosophy of the systems approach is gaining prominence. It is becoming evident to industrial managers, for example, that the manufacturing interval cannot be reduced unless efforts to reduce it are coordinated, in a systemwise sense, with the activities of sales, accounting, engineering, and materials ordering.

Our interest is focused on production systems. Discussion of production systems, however, will be preceded by a brief history of the development of production and its management.

Historical Background

Man has always produced. The study of production and production systems is, in a sense, a study of human life. For thousands of years man fashioned primitive tools of bone and rock to survive his savage environment. In comparatively recent times, having domesticated animals and settled into an agrarian way of life, man produced more refined tools, clothing, and housing. He became an artisan, a skilled craftsman; eventually he settled in towns and cities. In the Middle Ages individual craftsmanship rose to a peak in the guilds. "Products" like gunpowder, the long bow, and the printing press continued to alter man's way of life.

In the 18th century there arose a phenomenon of production that was to rupture man and his past as perhaps nothing else has ever done: the industrial revolution. New sources of power like the steam engine displaced muscle power; man could not sell his muscle power cheaply enough to compete. The house loom gave way to the mechanical loom, which grew larger and more formidable every year and became concentrated in factories. Industrial complexes arose; capitalism and the mass proletariat were born. Man as a worker lost most of the individuality he had possessed.

At the beginning of the 20th century, Henry Ford introduced the *assembly line* and *mass production* emerged. It is important to grasp the full meaning of "mass production"; it is neither production for the masses, although this may be an outcome, nor production in the millions. Mass production requires that like parts of an assembly line be interchangeable and that all parts be replaceable, characteristics which permit *production and maintenance* of large quantities. The assembly line shattered any pride man had left in what he produced since it necessitated the decomposition of the total task into its minutest elements and the subsequent re-grouping of these elements according to norms of production totally unrelated to the individual.

In the early 1940's the *electronic computer* was developed and again man found himself displaced by the machine in an area of production. The computer can handle all "programmable tasks," i.e., tasks that are well defined from procedural and structural points of view, more quickly and more economically than human beings. Job displacement due to computers is in evidence today and will be more prevalent in the future. Armies of "white-collar" employees—clerks, dispatchers, record-keepers, etc.—have been superseded by the computer, and perhaps more poignantly, each year tens of thousands of such "white-collar" employees are never hired in the first place.

The Management of Production Systems

Under the elementary or individualistic forms of production, the acts of producing and the management of production were simple and were handled by one person. These conditions persisted through the early stages of the industrial revolution. The successful entrepreneur was a "self-made" man who started small and grew wealthy and powerful. Even when his enterprise expanded, he retained absolute control of the functions and processes of production, knowing, usually by first name, every person in his employ, and carrying in his head, or attempting to carry, all the personal, financial, accounting, inventory, and productivity information needed for the function of business.

Naturally, as production increased and the firm expanded, *it was not possible for one man or a handful of men to maintain a constant vigil on daily events, formulate managerial decisions, and initiate action.* In large organizations a pyramidal or, to use another word, a hierarchical structure, with responsibility and authority delegated to subordinates, began to take shape.

It is a common observation that the amount of information (in the sense of intelligence) created and transmitted among a group of N people is at least of the order of 2^N if every member of the group is to maintain complete knowledge of every other member's activities. In practice, every member need not have such complete information for the group to achieve success, nor does he even desire such knowledge. The hierarchical type of organization further limits the amount of information transmitted. According to Simon,[†] it is perhaps the most efficient type of organization in this information-limiting respect. Simon further conjectures that the

[†] Herbert A. Simon, *The New Science of Management Decision*, Harper, New York, 1960.

need to limit the quantity of information may be a primary reason for the prevalence of the hierarchical type of organization. Two factors account for this reduction in information. First, if a group of size N is divided into k subgroups of sizes $n_1, n_2, \ldots, n_k$, then even under conditions of complete knowledge within any subgroup the total amount of information transmitted is proportional to $\Sigma_{i=1}^{k} 2^{n_i}$ which is much smaller than 2^N. Second, the various levels of the heirarchical structure act as filters to the information generated at or below their levels. Only a small fraction, and oftentimes a minute fraction, of the information generated within a group is transmitted to higher levels.

The advent of the electronic computer may, once more, radically change the picture, this time in the direction of the past. That is, it is once again possible for one man, the manager, or a small group of men, to possess *all* the information necessary for production. If the "original occurrences" that constitute the minute-by-minute activities of production are captured at their source, an electronic data-transmission and computation system is capable of analyzing such information, summarizing the analysis, and presenting the results of the analysis to management with minimum error and time lag. Today, centralized decision-making is not only feasible but also practical, as evidenced by the various defense command systems, airline reservation systems, production control systems, etc., already in existence.

Thus, while the first half of the 20th century witnessed the division of the large production enterprise for purposes of management and control, it may well be that the second half of the century will witness the reversal of the process, with small semiautonomous units being made into larger units.

This centralization of information and decision-making has two profound consequences. First, it makes possible the study of a production system as a whole, which is in direct contrast to the former practice of studying fragmented, artificially compartmentalized activities. Second, it means that a decision's area of impact is greatly enlarged. Consequently, the decision should be arrived at in a *rational* fashion whenever available data permit. In these circumstances the manager's responsibility is increased, as well as his need for more refined tools for reaching such decisions. At the outset, we wish to make one point clear: the performance of the manager is measured by the *results* he achieves rather than by the type of decisions he makes or by the approaches he uses. In this respect management is no different from other fields: the elegance of the engineer's mathematical treatment is really irrelevant if the bridge collapses or the airplane falls in flames. A manager's decision to stabilize production at the expense of increasing inventory might be based on the best statistical and other data available and yet may spell disaster for a

firm should the market decline. The manager cannot hide behind justi-
fications of his decisions, though he welcomes assistance in reaching such
decisions.

Attempts have been made and will continue to be made to assist the
manager in formulating problems and reaching "correct" decisions. *Scientific management*, which dates back to 1881 and is usually credited to
F. W. Taylor and Henry R. Towne, was an early attempt to construct
such aids in the area of work measurement and performance evaluation.
Particularly after World War II, great impetus was given to the analysis
of managerial systems by advances in the fields of economics, statistical
analysis, operations research, and management science. The latter two
areas are commonly regarded as the basic sources of methodologies and
techniques for the analytical study of production systems.

It is the purpose of this book to introduce such concepts, and to provide
the practitioner with the framework of analysis and synthesis and the
mathematical structures that may be applied in each situation. We propose to accomplish this objective by first discussing the general principles
involved and then illustrating each principle with different production
problems and the approaches that have been proposed for their solution.

Our discussion springs from the vantage point of the operational system
itself: its characteristics, variables, constraints, objective, etc. But it is
rather difficult, beside being ill-advised to separate the qualitative statement of the problem from the quantitative methods of its solution. To be
sure, insight into the problem is limited by the analyst's knowledge of the
available quantitative approaches of study. And conversely, any deep
understanding of the power of a mathematical theory can be gained only
through exposure to problems to which the theory is applicable.

In the next section, §2, we briefly outline the framework of the analytical
study of production systems. This is followed, in §3, with a discussion of
the concept of models and modeling techniques. Section 4 presents an
important, and often overlooked, component of the model of any system,
namely, the criterion for decision. In §5 we discuss the levels of decision
in operational systems; and finally, in §6, we contrast the requirements on
the performance of a component of a system with the requirements on the
performance of the system as a whole.

The fact of the matter is that the frontiers of the area which Simon
called "programmed decisions,"[†] i.e., decisions which are subject to logical and quantitative analysis, are expanding due to the application of
searching analysis to operational problems which remained hitherto only
qualitatively studied. The foundation of such analysis is mathematical in
nature.

[†]Op. cit. pp. 14–20.

§2. STEPS OF THE ANALYTICAL STUDY OF PRODUCTION SYSTEMS

We can summarize the steps of the analytical study of production systems as follows:

2.1 Initiation of System Studies

This phase concerns itself with describing in a general way the problems to be faced and the barriers to overcoming those problems. In this phase, ideas are generally nebulous and expression is vague. The statement of a problem may take the following form: in order to strengthen defenses against germ warfare, can we develop a system that protects against carriers on land, sea, or air? Or: it is obvious that our managers are not usually fed correct information, and if they are, the information often comes too late for effective action. Can something be done to keep our managers "ahead of the game"?

2.2 Feasibility Studies

A feasibility study is undertaken to determine the *technical* and *economic* feasibility of a proposed change. Data from the study determine whether a full scale systems study is to be undertaken or, more often, to what degree it is to be undertaken. A feasibility study has the following features: (1) It is normally of short duration. It is at least an order of magnitude shorter than the total system study. (2) It is characterized by its low cost since it represents, in effect, the amount of money management is willing to spend even if nothing comes of it. (3) It is undertaken when there is a question of either forging ahead or discontinuing an idea. Naturally, if the decision to carry out the full scale study is already made for political, prestige, or other reasons, feasibility studies are not pertinent.

A system's *worth* and its disadvantages are revealed by a feasibility study. Sometimes, the worth of an activity, or its utility, is easily quantifiable. It may be measured in savings in dollars, personnel, equipment, material, time, space, etc.. It may also be measured in terms of an increased ability for taking advantage of special opportunities and markets. In areas where human values are of critical importance, however, e.g., in defense, customer service, supervisory functioning, etc., the benefits of a system are not easily measured.

2.3 The Systems Study

This is the active undertaking of the development of a system when such development has been deemed feasible and necessary. The following steps are usually included:

Problem Definition

This is the determination of the nature of the factors giving rise to the problem and of the nature of the problem itself. Of course, this step has been partially covered in phases 2.1 and 2.2 above. None of the steps outlined here are "one shot" activities; rather, they occur in a continuum and are constantly being improved and sharpened in focus.

Model Construction

Because certain aspects of the system may lend themselves to formal treatment, a model of such components and of their modes of interaction with other components should be constructed. A discussion of modeling is presented below in §3. Inherent in any model is the choice of a criterion of performance, a choice which is partially determined by the manner in which the problem has been defined.

Derivation of Solution

The model is used in a continuing process of synthesis followed by analysis and testing, which lead to improved synthesis and further analysis. A solution is reached when it is felt that the answer obtained at a certain stage is the best relative to the established criteria.

Validation

In the context of hardware systems, e.g., radar detection, microwave transmission, etc., the question of validation is usually interpreted in a very specific manner. In such systems, solutions are usually obtained for components and for more or less isolated problems. The process of validation is then understood to be the process of verification of the behavior of the various components as an integrated system. It is usually carried out in steps: components are tested together in subsystems which are, in turn, combined in higher-order subsystems until the whole system is tested as a working unit.

On the other hand, in the context of conceptual systems such as we will be dealing with throughout this book, the question of validation takes on a different light. First, there is the problem of validating the model itself. By this we mean proving that the model is a true representation of the system under study. In other words, this is the problem of satisfying oneself that the model *behaves* in the same fashion as the real-life system. Second, there is the problem of validating the *solution*, i.e., demonstrating that the solution derived from the model satisfies the stated criterion (or criteria).

The problem of validation, with the two aspects stated above, is certainly not unique to the study of what we termed "conceptual systems," but is encountered in many phases of science and engineering. For instance, consider a small scale model of an airplane wing which is constructed for testing in a wind tinnuel. It is necessary to ascertain first that the model possesses certain characteristics, e.g., surface friction, identical to the airplane wing. And, second, it is necessary to verify any "solution" arrived at, e.g., ratio of length to width for minimum drag, under actual operating conditions.

Model validation takes different forms depending on the nature of the model itself. Invariably it involves subjecting the model to certain input conditions and comparing its output with the output of the actual system (or some predetermined output if the system does not exist). The two outputs must be comparable as the minimum prerequisite for the model to be considered a valid representation of the system.

The environment in which a model is constructed also relates directly to its validity. For example, a model which is valid for the researcher need not be valid for the manager, and vice versa.

The process of validation of the solution derived from the model requires great care since it can be misleading if not correctly done. Here, one cannot escape the onus of methodology. In general, there are three possible approaches.

Comparison with Past Performance. If the solution purports to optimize the performance of the system relative to a given criterion, it is always possible to compare past performance of the system to the performance that would have been obtained if the new solution were applied. In fact, it is possible to compare the performance under the new solution with the performance under any other alternative proposal. The superiority of the new solution over other alternatives can be considered as a verification of its validity.

There are three drawbacks to this approach. First, the system under study may not be in existence, and hence have no past. But even if the system were in existence, the second objection might shatter the halo of confidence generated by the results of validation. For, in all probability, the model has been constructed after careful study of past performance of the system and its environment. It is therefore to be expected that the new solution based on the model would be most successful when applied to this same past history. In fact, it would be strange indeed if such superiority were not easily demonstrable.

In many instances stochastic, i.e., probabilistic, variation is an important aspect of the inputs (or, in general, the exogenous environment) to the system. For example, the demand for a product, the pattern of arrival of airplanes at an airport, and the atmospheric conditions affecting the flight of a missile, etc., are all exogenous factors affecting their respective systems in a stochastic fashion. But when we evaluate the performance of the system over a past period, all the inputs are known with certainty and a very important element of the decision process has thus been eliminated. This is true unless, of course, it is possible to recreate the past with all its stochastic uncertainty.

In any case, whether or not the past is recreated, comparison and subsequent decision would be based on *one set of input data*, which is highly objectionable. This is the third important criticism levied against this method of validation. Managers of many production systems hesitate to make major policy decisions on the basis of such meager proof.

In order to counteract these weighty arguments the next approach has been suggested.

Comparison with Future Performance. Once a solution is obtained or different solutions are derived from different models, the performance of the system may be compared under different alternatives *from then on*. It is immaterial which solution is actually put into practice and which alternatives are compared to it "on paper." The important thing is that all alternatives are subjected to identical exogenous inputs.

This approach seems to answer the objections raised against the previous approach, except for the following three considerations. First, if the system does not exist the method is infeasible. Second, it may take too long and cost too much to arrive at a conclusion. And third, the comparison is again based on *one* set of input data and no conclusions can be drawn concerning other sets of input data.

Comparison Through Simulation. The third approach to validation is through Monte Carlo simulation which may or may not require the use of computers. This approach can satisfy all previously raised objections, especially since repeated Monte Carlo experimentation satisfies the requirement of testing under different and randomly chosen exogenous inputs.

We devote a good part of Chapter 7 to the discussion of the technique of simulation and Monte Carlo methods. Suffice it to say that while this approach certainly has the potential of answering all questions, it generates some problems of its own which may seriously detract from its contribution.

2.4 Implementation

This is the putting into practice the results of the systems study. Implementation is usually divided into two phases.

Preliminary

This activity, depending on the system under study, can have different forms—a pilot plant, a prototype product, a parallel run, a partial implementation on existing production facilities, etc.

Full Scale

This is complete construction and conversion to the new system.

We emphasize the fact that none of the above steps 2.1 through 2.4 are "concrete steps" with defined beginnings and endings. Rather, almost every activity is present throughout the study from inception of the idea to the "ribbon cutting" process.

2.5 Maintenance Engineering

This takes into account the fact that a system is never "complete"; rather, a system is a living animal which undergoes constant change throughout its life. Hence, full scale implementation does not imply termination of all activities. It merely signals the cessation of all *major design activities* until a new systems study is initiated to replace or supersede the old.

This necessitates the continuing maintenance of the system in at least two respects: (1) introducing improvements and minor changes, and (2) continuing the vigil on the validity of the system's performance. Should the change in the environment be radical enough to invalidate the solutions previously arrived at, the time is then ripe for initiating a new systems study.

It is our contention that failure of the majority of systems can be traced directly to delinquency in the area of maintenance engineering. We cannot overemphasize the importance of this function for the *continuing* success of the solutions arrived at.

§3. MODELS OF SYSTEMS

3.1 General Discussion

In §2 we mentioned that, subsequent to the definition of the problem, a model is constructed for the system as a whole and for individual components of the system. The concept of modeling will now be discussed in greater detail.

First, we wish to emphasize that modeling is not a new activity. From the dawn of history man has used models to *represent objects or ideas*. From the simplest act of communication, perhaps the charting of animal images in the sand, to the most complex, e.g., the building of massive tombs and monuments that embody the ethos of an entire culture, man has used models to express his meaning. Science, in general, is based on the notion of modeling, and the progress of science is the progress of modeling of natural phenomena and ideas.

A model is constructed so that it can be manipulated to reveal the inner workings of the system or phenomena it represents. Successful models aid in solving problems because they equip us to evaluate or predict the consequences and utility of different policy decisions. A secondary aspect of model construction is that it provides a concrete description of what we have in mind.

Model construction is, in a sense, an art. First, it requires a rigorous adherence to purpose; the objective of a study must constantly be kept in mind so that a model appropriate to it will result. For example, if the objective is to show what a new car design looks like, it is enough to have a wooden scale model of the real car. But if the objective is to study the stability of a new car design on rough terrain, a wooden scale model of the car is useless. In such a case, an analog computer might be the best tool for constructing the model. Secondly, model construction is an artful balancing of opposites. On the one hand, the model must be simple enough to manipulate, which means that it must necessarily be an *abstraction* from reality; on the other, the model must be complex enough to mirror the system it actually represents. Achieving this balance requires subtlety and skill.

3.2 Classification of Models

Various classifications of models have been offered in the literature. We prefer the classification given by Churchman, Ackoff and Arnoff,[†] which we summarize below.

There are three "pure" types of models: iconic, analog and symbolic. An *iconic* model "looks like" the object it represents, such as a model of an airplane (scaled down) or a model of the atom (scaled up). An *analog* model substitutes one property for another; the problem is solved in the substituted state and finally the solution is translated back to the original dimensions or properties. An excellent illustration of analog model is the slide rule in which the physical property measured is represented by lengths along a logarithmic scale. An electronic analog computer may represent the compression force in a helical spring by the increase in voltage potential in a network. *Symbolic* or *mathematical* models are by far the most important type of models. This is only natural since they are the most abstract and hence the most general. In these models a symbol, such as y or α, represents a quantity such as distance or marginal gain.

Models of systems are usually a combination of two or more of the three "pure" types discussed above, depending on the complexity of the system. Any system or subsystem may be represented by several models

[†] C. West Churchman, R. L. Ackoff and E. L. Arnoff, *Introduction to Operations Research*, Wiley, New York, 1957, Chapter 7.

which range in complexity and sophistication from the elementary to the complex and from the iconic to the symbolic. In fact, it is a rare event indeed to have one model constructed for a system or a component. Usually, simple models lead to complex models, in the same way that simple experiments shed light on the construction of more complex experiments.

The concept of modeling, which is so evident and self-explanatory in the case of hardware systems, seems to be difficult to grasp in the case of conceptual systems. This need not be the case since the concept is really based on two elementary notions which were discussed above and which we summarize as follows:

1. A model is a representation, which can be made simple or complex depending on the factors which the analyst wishes to consider and on the assumptions he makes concerning these factors.
2. A model is manipulated to arrive at a solution.

There is really no substitute for learning by doing. Consequently, suppose we consider a specific problem and its environment—say the problem of *inventory control*—and proceed to construct mathematical models. First, we shall start with an extremely simple model by disregarding many of the characteristics of real-life situations. Then gradually we enrich our arguments, and, in the process, complicate the models, by taking into account more and more of the real-life factors.

In this manner the reader can perceive the intimate relationship between the assumptions made, the model constructed, and the solution arrived at. At the termination of this series of models the reader is urged to project the analysis into areas of even more general consideration. Inventory management is a very fertile field of study, and several excellent books available on the subject are listed at the end of the chapter. In any of these books may be found different, and perhaps more elaborate, models.

3.3 Examples of Models

One of the most fertile fields of study in production systems is the theory of inventory management. In the context of inventory systems we give three illustrations of models which range from the very simple to the complex.

Deterministic Constant Rate of Demand

The most elementary model of inventory systems, and incidentally one that has a long and honorable history dating back to 1915, assumes that reality can be approximated by:

1. Continuous known rate of demand, R units/unit time.
2. Infinite planning horizon, i.e., an infinite duration of the process.

3. Satisfaction of all demand—i.e., no stockouts or late deliveries are permitted. This restriction can also be interpreted to mean the assumption of infinite cost for late deliveries.
4. Immediate delivery of replenishments, i.e., no lead time.
5. One item in inventory or, alternatively, no interaction among the items if there are more than one.
6. Two costs are involved in the management of stock: (1) the cost of investment, assumed proportional to the *average* quantity in stock, and (2) the cost of ordering and receiving, which is incurred each time an order or a receival occurs and is independent of the quantity ordered or received.
7. Cost of the item, a constant independent of time and quantity ordered.

Using these assumptions and simplifications, we can determine the most economic ordering quantity, say Q^*, and the timing of its receipt to minimize the total cost of inventory management.

Let A be the cost of placing and receiving a quantity Q; c the unit cost of commodity; R the total requirement per unit time; and h the cost of investment per unit per unit time (the unit time may be one year, for example). The total average cost of inventory management is given by

$$TAC = R A/Q + h Q/2. \qquad (1\text{-}1)$$

The first term is the cost of ordering (per unit time) and the second term is the cost of *average investment*, when a quantity Q is ordered at regular intervals of duration t_0. The variation in inventory level is represented in Fig. 1-1a while the TAC is represented in 1-1b. Obviously, $t_0 = Q/R$. The optimal ordering quantity Q^* is obtained by differentiating Eq. (1-1) with respect to Q, the only variable in the equation, and equating to zero. We obtain

$$Q^* = \sqrt{2RA/h} \quad \text{and} \quad TAC = \sqrt{2RAh}. \qquad (1\text{-}2)$$

The mathematical model of the problem is composed of Fig. 1-1a and Eq. (1-1). Manipulation of the model by differentiation (or graphical

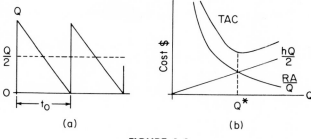

(a)   (b)

FIGURE 1-1

plotting in Fig. 1-1b) yields the optimal solution Q^*. Formally speaking, the problem has been "solved."

From a practical point of view, however, we must recognize that this model is a drastic simplification of real-life situations. It is not difficult to encounter situations in which one (or several) of the above assumptions is simply not true and any conclusions based on it entail gross errors. In the model of deterministic demand with back orders and the model of deterministic variable demand discussed below we relax some of the assumptions that were necessary for the development above. However, we wish to remark that we have gained great insight into inventory costs even from this elementary model. Indeed, from Eq. (1-2) it is obvious that the cost of inventory management is proportional to the *square root of demand*, a fact usually not fully understood by managers of inventory stocks.

Deterministic Demand with Back Orders

Perhaps the simplest extension of the deterministic constant rate demand model is in systems in which assumption (3) of the model is not true, i.e., we no longer insist on satisfying all customer demand on time, but accept *back orders* at a finite penalty π per unit per unit time. The fluctuation of the level of stock when the quantity ordered is Q is shown in Fig. 1-2.

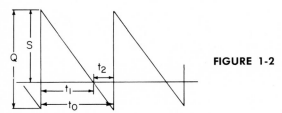

FIGURE 1-2

Our objective is still to determine the optimal ordering quantity Q^* that should be received at regular intervals of duration t_0. But now, receival of a quantity Q raises the level of inventory to S: the difference $(Q - S)$ is assumed to be instantaneously consumed to satisfy back orders.

It is obvious that $t_1 = S/R$ and $t_2 = (Q - S)/R$, while t_0 still equals Q/R. Now, the total average cost per unit time is

$$TAC = \frac{R}{Q}\left\{A + h\left(\frac{S}{2}\right)t_1 + \pi\left(\frac{Q - S}{2}\right)t_2\right\}$$

$$= \frac{RA}{Q} + \frac{hS^2}{2Q} + \frac{\pi(Q - S)^2}{2Q}. \tag{1-3}$$

To determine the optimal Q and S, we take partial derivatives of Eq. (1-3) and equate to zero,

$$\frac{\partial(TAC)}{\partial Q} = \frac{-RA}{Q^2} - \frac{hS^2}{2Q^2} + \frac{\pi(Q-S)}{Q} - \frac{\pi(Q-S)^2}{2Q^2} = 0,$$

and

$$\frac{\partial(TAC)}{\partial S} = \frac{hS}{Q} - \frac{\pi(Q-S)}{Q} = 0,$$

yielding

$$Q^* = \sqrt{\frac{2RA}{h}} \sqrt{\frac{h+\pi}{\pi}}, \tag{1-4}$$

$$S^* = \sqrt{\frac{2RA}{h}} \sqrt{\frac{\pi}{h+\pi}}, \tag{1-5}$$

and

$$TAC^* = \sqrt{2RAh} \sqrt{\frac{\pi}{h+\pi}}. \tag{1-6}$$

Two brief remarks should be made. First, the removal of a simplifying assumption has led to a more complicated model. Second, the solution of the deterministic constant rate demand model discussed above can be derived from this deterministic demand with back orders model by allowing π to approach infinity.

Deterministic Variable Demand

A more realistic view of some real-life inventory situations involves the rejection of two assumptions of the deterministic constant rate demand model: the assumption of equality of demand from period to period (assumption (1)), and the assumption of planning for an infinite horizon (assumption (2)). We still assume that the demand is *deterministic* but we allow it to vary from period to period, and we limit our planning to a finite horizon of N periods.

This seemingly innocent generalization of the simple deterministic constant rate demand model in fact requires a completely fresh look at the problem and leads, as will be seen presently, to a *dynamic programming* model of the system.

Let I_t be the inventory at the *end* of period t, with I_0 the initial inventory; h_t the cost of investment per unit of inventory *carried forward to period* $t+1$, i.e., we are basing the cost of inventory on the end-of-period inventory; A_t the cost of ordering in period t; q_t the amount ordered (still assuming instantaneous delivery); and r_t the known requirement for

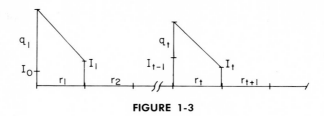

FIGURE 1-3

period t (see Fig. 1-3). Now, it is obvious that the end-of-period inventory is given by

$$I_t = I_{t-1} + q_t - r_t. \tag{1-7}$$

It is equally obvious that the only decision to be made at the beginning of each interval is the determination of the magnitude of q_t. Clearly, q_t is constrained between 0 and $\Sigma_{j=t}^{N} r_j$, i.e., $0 \le q_t \le \Sigma_{j=t}^{N} r_j$.

The total cost of inventory management is then given by

$$TC = \sum_{t=1}^{N} \{\delta(q_t) \cdot A_t + h_t I_t\} + h_0 I_0 \tag{1-8}$$

where $\delta(q_t) = 0$ if $q_t = 0$ and $= 1$ if $q_t > 0$, and the starting inventory is I_0. Define

$$f_1(I_0) = \min_{\substack{\{q_t\}\ge 0 \\ I_{t-1}+q_t \ge r_t}} \sum_{t=1}^{N} \{\delta(q_t) \cdot A_t + h_t I_t\}. \tag{1-9}$$

The second constraint under the minimum operator is to satisfy the no-stockout condition. Now consider the Nth period with any given starting inventory I_{N-1}; we have

$$f_N(I_{N-1}) = \min_{\substack{q_N \ge 0 \\ I_{N-1}+q_N = r_N}} \{\delta(q_N)A_N\}. \tag{1-10a}$$

For any given I_{N-1} the optimal policy, q_N^*, can be very easily determined. In fact, it is not difficult to see that if $0 < I_{N-1} < r_N$ then $q_N^* = r_N - I_{N-1}$ and $f_N = A_N$ while if $I_{N-1} \ge r_N$ then $q_N^* = 0$ and $f_N = 0$. This is the "solution of the one-stage problem." Notice its conditional dependence on I_{N-1}. In the penultimate period,

$$f_{N-1}(I_{N-2}) = \min_{\substack{q_{N-1},q_N \ge 0 \\ I_{N-2}+q_{N-1}\ge r_{N-1} \\ I_{N-1}+q_N=r_N}} \{\delta(q_{N-1})A_{N-1} + \delta(q_N)A_N + h_{N-1}I_{N-1}\} \tag{1-10b}$$

which, remembering Eq. (1-7), can be reduced to

$$f_{N-1}(I_{N-2}) = \min_{\substack{q_{N-1} \geq 0 \\ I_{N-2}+q_{N-1} \geq r_{N-1}}} \{\delta(q_{N-1})A_{N-1} + h_{N-1}(I_{N-2} + q_{N-1}$$

$$- r_{N-1}) + f_N(I_{N-2} + q_{N-1} - r_{N-1})\} \tag{1-10c}$$

Notice first how the solution of the two-stage problem depends on the solution of the one-stage problem, $f_N(I_{N-1})$. This is characteristic of the dynamic programming approach. Second, the evaluation of the optimal two-stage solution, (q^*_{N-1}, q^*_N), is straightforward, though more complicated. In particular, it is easy to verify that under the conditions of the problem the optimal ordering policy is given by

$$f_{N-1}(I_{N-2}) = \begin{cases} h_{N-1}(I_{N-2} - r_{N-1}) & \text{if } I_{N-2} \geq r_{N-1} + r_N; \\ h_{N-1}(I_{N-2} - r_{N-1}) + A_N & \text{if } r_{N-1} \leq I_{N-2} < r_{N-1} + r_N; \\ \min \left\{ \begin{array}{c} A_{N-1} + h_{N-1}r_N \\ A_{N-1} + A_N \end{array} \right\} & \text{if } I_{N-2} < r_{N-1} \end{cases}$$

and

$$q^*_{N-1} = q^*_N = 0 \quad \text{if } I_{N-2} \geq r_{N-1} + r_N;$$

$$\left\{ \begin{array}{l} q^*_{N-1} = 0; \\ q^*_N = r_N - (I_{N-2} - r_{N-1}) \end{array} \right\} \quad \text{if } r_{N-1} \leq I_{N-2} < r_{N-1} + r_N$$

$$\left\{ \begin{array}{l} q^*_{N-1} = r_{N-1} + r_N - I_{N-2}; q^*_N = 0 \\ q^*_{N-1} = r_{N-1} - I_{N-2}; q^*_N = r_N \end{array} \right\} \quad \text{if } I_{N-2} < r_{N-1}$$

Again, notice the conditional nature (on I_{N-2}) of the two-stage solution. Naturally, while the calculations remain straightforward, from now on they do get involved as we move backwards to periods $N - 2, N - 3, \ldots,$ 2,1.

In general, we have the *functional equation*

$$f_t(I_{t-1}) = \min_{\substack{q_t \geq 0 \\ I_{t-1}+q_t \geq r_t}} \{\delta(q_t)A_t + h_t(I_{t-1} + q_t - r_t)$$

$$+ f_{t+1}(I_{t-1} + q_t - r_t)\} \tag{1-10d}$$

Consequently, it is possible to compute f_t starting at $t = N$ as a function of I_{t-1} ultimately deriving $f_1(I_0)$ and thereby obtaining an optimal solution.

The dynamic programming formulation of Eq. (1-10) is rather general and does not take cognizance of the special structure of the problem under our assumed conditions. Capitalizing on this special structure results in an extremely efficient computational scheme. We state without proof, but with a brief explanation, the five theorems that lead to such an efficient computational algorithm.   The reader is urged to refer to the original paper by Wagner and Whitin[†] for the proofs.

Theorem 1: There exists an optimal program such that
$I_{t-1}q_t = 0$ for all t.

Since both I_{t-1} and q_t must be ≥ 0, the theorem implies that for an optimal program *either or both* must be equal to zero. In other words: if the inventory entering a period is > 0, then nothing should be ordered ($q_t = 0$), and conversely, if something is ordered ($q_t > 0$), then the inventory at the beginning of the period must $= 0$. It is also possible that both I_{t-1} and $q_t = 0$, e.g., when $r_t = 0$.

Theorem 2: There exists an optimal program such that for all t, either $q_t = 0$ or $q_t = \Sigma_{j=t}^{k} r_j$ for some k, $t \leq k \leq N$.

In other words, the amount ordered, q_t, is either 0 or exactly equal to the sum of demand in one or more periods—it cannot include a fraction of the demand in any period.

Theorem 3: There exists an optimal program such that if r_{t_2} is satisfied by some q_{t_1}, $t_1 < t_2$, then all demands r_j, $j = t_1 + 1, \ldots, t_2 - 1$, are also satisfied by q_{t_1}.

This theorem states that if, for example, we order a quantity q_3 in the third period to satisfy the demand in the eighth period, then q_3 must also satisfy all the intermediate demands: r_4, r_5, r_6, and r_7. It is not possible for an optimal solution to have it otherwise, viz., it is not possible that the optimal solution will dictate that q_3 contains r_8 but that the demand in the fifth period, say, is satisfied by a separate receival in the fifth or some prior period.

Theorem 4: Given that in the optimal solution for the N-period horizon $I_t = 0$ for period t, it is optimal to consider periods 1 through t by themselves.

Translated, this theorem means that if the *optimum* for the N-period horizon turned out to make the starting inventory in period $t + 1$ equal to 0, then we could have considered periods 1 to t by themselves and calculated *their* optimum, and periods $t + 1$ to N by themselves and calculated their optimum. The important fact is that the optimum for the whole N-period horizon would be the sum of the two subhorizon optima. Thus, we do not sacrifice any optimality by dividing the planning horizon,

[†]H. M. Wagner and T. M. Whitin, "Dynamic Version of the Economic Lot Size Model," *Management Science*, Vol. 5, No. 1, October 1958, pp. 89–96.

but we gain a lot in speed of computation since this latter varies with the *square* of the number of periods involved, as will be shown below.

> *Theorem 5: The Planning Horizon Theorem.* If in the forward algorithm the minimum cost at period t_2 occurs for $q_{t_1} > 0$, $t_1 \leq t_2$, then in periods $t > t_2$ it is sufficient to consider only periods j so that $t_1 \leq j \leq t$. In particular, if $t_1 = t_2$, then it is sufficient to consider programs so that $q_{t_2} > 0$.

The interpretation of this theorem and its implications to the algorithm for calculating the optimal policy are fundamental and deserve close attention.

We begin by explaining the terms "forward algorithm" mentioned in the theorem. It is well known in the theory of dynamic programming that, in deterministic systems, an optimal policy can be determined by either one of two approaches. The first, called the backward algorithm, evaluates the optimum of the *last stage*, stage N, as a function of the state of the system at the beginning of stage N. Then the algorithm moves backwards to the penultimate stage, stage $N - 1$, and evaluates the optimal policy of the *last two stages* as a function of the state of the system at the beginning of the $(N - 1)$st stage. The algorithm continues its backwards movement until stage 1 is reached. This is essentially what Eqs. (1-10a) to (1-10c) purport to do.

The second approach, called the forward algorithm, starts with evaluating the optimal policy of arriving at each possible state at the end of the *first* stage, stage 1. This set of optimal policies is used by moving forwards in a stepwise fashion to determine the optimal policy to arrive at each state of the second, third, etc., stages until the final stage, stage N, is reached.

The question as to which algorithm to use, the forward or the backward, is difficult to answer in general. Each problem must be considered in the light of computational efficiency, which varies from problem to problem. In the present dynamic programming formulation it turns out that the forward algorithm is better.

Now, the theorem can be interpreted relative to Fig. 1-4. It states that if at period t_2 the optimum (over the subhorizon 1 to t_2) occurs with

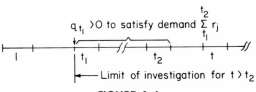

FIGURE 1-4

$q_{t_1} > 0$, $t_1 \leq t_2$, then in periods $t > t_2$ it is sufficient in the evaluation of the optimum for the subhorizon 1 to t to consider alternative policies only in the periods j, $t_1 \leq j \leq t$.

We illustrate the forward algorithm for the case $h_t = h$, a constant independent of time. We assume $I_0 = 0$; (otherwise we must reduce the demand in successive periods until all initial inventory is exhausted). Clearly, considering the first period by itself, if $r_1 > 0$ we must place an order for *at least* r_1. Let $C^*(t)$ denote the *minimal cost* of inventory management for the subhorizon of periods 1 to t. Then obviously

$$C^*(1) = A_1$$

i.e., for a one-period subhorizon with requirement r_1, the optimal, i.e., minimum cost, policy is the only policy possible, namely to order $q_1^* = r_1$. No inventory will be on hand at the end of the period and the only cost involved is the cost of ordering and receiving, A_1.

Consider next the planning subhorizon consisting of the first two periods. There are exactly *two* possible ways of satisfying the demand: either order in the second period $q_2 = r_2$ and use the optimal policy for the first period subhorizon already determined above, or order in the first period $q_1 = r_1 + r_2$ and carry inventory in the second period. The two alternative policies are represented in Fig. 1-5.

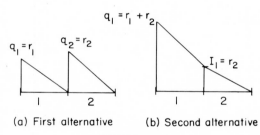

(a) First alternative   (b) Second alternative

FIGURE 1-5

Let $B_i(2)$ denote the value of the cost function for the ith alternative policy in the second period. Clearly,

$$B_1(2) = A_1 + A_2, \qquad B_2(2) = A_1 + hr_2$$

and

$$C^*(2) = \min [B_1(2); B_2(2)].$$

In general, it is easy to see that in the jth period there are exactly j alternative policies with respective costs

$$B_1(j) = A_j + C^*(j - 1)$$
$$B_2(j) = A_{j-1} + hr_j + C^*(j - 2), \text{ etc.,}$$

and finally
$$B_j(j) = A_1 + h(r_2 + 2r_3 + 3r_4 + \cdots + (j - 1)r_j).$$
Thus we have
$$C^*(j) = \min_i [B_i(j)] \qquad\qquad (1\text{-}11)$$
The solution of the optimal ordering and storage pattern is given by
$$C^*(N) = \min_i [B_i(N)] \qquad\qquad (1\text{-}12)$$
Theorem 5 is invoked whenever applicable to reduce the number of alternative policies investigated at each step of the iterations.

Numerical Example.   Suppose that it is desired to evaluate the optimal ordering policy for an item with the following parameters: $h = \$0.0005$ per month per unit and $A_1 = A_2 = A_3 = \$15$, $A_4 = \cdots = A_7 = \$10$, and the demand in units over a seven month planning horizon is $r_t = \{3{,}000;\ 10{,}000;\ 5{,}000;\ 2{,}000;\ 5{,}000;\ 3{,}000;\ 4{,}000\}$.

The steps of iteration proceed as follows:

Stage 1:

$$\underline{C^*(1) = A_1 = 15} \qquad\qquad\qquad\qquad q_1^* = 3$$

Stage 2:

$$B_1(2) = A_2 + C^*(1) = 30$$
$$B_2(2) = A_1 + hr_2 = 15 + 0.0005 \times 10{,}000 = 20$$
$$\therefore \underline{C^*(2) = 20} \qquad\qquad\qquad\qquad q_1^* = 13$$

Stage 3:

$$B_1(3) = 15 + C^*(2) = 35$$
$$B_2(3) = A_2 + hr_3 + C^*(1) = 15 + 0.0005 \times 5{,}000 + 15 = 32.50$$
$$B_3(3) = A_1 + h(r_2 + 2r_3) = 15 + 0.0005(10{,}000 + 10{,}000) = 25$$
$$\therefore \underline{C^*(3) = 25} \qquad\qquad\qquad\qquad q_1^* = 18$$

Stage 4:

$$B_1(4) = A_4 + C^*(3) = 35$$
$$B_2(4) = A_3 + hr_4 + C^*(2) = 36$$
$$B_3(4) = A_2 + h(r_3 + 2r_4) + C^*(1) = 34.50$$
$$B_4(4) = A_1 + h(r_2 + 2r_3 + 3r_4) = 28$$
$$\therefore \underline{C^*(4) = 28} \qquad\qquad\qquad\qquad q_1^* = 20$$

Stage 5:

$$B_1(5) = A_5 + C^*(4) = 38$$
$$B_2(5) = A_4 + hr_5 + C^*(3) = 37.50$$
$$B_3(5) = A_3 + h(r_4 + 2r_5) + C^*(2) = 41.00$$
$$B_4(5) = A_2 + h(r_3 + 2r_4 + 3r_5) + C^*(1) = 42.00$$
$$B_5(5) = A_1 + h(r_2 + 2r_3 + 3r_4 + 4r_5) = 38$$
$$\therefore \underline{C^*(5) = \$37.50}$$

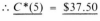

Stage 6:

$$B_1(6) = A_6 + C^*(5) = 47.50$$
$$B_2(6) = A_5 + hr_6 + C^*(4) = 39.50$$
$$B_3(6) = A_4 + h(r_5 + 2r_6) + C^*(3) = 40.5$$
$$\therefore \underline{C^*(6) = \$39.50}$$

Stage 7:

$$B_1(7) = A_7 + C^*(6) = 49.50$$
$$B_2(7) = A_6 + hr_7 + C^*(5) = 49.50$$
$$B_3(7) = A_5 + h(r_6 + 2r_7) + C^*(4) = 43.50$$

$\therefore \underline{C^*(7) = \$43.50}$, which is the *minimum cost*, and the optimal ordering policy is given by:

$$q_1^* = r_1 + r_2 + r_3 + r_4 = 20{,}000 \text{ units}$$
$$q_5^* = r_5 + r_6 + r_7 = 12{,}000 \text{ units.}$$

The fluctuation in inventory levels is depicted in Fig. 1-6.

Notice that we have invoked Theorem 5 (the Planning Horizon theorem) in the calculations at Stage 6. This was possible because the optimal pattern of the five-period subhorizon yielded an order q_4^* to be

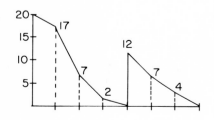

FIGURE 1-6 Inventory Fluctuation for Optimal Policy

received at the beginning of period 4. Consequently, in calculating the optimal ordering pattern in the six-period planning subhorizon we *need not evaluate alternatives earlier than the 4th period.* This reduces the number of alternatives at Stage 6 to three instead of six, and of course reduces the number of calculations in all subsequent stages (of which we had only one, Stage 7).

Also, the optimal pattern of ordering for the seven-period planning horizon divides the total horizon into two subhorizons of unequal lengths. The first subhorizon comprises periods 1 through 4, and the second subhorizon comprises periods 5 through 7. The terminal inventory at the end of each subhorizon is, naturally, zero. According to Theorem 4, we would obtain the same optimal cost if we treated each subhorizon individually. We emphasize that this significant characteristic is the property of the manner in which the *optimal* solution for the *total horizon* divided the horizon, and not of any intermediate stage.

Finally, we briefly make the following two remarks. First, while the model of deterministic demand with back orders represented a mild complication of the basic deterministic constant rate of demand model, the elimination of the assumption concerning equal demand from period to period necessitated a completely different formulation and a much more complex model. Second, the dynamic programming algorithm is incomparably better than brute force enumeration. In a planning horizon of N periods, enumeration requires investigating 2^{N-1} alternative policies while dynamic programming requires a *maximum* of $N(N + 1)/2$ calculations (if in no period can we invoke Theorem 5).

Other Inventory Models

Undoubtedly other inventory models can be constructed which assume, or do not assume, any of the seven basic assumptions listed under the deterministic constant rate of demand model. The models are different, and their degree of complexity is dependent on the simplifying assumptions made in each case.

Some of these models are left as exericses to the reader at the end of this chapter; see problems (6) to (11). Other models are treated in other parts of the book because they serve also as illustrations for other concepts besides the concept of modeling. For example, in Chapter 3, §3, we discuss an inventory model in which we take into account the *interaction* among the items in inventory (see assumption (e) of the deterministic constant rate of demand model above). In the problems of the same chapter we discuss a central and subsidiary inventory system. Queueing theory, which is discussed in Chapter 5, is, in fact, a study of in-waiting inventory systems of a more general character. In the first section of that chapter we discuss, for example, a specific inventory problem concerning the "buffer" inventories required between two operations whose output is stochastically varying.

The profusion of inventory models in all their varied aspects is due to the simple fact that many systems can be *interpreted* as inventory systems. A moment's reflection verifies that many allocation, assignment, investment, and other problems can be thus interpreted. The "stocks" in each case vary; they can be energy, men, time, money, or any other resource.

§4. CRITERIA FOR DECISION

4.1 Explicit Statement of Criterion

Optimization is always relative to a criterion or a set of criteria, implicit or explicit. One choice is "better" than another only in the sense that it satisfies a criterion to a greater extent. To be sure, as will be seen presently, a decision may be "best" relative to one criterion but very bad indeed relative to another.

Human endeavors generally have objectives. The following is a partial list of such objectives.

1. *Profit:* (or its antithesis, *cost*)—immediate or future.

2. *Quality*: this refers to the "is-ness" of the product or service, its content or composition. Quality may be the result of specifications on manufacturing tolerances, chemical composition, surface finish, etc..

3. *Performance*: this refers to the "what" and "how" of the behavior of the product or service. It may be described by reliability, interchangeability, interference with other components (heat, maintenance, etc.), durability (i.e., longevity), and so forth.

4. *Adaptability to change*: (or its opposite, *rigidity of design*) an objective infrequently recognized but one that is present, nevertheless, in almost every design.

5. *Safety.*

6. *Time:* this refers to such items as target dates that must be met, changes that must be incorporated at fixed intervals, etc..

7. *Aesthetic*: this refers to such qualities as beauty, tranquility, harmony, etc..

8. *Quantity.*

In a sense, the above objectives determine the *value system* by which the endeavor is conducted. The statement of the criterion is an unambiguous specification of the aspect or aspects of the objective(s) against which the decision is to be measured and the choice of the course of action is to be made. For example, if the *objective* is profit, the criterion specifies which kind of profit we are interested in: immediate profit, long-run average profit, minimum profit, etc.. Clearly, successful resolution of the problem demands statement of the criterion as well as the objective.

Since we are concerned with rational decisions, i.e., rational choices among alternatives, the *explicit statement of the criterion* (or criteria) used is mandatory, irrespective of questions of *measurability*.

4.2 Importance of Criterion

The choice of the criterion is fundamental to the design of any system or subsystem for at least two reasons:

First, it affects the *design and manipulation of the model*. We recall from our discussion in the previous section that the model is constructed with the criterion in mind. It may prove costly indeed if the model were constructed and it is then discovered that it does not yield the desired result, especially if the manipulation of the model is restricted to satisfying the given criterion.

An example may help drive the point home. Suppose it is desired to control the flow of work in a progressive-assembly shop. Suppose also that the stated objective is to minimize the overtime and idle time costs of operation, as well as smooth manpower requirements over a finite planning horizon. Obviously, the model as well as the operational design of the system will ignore such important cost sources as *inventory* of raw material and finished products. It is conceivable and highly probable that neither the model nor the operational system can accomodate the optimization of the *total system* of inventory and manufacturing shop should that be deemed necessary later on.

Second, the wrong criterion *leads to wrong conclusions*. This is self-evident and requires no elaboration. However, for a demonstration of such a result, see the examples on the evaluation of new projects presented below.

It is a rare event indeed in which the design of a system is undertaken realtive to *one* criterion. In the overwhelming majority of the cases we wish to optimize relative to *two or more* criteria. For example, we may wish to maximize long-run expected profit and also minimize the variability about such expectation. Or we specify that a dynamic system must be stable, fast-responsive, with minimum variability and minimum cost. Sometimes the criteria are conflicting; we may, for example, be concerned with minimizing both inventory *and* production fluctuations. Oftentimes one decision, say decision A, is high on one criterion but low on another, while another decision, B, is quite the opposite. Several questions immediately present themselves concerning performance optimization. These questions arise naturally and are usually formulated as the measurement of utility of an item or an activity. The study of utility functions and multiple criteria are well beyond our scope, but we briefly mention three possible approaches.

The first is to combine the various measures in one grand measure by weighting them in some linear or nonlinear fashion. In essence this is what we did in the three inventory models discussed in the previous section. Any specific pattern of ordering $\{q_t\}$, $t = 1,\ldots, N$, results in *two* measures: the cost of ordering and the cost of storing. One pattern may be high on one cost and low on the other; another pattern may behave in quite the opposite manner. In order to be able to choose among the infinite number of possible patterns and quantities, the two measures were added linearly (with unity weights) in an overall objective function; see Eqs. (1-1), (1-3), and (1-8). This approach is extensively used, especially when the relative importance (weight) of each measure is known.

The second approach is to optimize one measure relative to a *primary* criterion, and among the set of optima thus determined, optimize relative to a *secondary* criterion, and so on, until either the measures are exhausted or we possess only one optimal relative to a subset of the measures. In effect, this approach gives a large weight to the primary measure so that it dominates all the other measures. When a set of optima relative to this criterion is determined, it assigns a large weight to the secondary measure, etc.

The third approach, which is frequently used in the case of two measures, is to fix the level of one of them and optimize relative to the other measure. For example, different priority rules in so-called "job shops" result in different behavior where behavior is measured by a vector of characteristics such as: job lateness, size of queues at the different operations, average waiting time in each queue, machine utilization, etc. Suppose for a moment that we are interested in only two measures: lateness and machine utilization. Clearly, these two measures are diametrically opposed to each other in the sense that one is minimized if the other is maximized. But we can proceed as follows: for a given acceptable average job lateness (or machine utilization), choose the priority rule which maximizes machine utilization (minimizes lateness).

With the above remarks in mind, we proceed now with examples of different criteria that have been proposed and examples of some of the operational contexts in which they were applied.

4.3 Criteria for Deterministic Systems

In our discussion of the various criteria suggested and used in practice we distinguish between deterministic and nondeterministic systems. The difference between the two will become evident from our discussion of each individual criterion in both categories. In certain instances, such as the maximum expected profit in the probabilistic case and the maximum average profit in the deterministic case, one criterion is a simple extension of the other into the domain of stochastic processes. However, this is not always the case; there is, for example, no deterministic equivalent to the "minimum-variance" criterion in probabilistic systems.

In this section, we deal with criteria for deterministic systems; the following section treats criteria for nondeterministic systems.

Our presentation will proceed in the following manner. We shall state the criterion and discuss its significance and then follow, where it is advantageous, with an example of the criterion's application in practical problems. Thus, two results are achieved simultaneously: we illustrate the use of the proposed criterion and we present an application which utilizes the criterion in the definition of the model. The reader should study each application critically, especially from the point of view of the relevance of other criteria and the effects of changing the criterion on the solution obtained.

The criteria discussed are:

Maximum total profit.
Maximum present worth.
Minimum absolute value (of error).

Maximum total (or Average) Profit (Minimum cost)

This is a familiar and well-known criterion which we have adopted in the inventory models of the previous section. In the first two of these models we assumed an infinite planning horizon, and the criterion was to minimize the average total cost of inventory management. In the third inventory model a finite planning horizon was assumed, and the criterion was to minimize the total cost over the horizon.

We shall encounter this criterion frequently in future models of systems (e.g., every deterministic linear programming model uses this criterion as its objective function). For the moment, however, we give an illustration from the rather fertile and largely unexplored field of optimal facility planning.

Example: An Optimal Location-Allocation Problem

The problem of optimal location-allocation boasts a long and rather sophisticated history. It is usually demonstrated with the so-called "warehousing problem," the point of which is to determine optimally the number of warehouses, their locations, and the allocation of demand to each warehouse, given all the pertinent data on the producing factories as well as on the consuming centers. We shall discuss this problem in a later chapter.[†]

[†] See Chapter 7, §3.4.

The general problem of optimal facility planning can be formulated in the following terms: *given* the location of each consuming center, together with its demand and the costs of shipping from any place to each center, *find* the number, location, and capacity of each new source that must be provided in order to minimize the total cost of operation. Of course, the terms "location," "consumer," and "capacity" should be considered as generic rather than literal. For example, "location" need not be physical but may occur *in time*; a "consuming center" need not be consuming anything but may interact with the new facility, etc.

The general problem as presented above is of formidable dimensions. We can simplify it by restricting it to the determination of the *number* and *location* of the new facilities and by making the necessary assumptions concerning the absence of capacity limitations and the independence of cost of production of either capacity or location, etc.. Though simplified, the problem is certainly not trivial. In passing, we should note the difference between the problem stated here and the well-known Transportation problem of linear programming.

Suppose that the total cost of production and allocation is composed of two major costs: (1) the cost of providing the resources, which is a function of their number m, say $g_1(m)$; and (2) the cost of distribution, assumed to be proportional to the distance between the source and destination, and independent of the quantity distributed. Let $g_2(m)$ be the *minimum* cost of distribution for a given number of sources, m. The total cost is then given by

$$C = g_1(m) + g_2(m)$$

and is a function of m. Assuming, for simplicity, that both g_1 and g_2 are continuous in m, the optimal value of m is obtained from

$$\frac{dC}{dm} = \frac{d}{dm} g_1(m) + \frac{d}{dm} g_2(m) = 0.$$

The determination of $g_1(m)$ is usually not difficult, at least from a conceptual point of view, though it requires large amounts of empirical data which, in many cases, may not be available but can be estimated with a reasonable degree of accuracy. On the other hand, the determination of the minimal cost function $g_2(m)$ poses certain difficulties.

Since we assumed that the cost of distribution is proportional to the distance between source j and destination i, let (X_{D_i}, Y_{D_i}) denote the location of consuming center i and (X_j, Y_j) denote the location of source j, and let

$$\psi(i,j) = w_{ij} \sqrt{(X_{D_i} - X_j)^2 + (Y_{D_i} - Y_j)^2}$$

be this cost where w_{ij} is the constant of proportionality. Any allocation of n destinations to m sources can be given by a matrix $[\alpha_{ij}]$ with $\alpha_{ij} = 1$ if destination i is allocated to source j, and $\alpha_{ij} = 0$ otherwise.

For example, if there are four destinations and two sources, the following matrices illustrate three of the possible seven allocations. For an exercise, the reader should determine the other four allocations.

$$
\begin{array}{c}
 \\
1 \\
2 \\
3 \\
4
\end{array}
\begin{array}{cc}
a & b \\
\end{array}
\begin{bmatrix}
1 & \\
 & 1 \\
1 & \\
 & 1
\end{bmatrix}
\qquad
\begin{array}{cc}
a & b \\
\end{array}
\begin{bmatrix}
1 & \\
1 & \\
1 & \\
 & 1
\end{bmatrix}
\qquad
\begin{array}{cc}
a & b \\
\end{array}
\begin{bmatrix}
1 & \\
 & 1 \\
 & 1 \\
1 &
\end{bmatrix}
$$

In the first pattern $\alpha_{11} = 1$, which means that destination 1 is allocated to source a, etc.. It can be shown that, in general, there are

$$
S(n,m) = \frac{1}{m!} \sum_{k=0}^{m} \binom{m}{k} (-1)^k (m - k)^n
$$

different allocation matrices, assuming that all sources are indistinguishable (with respect to product, capacity, service, etc.). In essence this is the problem of the number of ways of placing n different objects in m indistinguishable cells with no cell empty.

Now, for any *given allocation*, the total cost of distribution is

$$
\phi(m) = \sum_{j=1}^{m} \sum_{i=1}^{n} \alpha_{ij} \cdot w_{ij} \sqrt{(X_{D_i} - X_j)^2 + (Y_{D_i} - Y_j)^2}. \tag{1-13}
$$

Of course we are faced with the problem of the optimal determination of the *allocation*, $[\alpha_{ij}{}^*]$, and the *location* $\{(X_j^*, Y_j^*)\}$, that minimize $\phi(m)$. This would yield $g_2(m)$.

Differentiating Eq. (1-13) partially with respect to X_j and Y_j and equating to zero, we obtain

$$
\frac{\partial \phi}{\partial X_j} = 0 = \sum_{i=1}^{n} \frac{\alpha_{ij} w_{ij}(X_{D_i} - X_j)}{\sqrt{(X_{D_i} - X_j)^2 + (Y_{D_i} - Y_j)^2}}
$$

$$
\frac{\partial \phi}{\partial Y_j} = 0 = \sum_{i=1}^{n} \frac{\alpha_{ij} w_{ij}(Y_{D_i} - Y_j)}{\sqrt{(X_{D_i} - X_j)^2 + (Y_{D_i} - Y_j)^2}} \tag{1-14}
$$

Let $D_{ij} = \sqrt{(X_{D_i} - X_j)^2 + (Y_{D_i} - Y_j)^2}$, then Eqs. (1-14) become

$$
\sum_{i=1}^{n} \{\alpha_{ij} w_{ij} (X_{D_i} - X_j)/D_{ij}\} = 0
$$

$$
j = 1, \ldots, m \tag{1-15}
$$

$$
\sum_{i=1}^{n} \{\alpha_{ij} w_{ij} (Y_{D_i} - Y_j)/D_{ij} = 0.
$$

This set of simultaneous equations must be solved $S(n,m)$ times and the optimum determined as the minimum of the set of minima thus obtained.

Equations (1-15) can be solved iteratively in the following way. Rewrite the equations as:

$$X_j = \frac{\sum_{i=1}^{n} (\alpha_{ij} w_{ij} X_{D_i}/D_{ij})}{\sum_{i=1}^{n} (\alpha_{ij} w_{ij}/D_{ij})}$$

$$j = 1, \ldots, m$$

$$Y_j = \frac{\sum_{i=1}^{n} (\alpha_{ij} w_{ij} Y_{D_i}/D_{ij})}{\sum_{i=1}^{n} (\alpha_{ij} w_{ij}/D_{ij}).}$$

Let the superscript denote the iteration number

$$X_j^{k+1} = \frac{\sum_{i} (\alpha_{ij} w_{ij} X_{D_i}/D_{ij}^k)}{\sum_{i} (\alpha_{ij} w_{ij}/D_{ij}^k)}$$

$$j = 1, \ldots, m$$

$$Y_j^{k+1} = \frac{\sum_{i} (\alpha_{ij} w_{ij} Y_{Di}/D_{ij}^k)}{\sum_{i} (\alpha_{ij} w_{ij}/D_{ij}^k)}$$

A convenient starting value of $D_{ij}{}^0$ is obtained as the weighted mean co-ordinates,

$$X_j{}^0 = \frac{\sum_{i} \alpha_{ij} w_{ij} X_{D_i}}{\sum_{i} \alpha_{ij}}$$

$$j = 1, \ldots, m$$

$$Y_j{}^0 = \frac{\sum_{i} \alpha_{ij} w_{ij} Y_{D_i}}{\sum_{i} \alpha_{ij}}$$

As an illustration of the above procedure, consider the case with $n = 7$ destinations and $m = 2$ sources. The locations of the 7 destinations are given by the coordinates: (15, 15), (5, 10), (10, 27), (16, 8), (25, 14), (31, 23), and (22, 29) with $w_{ij} = 1$ for all i and j. There are $S(7, 2) = 63$ possible allocations which were solved to determine the optimal source locations, which are shown in Fig. 1-7 as points O_1 and O_2.

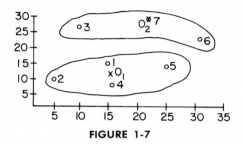

FIGURE 1-7

This approach is exact but unfortunately requires a large number of calculations which may prove impossible even for the largest electronic computer. This occurs in spite of the drastically simplifying assumptions which were made concerning linearity of costs with distance, independence of cost from quantity shipped, homogeneity of product (no questions of product mix), etc..

Clearly, what is needed for the solution of large scale practical problems is some heuristic approach, i.e., some logical rule of thumb, which eliminates many of the alternatives at the outset, leaving only a small subset of alternatives to be searched for the optimal, or near-optimal, solution.

Before describing examples of such heuristic approaches, we should note that if the locations of the sources are known, the problem of allocation is trivially simple since it involves assigning each consuming center to the nearest source. On the other hand, for any given *allocation*, the optimal locations of the sources are determined in a fairly straightforward fashion utilizing the extremal Eqs. (1-14) above. This suggests that a reasonable heuristic approach would be the following. Using *a priori* reasoning, determine a set of alternative location patterns of the *m* sources. In many instances, this is fairly easy to do since many locations are ruled out because of geographic or other reasons (the necessity to be close to a sea port, inaccessibility in the winter, etc.). For each pattern a minimum cost allocation is determined. The minimum among these minima is then chosen for detailed analysis by the extremal Eqs. (1–14) to determine the exact optimal location under the specified allocation. If the location thus determined coincides with the assumed location, this may be taken as a strong indication of optimal, or near-optimal, solution. Otherwise, successive approximating schemes may be used. Of course, there is always the possibility of some location pattern other than the minimum chosen above yielding a minimum cost (after optimizing its location) which is still lower than that previously obtained. Unfortunately, there is no way to guarantee against such an occurrence except by exhaustive enumeration.

Another heuristic approach, which has been used by Cooper,[†] is as follows. At the outset assume that the location of the m sources *will coincide with the location of m of the destinations.* But which m? Form all possible choices of m out of n locations, and there are $\binom{n}{m} = n!/m!(n - m)!$ such choices. For each choice, calculate the minimum cost allocation. The minimum among these minima is to be treated according to the extremal Eqs. (1–14) to determine the optimal location under the assumed allocation. Naturally, the success of this approach is dependent on the magnitude of $\Sigma_{m=1}^{\overline{m}} \binom{n}{m}$, where $\overline{m}$ is the upper limit on the number of sources, $\overline{m} \leq n$. Usually $\overline{m}$ is $\leq \dfrac{n}{2}$.

Although there is no guarantee that this approach will in fact yield the exact optimum (as derived from the model described above), Cooper reports that in every case he tried (with $n = 7$, $m = 2$) the optimum coincided with the exact solution. This does not constitute a proof of the procedure's optimality, but is certainly encouraging.

In general, heuristic approaches to large scale practical problems have favored lines of attack which start with a small set of possible location patterns—since, as we explained before, these are usually limited in number to no more than 100 in the majority of cases—and optimize the objective within this set.

Maximum Present Worth

Our second example of criteria for decision is taken from the fields of capital investment and replacement policy. To place our discussion in its proper perspective, a slight detour at this point is necessary.

In a going concern situations often arise where a new activity which involves an outlay of capital is contemplated. And, in the majority of cases, more than one alternative course of action is open to management, which is called upon to decide among these alternatives. We shall assume that decision is based solely on the economic aspects of the alternatives.

Analysis usually begins with a detailed evaluation of the necessary outlays of capital over a period of time and the expected income over the

[†] Leon Cooper, "Location-Allocation Problems," *Operations Research*, Vol. 11, No. 3, May–June 1963, pp. 331–343.

same finite planning horizon for each alternative. For the sake of concreteness, let Q_t denote the *net income* assumed to be realized at the *end* of period t; $t = 1, 2, \ldots, n$. (A negative Q would indicate an *outlay* of capital.) With the knowledge of $\{Q_t\}$, management is called upon to choose the "best" undertaking or project.

To this end, management needs a criterion for decision, and unfortunately (or perhaps fortunately!) there is an abundance of such criteria, each with its advocates and each open to criticism. We will enumerate and briefly explain four such criteria, starting with the criterion cited as the title of this section: The Present Worth (PW) Criterion.

It is axiomatic in economic analysis to recognize the differential value of money over time. Specifically, a dollar available now is worth more than a dollar available a year from now. This is so even when factors like inflation are disregarded because we may assume that it is *always* possible to invest an available dollar at some market interest rate, $i > 0$, so that at the end of one year we would have accumulated $(1 + i)$ dollars. This is necessarily preferable to the income of just one dollar at the end of the same year. (Incidentally, $(1 + i)$ is called the compound interest rate, $1/(1 + i)$ the discount rate, and $Q_t/(1 + i)^t$ the discounted cash flow.) Extending the argument to any arbitrary set of income $\{Q_t\}$, and any set of interest rates, i_t, $t = 1, \ldots, n$, we can immediately see that the total accumulated sum at the *end* of the planning horizon is given by

$$S_n = Q_0 \prod_{t=1}^{n} (1 + i_t) + Q_1 \prod_{t=2}^{n} (1 + i_t) + \cdots + Q_{n-1}(1 + i_n) + Q_n.$$

Clearly, instead of talking about future accumulation of capital, we can always reverse the argument and talk about the *present worth* of such future receipts:

$$P = Q_0 + \frac{Q_1}{1 + i_1} + \frac{Q_2}{(1 + i_1)(1 + i_2)} + \cdots + \frac{Q_n}{\displaystyle\prod_{t=1}^{n}(1 + i_t)}$$

where P measures such present worth. Note that if we multiply both sides of the equation by $\prod_{t=1}^{n}(1 + i_t)$ we would obtain

$$P \prod_{t=1}^{n}(1 + i_t) = Q_0 \prod_{t=1}^{n}(1 + i_t) + Q_1 \prod_{t=2}^{n}(1 + i_t) + \cdots + Q_n.$$

Comparing the right hand side of this equation with the right hand side of the equation defining S_n we immediately see that

$$S_n = P \prod_{1}^{n}(1 + i_t).$$

This yields the following interpretation of P: it is the amount of the immediate investment which would accumulate a total sum equal to S_n at the end of the n-period planning horizon. Consequently, if two projects A and B are competing with each other, then A is preferred to B if $P_A > P_B$.

For example, consider the data in Table 1-1 for two mutually exclusive alternatives, assuming an interest rate $i_t = 6\%$ per period for all t:

TABLE 1-1

End of Period	Actual Cash Flow		Discounted Cash Flow	
	Alternative A	Alternative B	Alternative A	Alternative B
0	-500	-500	-500	-500
1	200	100	188.68	94.34
2	200	220	178.00	195.80
3	120	200	100.75	167.92
4	300	220	237.63	174.26
		Total	205.06	132.32

The present worth of each alternative is evaluated by discounting the cash flow at the given interest rate of 6% and summing. For example, an income $Q_{B2} = \$220$ is discounted by $1/(1 + 0.06)^2 = 0.89$; and the present worth of Q_{B2} is given by $220 \times 0.89 = \$195.80$ as shown. Evidently, while both projects require the same immediate investment ($= \$500$), project A is preferred to project B.

The major objection to the PW criterion is that it requires complete knowledge of future income $\{Q_t\}$ *and* future interest rates $\{i_t\}$. Anticipation of the situation when future interest rates are not known with certainty has led to attempts to develop a method for measuring the desirability of a proposed productive investment project independent of the future interest rates $\{i_t\}$. The "*Internal Rate of Return*" (IRR) criterion purports to achieve such an objective.

The IRR is defined in the following fashion. For a given proposed productive investment project, define a set of rates of return, called the *internal* rates of return, ρ_t, $t = 1, \ldots, n$, as any set of interest rates which will reduce the discounted sum of the *net* incremental returns from the project to a present worth of zero. That is

$$0 = Q_0 + \frac{Q_1}{(1 + \rho_1)} + \frac{Q_2}{(1 + \rho_1)(1 + \rho_2)} + \cdots + \frac{Q_n}{\prod_{t=1}^{n}(1 + \rho_t)}.$$

Since the ρ's are interest rates, they must satisfy the requirement

$$-1 < \rho_t < \infty .$$

(A negative interest rate implies capital depletion rather than capital accumulation.) In most of the applications, the special set or sets of ρ's for which $\rho_t = \rho$ for all t are selected, assuming that such a set exists. In other words, the internal rate of return ρ is defined as the value which satisfies the equation

$$0 = Q_0 + \frac{Q_1}{(1 + \rho)} + \frac{Q_2}{(1 + \rho)^2} + \cdots + \frac{Q_n}{(1 + \rho)^n}$$

so that $-1 \leq \rho < \infty$.

Notice that if we multiply both sides by $(1 + \rho)^n$ we obtain

$$0 = Q_0(1 + \rho)^n + Q_1(1 + \rho)^{n-1} + \cdots + Q_{n-1}(1 + \rho) + Q_n.$$

Again, if the right hand side of this equation is compared with the right hand side of the equation defining S_n, an interpretation of ρ is readily available: it is the *imputed* rate of return which results in zero capital accumulation at the end of an n-period planning horizon. In other words, at an internal rate of return equal to ρ, all expenditure is recovered *with interest*, at a rate equal to ρ.

Now, if we likewise assume that the *market* rates of return, $\{i_t\}$, are in fact equal to a single constant i for the planning horizon, then the equality $i = \rho$ would indicate that the *present worth* P for the project is exactly zero. Hence, it is assumed that a $\rho > i$ indicates a worthwhile project since it seems that it will make net incremental returns to the firm on its invested capital at a rate of interest higher than the market rate of interest. Likewise, a $\rho < i$ indicates an undesirable project. Moreover, project A would be preferred to project B if $\rho_A > \rho_B$.

We recall that the IRR criterion was used in an effort to avoid relying on the estimates of the market rates of returns, $\{i_t\}$. To be sure, the evaluation of ρ, or for that matter the evaluation of the set $\{\rho_t\}$, is accomplished without knowledge of market rates of interest, $\{i_t\}$. It is claimed, consequently, that it is sufficient for a decision to be made to have an idea about the *range* of variation of $\{i_t\}$.

But the IRR criterion is not without its drawbacks. First, the IRR approach may yield *more than one value* of ρ satisfying the defining equation. Under such circumstances, it is not clear what the "true" internal rate of return is. For example, consider a project which has the following pattern of net receipts (a negative Q_t indicates an outlay of capital),

$$Q_0 = -1, Q_1 = 6, Q_2 = -11, Q_3 = 6$$

and has internal rates of return $\rho = 0$, 1, and 2. (The reader can satisfy himself that each of the above three values of ρ satisfies the defining equation $0 = -1 + 6/(1 + \rho) - 11/(1 + \rho)^2 + 6/(1 + \rho)^3$.) The problem lies in choosing the "correct" internal rate of return to be adopted. Moreover, if $i = 0.50$, there arises a question as to whether this project is good (both $\rho = 1$ and $\rho = 2$ are > 0.50) or bad ($\rho = 0$ is < 0.50).

Second, even in situations for which ρ is unique, a further difficulty arises in the application of the IRR method. It is possible to encounter problems in which two projects, A and B, are being compared wherein A is preferred to B according to the PW criterion and B is preferred to A according to the IRR criterion! An example of such a situation is given in Table 1-2, where the present worth of the two projects is evaluated at $i = 0.50$. The contradiction here is disconcerting because both projects

TABLE 1-2

		Project A	Project B
	Q_0	-1	-1
	Q_1	1	2
	Q_2	4	2
IRR:	ρ	1.562	1.732
PW:	P	1.444	1.222

are evaluated by the same value system, namely, their economic worth over a finite horizon, and both criteria utilize the same economic data, i.e., the net returns over the planning horizon. How are we to decide which of the projects is superior?

To select one of the projects over the other, we must first thoroughly understand the meaning of the "internal rate of return." Hindsight reveals some rather subtle relationships that should have been evident to us from the very definition of $\{\rho_t\}$.

In the discussion immediately following the equation which defines ρ we interpreted the IRR as the imputed interest rate at which all expenditure is recovered *with interest* at a rate equal to ρ. Pursuing this line of reasoning a little further, let U_t be the unrecovered investment at the end of period t. Then, by definition,

$$U_t = U_{t-1}(1 + \rho_t) - Q_t.$$

That is, the unrecovered investment, U_t, at the end of period t is equal to the unrecovered investment, U_{t-1}, at the beginning of period t (or equivalently, at the end of period $t - 1$), plus an interest payment, minus the net revenue, Q_t, accruing at the end of period t. It is easy to show through recursive substitution in the above equation for $t = 1, 2, \ldots, n$ that the equation is indeed the defining equation for $\{\rho_t\}$.

Now, for simplicity, let $n = 2$; i.e., consider a project whose span of life is only two periods. And for concreteness, consider a project whose net returns over a two-period horizon are:

$$Q_0 = -1, Q_1 = 3, Q_2 = -1.$$

From the defining equation

$$0 = Q_0 + \frac{Q_1}{(1 + \rho_1)} + \frac{Q_2}{(1 + \rho_1)(1 + \rho_2)},$$

it is easy to deduce that

$$\rho_2 = \frac{Q_2}{(1 + \rho_1)(-Q_0) - Q_1} - 1 = \frac{-1}{\rho_1 - 2} - 1.$$

We have one equation in two variables; hence, any one variable can be determined arbitrarily, and the other variable will have a corresponding value. Table 1-3 depicts some typical values of ρ_1 and ρ_2 in the range of interest.

TABLE 1-3

ρ_1	ρ_2
-1	-0.667
-0.618	$-0.618 \rightarrow \rho_1 = \rho_2$
0	-0.50
0.50	-0.333
1.00	0
1.618	$1.618 \rightarrow \rho_1 = \rho_2$
1.8	4

Note that if we limit considerations to the usual internal rate of return $\rho = \rho_1 = \rho_2$, there are two such values, namely $\rho = -0.618$ and $\rho = 1.618$. The meaning of these two internal rates of return may be understood if we evaluate the unrecovered investment at the end of each period $t = 0, 1, 2$ as in Table 1-4.

TABLE 1-4

t	Q_t	U_{t-1}	ρU_{t-1}	U_t	Q_t	U_{t-1}	ρU_{t-1}	U_t
	$\rho = -0.618$				$\rho = 1.618$			
0	-1	$-$	$-$	1	-1	$-$	$-$	1
1	3	1	-0.618	-2.618	3	1	1.618	-0.382
2	-1	-2.618	1.618	0	-1	-0.382	-0.618	0

Consider the last column under each ρ. Note that the unrecovered investment is *positive* at the end of period 0, becomes *negative* at the end of period 1, and, of course, by definition of ρ, becomes zero at the end of period 2. The sign of the unrecovered investment U_t indicates the position of the firm vis-à-vis the project. A *positive* U_{t-1} means that the firm is a *lender* to the project during period $t - 1$, while a *negative* U_{t-1} means that the firm is a *borrower* from the project during period $t - 1$. Consequently, ρU_{t-1} represents money *earned* by the firm when $U_{t-1} > 0$, but it represents money *paid* by the firm when $U_{t-1} < 0$. Hence, during periods t, when the firm is a lender to the project, it is desirable for ρ_t to be large, but during periods t, when the firm is a borrower from the project, it is desirable for ρ to be small.

Consequently, in the special case for which $\rho_t = \rho$, a constant for all t, it cannot be said that the project should be undertaken if $\rho > i$ or $\rho < i$. According to our discussion above, ρ_t should be sometimes $> i$ (lender situation) and sometimes $< i$ (borrower situation). This conclusion is in direct contradiction to the first common use of the IRR approach.

Applying this conclusion to the particular example of Tables 1-3 and 1-4, and assuming a market interest rate $i = 0.5$, the project is worthwhile. There is, in fact, a considerable range of values of $\rho_1 > 0.5$ and $\rho_2 < 0.5$, as Table 1-3 demonstrates.

We still have to explain the possibility of opposite ranking of projects by the PW and IRR criteria. Let us return, then, to the two projects, A and B of Table 1-2. The fundamental difficulty in using the IRR approach may be seen if we insert the data for projects A and B in the unrecovered investment formula, obtaining the results shown in Table 1-5.

TABLE 1-5

	Project A; $\rho = 1.562$				Project B; $\rho = 1.732$			
t	Q_t	U_{t-1}	ρU_{t-1}	U_t	Q_t	U_{t-1}	ρU_{t-1}	U_t
0	-1	—	—	1	-1	—	—	1
1	1	1	1.562	1.562	2	1	1.732	0.732
2	4	1.562	2.438	0	2	0.732	1.268	0

In each of these cases, the firm would remain a *lender* to the project during both periods 1 and 2, and hence ρU_{t-1} represents income to the firm. Obviously, it is desirable to have ρ as large as possible. However, note that the unrecovered investment, U_1, at the end of period 1 is *not* the same for the two projects. This is crucial from two points of view:

1. The prospective interest payments from the projects to the firm during the second period are based upon their respective U_1's. Hence, the internal rates of return, ρ_A and ρ_B, are not comparable during period 2

simply because they are based on two different principals. Since, in general, no two projects have the same U_t at the end of any period except perhaps the first (U_n always $= 0$), the internal rates of returns are not comparable.

The argument for the incomparability of the two internal rates of return, ρ_A and ρ_B, can be made even more plausible when stated in the following way. ρ presumably measures the imputed interest on the unrecovered investment at the end of period t. Since the net income in period $t = 2$ was 4 for project A but only 2 for project B, we can consider the one-period investment problem with the following data:

	Project A	Project B
Initial investment	1.562	0.732
Net income	4.0	2.0

Which is the better project? Evidently, ρ is the solution of the equation

$$U_2 = U_1(1 + \rho) - Q_2 = 0$$

or

$$\rho = \frac{Q_2 - U_1}{U_1}$$

which yields

$$\rho_A = \frac{4 - 1.562}{1.562} = 1.562$$

and

$$\rho_B = \frac{2 - 0.732}{0.732} = 1.732.$$

It is not immediately obvious why one should attach any special importance to the difference between ρ_A and ρ_B, especially in view of the fact that the two Q_2's *and* the two U_1's are different.

2. An even more basic assumption underlying the concept of the IRR is that since both projects require the same capital investment of 1 unit and have the same span of life, $n = 2$, a value $\rho_B = 1.732 > \rho_A = 1.562$ results in that project B is preferred to A. But this implies that the investment of 1 unit in A and B will be converted at the end of period 2 into

$$S_A = 1 + 1(1.562) + (1 + 1.562)(1.562) = 6.562$$

and

$$S_B = 1 + 1(1.732) + (1 + 1.732)(1.732) = 7.464$$

respectively. However, an implication of this reasoning is that the net incremental return, Q_1, from either project, would be reinvested during period 2 at the same rate of return which the project itself is earning— 1.562 for A and 1.732 for B. But this is patently self-contradictory. For, if an opportunity always exists at the high rate of 1.732 (at which the receipts of B are reinvested) then there is no reason at all for investing the receipts from A at an inferior rate of only 1.562. On the other hand, if no such lucrative opportunities exist, then receipts from both projects should be reinvested at the market rate of interest, which was assumed to be $i = 0.5$ above!

The fact that projects A and B cannot be ranked independently of the possibilities for the reinvestment of funds external to the project can be demonstrated in still another way. For each project we can construct a table of typical values of ρ_1 and ρ_2 similar to Table 1-3. Such analysis is shown in Table 1-6. Notice that the usual internal rate of return $\rho = \rho_1 = \rho_2$ is only one special pair of an infinite number of possible pairs (ρ_1, ρ_2) for each project. The possible sets of pairs of internal rates of return for each project are compared with the market rates of return (i_1, i_2) and a decision is made concerning the profitability of each project. Under such a scheme the points at which $\rho = \rho_1 = \rho_2$ for each project have no special significance.

TABLE 1-6

Project A		Project B	
ρ_1	ρ_2	ρ_1	ρ_2
∞	-1	∞	-1
4	0	3	0
2	1	2	1
1.562	1.562	1.732	1.732 $\rightarrow \rho_1 = \rho_2$
1	3	1.50	3
0.50	7	1.25	7
0	∞	1	∞

By now it must be evident that the IRR criterion is open to serious questions. Our discussion above can only cast a deep shadow of doubt on the validity of the approach. In fact, we have demonstrated that the IRR approach cannot escape (which it originally claimed it could) the onus of evaluating the market interest rates $i_1, \ldots, i_n$. Yet, there is no question of the need to construct a measure of the rate of economic benefit accruing from a project which is "internal" to the project, i.e., which is independent of the market rate of interest, $\{i_t\}$.

The following suggestion, which does not pretend not to require information on the market rate of interest, $\{i_t\}$, was advanced recently by Solomon[†] as a correction to the IRR method. Let Q_0 be the initial investment and Q_1, Q_2,..., Q_n the net receipts over an n-period planning horizon. Then the "*Average Rate of Return*," (ARR), is defined as that rate of interest on the initial investment which would give the same total wealth at the end of n periods as would the net incremental returns Q_1, Q_2,..., Q_n from the project together with the assumed reinvestment at *market* rate. Mathematically, the ARR is designated by r and is given as the solution to the equation

$$0 = Q_0(1 + r)^n + Q_1 \prod_1^n (1 + i_t) + Q_2 \prod_2^n (1 + i_t) + \cdots + Q_n; Q_0 < 0.$$

Under this criterion, project A is preferred to B if $r_A > r_B$. It is easy to show that the ARR criterion is consistent with the PW criterion, i.e., that the two criteria will never yield conflicting conclusions. Since we have previously concluded that the PW method is superior to the IRR method, the ARR approach is also preferred to the IRR.

We conclude the discussion by briefly presenting two other criteria for decision in investment problems.

One popular criterion is the "*Equivalent Annual Return*" criterion which is a redistribution of the present worth of a project over n equal receipts which include interest. For a set of net receipts Q_0, Q_1,..., Q_n, and market interest rate, i, over the planning horizon,

$$P = \sum_{t=0}^n Q_t(1 + i)^{-t} = \frac{R}{(1 + i)} + \frac{R}{(1 + i)^2} + \cdots + \frac{R}{(1 + i)^n}$$

$$= R \sum_{t=1}^n (1 + i)^{-t} = \frac{(1 + i)^n - 1}{i(1 + i)^n} R.$$

Then $R = [i(1 + i)^n / \{(1 + i)^n - 1\}] P$. Obviously, the Equivalent Annual Return Criterion is consistent with the PW criterion since it is proportional to it.

Another common criterion, the "*Economic Life*," states that there is a length of life for which the cost of operation of a facility will be at a minimum. Where replacements are repeated and their history is known, the economic life of a facility can be determined. This condition is approximated in automotive vehicles, prime movers, machine tools, etc., during

[†]Ezra Solomon, "The Arithmetic of Capital Budgeting Decisions," *Journal of Business*, Vol. 24, No. 2, April 1956.

periods of stable economy. The determination of Economic Life has practical applications when cost patterns of successive replacements are similar. This is most likely to occur with short-lived facilities and where there are a number of similar units whose service characteristics can be averaged. In the absence of such cost data, decision must be made on estimates which are, naturally, prone to error.

To summarize: decision for investment purposes can be made relative to any one of several criteria. We have discussed a few such criteria and analyzed in some detail objections raised against the internal-rate-of-return criterion. This served to illustrate, once more, the central importance of the criterion in decision processes. For a more detailed discussion of investment and replacement policies, the reader is urged to consult the references cited at the end of the chapter.

Minimum Absolute Value

Minimization of the absolute value of the error usually presents itself in two forms: minimization of the *sum* of absolute value of the errors throughout the process, which we discuss here, and the minimization of the absolute value of the *terminal* error, which we discuss below.

Intuitively speaking, the minimization of the sum of the absolute errors is a more appealing criterion than, and in many instances is preferred to, the minimum-squared-error criterion discussed below. It is equally true, however, that the mathematical manipulation of the resulting objective function is oftentimes very difficult. As an exercise, the reader should attempt to derive the optimal coefficients a and b in the linear regression example presented below using the minimization of the Σ(absolute deviations) as the criterion instead of the minimization of the Σ(deviations)^2.

Example: A Location Problem

Consider the following problem: suppose we want to locate a new machine in a plant where there are n existing machines. This new machine interacts with each of the old ones, and the degree of interaction with machine j is measurable and equal to A_j. The constant A_j may measure the expected frequency of traversing the distance between the new machine and old machine j. Alternatively, A_j may measure the number of units of a product mix that have both machines in their manufacturing specifications. As a third interpretation, there may be no machines at all, and A_j may measure the relative frequency of communication (verbal or otherwise) between a new "operator" and old "operator" j. Assuming cost to be proportional to the distance from machine j and the constant of proportionality to be given by the degree of interaction, find the optimal location of the new machine.

The principles involved in such an optimization process can best be il-

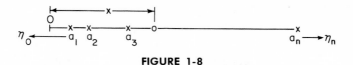

FIGURE 1-8

lustrated by the simple case in which all the existing machines are located along a straight line (say along an aisle) at distances $0 \leq a_1 < a_2 < a_3 < \ldots < a_n$ from some arbitrary origin. Obviously the new machine will be located along the same line, say at distance x from the origin (see Fig. 1-8). Mathematically, we wish to minimize

$$F = \sum_j A_j |x - a_j|, \qquad A_j > 0$$

subject to the known relationship among the a_j's.

To render the main result of the treatment below more meaningful and to give the reader some insight into the handling of absolute measures, we consider first the simple case of only two old machines with $a_1 = 0$ and $a_2 > 0$ (see Fig. 1-9). If the new machine is placed at a distance x from

FIGURE 1-9

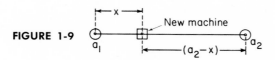

a_1, the objective would be to minimize $F = A_1 |x - 0| + A_2 |x - a_2| = (A_1 - A_2)x + A_2 a_2$. Evidently, since $A_2 a_2$ is a constant independent of x, the optimal location of the new machine is determined solely by the sign of $A_1 - A_2$ and is independent of the value of a_2. In particular, if $A_1 - A_2 > 0$, x is to be made as small as possible, $x \equiv a_1$; if $A_1 - A_2 < 0$, x should be made as large as possible, $x \equiv a_2$; and if $A_1 = A_2$, x can take on any value *between* a_1 and a_2.

These results may contradict the reader's immediate impulse to place the new machine at the "center of gravity" with weights A_1 at a_1 and A_2 at a_2, which is an optimal solution relative to a different criterion (which?).

In the general case of n old machines, the placement of the new machine between old machines j and $j + 1$ means that optimal location x is independent of $\{a_j\}$, $j = 1, \ldots, n$. The following treatment yields the optimal pair of old machines between which the new machine is to be placed.

Let $\eta = 0$ denote the half line to the left of a_1 (extending to $-\infty$), and let $\eta = n$ be the half line to the right of a_n (extending to $+\infty$).[†] Then for

---

[†] This is an abbreviated way of stating "... the half-line to the left of the machine located at a $_1$," etc..

some integer, $\eta, 0 \leq \eta \leq n$,

$$F = \sum_{j=1}^{\eta} A_j |x - a_j| + \sum_{\eta+1}^{n} A_j |x - a_j|$$

and if

$$a_\eta \leq x \leq a_{\eta+1},$$

then

$$F(\eta) = \sum_{1}^{\eta} A_j(x - a_j) + \sum_{\eta+1}^{n} A_j(a_j - x)$$

$$= x\left\{ \sum_{1}^{\eta} A_j - \sum_{\eta+1}^{n} A_j \right\} + \left\{ -\sum_{1}^{\eta} A_j a_j + \sum_{\eta+1}^{n} A_j a_j \right\}$$

$$= x M(\eta) + D(\eta),$$

with $M(\eta)$ and $D(\eta)$ defined as the quantities between the braces, respectively. Suppose $x \geq 0$, then for $0 \leq x \leq a_1, (\eta = 0)$,

$$F(0) = -x\sum_{1}^{n} A_j + \sum_{1}^{n} A_j a_j = x M(0) + D(0)$$

but for

$$x \geq a_n(\eta = n),$$

$$F(n) = x\sum_{1}^{n} A_j - \sum_{1}^{n} A_j a_j = x M(n) + D(n).$$

Since $x \geq 0$, we conclude that $M(0) < 0$ and $M(n) > 0$. Also, it is easy to show that

$$M(\eta) = M(\eta - 1) + 2A_\eta.$$

Therefore, $M(\eta)$ is a step function, monotonically increasing from a negative to a positive value. We distinguish between two cases, represented graphically in Fig. 1-10. It is obvious that for $M(\eta) < 0$, $a_\eta \leq x \leq a_{\eta+1}$, we have

$$F_{\max}(\eta) = M(\eta)a_\eta + D(\eta)$$

$$F_{\min}(\eta) = M(\eta)a_{\eta+1} + D(\eta)$$

and therefore,

$$F_{\min}(\eta - 1) = M(\eta - 1)a_\eta + D(\eta - 1)$$

$$= F_{\max}(\eta) = F_{\min}(\eta) + M(\eta)(a_\eta - a_{\eta+1})$$

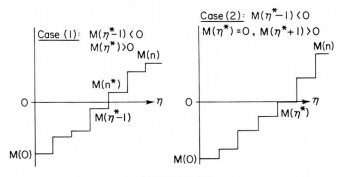

FIGURE 1-10

Consequently,

$$F_{\min}(\eta - 1) > F_{\min}(\eta),$$

the difference being equal to $M(\eta)(a_\eta - a_{\eta-1})$. Similarly, it is easily shown that for $M(\eta) > 0$,

$$F_{\min}(\eta + 1) > F_{\min}(\eta)$$

and the difference is equal to $M(\eta)(a_{\eta+1} - a_\eta)$.

Since, in case (1), Fig. 1-10, $M(0) < \ldots < M(\eta^* - 1) < 0$ and $0 < M(\eta^*) < \ldots < M(n)$, F is minimum at $x^* = a_\eta^*$. The numerical value of η^* is evaluated from the two inequalities

$$M(\eta^* - 1) = \sum_1^{\eta^*-1} A_j - \sum_{\eta^*}^n A_j < 0$$

i.e.,

$$\sum_1^{\eta^*-1} A_j < \sum_{\eta^*}^n A_j \quad \text{or} \quad \sum_1^{\eta^*-1} A_j < \tfrac{1}{2} \sum_1^n A_j$$

and

$$M(\eta^*) = \sum_1^{\eta^*} A_j - \sum_{\eta^*+1}^n A_j > 0$$

i.e.,

$$\sum_1^{\eta^*} A_j > \sum_{\eta^*+1}^n A_j \quad \text{or} \quad \sum_1^{\eta^*} A_j > \tfrac{1}{2} \sum_1^n A_j$$

In case (2) of Fig. 1-10, $\sum_1^{\eta^*+1} A_j = \sum_1^{\eta^*} A_j = \tfrac{1}{2} \sum_1^n A_j$, and x^* is any value in the range $a_{\eta^*} \le x^* \le a_{\eta^*+1}$.

Notice that the optimal location x^* seems to be determined *independently* of the measures $\{a_j\}$. This is not quite true. What happens is that x^* is arrived at in two separate steps: the first step determines the interval (a_{n^*}, a_{n^*+1}) in which the new machine is to be placed. This is certainly dependent on the values $\{a_j\}$ as well as on $\{A_j\}$. The second step is to search for the optimal x^* within this interval, and this is independent of $\{a_j\}$.

Up to the present, our discussion has been limited to the *one dimensional* case. In two or three dimensions, the rectangular movement is retained (i.e., interaction is assumed to run parallel to the coordinate axes as, for example, in the case of material moved along aisles) and we have:

$$\text{minimize } F = \Sigma A_j |x - a_j| + \Sigma B_j |y - b_j| + \Sigma C_j |z - c_j|$$

Each summation is now minimized independently following the above procedure.

4.4. Criteria for Nondeterministic Systems

In the study of criteria for nondeterministic systems, many writers have stressed the difference between decision under *risk* and decision under *uncertainty*: the former assumes knowledge of the probability distribution function of the variable or variables involved, while the latter assumes complete ignorance concerning probabilities. The distinction is certainly helpful from pedagogical and classificatory points of view, though it may sometimes lead to confusion. This is the case, for example, in Laplace's rule of insufficient knowledge discussed below: it transforms decision under uncertainity to decision under risk by assigning probabilities in an arbitrary (though logical) fashion.

Without getting entangled in the pros and cons of such classification, we present below some criteria proposed for nondeterministic systems. The first six criteria may be considered examples of criteria for decision under risk, while the last four examples of criteria under uncertainty.

The criteria discussed are:
1. Minimization of the mean squared error
2. Minimization of terminal loss
3. Maximization of expected gain
4. Optimizing the probability of a specific event
5. Optimizing relative to the most likely future state
6. Satisfising to a known aspiration level
7. Minimizing the maximum deviation
8. The Laplace Criterion
9. The Minimax regret criterion
10. The Hurwicz Criterion

Minimization of the Mean Squared Error (Minimum-Variance)

It is certainly difficult to find a criterion that is used more profusely in the various branches of science, engineering, and mathematics than the minimum mean-squared-error criterion. Indeed, it is a standard criterion in the analysis and synthesis of stochastic systems, as the few examples presented below attempt to demonstrate. Perhaps the main attraction of this criterion is its mathematical tractability, an important asset indeed.

It is also used as a criterion in nonstochastic systems, for the minimization of the mean squared error (or equivalently, minimization of the sum of squared error) need not be confined in its application to stochastic systems, but can be equally used as a criterion for *deterministic* systems. Then, we need not be concerned with "error" per se, but with any other characteristic of the system.

As an example, consider the machine location problem discussed on p. 42. Instead of adopting the minimum absolute value of weighted distances as our criterion, we could have adopted the minimum weighted sum (or mean) of the squares of distances between the old machines and the new one. Using the same notation as in that machine location problem, the objective function would be replaced by

$$\text{minimize } F = \sum_j A_j (x - a_j)^2.$$

It is left to the reader to determine the optimal location of the new machine under this criterion and to compare the mathematical development with that presented on p. 44. (See also problem 12 at the end of the chapter.)

In the context of stochastic (or probabilistic) systems, an almost unlimited fund of examples is available on which to draw. Three such examples are included.

Example: Curve Fitting.

A standard problem in statistics, econometrics, engineering, and almost every branch of science based on empirical studies is the following: given N "points" $(x_1, y_1), (x_2, y_2), \ldots, (x_N, Y_N)$ where x_i is the value of the *independent* variable and y_i is the corresponding value of the *dependent* variable, can we represent the functional dependence of y on x as a polynomial of degree $n < N - 1$? Naturally, we seek the "best" representation, where "goodness" is measured relative to the "least-squares" criterion.

There are several important practical reasons for discovering such functional relationships between two variables. Foremost among these are: (1) the functional relationship may *reveal* some unknown *structure* of the underlying cause-and-effect system; (2) the analytical expression is

tractable in further mathematical analysis; and (3) the functional relationship is used to *forecast* the response of the system to any given input.

The simplest, nontrivial polynomial is, of course, of the first order,
Fig. 1-11,

$$y_i' = a + bx_i.$$

y_i' represents the "true" value of the dependent variable if the system is
error free. Since the actual reading obtained was y_i, the difference

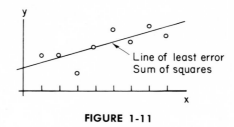

FIGURE 1-11

$(y_i - y_i')$ represents the random error or deviation from the (hypothetical)
ideal,

$$e_i = y_i - y_i' = y_i - (a + bx_i)$$

and the sum of the squared-error is a function of the unknown parameters
a and *b*,

$$G(a,b) = \sum_i e_i^2 = \sum_i [y_i - (a + bx_i)]^2$$

We must determine *a* and *b* in an optimal fashion, i.e., to minimize *G*.
Taking partial derivatives and equating to zero we obtain

$$\frac{\partial G}{\partial a} = \sum 2[y_i - (a + bx_i)][-1] = 0$$

i.e.,

$$\sum y_i = Na + b \sum x_i \tag{1-16a}$$

$$\frac{\partial G}{\partial b} = \sum 2[y_i - (a + bx_i)] \ [-x_i] = 0$$

i.e.,

$$\sum x_i y_i = a \sum x_i + b \sum x_i^2 \tag{1-16 b}$$

Eqs. (1-16a) and (1-16b) are the well-known "normal equations" which are solved to yield

$$a = \frac{\sum y_i \sum x_i^2 - \sum x_i \sum x_i y_i}{N \sum x_i^2 - \left(\sum x_i\right)^2}, \quad b = \frac{N \sum x_i y_i - \sum x_i \sum y_i}{N \sum x_i^2 - \left(\sum x_i\right)^2}.$$

For computing purposes, it is much more convenient to take the origin of the x, y coordinates at the point $(\bar{x}, \bar{y})$, where $\bar{x} = \frac{1}{N} \Sigma x_i$ and $\bar{y} = \frac{1}{N} \Sigma y_i$;

$$y_i' - \bar{y} = a + b(x_i - \bar{x}).$$

Following the same procedure as above we obtain

$$a^* = 0 \quad \text{and} \quad b^* = \frac{\sum (v_i - \bar{y})(x_i - \bar{x})}{\sum (x_i - \bar{x})^2} \tag{1-17}$$

and the straight line is given by

$$y_i' - \bar{y} = b^*(x_i - \bar{x}).$$

Needless to say, the approach is applicable to any polynomial of order $n < N - 1$,

$$y_i = a_0 x_i^n + a_1 x_i^{n-1} + \cdots + a_n$$

In this case, we take $n + 1$ partial derivatives and solve for the optimal set $a_0^*, a_1^*, \ldots, a_n^*$.

As was mentioned, least squares estimates of regression curves—as the above lines are called—are extensively used in forecasting. The rationale for their use rests on certain assumptions concerning the stochastic behavior of the assumed *random* error. But we do not have to go into such detailed analysis here. We wish only to note such use and make a few remarks concerning forecasting· in general. We shall refer again in Chapter 6 to another method of forecasting called "exponential smoothing." The reader is encouraged to compare the two approaches concerning computational ease and speed of response to a changing environment.

Generally speaking, two properties are desirable in any forecasting technique. First, if the underlying causation system remains stationary, i.e., if no sudden and definite variation in the level of any of the factors affecting the system occurs, then the *average* of the process should be estimated since all deviations from the average are *random* and hence unpredictable. On the other hand, should a definite variation in the system occur (an "assignable cause" in the parlance of statistical quality control),

the forecasting technique must "catch up" with the fact and predict performance based on the new environment. These two desired objectives
can be summarized as follows: we want the forecasting technique to exhibit stability in the face of "noise" but to react with minimum time delay
to any change in the causation system. It is interesting to speculate on the
behavior of such regression lines under differently changing environments.

Example: Estimating the Mean of a Population

The following problem in statistical inference is often encountered. If
$x_1, x_2, \ldots, x_n$ are the values obtained in a random sample of size n from
a population with mean μ, unknown, and variance σ^2, also unknown,
what is the "best" estimate of μ? If we restrict ourselves to the class of
linear estimates—and naturally we are interested in *unbiased* estimates,
i.e., estimates whose mathematical expectation is the unknown parameter
μ—what is the *minimum-variance* estimate?

Let S be the statistic estimating μ, and let

$$S = a_1 X_1 + a_2 X_2 + \cdots + a_n X_n$$

so that

$$a_1 + a_2 + \cdots + a_n = 1 \tag{1-18}$$

i.e., S is a *smoothed* average of the observations.

Here $X_1, \ldots, X_n$ are random variables with the given but unknown
distribution. Clearly, S is unbiased since

$$\mathcal{E}(S) = \sum_i a_i \, \mathcal{E}(X_i) = \mu \sum_i a_i = \mu.$$

Now, the variance of S is given by

$$\mathrm{Var}\,[S] = \sum_i a_i^2 \,\mathrm{Var}\,[X_i]$$

$$= \sum_i a_i^2 \sigma^2 \tag{1-19}$$

Thus, we wish to minimize Eq. (1-19) subject to the constraint of
Eq. (1-18). The answer is given by

$$a_i = \frac{1}{n}$$

whence

$$S = \frac{1}{n}(X_1 + X_2 + \cdots + X_n) = \overline{X},$$

the arithmetic mean.

Incidentally, the problem of maximizing the quadratic function of Eq. (1-19) subject to the linear constraint of Eq. (1-18) can be treated either by the method of dynamic programming or by the method of Lagrange multipliers.

Example: Wiener's Optimal Filter of Statistical Input

Our third example is drawn from the field of communications engineering and deals with the optimal design of filters, where optimality is measured against the least-squares (or minimum-variance) criterion. This approach was first proposed independently by Wiener[†] and by Kolmogoroff in 1941 and has formed the foundation of the design of such systems.

FIGURE 1-12 $f_i(t) \longrightarrow \boxed{g(t)} \longrightarrow f_0(t)$

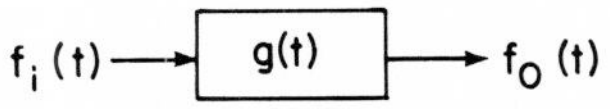

Suppose that a time-varying signal $f_i(t)$ is the input to a system whose impulse response is $g(t)$, resulting in output $f_o(t)$. (See Fig. 1-12.) That is, the output of the system is related to the input by the well-known convolution integral

$$f_o(t) = \int_0^t f_i(\tau) g(t - \tau) d\tau.$$

Let the *desired output* be $f_d(t)$. Then, the average squared error (between actual and desired outputs) is given by

$$\overline{e^2} = \lim_{T \to \infty} \frac{1}{2T} \int_{-T}^{T} [f_o(t) - f_d(t)]^2 dt,$$

where the bar over the square of e indicates the time average. It is desired to design the system, i.e., decide upon the optimal response $g^*(t)$, which minimizes e^2.

It is possible to carry out the analysis for the minimization of $\overline{e^2}$ with respect to $g(t)$ in either the time or the complex-frequency domain. Although the details of the analysis are straightforward, we shall not pursue them here because they involve manipulations in the complex domain, which are introduced at a later point. Suffice it to say, that such analysis indicates that the optimal filter is a function *only* of the *correlation functions* (auto- and cross-correlation functions) of the input and output. This is a startling result which we shall use later in our study of feedback control systems. Needless to say, this result is a direct consequence of the criterion adopted.

[†]Norbert Wiener, *The Interpolation, Extrapolation, and Smoothing of Time Series*, Wiley, New York, 1950.

Minimization of Terminal Loss

This criterion is adopted whenever the intermediate errors in a process are immaterial but the final error or deviation is decisive. If decision d_i gives rise to terminal error e_i, then the optimal decision d^* yields the min $\{e_i\}$. In stochastic processes we may be interested in minimizing the *expected* terminal error or loss.

Oftentimes the same problem can be formulated as optimization with respect to this criterion or to some other criterion; the difference is more semantic than real. An example is the machine sequencing problem treated in Chapter 4, §9. This problem is usually stated as the minimization of *total completion time* of n jobs on m machines. Equivalently, we can ask for *minimizing the error* (i.e., time lag) between the completion *of the terminal event* and some known lower bound on the total time for completion.

Needless to say, the same comment applies to other criteria. A reformulation of the problem—together with a change in the criterion—is sometimes more of a rewording of the objective than a fundamental change in the problem, and the same result is achieved. Another instance of the comment is the inventory example given below. The problem is formulated as the minimization of the terminal expected cost; it could well be formulated as the minimization of the expected cost of a one-stage inventory process. The criterion may also be stated as the maximization of some terminal state variable. For example, one of the problems of putting a satellite into orbit is to maximize the terminal (i.e., at burnout) horizontal velocity subject to certain constraints.

A common example of application of the minimum-terminal-error criterion is provided by Vajda.[†] A man wishes to cross a river in a boat; (see Fig. 1-13). The velocity of the boat is a constant c, and at a distance x from the starting position the current velocity is v_x. What is his optimal direction of movement, θ_x^*, at every distance x to minimize his terminal distance downstream from the starting position? The solution to this problem is a straightforward application of the theory of dynamic programming and is left as an exercise for the reader.

As an illustration of the application of the criterion we discuss in greater detail a terminal inventory problem treated by Hadley and Whitin.[‡]

Example: Optimal Terminal Inventory[*]

Stored items subject to obsolescence present the peculiar problem of a loss incurred when the item is not utilized. The problem is encountered

[†] S. Vajda, *Mathematical Programming*, Addison-Wesley, Reading, Mass., 1961, p. 251.
[‡] G. Hadley and T. M. Whitin, "An Optimal Final Inventory Model," *Mgt. Sc.*, Vol. 7, No. 2, Jan. 1961, pp. 179–183.
[*] This example may be skipped on first reading.

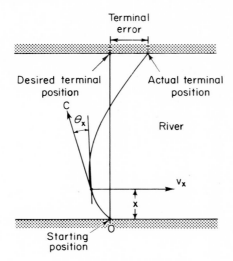

FIGURE 1-13

most frequently in the context of spare parts for specialized machinery. The demand is probabilistic with a very low rate, and beyond a certain period of time—specifically, the expected useful life of the equipment— the spare parts are useless except for resale as scrap. When the operating system involves several units of such equipment, the dynamic aspect of maintaining a stock of spare parts continues until no further new equip- ment is purchased. Obsolescence enters into the picture in the last stage of the process. It is desired to determine, in an optimal fashion, the final inventory, i.e., the inventory to be held on hand when it is known that no further replenishments will be made. The criterion is to minimize the *expected* cost of this terminal inventory.

Assume the cost function to be composed of a loss c_0 per unit of inven- tory at the time of obsolescence, a cost of investment h per unit per unit of time, and a stockout penalty π per unit per unit time. In the usual circumstances $h < c_0 < \pi$.

We also assume the demand for the item to be Poisson distributed with mean rate λ, constant over time. The date of obsolescence is also as- sumed known and fixed, T.

Let $p(x, \lambda t)$ denote the probability that x units are demanded in a period of length t, $0 \leq t \leq T$. That is,

$$p(x, \lambda t) = \frac{(\lambda t)^x e^{-\lambda t}}{x!}.$$

The expected cost with N units on hand is given by

$$\mathcal{E}C(N) = c_0 \sum_{x=0}^{N-1} (N - x)\, p(x,\lambda T) + h \int_0^T \sum_{x=0}^{N-1} (N - x)p(x,\lambda t)\, dt$$

$$+ \pi \int_0^T \sum_{x=N}^{\infty} (x - N)\, p(x,\lambda t)\, dt \qquad\qquad (1\text{-}26)$$

If N^* is the optimal final inventory, we must have $\mathcal{E}C(N^*) < \mathcal{E}C(N^* - 1)$ and $\mathcal{E}C(N^*) < \mathcal{E}C(N^* + 1)$. Define the operator Δ as

$$\Delta\mathcal{E}C(N) = \mathcal{E}C(N + 1) - \mathcal{E}C(N).$$

Then if N^* is optimal, it must be true that

$$\Delta\,\mathcal{E}C(N^* - 1) < 0 \qquad \text{and} \qquad \Delta\mathcal{E}C(N^*) \geq 0.$$

Obviously N^* is the largest N for which $\Delta\mathcal{E}C(N^* - 1) < 0$ (if $\Delta\mathcal{E}C(N) = 0$ then either N or $N + 1$ is optimal). From Eq. (1-26)

$$\Delta\mathcal{E}C(N - 1) = c_0 \sum_0^{N-1} p(x,\lambda T) + h \int_0^T \sum_0^{N-1} p(x,\lambda T)\, dt$$

$$- \pi \int_0^T \sum_N^{\infty} p(x,\lambda t)\, dt. \qquad\qquad (1\text{-}27)$$

But $\displaystyle\int_0^T p(x,\lambda t)\, dt = \int_0^T \frac{(\lambda t)^x e^{-\lambda t}}{x!}\, dt = \frac{\lambda^x}{x!} \int_0^T t^x e^{-\lambda t}\, dt.$ Integrating the last expression by parts we obtain

$$- \frac{1}{\lambda} \frac{(\lambda T)^x}{x!} e^{-\lambda T} + \frac{\lambda^{x-1}}{(x - 1)!} \int_0^T t^{x-1} e^{-\lambda t}\, dt.$$

The second term is of identical form to the integral we started with; hence successive integration leads to the series

$$- \frac{1}{\lambda} \frac{(\lambda T)^x}{x!} e^{-\lambda T} - \frac{1}{\lambda} \frac{(\lambda T)^{x-1}}{(x - 1)!} e^{-\lambda T} - \cdots$$

$$- \frac{1}{\lambda} (\lambda T) e^{-\lambda T} + \int_0^T e^{-\lambda T}\, dt,$$

which immediately yields

$$\int_0^T p(x,\lambda t)\, dt = \frac{1}{\lambda} \sum_{u=x+1}^{\infty} p(u,\lambda T).$$

We can now simplify Eq (1-27) to

$$\Delta \mathcal{E} C(N - 1) = c_0 \sum_{0}^{N-1} p(x, \lambda T) + \frac{h}{\lambda} \sum_{x=0}^{N-1} \sum_{u=x+1}^{\infty} p(u, \lambda T)$$

$$- \frac{\pi}{\lambda} \int_{0}^{T} \sum_{N}^{\infty} p(x, \lambda t) \, dt$$

Expanding the double summations it is easy to see that

$$\Delta \mathcal{E} C(N - 1) = c_0 \sum_{u=0}^{N-1} p(u, \lambda T) + \frac{h}{\lambda} \sum_{u=0}^{N} u \cdot p(u, \lambda T) + \frac{hN}{\lambda}$$

$$\cdot \sum_{u=N+1}^{\infty} p(u, \lambda T) - \frac{\pi}{\lambda} \sum_{u=0}^{\infty} u \cdot p(N + u, \lambda T).$$

But

$$\sum_{u=0}^{N} u \cdot p(u, \lambda T) = \sum_{u=0}^{N} \lambda T \cdot p(u - 1, \lambda T) = \lambda T \left[\sum_{u=1}^{N} \frac{(\lambda T)^{u-1}}{(u - 1)!} e^{-\lambda T} \right]$$

$$= \lambda T \left[1 - \sum_{u=N}^{\infty} p(u, \lambda T) \right] = \lambda T - \sum_{u=N}^{\infty} \lambda T \cdot p(u, \lambda T)$$

$$= \lambda T - \sum_{u=N}^{\infty} \frac{(\lambda T)^{u+1} e^{-\lambda T}}{u!} = \sum_{u=N+1}^{\infty} u \cdot p(u, \lambda T),$$

which leads to the further simplification

$$\Delta \mathcal{E} C(N - 1) = c_0 \sum_{u=0}^{N-1} p(u, \lambda T) + hT \left[1 - \sum_{u=N}^{\infty} p(u, \lambda T) \right] + \frac{hN}{\lambda}$$

$$\cdot \sum_{u=N+1}^{\infty} p(u, \lambda T) - \frac{\pi}{\lambda} \left[\lambda T \sum_{u=N}^{\infty} p(u, \lambda T) - N \sum_{u=N+1}^{\infty} p(u, \lambda T) \right].$$

Since $\sum_{u=0}^{\infty} u \cdot p(N + u, \lambda T) = \sum_{u=N+1}^{\infty} (u - N) p(u, \lambda T) = \lambda T \sum_{u=N}^{\infty} p(u, \lambda T)$

$- N \sum_{u=N+1}^{\infty} p(u, \lambda T)$, we finally have

$$\Delta \mathcal{E} C(N - 1) = c_0 - c_0 \sum_{u=N}^{\infty} p(u, \lambda T) + h T - h T \sum_{u=N}^{\infty} p(u, \lambda T)$$

$$+ \frac{h N}{\lambda} \sum_{u=N}^{\infty} p(u, \lambda T) - \frac{h N}{\lambda} p(N, \lambda T) - \pi T \sum_{u=N}^{\infty} p(u, \lambda T)$$

$$+ \frac{\pi N}{\lambda} \sum_{u=N}^{\infty} p(u, \lambda T) - \frac{\pi N}{\lambda} p(N, \lambda T)$$

$$= A(T) - B(N, T) + D(N, T) \tag{1-28}$$

where

$$A(T) = (c_0 + h T) \left[1 - \sum_{u=N}^{\infty} p(u, \lambda T) \right]$$

$$B(N, T) = \frac{N(h + \pi)}{\lambda} p(N, \lambda T)$$

$$D(N, T) = \left[\frac{N(h + \pi)}{\lambda} - \pi T \right] \sum_{u=N}^{\infty} p(u, \lambda T).$$

A, B and D can be evaluated using Poisson tables. The optimal N^* is the largest N for which Eq. (1-28) is ≤ 0.

It is obvious that the optimal final inventory varies with T, the time to obsolescence. Fig. 1-14 depicts such a functional relationship for the following values of parameters: $c_0 = \$200$, $\pi = \$900$, $h = \$0.10$ and $\lambda = 0.01$. Such a curve can be utilized in determining the quantity of replenishment throughout the last phase of the life of the system.

Maximization of Expected Gain

Maximization of expected gain is a straightforward generalization of its deterministic counterpart, the maximization of average gain (over time). Implicit in the criterion is the notion of repeated trials. It is sometimes difficult to justify the adoption of this criterion when this repeated-trials premise is challenged.

No examples of the application of this criterion will be given since we shall encounter it quite frequently in future studies. A few inventory problems are given as exercises for the reader at the end of the chapter.

Optimizing the Probability of a Specific Event

In certain processes attention is usually—but not exclusively—focused on a specific event such as the occurrence of a defective unit, the occur-

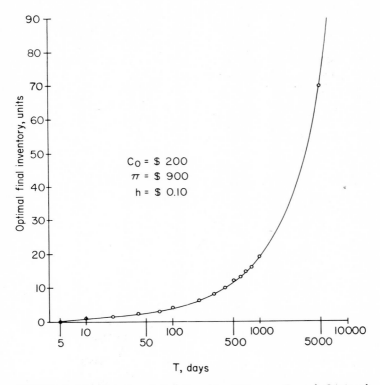

FIGURE 1-14   Functional Relationship Between T and Optimal Inventory

rence of overflow, the shifting of frequency from one section of the spectrum to the other, the attaining of a certain altitude in flight, etc.. The event of interest occurs with a certain probability, e.g., α. It is desired to choose the decision—or design the process—that minimizes (or maximizes) α, depending on whether it is an undesirable or a desirable event.

Example: Determination of Buffer Inventories

Consider the following inventory problem.   Demand for item i, y_i, is uniformly distributed about a known average μ_i and with range $2d_i$. That is, the density function of y_i is of the form

$$f_i(y) = \begin{cases} 1/2d_i & \text{if} \quad \mu_i - d_i \leq y_i \leq \mu_i + d_i \\ 0 & \text{otherwise} \end{cases}$$

Because of the continuing nature of the demand, the average quantity of replenishment in period t, q_{it}, is set at a constant level $q_{it} = \mu_i$ for all t. That is, assuming stationarity of the demand distribution function, and assuming the independence of demand in any period of past or future demand, the average supply is set equal to the average demand. Let B_i be the buffer inventory (i.e., safety stock) of item i. We shall assume that any deviation of the actual inventory at the beginning of the period from B_i is absorbed in the replenishment quantity $q_{it} = \mu_i$ so that the starting buffer inventory in each period is exactly B_i.

Finally, suppose that we have a restriction on the aggregate average capital investment which we do not want to exceed. The problem is to determine the optimal buffer inventories $\{B_i\}$, $i = 1, 2, \ldots, n$, which *minimize the probability α of a stock-out condition* on any item. That is, we wish to minimize α in

$$\alpha = P(y_i > B_i + q_i) \qquad\qquad i = 1, \cdots n \qquad (1\text{-}29)$$

so that

$$\sum_i c_i(q_i/2 + B_i) \le I \qquad\qquad (1\text{-}30)$$

where c_i is the cost of item i, $(q_i/2 + B_i)$ is the average units in inventory of item i, and I is the upper limit on the average invested capital.

But the probability $P(y_i \ge B_i + q_i) = \dfrac{d_i - B_i}{2d_i}$. Also, it is obvious that if the constraint on the total average investment is limiting, the inequality of Eq. (1-30) will be satisfied as *equality*. Hence, the problem is reduced to

$$\text{Minimize } \alpha \qquad\qquad (1\text{-}31)$$

so that

$$B_i + 2d_i\alpha = d_i \qquad\qquad i = 1, \cdots, n \qquad (1\text{-}32)$$

and

$$\sum_i c_i B_i = I - \sum_i c_i q_i/2 = L \qquad\qquad (1\text{-}33)$$

In Eqs. (1-32) and (1-33) we have transformed the probabilistic statement of (1-29) and (1-30) to the equivalent deterministic statements. Since this is a system of $(n + 1)$ independent equations in $(n + 1)$ unknowns, (the n B_i's and α), it yields a unique solution if one exists. The question of minimization of α is irrelevant since the convex set of the linear program specified by Eqs. (1-31) to (1-33) degenerates to one point.

In matrix form we have

$$
\begin{bmatrix}
1 & \cdot & \cdot & \cdot & \cdot & \cdot & 0 & 2d_1 \\
\cdot & & & & & & & \cdot \\
\cdot & & & & & & & \cdot \\
\cdot & & & & & & & \cdot \\
0 & \cdot & \cdot & \cdot & \cdot & \cdot & 1 & 2d_n \\
c_1 & \cdot & \cdot & \cdot & \cdot & \cdot & c_n & 0
\end{bmatrix}
\begin{bmatrix}
B_1 \\ \cdot \\ \cdot \\ \cdot \\ B_n \\ \alpha
\end{bmatrix}
=
\begin{bmatrix}
d_1 \\ \cdot \\ \cdot \\ \cdot \\ d_n \\ L
\end{bmatrix} ;
$$

The inverse of the square matrix is immediately available as

$$
\frac{-1}{b}
\begin{bmatrix}
(b - c_1 d_1) & - c_2 d_1 & \cdot & \cdot & \cdot & \cdot & \cdot & - c_n d_1 & d_1 \\
- c_1 d_2 & (b - c_2 d_2) & & & & & & - c_n d_2 & d_2 \\
\cdot\cdot & & & & & & & & \cdot \\
\cdot\cdot & & & & & & & & \\
\cdot & & & & & & & & \cdot \\
- c_1 d_n & - c_2 d_n & & & & & & (b - c_n d_n) & d_n \\
\dfrac{c_1}{2} & \dfrac{c_2}{2} & \cdot & \cdot & \cdot & \cdot & \cdot & \dfrac{c_n}{2} & \dfrac{-1}{2}
\end{bmatrix}
$$

where $b = \Sigma_i c_i d_i$. Therefore,

$$
B_i = \frac{1}{b} \left\{ (b - c_i d_i) d_i - \sum_{k \neq i} c_k d_i d_k + L d_i \right\} = \frac{d_i}{b} \cdot L \tag{1-34}
$$

and

$$
\alpha = \frac{1}{b} \left\{ \sum_i \frac{c_i}{2} d_i - \frac{L}{2} \right\} = \frac{1}{2} - \frac{L}{2b} \tag{1-35}
$$

Equations (1-34) and (1-35) bear interesting interpretations. d_i is the half-range of the distribution of demand and, for this particular distribution function, d_i is proportional to the standard deviation σ_i, (specifically, $d_i = \sqrt{3}\ \sigma_i$). Hence, the optimal rule is to apportion the available residual capital $L(= I - \Sigma_i c_i q_i / 2)$ in the ratio of the cost of one standard deviation to the sum of the costs of all standard deviations. Also, since α is ≥ 0, (being the probability of an event), we must have $1 - L/b \geq 0$, i.e.,

$$
I \leq b + \sum_i c_i q_i / 2 = \sum_i c_i (d_i + q_i / 2) \tag{1-36}
$$

which is a natural upper limit on the available capital if the restriction is to be "active" since the right hand side of Eq. (1-36) is the average cost of investment for 100% assurance against out-of-stock conditions.

Admittedly, the problem treated in this example is a drastic simplification of practical situations. However, as the discussion above indicates, the results obtained yield meaningful interpretations, to which we add one more remark. We seem to have ignored *cost* completely, since the criterion is relative to the *probability* of occurrence of stockout. However, cost values can be *imputed* from the solution obtained from probabilistic considerations *and vice versa*: if we were minimizing costs we could impute a probability of stockout to the solution. Naturally, the solution is optimal relative to only one objective, either probability or cost. This is a rather important point, and the reader is encouraged to develop the facility of imputing one measure from the optimal solution relative to another measure. (See also problem 6 at the end of the chapter.)

Optimizing Relative to the Most Likely Future State

According to this criterion the system may be in any one of several states, with a known probability of being in any particular state. We choose the state with the *highest probability* and act as though the system were *certain* to be in that state. Optimization then follows some other criterion.

Needless to say, this mode of behavior is subject to serious question. In the case of a large number of possible states, each with a small probability, the criterion requires that we ignore all states but one (whose probability may be of the order of 0.05) and act as though it were certain to occur! To many practical decision makers this may not be a satisfactory procedure. Also, there is the possibility of multi-modal probability distribution functions of states. That is, two or more states may have equal probabilities, in which case the criterion is ambiguous and breaks down completely.

"Satisfising" to a Known Aspiration Level

For a given "aspiration level" L, select the alternative which maximizes the probability that the outcome will be $\geq L$, assuming such an alternative exists. Another interpretation of the criterion is the following: for a given satisfactory level L concerning one measure of the behavior of the system, optimize relative to another measure.

Example: System Reliability

In many applications the performance of a system is satisfactory if it attains some given reliability figure R. The objective then is to optimize the performance of the system relative to another measure (e.g., relative to minimizing cost, total weight, etc.) so that the reliability of the system is still maintained $\geq R$. (Problem 20 at the end of the chapter is an application of this principle.)

Example: Statistical Hypothesis Testing

Another application of the criterion in a different field is to the resolution of problems of testing hypotheses. Suppose that a random sample of size n is taken from a normal population of unknown mean μ and known variance σ^2. We wish to test the hypothesis $H_0 : \mu = \mu_0$ against the alternative hypothesis $H_1 : \mu \neq \mu_0$, with the following proviso: if the true population mean is actually μ_0, we do not want to reject H_0 a proportion of the time greater than α_0 (usually set at 0.05 or 0.01). The probability α_0 is called the "size" of the test, and the error committed in rejecting H_0 *when it is in fact true* is called "error of type I." Of course, the only other type of error that can be committed in such a decision situation is to accept H_0 *when it is in fact false*. This is called "error of type II," and occurs with probability β.

Now, the problem is to design the test, i.e., decide upon the statistic to be used and the limits of acceptance and rejection of H_0 based on the given sample, to minimize β so that the size of the test α is $\geq \alpha_0$.

The reader is referred to any text on statistics for examples of the application of statistical hypothesis testing.

Minimization of the Maximum Deviation (or Expected Deviation)

Here it is assumed that each decision entails an error which varies deterministically or randomly between known limits. We wish to choose the criterion that minimizes the maximum possible such error.

This criterion was first suggested by Wald and investigated rather intensively in the field of statistical decision theory. By its very construct, the criterion is *pessimistic* since it guards against the worst possible consequence in every decision. We discuss below several attempts to dilute such pessimism. For the present, we illustrate the application of the criterion to a decision situation in the area of quality control.

Example: A Quality Control Problem

In many situations the outcome of a process (or the output of a system) is a chance variable which depends on uncontrollable parameter (or parameters). For instance, the "outgoing quality" of a product varies randomly depending on the average (i.e., long-run) percent defective p. The amount of an item in stock may vary randomly depending on supply, demand, and lead time variations; furthermore, if these variables are assumed to be Poisson distributed with means μ_s, μ_d and μ_l, respectively, then the expected "on hand" inventory is a function of these three parameters. The total cost of a service facility such as tool cribs in a large factory or runways in an airport, is composed of the cost of providing the facility plus the cost of any waiting time on the part of the customers. The demand on the services of the facility is usually stochastic in nature with a known or unknown distribution function. The total cost of service depends on the specific values of the parameters of the demand distribution function (e.g., the mean and variance).

Let us return to the quality control example. Suppose that production is in lots of size N and inspection is based on a sample of size n. The usual procedure is to inspect the n items in the sample. Then if c units or less are defective, the lot is accepted and if more than c units are defective, the lot is rejected. Here c is called the "acceptance number." Let P_a denote the probability of accepting a lot. With n fixed, P_a is clearly dependent on the average per cent defective p in the product as well as on the acceptance number c. Assume that any defectives in the sample are replaced with good units; the remaining $N - n$ units in each lot are passed with no further inspection if the lot is accepted, but are screened 100% if the lot is rejected.

According to this scheme when a lot is accepted, which occurs with probability P_a, on the average $p(N - n)$ defective units will be shipped to the customer. We define the Average Outgoing Quality as

$$AOQ = \frac{P_a p(N - n)}{N} = P_a p \left(1 - \frac{n}{N}\right). \tag{1-37}$$

We emphasize that Eq. (1-37) yields the average fraction defective in lots of size N subjected to the inspection plan described above. The actual number of defectives in any lot will vary in a random fashion.

For any given c the AOQ is a function of p only. If p is not constant over time, which is the case in practice, the AOQ will vary with the variation in p, $0 \le p \le 1$, yielding a curve of the form shown in Fig. 1-15. Naturally, if p is close to 0, the proportion of defectives in the outgoing lots will be close to zero. While if p is close to 1 the proportion of defectives in the outgoing lots will still be close to zero because the lots will be rejected and the defectives replaced through 100% inspection. The maximum ordinate of the curve represents the highest fraction defective attainable under the inspection plan and is called, naturally enough, the Average Outgoing Quality Limit—$AOQL$ for short.

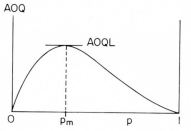

FIGURE 1-15

It is easy to see that the average number of units inspected ·per lot is equal to

$$I = n + (1 - P_a)(N - n).$$

Notice that P_a itself is a function of the fraction defective p for any given c. Suppose now that the average total operating cost, C, to the producing firm is composed of two parts: (1) the average cost of sampling, s, per unit sampled and (2) the average cost of replacing defective units shipped to the customer, r, per unit defective. Then,

$$C = s[n + (1 - P_a)(N - n)] + rN(AOQ)$$

with r usually $> s$.

If the producer wishes to operate conservatively he would adopt the minimax expected cost criterion. The problem then reduces to the choice of the sample size $n \leq \gamma N$, (the fraction γ represents an upper bound on the sample size, usually taken at 10 to 15%), and the acceptance number c, so that *the maximum expected cost is minimized for all* values of p, $0 \leq p \leq 1$.

The detailed calculation of such optimal decision is left as an exercise to the reader at the end of the chapter.

The Laplace Criterion

This criterion, as well as the following two criteria, is concerned with decision making in "one shot" decisions under conditions of uncertainty.

It is assumed that there are available m alternative decisions $d_1, \ldots, d_m$, and that the system may be in any one of n different states $s_1, \ldots, s_n$. If decision d_i is made and the state of the system (state of "nature," as it is usually called) turns out to be s_j, a reward (or penalty) $r(i, j)$ accrues to the decision maker. This is the case, for example, of the production manager who may either continue with current facilities (decision d_1) or purchase new facilities (decision d_2). The market may be in any one of three states: declining (state s_1), steady (state s_2), or expanding (state s_3). The consequence of any decision he makes and any market condition is a certain amount of profit (reward) which is, obviously, a function of both decision d_i and state s_j.

It is easy to see that the data can be reduced to a matrix format, in which the m rows represent the decisions and the n columns represent the states of "nature," and the entries in the body of the matrix are the rewards $r(i, j)$ for $i = 1, \ldots, m$ and $j = 1, \ldots, n$. The matrix is usually referred to as the "payoff matrix." The problem is to determine the optimal decision.

The Laplace criterion is based on the so-called "principle of insufficient reason." That is, since any one of the n states may ensue, assume they are *equally probable*, and then choose the decision that yields the *maximum expected reward* (or minimum expected loss).

For example, consider the following "payoff matrix:"

THE PAYOFF MATRIX

States Decisions	s_1	s_2	s_3	s_4	s_5
d_1	3	1	3	2	6
d_2	6	7	-5	8	0
d_3	3	4	-1	-2	9
d_4	3	3	2	-2	-1

(1-38)

There are five possible states, assumed equally probable, each with probability $1/5$. The expected gain from each decision is as follows:

Decision	Expected Gain
d_1	3
d_2	3.2
d_3	2.6
d_4	1.0

Hence the optimal decision is d_2.

The Minimax Regret Criterion

First suggested by Savage,[†] this criterion introduces the notion of "regret" which is the difference between the best possible payoff in any state and the actual payoff under the specific decision made. The optimal decision is the decision which minimizes the maximum possible regret.

Applying this criterion to the payoff matrix of (1-38), we first construct the regret matrix:

THE REGRET MATRIX

	s_1	s_2	s_3	s_4	s_5
d_1	3	6	0	6	3
d_2	0	0	8	0	9
d_3	3	3	4	10	0
d_4	3	4	1	10	10

The optimal decision is then d_1 since the maximum regret under d_1 (6 units) is less than the maximum regret under any other decision.

[†]L. J. Savage, "The Theory of Statistical Decision," *Journal of the American Statistical Association*, Vol. 46, pp. 56–67, 1951.

The Hurwicz[†] Criterion

This criterion is an attempt to give explicit expression to the subjective "degree of optimism." This latter is represented by a fraction α between 0 and 1. Under decision d_i the optimist would concentrate on the maximum reward $\bar{r}(i, j)$, while the pessimist would be concerned with the minimum possible reward, $\underline{r}(i, j)$. This criterion combines these two payoffs with weights α and $(1 - \alpha)$, respectively, and chooses as optimal the decision with the maximum weighted gain, $0 \leq \alpha \leq 1$.

As an example we utilize once more the payoff matrix of (1-38). The series of calculations with $\alpha = 0.8$ are given in Table 1-7:

TABLE 1-7.

Decision	$\bar{r}(i,j)$	$\underline{r}(i,j)$	$\alpha r + (1 - \alpha) r$
d_1	6	1	5
d_2	8	-5	5.4
d_3	9	-2	6.8
d_4	3	-2	2.0

According to this criterion the optimal decision is d_3.

It is instructive to compare the optimal decisions obtained *with the same payoff matrix* but under different criteria, particularly under the last four criteria. This is accomplished in Table 1-8.

TABLE 1-8.

Criterion	Optimal Decision	Payoff
Maxmin	d_1	1
Laplace	d_2	3.2
Minimax		
Regret	d_3	6
Hurwicz	d_3	6.8

A natural question to ask is: which criterion to adopt and which payoff to expect? Unfortunately, there is no answer to this question, since it is dependent on the strategic objectives of the system. We shall discuss this point in the following section.

§5. THE LEVELS OF DECISION

Production systems exhibit a wide range of complexity and varying degrees of sophistication. In the previous section we discussed some of the

[†]L. Hurwicz, "Optimality Criteria for Decision Making Under Ignorance," *Cowles Commission Discussion Paper, Statistics*, No. 370, 1951.

criteria used in designing such systems. In this section we discuss an important aspect of decision making, namely, the classification of the levels at which decisions are made in the *design and operation* of systems. The reader is urged to correlate these levels with our discussion in §2 relative to the steps of systems study.

In general, decisions can be classified as:

1. *Strategic*, i.e., goal-setting
2. *Tactical*, i.e., policy determining
3. *Technical*, i.e., operating.

At the outset we emphasize that the design of any system involves all three levels of decision, independent of the size of the undertaking. Moreover, the importance of the decisions follows the order of their listing above.

A *strategic* decision sets the objective and determines the goal (or goals) to be achieved. It is usually made at a high level of authority and responsibility and is to be credited with all the subsequent activities. Increasing production by 25%, doubling the Gross National Income over the next 5 years, and liquidating certain activities over a given period of time are all examples of strategic decisions. In the military field the decision made during World War II to destroy Nazi Germany first rather than Japan is a classic example of a strategic decision.

Even among strategic decisions there are different stages which we shall not enumerate. It is important to realize, however, that any decision on the *criterion* to be adopted in evaluating the performance of a system or a component is a strategic decision.

Once the objective and criterion (or criteria) are decided upon, a second level of activities takes place. These activities involve *tactical* decisions, viz., decisions that determine the course of action to be followed in order to optimize performance. Our treatment in the previous sections (as well as in future chapters) exemplifies tactical decisions. For instance, consider the model of Deterministic Variable Demand of §3 above. The analysis was undertaken to determine the *optimal ordering policy* $\{q_t{}^*\}$ relative to the already established criterion of minimizing total operating costs. In military operations, tactical decisions are exemplified by the design of the invading forces in Europe to achieve the already established objective of destroying Nazi Germany.

The third level comprises *technical* decisions, i.e., the decisions that launch and maintain the system in operating condition.

A system of statistical quality control furnishes an excellent everyday example of the three levels of decision discussed above. The strategic decision involves the determination of the "process capabilities," which is usually established after extensive testing and a reasonably long "shake down" period. Once the objective is set through the specification of the process capabilities, statisticians and engineers are involved in the determination of the minimum-cost sampling inspection scheme to be followed. This is the phase of tactical decisions. Finally, when the sampling plan is determined, the quality-control department takes over the responsibility of actually drawing the samples, plotting the control chart, carrying out the necessary tests of significance, and, naturally, alerting the responsible authorities should an "assignable cause" be suspected. This is the operational phase of the system.

Needless to say, no process or production system remains static throughout its life. Improvements occur perhaps through better inputs (such as better material) or through the availability of better technology. Then it is necessary to re-examine the whole system in view of the new developments. A systems study is initiated to determine new objectives, new policies for achieving such objectives, and new operating procedures for implementing the policies.

§6. COMPONENT VERSUS SYSTEM PERFORMANCE

An immediate consequence of adopting the systems approach is that action, decision, and performance are weighed in the context of their effect on the overall performance of the system. Consequently improving the performance of a component may be good, ineffectual, or actually harmful to the performance of the system as a whole.

Consider the following three examples:

1. Production-inventory systems oftentimes involve the function of *forecasting*. It is well known that there is a "penalty for ignorance," which the firm pays whenever the actual market deviates significantly from its estimates. Improved forecasts of business activities will almost always lead to *improved* total system performance. Naturally, there is a degree of accuracy of forecasts beyond which any expenditure of effort or money is not recovered. However, real-life firms are working with such poor forecasting tools that such a point is not likely to be achieved for some time.

2. Our second example is drawn from the field of electrical communication theory. Suppose that a system is receiving a continuous signal which varies with time. Then, if we are not interested in signal frequencies beyond a certain maximum frequency, f_m, we can "get away" with sampling the incoming signal at a rate equal to $2f_m$ (assuming the signal is of very long duration). This is the gist of the important Sampling Theorem in communication theory. Sampling the signal offers distinct advantages (less hardware involved, better future data processing, etc.) over working with the continuous signal. The important consequence of this theorem is that sampling at higher rates *does not enhance* the performance of the system.

3. In the early designs of airplanes, it was found that mechanical resistance to the movement of the "joystick" hampered, to some degree, the maneuverability of the airplane. Servo-systems were then introduced to reduce the required mechanical effort in moving the joystick. However, it was found that reducing the resistance beyond a certain limit caused the pilot to lose the "feel" of the airplane and actually resulted in adverse effects. The overall performance of the man-machine system was *reduced* by the excessive improvement in the servo-system.

When the *interaction* among components is considered, no single component can either dominate or be dominated by other components.

6.1 Some Important Measures of Dynamic System Performance

In §4 we discussed various goals and criteria of performance. In this section we add a few measures of dynamic performance. Generally speaking these are concerned with either the *transient* (i.e., short range) or the *steady-state* (i.e., long range) performance of the system.

Among transient measures are the *maximum overshoot*, the *time lag*, and the *damping* characteristics. These measures assume a step input at time zero. For an under-damped system, the output will overshoot and oscillate about the correct value which it eventually achieves if the system is stable (see Fig. 1-16). An over-damped system does not oscillate at all,

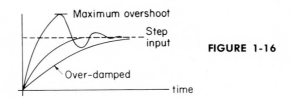

FIGURE 1-16

while a critically-damped system rises exponentially to the desired value. The time lag is usually measured by the system *time constant*, which is defined as the time required to reduce the error between the input and output to approximately 1/3 of its value.

Two important characteristics of steady-state performance are concerned with *stability* and the *steady-state error* between the output and the input. A system is absolutely stable if an error is eventually corrected. A system in which an error increases without bounds is absolutely unstable. On the other hand, the steady-state error measures the difference between the input and output after the system has been in operation for a long time. Naturally, the smaller the error the better the performance.

By necessity, our discussion of these characteristics is brief and sketchy.

We postpone a more elaborate discussion to Chapter 6 on feedback control systems.

COMMENTS AND BIBLIOGRAPHY

§1. For a general and brief discussion of the role of management from a historical point of view, see:

CLOUGH, DONALD J. *Concepts in Management Science*, Prentice-Hall, Inc., Englewood Cliffs, N. J., 1963, Chapter 2.

As an example of the new position and impact of computer technology on the function of production control, see the following application:

ELMAGHRABY, S. E., and R. T. COLE   "On the Control of Production in Small Job Shops," *Journal of Industrial Engineering*, Vol. 14, No. 4, July–August 1963, pp. 186–196.

A historical review of F. W. Taylor's "Scientific Management" and a critical analysis of its development is given in:

DAVIDSON, HAROLD O.   *Functions and Bases of Time Standards*, Special publication of the Institute of Industrial Engineers, 1957.

A projection of the role of the computer in the functions of management is found in:

SIMON, HERBERT. *The New Science of Management Decision*, Harper, New York, 1960.

A lucid discussion of the notions of management and science is given in:

DAVIDSON, HAROLD O. "The Management, Engineering, and Scientific Functions," *Journal of Industrial Engineering*, Vol. 11, No. 2, March–April 1960, pp. 120–124.

§2. The following book is an excellent introduction to the field of systems engineering:

HALL, ARTHUR D.   *A Methodology for Systems Engineering*, Van Nostrand, Princeton, N. J., 1962.

§3. The dynamic programming approach of Deterministic Variable Demand inventory model is due to:

WAGNER, HARVEY M., and THOMSON M. WHITIN   "Dynamic Version of the Economic Lot Size Model," *Management Science*, Vol. 5, No. 1, October 1958, pp. 89–91.

Also, see:

ZABEL, EDWARD.   "Some Generalizations of an Inventory Planning Horizon Theorem," *Management Science*, Vol. 10, No. 3, April 1964, pp. 465–471.

§4. The Location-Allocation problem presented as an example of the Maximum Total Profit criterion is adapted from:

COOPER, LEON. "Location-Allocation Problems," *Operations Research*, Vol. 11, No. 3, May–June 1963, pp. 331–343.

The comparison between the Present Worth Method and the Internal Rate of Return method for project evaluation is based on the lucid paper of:

BERNHARD, RICHARD H.   "Discount Methods for Expenditure Evaluation— A Clarification of Their Assumptions," *Journal of Industrial Engineering*, Vol. 13, No. 1, January–February 1962, pp. 19–27.

Excellent discussions of investment and replacement policies can be found in the following two books:

BIERMAN, C. H. and S. SMIDT   *The Capital Budgeting Decision*, Macmillan, New York, 1960.

MORRIS, W. T.   *The Analysis of Management Decision*, Irwin, Homewood, Ill., 1956.

Also, see:

KAPLAN, SEYMOUR   "A Note on A Method For Determining The Uniqueness Or Non-Uniqueness Of The Internal Rate of Return For A Proposed Investment," *the Journal of Industrial Engineering*, Vol. 16, No. 1, January–February 1965.

SOLOMON, EZRA.   "The Arithmetic of Capital Budgeting Decisions," *Journal of Business*, Vol. 29, No. 2, April 1956.

There are very few attempts to optimize systems relative to the "absolute-value" criterion. The example given is due to:

FRANCIS, R. L.   "A Note on the Optimum Location of New Machines in Existing Plant Layout," *the Journal of Industrial Engineering*, Vol. 14, No. 1, January–February 1963, pp. 57–59.

Examples of the use of various criteria in the field of statistics can be found in the excellent book:

WILKS, S. S.   *Mathematical Statistics*, Wiley, New York, 1962, Chapter 10.

Also, see:

SCHLAIFER, ROBERT.   *Introduction to Statistics for Business Decisions*, McGraw-Hill, New York, 1961.

The Minimax Regret (minimax risk) criterion was first suggested by Savage in

SAVAGE, L. J.   "The Theory of Statistical Decision," *the Journal of the American Statistical Association*, Vol. 46, 1951, pp. 55–67.

The Hurwicz criterion was first reported in

HURWICZ, L.   "Optimality Criteria for Decision Making Under Ignorance," *Cowles Commission Discussion Paper, Statistics*, No. 370, 1951 (Mimeographed).

A lucid discussion of these and other criteria and of questions of measurement of utility can be found in

LUCE, D. and H. RAIFFA.   *Games and Decisions*, Wiley, New York, 1957.

The study of the statistical design of control systems is the subject of numerous books in the field of electrical engineering. For an elementary introduction to the subject see

TRUXAL, JOHN G.   *Control Systems Synthesis*, McGraw-Hill, New York, 1955, Chapter 8.

For a more detailed (and formal) discussion of the problem of maximizing the terminal horizontal velocity of a satellite see:

BELLMAN, R. and S. DREYFUS   *Applied Dynamic Programming*, Princeton University Press, Princeton, N.J., 1962, Chapter VI, §10.

The example on the minimization of terminal inventory loss is due to:

HADLEY, G., and T. M. WHITIN   "An Optimal Final Inventory Model," *Management Science*, Vol. 7, No. 2, January 1961, pp. 179–183.

A lucid discussion of Markovian inventory systems (Problem 19) is given in:
STARR, M. K., and MILLER, D. W. *Inventory Control: Theory and Practice*, Prentice-Hall, Englewood Cliffs, N.J., 1962, pp. 130–142.

EXERCISES

1. Give three examples of systems you are familiar with in which it is desired to optimize relative to *two or more* criteria. For each example suggest a "reasonable" weighting factor of the various criteria and demonstrate how such weights can be used to reduce the objectives to a single one.

2. Suppose that a highway system must be constructed in your home state. List what you consider the most important objectives to be achieved by such a system. Rank the various objectives in the order of their importance—as you see it—in times of both peace and war. Specify, to the best of your ability, the operational criteria to be used in choosing among various contractors who are tendering for the project.

3. Analog computers are usually electronic. However, they need not be thus restricted. Give one example of a system that can be simulated by a *hydraulic* analog. Give another example of a system that can be simulated by a *pneumatic* analog.

4. Iconic models are usually used as visual aids. Mention at least three situations in which iconic models are constructed for purposes of engineering analysis (i.e., they are not merely visual aids). Mention briefly the reasons you believe lie behind their use in these studies.

5. Given that a large metropolitan area is in need of a large airport which can accomodate the increased future traffic, discuss briefly the steps of undertaking such a project, its objectives, limitations, operational criteria, etc.

6. In both of the following problems draw a graph showing the fluctuation of inventory. This should also assist you in developing the mathematical model.
   Construct a model for the determination of the optimal level of inventory to be carried at the beginning of an interval in which the demand y is *probabilistic* with known distribution function $f(y)dy$ and the costs involved are:
   (a) cost of disposal, c_d, proportional to the quantity remaining at the end of the period.
   (b) cost of shortage, π, proportional to the quantity short.
   Solve for the optimal inventory level relative to the minimum-expected-cost criterion.

7. The problem is similar to that in Problem 6 except that the cost structure is slightly different:
   (a) a cost of investment, c_1 per unit *per unit time*, proportional to the *average* inventory carried.
   (b) a cost of disposal, c_d, as in Problem 6.
   (c) cost of shortage, π, per unit *per unit time*, proportional to the average quantity short.
   Carry out the analysis except for the explicit evaluation of the optimal inventory level.

8. Referring to the Deterministic Variable Demand of §3.3, do the following:
   (a) Solve the numerical example with the cost of carrying inventory being proportional to average inventory rather than end-of-period inventory.
   (b) Extend the mathematical formulation to accept backorders, assuming a cost of $b/unit/unit time, and gradual consumption over each period.
9. A warehouse wishes to manage its inventory in an optimal manner to meet future demands for a stable commodity during the following year. The schedule of requirements is shown:

Month	1	2	3	4	5	6	7	8	9	10	11	12
Demand in Thousands	3	6	8	12	18	10	4	1	2	6	10	5

Because of the strong seasonal pattern of demand, the purchase price of the commodity fluctuates from month to month according to the following schedule:

Procurement
Cost/Unit $0.10 0.10 0.13 0.15 0.15 0.10 0.10 0.06 0.10 0.12 0.12 0.10

The selling price is catalog-fixed at $0.19/unit. It costs $0.0008/unit of end-of-month inventory.
   (a) Assuming that the costs of ordering and receiving a shipment are negligible, what is the optimal ordering policy?
   (b) If the cost of ordering and receiving is $10 per order, what is the optimal ordering policy?

Hint: To solve part (a) use simple marginal analysis (why?). For part (b) prove first that theorems 1 and 2 of Wagner and Whitin are still valid in the case of time dependent purchase price and constant inventory cost/unit.

10. Consider the demand in the first six periods of Problem 9

Period	1	2	3	4	5	6
Demand x 1000	3	6	8	12	18	10

Assume the cost of end-of-period inventory to be $0.02/unit, and assume the following quantity discount schedule

Quantity Purchased	0–999	1000–4999	5000–9999	10,000–19,999	>20,000
Unit Price	15¢	10¢	5¢	4¢	3.8¢

   (a) Formulate the functional equation of minimal total cost.
   (b) Reason, in a heuristic fashion, why the "planning horizon theorem" of Wagner and Whitin would not hold.
   (c) Solve for the optimal policy.

Hint: To narrow down the number of alternatives at each stage, show that if $I_{t-1} \geq r_t$, then no order will be placed at the beginning of period t, i.e., $q_t = 0$.

11. Set up a mathematical model to determine the optimal production quantity, Q^*, for a production-inventory system assuming a continuous consumption rate R units/year, and costs of machine set-up A/set-up, storage cost c_1/unit of average inventory/year, and backorder cost c_0 unit of average stockouts/year, such that *shortages never exceed s* units.

(a) Solve for the optimal Q^* given the following set of values: $R = 12{,}000$, $A = \$25$, $c_1 = \$0.02$, $c_0 = \$0.10$ and $s = 100$ units.

(b) Would it make any difference to the answer if s was set equal to 1400 units? What would the optimal policy be in this case?

(c) Is there any relationship between the optimal s (assuming it can be chosen at will between 0 and ∞) and the cost of understorage c_0?

12. Consider the following machine location problem. It is desired to locate a new machine, X, among seven old machines all of which are arranged along one aisle. The degree of exchange of product between X and old machine j, as well as the distance of j from some arbitrary origin are given in the following table:

Old Machine No.	1	2	3	4	5	6	7
Measure of Interaction A_j	5	3	7	14	2	10	30
Distance from Origin a_j	0	2	5	7	10	12	17

(a) What is the optimal location of X, say x, if the objective is the minimize $\Sigma_j A_j |x - a_j|$

(b) What would be the value of the optimal x if the objective is to minimize $\Sigma_j A_j (x - a_j)^2$?

13. Suppose that the interaction between the new machine and old machine j in problem 12 above is a random variable approximately normally distributed with mean μ_j and variance σ_j^2. What is the optimal location of X which minimizes the total *expected* cost if the latter is assumed equal to $A_j \times$ (distance)^2? What is the optimal location of machine X that minimizes the *variance* of the total cost?

14. Referring to the sections on the Maximum Total Profit and the Minimum Absolute Value criteria, discuss the applicability of other criteria to the examples given.

15. Prove that the present worth criterion as defined by the equation $P = Q_0 + Q_1/(1 + i_1) + Q_2/(1 + i_1)(1 + i_2) + \cdots + Q_n/(1 + i_1)\cdots(1 + i_n)$ is equivalent to the average rate of return as defined by the equation $Q_0(1 + r)^n = Q_1 \Pi_2^n (1 + i_t) + Q_2 \Pi_3^n (1 + i_t) + \cdots + Q_n$.

16. A sampling inspection plan is to be installed on lots of size $N = 1000$ units. Extensive studies on the average percent defective indicated that it varies randomly between .05 and 0.25. Inspection is not destructive, and defective units are replaced in the sample and in rejected lots. The cost of inspection is $\alpha = \$0.15$ per unit and the cost of replacing a defective unit on the customer's premise is $\beta = \$0.55$.

(a) If the sample size $n = 40$, what is the minimax value of the acceptance number c? What is the value of the optimal total cost?

(b) What are the minimax values of n and c if n can be 40, 50, or 60? What is the optimal cost?

17. In Problem 16, if it is known that the percent defective p is *uniformly distributed* between the two values given, would the minimax criterion still be your choice? Why?

Feel free to suggest another criterion (or criteria) which you consider as more "logical." What would be the answer to part (a) of Problem 16 under the new criterion (or criteria)?

18. The manager of a storeroom knows that demand for his product has the following distribution function

d	0	1	2	3	4	5
$p(d)$	0.1	0.3	0.15	0.15	0.2	0.1

If ordering costs $10 per order, and the inventory carrying charges are $6 per terminal inventory, what is his optimal policy concerning the quantity he should start with assuming a profit of $20 per unit sold, under each of the following criteria:

(a) Laplace

(b) Maximin profit

(c) Minimax regret

What criterion would you adopt as most "reasonable," given the data of the problem?

19. Suppose the manager of the storeroom of Problem 18 has decided upon the following reordering policy (lead time $= 0$)

Stock Level	Order
0	5
1	3
2, 3, 4, 5	0

The level of inventory is now a Markovian process. Determine his long-run expected profit.

20. A system is composed of four stages in series, each stage comprising one or more identical components in parallel. The total operation of the system is dependent on the functioning of each stage—failure of any stage means failure of the whole system. The parallel-component arrangement in any stage is really a device to introduce redundancy in order to achieve a certain minimum level of overall system reliability. Let p_i be the availability (= Probability of component or system being operational) of a component in stage i, and c_i its cost, $i = 1, 2, 3, 4$. Given the following system availability requirement: $R = 0.99$ (reliability level), determine the *least-cost configuration* (i.e., degree of redundancy at each stage) that yields a total availability $A \geq R$ when the other parameters have the following values:

Stage	1	2	3	4
Component Cost	1.2	2.3	3.4	4.5
Component Availability	0.8	0.7	0.75	0.85

Hint: Use a dynamic programming approach.

21. Consider the following "newsboy" problem. He orders a quantity q_1 of a magazine at the beginning of a month @8¢/copy. Demand during the first ten days of the month is probabilistic with the following distribution:

d_1	80	150
$p(d_1)$	3/4	1/4

A magazine is sold @15¢/copy. On the 10th of the month he has the chance to order more copies @6¢/copy, or return any unsold copy @4¢/copy. There is a flat fee of delivery on the 10th of $2.00. Let q_2 denote the quantity ordered (or returned) on the 10th. Demand during the last 20-day period is probabilistic with the following distribution function:

d_2	20	50	60
$p(d_2)$	5/8	1/4	1/8

Any unsold magazines are returned at the end of the month @2¢/copy. Formulate the functional equation of a dynamic programming model and determine the optimal policy (q_1^*, q_2^*) which maximizes his expected profit? What is the value of this policy?

22. A company has an opportunity to engage in a venture for which the following disbursements and receipts are in prospect:

Year End	Disbursements	Receipts
	(x1000)	(x1000)
0	3,200	0
1	650	840
2	650	1,000
3	400	2,500
4	400	1,800

Determine the desirability or otherwise of the venture on the basis of:
(a) Present worth amount with market interest rate at 5% and at 10%.
(b) Internal rate of return.
(c) Equivalent annual amount with interest rate at 5%.

23. The *Capitalized Value* criterion is an alternative criterion favored in some quarters dealing with long-term opportunities, such as highway, railway, electric power and other developments. On a capitalized basis, the income and disbursements will be calculated as though they will continue in perpetuity. In the case of equipment of a shorter span of life, it is assumed that the equipment will be replaced by an identical unit and that the history of disbursements and income will be repeated.

The capitalized basis of evaluation consists of finding a single amount in the present whose return (on the compounded accumulated capital) at the end of each year at a given rate of market interest will be equal to the net difference of receipts and disbursements assuming perpetuity.

Show that if the equivalent annual disbursements for a project are D, and the equivalent annual income is I, then the capitalized value, C, of the project is given by $C = (I - D)/i$ where i is the given market interest rate.

Using the data of Problem 22, determine the capitalized value of the net receipts.

Finally, show that the Capitalized value criterion is consistent with the Present Worth criterion.

24. A company is a large consumer of stationery, and consumes 1,500,000 sheets a year. The sheets are purchased "blank" and 1,200,000 sheets are drilled with holes for binding, the remaining 300,000 sheets have their corners rounded. Both operations are currently subcontracted at a cost of 40¢ for drilling and 30¢ for cutting, per thousand sheets. In re-evaluating its position, two alternative courses of action were suggested. Alternative A consisted of the purchase of a paper drill for $480 and alternative B consisted of purchasing a combination paper drill and corner cutter for $630. The relevant data on the two proposals are summarized in the following table:

	Proposal A	Proposal B
Life	10 years	10 years
Annual Cost Including Labor to Drill	$50	$60
Annual Labor to Cut Corners	–	25
Salvage Value	40	60

Assume that depreciation is on a straight-line basis. (If C is the cost of the asset, L its salvage value, n is the estimated life of the asset in years, and i is the interest rate, then "straight-line" depreciation allowance is the amount of money to be withheld from the useful services of the asset at the end of each year for the life period of the asset so that at the end of its life the capital invested as well as interest on the unrecovered capital each year are completely recovered. A good approximation is

$$(C - L)\left[\frac{1}{n} + \left(\frac{n + 1}{n}\right)\frac{i}{2}\right] + Li \ .$$

Which is the better alternative, A or B? Could you suggest another alternative or alternatives? State your reasons.

25. Management is always faced with new proposals for expansion, improvement of current activities, new investment possibilities, etc. If you were to advise management on the ways and means for checking the worth of these proposals and on their functional behavior, what proposals would you make? (List all methods of validation and verification in all possible circumstances, such as

proposals concerning systems in existence or systems which are still non-existent: proposals which affect personnel, etc.).

26. A tire company plans to carry inventory into their peak sales period, as their sales will exceed their regular time capacity to manufacture tires. Their cost structure is composed of three costs:

Cost of Storing Tires:	10¢/Tire Per Year
Cost of Understock:	50¢ Additional Cost/Tire
	(In order to manufacture
	on overtime)
Cost of Disposal:	12¢/Tire
	(This is, in fact, the
	discounted cost of
	carrying inventory
	thereafter.)

The company estimates their probable sales (in units) during the peak period, in addition to regular time production capacity, to be represented with the following "triangular" probability distribution:

$$f(x) = \begin{cases} \dfrac{(x - 600)}{54 \times 10^4} & \text{for } 600 \le x \le 1200 \\[2ex] \dfrac{(2400 - x)}{108 \times 10^4} & \text{for } 1200 \le x \le 2400 \\[2ex] 0 & \text{Otherwise} \end{cases}$$

(a) Determine the optimal number of tires to store (to minimize average total cost). Compare your result with the cost of storing the average demand.

(b) Suppose the company wishes to "look ahead" *two* seasons instead of one, and that there is a set-up cost for production. Would your approach for determining the optimal stock be the same (assume the company can produce next year also)? Namely, would you consider treating each period separately or would you be forced to treat both periods simultaneously? Discuss the factors leading to your decision. Suggest an approach.

CHAPTER 2 / # The Graphic Representation of Systems

§1. INTRODUCTION

1.1 Descriptive vs. Analytical Representation

The distinguishing aspect of a system—as opposed to an individual component—is the interaction among its various components. The mode of this interaction, its genre and direction determine the structure of the system. The engineer, in his analysis or synthesis of systems, is ultimately concerned with such structure. Insight into the cause-and-effect relationships and into the performance of the system as a whole can be gained only through such knowledge. In fact, the determination of the structure of the system is a prelude to the framing of the problem for quantitative analysis.

Graphic methods for representing activities and relationships are not novel. Engineers of various disciplines have always resorted to graphic portrayals of physical phenomena, of machinery and "hardware" systems, and of conceptual relationships. However, to the designer of productive systems the available graphic techniques have been, as late as the early fifties, merely a different "language" that may offer the clarity usually associated with pictorial exhibits but do not enhance the fundamental understanding of the structure or of the dynamic behavior of the system.

In essence, these techniques were intended for charting activities on the macro- or micro-scale. For example, the *Process Flow Chart* (or *Flow Diagram*), is a graphic portrayal of the various activities encountered in the process of manufacturing a product. It is a permutation of four basic activities: Operation, Inspection, Transportation, and Storage. Each activity is represented by a different symbol as shown in Fig. 2-1. The analysis of existing or prospective operations defines the sequence of activities; the verbal description is then translated into its pictorial image.

Note that the definition of the basic symbols or "words" of this pictorial language is really a matter of taste. We may define an "operation"

Operation   Inspection   Transportation Storage

FIGURE 2-1 The Four Basic Symbols of Process Flow Charts

to encompass all the activities that operate on a product to change its physical content, or we may divide these activities into two or more subsets such as "operations that add material" (e.g., assembly operations), "operations that subtract material" (e.g., machine cutting), and "operations that do not change material content" (e.g., heat treatment). One may then choose a different symbol for each subset of operations and create a different "language." The variety of such languages is limited only by the imagination of the analyst and can certainly be different from one production process to another.

Similar remarks can be made about the other graphic techniques: Gantt charts, Operator Motion-Analysis charts, and Multiple-Activity charts. We refer the interested reader to any of the several books on Motion and Time Study or to Chapter 3 in Bowman and Fetter's book listed at the end of the chapter.

Recent advances in the engineering science of control systems and in the mathematical theory of probability have enriched the field of graphic representation with new and powerful techniques. In this chapter we shall discuss three techniques which have proven to be of great value in the study of the structures of systems: the *block diagram*, the *signal flow graph*, and the *activity network*. The first two techniques define the functional relationships among the components; the third technique defines temporal relationships.

We wish to emphasize that these techniques should be viewed as the system designer's tools—to be utilized whenever appropriate or advantageous. Thus, there is no fundamental difference, apart from symbolism, between a signal flow graph and a block diagram, and nothing prevents a block diagram from being redrawn as a signal flow graph or vice versa, (nothing, that is, except the utility of the the technique adopted and its ease of manipulation under the special circumstances of the model). One encounters a similar choice in the study of physical systems: in one instance we may view light according to Newton's corpuscular theory, and in another instance we may wish to view it according to Maxwell's electromagnetic wave theory. The choice of a vantage point is a matter of convenience rather than a matter of strict adherence to a predetermined set of rules.

§2. BLOCK DIAGRAMS

2.1. Representation of Functional Relationships

The generic unit of a block diagram is the fundamental block shown in Fig. 2-2. The "Functional Relationship" of the block relates the output to the input in a functional manner:

$$\theta_0(t) = \int_0^t \theta_i(\tau) g(t - \tau) \, d\tau \tag{2-1}$$

where $g(u)$ is the impulse response of the block.

Now define the (one-sided) Laplace transform[†] of a function $f(t)$ as

$$\mathcal{L}[f(t)] = \int_0^\infty f(t) e^{-st} \, dt$$

where $s = \sigma + j\omega$ is a complex variable, $j = \sqrt{-1}$. Then taking the Laplace transform of both sides of the equation, we have

$$\theta_0(s) = \theta_i(s) G(s); \tag{2-2}$$

$G(s)$ is called the *transfer function* of the block.

FIGURE 2-2   The Fundamental Block

We wish to draw a sharp distinction between block diagramming as presented here, which represents a precisely defined mathematical formulation, and some other uses of block diagramming which may be found in the literature. For example, the organization chart of a company is sometimes presented in a "block diagram" form. The reader should realize that the organization is "blocked" for drawing convenience, that there is no mathematical relationship between inputs and outputs of any block, and that, therefore, such diagrams are excluded from our discussion.

It immediately follows from Eq. (2-2) that in a cascade of such blocks, as in Fig. 2-3, the output $\theta_0(s)$ is given by $\theta_0(s) = \left\{ \prod_{k=1}^{4} G_k(s) \right\} \theta_i(s)$, where

[†] For a more detailed treatment of Laplace transform together with examples, see §2 of Chapter 6.

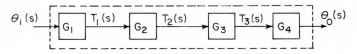

FIGURE 2-3   A Cascade Block Diagram

$\prod_k$ denotes the product over the values of k, and that any intermediate out-

put such as $T_3(s) = \left\{ \prod_{k=1}^{3} G_k(s) \right\} \theta_i(s)$. It is obvious that each block is

independent of other blocks in its action in the sense that its transfer function is *invariant* under conditions of coupling with other blocks. This is a fundamental property of block diagrams. In fact, a fundamental block can be defined as the smallest noninteracting (i.e., invariant) component of a system. However, the engineer is not obligated to draw block diagrams which are constituted solely of such simple fundamental blocks. If no need exists for maintaining the identity of the individual components, a "compound" block can be drawn that represents the functional relationship of several simple blocks. The process of compounding terminates when the output(s) is given directly in terms of the input(s). To be sure, we can represent the cascaded system of Fig. 2-3 by the simple transfer function of Fig. 2-4.

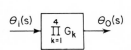

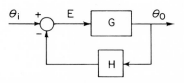

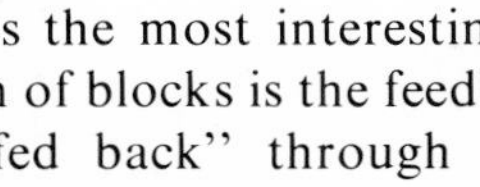

**FIGURE 2-4   Equivalent   Block   to
Fig. 2-3.**

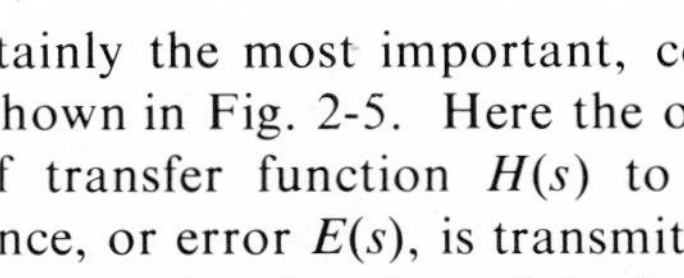

FIGURE 2-5   Basic Feedback Loop

Perhaps the most interesting, and certainly the most important, configuration of blocks is the feedback loop shown in Fig. 2-5. Here the output is "fed back" through a block of transfer function $H(s)$ to be compared with the input, and the difference, or error $E(s)$, is transmitted forward through G. The output of such a system is a function of the input and of itself, and can be obtained from the set of simultaneous equations

$$\theta_0(s) = E(s)G(s)$$

$$E(s) = \theta_i(s) - \theta_0(s)H(s)$$

i.e.,

$$\theta_0(s) = \frac{G(s)}{1 + G(s)H(s)} \cdot \theta_i(s). \qquad (2\text{-}3)$$

Thus, the equivalent transfer function of the system is $G/(1 + GH)$; also, as $G \to \infty$, $\theta_0 \to \theta_i$, but as $H \to \infty$, $\theta_0 \to 0$.

The objective of block diagramming, or for that matter of any graphic technique, is to achieve the characterization of the output(s) in terms of the input(s). Naturally, block diagramming is not an end in itself but a step in the analysis of the system performance. Such analysis is normally achieved through simplification and reduction of the original block diagram to determine the overall transfer function. The algebraic manipulations to achieve such an end are best illustrated by an example.

Consider the block diagram of Fig. 2-6. We want to determine the output, θ_0, in terms of the two inputs θ_{i_1} and θ_{i_2}. By inspection we can write

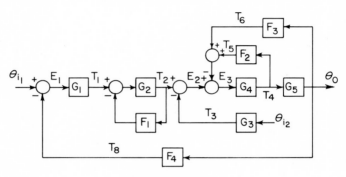

FIGURE 2-6

the following equations, making use of the basic feedback loop of Eq. (2-3):

$$E_1 = \theta_{i_1} - T_8 = \theta_{i_1} - \theta_0 \cdot F_4$$

$$T_1 = E_1 \cdot G_1$$

$$T_2 = \frac{G_2}{1 + F_1 G_2} \cdot T_1$$

$$E_2 = T_2 - T_3 = T_2 - \theta_{i_2} \cdot G_3$$

$$E_3 = E_2 - (T_5 + T_6) = E_2 - T_4 \cdot F_2 - \theta_0 \cdot F_3$$

$$T_4 = E_3 \cdot G_4$$

$$\theta_0 = T_4 \cdot G_5.$$

Eliminating all intermediate outputs T_1, T_2, T_4, we obtain

$$\theta_0 = \frac{(G_1 G_2 G_4 G_5) \cdot \theta_{i_1} - G_3 G_4 G_5 (1 + F_1 G_2) \cdot \theta_{i_2}}{(1 + G_4 F_2)(1 + F_1 G_2) + G_1 G_2 G_4 G_5 F_4 + G_3 G_4 G_5 (1 + F_1 G_2)},$$

$$(2-4)$$

which can be decomposed into

$$\theta_0 = \frac{G_1 G_2 G_4 G_5}{R} \cdot \theta_{i_1} - \frac{G_3 G_4 G_5 (1 + F_1 G_2)}{R} \cdot \theta_{i_2}$$

where R is the denominator of Eq. (2-4). This form reveals the relationship of θ_0 and the two inputs θ_{i_1} and θ_{i_2}, and can be depicted as in Fig. 2-7.

FIGURE 2-7   Equivalent Block Diagram to Fig. 2-6

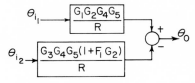

The following three examples illustrate the use of block diagrams in three different engineering disciplines.

2.2 Example: Motor Drive Control

Figure 2-8 is the block diagram of a motor-drive system with first-derivative input control, i.e., the input torque to the motor is the sum of the amplified error, $E(s)$, and the rate-of-change of the input, $K_2 s \theta_i(s)$. The block diagram shows the output, θ_0, as the input to the load (of transfer function $Js^2 + fs$). This is purely for notational convenience since the load is in reality the inertia J and the friction f of the motor. Both factors are functions of the output angle θ_0, hence the torque applied to the motor is equal to the resistance of the motor ($=$ inertia (Js^2) + friction (fs)). The algebraic equations relating the various components of the system are

$$E = \theta_i - \theta_0$$
$$T = K_1 E + K_2 s \theta_i$$
$$T = (Js^2 + fs)\theta_0,$$

hence

$$\theta_0(s) = \frac{K_1 + K_2 s}{Js^2 + fs + K_1} \cdot \theta_i(s).$$

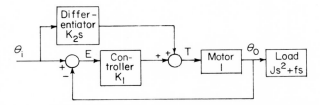

FIGURE 2-8   Proportional-Error Correction with First Derivative Input Control

2.3 Example: Production-Inventory System

Insight into the dynamic behavior of economic systems can sometimes be gained by representation into block diagram form. Figure 2-9 depicts a production-inventory system in which it is desirable to maintain a specified level of inventory I_0 on hand at all times. The sales S are satisfied from production P and available inventories I. Any deviation of actual inventory I from the desired level I_0 gives rise to the error E. The

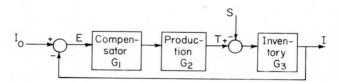

FIGURE 2-9 **Simple Production-Inventory System**

"Compensator" is in fact a decision-making mechanism that determines the desired increase or decrease in production based on the value of E. The production facilities react to such commands in a fashion determined by the characteristics of the facilities. Production adds to inventory and Sales subtract from it. It is easily seen that

$$E = I_0 - I$$

$$T = E \cdot G_1 G_2$$

$$I = (T - S)G_3,$$

hence

$$I = \frac{G_1 G_2 G_3}{1 + G_1 G_2 G_3} \cdot I_0 - \frac{G_3}{1 + G_1 G_2 G_3} \cdot S$$

as depicted in Fig. 2-10. The study of the dynamic behavior of production-inventory systems along these lines will be pursued later on; see Chapter 6 on feedback control systems.

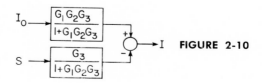

FIGURE 2-10

2.4 Example: A Chemical Plant[†]

A chemical plant produces urea $[CO(NH_2)_2]$ which is used in the manufacture of plastics. The main components of the system are the vacuum evaporator which removes water from a urea-water mixture, and a prill tower. Concentrated urea is pumped from the evaporator to the prilling tower where a solid product is formed. The evaporator pressure and temperature are controlled to keep suction pressure on the feed pump. The flow of steam to the jet ejector was set by the temperature controller. Air loading of the vacuum ejector is controlled by the vacuum controller.

Originally, however, the system was designed differently; it had, particularly, different level control and pressure control in the prill tower. Analysis through analog simulation revealed the instability of the system, which in turn resulted in the revised design described above and presented schematically in Fig. 2-11.

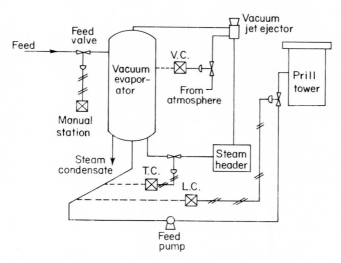

FIGURE 2-11   Schematic of Urea Production

Without going into the detailed chemical engineering aspects of analysis to determine the dynamic behavior of the various components of the system, the block diagram shown in Fig. 2-12 was finally achieved. Further analysis by analog simulation revealed some important aspects of the behaviour of the total system. For example, it was discovered that the level control system (on the evaporator) is unable to cope with high frequency

[†] D. E. Johnson, "Simulation and Analysis Improve Evaporation Control" *Journal of the Instrument Society of America*, Vol. 7, No. 7, pp. 46–49, July, 1960.

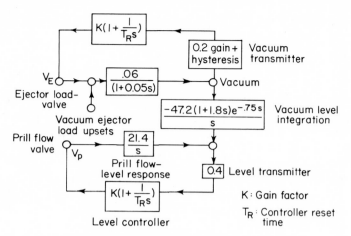

FIGURE 2-12   Block Diagram Representation

disturbances of about one cycle per minute. Furthermore, extremely strong interaction between vacuum and level in evaporator was detected; previously this interaction had gone undetected by plant measurements. As a result of such analysis the plant engineers could make positive recommendations to improve the performance of the system. For example, they recommended the installation of a more sensitive vacuum control system and the placement of the pressure regulator on the steam line to ejector.

This application is illustrative of the wide use of block diagramming in the study of the dynamic behavior of systems in the chemical engineering field.

2.5 Limitations of Block Diagrams

The three examples discussed above were drawn from three different engineering disciplines—electrical, industrial and chemical engineering, respectively—and demonstrate the power and extent of applicability of the technique of block diagramming. The first example dealt with an electro-mechanical system; the second, with a production-inventory system, and the third with a control system for a chemical process. In each context the transfer functions of individual components were evaluated and the components then linked together in a system that simulates the input-output relationships among the components.

However, block diagrams are not without their limitations. In brief, the following objections were levied against block diagrams: (1) the assumption of invariance (of the transfer function) is sometimes erroneous;

(2) it is sometimes difficult to isolate noninteracting elements; (3) there exists the possibility of concealing some important characteristics within the walls of the block; (4) once a block is drawn, the designer loses contact with the flow of signal or information inside the block which, in turn, may limit the insight he may gain into the operation of the block; (5) inputs and outputs are not the only signals present in the system, but signals inside any block are obscured, and consequently, it is not possible to study the reaction of the system to variations within any one of the signals.

In an attempt to answer some of these objections, S. J. Mason originated the signal flow graph. The following section is devoted to a discussion of this procedure.

§3. SIGNAL FLOW GRAPHS*

3.1 Definition of the Generic Element

In essence, signal flow graphs (and, for that matter, block diagrams) are network representations of simultaneous linear equations. The study of such systems derives its importance from the fact that the behavior of many physical systems can be described by ordinary integro-differential equations. Through the use of transform theory (Fourier and Laplace transforms), they can be reduced to a set of algebraic equations.

One can always work in the purely algebraic domain if one is willing to sacrifice two important advantages of graphic representation. First, as was mentioned before in §1, the mathematical equations of a system are essentially quantitative relations among the variables and not a representation of the *structure* of the system. Second, the graphic representation oftentimes suggests fundamental relationships among the variables independent of the essence of the elements but dependent on the *topology* of the graph, i.e., the manner in which the elements are interconnected. For the moment, we are concerned with the representation of such systems as signal flow graphs.

FIGURE 2-13 Generic Element in Signal Flow Graphs

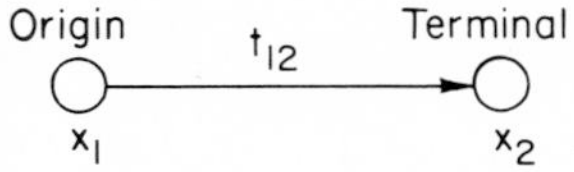

The generic element of signal flow graphs is shown in Fig. 2-13. It consists of a *directed arc*, or an arrow, connecting two nodes x_1 (origin) and x_2 (terminal). The branch is said to be of "transmittance" t_{12} meaning that the value of the node x_1 is multiplied by t_{12} as it is transmitted

---

* This section may be omitted on first reading.

through the branch such that the variable represented by the node x_2 is
equal to $x_1 \cdot t_{12}$.

In general, more than one arc may leave any node, and more than one
arc may terminate at any node. In the former case, the value of the node
is multiplied by the transmittance of each arc emanating from it, while in
the latter case, the value of the node is equal to the *sum* of all the inputs
into it.

By convention, a *sink* is a node with no arcs leaving it, and an *origin* is a
node with no arcs entering it. A system may have any number of origins
and sinks but must have *at least* one origin and one sink.

The equation $x_2 = a_1 x_1 + a_3 x_3$ can be represented as in Fig. 2-14a;
the equation $x_3 = b_0 x_0 + b_1 x_1 + b_2 x_2$ can be represented as in 2-14b.
The set of two linear equations is represented in 2-14c.

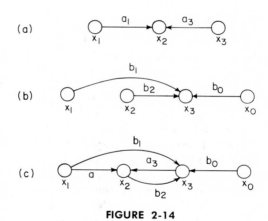

FIGURE 2-14

From the basic definition of the generic element, it immediately follows
that:

1. Each node represents a variable; each node has a value.
2. The value of the node (i.e., variable) is transmitted through all arcs
   leaving the node.
3. The arrow along any arc indicates the direction of flow of the signal
   (information, goods, etc.).
4. The signal along any arc is equal to the value of the originating node
   (variable) multiplied by the transmittance of the arc.
5. Any number of arcs may lead into a node or leave a node.
6. The value of the node (variable) is the sum of all signals along the
   arcs leading to the node.

3.2 The Reduction of Signal Flow Graphs

The graphic algebra utilized to reduce a signal flow graph to a residual graph showing only the nodes of interest proceeds according to a few simple rules which are derived from the basic properties enumerated above. For example, it is obvious that for two branches in series, as in Fig. 2-15a, $x_2 = x_1 \cdot t_{12}$ and $x_3 = x_2 \cdot t_{23} = x_1 \cdot t_{12} \cdot t_{23}$; thus node x_2 can be eliminated to obtain the equivalent residual graph shown. In the case of two arcs in parallel, as in 2-15b, $x_2 = x_1(t_1 + t_2)$, and the equivalent graph is evident.

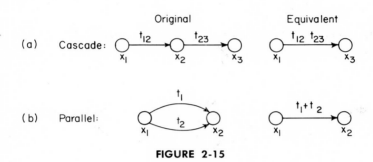

FIGURE 2-15

The table in Fig. 2-16 gives six more rules of reduction. We briefly explain a few. The complete reduction of the *feedback loop* of 2-16b is accomplished in Fig. 2-17 in three steps: first the reduction of the feedback loop to a self-loop, then the elimination of the self-loop, and finally the elimination of the middle nodes. The first step follows from the two equations

$$x_2 = x_1 \cdot t_{12} + x_3 \cdot t_{32}$$

$$x_3 = x_2 \cdot t_{23}$$

which, upon eliminating x_2, yields,

$$x_3 = x_1 \cdot t_{12} \cdot t_{23} + x_3 \cdot t_{32} \cdot t_{23}. \tag{2-5}$$

The reduction of the *self-loop* around x_3 follows immediately from Eq. (2-5):

$$x_3(1 - t_{23} \cdot t_{32}) = x_1 \cdot t_{12} \cdot t_{23}$$

i.e.,

$$x_3 = x_1 \frac{t_{12} \cdot t_{23}}{1 - t_{23} \cdot t_{32}}.$$

Eliminating node x_3 yields the equivalent graph shown.

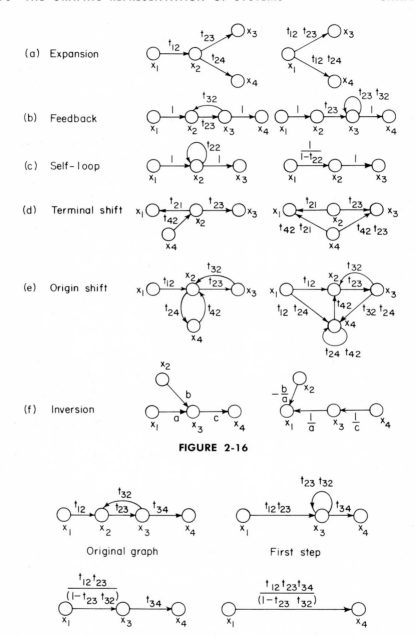

(a) Expansion

(b) Feedback

(c) Self-loop

(d) Terminal shift

(e) Origin shift

(f) Inversion

FIGURE 2-16

Original graph

First step

Second step

Equivalent graph

FIGURE 2-17

Terminal shift, rule (d) in Fig. 2-16, removes an arrow from the node of incidence. Notice that an arc is required between x_4 and every node dependent on the node of incidence x_2. *Origin shift*, rule (e) in Fig. 2-16, removes the *start* of an arc from the node of incidence and replaces it with arcs and self-loops that preserve the original relationships. *Inversion* is the reversal of the direction of a branch, which implies that the variable at the end of the branch is to be defined in terms of an equation different from the one used in the original graph. An arc of transmittance *a* terminating in node *x* can be inverted (1) by reversing the arrow on the arc and dividing by its transmittance, (2) by moving the terminals of the branches that were converging on node *x* so as to keep them converging in the new graph, and (3) by dividing the transmittance of these branches by the initial transmittance of *a* and changing their signs. When all the arcs along a path are inverted, the path is said to be inverted.

The set of rules presented in Fig. 2-16 leads to a systematic stepwise reduction of complicated graphs. Perhaps the best guides to the procedure of graph reduction are insight into the problem and familiarity with the procedure of reduction. Incidentally, the same original graph may be reduced to different residual graphs depending on the interest of the analyst, as exemplified in Fig. 2-18. Mason, to whom the theory of signal

Original graph   Reductions

FIGURE 2-18

flow graphs is credited, proposed a rather simple and straightforward rule for reducing complicated graphs. We shall discuss the rule after presenting an example demonstrating the use of the technique.

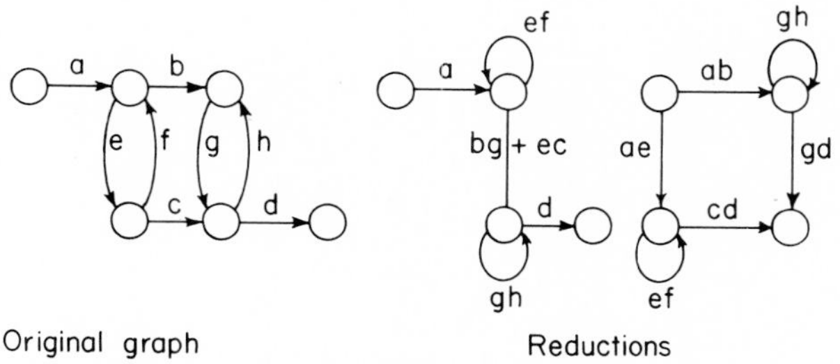

Example: Gambler's Ruin

The classical ruin problem is as follows: a gambler and his adversary have a total of *a* dollars. The game starts with the gambler having *b* dollars and his adversary $(a - b)$ dollars. At each play the gambler either loses one dollar with probability *q* or gains one dollar with probability *p*. Naturally, $p + q = 1$. The game ends when the gambler either loses the *b* dollars to his opponent or his capital is increased to a leaving his adversary penniless.

If x_b represents the probability that the gambler will be ruined when he possesses b dollars, then clearly,

$$x_b = p \cdot x_{b+1} + q \cdot x_{b-1}. \tag{2-6}$$

Since he cannot be "ruined" when he gains all the money, $x_a = 0$. On the other hand, if his capital is reduced to zero he is certainly ruined, therefore, $x_0 = 1$.

With the definition of the end points it can be shown that the system of equations in Eq. (2-6) admit a unique solution and that if $\bar{x}_b$ represents the probability of winning when he possesses b dollars, then $\bar{x}_b = 1 - x_b$. Here we illustrate the solution of the problem by signal flow graph methods. For this purpose, let x_i denote his probability of ruin when he possesses i dollars, and let $a = \$4$ and $b = \$1$. Then Eq. (2-7) reads:

$$x_0 = 1$$

$$x_1 = p \cdot x_2 + q \cdot x_0 = px_2 + q$$

$$x_2 = p \cdot x_3 + q \cdot x_1 \tag{2-7}$$

$$x_3 = p \cdot x_4 + q \cdot x_2 = q \cdot x_2$$

$$x_4 = 0$$

and can be depicted as in Fig. 2-19. The steps of reduction are shown in Fig. 2-20(a) to (d). Hence, $x_1 = q/[1 - pq/(1 - pq)] = q(1 - pq)/$

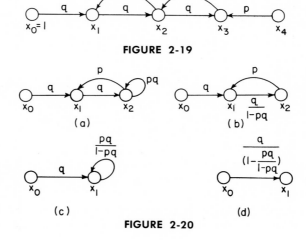

FIGURE 2-19

(a)   (b)

(c)   (d)

FIGURE 2-20

$(1 - 2pq)$, which is the required probability that starting with $b = \$1$ against an adversary possessing $a - b = \$3$ the gambler will be ruined. Notice that if the game is "fair" $p = q = \frac{1}{2}$ and $x_1 = \frac{3}{4}$, as is intuitively expected.

3.3 Mason's Rule

In the case of complicated graphs, the step-by-step method of reduction followed above is cumbersome and prone to error. Mason[†] proposed a rule for reducing such graphs. In spite of its formidable appearance, the rule is rather simple and straightforward.

In a network composed of several sources, nodes, and sinks, the transmittance from a source to a sink is given by

$$T = \sum_j \pi_j \frac{\Delta j}{D}$$

where π_j is the transmittance along the jth forward "path." The weighing factor Δ_j / D is to be explained presently. (A "path" is a connected graph in which each node appears only once and all arrows lead from the start node to the terminal node. A "loop" is a path in which the source appears twice each time the loop is traversed.)

Let $L_1, L_2, \ldots, L_n$ represent the loops present in the graph. Then,

$$D = 1 - \sum_i L_i + \sum_{i,j} L_i \cdot L_j - \sum_{i,j,k} L_i \cdot L_j \cdot L_k + \cdots$$

where each multiple summation extends over *nonadjacent loops*. If the forward path π_j is removed—which implies the removal of all nodes and branches along the path—the remaining network will contain the loops $L_1, L_2, \ldots, L_m; m \leq n$. Then,

$$\Delta_j = 1 - \sum_i L_i + \sum_{i,j} L_i \cdot L_j - \cdots$$

where each multiple summation extends over nonadjacent loops of the remaining network. The value of a sink is the sum of all branches feeding into the sink.

An example should help clarify the rule. Consider the graph of Fig. 2-21. There are three forward paths and four loops. The reader can easily verify the following:

$$\pi_1 = a\, b\, c\, d\, e \qquad \Delta_1 = 1$$

$$\pi_2 = f\, g\, e \qquad \Delta_2 = 1 - bh - ci$$

[†] S. J. Mason, "Feedback Theory: Some Properties of Signal Flow Graphs," *Proceedings of the Institute of Radio Engineers*, Vol. 41, Sept., 1953, pp. 1144–1156.

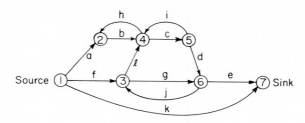

FIGURE 2-21

$$\pi_3 = k \qquad \Delta_3 = 1 - (bh + ci + gj + \ell cdj) + (gjbh + gjci)$$

$$\pi_4 = f\ell cde \qquad \Delta_4 = 1$$

and $D = 1 - bh - ci - \ell cdj - gj + bhgj + cigj$.
Hence, the transmittance $t_{1,7}$ is given by

$$t_{1,7} = \{abcde + fge[1 - (bh + ci)] + k[1 - (bh + ci + gj + \ell cdj)$$

$$+ (gjbh + gjci)] + f\ell cde\}/\{1 - (bh + ci + gj + \ell cdj)$$

$$+ (bhgj + cigj)\}$$

For further examples on Mason's rule the reader is referred to Hall and Miskhin and Braun, cited at the end of the Chapter.

Example: Gambler's ruin: Different Treatment

The problem of the gambler's ruin discussed in the first Example can be treated from a different point of view. Let the nodes represent the amount of money possessed by the gambler at any time (rather than the probability of ruin as before), so that his state is represented by the node y_i when he possesses i dollars.

If the gambler starts, as before, with one dollar, then his state is represented by node y_1. He can lose his dollar (with probability q) and thus move to node y_0, at which time the game terminates, or he may win a dollar (with probability p) and thus move to node y_2. At node y_2 he may lose one dollar and return to his original status of y_1, or he may again win one dollar and move to state y_3, and so on.

Suppose that each play consumes one time unit. Then the amount of money in the gambler's possession is a time series which is a *random* time series. In fact, the very duration of the series is a random variable.

Another way to characterize the process is as a "*random walk*" process in which each play is *one* step since the gambler can gain or lose only one dollar; the step is to the "right" if he gains one dollar and to the "left" if he loses one dollar. Random walk processes are excellent mathematical models for many physical processes in which stochastic variation exists.

The reader is referred to the excellent exposition of Feller listed at the end of this chapter.

For our present purposes, we wish to be able to count the number of periods, or steps, required to move from one state to another. To this end, we define the *generating function* of a time series $a_1, a_2, a_3, \ldots,$ as

$$A(z) = a_0 + a_1 z + a_2 z^2 + a_3 z^3 + \cdots = \sum_{t=0}^{\infty} a_t z^t.$$

$A(z)$ is, in fact, the *z-transform* of the time series $\{a_t\}$ and will be discussed in greater detail in Chapter 6. We shall always refer to it as such.

Then, from any state y_i the gambler can move *in one step* either to state y_{i+1} (with probability p) or to state y_{i-1} (with probability q) and the probability of moving to any other state is zero. Consequently, the z-transform of these transitions is simply pz for movement to y_{i+1} and qz for movement to y_{i-1}.

The complete signal flow chart—assuming $a = \$4$—can be easily drawn as in Fig. 2-22.

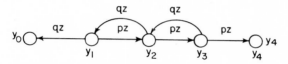

FIGURE 2-22 Signal-Flow Graph of Gambler's Movement

For clarity of exposition, we shall redraw the graph as shown in Fig. 2-23. The reader can easily verify that, except for the node 0 and the branch $(0y_1)$, this graph is isomorphic with the graph of Fig. 2-22. We have introduced the fictitious origin 0 and the branch $(0y_1)$ whose transmittance is unity and of zero duration in order to represent the "start of the game."

It is now evident that there is one source 0 and two sinks: y_0 and y_4. Consider first the transmittance between 0 and y_0. There is only one forward path $\pi_1 = 0, y_1, y_0$ whose transmittance is qz. There are two

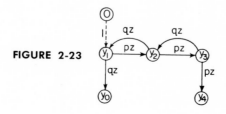

FIGURE 2-23

loops: y_1, y_2, y_1 and y_2, y_3, y_2. Thus, $L_1 = pqz^2 = L_2$, and $D = 1 - 2pqz^2$. Removal of the forward path leaves L_2 intact; therefore, $\Delta_1 = 1 - pqz^2$. Hence

$$T_{0,y_0} = \frac{qz(1 - pqz^2)}{1 - 2pqz^2}.$$

Next, the transmittance between 0 and y_4 can be easily evaluated since we have only one forward path $\pi_2 = 0, y_1, y_2, y_3, y_4$ whose transmittance is $p^3 z^3$. Removal of this path cancels all loops, hence $\Delta_2 = 1$. Hence,

$$T_{0,y_4} = \frac{p^3 z^3}{1 - 2pqz^2}.$$

As a check on our calculations, we evaluate the transmittances as time $\rightarrow \infty$, i.e., as $z \rightarrow 1$:

$$T_{0,y_0} \rightarrow \frac{q(1 - pq)}{1 - 2pq} \text{ and } T_{0,y_4} \rightarrow \frac{p^3}{1 - 2pq}; \; T_{0,y_0} + T_{0,y_4} = 1,$$

indicating that the probability of either ruin or winning the game is necessarily equal to one for a game of long enough duration.

Example: An Inventory Problem

Suppose that the manager of a warehouse knows that the demand per period for his product has the following probability distribution function:

d	0	1	2	3
$p(d)$	0.10	0.40	0.30	0.20

He adopts the following ordering policy: at the beginning of each period he checks his "on hand" inventory and orders only if he has nothing in stock. The quantity ordered is $q = 3$ units. Assuming *instantaneous delivery*, there are, in fact, only three states: x_1, x_2, and x_3, corresponding to the number of units in inventory.

In order to express the continuation of the process for a long period of time, we again utilize the z-transform of the transition probabilities. The signal flow graph is as shown in Fig. 2-24.

Suppose that we are interested in the probability of being in state x_3 (presumably because we can then calculate the average number of orders per year). Introduce the dummy origin $y_0(= 1)$ and the dummy transition (y_0, x_3)—shown dotted in Fig. 2-24—with transmittance *unity*. Then, if we reduce the graph to the single transmittance (y_0, x_3) it would yield the desired expression.

We remark that the graph in Fig. 2-24 contains 6 loops: three self-loops

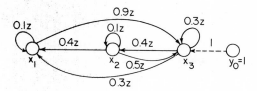

**FIGURE 2-24 Signal Flow Graph For In-
ventory Problem**

and three feedback loops. These are set forth in Fig. 2-25. Between nodes y_0 and x_3 there is only one forward path of transmittance $\pi_1 = 1$. Eliminating node x_3 leaves only the two self-loops about x_1 and x_2; whence

$$\Delta_1 = 1 - 0.2z + 0.01 z^2.$$

From the definition of D in Mason's rule, we have

$$D = 1 - 0.5z - 0.4z^2 - 0.1z^3.$$

Therefore,

$$T_{y_0,x_3} = \frac{1 - 0.2z + 0.01z^2}{1 - 0.5z - 0.4z^2 - 0.1z^3}$$

which, by long division, yields

$$T_{y_0,x_3} = 1 + 0.3z + 0.56z^2 + 0.50z^3 + 0.504z^4 + 0.508z^5 +$$
$$+ 0.5056z^6 + 0.5064z^7 + \cdots$$

Hence, if the system starts in state x_3, the probability that it will *return* to x_3 after k number of periods, $p_{y_0,x_3}(k)$, is given by the coefficient of z^k in the above series. Incidentally, the steady-state probability of being in

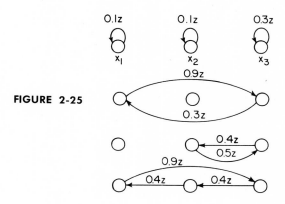

FIGURE 2-25

state x_3 is easily evaluated from the theory of Markov Processes to be 0.50625. We can see that the coefficient of z^k in the above series approaches the steady-state probability remarkably fast, the error being less than $1/30\%$ at $k = 7$ periods. Also, we remark that

$$T_{y_0,x_3}\big|_{z=1} = \sum_{k=0}^{\infty} p_{y_0,x_3}(k) \to \infty$$

which is in accordance with the fact that x_3 is a *recurrent* event with mean recurrence time $< \infty$.

It is interesting to evaluate the transmittances T_{y_0,x_1} and T_{y_0,x_2}. Since there is only one forward path, of transmittance $\pi_2 = 0.4z$, between nodes y_0 and x_2, we immediately obtain

$$T_{y_0,x_2} = \frac{0.4z(1 - 0.1z)}{D} = \frac{0.4z - 0.04z^2}{D}.$$

However, there are *two* paths between nodes y_0 and x_1 with

$$\pi_{3,1} = 0.16z^2, \qquad \Delta_{3,1} = 1$$

and

$$\pi_{3,2} = 0.3z, \qquad \Delta_{3,2} = 1 - 0.1z,$$

whence

$$T_{y_0,x_1} = \frac{0.16z^2}{D} + \frac{0.3z(1 - 0.1z)}{D} = \frac{0.3z + 0.13z^2}{D}.$$

Now, at any time t the system must be in one of the three states x_1, x_2, or x_3. This is borne out by the sum

$$T_{y_0,x_1} + T_{y_0,x_2} + T_{y_0,x_3} = \frac{1 + 0.5z + 0.1z^2}{1 - 0.5z - 0.4z^2 - 0.1z^3}$$

$$= 1 + z + z^2 + z^3 + \cdots.$$

§4. ACTIVITY NETWORKS

4.1 Need for Activity Networks

While the two methods of representation outlined above had their origin in the fields of electrical feedback control and electrical networks, the third method we are about to discuss emanated from the field of military and industrial Operations Research. As such, it represents the first concrete attempt at the graphical representation of systems encountered in the areas of industrial engineering, economics, and operations research, and at defining, in a mathematical sense, the relationships among the various components of the system.

The need for such representation arose from the lack of a tool available to management for the control of a multitude of interdependent activities in a *project type* production. We digress for a moment to explain the problem in its general industrial context.

Three factors already in existence as a result of several centuries of human productivity and social change reinforced each other in giving dominance to a special type of human activity, namely, the *project type* production. These factors are, in the order of their importance: *first*, the extremely rapid rate of scientific, engineering, and technological advances which increases the rate of obsolescence among existing (or even contemplated) products and services. *Second*, the industrial might of modern giants which makes possible the translation of ideas into product, relatively speaking, within a very short span of time. And *third*, a social structure which is receptive to such change.

The project type production, in which a host of associated activities are undertaken with the purpose of providing a product or a service for a short span of time, does not make obsolete previously established modes of production (such as mass production). Rather it represents a significant mode of behavior, in some cases a dominant one (such as in the military section of production) which exerts a definite and large influence on the theory and practice of management. Perhaps most significant among such effects is the fact that the project must *start* right and *continue* within the prescribed limits simply because there is no time for a prolonged "shake-down" trial-and-error period.

In the development of large scale systems—such as a microwave system for the transmission of telephone and television signals across the continent—management has long been seeking a systematic approach that permits it to control, in an effective fashion, the allocation of scarce resources and to monitor the progress of the project itself. On the other hand, directives from upper management to reschedule to earlier completion dates certain phases of the project or to keep expenditures (or the allocation of other scarce resources such as manpower) within certain bounds were frequently misinterpreted by overzealous executives. The fault usually lay in the fact that such general directives were not translatable into operational rules simply because of the absence of any mechanism that effects such translation.

The problem naturally resolves itself into a problem of *scheduling* activities of known sequence (the latter is usually determined by the technology of the process) subject to *availability restrictions* (of scarce resources) in such a fashion as to *optimize certain economic criteria*.

Attempts to resolve this problem have resulted in two similar approaches, apparently arrived at independently: the PERT-network approach (for Program Evaluation and Review Technique) and the CPM approach (for Critical Path Method). Both approaches rely heavily on diagramming the system in a network form, and both attempt to analyze the scheduling aspect of the problem. Kelley[†], who is generally credited with the CPM approach, later cast the scheduling problem in a parametric linear programming form. But his objective was still restricted to finding the optimal completion time for each phase of the project. To date, the general problem of scheduling interdependent activities to capacity restrictions with the objective of minimizing an overall economic criterion has not been resolved.

Both PERT and CPM techniques have extensive applications in industrial and military systems, and several extensions and reformulations of both techniques have appeared in the literature during the past three years. (See the references cited at the end of the Chapter.)

4.2 Elements of Activity Networks

A project is considered to be composed of *activities* (represented by arcs) and *events* (represented by nodes). An arc leading from one node to another is *directed* and represents the activity that *must* take place after the occurrence of the first node in order for the second node to obtain. The direction of the arrow determines the *precedence relationship* between the two nodes. An event is considered to be a well-defined occurrence in time, and the precedence relationship is transitive among the nodes.

The result of such representation is a directed network with the following characteristics (see Fig. 2-26):

1. The events (nodes) are numbered so that an activity (an arc) always leads from a small number to a larger one.

2. Each node must have at least one arc leading into it and one arc going out of it except the *origin* (node 1) and the *terminal* (node N). The former has only arcs leading out of it and the latter arcs leading into it.

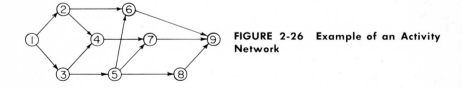

FIGURE 2-26   Example of an Activity Network

[†]J. E. Kelley, Jr., "Critical Path Planning and Scheduling: Mathematical Basis," *Operations Research*, Vol. 9, No. 3, 1961, pp. 296–320.

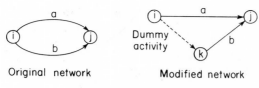

Original network   Modified network

FIGURE 2-27

For machine computation, any two nodes may be connected by, at most, one arc. This constraint can be satisfied in one of two ways: either combine the two or more activities in one comprehensive activity or, better still, use *dummy activities* and *dummy events* of zero duration and utility, shown in Fig. 2-27. The introduction of such dummy activities is useful in resolving this and other situations, as we shall see below.

3. By construction, the network contains no loops, i.e., in any forward path from origin to terminal each node appears once and only once.

4. Since the precedence relationship is transitive, each event along a path must have all preceding events and activities completed before it can be realized.

It sometimes happens that an activity c is a successor to two activities a and b, but activity b has a successor, d, which is *not* a successor of activity a. That is, if the symbol $<$ indicates precedence, then we have $a < c$, $b < c$, $b < d$. Then, if we draw the network as in Fig. 2-28(a), c will bear

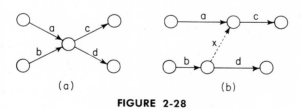

(a)   (b)

FIGURE 2-28

the correct relationship to a and b but d is made dependent on a, which is erroneous. The correct representation is shown in (b) in which x is a *dummy activity* of zero duration and utility.[†]

4.3 Activity Time Estimates

Activity networks are a tool for planning and control. Therefore, the network is constructed *before* (or at the latest in the early stages of) the project realization.

[†] If the reverse notation is used so that *nodes* represent *activities* and *arcs events*, dummy activities are no longer necessary to represent accurately the precedence relationships among events; see Levy, Thompson and Wiest, cited at the end of the chapter.

In order to determine the projected total elapsed time from the start of the project to its termination, estimates of the time required by the various activities are necessary.

In certain instances an estimate of the duration of an activity can be made with a fair degree of confidence in its precision. Under such circumstances, we shall denote the estimate by T_{ij} and assume that it is known with certainty. The subscripts i and j indicate that the time estimate refers to the arc joining nodes i and j and is directed from i to j.

However, in many other instances it may be extremely difficult to state with an equal amount of certainty the duration of an activity that is not to be realized except at some future time. This may be due to several reasons including the possibility that the activity is a research study whose duration is unknown even to the experts in the field. Under such circumstances, one can reasonably expect some form of limits, both upper and lower, on the duration of the activity. For this reason, let

b_i denote a *pessimistic* estimate of the time, which is defined as the duration not to be exceeded;

m_i the *most likely* duration, or the mode of the distribution of the duration; and

a_i the *optimistic* estimate which may be realized if all the factors worked perfectly together and is not supposed to be bettered.

In order to be able to manipulate these time estimates mathematically, we make the following two assumptions:

Assumption 1: The distribution function of the actual duration of the activity, y_{ij}, is unimodal.

Assumption 2: The distribution function can be approximated by the Beta-distribution, i.e., $f(y) = K(y - a)^\alpha (b - y)^\beta$ where α and β are two parameters that are chosen to satisfy the definitions of a, b, and m above (see Fig. 2-29).

The above definitions and assumptions lead to the following approximations:

$$\mathcal{E}(y_{ij}) = T_{ij} \simeq \frac{1}{6}(a + 4m + b) \tag{2-8a}$$

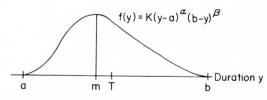

FIGURE 2-29   Fitting   a   Beta-Distribution   to   Data

and the variance of the duration by

$$\text{Var}(y_{ij}) = \sigma_{ij}^2 \simeq \frac{(b-a)^2}{36} \tag{2-8b}$$

In order to be able to make some probability statements concerning the time of completion of any event, we need to make two further assumptions:

Assumption 3: The activities are *independent*.

Assumption 4: If t_i represents the time at which node i obtains, we assume that t_i is *normally* distributed.

These two assumptions lead directly to the following results. If nodes $1, 2, \ldots, N$ lie on a path π, and k ranges over the branches $(1, 2), (2, 3) \ldots,$ $(N-1, N)$ of π which are in series,[†] then

$$\mathcal{E}(t_N) = \sum_{k \epsilon \pi} T_k \tag{2-9a}$$

and

$$\text{Var}(t_N) = \sum_{k \epsilon \pi} \text{Var}(y_k) = \sum_k \sigma_k^2 \tag{2-9b}$$

where the Var (y_k) is given by Eq. (2-8b). Also, the probability that event N will occur on or before a specified time $t_N(s)$ is given by

$$P_r\{t_N \leq t_N(s)\} = \phi \left\{ \frac{t_N(s) - \mathcal{E}(t_N)}{\sqrt{\text{Var}(t_N)}} \right\}$$

$$= \phi \left\{ \frac{t_N(s) - \sum_k T_k}{\sqrt{\sum_k \sigma_k^2}} \right\} \tag{2-10}$$

where the summation is understood to be over all branches in the path from node 1 to node N. $\phi(x)$ is the cumulative standard normal distribution function of x, i.e.,

$$\phi(x) = \int_{-\infty}^{x} (2\pi)^{-1/2} e^{-y^2/2} \, dy.$$

4.4 Earliest Time, Latest Time, and Slack Time

Equation (2-9a) defines the expected time of occurrence of event i (henceforth referred to as "time of event i") when *moving forward* from

[†] For the definition of "path," see page 93; moreover, we shall specify a path by either specifying its nodes, $\pi = 1, 2, \ldots, N$ or by specifying its arcs, $\pi = \{(1, 2), (2, 3), \ldots, (N-1, N)\}$.

the origin I (which is always assumed at time zero) to event i along some specific path π, say.

Suppose that more than one forward path leads from I to i. Denote the paths by $\pi_1, \pi_2, \ldots, \pi_r$. Corresponding to each path π_j we can evaluate, utilizing Eq. (2-9a), the expected time of event i. Let us denote this time by $T(\pi_j)$; then it is obvious that

$$t_i(E) = \underset{\pi_j}{\text{Max}} \{T(\pi_j)\} \tag{2-11}$$

gives the *earliest expected* time of event i, hence we designate it by $t_i(E)$ to emphasize this fact. For example, consider node 4 in Fig. 2-26. There are two forward paths leading to it: $\pi_1 = 1,2,4$ and $\pi_2 = 1,3,4$. Hence $t_4(E) = \text{Max} \{(T_{1,2} + T_{2,4}); (T_{1,3} + T_{3,4})\}$.

As the reader may suspect by now, certain events can be delayed with no effect upon the completion of the last event N. The latest time an event must be accomplished in order to avoid a delay in N is called the *latest expected completion* time, and will be denoted by $t_i(L)$. It can be determined by *moving backwards* from node N to the origin I, fixing the objective date of event N at $t_N(E)$ or some other specified time $t_N(s)$ and subtracting $\Sigma_k\, T_k$ along any backward path between N and i. Similarly, if more than one backward path exists between nodes N and i,

$$t_i(L) = t_N(E) - \underset{\pi_j}{\text{Max}} \left(\sum_{k \in \pi_j} T_k \right) \tag{2-12}$$

where the summation is taken over the activities of each path.

The difference,

$$t_i(L) - t_i(E) = S_i \tag{2-13}$$

is the *slack time* of event i. It represents the expected delay (in the mathematical sense) in the occurrence of event i that causes no delay in $t_N(E)$.

4.5 The Critical Path

Starting from the origin I and moving *forward* toward node N, we can evaluate, in a stepwise fashion, the earliest completion time, $t_i(E)$, for $i = 1, 2, \ldots, N$. This specifies the earliest expected completion time of the terminal, $t_N(E)$. In this process we apply Eqs. (2-9a) and (2-11).

Having determined $t_N(E)$, we can now move *backwards* toward the origin I to determine $t_i(L)$ for $i = N - 1, N - 2, \ldots, 1$, utilizing Eqs. (2-9a) and (2-12).

In these forward and backward movements there must be *at least one* path whose slack, as given by Eq. (2-13), is equal to zero. That is, there must be at least one sequence of nodes $I, \ldots, j, \ldots, N$ and the *connected path* of branches $(1,k), \ldots, (v,N)$ so that for each node j along this path $S_j = 0$. This is called the *critical path* for the simple reason that, along this path, denoted by π_c,

$$t_N(E) = \sum_{k \in \pi_c} T_k, \tag{2-14}$$

and an increase in any T_k would certainly cause an increase in $t_N(E)$.

It is evident that if management wishes to reduce the time of completion of the project it would do better to concentrate its efforts on activities that lie along the critical path(s). Since other activities do not affect $t_N(E)$, expenditure of effort on them would be wasteful.[†] This brings to light the fallacy of "across-the-board" speed-up of activities.

4.6 Numerical Example

In order to maintain the simplicity of the example, we shall assume that we are given the (deterministic) estimates of the duration of the activities, $\{T_k\}$, of the network shown in Fig. 2-30. They are also shown in matrix form as the T_k-matrix (Fig. 2-31).

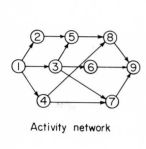

Activity network

FIGURE 2-30

	1	2	3	4	5	6	7	8	9
1	0	2	4	1					
2		0			4				
3			0	6	8	2			
4				0		12	5		
5					0			10	
6						0			11
7							0		4
8								0	7
9									0

T_k – Matrix

FIGURE 2-31

The steps of calculation of $t_i(E)$ and the determination of the critical path(s) are better understood with reference to the Slack Time Table shown in Table 2-1. This table is merely an organized manner of carrying out the steps previously discussed.

[†] Clearly, this is true until significant changes have been made in the activities along the critical path that cause $t_N(E)$ to be reduced to a point where a new critical path(s) is created that includes these activities.

TABLE 2-1   Slack Time Table

		A	B	C	D	E
	Node	$t_i(E)$	$t_i(B)$	$t_i(L)$	S_i	Critical Path
Origin	1	0	27	0	0	×
	2	2	21	6	4	
	3	4	23	4	⓪	×
	4	1	16	11	10	
	5	10	17	10	0	×
	6	12	11	16	4	
	7	13	4	23	10	
	8	20	7	20	0	×
Terminal	9	27	0	27	0	×

1. List the nodes of the network from origin I to terminal N.
2. Column A gives the earliest expected time of node i,

$$t_i(E) = \max_{j<i} [T_{ji} + t_j(E)] \qquad i = 1, 2, \cdots, N$$

where the maximum is taken over all nodes j (i.e., rows in the T_k-matrix) which are connected to node i by an arc (j, i). Notice that $t_i(E)$ is calculated in a stepwise fashion starting with node I and ending in node N. For example,

$$t_5(E) = \max [T_{2,5} + t_2(E); T_{3,5} + t_3(E)]$$

$$= \max [(4 + 2); (6 + 4)] = 10$$

which is the entry opposite node 5 in Column A.

3. Having obtained $t_N(E)$, move backwards toward the origin and calculate for each node i

$$t_i(B) = \max_{j>i} [T_{ji} + t_j(B)] \qquad i = N - 1, N - 2, \cdots, I \qquad (2\text{-}15)$$

where $T_{ji} = T_{ij}$ and enter $t_i(B)$ in Column B. In Eq. (2-15) the maximum is taken over all nodes $j > i$ which are connected to node i by an arc. For example, having obtained $t_9(B) = 0$, $t_8(B) = 7$, $t_7(B) = 4$, and and $t_6(B) = 11$ (which are self-evident), we have

$$t_5(B) = T_{8,5} + t_8(B) = 10 + 7 = 17$$

and

$$t_4(B) = \max [T_{8,4} + t_8(B); \quad T_{7,4} + t_7(B)]$$

$$= \max [(5 + 7); \quad (12 + 4)] = 16$$

as shown in Table 2-1.

4. Enter in column C: $t_N(E) - t_i(B) = t_i(L)$, which is the latest start time.

5. In column D evaluate the slack

$$S_i = t_i(L) - t_i(E) \geq 0. \tag{2-16}$$

For example, $S_3 = 6 - 2 = 4$ and $S_7 = 23 - 13 = 10$

6. In column E enter an × wherever $S_i = 0$. The nodes (i.e., rows) thus marked must form a connected path from I to N and define the critical path, which is shown in double lines in Fig. 2-32. Opposite each node we have entered three numbers which are copied directly from the table: the first number is $t_i(E)$; the second is $t_i(L)$; and the last is S_i.

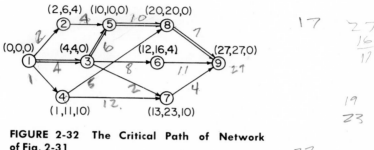

FIGURE 2-32   The Critical Path of Network of Fig. 2-31

Notice that each node that is not along the critical path has a slack time > 0.

If we were also given the set of optimistic and pessimistic time estimates of each activity, $\{a_k, b_k\}$, we would have calculated the Var $[t_9(E)]$ by Eq. (2-9b). Then it would have been a simple matter to evaluate the probability of completing the project at any specified time $t_9(s)$. (See Exercise 9 at the end of chapter.)

4.7 A Flow-Network Interpretation for Determination of the CP

Activity networks which are of concern to us here possess no "flow" of any uniform commodity through them. In fact, the network is a representation of a heterogeneous number of activities or tasks that combine to realize certain events.

However, it is possible to view the network as a *flow-network* in which a unit flow enters at the origin I and exits at the terminal N. The time of each activity, T_{ij}, can then be interpreted as the time of transportation of the unit commodity from node i to node j (or as the cost of such transportation). Naturally, all intermediate nodes act as "transshipment" centers and, in order to conserve the total flow through the network, the "input" to each node must equal the "output." Under such interpretation, determining the critical path is equivalent to determining the maximum transportation route (or cost) from I to N. The advantage of such interpretation is twofold: first, a linear programming formulation—and in particular a dual algorithm—is immediately available, and, second, the whole body of literature on network flows and LP can be utilized to answer any other questions (such as sensitivity analysis) which are deemed of interest in the study of such networks.

The approach is best illustrated with reference to an example. Consider the activity network shown in Fig. 2-33. The duration of each activity, T_{ij}, is indicated on each branch. A unit flow is imposed on the origin as

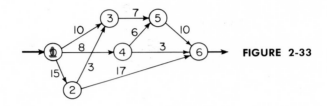

FIGURE 2-33

input and on the terminal as output. Each arrow (i,j) has its "tail" incident on some node i and its "head" incident on node j. Such a branch is represented by the column vector $V_{ij} = < 0, 0, \ldots, 1, 0, \ldots, -1, \ldots, 0 >$ of N entries where the $+1$ is in the ith position and the -1 in the jth position and the rest of the entries are zeros.

Let $X_{ij} \geq 0$ denote the nonnegative flow along branch (i,j). Then we wish to

$$\text{Maximize } 15X_{12} + 10X_{13} + 8X_{14} + 3X_{23} + 17X_{26} + 7X_{35} + 6X_{45}$$
$$+ 3X_{46} + 10X_{56}$$

subject to the restriction that, for each node i, the total input flow is equal to the total output flow. That is, with reference to Fig. 2-33.

$$
\begin{array}{llllllll}
X_{12} & +X_{13} & +X_{14} & & & & & = 1 \\
-X_{12} & & & +X_{23} & +X_{26} & & & = 0 \\
& -X_{13} & & -X_{23} & & +X_{35} & & = 0 \\
& & -X_{14} & & & & +X_{45} & +X_{46} & = 0 \\
& & & & & -X_{35} & -X_{45} & & +X_{56} = 0 \\
& & & & -X_{26} & & & -X_{46} & -X_{56} = -1
\end{array}
$$

(2-17)

In matrix notation we have

$$\text{Maximize } \Sigma \; T_{ij} \cdot X_{ij}$$

such that $V \cdot X = V_0$ where V is the matrix formed from the column vectors V_{ij}, X is the column vector $<X_{ij}>$ and V_0 is the column vector of imposed flow $V_0 = <1, 0, \ldots, 0, -1>$.

The solution of the LP problem is readily obtained through the dual formulation. Let $w_1, \ldots, w_6$ be the dual variables. Then the dual problem is to

$$\text{Minimize } w_1 - w_6$$

subject to:

w_1 $-w_2$				≥ 15	(2-18a)
w_1	$-w_3$			≥ 10	(2-18b)
w_1	$-w_4$			≥ 8	(2-18c)
w_2 $-w_3$				≥ 3	(2-18d)
w_2		$-w_6$		≥ 17	(2-18e)
w_3	$-w_5$			≥ 7	(2-18f)
w_4 $-w_5$				≥ 6	(2-18g)
w_4	$-w_6$			≥ 3	(2-18h)
w_5 $-w_6$				$\geq 10.$	(2-18i)

Since, in the dual formulation, each inequality contains two and only two variables, the minimization can be achieved by inspection in one scanning of Eqs. (2-18a) to (2-18i). In particular, if we put $w_1 = 0$, then we have, successively,

$w_2 = -15$ to satisfy   (2-18a)

$w_3 = -18$ to satisfy   (2-18d)

$w_4 = -8$ to satisfy   (2-18c)

$w_5 = -25$ to satisfy   (2-18f)

$w_6 = -35$ to satisfy   (2-18i).

The optimal of the dual problem is given by $w_1 - w_6 = 35$.

According to a well-known result of the Complementary Slackness theorem of LP, each inequality of Eq. (2-18) satisfied as inequality must have its corresponding variable $= 0$. Moreover, this relationship uniquely determines the optimal solutions of the primal problem, $\{X_{ij}^*\}$. Finally, the optimal of the primal thus calculated must equal the optimal of the dual.

From our solution of the dual problem, it is easily seen that the following inequalities are satisfied as equalities: (2-18a), (2-18c), (2-18d), (2-18f), and (2-18i).   Hence, variables X_{12}, X_{14}, X_{23}, X_{35}, and X_{56} are ≥ 0. Putting the other variables in Eq. (2-17) equal to 0 we obtain:

$$
\begin{array}{rcl}
X_{12} + X_{14} & = & 1 \\
- X_{12} \qquad + X_{23} & = & 0 \\
- X_{23} + X_{35} & = & 0 \\
- X_{14} & = & 0 \\
- X_{35} + X_{56} & = & 0 \\
- X_{56} & = & -1.
\end{array}
\tag{2-19}
$$

Eqs. (2-19) yield the unique solution:

$$X_{12} = X_{23} = X_{35} = X_{56} = 1; X_{14} = 0.$$

To be sure, $\Sigma X_{ij} T_{ij} = 35$, as before. Notice that:

(1) The number of variables $\{X_{ij}\}$ is equal to the number of branches. However, there are exactly N dual variables, w_i, which correspond to the number of nodes in the network.

(2) The branches corresponding to the optimal solution of the primal problem of Eq. (2-17) define a "spanning tree;" i.e., they define a graph that contains one and only one branch incident on any node, and all nodes of the graph are connected. See Fig. 2-34.

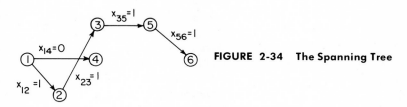

FIGURE 2-34   The Spanning Tree

(3) The chain from origin to terminal is unique and defines the critical path, i.e., there is no other chain between nodes 1 and 6 so that $\Sigma T_{ij} \cdot X_{ij} > 35$.

(4) Alternate optimal solutions to the LP of Eq. (2-17) define alternate spanning trees of the network of Fig. 2-33. For example, if the duration $T_{2,6}$ of activity (2,6) were 20 rather than 17, it is obvious that the path 1, 2, 6 would be another CP (of duration 35 units). In the LP formulation this would have manifested itself in that more of the dual inequalities of

Eq. (2-18) would be satisfied as equalities. In particular, with $T_{26} = 20$, inequality (2-18e) would have been satisfied as equality, which in turn would have caused the variable X_{26} to appear in the system of Eqs. (2-19). It is left to the reader to verify that the new set of Eqs. (2-19) is satisfied *only* by two sets of values; the set obtained above and the set

$$X_{12} = X_{26} = 1; \quad X_{14} = X_{23} = X_{35} = X_{56} = 0,$$

which defines a different spanning tree.

4.8 Estimating the Optimal Duration of a Project

A natural question that is asked by project managers and project co-ordinators is: how much time *should* be allowed each activity and what is the *best target time* for the completion of the whole project? Such a question necessarily presumes the existence of different possible durations for some, if not all, of the activities in the project. Such an assumption is not unrealistic. The majority of the activities encountered in the industrial, governmental, and military projects can be accomplished in shorter or longer durations by increasing or decreasing the resources (such as facilities, manpower, or money) available to them.

The following attempt to answer this question is due to Kelley.[†] Let (i,j) denote an activity in the project, and let A be the set of all such activities. Suppose that for activity (i,j) there are two extreme durations: d_{ij} and D_{ij} with $d_{ij} \leq D_{ij}$. The interpretation of the time d_{ij} is that it is the fastest possible time of the activity without incurring prohibitive costs or changing the very nature of the project. D_{ij} is the minimum-cost duration: it represents the time the activity would take if we wished to minimize the cost of that individual activity.

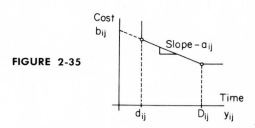

FIGURE 2-35

Let the cost of the activity be a linear function of its duration, y_{ij}, and be given by

$$c_{ij} = b_{ij} - a_{ij} \cdot y_{ij}$$

[†]J. E. Kelley, "Critical Path Planning and Scheduling: Mathematical Basis," *Operations Research*, Vol. 9, No. 3, 1961, pp. 296–320.

where b_{ij} and $a_{ij} \geq 0$ are constants, as shown in Fig. 2-35. Naturally, y_{ij} is restricted by

$$d_{ij} \leq y_{ij} \leq D_{ij}. \qquad (2\text{-}20)$$

If t_j represents, as before, the realization time of event j, then

$$t_j \geq t_i + y_{ij} \qquad i < j, \ (i,j) \epsilon A \qquad (2\text{-}21)$$

for every i and j. Restrictions in Eq. (2-21) simply state that if event i occurs before event j then the latter can obtain at least y_{ij} time units later.

Now we can state the problem as: Minimize $\Sigma_{(i,j)\epsilon A} c_{ij}$ subject to restrictions in Eqs. (2-20) and (2-21) and such that

$$t_N = \lambda. \qquad (2\text{-}22)$$

This last equation defines the desired duration of the project as equal to $\lambda > 0$.

This is an LP formulation which is different from the previous (i.e., flow-network) formulation in that our objective here is to minimize the total cost of the project for a specified completion time.

In particular, this is a *parametric LP problem*. If λ is varied from $\underline{\lambda} = \underline{t}_N = \{t_N(E) \mid y_{ij} = d_{ij}\}$ to $\overline{\lambda} = \overline{t}_N = \{t_N(E) \mid y_{ij} = D_{ij}\}$ we obtain a total cost which is a function of the parameter λ. Kelley has shown that the cost function thus generated is a convex, piecewise linear function of λ, as shown in Fig. 2-36. The optimal duration λ^* corresponding to any level of expenditure can be obtained directly from such a relationship. The literature on techniques for solving such a parametric LP yields the method for generating the cost function and choosing λ^* (see Kelley in the references cited at the end of the chapter). However, in the following section we describe a flow-network algorithm which obviates the need to

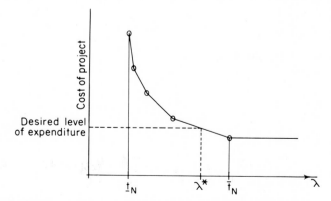

FIGURE 2-36   Variation of Total Project Cost With Duration λ

resort to such general procedures and which results in great savings in time and computing effort.

4.9* A Flow-Network Algorithm for the Determination of Project Duration-Cost Curve

It is axiomatic in the solution of mathematical models of real-life problems that general algorithms are utilized only as a last resort when all short-cuts and special solutions have failed. Therefore, applying the general parametric linear programming theory to the determination of the optimal time-cost problem may be wasteful in view of the special structure of the problem stated in Eqs. (2-20) to (2-22).

Such special structure was capitalized upon by Fulkerson[†] who developed a rather simple and elegant flow-network algorithm for the determination of the complete parametric cost curve of Fig. 2-36.

In spite of the simplicity of the algorithm, its explanation is lengthy. We devote this section to the explanation.

First, we restate the problem of Eqs. (2-20) to (2-22) in the following form:

$$\text{Maximize} \quad P(\lambda) = \Sigma \, a_{ij} \, y_{ij} \tag{2-23}$$

subject to

$$t_i + y_{ij} - t_j \leq 0 \qquad \text{for all } (i,j) \, \epsilon A \tag{2-24}$$

$$-t_1 \qquad \quad + t_n \leq \lambda \tag{2-25}$$

$$y_{ij} \qquad \leq D_{ij} \qquad \text{all } (i,j) \tag{2-26}$$

and

$$- y_{ij} \qquad \leq -d_{ij} \qquad \text{all } (i,j) \tag{2-27}$$

We give a numerical example to illustrate the mathematical formulation of Eqs. (2-23) to (2-27). This example, which is shown in Fig. 2-37, will be the vehicle for illustrating the different steps of the procedure.

Arc	d_{ij}	D_{ij}	a_{ij}
1,2	4	6	8
1,3	4	8	9
1,4	3	5	3
2,4	3	3	∞
2,5	3	5	4
3,6	8	12	20
4,6	5	8	5
5,6	6	6	∞

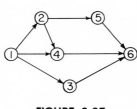

FIGURE 2-37

---

*Section can be omitted on first reading.
[†] D. R. Fulkerson, "A Network Flow Computation for Project Cost Curve," *Management Science*, Vol. 7, No. 2, 1961.

The primal formulation of Eqs. (2-23) to (2-27) can be exhibited in matrix form as shown in Table 2-2:

TABLE 2-2

y_{12}	y_{13}	y_{14}	y_{24}	y_{25}	y_{36}	y_{46}	y_{56}	t_1	t_2	t_3	t_4	t_5	t_6		Dual Variable
1								1	−1					≤ 0	f_{12}
	1							1		−1				≤ 0	f_{13}
		1						1			−1			≤ 0	f_{14}
			1						1		−1			≤ 0	f_{24}
				1					1			−1		≤ 0	f_{25}
					1					1			−1	≤ 0	f_{36}
						1					1		−1	≤ 0	f_{46}
							1					1	−1	≤ 0	f_{56}
								−1					1	≤ λ	v
1														≤ D_{12}	g_{12}
	1													≤ D_{13}	g_{13}
		1												≤ D_{14}	g_{14}
			1											≤ D_{24}	g_{24}
				1										≤ D_{25}	g_{25}
					1									≤ D_{36}	g_{36}
						1								≤ D_{46}	g_{46}
							1							≤ D_{56}	g_{56}
−1														≤ $-d_{12}$	h_{12}
	−1													≤ $-d_{13}$	h_{13}
		−1												≤ $-d_{14}$	h_{14}
			−1											≤ $-d_{24}$	h_{24}
				−1										≤ $-d_{25}$	h_{25}
					−1									≤ $-d_{36}$	h_{36}
						−1								≤ $-d_{46}$	h_{46}
							−1							≤ $-d_{56}$	h_{56}
a_{12}	a_{13}	a_{14}	a_{24}	a_{25}	a_{36}	a_{46}	a_{56}	0	0	0	0	0	0		

Next, consider the dual program of Eqs. (2-23) to (2-27). Assign the dual variables f_{ij}, v, g_{ij} and h_{ij} to constraints (2-24) to (2-27), respectively. Then the dual linear program is given by

$$\text{Minimize } \lambda v + \sum_{(i,j)} D_{ij} g_{ij} - \sum_{(i,j)} d_{ij} h_{ij} \tag{2-28}$$

subject to

$$f_{ij} + g_{ij} - h_{ij} = a_{ij} \quad \text{all } (i,j) \in A \tag{2-29}$$

and

$$\sum_j (f_{ij} - f_{ji}) = \begin{cases} v & i = 1 \\ 0 & i \neq 1, N \\ -v & i = N \end{cases} \tag{2-30}$$

Here, all the variables are nonnegative, and equalities are imposed because the primal variables were not explicitly constrained in sign.

In passing we remark that Eqs. (2-30) are "flow conservation constraints" since they state that if f_{ij} is interpreted as the flow in arc (i,j) from i to j then the flow *into* node 1 is v, the flow *out* of node N is v, and the total input flow at any intermediate node is equal to the total output flow.

Since the objective is to minimize Eq. (2-28), it immediately follows from constraints (2-29) that *at the minimum* either g_{ij} or h_{ij} must be equal to zero. Hence we may assume from the beginning that

$$g_{ij} = \max [0; a_{ij} - f_{ij}] \qquad\qquad (2\text{-}31)$$

$$h_{ij} = \max [0; f_{ij} - a_{ij}]. \qquad\qquad (2\text{-}32)$$

The reader conversant with the theory of networks of flow (cf. Chapter 4, §6) will immediately recognize g_{ij} as the "residual capacity" in arc (i,j) when a_{ij} is interpreted as the arc's capacity and f_{ij} is the flow in the arc; h_{ij} is recognized as the "reverse capacity" in the *directed* arc (i,j) in excess of a_{ij}.

Moreover, since a_{ij} is a given constant, it follows from Eq. (2-31) that g_{ij} is linear in f_{ij} for f_{ij} in the region 0 to a_{ij}, while h_{ij} is linear in f_{ij} for any $f_{ij} \geq a_{ij}$. The two variables can be sketched as in Fig. 2-38 as functions of the flow f_{ij}.

Therefore, the objective function of Eq. (2-28) can be written as

$$\text{Minimize } \lambda v + \sum_{(i,j)} D_{ij} \cdot \text{Max} [0; a_{ij} - f_{ij}]$$

$$- \sum_{(i,j)} d_{ij} \cdot \text{Max} [0; f_{ij} - a_{ij}] \qquad\qquad (2\text{-}33)$$

The first term λv is linear in $v \geq 0$; the second term is linear in f_{ij} for $0 \leq f_{ij} \leq a_{ij}$; while the third term is linear in f_{ij} for $f_{ij} \geq a_{ij}$. Consequently, the objective function is piecewise linear in f_{ij}. Denote the flow in the first region by $f_{ij}^{(1)}$ and in the second region by $f_{ij}^{(2)}$ (actually $= f_{ij} - a_{ij} \geq 0$). Then we can substitute in the objective function $\Sigma D_{ij}(a_{ij} - f_{ij}^{(1)})$ for the first summation, and $\Sigma d_{ij} f_{ij}^{(2)}$ for the second summation. Thus we obtain, after eliminating the constant term $\Sigma D_{ij} a_{ij}$, the dual

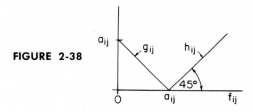

FIGURE 2-38

program

$$\text{Minimize } \lambda v - \Sigma D_{ij} f_{ij}^{(1)} - \Sigma d_{ij} f_{ij}^{(2)} \tag{2-34}$$

subject to:

$$\sum_{j,k} [f_{ij}^{(k)} - f_{ji}^{(k)}] = \begin{cases} v & \text{for } i = 1, \\ 0 & i \neq 1, N \\ -v & i = N \end{cases} \tag{2-35}$$

$$f_{ij}^{(1)} \leq a_{ij} \qquad\qquad \text{for all } (i,j) \, \epsilon \, A \tag{2-36}$$

and

$$f_{ij}^{(k)}, v \geq 0, k = 1,2. \quad \text{for all } (i,j) \, \epsilon \, A \tag{2-37}$$

This program has the following interpretation. In a network of N nodes *two arcs* now replace the single arc (i,j). The first of these two arcs has a capacity a_{ij}, while the second arc is not limited in capacity. The problem is to construct a flow $f_{ij}^{(k)}$ from node 1 to node N in the new network which minimizes Eq. (2-34) subject to the "flow conservation" constraints of Eq. (2-35).

To illustrate, we return to the primal program of Eqs. (2-23) to (2-27). The corresponding dual program of Eqs. (2-28) to (2-30) can be easily constructed from the matrix form. The enlarged network corresponding to Fig. 2-37 is shown in Fig. 2-39, it being understood that the capacity is

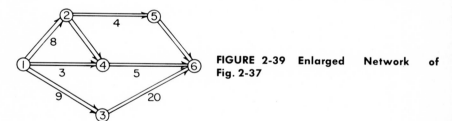

FIGURE 2-39   Enlarged   Network   of Fig. 2-37

infinite when not stated on the arc. For example, both arcs joining nodes 2 and 4 and 5 and 6 have infinite capacities. This is so because in the primal program the cost of reducing the duration of either activity was infinite.

The algorithm for determining the duration-cost function closely follows the reasoning of maximal-flow determination.[†] For simplicity of exposition we shall divide the presentation into five steps:

    1. Determining the maximum duration $(\bar{\lambda})$.
    2. Determining the feasibility of $\lambda < \bar{\lambda}$.

[†] cf. Chapter 4, §4.

3. Labeling for minimum cost activities.
4. Effecting the reduction: The Node Time Change Routine.
5. Reverse labeling.

The last step is an important complication induced by the directedness of activity networks. The steps of iteration will be illustrated utilizing the network of Fig. 2-37 (or its enlarged form of Fig. 2-39).

Step 1: Determining the Maximum Duration $\overline{\lambda}$. $(= \overline{t_N}(E) \mid y_{ij} = D_{ij})$.

Put all $y_{ij} = D_{ij}$ and determine $\overline{t}_i(E)$, the earliest completion time of all nodes $i = 1 \ldots, N$, by any one of several methods explained before (see §4.5 and §4.7).

For convenience of notation and clarity of exposition, we adopt the format of Fig. 2-40. We exhibit only one arc of capacity a_{ij} (finite or infinite), it being understood that a second arc of infinite capacity also exists and will be introduced when needed. Also, we present the two limit durations D_{ij} and d_{ij} as a column vector $<D_{ij}, d_{ij}>$, and the two quantities $f_{ij}^{(k)}$ and a_{ij} (or ∞) as a row vector $(f_{ij}^{(1)}, a_{ij} - f_{ij}^{(1)})$ or $(f_{ij}^{(2)}, \infty)$. Each node is represented by a circle bearing two numbers: the node number i and its $t_i(E)$.

In the starting network of Fig. 2-40, all $f_{ij} = 0$. We can easily see that $\overline{\lambda} = \overline{t}_6 = 20$, and that the critical path (CP) is $1, 3, 6$.

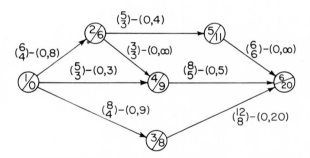

FIGURE 2-40 $t_i(E)$ and Starting Flow $f_{ij} = 0$

Step 2: Determining Feasibility of $\lambda < \overline{\lambda}$

Label the origin, node 1, with $(\infty, 0)$. In general, a node j is labeled, when possible, with (q_j, i) where q_j denotes the amount of flow that can be made available at j from node i through increased flow in the arc (i,j), and i is the preceeding node from which such flow originates. Check each arc originating from node 1 for the relationship

$$s_{1j}^{(2)} = d_{1j} - t_j = 0 \tag{2-38}$$

Here $s_{ij}^{(2)}$ represents the possible reduction in the duration of activity $(1,j)$ and we have written t_j in short for $t_j(E)$. Any node j for which Eq. (2-38) holds should be labeled $(\infty, 1)$. In general, for any node i which is labeled with ∞, check all nodes j connected with it for

$$s_{ij}^{(2)} = t_i + d_{ij} - t_j = 0 \tag{2-39}$$

If Eq (2-39) holds for j, label it with (∞, i). Continue the process until one of two conditions obtain: (1) the terminal N cannot be labeled, or (2) N can be labeled with ∞. In the first eventuality it *is possible* to reduce λ; consequently, go to the labeling routine below. In the second eventuality it is not possible to reduce λ and so terminate the analysis.

In either case, maintain the labeling of the nodes with ∞ throughout all subsequent analysis.

Step 3: Labeling for Minimum Cost Activities

Start with the origin, node 1 (which is always labeled with $(\infty, 0)$). For any labeled node i check all nodes j connected with i so that either

$$s_{ij}^{(1)} = t_i + D_{ij} - t_j = 0 \tag{2-40}$$

and

$$f_{ij} < a_{ij}$$

or

$$s_{ij}^{(2)} = t_i + d_{ij} - t_j = 0. \tag{2-41}$$

If Eq. (2-40) holds, label node j with (q_j, i) where

$$q_j = \min \{q_i; a_{ij} - \overline{f_{ij}^{(1)}}\} \tag{2-42}$$

If Eq. (2-41) holds, label node j with (q_i, i). Continue the labeling until one of the following two conditions obtains: (a) the terminal N cannot be labeled (called *nonbreakthrough*)—go to "Node Time Change Routine" described in Step 4; or (b) terminal N is labeled (called *breakthrough)*—go to "Flow Change Routine" described below.

> *Discussion.* Consider eventuality (a). Whenever (a) obtains it must be because $f_{ij} = a_{ij}$ for all arcs satisfying $s_{ij}^{(1)} = 0$. Recalling that the flow f is, in fact, cost, it follows that when condition (a) obtains the maximum flow into N has been achieved under the existing node times $t_i(E)$. The only way to increase the flow into N (i.e., incur higher cost) is through a reduction in some $t_i(E)$'s. This is precisely what the Node Time Change Routine purports to achieve.
>
> Next, consider eventuality (b). Since a breakthrough has been achieved, the flow from 1 to N can be increased by the amount indicated in the labeling of N. By construction, see Eq. (2-42), this flow must be the minimum capacity (i.e., cost) in some critical path. The Flow Change Routine performs such increase in flow.

To illustrate, we apply Steps 2 and 3 to the network example, proceeding from Fig. 2-40. The origin is labeled $(\infty,0)$. Since no node connected with 1 has $s_{ij}^{(2)} = 0$, no other node can be labeled with ∞, i.e., condition (a) obtains and no breakthrough is possible. This establishes the feasibility of $\lambda < \overline{\lambda}$.

Node 1 is connected to nodes 2, 3 and 4. Since $s_{1j}^{(1)} = 0$ for $j = 2$, 3, and $f_{12} = f_{13} = 0 < a_{1j}$, the conditions of Eq (2-40) are satisfied and nodes 2 and 3 can be labeled. We have

$$q_2 = \min\{\infty;\quad 8 - 0\} = 8; \quad \text{hence } 2 \text{ is labeled } (8,1);$$

$$q_3 = \min\{\infty;\quad 9 - 0\} = 9; \quad \text{hence } 3 \text{ is labeled } (9,1).$$

Node 2 connects with nodes 4 and 5. Notice that $s_{24}^{(2)} = 0$, i.e., the condition of Eq. (2-41) is satisfied for 4, and $s_{25}^{(1)} = 0$ with $f_{25} = 0 < a_{25}$, i.e., the conditions of Eq. (2-40) are satisfied for 5. Consequently, both nodes can be labeled as shown in Fig. 2-41.

At this juncture we are free to either proceed with nodes 4 and 5 just labeled and investigate the labeling of nodes connected with them, or return to node 3 which was labeled from 1 and investigate the labeling of nodes connected with it. It is advisable to be systematic in the procedure, and we prefer to scan all nodes previously labeled before proceeding with the newly labeled nodes.

Consequently, we investigate node 3. The only node connected to 3 is the terminal 6, and

$$s_{36}^{(1)} = 0, f_{36} = 0 < 20.$$

Consequently, node 6 can be labeled. We have

$$q_{36} = \min\{9;\quad 20 - 0\} = 9,$$

and the labeling of 6 is $(9,3)$—a breakthrough.

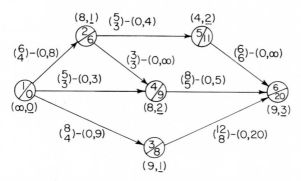

**FIGURE 2-41 Labeling According to Step 2.
Breakthrough**

The Flow Change Routine. This routine is to be applied whenever a breakthrough has occurred. Start with node N. For any labeled node j with label (q_j, i) increase the flow f_{ij} by q_N, reduce the residual capacity in the arc (i,j) by q_N, and erase the labeling of j. Continue this process until I is reached.

Step 4. Effecting the Reduction: The Node Time Change Routine

This routine is to be applied whenever a breakthrough did *not* occur. The nodes of the network can be divided into two mutually exclusive and totally exhaustive sets: the labeled nodes (including those labeled with ∞) and the unlabeled nodes. Let Z be the set of arcs $\{(i,j)\}$ so that one node is labeled and the other is not labeled. By necessity, the set Z is a *cut set*, i.e., it separates node I from node N. Moreover, Z contains two mutually exclusive (but not necessarily exhaustive) subsets:

$$Z_1 = \{(i,j) \mid i \text{ labeled}, j \text{ unlabeled}, s_{ij}^{(k)} < 0\}$$

and

$$Z_2 = \{(i,j) \mid i \text{ unlabeled}, j \text{ labeled}; s_{ij}^{(k)} > 0\}.$$

Ignore all arcs of Z_1 where the equality $s_{ij}^{(k)} = 0$ holds, $k = 1$ or 2. Define

$$\delta_1 = \min_{Z_1} [-s_{ij}^{(k)}], s_{ij}^{(k)} < 0$$

$$\delta_2 = \min_{Z_2} [s_{ij}^{(k)}], s_{ij}^{(k)} > 0 \tag{2-43}$$

and put

$$\delta = \min(\delta_1, \delta_2). \tag{2-44}$$

For all *unlabeled* nodes change the node times $\{t_j\}$ to $\{t_j - \delta\}$. Discard all labels other than ∞ and return to Step 3.

> *Discussion.* We recall that the "capacity" a_{ij} is in fact the marginal cost of the primal problem. A breakthrough results in increasing the "flow" into N by the minimum "capacity" along a CP, i.e., it determines the minimum-cost activity along one CP. As long as breakthrough is possible, the Flow Change Routine saturates the "capacity" of one activity along a CP. The set composed of these saturated minimum-cost activities represents the arcs whose duration must be reduced, and the cost of such reduction is guaranteed to be minimal.
>
> When a nonbreakthrough condition obtains it must be because the CP's have been exhausted. The Node Time Change Routine then proceeds to reduce the length of all CP's *simultaneously* by the maximum possible amount. This is the amount δ. It represents the possible reduction in all CP's before either another path becomes critical or an activity has been reduced to its lower bound, d_{ij}.

Notice that the ∞-labeling permits the procedure to select the next-cheapest activity along a CP whenever the cheapest activity has reached it lower limit, d_{ij}.

To illustrate, we proceed with the example where we left it in Fig. 2-41. Since a breakthrough was obtained, we utilize the Flow Change Routine to obtain Fig. 2-42. Notice that the path *1, 3, 6* is the only CP, and that the "flow" of 9 through this path denotes the cost of the cheapest activity along the path.

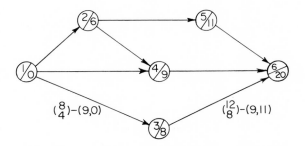

FIGURE 2-42   Result of Flow Changing Routine in CP 1, 3, 6

We start the labeling procedure anew, and we immediately obtain Fig. 2-43 in which no breakthrough is possible. We go to the Node Time Change Routine. Notice that arcs (1,3), (4,6) and (5,6) constitute the cut set Z since each arc has one of its terminal nodes labeled and the other

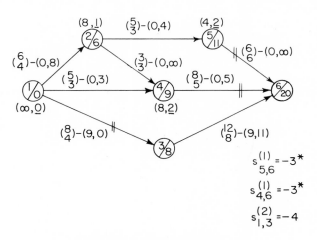

$$s^{(1)}_{5,6} = -3^*$$

$$s^{(1)}_{4,6} = -3^*$$

$$s^{(2)}_{1,3} = -4$$

FIGURE 2-43   No Breakthrough

node not labeled. Also, all arcs of Z are in Z_1; the subset Z_2 is empty:

$$s_{5,6}^{(1)} = 11 + 6 - 20 = -3 = s_{5,6}^{(2)}$$

$$s_{4,6}^{(1)} = 9 + 8 - 20 = -3 > s_{4,6}^{(2)}$$

$$s_{1,3}^{(2)} = 0 + 4 - 8 = -4 \quad (s_{1,3}^{(1)} = 0).$$

Consequently, $\delta = 3$. The only unlabeled nodes are 3 and 6. We reduce their times by 3 to yield the network of Fig. 2-44.

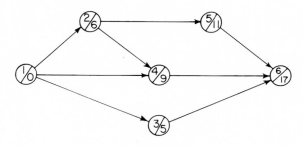

FIGURE 2-44

The alert reader will remark that the reduction of 3 time units was in activity $(1,3)$, which is the cheaper of the two activities constituting the CP $1, 3, 6$. Also, the reduction of 3 time units was the maximum possible before two other paths, (namely $1, 2, 4, 6$ and $1, 2, 5, 6$) become critical.

The network example of Fig. 2-40, which has been serving as our vehicle of illustration, was contrived to be simple. Unfortunately, it does not illustrate the realization of the subset Z_2 and the interpretation of that eventuality. To this end we utilize another network whose capacities and labeling are shown in Fig. 2-45. The cut set $Z = \{(1,3), (3,4), (4,6), (5,6)\}$,

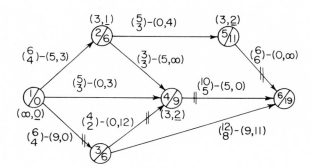

FIGURE 2-45

with $Z_1 = \{(1,3), (4,6)\ (5,6)\}$ and $Z_2 = \{(3,4)\}$. This is so because

$$s_{5,6}^{(1)} = 11 + 6 - 19 = -2 = s_{5,6}^{(2)} \qquad 5 \text{ labeled, } 6 \text{ not labeled}$$

$$s_{4,6}^{(2)} = 9 + 5 - 19 = -5 \qquad (s_{4,6}^{(1)} = 0), 4 \text{ labeled, } 6 \text{ not labeled}$$

$$s_{1,3}^{(2)} = 0 + 4 - 9 = -2 \qquad (s_{1,3}^{(1)} = 0), 1 \text{ labeled, } 3 \text{ not labeled}$$

but

$$s_{3,4}^{(1)} = 6 + 4 - 9 = 1 > s_{3,4}^{(2)} (= -1), 4 \text{ labeled, } 3 \text{ not labeled}$$

If arc $(3,4)$ were not included in Z, the latter would not constitute a cut set. In this case, $\delta_1 = 2$, $\delta_2 = 1$ and $\delta = 1$.

We return to the network of Fig. 2-44 and proceed with the calculations of Step 3, but with less detailed explanation. The following iterations are shown in Figs. 2-46 to 2-49.

Discussion. We pause for a moment to elaborate on a new phenomenon in the labeling of Fig. 2-49. Node *3* is labeled with ∞ and at the same time a breakthrough occurred. Following our previous interpretation of the label, the cost of shortening activity $(1,3)$ must be infinite, and yet a reduction in the time of CP *1, 3, 6* is possible! This seems logical since activity $(1,3)$ has

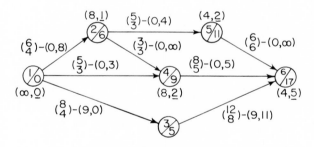

FIGURE 2-46 Breakthrough

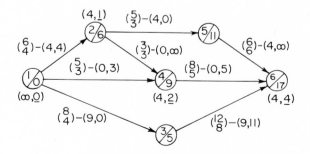

FIGURE 2-47 Breakthrough

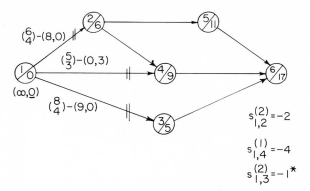

FIGURE 2-48   No Breakthrough

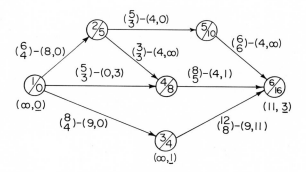

FIGURE 2-49   Breakthrough

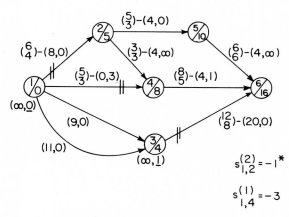

FIGURE 2-50   No Breakthrough

been shortened to its lower limit and no further reduction is permissible. However, activity (3,6) can be shortened—at a cost of 11 units per unit reduction. Hence the breakthrough with labeling 11 at 6.

It is at this point that we utilize the second arc of infinite capacity between nodes 1 and 3. The drawing of these arcs, it is to be recalled, was forfeited to keep the diagrams uncluttered. Now it is evident that the second arcs of infinite capacity by which the original network was augmented were only a device to permit shortening, whenever needed, the second-cheapest, third-cheapest, etc., activities along a CP. In Fig. 2-50 above we utilize the second arc between nodes 1 and 2.

We proceed with the labeling and shortening in Fig. 2-50 to 2-54.

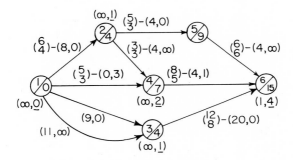

FIGURE 2-51   Breakthrough

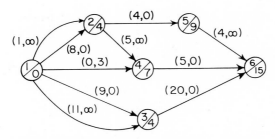

FIGURE 2-52   Increasing the Flow by Introducing Second Arc Joining Nodes 1 and 2

In Fig. 2-54 we finally achieved labeling node 6 with ∞, which signals the termination of the procedure. To be sure, each activity along the CP 1, 2, 5, 6 is at its lower limit, d_{ij}.

We summarize, in the following Table 2-3, the results obtained: If we take the cost of completing the project with all activity times set equal to D_{ij} as our datum, the project duration-cost curve would be as shown in Fig. 2-55, (compare with Fig. 2-36).

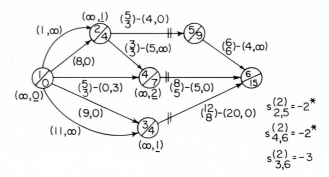

FIGURE 2-53   No Breakthrough

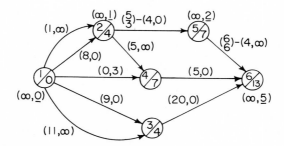

FIGURE 2-54   Breakthrough with ∞-Labeling

TABLE 2-3

Cycle Number	$t_6(E)$	$\Sigma_i f_{i6}$	δ	Increase in Cost $\delta \times \Sigma f_{i6}$	Cumulative Increase in Cost
1	20	9	3	27	27
2	17	17	1	17	44
3	16	28	1	28	72
4	15	29	2	58	130
5	13	∞	∞	Termination	

Step 5: Reverse Labeling

Project networks are *directed* networks, a characteristic which demands special interpretation of the notion of "capacity." In particular, if the capacity of a directed arc is a_{ij} along the direction of the arrow $i \rightarrow j$, it is considered 0 in the reverse direction, $j \rightarrow i$. However, once flow $f_{ij} > 0$ exists from i to j, a "capacity" of $r_{ji} = 0 - (-f_{ij}) = f_{ij}$ is created in

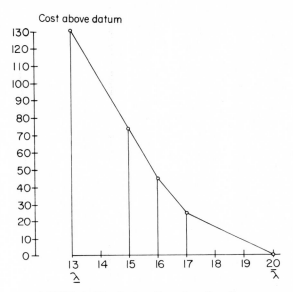

FIGURE 2-55 Project Duration-Cost Curve

the direction j to i. This fictitious capacity obviously represents the limit to flow reversal,[†] see Fig. 2-56.

Consequently, these properties must be taken into account when determining the maximal flow between origin and terminal, otherwise something less than the true maximal flow will result.

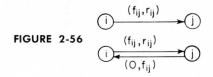

FIGURE 2-56

Consider, for example, the network of Fig. 2-57. Straightforward application of Steps 1 through 4 leads to the sequence of diagrams shown in Figs. 2-57 through 2-60. We wish to discuss the labeling of Fig. 2-60 in greater detail.

It is easy to see that node *2* can be labeled from node *1*. However, node *3* cannot be labeled from *1* because $f_{13} = a_{13}$; neither can node *4* (since $s_{1,4}^{(1)}$, $s_{1,4}^{(2)} \neq 0$). Next, consider node *2*. We can label both nodes *4* and *5*, but *6* cannot be labeled from either *4* or *5*. Presumably, a nonbreakthrough condition has been reached.

[†] See Chapter 4, §6 for a more detailed discussion of maximal flow in directed networks.

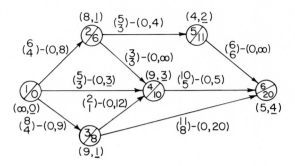

FIGURE 2-57

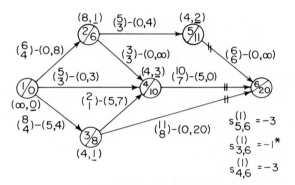

FIGURE 2-58   No Breakthrough

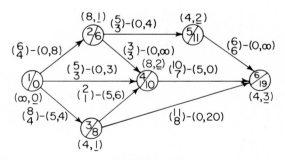

FIGURE 2-59

However, such is not the case. Consider arc (3,4). A flow of 5 units exists in the direction $3 \to 4$, and this flow can be reversed. According to our previous interpretation of flow reversal we should be able to label node *3* from *4*. Therefore, to the conditions in Eqs. (2-40) and (2-41) we

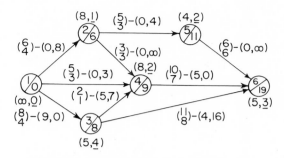

FIGURE 2-60   Example of Reverse Labeling

add the following condition. If i is labeled and j is not labeled so that

$$s_{ji}^{(1)} \text{ or } s_{ji}^{(2)} = 0 \quad \text{and} f_{ji}^{(1)} \text{ or } f_{ji}^{(2)} > 0, \tag{2-45}$$

then label j with (q_j, i) where

$$q_j = \min [q_i, f_{ji}^{(k)}]. \tag{2-46}$$

The conditions in Eq. (2-45) are satisfied for node 3 since $s_{3,4}^{(2)} = 8 + 1 - 9 = 0$ and $f_{34}^{(1)} = 5$. Therefore, node 3 can be labeled with $(5,4)$.

When 3 is labeled from 4, node 6 can be labeled from 3, and the result is a *breakthrough*. Carrying out the flow change according to the labels of Fig. 2-60 results in the flow of Fig. 2-61.

Notice that the overall result of the reversal of flow in arc $(3,4)$ is equivalent to the diversion of some flow from its original path in order to accomodate the new flow. This easily can be gleaned from a comparison of Figs. 2-60 and 2-61.

From this point on the iterations follow the usual pattern and will not be pursued any further.

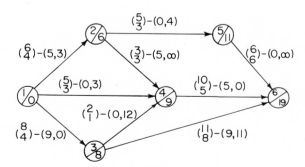

FIGURE 2-61

4.10 Comments on Activity Networks

Our study of the analysis of activity networks is incomplete without some general comments on few of the theoretical formulations and practical aspects of the procedures outlined above.

The Adequacy of Representation

A careful study of PERT, CPM, and other varieties of the same genre reveals that the conceptual model for such networks is severely restricted from a *logical* point of view and in many instances falls short of adequately representing a wide variety of research and development activities. For example, there is an implicit determinateness in the existence of all events and activities—a determinateness which is exemplified by relationships such as Eq. (2-11). To see this, consider Fig. 2-62. Both

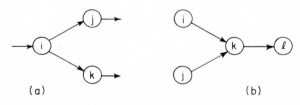

(a)   (b)

FIGURE 2-62

activities (i,j) and (i,k) in part (a) of the figure *must* be undertaken after event i occurs. On the other hand, in part (b), both activities (i,k) and (j,k) *must* be completed before event k obtains. In fact, activity (k,ℓ) cannot take place except after the completion of both activities (i,k) and (j,k). The terminal event N of a network occurs after all project activities and events have taken place.

Needless to say, industrial and economic systems abound with different logical classes of events, uncertain activities, etc., which cannot be handled by the above approach.

For instance, suppose that node i in Fig. 2-62a represents the event: submitting price quotations on projects A and B. Furthermore, suppose that there is a reasonable chance of winning a contract on either project A or B, *but not on both*. How can we represent such eventualities? Obviously, the PERT-CPM approach is not adequate unless we are willing to construct an activity network for each possible turn of events—a procedure which is at best clumsy and at worst computationally infeasible.

As another illustration, suppose that node k in Fig. 2-62b represents an event which occurs if *either* activity (i,k) *or* activity (j,k) *or both* occur. Such is the case, for example, in research projects in which a problem is attacked on more than one front. Again it is evident that the traditional approach is incapable of representing such an "either-or" logical relationship.

Research on expanding the concepts of activity networks to cope with these and other logical relationships is continuing under the heading of "generalized activity networks." The interested reader is referred to the references cited at the end of the chapter for suggested approaches to the representation of such systems.

The Problems of Limited Resources

It was pointed out in the introduction to this section that, basically, activity networks are management tools intended to answer questions of *analysis* and *synthesis* relative to projects involving a multitude of activities and drawing upon a variety of resources.

The determination of the critical path, the second critical path, etc., up to the kth critical path; the determination of slack time for each activity or event; the determination of earliest start and completion times, as well as the latest start and completion times are all examples of *analysis* in the context of activity networks. They are so designated because they are derived *after* the structure of the network is given.

On the other hand, we have seen an example of *synthesis* in the determination of the optimal activity times for a given cost value. It is interesting to remark that the synthesis problem required a more advanced treatment than the analysis problems. This is generally true. But the reader must realize that *all* our previous treatment, concerning both analysis and synthesis problems, was dealing with *scheduling* or *temporal* relationships among the activities and events.

Needless to say, temporal questions are not the only questions of concern to management. In fact, in some instances they may not even be the most important questions, being overshadowed by problems of the optimal allocation of scarce resources.

These problems arise naturally in any project in one of two forms:

1. It may be that management has fixed amounts of each resource which it cannot exceed, or does not desire to exceed, and wishes to evaluate the impact of such scarcity in the resources on performance (as measured, for example, by the total duration of the project, or by the maximum delay in certain activities, etc.).

2. It may be that management has a more or less free hand in acquiring (or securing) any amounts of the necessary resources, and the question is: what are the optimal amounts to be acquired to achieve a given target date? Naturally, optimality will have to be defined relative to a well-specified criterion.

Before proceeding further, we should clarify the type of resources we are concerned with here. Generally speaking, these are labor, engineering and management skills; machinery; equipment and productive units; facilities such as stores and receiving docks; and, finally, capital in its different forms. In spite of the radical differences in the nature of these resources, it is evident that *for the purposes of our present analysis* they can be treated in the same manner. For example, suppose that management knows that because of its other financial commitments it will not be able to borrow more than $1.5 million over the next year to meet its cash requirements. Clearly, this figure of $1.5 million can be treated as a limited capacity on borrowing for cash needs in the very same way that productive capacity of a piece of equipment over the next year is treated. Henceforth, we need not identify the various resources beyond a label to distinguish one from the other.

The problems of resource considerations in PERT-CPM type analysis have thus far defied rigorous mathematical treatment and optimal solutions. Heretofore, one has had to be content with approximate "solutions" and heuristic "common-sense" approaches. We shall describe some of these approaches below, but first investigate the reasons for this state of affairs.

Difficulties in Resolving the Resource Problem. Two reasons stand out as the causes for the current uncertainty and lack of a definitive solution to these problems. These reasons can be summarized under two general headings: the difficulty of *statement* of the problem and the difficulty of *formulating* a mathematical model even if a complete and clear statement were possible.

(a) *Difficulties in the Statement of the Problem.* First of all, the same comments previously made concerning the difficulties encountered in estimating the *duration* of an activity (see page 102) can be repeated almost verbatim relative to estimating the projected *consumption* of the various resources, especially if the activity in question is a gross activity, in the sense that it was not subdivided into its elementary components.

This is true for several good reasons. Oftentimes, only a subset of the resources are required for the full duration of the activity; the other resources are needed for only a fraction of that duration. The analyst must then choose between subdividing the activity according to the combination of resources required at any point of time, which may lead to a prohibitively complicated network, or leaving the activity as a unit, a course of action which must lead to a gross exaggeration of the total requirements!

It is generally recognized, though very rarely explicitly stated, that the time estimates of an activity are based on subjective knowledge of the availability of resources. The functional relationships between these two variables may not be known, which in no sense vitiates their existence. It immediately follows that subdividing the activity in correspondence to its resource requirements at various points of time may change the time estimates of the subdivisions, which in turn may affect the resource requirements! A vicious cycle results which may disrupt any possibility of obtaining meaningful results.

Another major roadblock to a clear and precise statement of the problem is the fact that an activity can usually be *started*, and possibly *maintained* for a long time, with fewer resources than are ideally needed. In other words, the statement of resource requirements is inherently subject to a "band of indifference," in which duration is not affected, and another wider band of feasibility at the price of prolonged duration of the activity. If the functional relationship between resource availability and the duration were known, analysis similar to the duration-cost analysis could be conducted. In general, this functional relationship is not defined, as was stated above. Moreover, activities which require more than one resource would require a completely different treatment from those activities which require only one resource.

The minimum requirement of a resource to start an activity is called "threshold." If the various resources are totally independent, the threshold of an activity which requires a combination of resources (e.g., an assortment of skills) would be the threshold of its most limiting resource. Unfortunately, the possibility of resource substitution (e.g., labor of one skill substituting for labor of another skill for a period of time) plays havoc with the concept of threshold for complex activities.

Leaving, for a moment, the problems centered around the activity, we find that difficulties are encountered on a completely different plane. In particular, the capacities of the various resources are set arbitrarily. A more meaningful statement would be a cost-capacity level functional relationship, but this is difficult to obtain. The result is the existence of a threshold on the high side of the specified capacity, which we shall call "margin," over and above the threshold (on the lower side of the requirements of an activity) mentioned in the previous paragraph. This "extra margin" of availability of resources is oftentimes present in the form of overtime capacity, possible temporary acquisitions, or shifting in the resource labeling (e.g., from one skill to another). Consequently, if at any point of time the stated capacity of one or several resources is exceeded, the analyst must recognize the ever-present possibility of relaxing the constraint(s). The limits to such relaxation are, necessarily, dependent on the set of resources in question, and cannot be stated in advance.

Finally, there is an implicit, and incorrect, assumption that an activity is an individual entity. This may be true from certain points of view, (e.g., precedence relationships) but need not be true from the point of view of resources. It is conceivable, and by no means rare, that an activity can be carried out intermittently so that its demand on the resources is also intermittent. The question, of course, is the statement of this fact within the framework of activity networks, especially if an activity *may* be (but *need not* be) split only at a finite number of points. The combinatorial character of the various possibilities that present themselves in the case of several activities demanding the same resources at the same time can easily be seen.

(b) *Difficulties in the Formulation of the Mathematical Model.* Unfortunately, it seems that even if the problem were correctly and precisely stated, it would be very difficult indeed to give a reasonably comprehensive mathematical model which would incorporate the various variables in a *solvable* formulation. This is perhaps due to four factors acting individually or in unison to limit the power of analytical models.

First, there is the interdependence of activities (due to sharing the same resources in an *efficient* manner), the dependence on the manner in which an activity is subdivided, and the dependence on available resource capacities; all three dependencies are basically nonlinear in character. Thus, even if the functional relationships describing all three instances of interrelationships were determined, there would still remain the task of combining these individual relationships into a meaningful whole.

Second, it is oftentimes difficult to ascertain the objectives of management, particularly when these objectives are poorly formulated and far from crystallized in management's own mind. For example, the objective may be any one of the following three:

1. Minimize total project cost assuming unlimited availability of the various resources *at a price*. The price may or may not be linear with the quantity ordered. But clearly the trade-off here is between small capacities with a long project duration and large capacities with short duration.
2. Minimize the duration of project under limited capacity levels.
3. "Level" the resources' consumption while achieving a specified target completion date.

Oftentimes, management is desirous of "having its cake and eating it too," in the sense that it specifies the minimization of all three variables— total duration of project, capacity levels, and variation about the average usage.

Third, the freedom of subdividing some activities, combined with the freedom of scheduling an activity within an interval equal to its duration plus the activity's slack time, gives rise to a combinatorial problem of formidable magnitude. In the heuristic approaches currently proposed for the problem of resource allocation, examples of which are discussed below, some arbitrary ranking rule is usually adopted to break the ties among contending activities and thus get rid of the combinatorial problem.

Fourth, and finally, the notions of "threshold" and "margin" are necessarily subjective in nature, and their incorporation into a model is difficult if not impossible. For example, if more than one activity competes for the same scarce resources, can we *start* more than one activity at the threshold, or should we devote the resources to fewer activities? How would this affect the duration of the project in both cases? As another example, suppose an activity which started with a partial crew is stopped —how much of this activity is accomplished?

The above discussion is not intended to discourage the reader from undertaking active research and investigation to solve the problem of optimal resource allocation. On the contrary, it is intended to encourage such work by clearing away difficulties and by pointing out possible pitfalls. Needless to say, any attack on the problem must start with simplifying assumptions. The qualitative discussion presented above should assist in the choice of the necessary assumptions to render the problem analytically tractable.

Next, we briefly sketch two approaches used to determine "better" resource allocations.

Samples of Heuristic Approaches. Needless to say, absence of rigorously proven mathematical solutions opens the door to heuristic algorithms. These are, in the final analysis, the application of common sense "rules of thumb"—whose number and variety are limited only by the ingenuity of the investigator. Consequently, there exists at present a good number of such approaches, some of which are cited at the end of the chapter. There is little doubt that the number of heuristic approaches will increase as more and more investigators are attracted to this field. However, we shall content ourselves with the two approaches originally put forth by Kelley[†], namely, the *serial* method and the *parallel* method. Both approaches begin where the CP analysis leaves off, so that at the start of application of either approach it is assumed that we have available the earliest and latest completion times of each event and the slack time in each activity, as well as the CP's. Moreover, both approaches assume limited resources specified at the start of the project.

(a) *The Serial Approach.* It derives its name from the fact that activities are considered sequentially, starting at the originating node and proceeding in a stepwise fashion towards the last node N.

The activities are ranked in some order—e.g., in order of ascending arrow head (or arrow tail). They are then scheduled in that order and

[†] J. E. Kelley, "The Critical Path Method: Resources Planning & Scheduling," Chapter 21 of *Industrial Scheduling*, Muth & Thompson, Eds., Prentice Hall, 1963.

also according to the availability of resources. An activity whose turn it is to be scheduled but which requires unavailable resources is passed over for other activities which can be scheduled with available resources. The delay in an activity may or may not cause a delay in the termination time of the project, depending on the available slack time of the activity.

In spite of the apparent simplicity of the procedure, its application involves problems of its own. For example, if the activities are ranked according to the number of the arrow head, two disturbing phenomena occur: (1) since the numbering of the nodes is not unique, different numbering would lead to different ranking which, in turn, leads to different resource utilizations and project durations; (2) the ranking is not unique when more than one arc impinges on the same node. Then it is necessary to have a secondary ranking. This may be based on the slack time of the activities, the number of their originating nodes, the subjective feeling of the "importance" of the activity, or on some random rule.

It is conceivable that an activity can be delayed due to scarcity of the necessary resources beyond a limit which is considered "tolerable." Under such conditions, it may be deemed necessary to *acquire* more of the necessary resources, rather than delay the activity. Our discussion presented above concerning the "margin" on capacity limitations is pertinent in this respect. What is interesting is that now we are obliged to define what is meant by "acceptable" delay in each activity.

(b) *The Parallel Approach.* In this approach we consider one time interval and *all* the activities that *can* be scheduled during that interval. The activities are ranked in some fashion (again according to slack, terminal node, or starting node, etc.) and scheduled according to resource availability; otherwise, the activities are delayed. Then the next time interval is considered, etc..

This approach has the advantage of eliminating dependence on the numbering of the nodes, unless, of course, such numbers are again used for secondary ranking.

General Remarks. The problem of optimal resource allocation in project type activities is an important managerial problem, and until very recently little attention was paid to its resolution. Now the framework of PERT-CPM analysis seems to be the natural framework for resolving the problem. To date, the various attacks on the problem have resulted in heuristic approaches with varying degrees of success.

In the exercises at the end of the chapter, we give a problem which illustrates the difficulties encountered in this area even under no capacity limitations; see Exercise 10.

The Significance of the Assumptions Concerning the Distribution Function of y_{ij}

If the estimates of the duration of the activities, $\{y_{ij}\}$, are admittedly nondeterministic, i.e., if the variability of an estimate about its expected value cannot be ignored, it must be evident by now that assumptions 1 and 2 concerning the *form of the distribution* of y_{ij}, are not fundamental to the analysis of such networks, since only the first two moments of the distribution function are utilized in the subsequent analysis. The assumption of a Beta distribution function is highly convenient under the stipulation of three time estimates a, b, and m as defined above.

However, in some instances it would be equally "logical" to assume other forms of distribution functions. For example, if a and b represent the range of the possible durations of an activity, with all intermediate values $a \leq y \leq b$ equally likely, a uniform distribution over the closed interval $[a,b]$ would be adequate, as in Fig. 2-63. The expected value T would now equal $\frac{1}{2}(a + b)$ and Var $(y) = \frac{1}{3}(b - a)^2$. All subsequent derivations are not affected by the form of the distribution of y_{ij}.

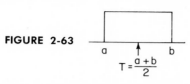

FIGURE 2-63

$$T = \frac{a + b}{2}$$

A more fundamental criticism of the approximation of Eqs. (2-8a) and (2-8b) was given by Grubbs[†], who showed that these approximations do imply a very restrictive relationship among the parameters α and β of the assumed beta-distribution. In particular, these two equations imply that $\alpha = 2 \pm \sqrt{2}, \beta = 2 \mp \sqrt{2}$ or $\alpha = \beta = 3$. Alternatively expressed, these approximations amount to an assumption that the beta-distribution has coefficient of skew equal to ∓ 0.707 or 0, respectively, which in turn, vitiates the assumption of independence of the three time estimates: a, m and b!

Probabilistic Considerations

Equation (2-10) yields the probability of project completion on or before any specified time $t_N(s)$. There are two pertinent comments concerning such probability statements. *First*, consider the case where several forward paths $\pi_1, \pi_2, \ldots, \pi_r$ lead from the origin 1 to node i as shown in Fig. 2-64. If $T(\pi_j)$ is the duration of path π_j, then we have, by Eq. (2-11),

$$t_i(E) = \max_{\pi_j} \{T(\pi_j)\}.$$

If the different paths are assumed to be independent—which is *not* true if any two paths share one or more branches—then $t_i(E)$ is the maximum of a finite set of random variables. The following remark refers to the case where $T(\pi_j)$ is assumed normally distributed with some mean $T(\pi_j)$ and

[†]Frank E. Grubbs, "Attempts to Validate Certain PERT Statistics, or 'Picking on PERT'," *Operations Research*, Vol. 10, No. 6, Nov.–Dec. 1962, pp. 912–915.

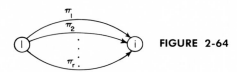

FIGURE 2-64

variance $\sigma^2(\pi_j)$. If $T(\pi_j)$ is *not* normally distributed, the remark holds *a fortiori*.

It is well known that the maximum of two or more normally distributed variables is *not* normally distributed. However, as pointed out by Clark[†], it can be *approximated* by a normally distributed variable; but the expected value and variance of this approximation are not those given by Eqs. (2-9a) and (2-9b).

In order to appreciate the extent of the error committed in Eqs. (2-9a) and (2-9b), the following Table 2-4 is extracted from Tippett[‡] whose more comprehensive table gives the mean and standard deviation of the maximum of n standard normal deviates. That is, if

$$Y = \text{Max}\{X_1, X_2, \cdots, X_n\}$$

where $X_1, X_2, \ldots, X_n$ are normally distributed with mean 0 and variance 1, then the mean and standard deviation of Y for various values of n are as given in Table 2-4.

TABLE 2-4   Mean and Standard Deviation of Y

n	1	2	3	4	5	6	7	8	9	10
$E(Y)$	0	0.5642	0.8463	1.0296	1.1630	1.2672	1.3522	1.4236	1.4850	1.5388
σ_y	1	0.8256	0.7480	0.7012	0.6690	0.6650	0.6260	0.6107	0.5978	0.5868

Interpreting Table 2-4 in the context of activity networks, we see that if four paths π_1, π_2, π_3, and π_4 lead from 1 to i in Fig. 2-64, and if the duration of each path is assumed to be normally distributed with mean $\overline{T}$ and variance σ^2, which are the same for all paths, then

$$\mathcal{E}[t_i] = 1.0296\overline{T}$$

and

$$\sigma_i = 0.7012\sigma$$

Had we applied Eqs. (2-9a) and (2-9b), we would have obtained $\mathcal{E}(t_i) = \overline{T}$ and $\sigma_i = \sigma$, respectively. The error committed is clearly not insignificant.

[†]Charles E. Clark, "The Greatest of A Finite Set of Random Variables," *Operations Research*, Vol. 9, No. 2, 1961.

[‡]L. H. C. Tippett, "On The Extreme Individuals and the Range of Samples Taken From a Normal Population," *Biometrika*, Vol. 17, 1925, pp. 364–377.

Clark has indicated a stepwise procedure that yields the estimates $\mathcal{E}[t_i]$ and σ_i^2 of the approximate normal deviate, taking correlations into account.

Second, it was pointed out by Healy[†] that the probability statement made concerning $t_N(E)$ is a function of the *subdivision of the activities*.

Engineers and managers who deal with real life problems realize that activities and events can, sometimes, be defined almost at will. That is, the degree of detail in defining the activities and events is not a consequence of unalterable inherent characteristics of the project but rather a result of (perhaps irrelevant) factors such as the time available for detailed analysis, who is responsible for the activity, and the analyst's tastes and preferences. Healy showed that if an activity is decomposed into several activities so that: (1) the expected time of the small activities add up to the expected time of the "parent" activity, and (2) the range of the small activities add up to the range of the "parent" activity, then the variance of the terminal event is necessarily decreased. Consequently, for the same specified $t_N(s)$ as before the subdivision, the probability statements would be different. Therefore, care should be taken in defining the activites and, above all, in interpreting the probability statements.

Critical Activities Vs. Critical Paths

The analysis of PERT (and CPM) focuses attention on the notion of critical *path*. However, it must be evident from the probabilistic structure of the model that any path is critical (in the sense that it is of longest duration) with a certain probability. Consequently, it seems meaningful to inquire about individual critical *activities* rather than about whole paths, where an activity is critical if it is common to one or more paths, each of which may be critical with a high enough probability.

The study of critical activities is appealing from another point of view. We recall that the main interest in evaluating the critical path is to determine the "bottleneck" activities, with the purpose of concentrating attention on such activities. Thus, sooner or later, we have to concern ourselves with individual activities. It is, therefore, logical to focus attention from the start on the critical activities as defined above.

The determination of the critical activities is not easy. We suggest two approaches: (1) evaluate the first k critical paths (i.e., the longest, the second longest, etc., up to the kth longest) and define the set of activities common to r or more such paths as critical; (2) use Monte Carlo simulation to determine k critical paths and define the set of activities common to r or more such paths as critical.

[†]Thomas Healy, "Activity Subdivision and PERT Probability Statements," *Operations Research*, Vol. 9, No. 3, 1961, pp. 341–348.

An illuminating discussion of the second approach is found in Van Slyke's article cited at the end of the chapter.

The Utility of Activity Networks

Practical applications of activity network analysis indicate that their greatest contribution lies in the systematic fashion in which the project is analyzed.

In order to be able to draw the network, however crudely, every contributor to the project is forced to think ahead, enumerate, organize, and evaluate each activity and event individually and in relation to other components of the project. This, plus the fact that the network provides a common "road map" for all participants in the project—who may be physically separated—reduces the problems of communication and control.

Thus, even when stripped of all their mathematics, activity networks do provide a representation of systems that has significantly contributed to the success of many large-scale projects.

§5. OTHER GRAPHIC REPRESENTATIONS

In this chapter we discussed in some detail three graphic representations of systems: block diagrams, signal flow graphs, and activity networks.

By now the reader must realize that all three representations are in fact *network* representations. The difference among them lies in the mathematical definition of the arcs, the nodes, (or blocks) and the relationships among them.

In the first representation (§2), a signal is assumed to flow through the network. The node (in this case a block) represented a transformation of the signal. The arc leaving the node thus contained the transformed signal, which is acted upon by another node, etc..

In the second representation (§3), the transformation of the signal occurred on the arc; the node represented the value of the transformed signal.

In the third representation (§4), the directed arc represented a precedence relationship between its terminal nodes. Each arc thus defined an activity, and the parameters of each activity gave its duration, the consumption of scarce resources, etc.

Needless to say, these three representations do not exhaust the different possible definitions of arcs and nodes. One can safely say that there is an inexhaustible number and variety of such definitions that can be accorded to a graph.

In Exercise 13 at the end of this chapter, we let a graph represent the "bill-of-materials" for an assembly. In this case the nodes represent commodities, and an arc represents the "go into" relationship between its terminal commodities (nodes).

In chapter 4, §15 we let the graph represent the process of assembly. The nodes of the graph represent operations, and the arcs represent precedence relationships imposed by technological requirements.

Chapters 4 and 5 are devoted to flow networks and queue networks, respectively. The distinction between the two lies in the deterministic nature of flow in the first and the stochastic nature of flow in the second.

We reiterate, at the expense of being redundant, that the graphic representation of systems is an *aid* to analysis and synthesis, and a valuable aid indeed. The reader should satisfy himself that in each of the above-mentioned applications, the system could be equally represented by either differential equations, algebraic linear equations, or matrices of different kinds, etc.—represented, that is, in a formal mathematical manner, but not without a great loss of insight and facility of solution.

COMMENTS AND BIBLIOGRAPHY

§1. An extensive discussion of graphic techniques which, in essence, are of the first type can be found in:

BOWMAN, E. H. and R. B. FETTER   *Analysis for Production Management*, Homewood, Ill., Irwin, 1961, Chapter 3.

Similar techniques can be found in several books on plant layout and motion and time study.

§2. The full utility of block diagramming will be in evidence in our discussion of feedback control systems, Chapter 6. We mention here a reference on the subject; more references are cited in the chapter on feedback:

THALER, G. J. and R. G. BROWN   *Servomechanism Analysis*, New York, McGraw-Hill, 1953.

§3. Signal flow graphs have a very recent history, dating back to the paper by:

MASON, S. J.   "Feedback Theory: Some Properties of Signal Flow Graphs," *Proceedings of the Institute of Radio Engineers*, Vol. 41, September 1953, pp. 1144–1156.

The subject is discussed in the following books:

HALL, A. D.   *A Methodology for Systems Engineering*, Princeton, N. J., Van Nostrand, 1962, pp. 356–374.

MISHKIN, E. and L. BRAUN, JR., eds.   *Adaptive Control Systems*, New York, McGraw-Hill, 1961, pp. 35–39.

TRUXAL, JOHN G.   *Control System Synthesis*, New York, McGraw-Hill, 1955, Chapter 2.

An excellent introduction to Random Walk and Markov Processes is given in:

FELLER, W.   *Introduction to Probability Theory and Its Application*, New York, Wiley, 1957.

Also see:

HOWARD, R. A.   "Control Processes," *Notes on Operations Research*, Cambridge, Mass., The Technology Press, 1959, pp. 128–149.

A discussion of the place of signal flow graphs in the context of Graph Theory is found in:

SESHU, S. and M. B. REED *Linear Graphs and Electrical Networks*, Reading, Mass., Addison-Wesley, 1961.

§4. A large bibliography exists on Activity Networks. The original ideas are contained in:

KELLEY, J. E., JR. and M. R. WALKER "Critical Path Planning and Scheduling," *Proceedings of the Eastern Joint Computer Conference*, 1959, pp. 160–172.

MALCOLM, D. G., J. H. ROSEBOOM, C. E. CLARK and W. FAZER "Application of a Technique for Research and Development Program Evaluation," *Operations Research*, Vol. 7, No. 5, 1959, pp. 646–669.

The flow-network interpretation is from:

CHARNES, A. and W. W. COOPER "A Network Interpretation and a Directed Subdual Algorithm for Critical Path Scheduling," *Journal of Industrial Engineering*, Vol. 13, No. 4, July–August 1962, pp. 213–219.

The Linear Programming Model for the estimation of the optimal duration of a project is due to:

KELLEY, J. E. "Critical Path Planning and Scheduling: Mathematical Basis," *Operations Research*, Vol. 9, No. 3, 1961, pp. 296–320.

The network flow algorithm for the determination of the duration-cost curve is given in:

FORD, L. K. and D. R. FULKERSON *Networks of Flow*, Princeton, N. J., Princeton University Press, 1962, Chapter 3.

FULKERSON, D. R. "A Network Flow Computatuion for Project Cost Curve," *Management Science*, Vol. 7, No. 2, January 1961, pp. 167–178.

The comments on the probabilistic considerations are adapted from:

CLARK, C. E. "The Greatest of a Finite Set of Random Variables," *Operations Research*, Vol. 9, No. 2, March–April 1961, pp. 145–162.

TIPPETT, L. H. C. "On the Extreme Individuals and the Range of Samples Taken from a Normal Population," *Biometrika*, Vol. 17, 1925, pp. 364–377.

See also:

CLARK, C. E. "The PERT Model for the Distribution of an Activity Time," (Letter to the Editor), *Operations Research*, Vol. 10, No. 3, 1962, pp. 405–406.

HEALY, T. "Activity Subdivision and PERT Probability Statements," *Operations Research*, Vol. 9, No. 3, 1961, pp. 341–348.

For further comments on PERT see:

GRUBBS, F. E. "Attempts to Validate PERT Statistics or 'Picking on PERT,'" (Letter to the Editor), *Operations Research*, Vol. 10, No. 6, November–December 1962, pp. 912–915.

POCOCK, J. W. "PERT As An Analytical Aid for Program Planning—Its Payoffs and Problems," *Operations Research*, Vol. 10, No. 6, November–December 1962, pp. 893–903.

ROSEBOOM, J. H. "Comments on a Paper by Thomas Healy," (Letter to the Editor), *Operations Research*, Vol. 9, No. 6, November–December 1961, pp. 909–910.

VAN SLYKE, R. M. "Monte Carlo Methods and the PERT Problem," *Operations Research*, Vol. 11, No. 5, September–October 1963, pp. 839–860.

A general mathematical formulation of PERT is given in:

LEVY, F. K., G. L. THOMPSON and J. D. WIEST "Mathematical Basis of the Critical Path Method," *Industrial Scheduling*, J. F. Muth and G. L. Thompson, eds., Englewood Cliffs, N. J., Prentice-Hall, 1963, Chapter 22. Chapters 20 and 21 of the same reference are general discussions of PERT. In particular Chapter 20, "Introduction to the Critical Path Method," gives a lucid introduction to the subject with the role of nodes and branches reversed.

MACCRIMMON, K. R. and C. A. RYAVEC. "An Analytical Study of PERT Assumptions," *Operations Research*, Vol. 12, No. 1, January–February 1964, pp. 16–37.

The treatment of activity networks containing different logical relationships can be found in:

ELMAGHRABY, S. E. "An Algebra for the Analysis of Generalized Activity Networks," *Management Science*, Vol. 10, No. 3, April 1964, pp. 494–514.

The problem of resource allocation is treated in the following references:

BURGESS, A. R. and J. B. KILLEBREW "Variations in Activity Level on a Cyclic Arrow Diagram," *Journal of Industrial Engineering*, Vol. 13, No. 2, March–April 1962, pp. 76–83.

DEWITTE, L. "Manpower Leveling of PERT Networks," *Data Processing for Science/Engineering*, Vol. 2, No. 2, 1964, pp. 29.

KELLEY, J. E. "The Critical Path Method: Resources Planning and Scheduling," *Industrial Scheduling*, Muth and Thompson, eds., Englewood Cliffs, N. J., Prentice Hall, 1963, Chapter 21.

LEVY, F. K., G. L. THOMPSON and J. D. WIEST "Multi-Ship, Multi-Shop Workload Smoothing Program," *Naval Research Logistics Quarterly*, Vol. 9, No. 1, 1963, pp. 37–44.

MIZE, J. H. "A Heuristic Scheduling Model for Multi-Project Organizations," Ph.D. thesis, Lafayette, Ind., Purdue University, August 1964.

MOSHMAN, J., J. JOHNSON and M. LASFER "RAMPS—A Technique for Resource Allocation and Multi-Project Scheduling," *Proceedings 1963 Spring Joint Computer Conference, Detroit, Michigan*, Baltimore, Md., Books Inc., pp. 17.

EXERCISES

1. Reduce the following signal flow graphs to one (s,t) elements.

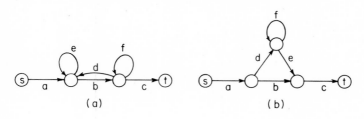

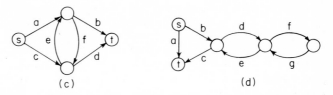

(c)   (d)

2. Consider the following inventory problem: Demand per period is probabilistic with the following distribution function,

d	0	1	2	3
$p(d)$	0.1	0.3	0.4	0.2

When the stock level is reduced to *one or zero*, a quantity of three units is ordered. The supplier lead time is *one period*. Sketch the signal flow graph representing the system and derive the transmittance T_{x_0,x_3} assuming the system starts in state x_0 (the state x_i represents i units in inventory).

3. A machine is in one of two states: operative or failed. The probability that it fails in a unit time period is 0.05, and the probability that it will be repaired in a unit time interval is 0.60.

   Draw the signal flow graph representing the system and deduce the probability of being in the *failed* state in the 4th period of time.

4. A model of heat diffusion due to Ehrenfest can be described as follows: there are two containers I and II and a particles distributed in them. At time n a particle is chosen at random and removed from its container to the other. The state of the system is determined by the number of molecules in I, and is represented by E_k when there are k particles in I. The system can then move from state E_k to either state E_{k-1} or E_{k+1} with corresponding probabilities k/a and $(a - k)/a$. Construct the Markov stochastic matrix for such a model assuming $a = 4$. (Note that in this case there are five states.) Draw the signal flow graph and calculate the probability of being in state E_0 at the 7th experiment assuming the system started in state E_3.

5. Progress of work in a shop producing electromechanical equipment is in the following sequence. There is a series of operations that terminate at an inspection station I. Inspected units are dispatched to one of two areas: a further testing operation, T, or to an adjustment operation, J. Units in the test area are either accepted and sent to J or rejected and sent to a separate repair area, R. From the repair area material flows back to be tested. After adjustment in J, the units are packed and delivered to the store.

   (a) Draw a signal flow graph and assume the necessary probabilities and times of transfer.

   (b) Determine the average time of completion of any unit.

6. Suppose that it is desired to install an inventory control system in a plant of 5,000 employees, $40 million annual sales and approximately 250 different major products. If you were designated as the project engineer, how would you construct a PERT network of the various activities and events which would constitute such a project from start to finish? Consider the system in as much detail as possible.

Evaluate the critical path and suggest possible improvements.

7. Mention at least two objections to the Linear Programming model for the determination of the optimal duration of a project.

   (*Hint*: Relative to: the determination of the kth critical path; earliest and latest completion times; slack times; two or more critical paths.)

8. Healy's remarks (see "Probabilistic Considerations") concerning the dependence of probability statements on the subdivision of the activities are themselves subject to criticism. Discuss his assumptions and determine if his conclusions are predetermined by his assumptions. Can you suggest alternate assumptions which would eliminate such dependence?[†]

9. The following are estimates (in weeks) of activity times. Opposite each activity are given three numbers which represent the optimistic, most likely and pessimistic estimates, respectively.

   (a) Draw the PERT network.
   (b) Determine the critical path by the tabular method.
   (c) Determine the probability of completing the project five weeks earlier. Interpret such probability.
   (d) Suggest a general algorithm for determining the kth critical path in directed networks with no loops, such as in PERT.
      (Hint: use a combinatorial approach or a dynamic programming approach.)
   (e) Determine the sequence of activities that constitute the second and third critical paths, i.e., the paths with the *second* and *third* longest duration.
   (f) Based on the first, second, and third CP's, determined in (e), determine the four most critical activities. Explain your reasons for choosing these four activities.

Activity	Times	Activity	Times	Activity	Times
(1, 2)	3, 4, 8	(6, 16)	1, 3, 8	(11, 16)	1, 4, 8
(1, 3)	1, 2, 3	(6, 20)	0, 3, 10	(11, 19)	1, 3, 10
(1, 6)	0, 2, 10	(7, 8)	1, 2, 3	(12, 20)	2, 4, 5
(1, 8)	3, 3, 3	(7, 11)	4, 10, 21	(13, 17)	5, 11, 22
(2, 3)	6, 15, 16	(7, 12)	3, 9, 16	(13, 18)	4, 10, 17
(3, 4)	5, 10, 20	(7, 15)	4, 9, 19	(14, 15)	5, 11, 21
(3, 9)	3, 7, 10	(8, 9)	2, 6, 9	(14, 19)	3, 7, 10
(3, 16)	1, 8, 14	(8, 18)	1, 7, 13	(15, 17)	2, 8, 15
(4, 7)	1, 3, 8	(9, 10)	1, 2, 7	(15, 18)	2, 5, 6
(4, 11)	10, 11, 14	(9, 13)	9, 11, 15	(15, 19)	8, 11, 12
(4, 16)	2, 5, 9	(9, 19)	1, 4, 10	(15, 20)	0, 3, 11
(5, 7)	10, 12, 17	(10, 12)	8, 10, 15	(16, 19)	7, 11, 17
(5, 10)	2, 6, 8	(10, 13)	1, 5, 7	(17, 20)	2, 6, 8
(6, 7)	3, 4, 5	(10, 20)	1, 3, 4	(18, 19)	1, 5, 9
(6, 8)	2, 6, 8	(11, 13)	2, 6, 8	(19, 20)	1, 5, 10

10. The following network gives the precedence relationship among activities, and the table gives the expected duration of each activity together with its demands on two scarce resources.

[†]Roseboom, *Operations Research*, Vol. 9, No. 6, 1961.

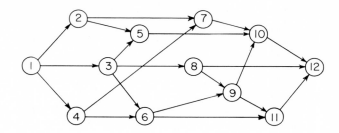

Activity	Duration	Resources I	II	Activity	Duration	Resources I	II
(1, 2)	12	3	—	(5, 10)	19	17	—
(1, 3)	10	2	—	(6, 9)	30	6	13
(1, 4)	11	—	4	(6, 11)	22	10	—
(2, 5)	6	—	—	(7, 10)	7	—	—
(2, 7)	5	2.1	—	(8, 9)	2	—	1
(3, 5)	4	—	1.3	(8, 12)	14	6	6
(3, 6)	15	2	2	(9, 10)	14	—	7
(3, 8)	31	3	14	(9, 11)	10	2	2
(4, 6)	6	1	—	(10, 12)	16	8	1
(4, 7)	18	5	5	(11, 12)	15	5	5

(a) Determine the critical path.

(b) Determine resource requirements assuming primary ranking on i and secondary ranking on j (for activities (i, j_1), (i, j_2) ... starting from node i).

(c) Attempt leveling of both resources by any technique you develop. State your procedure explicitly (i.e., in algorithm format) and the final results of leveling using your procedure.

11. In the network of Problem 10, determine the second and third critical paths, i.e., the second longest and the third longest paths from node 1 to node 12 (see Problem 9). Based on these three paths, which activities would you consider as critical activities?

12.

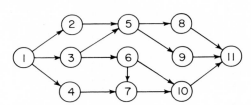

In the above network, some of the activities can be performed in shorter or longer durations, depending on the desired completion time of the project and the total level of expenditure desired. The following table gives the pertinent data.

Activity	Shortest Duration d	Longest Duration D	Unit Increase in Cost c
1, 2	6	12	4
1, 3	1	6	2
1, 4	2	5	13
2, 5	5	5	∞
3, 5	1	1	∞
3, 6	2	5	4
4, 7	6	12	2
5, 8	4	7	20
5, 9	1	4	12
6, 7	3	3	∞
6, 10	3	4	9
7, 10	6	11	2
8, 11	3	5	10
9, 11	5	10	11
10, 11	2	7	4

(a) Determine the critical path assuming all activities are at their minimum duration d.

(b) Determine the critical path assuming all activities are at their maximum duration D.

(c) Determine the project duration-cost curve following the Fulkerson procedure of §4.9.

(d) Compare the value of λ at the various "break points" with the duration of critical paths in the network.

13. The "bill-of-material" of any final assembly defines the quantity q_{ij} of commodity i required for the production of a *unit* of commodity j. The numbers $\{q_{ij}\}$ can be arranged in a matrix form as shown in the following example:

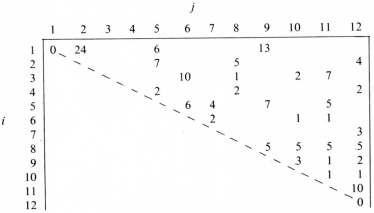

The Next-Assembly Matrix Q

Here, we have one assembly, number *12*. All other commodities are either raw material (such as commodities *1,3* and *4*) or subassemblies (such as commodities 5 to *11*). Notice that the commodities are numbered such that if commodity i is needed for the production of commodity j, then i is numerically smaller than j. Consequently, the matrix Q is triangular.

(a) Draw a network representation of the Next-Assembly matrix Q, in which the nodes represent the commodities and the arcs the relationship "go into." Each arc will have a number, q_{ij}, and is *directed* from i to j.

(b) Let T_{ij} denote the *total* quantity required of commodity i for assembly (or subassembly) j. Show that

$$T_{ij} = \Sigma_k q_{ik} T_{kj} \text{ with } T_{ii} = 1.$$

From which deduce that the matrix $T \equiv \{T_{ij}\}$ is given in terms of the matrix Q by

$$T = (I - Q)^{-1}$$

(c) Due to the triangularity of the matrix Q, the inverse $(I - Q)^{-1}$ can be easily obtained through elementary vector operation. Suggest such a scheme of calculation and utilize it to obtain the matrix T corresponding to the above-given Q.

(d) In some instances, a fraction of the end product is utilized as input to some subassembly, which is ultimately used for the production of the end product. (E.g., a small fraction of the electricity generated is used for field excitation.) Under such conditions, the matrix Q is no more triangular. The question then arises: does the matrix T exist and is it realizable? (T exists if each T_{ij} is ≥ 0, and is realizable if $T_{ii} \geq 1$.)

Suggest a necessary and sufficient condition for the existence and realizability of T.

14. The following data pertains to a project of 11 activities and 7 events.

Activity	D_{ij}	d_{ij}	a_{ij}
1,2	10	7	5
1,3	8	6	7
1,4	13	6	6
2,4	6	6	∞
2,7	28	20	9
3,4	5	3	8
3,6	23	15	11
4,5	8	3	3
5,6	9	4	8
5,7	10	6	10
6,7	7	5	6

Determine the optimal cost-duration curve and deduce the optimal duration of each activity in the project to yield a completion time $\lambda = 31$.

15. A useful approach to the study of PERT is through Monte Carlo simulation. Recalling that the duration of each activity is assumed a random variable y_{ij} with some probability distribution function, we can define a *realization of the project* as the network of the project with a fixed value for the duration of each arc in the network. For a particular realization of the network it is easy to determine the critical path (CP) whose length is the project duration.

A sample point (through Monte Carlo sampling) is then a realization of the project. Repeated sampling yields all the statistical information desired concerning the scheduling aspects of the project, such as the probability distribution function of completion times, the criticality of an activity (i.e., the probability that the activity lies on a CP), the criticality of a path (i.e., the probability that a path is critical), etc.

Suppose that it is desired to estimate, through Monte Carlo simulation, the mean duration of the project so that with probability 0.95 our estimate of the mean is within $\sigma_t/50$ of the true mean, where σ_t is the standard deviation of the project duration.

What is the minimum size of sample necessary?[†]

16. Referring to the previous problem, consider a specific activity a. For any realization of the project, activity a is either on the CP or it is not. The proportion of times in which a falls on the CP is a reasonably good measure of the criticality of this particular activity. We denote the probability of activity a falling on the CP by p, the parameter of the binomial distribution.

What is the minimum sample size needed to estimate p within 0.01 of its true value with probability 0.95?[†]

17. Table 2-5 on page 150 gives the data for a steam calender and pipeline maintenance project. The three time estimates under a, m, and b are the optimistic, most likely, and pessimistic estimates, respectively.

    (a) Determine, through a PERT formulation, the *expected* completion time of the project and the estimated variance of the duration of the project based solely on the CP.

    (b) What is the probability that the project will be completed in 250 hours or less?

    (c) If you were asked to place bounds on the duration of the project, what would your answer be?

    (d) Using the cost data given, what is the optimal duration of each activity to complete the project in exactly 250 hours?

18. Show that the Flow-Network Algorithm for the determination of project cost-duration curve, §4.9, need not be applied to the original network but only to a reduced network in which all paths of duration shorter than $\lambda_{min} = \{t_N(E) \mid y_{ij} = d_{ij}\}$ for all (i,j) have been removed.

[†]Van Slyke, *Operations Research,* Vol. 11, No. 5, 1963.

TABLE 2-5

Activity No.	Prede-cessor Activity Nos.	Description of Activity	Time (hours)			Cost (dollars)	
			a	m	b	Normal	Crash
101	—	Inspect and measure pipe	2	4	5	16	22
102	—	Devlp. cal. mtls. list	3	6	8	18	25
103	101	Make drawings of pipe	2	3	5	12	18
104	—	Deactivate line	7	8	10	8	14
105	102	Procure calendar parts	120	244	320	12	35
106	102	Assemble calender work crew	6	8	9	20	30
107	103	Devlp. matl. list (pipe)	3	4	7	10	13
108	104,105,106	Deactivate calender	4	4	5	3	3
109	107	Procure valves	136	220	280	10	20
110	107	Procure pipe	136	200	240	10	22
111	107	Assemble work crew (pipe)	4	6	7	16	20
112	108	Tie off warps	1	2	3	3	8
113	110,111	Prefab pipe sections	20	40	50	120	240
114	111	Erect scaffold	6	12	15	30	65
115	112	Disassemble calender	4	10	14	90	210
116	112	Empty and scour vats	2	3	5	6	9
117	104,114	Remove old pipe	18	30	38	180	300
118	115	Repair calender	35	70	98	650	1500
119	113,117	Position new pipe	6	8	12	50	110
120	118	Lubricate calender	3	5	6	10	22
121	109,119	Position new valves	5	7	10	66	100
122	119	Weld new pipe	6	8	11	50	60
123	120	Reassemble calender	18	22	24	200	270
124	123	Adjust and balance calender	6	8	14	80	95
125	121,122	Insulate pipes	15	20	30	60	75
126	121,122	Connect pipes to boiler	3	4	5	24	30
127	121,122,123	Connect pipes to calender	7	8	11	48	50
128	116,124	Refill vats	1	1	1	2	2
129	125,126	Remove scaffold	3	4	4	16	18
130	126	Pressure text	5	6	9	15	16
131	128	Tie in warps	3	4	5	8	10
132	127,131	Activate calender	2	2	3	14	14
133	129,130,132	Clean up	3	4	5	15	18

Describe a procedure by which such paths can be determined and removed at the beginning of the analysis.

19. Consider the earliest completion time of a project, $t_N(E)$, as determined by the length of the critical path when the duration of each activity is taken to be the *average* duration (Eq. (2.8a)). Is $t_N(E)$ unbiased, optimistic, or pessimistic relative to the true average duration of the project?[†]

[†]Fulkerson, *Operations Research*, Vol. 10, No. 6, 1962.

CHAPTER 3

Modes of Component Interaction

§1. INTRODUCTION

We have often repeated that the distinguishing aspect of a system is the fact that it is a collection of *interacting* components. In this chapter we propose to discuss in greater detail the modes of interaction met in practice. In particular, we shall define two modes of interaction: *stationary* and *dynamic*.

By *stationary interaction* we mean interaction in which time is not a dimension. Specifically, whenever all the components of the system are in existence at the same time and their modes of interaction are well-defined so that time is no factor in either the existence of any input or output or in the existence of the components themselves, we shall refer to such an interaction as "*stationary*."

An example should help make this rather lengthy definition clear. Consider the following problem. We wish to produce two items, 1 and 2, on two machines, M_1 and M_2, and maximize the profit accruing from their sales. Let a_{ij} represent the manufacturing time per unit of item i on machine j, and let c_1 and c_2 be the profit per unit of items 1 and 2, respectively. Then we wish to

$$\text{Maximize } c_1 x_1 + c_2 x_2 = z \tag{3-1}$$

subject to the available capacity constraints on the two machines,

$$a_{11} x_1 + a_{21} x_2 \leq b_1$$

and $\hspace{13cm}$ (3-2)

$$a_{12} x_1 + a_{22} x_2 \leq b_2$$

where x_1 is the quantity produced of item 1, x_2 is the quantity produced of item 2, and b_1 and b_2 are the available capacities of the two machines, respectively.

This is a straightforward linear programming problem whose solution is readily available. It exemplifies our definition of stationary interaction;

we have recognized a system of two products competing for the time available on two machines. The interaction between these two components is defined by the inequalities of Eq. (3-2). The criterion of optimality is also well defined by the objective function Eq. (3-1). The decision—represented by the numerical values assigned to x_1 and x_2—is a "one shot" decision. This is true even though the decision may be applied day after day for the next year. In brief, the dimension of time which calls for a sequential type of decision is completely absent.

We are now in a position to define *dynamic interaction*. By this we mean interaction *over time* either because the components of the system are realized over time or because the inputs and outputs of the system—or portions thereof—are realized over time. Usually, dynamic interaction is associated with stochastic processes.

The majority of problems encountered in practice are dynamic in nature. Consequently, there seems to be a natural tendency for systems to be defined with dynamic interaction. One shot decisions are rare since time plays an important role in systems design. However, it is sometimes possible to formulate a dynamic problem as a stationary one. This should in no way obscure the dynamic nature of the system or the mode of interaction among the components.

Of course, the converse may also be true, i.e., a system which in its natural context gives rise to stationary interaction may be reformulated as a dynamic system. In many instances this is done for computational ease; oftentimes it is undertaken to illustrate a specific dynamic approach.

§2. ILLUSTRATION OF DEFINITIONS: THE "CATERER" PROBLEM

A good illustration, which, incidentally, serves also to illustrate dynamic interaction, is the so-called "caterer" problem. It is a paraphrasing of an airplane engines repair problem and is usually stated as follows: a caterer has to provide clean napkins for N consecutive days with r_i dinners served on day i. He has the choice of buying new napkins or sending soiled napkins to either a fast laundry service or to a slow laundry service. The different decisions entail different costs. What is his optimal policy?

Denote the duration of the slow service by p and the duration of the fast service by q. Let S be the total napkins purchased new at a cost of a per napkin. Denote the number of napkins sent to the fast laundry on the ith day by u_i at a cost of b per napkin, and the number of napkins sent to slow laundry by v_i at a cost of c per napkin. Finally, let w_i denote the soiled napkins which are disposed of in day i and assume the cost of disposal to be zero.

For the sake of clarity of exposition, and in order to avoid losing the reader in a maze of complicated and lengthy notation, we shall limit our discussion to the case where $p = 3$ and $q = 1$. Extension of the theory to arbitrary p and q is straightforward.

First, let us delineate the system under study and investigate the stationarity of the interaction. The system in question is defined by the following five components:

1. The source of new napkins, which is assumed infinite.
2. The fast service laundry, assumed to be of infinite capacity.
3. The slow service laundry, also assumed to be of infinite capacity.
4. The set of requirements $\{r_i\}$, $i = 1, \ldots, N$, assumed known deterministically.
5. The decision rule—a "black box" which determines the number of napkins to be purchased new and the number of napkins sent each day to either the fast or slow laundries or disposed of completely.

These five components interact; their modes of interaction are well defined and are depicted in a schematic fashion in Fig. 3-1.

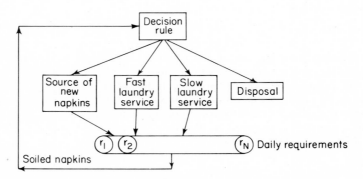

FIGURE 3-1 Schematic Representation of Caterer Problem

Our next task is to determine upper and lower limits on S, the number of new napkins. It is easy to see that if soiled napkins are available on the pth day from the slow service, the caterer would not have to purchase new more than the largest of the total requirements of p successive days. Therefore, $S \leq \max \{r_j + r_{j+1} + \ldots + r_{j+p-1}; j = 1, \ldots, N - p + 1\}$. It is also easy to see that he must purchase new at least the maximum total requirements for q days, i.e., $S \geq \max \{r_j + r_{j+1} + \ldots + r_{j+q-1}; j = 1, \ldots, N - q + 1\}$. Specifically, for $p = 3$ and $q = 1$,

$$\text{Max } \{r_j; j = 1, \cdots, N\} \leq S \leq \text{Max } \{r_j + r_{j+1} + r_{j+2}; j = 1, \cdots, N - 2\}.$$

2.1 Interpretation as Stationary Interaction: A Transportation Model

We now formulate a *transportation model* for the caterer problem. The "sources" are: (1) the source of new napkins and (2) the soiled napkins at the end of each day. The "destinations" are: (1) the required napkins over the N days and (2) the disposal activity. The costs of "transportation" are: (1) \$$a$, from the source of new napkins to any destination except disposal; (2) \$$b$, from any day i to days $i + 1$ or $i + 2$; (3) \$$c$ from day i to day $i + 3$ and thereafter; (4) zero from any day, including New, to disposal; and finally, (5) a very large cost, say ∞, from day i to day j for $j \leq i$, (in order to inhibit any solution in which soiled napkins are made available before they are used). The "transportation cost matrix" is depicted in Table 3-1.

TABLE 3-1   The Cost Matrix of Transportation Model

	Days						Disposal	Availability
	1	2	3	4	$\cdots$	N		
New	a	a	a	a	$\cdots$	a	0	S
day 1	∞	b	b	c	$\cdots$	c	0	r_1
2	∞	∞	b	b	$\cdots$	c	0	r_2
.	.					.	.	.
.	.					.	.	.
.	.					.	.	.
n	∞	∞	∞	∞	$\cdots$	∞	0	r_n
Reqts.	r_1	r_2	r_3	r_4	$\cdots$	r_N	S	$S + \Sigma r_i$

Algebraically, if s_i is the number of new napkins purchased for day i, $\sum_i s_i = S$, then we wish to

$$\text{Minimize } C = aS + b \sum_i (u_{i,i+1} + u_{i,i+2})$$

$$+ c \sum_i \sum_{t=i+3}^{N} v_{i,t} \tag{3-3}$$

subject to the demand constraints

$$s_1 = r_1, s_2 + u_{1,2} = r_2, s_3 + u_{1,3} + u_{2,3} = r_3$$

$$\tag{3-4}$$

$$s_i + u_{i-2,i} + u_{i-1,i} + \sum_{t=1}^{i-3} v_{t,i} = r_i, i = 4, \ldots, N$$

and also subject to the availability constraints

$$u_{i,i+1} + u_{i,i+2} + \sum_{t=i+3}^{N} v_{i,t} = r_i, i = 1, \ldots, N. \tag{3-5}$$

As a numerical example, consider the following data:

Requirements $\{r_i\} = \{120, 60, 70, 100, 90, 70, 110\}$

Costs: $a = \$0.30$, $b = \$0.15$, $c = \$0.05$.

We immediately deduce that $120 \leq S \leq 270$. Assume $S = 270$, and let the starting allocation be as shown in Table 3-2. Notice that this allocation minimizes the number of new napkins purchased. The physical interpretation of Table 3-2 in terms of quantities purchased and sent to fast and slow laundries, and disposed of is given in Fig. 3-2.

TABLE 3-2   Initial Program

	1	2	3	4	5	6	7	D	
New	120							150	270
1		60	60						120
2			10	50					60
3				50	20				70
4					70	30			100
5						40	50		90
6							60	10	70
7								110	110
	120	60	70	100	90	70	110	270	

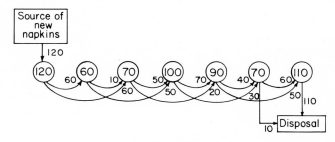

FIGURE 3-2

Obviously, the positive entry in the first row and last column of Table 3-2 is meaningless (since it implies the disposal of new napkins) and should be omitted in the evaluation of the physical flow of napkins. The cost of this program is $111.00.

The minimization of the total cost of Eq. (3-3) is a straightforward application of any one of several known algorithms for the solution of the Transportation problem of Linear Programming. The optimal program is shown in Table 3-3, and its physical interpretation is given in Fig. 3-3.

TABLE 3-3 Optimal Program

	1	2	3	4	5	6	7	D	
New	120	60	70					20	270
1				100	20				120
2					60				60
3						70			70
4					10	90			100
5						20	70		90
6							70		70
7							110		110
	120	60	70	100	90	70	110	270	

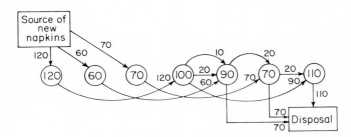

FIGURE 3-3 Interpretation of Optimal Program

The cost of this program, again ignoring the upper right hand entry, is $96.50.

2.2 Interpretation As Dynamic Interaction. A Dynamic Programming Model

Having treated the caterer problem as stationary interaction, we now interpret the problem as dynamic interaction, i.e., as a system in which *time* plays a role in the making of decisions.

Let y_i denote the totality of clean napkins available from all sources at the beginning of day i, and z_i the quantity of clean napkins left over at the end of day i. Obviously, $z_i = y_i - r_i$. Equally obvious, if we ignore disposal for the moment, Eq. (3-5) reduces to $u_i + v_i = r_i$. Consequently, we can substitute for u_i in the objective function, Eq. (3-3), to obtain an equation which is only a function of S and the v_i's of the form:

$$C = K + (a + d - b)S - (b - c) \sum_{i=1}^{N} v_i. \tag{3-6}$$

Here, $K = b \sum_{i=1}^{N} r_i$, and d is the cost of disposal per unit.

Now, since we assume that no cost of inventory is incurred we can assume that all S clean napkins are purchased at the beginning of the planning horizon. Therefore, on day i, previously-made decisions have determined the values of S, $v_1, v_2, \ldots, v_{i-1}$; and the value of y_i is known. The immediate problem then is to determine v_i optimally, since this determines u_i as well as z_i, and, together with previously-determined v's (and u's), these values will also determine y_{i+1}, the quantity of clean napkins available at the beginning of day $i + 1$. The situation then repeats for the duration of the planning horizon. Our problem is, of course, to determine both S^* and $\{v_i^*\}$ in an optimal manner, i.e., to minimize Eq. (3-6).

We shall not carry out such optimization, referring the reader to Problem 2 at the end of the chapter. There, the reader is asked to formulate a dynamic programming model which is solved iteratively in terms of S until, finally at the last stage, S and the v_i's are determined optimally. In this formulation the *reasoning* is sequential over the days in the planning horizon, which is typical of dynamic interaction. Of course, the solution still remains one shot and independent of time.

Having defined both stationary and dynamic interaction, and having illustrated both by a simple problem which can be given either interpretation (with varying degrees of insight and computational ease), we devote the remainder of this chapter to illustrating both types of interaction with examples of operational systems. These examples are drawn from the areas of inventory, production–inventory, and transportation systems.

§3. STATIONARY INTERACTION: CONSTRAINED INVENTORY SYSTEMS—DETERMINISTIC DEMAND

The classical approach to the determination of economic ordering quantities (EOQ) assumes that each item in inventory is independent of the others and hence can be treated separately.[†] Consequently, the optimal average total inventory is the sum of the individual optima and is given by

$$\tfrac{1}{2} \sum_i Q_i^* = \tfrac{1}{2} \sum_i \sqrt{\frac{2R_i A_i}{h_i}} \tag{3-7}$$

where Q_i^* is the EOQ for item i, R_i the total yearly requirements, A_i the cost of placing an order (or "setting up" for production), and h_i the cost of holding one unit of inventory per unit time. This model assumes no lost sales and has *a uniform rate* of demand throughout the year. The square-root expression in Eq. (3-7) is well known and has a rather long and honorable history dating back to 1915 (see Fig. 3-4).

[†] cf., Chapter 1, §3.3.

FIGURE 3-4

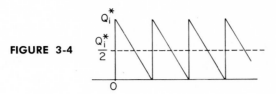

Recently, more attention has been focused on the fact that in reality the items may interact. Such interaction may emanate from various sources:

1. If the replenishments to inventory are realized through orders placed on a producing shop, it is possible that due to the capacity limitations on the various production facilities the replenishments can be only partially fulfilled. The capacity of the producing shop is then a limitation on the various quantities produced.

2. Under the specifications of the model, the average total investment is $\Sigma c_i \cdot Q_i^*/2$, where c_i is the unit purchase price of commodity i. It is possible that management cannot tolerate such an outlay of capital and sets an upper limit I^* which the average investment is not permitted to exceed. In such a case, the items in inventory are, in effect, competing with each other for the consumption of a limited resource which is the investment dollar. Any optimizing procedure must take such interaction into account.

3. It is evident that capital outlay in inventory need not be the only restriction. Others—floor space, gross weight, total volume, etc.—may also be restricting.

In all these situations the items interact: "favoring" one item (by increasing its average investment, allocating more space, etc.,) can occur only "at the expense" of some other item.

We shall illustrate the treatment of such constrained deterministic inventory systems by solving for the optimal Q_i^* assuming only one restriction, say the total average investment.

The problem can be stated as follows: determine economic ordering quantities $\{Q_i^*\}$ for n items so that

$$\Sigma c_i \frac{Q_i}{2} \leq I^*,\tag{3-8}$$

rewritten as $I^* - \Sigma c_i \dfrac{Q_i}{2} \geq 0$. Define the Lagrange multiplier λ as follows:

$$\lambda < 0 \quad \text{if} \quad I^* - \Sigma c_i \frac{Q_i}{2} = 0$$

$$\lambda = 0 \quad \text{if} \quad I^* - \Sigma c_i \frac{Q_i}{2} > 0.$$

Therefore $\lambda(I^* - \Sigma_i c_i Q_i/2)$ is *always* $= 0$; hence, addition of this term to any cost equation does not alter the equation. In particular, we add it to the total variable cost equation to obtain

$$C = \Sigma_i \frac{R_i}{Q_i} \cdot A_i + \Sigma_i h_i \frac{Q_i}{2} + \lambda \left(I^* - \Sigma_i c_i \frac{Q_i}{2} \right). \tag{3-9}$$

The first term is the yearly cost of ordering and the second term is the yearly cost of average investment.

Although the total yearly cost has not changed by such addition, the partial derivative of the cost with respect to the quantity ordered of each item, Q_i, has certainly changed to

$$\frac{\partial C}{\partial Q_i} = -\frac{R_i}{Q_i^2} \cdot A_i + \frac{h_i}{2} - \lambda \frac{c_i}{2}. \tag{3-10}$$

The last term, $-\lambda c_i/2$, has arisen because of the Lagrangian addition.

We digress for a moment to explain an elementary property of minimization (or maximization) of analytic bounded functions subject to constraints. The minimum of a function such as Eq. (3-9) whose variables (the Q_i's) are restricted by inequalities or equalities such as Eq. (3-8) is attained either within the domain of definition of the variables, as in Fig. 3-5(a), or at the boundary of the domain, as $F_1(x)$ in Fig. 3-5(b).

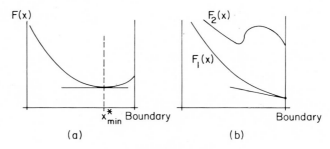

FIGURE 3-5

Clearly, if the minimum is attained within the domain, the restriction is *not limiting*. For the restriction to be "active," case (b) must obtain. Then, the derivative of the function at the boundary must be ≤ 0. It is equal to 0 in the very special case where the restriction occurs exactly at the unrestricted minimum as shown dotted in (a). In this discussion we have considered only "well-behaved" functions—functions such as $F_2(x)$ in (b) are much more complicated.

Returning now to the partial derivative in Eq. (3-10), we put $\partial C/ \partial Q_i \leq 0$ to obtain

$$Q_i^* \leq \sqrt{\frac{2R_i A_i}{h_i - \lambda c_i}}. \tag{3-11}$$

All the parameters of Eq. (3-11) are known except λ. Of course, for $\lambda = 0$, Eq. (3-11) reduces to Eq. (3-7). However, we know that if the restriction is "active" $I^* - \Sigma_i c_i Q_i^*/2 = 0$ and hence, λ is strictly < 0.

The evaluation of the Lagrange multiplier λ and of the optimal $\{Q_i^*\}$ follows an iterative procedure in which we assign λ a value < 0 and calculate the resulting $\{Q_i\}$; then we check that Eq. (3-8) is satisfied *as equality*. If this is not the case, we assign another value to $\lambda < 0$ and repeat the process until the set $\{Q_i^*\}$ is obtained which satisfies Eq. (3-8) as equality. If no such values are reached this is an indication that Eq. (3-8) is not limiting and the optimal $\{Q_i^*\}$ is given by Eq. (3-7).

The search for λ and $\{Q_i^*\}$ is carried out in a systematic fashion. For example, assign different values of $\lambda < 0$ in an increasing fashion, plot the resulting $\Sigma_i c_i Q_i/2$, and then interpolate for λ^* that satisfies Eq. (3-8) as equality.

If m restrictions such as (3-8) occur, then we define the set of Lagrange multipliers $\lambda_1, \lambda_2, \ldots, \lambda_m$, formulate the Lagrangian equation as in Eq. (3-9), and proceed formally with the partial differentiation. Although the procedure is straightforward from a conceptual point of view, it is quite involved from the mathematical as well as the computational point of view.[†]

Interpretation of the Lagrange Multiplier λ.

Suppose that in the above problem we were given the earning power, $\$\epsilon$, per dollar of capital in the free market. Since the average total investment is $\Sigma_i c_i Q_i/2$, (assuming that the available capital is I^*), the average uncommitted capital is $I^* - \Sigma c_i Q_i/2 \geq 0$. This average "free capital" would earn $\$\epsilon$ per dollar, or a total of $\epsilon(I^* - \Sigma_i c_i Q_i/2)$. The total variable cost of inventory management would now become

$$C = \sum_i \frac{R_i}{Q_i} A_i + \sum_i h_i \frac{Q_i}{2} - \epsilon \left(I^* - \sum_i c_i \frac{Q_i}{2} \right); \tag{3-12}$$

the last term is subtracted from the cost because it is *income*.

[†]Problems of existence of a solution arise due to the fact that two restrictions may be conflicting. Also, search techniques in two or more dimensions are cumbersome and time consuming, usually requiring the use of computers.

Compare now Eqs. (3-9) and (3-12). It is immediately evident that $\epsilon = -\lambda$; i.e., the Lagrange multiplier λ is the *imputed cost of capital*. In other words, $-\lambda$ is the imputed gain of uncommitted capital. It is "imputed" because it is *derived* from the restriction rather than determined externally to the system.

An interesting question that arises in this connection is the following: suppose we solve Eq. (3-9) for λ^* and find that $-\lambda^* > \epsilon$; what is the significance of this result? A moment's reflection indicates that λ is the "internal price" of money. If the "internal price" is higher than the external (i.e., market) price it would be more economical for the firm to borrow capital at the cost of $\$\epsilon$ per dollar. This would relax the restriction of Eq. (3-8) and consequently reduce the absolute value of λ. Borrowing is discontinued when $\epsilon = -\lambda$.

§4. STATIONARY INTERACTION: PRODUCTION—INVENTORY SYSTEMS

In the previous sections we gave examples of stationary interaction *within a function*, e.g., inventory. In this section we give an example of stationary interaction among components in *two functions*: production and inventory.

Systems in which both functions of production and inventory are found exist in abundance. In fact, every manufacturing enterprise also performs, to some degree, the function of inventory. The majority of production systems met in practice comprise the two functions although, sometimes, the subtleties of operations may obscure the nature of the functions undertaken (e.g., transportation is, in fact, inventory in transport between two manufacturing processes, though it is rarely recognized, let alone treated, as such). It is obvious that the control of both functions—i.e., defining the system to encompass the interacting components in both areas—affords a better utilization of the available resources.

The following problem is constantly faced by managers of production systems: what is the minimal-cost policy to satisfy a *known* demand over a *finite* planning horizon?[†] The manager has the choice of any combination of the following "pure" strategies:

1. Maintain the labor force constant and absorb demand fluctuations by accumulating and depleting inventories. This policy usually entails large capital outlays in inventories with the associated *oppor-*

[†] In practice, of course, the demand is not perfectly known, nor is the planning horizon finite. However, the assumption of certainty is made for simplicity of solution. The second assumption is very nearly true since the distant future bears little or no influence on current decisions. For further discussions of the models presented, the reader is referred to the references at the end of the chapter.

tunity costs, i.e., the costs of forfeiting profit because of investment in inventory.

2. Maintain investment in inventory at a minimum level consistent with emergency requirements and vary the labor force through hiring and layoffs to correspond to the fluctuating demand. This policy entails the *out-of-pocket* expenses of recruiting, interviewing, hiring, training, etc., whenever an employee is hired and the usual costs associated with layoffs such as compensation, changes in data processing information (e.g., payroll), loss of efficiency, etc., whenever an employee is laid off.

3. Vary the utilization of manpower by overtime work or by permitting idle time (or diversion of effort to maintenance, house cleaning, etc.) while maintaining a constant labor force. This policy also entails the obvious *out-of-pocket* and *opportunity costs*.

Naturally, the manager uses a mixture of these pure strategies. All three parameters—the size of the labor force, the size of inventory, and the amounts of over and idle time—are allowed to vary. The problem is: what is the optimal pattern of *aggregate* variation of all three parameters?

4.1 Review of Current Approaches

The literature is replete with various ingenious approaches to this problem. We refer the interested reader to a recent book by Hanssmann on the subject and the list of references cited therein.

However, we wish to single out one approach by Holt, Modigliani, and Muth, hereafter referred to as HMM, which we believe merits special attention for two important reasons. First, the concepts involved in the approach are simple and plausible. Second, the model was implemented in practice—a distinguishing element not shared by the majority of the other formulations. Let

r_t = demand requirement for period t, measured in some convenient unit such as hours of direct labor.

W_t = number of workers in period t.

I_t = net aggregate inventory at the end of period t, measured in hours (of direct labor).

P_t = production during period t, in hours.

$C_{1t}, C_{2t}, \ldots$ = various costs.

$a_1, a_2, \ldots$ = constants.

Assume that the costs incurred in varying production, inventory, and work force can be *approximated by linear or quadratic* functions, i.e., by functions of the form $y = ax + b$ or $y = ax^2 + bx + c$. This is the only basic assumption to be made in this model. Other approximating assumptions will be introduced as needed but, as will be seen, their need is derived from this assumption.

The plausibility of the assumption rests on the intuitively appealing notion that "small variations do not cost much but large ones do." For example, if one worker is hired a certain cost is incurred. However, the hiring of 20 workers involves more than 20 times the cost of the individual hiring. We now present a simplified version of the HMM model.

Costs of labor can be represented by

$$C_{1t} = a_1 W_t + a_2(W_t - W_{t-1})^2, \tag{3-13}$$

an equation composed of a linear and a quadratic term. The linear term represents the cost of employing W_t workers on regular time; the quadratic term measures the cost of changing the number of workers from period to period.

Costs associated with manipulating the level of production can be represented by

$$C_{2t} = a_3 P_t - a_4 W_t + a_5(P_t - a_6 W_t)^2, \tag{3-14}$$

again an equation of linear and quadratic terms. The formulation of this equation warrants some elaboration since it involves costing three modes of variation. The first is the variation of the *minimum* cost with production rate, assumed quadratic of the form

$$\text{minimum cost} = k_1 P^2 + k_2 P + k_3.$$

The second is the variation of the optimal work force, W_{0t}, with the production rate,

$$W_0 = k_4 P + k_5.$$

The third is the cost of the deviation of the actual work force, W_t, from the ideal work force, W_{0t}, assumed quadratic,

$$k_6(W - W_0)^2.$$

The actual cost, C_{2t}, is given, strictly speaking, by $k_6(W_t - W_{0t})^2 + k_1 P^2 + k_2 P + k_3$, with the value of W_{0t} substituted in terms of P_t from above.

Costs associated with inventory variation are represented by

$$C_{3t} = a_7(I_t - a_8 r_t)^2, \tag{3-15}$$

a quadratic equation, where $a_8 r_t$ represents some ideal inventory level for the demand rate r_t. Again, the expanded form of Eq. (3-15) is a function of two modes of variation: the cost of optimal inventory necessary for any level of demand and the cost of variation of actual inventory from the optimal. It can be easily shown that the ideal inventory varies as the *square root* of the rate of demand. Within a small range the square root relationship can be approximated by a linear relationship, hence the term $a_8 r_t$ in Eq. (3-15).

The total cost function is the sum of the costs in Eqs. (3-13) to (3-15) over the planning horizon,

$$C = \sum_1^N [a_1 W_t + a_2(W_t - W_{t-1})^2]$$

$$+ \sum_1^N [a_3 P_t - a_4 W_t + a_5(P_t - a_6 W_t)^2]$$

$$+ \sum_1^N [a_7(I_t - a_8 r_t)^2]. \qquad (3\text{-}16)$$

Naturally, inventory and production are related by

$$I_t = I_{t-1} + P_t - r_t. \qquad (3\text{-}17)$$

We wish to minimize Eq. (3-16) subject to the relation Eq. (3-17). The standard technique is to form the Lagrangian equation

$$G = C + \lambda(I_t - I_{t-1} - P_t + r_t), \qquad (3\text{-}18)$$

where λ is the Lagrange multiplier. Differentiate Eq. (3-18) partially with respect to the unknown variables W_t, I_t and λ. After some algebraic manipulation we obtain a system of $N - 1$ equations in $N + 1$ unknowns, W_1 to W_{N+1}, which can be solved after specifying the end conditions W_N and W_{N+1}. Substitution in the original system of equations yields the variables P_1 to P_N. The final result is of the form.

$$P_t = \sum_1^N \alpha_i r_i + \ell_1 W_{t-1} + \ell_2 I_{t-1} + \ell_3$$

$$W_t = \sum_1^N \beta_i r_i + \ell_4 W_{t-1} + \ell_5 I_{t-1} + \ell_6 \qquad (3\text{-}19)$$

where the α's and β's and ℓ's are constant coefficients.

This has been, by necessity, a rather sketchy outline of the approach. It does provide, however, some insight into the structure of the model and the various assumptions made. It also gives some indication of the required empirical data and the amount of analysis necessary to construct the model and obtain the final coefficients of Eq. (3-19). It also gives a hint of the analysis necessary to vary some of the parameters due to environmental changes or to check the sensitivity of the model to certain cost coefficients.

4.2 A Linear Programming Model

We now present a different approach to the same problem. Specifically, we formulate a linear programming model which, as we shall presently see, offers three advantages over the HMM model: (1) it does not require the assumption concerning the quadratic variation of costs; (2) it is a much simpler model to construct and to manipulate and is much easier to maintain in an operating environment; and (3) it places at the disposal of the manager the whole power of LP theory, which he may utilize to advantage.

In addition to the symbols defined before, we need the following:

X_t = hours of regular-time production in period t.
Y_t = hours of overtime production in period t.
a = cost of regular-time production per hour.
b = cost of overtime production per hour (usually taken = $1.5a$).
e = cost of idle time per hour.
h = cost of hiring per employee added.
ℓ = cost of layoff per employee laid off.
i = cost per unit period (say one month) of one unit of end-of-period inventory (measured in the common unit of hours of production).

Since the program of production and inventory is computed well in advance of the actual production period there is no question of lead time between decision and implementation.

Let A_t denote the number of hours of regular time available per employee in period t. If the period is taken, as is commonly the case, to be one calendar month, A_t represents the available capacity of regular-time working hours—adjusted by some average efficiency factor—per direct employee. A_t need not be constant from period to period; in fact, it will vary depending on vacations, shut-downs, maintenance requirements, etc.. Therefore, $A_t W_t$ represents the available capacity, in hours, of the work force. Obviously,

$$X_t \leq A_t \cdot W_t \quad \text{or} \quad X_t - A_t W_t + S_{1t} = 0, \tag{3-20}$$

i.e., total production on regular time cannot exceed available capacity. Consequently, the slack variable S_{1t} represents *idle time*.

Let B_t denote the number of O.T. hours available per employee in period t. Normally, B_t is between $0.20\,A_t$ and $0.25\,A_t$. By a similar argument to the above we have

$$Y_t \leq B_t \cdot W_t, \text{ i.e., } Y_t - B_t \cdot W_t + S_{2t} = 0. \tag{3-21}$$

We now need a counterpart to Eq. (3-17) relating inventory to production. We have

$$I_t = I_{t-1} + X_t + Y_t - r_t \geq 0 \tag{3-22}$$

which specifies that the inventory at the end of period t must be the sum of the starting inventory and production (on regular and overtime) minus the sales during the same period (see Fig. 3-6). Since we wish to satisfy all customer demand, I_t must be ≥ 0.

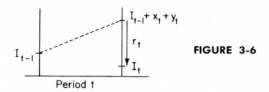

FIGURE 3-6

Period t

Finally, the change in the size of the work force is given by $(W_t - W_{t-1})$, which is > 0 or < 0 depending on whether $W_t > W_{t-1}$ or $W_t < W_{t-1}$. Since any number, positive or negative, can be represented as the difference between two *nonnegative* numbers, we put

$$W_t - W_{t-1} = U_t - V_t \tag{3-23}$$

where U_t represents the increase in the work force and V_t the decrease. If the left hand side of Eq. (3-23) is > 0, U_t is > 0 and $V_t = 0$; conversely, if the left hand side of Eq. (3-23) is < 0, U_t is $= 0$ and $V_t > 0$. Of course the same difference $(W_t - W_{t-1})$ can be represented by an infinite number of different values of U_t and V_t by simply adding the same constant to both. However, since we incur a cost whenever either U_t or V_t is > 0, the *minimum cost* program will not contain both at positive levels.

We now formulate the objective function. It is composed of costs of: (1) hiring, (2) layoff, (3) regular-time production, (4) O.T. production, (5) idle time, and (6) inventory carrying charges. Denoting the cost in period t by C_t we have,

$$C_t = h \cdot U_t + \ell \cdot V_t + a \cdot X_t + b \cdot Y_t + e \cdot S_{1t} + i \cdot I_t. \tag{3-24}$$

Our problem has been reduced to determining the unknown variables X_t, Y_t, W_t, U_t, V_t, and I_t that minimize $\Sigma_1^N C_t$. This is a straightforward linear programming problem for which algorithms for solution are available.

Since the number of employees is integral, we can restrict the solution to integer W_t, U_t, and V_t. The resultant would be a *mixed linear program*, since only some of the variables are restricted to be integers while the

others can be nonintegers. This restriction is, in the final analysis, unnecessary. The accuracy (or rather the lack of it) of the data with which
we are dealing—relative to expected demand, cost coefficients, etc.—
renders such a refinement meaningless. Moreover, a fraction employee
need not be infeasible since the same employee can be shared by more
than one function. In view of the fact that computer programs for solving
large-scale mixed linear programming problems are still in the develop-
mental stage, it is advisable to ignore, at least for the time being, such a
desired result.

Some simplification of the formulation given in Eqs. (3-20) to (3-23) is
possible, with a reduction in the number of original variables. Let the
starting inventory be I_0; then, from Eq. (3-22) we have, recursively,

$$I_1 = I_0 + X_1 + Y_1 - r_1$$

$$I_2 = I_0 + X_1 + X_2 + Y_1 + Y_2 - r_1 - r_2$$

and in general,

$$I_t = I_0 + \sum_1^t X_i + \sum_1^t Y_i - \sum_1^t r_i \geq 0$$

i.e.,

$$\sum_1^t X_i + \sum_1^t Y_i - S_{3t} = \sum_1^t r_i - I_0 \tag{3-25}$$

where S_{3t} represents the excess cumulative production over demand
requirements, i.e., the end-of-period inventory.

Having eliminated I_t from all restrictions, we substitute in the criterion
function to obtain

$$C_t = h \cdot U_t + \ell \cdot V_t + a \cdot X_t + b \cdot Y_t + e \cdot S_{1t} + i \cdot S_{3t}. \tag{3-26}$$

To summarize, we wish to

$$\text{Minimize } C = \sum_1^N C_t \text{ as given by Eq. (3-26)}$$

subject to the following constraints

$$X_t - A_t \cdot W_t + S_{1t} = 0 \tag{3-27}$$

$$Y_t - B_t \cdot W_t + S_{2t} = 0 \tag{3-28}$$

$$W_t - W_{t-1} - U_t + V_t = 0 \tag{3-29}$$

$$\sum_1^t X_i + \sum_1^t Y_i - S_{3t} = \sum_1^t r_i - I_0, t = 1, \ldots, N. \tag{3-30}$$

The size of the resulting linear program is rather modest: we have $4N$ equations in $5N$ original variables.

Model Enrichment

The basic model presented above can be enriched in several ways to take into account, in an explicit fashion, other managerial restrictions or to incorporate certain cost factors. We briefly discuss a few such extensions.

Increasing Marginal Cost of Hiring and Layoff. We recall that the plausibility of the quadratic approximation to the costs of hiring and layoffs used in the model of HMM rested on the intuitive feeling that a "small change does not cost as much as a large one." Such relationship can be readily incorporated in our linear programming model. Let the cost of hiring be h_1 per man for $0 \le U \le m_1$ and h_2 be the cost of hiring per man for $U \ge m_1$ where $h_2 > h_1$. Similarly for layoffs: ℓ_1 is applicable in the range $0 \le V \le m_2$ and ℓ_2 in the range $V \ge m_2$; $\ell_2 > \ell_1$. Graphically, the costs of changing manpower are as shown in Fig. 3-7.

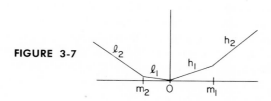

FIGURE 3-7

Naturally, the linear programming formulation must be changed to incorporate these new factors. Let U_{1t} represent hiring in the first range and U_{2t} represent hiring in the second range. Similarly for V_{1t} and V_{2t}. Then we have

$$C_t = h_1 \cdot U_{1t} + h_2 U_{2t} + \ell_1 \cdot V_{1t} + \ell_2 \cdot V_{2t}$$
$$+ a \cdot X_t + b \cdot Y_t + e \cdot S_{1t} + i \cdot S_{3t}. \qquad (3\text{-}31)$$

To the system of restrictions (3-27), (3-28), and (3-30) we must add

$$U_{1t} \le m_1; \text{i.e., } U_{1t} + S_{4t} = m_1 \qquad (3\text{-}32)$$

$$V_{1t} \le m_2; \text{i.e., } V_{1t} + S_{5t} = m_2 \qquad (3\text{-}33)$$

and modify Eq. (3-29) to read

$$W_t - W_{t-1} - U_{1t} - U_{2t} + V_{1t} + V_{2t} = 0. \qquad (3\text{-}34)$$

Notice that no explicit restrictions on U_{2t} or V_{2t} are required. This is due to the fact that both U_{2t} and V_{2t} are *priced higher* than U_{1t} and V_{1t}.

Hence, the optimizing procedure will not increase either of U_{2t} or V_{2t} without first exhausting all of U_{1t} or V_{1t}, according to whether we are increasing or reducing the labor force.

The restrictions Eqs. (3-32) and (3-33) are upper bounds on the variables $\{U_{1t}\}$ and $\{V_{1t}\}$. Dantzig[†] has shown a method by which such restrictions *need not* be explicitly stated. This would mean that the desired objective is achieved *without increasing the number of constraining equations*, an important advantage indeed. The number of *original variables*, however, will increase by $2N$ for each division of the real axis.

Limitations on the Freedom to Hire and Layoff.   We can incorporate, in a straightforward manner, any restriction on the *number* of employees hired or laid off as well as on the *timing* of such action. For example, if we specify that

$$U_t \le f_1 \cdot W_{t-1}$$
$$V_t \le f_2 \cdot W_{t-1},$$

we limit the number of hirings and layoffs to specified fractions f_1 and f_2 of the labor force. On the other hand, if we put

$$W_t - W_{t-1} \le n \quad \text{for} \quad t = t_{01}, t_{02}, \cdots, t_{0k},$$

we bound the possible increase in periods $t_{01}, \ldots, t_{0k}$ to no more than n individuals.

Optimizing Relative to Product Groups.   Our formulation optimizes the *aggregate* production, inventory, and labor force. This was done for simplicity of exposition and to maintain the continuity of discussion from the model of HMM. It is obvious, however, that the linear programming formulation offers a degree of freedom which is not possible with the previous model. In particular, we can optimize the objective function, taking into account the individual requirements of products or groups of products.

If we redefine the variables as X_{jt}, Y_{jt}, W_{jt}, U_{jt}, and V_{jt} to represent their respective quantities *relative to product j*, we can immediately see that with the proper definition of the cost parameters, the problem would become:

$$\text{Minimize } C = \sum_{j,t} C_{jt}$$

where $C_{jt} = h_j \cdot U_{jt} + \ell_j \cdot V_{jt} + a_j \cdot X_{jt} + b_j \cdot Y_{jt} + e_j \cdot S_{j1t} + i \cdot S_{j3t}$ subject to the restrictions

$$X_{jt} - A_{jt} \cdot W_{jt} + S_{j1t} = 0, \quad j = 1, \ldots, m$$

[†]G. B. Dantzig, "Upper Bounds, Block Triangularity and Secondary Constraints," *Econometrica*, Vol. 23, No. 1, Jan. 1955, pp. 174–183.

$$Y_{jt} - B_{jt} \cdot W_{jt} + S_{j2t} = 0$$

$$W_{jt} - W_{j,t-1} - U_{jt} + V_{jt} = 0$$

$$\sum_1^t X_{jt} + \sum_1^t Y_{jt} - S_{j3t} = \sum_1^t R_{jt} - I_{oj}, t = 1, \ldots, N.$$

The size of the program is necessarily expanded to $4mN$ restrictions in $5mN$ original variables.

Conclusion

The linear programming formulation given above seems to be an extremely powerful model for optimal smoothing of production, inventory, and work force. In casting the problem in this formulation we make available to the analyst and the manager the various powerful techniques of the theory of linear programming such as: sensitivity analysis by parametric programming, valuation of scarce resources by the shadow prices, etc.. The availability of the computer programs that solve linear programming problems relieves management from the decision of investing in the "software." On the other hand, the size of the program makes it feasible on rather small computers, such as the IBM 1620 with 20,000 core memory units.

Active research is currently undertaken for the solution of large-scale *integer* and *mixed* programming problems. Undoubtedly, it is only a matter of time before these computer codes are available. Then, the model can be cast with the integer requirements and the optimal solution obtained directly, not just approximately.

With these comments in mind, one might question the utility of the HMM model. The following is an important property of the latter model which is *not* shared by the linear programming approach. If the demand is stochastic (which, realistically, is almost always the case), and if the objective is to minimize the *expected cost* over the planning horizon, and if the costs are, in fact, quadratic, then the HMM decision rule is *optimal*. The utility of the model is directly dependent on the realization of the three if's mentioned in the previous sentence. The proof of this property was given by Simon in the reference cited at the end of the chapter.

Finally, it is worth remarking that in spite of the fact that we presented, above, a model of stationary interaction, application of the model in real life situations will necessarily lead to a *dynamic* model. This is so because planning production, inventory, and work force is not a static or one shot activity, but is undertaken periodically and takes into account the latest available data on these and other factors. This element of feedback is the essential characteristic of dynamic interaction, as will be seen presently.

§5. STATIONARY INTERACTION: A CLASS OF PRODUCTION OPTIMIZATION PROBLEMS*

There exists a certain class of production problems which entail indivisibilities in the activities as well as nonlinearities in costs and seem to present formidable obstacles to quantitative optimization. On the surface, one would expect a nonlinear model of the system or, at best, an enumerative approach which, in almost all real-life problems, promises to be prohibitively time consuming.

However, results of research conducted within the past ten years reveal that such problems can be cast in a *linear programming* formulation. The advantages of such a model are obvious. However, the one important disadvantage turned out to be the unwieldly size of the resulting LP, especially in the number of variables (columns) of the Simplex tableau. The reason for such occurrence is that each variable represents an indivisible activity and the manner in which such activities are generated is combinatorial in nature. The number of activities can easily run into the hundreds of millions.

For some time the prospects for the successful resolution of practical problems seemed bleak indeed. However, an ingenious approach which avoids such a combinatorial trap was proposed in 1961 by Gilmore and Gomory. The approach is based in part on a notion implicit in the work of Ford and Fulkerson[†] concerning multicommodity network flows and of Dantzig and Wolfe[‡] on the Decomposition Principle of LP.

The concepts involved in the formulation of the LP models are both novel and important. The approach to solutions is intriguing. We devote this section to a detailed exposition of both.

First, we motivate the development by explaining the various problems as they arise in their practical context. Then we detail the Gilmore-Gomory approach and illustrate its applicability to the other problems.

5.1 A Machine-Loading Problem

The following managerial problem is faced by many fabricating shops. It is desired to manufacture a large number of products which are demanded in specific quantities, and each product requires a known set of producing facilities in a given sequence. Due to the size of the end products (or their perishability, or constitution, etc.) in-waiting inventory is

---

[*] May be omitted on first reading.
[†] L. R. Ford and D. R. Fulkerson, "Suggested Computation for Maximal Multi-Commodity Network Flows," *Management Science*, Vol. 5, No. 1, Oct. 1958, pp. 97–101.
[‡] G. B. Dantzig and P. Wolfe, "Decomposition Principle for Linear Programs," *Operations Research*, Vol. 8, No. 1, Jan–Feb. 1960, pp. 101–111.

not permitted, (or can be neglected). It is desired to determine the optimal program of fabrication which satisfies the demand and stays within available capacities of the various producing facilities.

A concrete example should be illuminating. Consider a sheet-fabricating shop which contains several classes (i.e., types) of presses of varying capabilities and production rates. Any class may contain more than one press, but within a class the various presses are assumed indistinguishable.

The input to the shop is in the form of large metal sheets; the output is the sheets cut to size. Due to space limitations and the size of the product, a queue of jobs is not permitted to form at any operation. Since any finished sheet may require a sequence of operations on different classes of presses, an immediate consequence of the above restriction is that a product is loaded on the shop (i.e., released for production) if, and only if, *all its producing facilities are free*. This simple factor distinguishes the current problem from the traditional job-shop type mode of operation.

Two more points regarding the technology of production are worth noting. First, for a specific operation on a specific product, two or more classes of presses may be equally good. This gives rise to *groups* of press classes. For example, Table 3-4 gives the classes of presses and the num-

TABLE 3-4

Press Class	No. of Presses
A	3
B	5
C	5
D	4
E	1
H	2

ber of presses in each class. Table 3-5 gives a sample of product "layout sheets," and Table 3-6 gives the groups of press classes appearing in such layout sheets. Second, more than one product may be fabricated in the shop simultaneously provided the products do not overlap on any individual press. No sequencing of the different jobs on the same press is undertaken.

Notice that when a part is "loaded on the shop," i.e., released for production, it occupies all the presses designated in its layout sheet *at the same time*, so that the loading of another part must satisfy the noninterference restriction. Therefore, the loading of the second part must be within the limitations of the "left-over" presses. If the second part is

TABLE 3-5 Sample of Product "Layouts"

Part No.	Operation Number	Classes of Presses	Set-up Time	Operation Time hrs/1000 Units	Rate of Production Units/hr.
1	1	BC	2.1	3.5	285
	2	B	1	4.7	213
	3	EBC	1.3	4.7	213
	4	BC	1	4.8	208
	5	ABC	1	5.2	192
	6	ABCD	1.5	5.6	178
	7	DH	1	5.6	178
	8	BC	1	6.3	158
	9	B	1	5.8	172
	10	BC	2	6.6	151[a]
	11	BC	2	5.4	185
	12	ABC	1	5.1	196
2	1	D	1.5	5.0	200
	2	ABC	1.3	5.8	172
	3	BC	2.0	5.4	185
	4	BC	1	6.8	161[a]
	5	DH	2.2	4.2	238
3	1	AB	1.0	2.1	476
	2	ABCD	2.0	4.7	213
	3	ABCD	1.4	5.3	189[a]
4	1	AB	1.4	4.1	243
	2	ABC	1.2	4.6	217[a]
5	1	D	1.0	3.9	256
	2	AB	1.8	4.1	243[a]
	3	BC	1.0	3.6	278
6	1	D	2.0	3.8	263
	2	D	1.8	4.0	250
	3	B	1.7	3.8	263
	4	BC	1.0	4.5	221[a]
7	1	ABC	1.0	5.6	178[a]
8	1	ABC	1.2	0.5	2,000[a]
9	1	BC	1.3	0.5	2,000
	2	ABC	1.2	0.6	1,667
	3	BC	1.0	0.55	1,815
	4	BC	1.5	0.69	1,450[a]
	5	AB	2.0	0.58	1,722
10	1	DH	1.0	4.2	238[a]

[a] The letter a denotes the bottleneck operation.

TABLE 3-6

Groups of Press Classes	No. of Presses in Group
B	5
AB	8
BC	10
ABC	13
ABCD	17
EBC	11
D	4
DH	6

loaded, similar reasoning indicates that a third part can be loaded only if it does not violate any of the "left-over" availabilities from the previous two parts, etc. This is continued until no more parts can be loaded. We then have a *maximal assignment*.

Since the left-over presses are a function of the part or parts previously loaded, the combinatorial nature of the maximal assignments should now be in evidence. Each maximal assignment is indivisible, and its productivity as well as press utilization are known.

The question of "left-overs" bears close scrutiny. Obviously, a group of press classes contains as many presses as its component press classes (or types). For example, Table 3-6 indicates that group ABC contains 13 presses, which is precisely the sum of press classes (types) $A(= 3) + B(= 5) + C(= 5)$. When a part is loaded it occupies a press of a certain class. Consequently, the availability of presses must be reduced by one in that class and in every group *which contains that class*. This is obvious, for example, in the case of operation 9 of part 1 listed in Table 3-5: it occupies

TABLE 3-7

Groups of Presses	No. of Presses in Group
B	5
AB	8
BC	10
ABC	13
EBC	11
ABCD	17
ABCE	14
D	4
DH	6
ABCDE	18
ABCDH	19
ABCDEH	20

one press of class B which reduces the availability in class B as well as in groups AB, BC, ABC, ABCD, and EBC. In order to keep the accounting straight, whenever there are two groups with one or more classes in common but one group is not wholly contained in the other (such as groups ABCD and DH) or both are not wholly contained in a third group, then designate an arbitrary *control group* containing exactly those classes indicated in the two overlapping groups. Consequently, we need four control groups: ABCE, ABCDE, ABCDH, and ABCDEH containing 14, 18, 19, and 20 presses, respectively. The complete list of groups and number of presses in each group is given in Table 3-7.

For example, in Table 3-8 we give the press class requirements for the ten products of Table 3-5.

TABLE 3-8   Press Requirements of Each Part By Class of Presses

Part No.	B	D	BC	DH	AB	ABC	EBC	ABCD
1	2	—	5	1	—	2	1	1
2	—	1	2	1	—	1	—	—
3	—	—	—	—	1	—	—	2
4	—	—	—	—	1	1	—	—
5	—	1	1	—	1	—	—	—
6	1	2	1	—	—	—	—	—
7	—	—	—	—	—	1	—	—
8	—	—	—	—	—	1	—	—
9	—	—	3	—	1	1	—	—
10	—	—	—	1	—	—	—	—

Now consider Part 1. It requires two presses of class B, five presses of group BC, and two presses of group ABC. Consequently, its total demand on group ABC is nine, since group ABC contains class B and group BC. Continuing in this fashion, we can easily construct the press group requirements for each part, shown in Table 3-9.

A maximal assignment is formed in the following fashion. Suppose we load Part 10. The staring and "left-over" capacities of the various press groups will be as shown in Table 3-10. It is immediately obvious that Part 9 can be loaded (Table 3-11).

Continuing in this fashion, we load Parts 8, 7, 6, 5, and 4. The "left-over" capacities will then be as shown in Table 3-12.

At this point, it seems that no other part listed in Table 3-9 can be loaded because group ABC is exhausted. However, the alert reader will notice that it is possible to load *two other lots* of Part 10 without exceeding the available "left-overs," since the two lots would require only two presses of group DH.

TABLE 3-9 Press Group Requirements

Part #		B	AB	BC	ABC	EBC	ABCD	ABCE	D	DH	ABCDE	ABCDH	ABCDEH
1	B-2	2	2	2	2	2	2	2	—	—	2	2	2
	BC-5	—	—	5	5	5	5	5	—	—	5	5	5
	DH-1	—	—	—	—	—	—	—	—	1	—	1	1
	ABC-2	—	—	—	2	—	2	2	—	—	2	2	2
	EBC-1	—	—	—	—	1	—	1	—	—	1	—	1
	ABCD-1	—	—	—	—	—	1	—	—	—	1	1	1
		2	2	7	9	8	10	10	—	1	11	11	12
2	D-1	—	—	—	—	—	—	—	1	1	1	1	1
	BC-2	—	—	2	2	2	2	2	—	—	2	2	2
	DH-1	—	—	—	—	—	—	—	—	1	—	1	1
	ABC-1	—	—	—	1	—	1	1	—	—	1	1	1
		—	—	2	3	2	4	3	1	2	4	5	5
3	AB-1	—	1	—	1	—	1	1	—	—	1	1	1
	ABCD-2	—	—	—	—	—	2	—	—	—	2	2	2
		—	1	—	1	—	3	1	—	—	3	3	3
4	AB-1	—	1	—	1	—	1	1	—	—	1	1	1
	ABC-1	—	—	—	1	—	1	1	—	—	1	1	1
		—	1	—	2	—	2	2	—	—	2	2	2
5	D-1	—	—	—	—	—	1	—	1	1	1	1	1
	BC-1	—	—	1	1	1	1	1	—	—	1	1	1
	AB-1	—	1	—	1	—	1	1	—	—	1	1	1
		—	1	1	2	1	3	2	1	1	3	3	3

Table 3-9 Continued

Part #		B	AB	BC	ABC	EBC	ABCD	ABCE	D	DH	ABCDE	ABCDH	ABCDEH
6	B-1	1	1	1	1	1	1	1	—	—	1	1	1
	D-2	—	—	—	—	—	2	—	2	2	2	2	2
	BC-1	—	—	1	1	1	1	1	—	—	1	1	1
		1	1	2	2	2	4	2	2	2	4	4	4
7	ABC-1	—	—	—	1	—	1	1	—	—	1	1	1
		—	—	—	1	—	1	1	—	—	1	1	1
8	ABC-1	—	—	—	1	—	1	1	—	—	1	1	1
		—	—	—	1	—	1	1	—	—	1	1	1
9	BC-3	—	—	3	3	3	3	3	—	—	3	3	3
	AB-1	—	1	—	1	—	1	1	—	—	1	1	1
	ABC-1	—	—	—	1	—	1	—	—	—	—	1	1
		—	1	3	5	3	5	5	—	—	5	5	5
10	DH-1	—	—	—	—	—	—	—	—	1	—	1	1
		—	—	—	—	—	—	—	—	1	—	1	1

TABLE 3-10

	B	AB	BC	ABC	EBC	ABCD	ABCE	D	DH	ABCDE	ABCDH	ABCDEH
Starting Availabilities	5	8	10	13	11	17	14	4	6	18	19	20
Consumption due to Loading	—	—	—	—	—	—	—	—	1	—	1	1
Left-Over Capacities	5	8	10	13	11	17	14	4	5	18	18	19

TABLE 3-11

	B	AB	BC	ABC	EBC	ABCD	ABCE	D	DH	ABCDE	ABCDH	ABCDEH
Consumption due to Loading	—	1	3	5	3	5	5	—	—	5	5	5
Left-Over Capacities	5	7	7	8	8	12	9	4	5	13	13	14

TABLE 3-12

	B	AB	BC	ABC	EBC	ABCD	ABCE	D	DH	ABCDE	ABCDH	ABCDEH
Left-Over Capacities	4	4	4	0	5	1	1	1	2	2	2	3

The problem of the simultaneous loading of two or more lots of the *same product* on the shop can easily be taken care of in the following fashion. For each part i determine the bottleneck operation. This is determined by the machine class or machine group whose capacity is limiting for this particular part. For example, for Part 1 of Table 3-6, machine group EBC is limiting (consequently the fifth operation is the bottleneck operation); for Part 2, machine group DH is limiting, and consequently the third operation is the bottleneck operation, and so forth. Next, determine the *maximum* number of lots of part i that can be processed simultaneously (this is easily determined from the bottleneck operation) and let it be denoted by k_i. For example, $k_1 = 1$, while $k_2 = 3$; etc.

Now define new products $i_2, \ldots, i_r$, where r is the smallest integer greater or equal to $\log_2 k_i$, and let the consumption of product i_m be 2^{m-1} times the consumption of product i, $2 \leq m \leq r$. For example, for product 2 we would define a new product 2_2 which goes through the same *sequence* of operations as Part 2 but requires 2 presses of class D, 4 presses of group BC, 2 of group DH, etc.

Once these fictitious products are defined, the construction of maximal assignments proceeds in the usual manner. Some of these assignments will include the new fictitious products which will represent, in conjunction with the original products, the desired simultaneous loading on the shop of two, three, etc., lots of the same product.

Pursuing the example of generating a maximal assignment, we see that the following assignment (see Table 3-13) exhausts shop capacity.

TABLE 3-13

Part No.	Rate of Production
4	217
5	243
6	221
7	178
8	2000
9	1450
10	3×238

We recapitulate. Starting with the production information of Table 3-5, we construct maximal assignments in the manner illustrated above. There may be a large number of such assignments. Each assignment produces certain quantities of some parts and fully utilizes only a subset of the available press classes. It is desired to find the optimal combination of maximal assignments, i.e., the combination that optimizes a given objective function and remains within the available capacity of the shop.

Notice that we are no longer dealing with individual products but with maximal assignments.

Now, to the mathematical formulation of the model. Let X_j be the number of hours devoted to the jth assignment; let a_{ij} be the number of units of product i produced by assignment j per unit time. Obviously, a_{ij} is given by the minimum number opposite part i in column 6 of Table 3-5, and was denoted by the letter a. Let parts 1 to r go into the manufacture of assembly 1 in quantities $t_1, \ldots, t_r$ per unit of assembly 1; and let parts $r + 1$ to s go into the manufacture of assembly 2 in quantities $t_{r+1}, \ldots, t_s$ per unit of assembly 2, etc.. Let $q_1 \geq 0$ be the minimum requirement of product 1, $q_2 \geq 0$ be the minimum requirement of product 2, etc.. Finally, let $y_1, y_2, \ldots, y_M$ be the quantities produced of assemblies 1, 2, ..., M *in excess of* the minimum requirements, at profits $p_1, p_2, \ldots, p_M$ per unit of assembly, respectively. Then we wish to

$$\text{Maximize} \sum_{m=1}^{M} p_m y_m \tag{3-35}$$

subject to demand constraints

$$\sum_j a_{ij} X_j = t_i(y_1 + q_1) \qquad \text{for } i = 1, \ldots, r$$

$$\sum_j a_{ij} X_j = t_i(y_2 + q_2) \qquad \text{for } i = r + 1, \ldots, s$$

$$\quad . \tag{3-36}$$

$$\quad .$$

$$\sum_j a_{ij} X_j = t_i(y_M + q_M) \qquad \text{for } i = v + 1, \ldots, w$$

and available time constraint

$$\sum_j X_j \leq H;$$

where H is the total time available.

The problem presented in (3-35) and (3-36) is an LP whose solution is "straightforward" except for the fact that the matrix of coefficients $\{a_{ij}\}$ has one column per assignment, and there is a very large number of these. Several systematic methods of generating the matrix of assignments have been proposed, and we are certain that the reader can devise his own method. We postpone the discussion of efficient algorithmic generation of such maximal assignments until after we have completed the discussion of the other applications.

We remark that the above formulation completely ignores the problem of set-up time either as a function of the assignment or of the sequence within and among assignments. Needless to say, the need to manufacture intermittently but consume continuously—which gives rise to EMQ problems (see §3.3 of Chapter 1)—interacts strongly with the problem of sequencing. We do not propose to enter into an elaborate discussion of this facet of the problem; the interested reader is referred to Salveson's paper cited at the end of the chapter.

5.2 Economic Lot-Size Manufacturing Problem

The following problem is often encountered by manufacturing shops whose production is in batches and the demand is significantly fluctuating over time.

Given a large number of products to be manufactured, and given delivery requirements for each of these products over the planning horizon, it is required to determine the quantities to be produced in each time period to satisfy the demand and remain within shop capabilities concerning regular time and overtime capacities.

In the subsequent treatment, the following simplifying assumptions are made:

1. We are concerned only with the general loading of the shop rather than with any internal scheduling or sequencing over the various facilities.

2. We ignore machine capacity limitations. It is assumed that if manpower limitations are satisfied, the plan is feasible on the available machines.

3. We do not consider in-waiting inventory cost, i.e., the cost of inventory waiting to be processed by any machine, *first*, because the cost is relatively minor, and second, the resulting model is simpler.

4. Set-up costs are incurred each time the item is produced and are constant over time.

The point of departure of the present problem from classical EOQ formulations lies in the following two considerations: first, the delivery requirements on each item are *specified by period* (and not in terms of a constant *rate*), with a significant variation in requirements from period to period,[†] and *second*, it is desired to take into account the gross production capability of the shop (at least to a first degree of approximation, as represented by manpower availability).

Let r_{it} be the delivery requirements of item i in period t, $i = 1, \ldots, m$ and $t = 1, \ldots, N$. Under the stipulation of *no backorders*, there are 2^{N-1} patterns of satisfying the demand for each item (since in each period we have the dichotomy: produce or do not produce, and the demand in a

---

[†]This aspect of demand was treated previously (see §3.3 of Chapter 1).

nonproducing period is satisfied from the nearest prior producing period). Since a set-up cost is incurred each time the item is produced, it can easily be shown that the optimal (i.e., cheapest) pattern of production must be among these 2^{N-1} different patterns (there may be more than one optimal pattern).

Consequently, if the total requirements of an item are to be split over a number of production lots, they must be split in one of these 2^{N-1} patterns.

For example, suppose we have requirements r_{i1}, r_{i2}, r_{i3} for item i over a 3-period horizon. Then the $2^2 = 4$ patterns of production are as shown in Table 3-14:

TABLE 3-14

	Production in			Binary Representation of Production Pattern
	Period 1	Period 2	Period 3	
Pattern 1:	$r_{i1} + r_{i2} + r_{i3}$	0	0	1, 0, 0
Pattern 2:	$r_{i1} + r_{i2}$	0	r_{i3}	1, 0, 1
Pattern 3:	r_{i1}	$r_{i2} + r_{i3}$	0	1, 1, 0
Pattern 4:	r_{i1}	r_{i2}	r_{i3}	1, 1, 1

The indivisibility characteristic of the problem should now be apparent: each pattern of production for each item gives rise to a known consumption of the scarce resources available (regular and overtime capacities). It is desired to find the feasible combination of such patterns which optimizes an objective function, such as minimize overtime or minimize total production and inventory cost.

Let X_{ij} be the fraction of the total requirement for the ith part to be supplied by the jth alternative pattern of production; H_t the maximum availability of regular time-man hours during the tth time period; H'_t the maximum number of overtime labor man-hours in period t; ℓ_t the number of hours of overtime labor consumed in period t; and finally, β_{ijt} the labor input (in man hours) required during period t in order to carry out the jth alternative pattern for part i.

Then, a possible linear programming model is:

$$\text{Minimize } \sum_t \ell_t \tag{3-37}$$

subject to:

demand constraints $\sum_j X_{ij} = 1$ $i = 1, \ldots, m$

regular time constraints $\sum_i \sum_j \beta_{ijt} X_{ij} - \ell_t \leq H_t \quad t = 1, \ldots, N$

$$(3\text{-}38)$$

overtime constraints $\qquad \ell_t \leq H_t' \qquad\qquad t = 1, \ldots, N$

and the usual nonnegativity constraints on all unknown variables

$\qquad X_{ij}, \ell_t \geq 0, X_{ij} = 0 \text{ or } 1.$

Again, the solution of the LP of Eqs. (3-37) and (3-38) is "straightforward" except for the fact that there are as many X_{ij}'s as there are patterns of production for the various products, which is of the order of $2^{N-1}m$, a number which can easily run into the millions. Again, we postpone to later the discussion of efficient computational techniques that avoid this complexity.

We make two pertinent remarks on the above LP model. First, while it takes into account the indivisible character of each pattern of production, it also accounts for the "all-or-nothing" character of set-up time since each pattern determines its required setup. Second, the applicability of the model is dependent on the requirement that X_{ij} *must be either 0 or 1*. In other words, it is meaningless to split demand between two or more patterns, since, for one thing, this would be more costly (because the new pattern would not be one of the 2^{N-1} patterns, but a convex combination of a subset). And for another, the set-up time (which is unique to each pattern) is nonlinear and fractions thereof would be equally meaningless.

Since the answer to the LP of Eqs. (3-37) to (3-38), is in general, nonintegral, the model seems to fall short of its objective.

However, all is not lost. Manne,[†] who is responsible for the above formulation, also shows that there can be *at most N* items whose production schedule calls for a convex combination of several production patterns—i.e., whose X_{ij}'s are fractions. If the number of items m is much larger than the number of periods N in the planning horizon, the necessary correction to the LP optimal solution can be done manually with no major effect on the overall shop load.

5.3 The Cutting Stock Problem

The cutting stock problem is rather common in the lumber, steel, paper, and other industries and can be stated as follows. Demand is realized for certain sizes, while supply is available in different, and usually larger, sizes. It is desired to cut the raw material in such a way as to satisfy the demand and minimize cost. The latter includes the cost of the cutting operation itself plus the *cost of waste*, called the *trim* cost.

For the sake of definiteness assume we are dealing with paper which is

[†]A. S. Manne, "Programming for Economic Lot Sizes," *Management Science*, Vol. 4, No. 2, January 1958, pp. 115–135.

available in unlimited quantities in stock lengths $L_1 \ldots, L_K$. Also, we assume that our problem is *one-dimensional*—two and three dimensional problems are beyond our scope. Therefore, the width of the stock available is equal to the width demanded—we are only interested in lengthwise cutting.

Suppose that demand is for lengths $\ell_1, \ell_2, \ldots \ell_m$, with max $\ell_i \leq$ some L_k and that length ℓ_i is demanded in quantity q_i.

Clearly, it is meaningless to lump all available stock in one total length which is to be cut to satisfy the desired demand, since such a simple-minded approach ignores the fact that the stock rolls are available only in definite lengths L_1 to L_K in the first place. The only alternative is to find a maximal cutting pattern for each stock length L_k, together with its con-comitant trim loss, and then attempt to find the optimal combination of such cutting patterns (see Fig. 3-8).

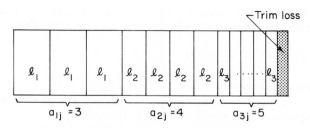

FIGURE 3-8   A Maximal Cutting Pattern

The alert reader will immediately recognize the correspondence between the maximal cutting pattern in the context of this problem and the maximal assignment of the machine loading problem of §5.1, or the production patterns of the manufacturing problem of §5.2 above. The discrete nature of each cutting pattern, as well as the combinatorial manner in which cutting patterns can be generated need no more elaboration.

The LP model for the cutting stock problem follows almost identical reasoning to the previously-mentioned two problems. Let a_{ij} denote the number of parts of length ℓ_i generated by pattern j, X_j the number of stock rolls cut in pattern j, and c_j the cost of cutting such a pattern (which includes trim loss). Then we wish to

$$\text{Minimize} \sum_j c_j X_j \tag{3-39}$$

so that

$$\sum_j a_{ij} X_j \geq q_i \text{ for } i = 1, \ldots, m \tag{3-40}$$

where q_i is the minimum quantity required of length ℓ_i.

Two factors contribute to the impracticability of a frontal attack on the LP model of Eqs. (3-39) and (3-40).   First, the astronomically large number of variables X_j, and second, the restriction to integers.   These are precisely the two complicating factors encountered before.

Consider the integer constraint first. Without this constraint the solution of Eqs. (3-39) and (3-40) is, in general, nonintegral. The fractional optimal can be rounded up or down to the nearest integer in some arbitrary but systematic fashion. The cost will increase, but if the nonintegral values are large, the changes in cost due to rounding off the fractions would be small. This is a cheap price to pay for being able to utilize the model. Henceforth, we shall assume that this is the approach used.

Finally, we come to grips with the question of a large number of activities. Because of the relevance of this discussion to the two previously mentioned problems, we underscore the discussion by treating it under a separate heading.

5.4   Efficient Generation of Activities

In all three problems briefly outlined in §5.1, §5.2 and §5.3, we have been faced with the same problem, namely, the large size of the A-matrix, the matrix of coefficients $\{a_{ij}\}$. As soon as we attempt *enumerating* all activities we run into the combinatorial trap which generates a tremendous number of such activities.

The way out of this dilemma is *not* to attempt to enumerate all activities. Rather, generate an activity (either a maximal assignment in §5.1, a production pattern in §5.2, or a maximal cutting pattern in §5.3) when, and only when, needed. By judicious choice of the activities to generate in order to improve on the current solution, and by avoidance of unprofitable activities, great gains in computational tractability can be made. This is basically the approach of Gilmore and Gomory,[†] which we now discuss with reference to the paper-cutting problem.

At any step of the Simplex iterations, we have a basis B of m activity vectors, say $B = \{P_1, \ldots, P_m\}$. B is an $m \times m$ matrix, and its inverse is denoted by B^{-1}. If $c_1, \ldots, c_m$ are the corresponding cost coefficients of the basis activities, then the marginal utility value $z_j - c_j$ of any nonbasis variable is given, in vector notation, by

$$C_B B^{-1} P_j - c_j$$

where C_B is the row vector $(c_1, \ldots, c_m)$.

Now, any nonbasis vector P_j is a candidate for introduction into the basis if its $z_j - c_j$ is > 0 (since we are minimizing), i.e., if . $C_B \cdot$

[†]P. C. Gilmore and R. E. Gomory, "A Linear Programming Approach to the Cutting Stock Problem," *Operations Research*, Vol. 9, No. 6, Nov.–Dec. 1961, pp. 849–859.

$B^{-1}P_j > c_j$. In the usual Simplex approach, we choose the vector P_k from among all such candidates so that $z_k - c_k = \max_{j \notin B} (z_j - c_j)$. But for any roll stock of length L, the cost c_k is approximately the same for any cutting pattern, and $C_B B^{-1}P_j - c_j$ is maximized if $C_B B^{-1}P_j$ is maximized. Moreover, any column vector P_j represents a cutting pattern. Consequently, at any stage of the Simplex iterations we are looking for a cutting pattern so that

$$\ell_1 a_1 + \ell_2 a_2 + \cdots + \ell_m a_m \leq L \qquad (3\text{-}41)$$

and

$$\text{maximize } C_B B^{-1}P_j = \pi_1 a_1 + \pi_2 a_2 + \cdots + \pi_m a_m \qquad (3\text{-}42)$$

where π is the vector of shadow prices (Simplex multipliers) $\pi = (\pi_1, \ldots, \pi_m) = C_B B^{-1}$. In Eqs. (3-41) and (3-42) we have, in fact, a small programming problem in which we wish to maximize the linear functional Eq. (3-42) subject to the single constraint of Eq. (3-41). It is, in fact, an integer LP problem and is known under several names: the "knapsack" problem, the "flyaway kit" problem, the "cargo loading" problem, and the "book stacking" problem. It can be formulated as a *dynamic programming* problem, and a solution is readily available in such formulation.

For, let $f_s(x)$ be the maximum of $\Sigma_{m=1}^s \pi_i a_i$ subject to the constraint $\Sigma_{m=1}^s \ell_m a_m \leq x$. That is, $f_s(x)$ represents the maximum of the objective function of Eq. (3-41) when s lengths remain to be cut and the remaining stock length is x. Then

$$f_s(x) = \max_r \{r\pi_s + f_{s-1}(x - r\ell_s)\} \qquad (3\text{-}43)$$

where $0 \leq r \leq [x/\ell_s]$ and the square brackets indicate the largest integer in x/ℓ_s; $0 \leq x \leq L$. Equation (3-43) is solved iteratively starting with $s = 1$ and terminating with $s = m$.

We remark that the only complete dynamic programming problem to be solved is for the longest L, since in the course of computing $f_m(L_{\max})$ one has automatically also computed the optimal cutting pattern under the current shadow prices (Simplex multipliers) $\pi_1, \ldots, \pi_m$ for all other lengths $\{L_k\}$, $k = 1, \ldots, K$.

Returning now to the subproblem of Eqs. (3-41) and (3-42), we compare $f_m(L_k)$ with c_k. If the inequality $f_m(L_k) = \Sigma_{i=1}^m \pi_i a_{ik}^* > c_k$ is satisfied for stock length L_k, the corresponding vector $P_k^* = <a_{ij}^*>$ is introduced into the basis of the parent problem of Eqs. (3-39) to (3-40) in the usual fashion. If the inequality is satisfied for more than one stock length L_k, the maximum inequality is chosen. If, however, the inequality is not satisfied for any stock length L_k, then the optimal of Eqs. (3-39) to (3-40) has been reached.

To sum up, the approach circumvents the problem of enumerating all feasible activities. It starts with any m activities as the basis for the LP model of Eqs. (3-39) to (3-40). It then evaluates the shadow prices (Simplex multipliers) $\pi_1, \ldots, \pi_m$ corresponding to this basis. Utilizing these multipliers, the subproblem of Eqs. (3-41) to (3-42) is solved, and this determines, in turn, the new cutting pattern to be introduced into the basis to improve the functional Eq. (3-39). The process is repeated with the new basis until no improvement in Eq. (3-39) is possible.

In spite of the tremendous saving in computing time realized by the above approach (over brute force enumeration of all activities), the computing effort is still not insignificant. Curiously enough, most of the effort is spent in a minor loop of the dynamic programming formulation of Eq. (3-43). This is the loop concerned with multiplying r by π_s, adding it to $f_{s-1}\,(x - r\ell_s)$, and evaluating the maximum over all r. This loop must be gone through $[L/\ell_s]$ times and then repeated as many times as the unit of measurement of L contains the smallest fraction in ℓ (8 if L is measured in inches and ℓ is specified to $1/8$ of an inch; 10 if ℓ is specified to 0.10 of an inch, etc.). The whole routine is then repeated m times if there are m lengths in order to solve one knapsack problem.

Gilmore and Gomory proposed a simplified procedure to speed up this phase of calculations. The procedure is based on the observation that *any* nonbasic vector P_j whose $z_j - c_j$ is > 0 is a candidate for introduction into the basis. Consequently, it is not necessary to evaluate the optimal solution of the knapsack problem; *any* solution with $\pi P_j > c_j$ is satisfactory for our purposes. However, the *optimal* solution of the original LP of Eqs. (3-39) to (3-40) is determined only through the *optimal* solution of the knapsack problem of Eqs. (3-41) to (3-42), as outlined above (to ascertain that no P_j exists where πP_j is $> c_j$).

We remark that the approach described above in dealing with LP problems which exhibit very "long" matrices—to wit, the concept of avoiding the complete enumeration of all column vectors of the LP matrix through the efficient generation of the activities, is an application of the well-known *Decomposition Principle* of LP.

It is also instructive to remark that the same *approach* is applicable to the other two problems stated in §5.1 and §5.2, though the precise formulation is different.

In the Machine-Loading Problem of §5.1, each column represented a maximal assignment. Applying the same reasoning of the Decomposition Principle, we find that the generation of maximal assignments can be stated either as an integer LP subject to the availability of presses in the various press groups or as a dynamic program subject to the same constraints. The precise formulation of this subprogram is left as an exercise to the reader (see Problems 13, 14, and 15 at the end of the chapter).

On the other hand, the problem of Economic Lot-Size Manufacturing of §5.2 yielded an LP formulation in which a column (of coefficients) represented a pattern of production. The application of the Decomposition Principle in this case is slightly more involved. In effect, it depends on the representation of any point in the convex set of feasible solutions as a convex combination of the *extreme* points of the set. A new column is then generated as the solution of a small (and rather trivial) LP. We shall not pursue this question any further here.

§6. DYNAMIC INTERACTION: A DISCUSSION

Having illustrated stationary interaction with several examples, we now turn to the illustration of dynamic interaction.

The distinguishing element between stationary and dynamic interaction is *time*: in the latter, components interact *over time* either because their *existence* occurs over time (i.e., not all the components are in existence at the same time) or their *quantitative measures* are known only over time.

It is perhaps worthwhile to dwell for a moment on the role of time in our studies.

In the study of systems, we are, basically, dealing with functional relationships among the components of the system. These relations are known. If they are not known, we conduct an analytical study of the behavior of the components and introduce the necessary assumptions and simplifications (such as linearity, convexity, upper bounds, etc.) that assist us in constructing models which yield the approximate functional relationships sought.

Through knowledge of such functional relationships and the inputs to the system we are able to solve the problems posed—whether they are problems of analysis (such as determining the outputs of the system) or problems of synthesis (such as optimizing certain characteristics of the outputs). Time need not enter into our consideration at all—even though some of the inputs and/or outputs occur over time. This is evidently so because the fact of occurrence over time is basically *irrelevant* to the study. For example, this was true in the Caterer problem studied in §2 above. The optimal strategy could be determined *at the outset* (or, of course, calculated day by day in a sequential fashion—the result would have been the same) in spite of the fact that an important element of the system, viz., the demand for clean napkins, was realized over time.

The above is true as long as the functional relationships, inputs, and outputs are all known deterministically, or can be assumed to be so. Under conditions of uncertainty in either the functional relationships among components or in the inputs to the system, we are forced to abandon the methodologies of stationary analysis and resort to dynamic analysis.

It is intuitively clear that, under conditions of uncertainty, time plays a major role, because it is not possible to ascertain *at the outset* the course of action of the system during its lifetime. Putting it differently, uncertainty forces us to formulate *decision policies* rather than make decisions. Our inability to foretell the exact state of the system forces us to wait. *In time* we will be able to ascertain the condition of the system and then determine the exact course of action based on our previously formulated policies.

Uncertainty introduces a radical change in our treatment of the interaction among the components. In essence, we make use of *feedback* (see Chapter 6), which is to say that we take cognizance of the status of the system (which is usually dependent on inputs and previously-made decisions) before making new decisions. In the deterministic case, however, feedback is not necessary.

To illustrate our discussion, consider the problem of optimal trajectory (see Fig. 3-9). Suppose it is required to optimize the path from 0 to X under guidance conditions. For the deterministic case, the optimal path

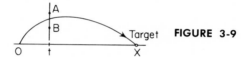

FIGURE 3-9

may be calculated, once and for all. It is immaterial whether it is determined in full before the flight takes place or calculated point by point during the flight itself, i.e., *in real time*. The result is the same trajectory. This is evidently a problem of stationary interaction.

Consider now the possibility of random errors in guidance that may cause the missile to deviate, at time t, to position A or B. Now, it is not possible to evaluate the optimal trajectory from 0 to X since we do not know, with certainty, where the missile will be at time t. Notice that, in all probability, the optimal path from position A (or position B) to X is no longer a return to the original (optimal) trajectory from 0 to X. The best we can do is formulate the optimal policy, namely, calculate the optimal trajectory from both A and B. But we must *wait* for the information of the actual position of the missile *at time t* before we decide on the action to be taken. Of course, we need not evaluate such policy *a priori*; we can always wait to time t and then decide on the optimal path. Time has figured very significantly in our behavior.

§7. DYNAMIC INTERACTION: THE OPTIMAL LOADING OF LINEAR MULTI-OPERATION SHOPS

A general class of shops exists which exhibit certain features concerning the flow of material from raw to finished products. We have termed this class "linear multi-operation" shops. Such shops are characterized by more than one operation (hence the "multi-operation") and by the absence of backtracking i.e., loops, in the flow of material from a starting to a finishing operation (hence the term "linear"). The designation does not imply, however, that each job passes through the shop with the same sequence of operations, which is the case in process industries or assembly lines. Nor does it imply that all jobs start and end at the same operation. For example, the following Fig. 3-10 exemplifies an L.M.O. flow shop. Note that a job may enter the shop at any one of the three operations designeated by "In," and the flow of material is from left to right.

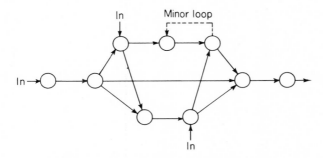

FIGURE 3-10   Linear Multi-Operation Flow

In actual practice, minor loops (such as repair work) may exist as shown in dotted lines, but usually these loops can be neglected because of their infinitesimal effect on the operations of the shop.

These specific characteristics of L.M.O. shops make it possible to construct a mathematical model for the optimal loading of the various operations taking capacity contraints into account. This section describes the mathematical model and construction of the control system.

The Problem

Suppose that loading of the various operations takes place at the beginning of regular intervals of time of duration Δ. Clearly, the set of jobs released to the shop (i.e., loaded on the various "In" operations) represents the input to the shop. Conceptually, we can consider all the products ordered by the customer for the duration of the planning horizon as queueing at a fictitious Operation 0 and competing for the limited shop capacity.

The *loading problem* is to determine at the beginning of each interval the load on each operation, i.e., *determine the list of jobs to be worked on during the next interval* Δ, *at each operation, in such a way as to achieve some explicitly stated objectives.* We shall assume that *all* job movements occur at the *end* of the period Δ.

The complexity of the problem is increased by the fact that the job processing time in any operation need not be an integer multiple of the review period. For example, consider a shop with only three operations in which the flow of work is as shown in Fig. 3-11. Some jobs follow the

FIGURE 3-11   A 3-Operations Shop

route 1–2–3; others bypass Operation 2. Suppose that the review period Δ is one week, that is to say, Operation 1 is loaded with new jobs at the beginning of each week. Assume also, for the sake of illustration, that the shop is empty at the beginning of week one. Clearly, at the end of the first week some of the jobs loaded on Operation 1 would be completed and shipped. The remaining jobs are either in Operation 2 or Operation 3, that is, if we assume perfect loading of Operation 1 so that there are no "leftovers."

At the beginning of week 2 we have to take into consideration, in loading Operation 1, the committed capacities in Operation 2 and 3 due to the jobs that are at these two operations, as well as make allowance for the jobs that will reach Operation 3 from the queue of jobs at Operation 2. It is evident, therefore, that starting with week 2 the jobs queueing at Operations 2 and 3 will be a mixture of jobs which were released to the shop in different weeks. That is to say, a mixture of jobs of different "ages" in the shop.[†] Fig. 3-12 is a schematic representation of the possible changing character of the load mix on the utilization of capacity in the three operations over a period of four weeks. Note that Operation 3 will still be working *in week 3* on some jobs released in week 1. The problem, of course, is to load Operations 1, 2, and 3 with jobs so that all three operations are fully loaded but not overloaded and optimize a given objective.

The Mathematical Model

Let k denote an operation number, $k = 1, \ldots, K$. Let X_{ik} denote the ith job in the queue at station k. We assume for the time being that any job is indivisible even though it may actually be constituted of several units. After loading, X_{ik} will be denoted by $\hat{X}_{ik}$ where $\hat{X}_{ik} = 1$ if X_{ik} were loaded on station k for the next interval Δ_1, and $\hat{X}_{ik} = 0$ if the job

---

[†]If the matrix of transition probabilities among operations is known, the steady-state condition can be easily calculated by the application of Renewal Theory; see Feller, cited at the end of the chapter.

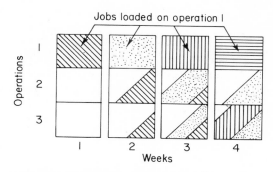

FIGURE 3-12   A Possible Flow of Jobs at Different Operations

were not loaded. Whenever there is no chance of error in identifying the operation to which we are referring, we shall drop the k in the subscript of X_{ik}. Let the length of the queue at operation k be N_k jobs, and let the manufacturing time for job X_{ik} be given by t_{ik} (= set-up time + processing time). Let $t_{ik}^0(\Delta_j) = t_{ik}$ if X_{ik} is *in* the queue of station k at time Δ_j, and let $t_{ik}^0(\Delta_j) = 0$, otherwise. Again, where there is no ambiguity, we shall drop the subscript k from t_{ik}^0 and N_k. We shall assume that time is measured in units of the loading interval Δ, with the first interval (from the present, whenever that may be) denoted by Δ_1, the second interval by Δ_2, etc. Clearly, at the beginning of each loading cycle, the first interval (for which we are loading the various operations) is Δ_1, the following interval is Δ_2, etc. Finally, let $C_k(\Delta_j)$ denote the *gross* capacity of operation k in period Δ_j.

For the time being we shall assume that the processing time of any job at any operation is less than or equal to Δ, the length of the review period. We shall discuss below the consequences of eliminating this assumption.

Ideally, the queue at each operation should be equal to the capacity of the operation for one period Δ. Under such conditions a job loaded in Operation 1 in period Δ_1 would "clear the shop" during period Δ_K at the latest (if the job is routed through all K operations), since each period would find the job advanced to the next queue.

In practice, this ideal situation can be approached but not realized. However, it sets the *objective* of our mathematical model, viz., the loading of operation k for period Δ_1 must strive to accomodate the capacities of operation $k + 1$ in period Δ_2, of operation $k + 2$ in period Δ_3, etc. We remark that such an orderly restriction is possible only because of the *linearity* of the shop as discussed in the Introduction.

Another important assumption of the basic model is that the progress of jobs in the shop takes place only at multiples of Δ. That is, a job completed at operation k remains at operation k until the next review period. Admittedly, this is a serious restriction on the movement of jobs, but by making Δ small enough we can, if we so desire, reduce the flow to near continuous for all practical purposes. A discussion of the factors entering into the determination of Δ is presented below.

Consider any operation, say operation k. The following Table 3-15 can be constructed, giving the jobs queueing *at* k and their processing times in the subsequent operation $k + 1, \ldots, K$.

TABLE 3-15

Jobs	Operation Number			
	k	$(k + 1)$	.....	K
X_1	t_{1k}	$t^0_{1(k+1)}$		t^0_{1K}
X_2	t_{2k}	$t^0_{2(k+1)}$		t^0_{2K}
X_3	t_{3k}	$t^0_{3(k+1)}$		t^0_{3K}
.	.	.		.
.	.	.		.
X_i	t_{ik}	$t^0_{i(k+1)}$		t^0_{iK}
.	.	.		.
.	.	.		.
.	.	.		.
X_{N_k}	t_{Nk}	$t^0_{N(k+1)}$		t^0_{NK}
Capacities	$C_k(\Delta_1)$	$C_{k+1}(\Delta_2)$		$C_K(\Delta_{K-k+1})$

If no jobs existed in operations $k + 1, \ldots, K$, our loading problem would reduce to the following: it is desired to assign 0 or 1 values to each variable X_i so that

$$\sum_i X_{ik} \cdot t^0_{ij}(\Delta_{j-k+1}) \leq C_j(\Delta_{j-k+1}) \quad k \leq j \leq K \tag{3-44}$$

and

$$\text{Maximize} \sum_i u_i(\Delta_1) X_{ik} \tag{3-45}$$

where $u_i(\Delta_1)$ is the utility of job i in period Δ_1.[†]

Equations (3-44) and (3-45) define an integer linear program where the variables are confined to the values 0 or 1. An algorithm for the solution

[†] The priority of the job has been suggested as a measure of its utility.

of such a linear program is given in the references cited at the end of the chapter.

Naturally, jobs do exist in the operations subsequent to operation k, and their effect on the loading of k in period Δ_1 must be determined.

We now make a remark which is fundamental to the understanding of the model: *The columns of Table 3-15 are removed from each other by a time span of length* Δ. Hence, to take a specific case, the effect of the jobs queueing at operation $k + 1$ is felt only in period Δ_2 because, by that time, jobs loaded on k would have progressed to $k + 1$ (or those among them destined to be processed in $k + 1$). Consequently, in loading operation k we must take into consideration the interaction with the *anticipated queue* at $k + 1$ in period Δ_2, the interaction at $k + 2$ in period Δ_3, and so forth. This implies that it is not possible to load operation k except after operations $k + 1$ through K have been loaded.

If a table similar to Table 3-15 is constructed for operation $k + 1$ it will become evident, by similar reasoning, that *it* cannot be loaded except after having loaded operations $k + 2$ through K. Therefore, we are led to the conclusion that we must load operation K first, which is relatively easy to accomplish. For operation K, our problem is to

$$\text{Maximize} \sum_i u_i(\Delta_1) X_{iK}$$

subject to the single restriction $\Sigma_i X_{iK} t_{iK}(\Delta_1) \leq C_K(\Delta_1)$.

This is the well-known "knapsack problem" which can be solved by the method of dynamic programming.

After loading operation K, suppose that some $\hat{X}_{iK} = 0$. This means that it was not possible to process all the jobs *at* K during the period Δ_1. The set of jobs $\{X_{iK} \mid \hat{X}_{iK} = 0\}$ constitutes the "leftovers" at K in period Δ_2. Denote these jobs by Y_ℓ, $\ell = 1, \ldots, n_K$.

Consider next the loading of operation $K - 1$ and the manner in which these "leftovers" at K will affect it. We construct the following Table 3-16: The jobs $X_1, \ldots, X_{N_{K-1}}$ are queueing *at* operation $K - 1$ in period Δ_1, and jobs $Y_1, \ldots, Y_{n_K}$ are the *anticipated queue* at operation K in period Δ_2. We now wish to Maximize

$$\sum_i u_i(\Delta_1) X_i + \sum_\ell u_\ell(\Delta_2) Y_\ell$$

subject to the constraints

$$\sum_i X_i t_{i(K-1)}(\Delta_1) \leq C_{K-1}(\Delta_1)$$

and

$$\sum_i X_i t_{iK}^0(\Delta_2) + \sum_\ell Y_\ell t_{\ell K}(\Delta_2) \leq C_K(\Delta_2).$$

TABLE 3-16

Jobs	Operation Number	
	$K-1$	K
X_1	$t_{1(K-1)}$	t^0_{1K}
X_2	$t_{2(K-1)}$	t^0_{2K}
.	.	.
.	.	.
.	.	.
$X_{N_{K-1}}$	$t_{N_{K-1}(K-1)}$	$t^0_{N_{K-1}K}$
Y_1	0	t_{1K}
.	.	.
.	.	.
.	.	.
Y_{n_K}	0	$t_{n_K K}$
Capacities	$C_{K-1}(\Delta_1)$	$C_K(\Delta_2)$

This linear program determines the values of $\{X_i\}$ and $\{Y_\ell\}$, which, in turn, determine the "leftovers" at $K-1$ in period Δ_2 and at K in period Δ_3. The procedure is now repeated for operations $K-2$, $K-3,\ldots,$ 3, 2, and 1. The loading of Operation 1 signals the end of the loading procedure.

Notice that we started, in Eqs. (3-44) to (3-45) and Table 3-15, by *looking forward* when loading Operation k to ensure "clear passage" for the loaded jobs through all subsequent operations in future periods. However, we ended by utilizing a *backward algorithm* that starts with Operation K and moves backwards to Operation 1. This is characteristic of multistage problems, especially in the theory of dynamic programming.

Dynamic Nature of the Control System

At the beginning of interval Δ_p, a "picture" of the queues at the various operations must be available to the loading procedure. We shall call this momentary picture the "Status" of the various jobs in the shop and "on order." If we assume that no activity occurs between the *end* of period Δ_{p-1} and the *start* of period Δ_p, the Status could be made available at any time in this interval. (Such is the case, for example, when Δ is one day, and the shop is closed at night. The Status can be reported at any time between the end of day Δ_{p-1} and the start of day Δ_p.) Otherwise, the Status must be made known immediately before the start of period Δ_p.

Since the Status at Δ_p uniquely determines the load on each operation during periods Δ_p, Δ_{p+1}, Δ_{p+2}, ..., Δ_{K-p+1} subject to the various (constant) requirements on the jobs and the limitations on the gross capacities, it is easily seen that "life starts afresh" with each new interval. Therefore, it is expedient to denote the intervals by Δ_1, Δ_2, ..., Δ_K, which we have done above.

It is equally clear that the only relationship between the Status at the beginning of period Δ_1 and Status at the beginning of period Δ_2 is the *Load* as specified for Δ_1. *If* the shop followed the specified Load meticulously, *if* the estimates of capacities and manufacturing times were known deterministically, and *if* no variation occured in the rate of defective units or in the shop "efficiency," the Status at Δ_2 could be determined with certainty. To be sure, under such conditions, the Status for all future periods could be determined with certainty.

In practice, however, these "if's" do not hold, and the Load for the period Δ_1 is only an objective to be approached, but is scarcely executed in its entirety.

The dynamic nature of the procedure should now be obvious. The Load for period Δ_1 is the input to which the shop reacts in a statistical fashion. The actual output of the shop is compared with the input to trigger off the necessary corrective actions and to establish the Status for period Δ_2. The loading procedure is applied to the Status to determine the Load for period Δ_2, and the cycle repeats. This operation can be depicted as a feedback control loop as shown in Fig. 3-13.

In Fig. 3-13, customer orders add to the "Jobs on Demand," while the final output of the shop subtracts from them. The result is the "Status" of jobs on demand and in the shop. The Status is the input to the loading procedure whose output, the Load, is the command given to the shop. The Output of the Shop is fed back to evaluate the Status, and the cycle repeats. The box entitled "Correcting Instructions" represents a smaller feedback loop which is concerned with changing the shop characteristics, such as capacity, if necessary.

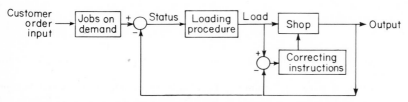

FIGURE 3-13   Feedback Loop Showing Dynamic Character of System

Comments

The mathematical model presented in this section can be enriched and complicated in several ways. For example, we have assumed that the operation time for each job, t_{ik}, is $\leq \Delta$; what if this is not true? Another implicit assumption in our treatment is that a job moves as a whole from one operation to another; i.e., there is no possibility of "lap-phasing," in which case parts of the job are operated upon simultaneously in different operations. From a practical point of view, lap-phasing is not only desirable but sometimes mandatory either to occupy production capacity which otherwise would be idle or to reduce manufacturing interval. How can such a mode of behavior be incorporated into the model?

A third practical consideration is the question of *job splitting* among two or more processing units which perform the same operation. This is a common sight in assembly shops, metal working shops, etc. Whenever the "job" contains more than one unit, the possibility of assigning two or more identical processing units presents itself as a time-saving and load-balancing device.

These and other generalizations are interesting and challenging problems from both theoretical and practical points of view. Unfortunately, space does not permit us to discuss them in full detail here; the interested reader is referred to the reference cited at the end of the chapter.

§8. DYNAMIC INTERACTION: THE HUB OPERATION SCHEDULING PROBLEM

The following problem arises in the context of commercial trucking operations. A common carrier is franchised to operate on certain routes between a central city—heretofore referred to as the hub and designated by 0—and a set of outlying cities—heretofore referred to as terminals and numbered 1 to N. All traffic is two way between the hub and terminals; no operation is permitted among the terminals (see Fig. 3-14). The distance between the hub and any terminal could be covered within a single scheduling period, which we shall take as one day.

Since the rates of transportation are fixed by Interstate Commerce Commission regulations, competition rests on service. The demand on

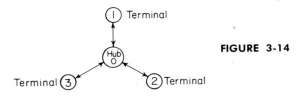

FIGURE 3-14

trucks is stochastic, a natural consequence of several independent random demands emanating from individuals and small businesses. The physical act of transportation normally takes place at night, and the demand for the current scheduling period is known *deterministically* by late afternoon. The demand for the next period, however, is known only probabilistically; no information is assumed known concerning demands farther into the future.

In essence, therefore, the company is operating under known and fixed demand for one period, and probabilistic demand for the following period; nothing is known beyond that. We shall refer to the former as the "current" or "immediate" demand, and to the latter as "future" or "next" demand.

Because of the uncertainty in future demand it is possible that the company might be caught short of trucks at one terminal while experiencing excess availability of trucks at another terminal. The company can cope with such a situation by following any of two courses of action, or both: (1) the company can move *empty* vehicles from any terminal to the hub or vice versa and (2) it can hold over shipments to the following day. The first course of action involves immediate out-of-pocket expenses; the second course of action involves a potential loss of customers in view of the kind of competition in existence.

Consequently, the following two *Rules of Operation* were strictly enforced by the company:

Rule 1: Trucks are loaded with available merchandise until either of the two (trucks or merchandise) is exhausted.

Rule 2: If there are fewer vehicles than needed at any terminal, the loads chosen to be held over are those incurring the minimum hold-over cost.

Fortunately, as we shall see in a moment, these two rules simplify the analysis to a great extent.

The problem facing the scheduler can then be stated as follows: could the shipping schedule for today, which includes loaded and empty vehicles as well as held-overs, be devised to minimize the expected cost of shipping for the two-period planning horizon (current and next period's)?

Again we pause for a moment to discuss the elements of the system under study and discern its dynamic nature. The system is composed of four elements: the cities, the scheduling policy, the fleet of transport vehicles, and the demand for its services. Due to the stochastic nature of the future demand and the uncertain character of the size of the fleet, the decision concerning the schedule on any specific day must be determined on the basis of the status of the last two elements mentioned above. Although the optimal *policy* is fixed, the decision takes place *in time* as the quantitative measures of the two components, the size of the fleet available and demand, are known.

Model of System

Let us denote by m_0 the set of all $N + 1$ cities *including* the hub, and by **m** the set of all N terminals, i.e., $m_0 \equiv \{0, 1, \ldots, N\}$ and $m \equiv \{1, 2, \ldots, N\}$. Let V_i be the total number of transport vehicles available at city i (ϵm_0) at the beginning of the current scheduling period. Let D_i denote the *outgoing demand* at $i(\epsilon m_0)$ and D_i' the *incoming demand* to $i(\epsilon m_0)$.[†] Obviously, since transportation is either from the hub to a terminal or from a terminal to the hub, the outgoing demand at the hub must be the incoming load at the terminals and vice versa; i.e.,

$$D_0 = \sum_{i \in m} D_i' \quad \text{and} \quad D_0' = \sum_{i \in m} D_i. \tag{3-46}$$

A similar notation applies to loaded transport vehicles. Let v_i be the number of *loaded* vehicles, i.e., shipments, departing from city $i(\epsilon m_0)$ and v_i' be the number of loaded vehicles arriving at city $i(\epsilon m_0)$. By the same token,

$$v_0 = \sum_{i \in m} v_i' = \min[V_0, D_0] \quad \text{and} \quad v_0' = \sum_{i \in m} v_i = \sum_{i \in m} \min[V_i, D_i]. \tag{3-47}$$

Next, let e_i be the *net* number of empty vehicles departing from city $i(\epsilon m_0)$. If e_i is negative, it is interpreted as vehicles *arriving* at city i. Naturally,

$$e_0 = \sum_{i \in m} - e_i \tag{3-48}$$

is the net number of empty vehicles departing from the hub (or arriving at the hub if e_0 is negative).

We recognize that the size of the fleet of transport vehicles is not constant. Additions, in the form of newly purchased, leased, rented or back-from-repair vehicles, as well as subtractions, in the form of temporary breakdowns, scheduled repairs, or vehicles sold, may change the number of vehicles available at each city almost daily. Therefore, let A_i denote the *net additions* to the vehicles at city $i(\epsilon m_0)$—a negative A_i denotes a *subtraction*. Note that V_i includes any A_i for the current scheduling period.

The following schematic, (Fig. 3-15) summarizes the symbology defined above.

We wish now to evaluate the number of "free" vehicles at each terminal at the end of the current schedule. This is the number of vehicles left "uncommitted" at the beginning of next period and will be available to meet future demand. Let u_i be the net uncommitted vehicles at city $i(\epsilon m_0)$.

[†]Our formulation assumes a uniform measure of "load" for both transport vehicles and customer demand.

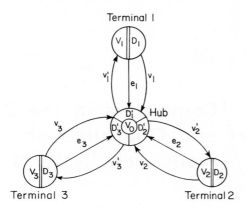

FIGURE 3-15

Notice that u_i can be evaluated with certainty by a simple bookkeeping operation for each city:

> [Uncommitted vehicles at end of current schedule]
>   = [Total vehicles available at the beginning of current period]
>   + [Vehicles received from all sources] − [Current demand]
>   − [Empty vehicles departing].

Or, in symbols,

$$u_i = V_i + v'_i + A_i - D_i - e_i \qquad i \epsilon \mathbf{m}_0 \tag{3-49}$$

subject to the equalities of Eqs. (3-46) to (3-48). Equation (3-49) is the "balance of vehicles" equation, similar to the net inventory equation one is so familiar with. It is interesting to note that our "inventory" here is the transport vehicles themselves.

We now make the following two remarks. First, u_i is known *deterministically*. Second, if u_i is negative ($u_i < 0$), it represents the number of loads that must be held over at the end of *next* period from current demand at i. Under such a condition, any future demand will worsen the situation since it will just add to the loads held over.

Naturally, we are interested in determining the *expected* number of loads to be held over at the end of next period's schedule. This is important because it is one of the two cost factors in our criterion function.

To this end, let $p_i(d)$ be the probability of future demand of magnitude d at city $i(\epsilon \mathbf{m}_0)$, and let

$$\overline{d_i} = \sum_{d=0}^{\infty} d \cdot p_i(d), \text{ the average demand at } i, \text{ and}$$

$$Q_i(k) = \sum_{d=k}^{\infty} p_i(d), \text{ the probability of demand } \geq k.$$

Let h_i denote the expected (i.e., average) number of loads held over at city i at the end of the next scheduling period. We must consider two cases:

Case (a): $u_i < 0$: According to our remark above, we are *certain* to hold over u_i loads. Any added demand will also be held-over. Hence,

$$h_i = -u_i + \sum_{d=0}^{\infty} d \cdot p_i(d) = \overline{d}_i - u_i > 0.$$

Case (b): $u_i \geq 0$: In this case u_i loads of the future demands will be transported, the remaining $(d - u_i)$-loads will be held over. The probability of such an eventuality is $p_i(d)$; hence,

$$h_i = \sum_{d \geq u_i}^{\infty} (d - u_i) \cdot p_i(d).$$

Adding and subtracting

$$\sum_{d=0}^{u_i-1} (d - u_i) p_i(d)$$

and simplifying the expression we obtain

$$h_i = \overline{d}_i - u_i + \sum_{d=0}^{u_i-1} (u_i - d) \cdot p_i(d) \geq 0 \qquad (3\text{-}50)$$

This expression differs from the previous expression for h_i only in the summation term. But when u_i is < 0, the summation term is meaningless and is put equal to 0. Hence, Eq. (3-50) gives h_i in both cases.

Decomposition of the Problem Into Three Versions

As was hinted above, the two Rules of Operation (see p.199) simplify the analysis to a great extent. For, on the face of it, it seems that we have three "decision parameters": $\mathbf{v} \equiv \{v_i\}$, $\mathbf{v}' \equiv \{v_i'\}$ and $\mathbf{e} \equiv \{e_i\}$. But, in fact, Rule (1) completely specifies $\mathbf{v}$, the set of the number of loaded vehicles departing from each city. In particular,

$$v_i = \min [V_i, D_i] \qquad i \epsilon \mathbf{m}_0 \qquad (3\text{-}51)$$

since we must schedule for departure all the loads for which vehicles are available. Consequently, $\mathbf{v}$ is no more a decision variable; neither is $v_0' = \Sigma_{i \epsilon \mathbf{m}} v_i$ by Eq. (3-47). In the following we shall be concerned only with $\mathbf{v}'$ and $\mathbf{e}$ and, in particular, we shall be concerned with the loaded vehicles scheduled for arrival at the terminals (since v_0' is completely determined by Eqs. (3-47) and (3-51)) and with the number of net empty vehicles departing from or arriving at the terminals (since e_0 is known once $\{e_i\}$, $i \epsilon \mathbf{m}$, is known (see Eq. (3-48)).

Next, we dispose of a trivial case. Suppose that

$$V_0 = D_0 \text{ and } V_i \leq D_i \text{ for all } i \epsilon \mathbf{m};$$

then the same Rule (1) completely determines the value of $\mathbf{v}'$ and $\mathbf{e}$:

$$v_i' = D_i' \quad \text{and} \quad e_i = 0 \quad \text{for all} \quad i \epsilon \mathbf{m}.$$

In this case, there are no decisions to make.

This leaves the following four mutually exclusive and, together with the trivial case above, collectively exhaustive cases:

Case (a): $V_0 < D_0$ and $V_i \leq D_i$ for each $i \epsilon \mathbf{m}$. It is immediately obvious that no empty vehicles are available, hence $\mathbf{e} = \mathbf{0}$. However, we must decide on $\mathbf{v}'$ optimally; this is the *"load-allocation problem."*

Case (b): $V_0 \geq D_0$ and $V_i > D_i$ for at least one $i \epsilon \mathbf{m}$. In this case, $v_i' = D_i'$ for all $i \epsilon \mathbf{m}$. However, the empty vehicles at the hub and at least one terminal must be allocated. This is the *"empty vehicle problem."*

Case (c): $V_0 \geq D_0$ and $V_i \leq D_i$ for each $i \epsilon \mathbf{m}$. Again, $v_i' = D_i'$ for $i \epsilon \mathbf{m}$. However, the empty vehicles at the hub must be allocated. This is an *"empty vehicle problem"* but of a simpler nature than Case (b).

Case (d): $V_0 < D_0$ and $V_i > D_i$ for at least one $i \epsilon \mathbf{m}$. In this case, there are some empty vehicles at some terminal(s) so that we must determine $\mathbf{e}$. Moreover, we must allocate the vehicles at the hub since $V_0 < D_0$. This is the *"mixed problem."*

Therefore, the four cases give rise to three distinguishable problems which will be treated separately. We wish to determine $\mathbf{v}'$ or $\mathbf{e}$, or both, optimally, i.e., to minimize a certain cost function. We proceed now to formulate this cost function.

The Criterion Function

At the outset we reiterate that our objective is to minimize costs over a planning horizon composed of only two periods: The current (today) and the next (tomorrow) periods.

There are *two types* of costs: the cost of moving empty vehicles between hub and terminal, and the penalty incurred due to holding shipments over to the next or following periods.

Let E_i be the cost of moving a vehicle empty between the hub and outlying terminal i. E_i is assumed constant independent of time or direction of movement. Since the number of empty vehicles moved over the same route is $|e_i|$, then the total cost of this activity is

$$\sum_{i \epsilon \mathbf{m}} E_i \cdot |e_i|. \tag{3-52a}$$

We shall divide the cost of holding shipments over the two-period planning horizon into two separately identifiable costs: the costs of holding shipments over the current period and the *expected* cost of holding shipments over the next period. The reason for such a division is obvious: the first cost is deterministically known, while the second is known only probabilistically (hence our resort to mathematical expectation).

The number of loads held over from the current to the next periods *at the outlying terminals* is fixed by Rule 1, while Rule 2 ensures that the penalty incurred is minimal. Since this is a fixed cost which is not subject to our decision, it can be ignored in the process of optimization.

However, the situation *at the hub* is different since Rules 1 and 2 specify the total outgoing loads ($v_0 = \Sigma_{i \epsilon \mathbf{m}} \, v_i' = \min \, [V_0, D_0]$) but leave the specification of the set $\{v_i'\}$, $i \epsilon \mathbf{m}$, to the scheduler. The determination of $\{v_i'\}$, $i \epsilon \mathbf{m}$, fixes the loads held over at the hub and, consequently, determines the cost incurred.

Let $\pi_{i \ell}$ denote the penalty of holding the ℓth load, $\ell = 1, \ldots, D_i'$, at the hub destined for the ith terminal. Without loss of generality, we number the loads so that $\pi_{i1} \geq \pi_{i2} \geq \ldots \geq \pi_{iD_i}$. According to Rule 2, the $v_i' (\leq D_i')$–loads sent out from the hub to terminal i must be the most expensive to hold over. Therefore, we must hold over loads number $v_i' + 1, v_i' + 2, \ldots, D_i'$ at a cost of $\Sigma_{\ell = v_i' + 1}^{D_i'} \pi_{i \ell}$. Summing over all terminals we obtain

$$\sum_{i \epsilon \mathbf{m}} \sum_{\ell = v_i' + 1}^{D_i'} \pi_{i \ell}. \tag{3-52b}$$

Finally, let H_i ($i \epsilon \mathbf{m}_0$) denote the average cost of holding over a load at city i for one period (one day). We have already derived, in Eq. (3-50), the expected number of loads thus held over. Therefore, we may write the cost over all cities as

$$\sum_{i \epsilon \mathbf{m}_0} H_i \cdot h_i. \tag{3-52c}$$

The total cost of operation is the sum of the three separate costs in Eqs. (3-52) given above. For ease of notation let $E_0 = \pi_{0 \ell} = 0$, then

$$C(\mathbf{e}, \mathbf{v}') = \sum_{i \epsilon \mathbf{m}_0} \left[E_i \cdot |e_i| + H_i \cdot h_i + \sum_{\ell = v_i' + 1}^{D_i'} \pi_{i \, \ell} \right]. \tag{3-53}$$

Our objective is to choose values $\mathbf{e}^*$ and $\mathbf{v}'^*$ so that Eq. (3-53) is minimized. To this end we define the two incremental "gain functions"

$$g(v_i') = C(v_i') - C(v_i' + 1) \tag{3-54}$$

and

$$G(e_i) = C(e_i) - C(e_i - 1). \tag{3-55}$$

Here, $C(v_i' + 1)$ is a shorthand notation for $C(e, \{v_k'\}, k \epsilon m_0, k \neq i, v_i' + 1)$; i.e., all decision variables (other than v_i') are left at their previous values and only v_i' is increased to $v_i' + 1$. The same interpretation is given $C(e_i)$. In essence, $g(v_i')$ is the unit incremental gain (negative cost) due to the increasing of v_i' to $v_i' + 1$. (This is the discrete analogue to marginal gain in functions of continuous variables.) Similarly, $G(e_i)$ is the incremental gain if e_i is decreased by one unit from e_i to $e_i - 1$, with all other variables unchanged. We now obtain explicit expressions for the two gain functions.

From Eq. (3-50),

$$h_i(\hat{e}_i'; \hat{v}_i') = \bar{d}_i - \hat{u}_i + \sum_{d=0}^{\hat{u}_i} (\hat{u}_i - d)p_i(d),$$

where the circumflex over the variables denotes the starting values corresponding to $\hat{e}_i$ and $\hat{v}_i'$. Hence,

$$h_i(\hat{e}_i - 1; \hat{v}_i') = \bar{d}_i - (\hat{u}_i + 1) + \sum_{d=0}^{\hat{u}_i} (\hat{u}_i + 1 - d)p_i(d)$$

and

$$h_i(\hat{e}_i; \hat{v}_i' + 1) = \bar{d}_i - (\hat{u}_i + 1) + \sum_{d=0}^{\hat{u}_i} (\hat{u}_i + 1 - d)p_i(d).$$

From Eq. (3-53) we have

$$C(\hat{e}, \hat{v}') = \sum_{i \epsilon m_0} \left[E_i |e_i| + H_i h_i(\hat{e}_i, \hat{v}_i') + \sum_{\ell = \hat{v}_i' + 1}^{D_i'} \pi_{i\ell} \right],$$

which yields

$$C(\hat{v}_i' + 1) = K + H_i h_i(\hat{e}_i; \hat{v}_i' + 1) + \sum_{\ell = \hat{v}_i' + 2}^{D_i'} \pi_{i\ell}$$

and

$$C(\hat{e}_i - 1) = K' + E_i |\hat{e}_i - 1| + H_0 h_0(\hat{e}_i - 1, \hat{v}_i'), + H_i h_i(\hat{e}_i - 1, \hat{v}_i'),$$

where K and K' represent all the terms of Eq. (3-53) not affected by the changes undertaken. We now substitute these values of C into $g(\hat{v}_i')$ and

$G(\hat{e}_i)$ to obtain

$$
\begin{aligned}
g(\hat{v}_i') &= H_i[h_i(\hat{e}_i; \hat{v}_i') - h_i(\hat{e}_i; \hat{v}_i' + 1)] + \pi_{i(\hat{v}_i' + 1)} \\
&= H_i Q_i(\hat{u}_i + 1) + \pi_{i(\hat{v}_i' + 1)} \quad\quad\quad\quad\quad\quad (3\text{-}56)
\end{aligned}
$$

and

$$
\begin{aligned}
G(\hat{e}_i) &= E_i[\,|\hat{e}_i| - |\hat{e}_i - 1|\,] + H_0[h_0(\hat{e}_i; \hat{v}_i') - h_0(\hat{e}_i - 1; \hat{v}_i')] \\
&\quad + H_i[h_i(\hat{e}_i; \hat{v}_i') - h_i(\hat{e}_i - 1; \hat{v}_i')] \\
&= H_i Q_i(\hat{u}_i + 1) - H_0 Q_0(\hat{u}_i) \pm E_i \quad \text{for } \hat{e}_i \gtrless 1. \quad (3\text{-}57)
\end{aligned}
$$

Recall that $Q_i(u_i) = \Sigma_{d=u_i}^{\infty} p_i(d)$; therefore

$$
\begin{aligned}
g(\hat{v}_i') - g(\hat{v}_i' + 1) &= H_i[Q_i(\hat{u}_i + 1) - Q_i(\hat{u}_i + 2)] + \pi_{i(\hat{v}_i' + 1)} - \pi_{i(\hat{v}_i' + 2)} \\
&= p_i(\hat{u}_i + 1) + \pi_{i(\hat{v}_i' + 1)} - \pi_{i(\hat{v}_i' + 2)} \geq 0 \quad (3\text{-}58)
\end{aligned}
$$

by the definition of the penalties π. Also,

$$
\begin{aligned}
G(\hat{e}_i) - G(\hat{e}_i - 1) &= H_i[Q_i(u_i + 1) - Q_i(u_i + 2)] \\
&\quad - H_0[Q_0(\hat{u}_i) - Q_0(\hat{u}_i - 1)] \\
&\quad + \begin{cases} 0 \text{ if } e_i \geq 2 \text{ or } e_i \leq 0 \\ 2E_i \text{ if } e_i = 1 \end{cases} \\
&= p_i(\hat{u}_i + 1) - (-p_0(\hat{u}_i - 1)) + \begin{cases} 0 \\ 2E_i \end{cases} \geq 0. \quad (3\text{-}59)
\end{aligned}
$$

We have just proven that $g(\hat{v}_i')$ is always $\geq g(\hat{v}_i' + 1)$, and $G(\hat{e}_i) \geq G(\hat{e}_i - 1)$; i.e., both gain functions are *nonincreasing* in their arguments. This is a very important property on which hinge the procedures outlined below.

The Load Allocation Problem ($V_0 < D_0$ and $V_i \leq D_i$ for all $i \in m$)

In the load allocation problem (Fig. 3-16) all $e_i = 0$, $i \in m_0$, but we must determine the vector v' in an optimal fashion subject to the two restrictions:

$$
v_i' = \min[V_0, D_i']
$$

and

$$
V_0 = \sum_{i \in m} v_i'.
$$

Hub D_i' v_i' Terminal i

FIGURE 3-16

TABLE 3-17 Cost and Other Data

		Hub	Terminals			
		0	1	2	3	4
Costs	Cost of Transportation Empty E_i	0	22	30	18	20
	Penalty for Holding over Current Period $\pi_{i\ell}$ $\ell=1$	—	150	140	120	120
	2	—	120	90	100	80
	3	—	80	60	40	60
	4	—	30	—	20	25
	Average Holding Cost H_i	100	40	60	50	40
Vehicles	Avail. Vehicles in Current V_i	9	4	3	7	4
	Net Arrivals in Next A_i	2	−1	0	1	−2
Demand	Outgoing Demand D_i	13	5	3	8	4
	Incoming Demand D_i'	20	4	3	4	2

	d	Hub 0	1	2	3	4
	0	0	0.1353	0.3679	0.0067	0.1353
	1	0.0005	0.2707	0.3679	0.0337	0.2707
	2	0.0023	0.2707	0.1839	0.0843	0.2707
	3	0.0075	0.1804	0.0613	0.1403	0.1804
	4	0.0190	0.0902	0.0153	0.1755	0.0902
Probability of "future" Demand $p_i(d)$	5	0.0378	0.0361	0.0031	0.1755	0.0361
	6	0.0630	0.0121	0.0005	0.1462	0.0121
	7	0.0901	0.0034	0.0001	0.1044	0.0034
	8	0.1126	0.0009		0.0653	0.0009
	9	0.1251	0.0002		0.0363	0.0002
	10	0.1251			0.0181	
	11	0.1138			0.0082	
	12	0.0948			0.0035	
	13	0.0729			0.0013	
	14	0.0520			0.0005	
	15	0.0348			0.0002	
	16	0.0217			0.0001	
	17	0.0127				
	≥18	0.0143				
Avge. Demand $\overline{d}_i$		10	2	1	5	2

In essence, we are allocating V_0 among the various terminals. Hence, we wish to retain (i.e., hold over) loads which incur the minimum penalty. Because of the nonincreasing character of the gain functions $g(v_i')$ for increasing v_i', these loads must be the "tail" loads, i.e., loads with the smallest $g(v_i')$'s.

The procedure to achieve optimal allocation is now obvious. We evaluate $g(v_i')$ for all $i \epsilon \mathbf{m}$ and assign V_0—loads in decreasing values of $g(v_i')$.

The procedure is best illustrated by a numerical example which we shall also utilize in the other two problems (the Empty Vehicle problem and the Mixed problem).

Suppose that a system comprises a hub and four outlying terminals. The pertinent cost and other data are given in Table 3-17. The demand is assumed Poisson distributed and "balanced" between hub and terminals (i.e., on the average, demand at the hub is equal to the total demands at the outlying terminals: $\bar{d}_0 = 10, \bar{d}_1 = \bar{d}_4 = 2, \bar{d}_2 = 1$ and $\bar{d}_3 = 5$). Notice that $D_0 = \Sigma_{i \epsilon \mathbf{m}} D_i'$ and $D_0' = \Sigma_{i \epsilon \mathbf{m}} D_i$ as specified by Eq. (3-46). Since $Q_i(u_i) = \Sigma_{d \geq u_i} p_i(d)$, we can easily construct Table 3-18 from the data of Table 3-17 for all values of u_i of immediate interest. In Table 3-18, we

TABLE 3-18   Values of $H_i Q_i(u_i + 1)$

		Hub	Terminals			
u_i	$u_i + 1$	0	1	2	3	4
<0	≤0	100	40	60	50	40
0	1	100	34.59	37.73	49.67	34.59
1	2	99.95	23.76	15.85	47.98	23.76
2	3	99.72	12.93	4.82	43.27	12.93
3	4	98.97	5.72	1.14	36.75	5.72
4	5	97.07	2.11	0.22	27.98	2.11
5	6	93.29	0.66	0.04	19.70	0.66
6	7	86.99	0.18	0	11.89	0.18
7	8	77.98	0		6.67	0
8	9	66.72			3.42	
9	10	54.21			1.59	
10	11	41.70			0	
11	12	30.32				
12	13	20.84				
13	14	13.55				
14	15	8.35				
15	16	4.87				
16	17	2.70				
17	18	1.43				

have actually calculated $Q_i(u_i + 1)$ directly, since this is the value needed in the g_i and G_i expressions.

Since $e_i = 0$ for all $i \epsilon \mathbf{m}_0$, then $u_i = V_i + v_i' + A_i - D_i$, a function of v_i'. Consequently $g(v_i') = H_i Q_i(u_i + 1) + \pi_{i(v_i'+1)}$ is also a function of v_i'. The following Table 3-19 gives the values of $g(v_i')$, and the 9 $(= V_0)$ highest gains are chosen for loading (shown underlined).

Therefore, the optimal schedule is:

Ship 3 loads to terminal 1, hold load 4 over,

    2   ''   2,   ''   3 '' ,

    2   ''   3,   ''   3,4'' ,

    2   ''   4, holding none over.

The optimal pattern of shipment is shown in Fig. 3-17.

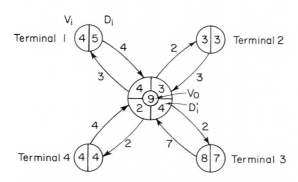

FIGURE 3-17 Optimal Schedule for the "Load Allocation" Problem

The Empty Vehicle Problem

In the empty vehicle problem ($V_0 \geq D_0$ and $V_i > D_i$ for at least one $i \epsilon \mathbf{m}$), the only decision variable to be determined in an optimal fashion is e, the number of empty vehicles moved between terminals and hub.

Let all e_i, $i \epsilon \mathbf{m}$, be set at their maximum values

$$\hat{e}_i = \max [0, V_i - D_i] \quad i \epsilon \mathbf{m}, \hat{e}_0 = -\sum_{i \epsilon \mathbf{m}} \hat{e}_i.$$

Suppose that $\hat{e}_i$ is reduced by unity to $\hat{e}_i - 1$ while all other $\hat{e}_k$, $k \neq i$, remain the same. Then clearly u_0 will be reduced by unity to $\hat{u}_0 - 1$ and u_i will be increased by unity to $\hat{u}_i + 1$. The net gain from such a reduction in $\hat{e}_i$ is given by Eq. (3-57). Because of the nonincreasing character of $G(e_i)$, the process of reduction is carried out in order of decreasing values

TABLE 3-19 Values of g(v'ᵢ)

		1			2			3			4	
v_i	u_1	$H_1Q_1(u_1+1)$	$g(v_1')$	u_2	$H_2Q_2(u_2+1)$	$g(v_2')$	u_3	$H_3Q_3(u_3+1)$	$g(v_3')$	u_4	$H_4Q_4(u_4+1)$	$g(v_4')$
0	-2	40	190	0	37.93	177.9	0	49.67	169.67	-2	40	160
1	-1	40	160	1	15.85	105.85	1	47.98	147.98	-1	40	120
2	0	34.59	114.59	2	4.82	64.82	2	43.27	83.27	—	—	—
3	1	23.76	53.76	—	—	—	3	36.75	56.75	—	—	—

Terminals

of $G(e_i)$ until either the empty vehicles are exhausted or the gain is ≤ 0. The remaining set of $\{e_i\}$ must be optimal.

We illustrate the approach with a numerical example which utilizes the data of Tables 3-17 and 3-18 but substitutes the values of V_i, D_i', and D_i given in Table 3-20. Notice that $V_0 > D_0$ and $D_0 = 13 = \Sigma_{i \in m} D_i$, and for terminal 3, $V_3 > D_3$. At $\{e_i\} = \{\hat{e}_i\}$, $i \in m$, the corresponding $\{\hat{u}_i\}$ can be evaluated using Eq. (3-49). The values of $\{\hat{e}_i\}$ and $\{\hat{u}_i\}$ are given in Table 3-20 which, for ease of reference, also contains the additions $\{A_i\}$.

TABLE 3-20

	Hub		Terminals		
	0	1	2	3	4
V_i	15	2	2	6	3
D_i	13	5	3	4	1
D_i'	13	4	3	4	2
A_i	2	-1	0	1	-2
$\hat{e}_i$	-4	0	0	2	2
$\hat{u}_i$	17	0	2	5	0

We start the procedure of unit decrement in e_i, $i \in m$, and evaluate $G(e_i)$, beginning with the starting solution $\hat{e}$. Since no terminal contains more than two vehicles, e_i ranges between 2 and -2.

At $\{e_i\} = \{\hat{e}_i\}$, $\hat{e}_0 = -4$ and $\hat{u}_0 = 17$. Hence, by Eq. (3-57),

$$G(\hat{e}_1 = 0) = H_1 Q_1(1) - H_0 Q_0(17) - E_1 = 34.59 - 2.70 - 22 = \quad 9.89$$

$$G(\hat{e}_2 = 0) = H_2 Q_2(3) - H_0 Q_0(17) - E_2 = \quad 4.82 - 2.70 - 30 = -27.88$$

$$G(\hat{e}_3 = 2) = H_3 Q_3(6) - H_0 Q_0(17) + E_3 = 19.70 - 2.70 + 18 = \quad 35.00$$

and

$$G(\hat{e}_4 = 2) = H_4 Q_4(1) - H_0 Q_0(17) + E_4 = 34.59 - 2.70 + 20 = \quad \underline{51.89}.$$

The maximum gain is $G(\hat{e}_4 = 2)$; therefore, e_4 is reduced by unity to 1. We remark that $H_0 Q_0(u_0)$ is a constant subtracted from $H_i Q_i(u_i + 1) \pm E_i$, $i \in m$, and hence can be ignored in evaluating the optimal choice. In Table 3-21 we let $G^0(e_i) = G(e_i) + H_0 Q_0(u_0)$.

Proceeding in identical fashion, we construct Table 3-21. The optimal choice of reductions is given by the underlined $G^0(e_i)$'s. There are exactly *six* underlined $G^0(e_i)$'s corresponding to the range of possible reductions without violating the restrictions on available empty trucks.

Finally, we determine the *absolute* worth of each reduction by including

TABLE 3-21   Calculation of $G(e_i) + H_0 Q_0(u_0)$

					Terminals							
	1			2			3			4		
e_i	u_1	$H_1 Q_1(u_1 + 1)$	$G^0(e_1)$	u_2	$H_2 Q_2(u_2 + 1)$	$G^0(e_2)$	u_3	$H_3 Q_3(u_3 + 1)$	$G^0(e_3)$	u_4	$H_4 Q_4(u_4 + 1)$	$G^0(e_4)$
2	—	—	—	—	—	—	5	19.70	37.70	0	34.59	54.59
1	—	—	—	—	—	—	6	11.89	29.89	1	23.76	43.76
0	0	34.59	12.59	2	4.82	−25.18	7	6.67	−11.33	2	12.93	−7.07
−1	1	23.76	1.76	3	1.14	−28.86	8	3.42	−14.58	3	5.72	−14.28

the term $-H_0 Q_0(u_0)$ in the evaluation:

$$G(e_4 = 2) = 54.59 - H_0 Q_0(17) = 54.59 - 2.70 = 51.89$$

$$G(e_4 = 1) = 43.76 - H_0 Q_0(16) = 43.76 - 4.87 = 38.89$$

$$G(e_3 = 2) = 37.70 - H_0 Q_0(15) = 37.70 - 8.35 = 29.35$$

$$G(e_3 = 1) = 29.89 - H_0 Q_0(14) = 29.89 - 13.55 = 16.34$$

$$G(e_1 = 0) = 12.59 - H_0 Q_0(13) = 12.59 - 20.84 = -8.75.$$

Since $G(e_1 = 0)$ is < 0, the reduction in e_1 (i.e., sending an empty vehicle from Hub to terminal 1) incurs a *loss* (negative gain) and should not be undertaken. No further analysis is necessary because of the nonincreasing character of $G(e_i)$. Hence, the optimal schedule is: $e_1 = 0$, $e_2 = 0$, $e_3 = 0$, $e_4 = 0$; i.e., no empty vehicles are moved.

The Mixed Problem

In the mixed problem ($V_0 < D_0$ and $V_i > D_i$ for at least one $i \epsilon m$), we must allocate the load at the hub, i.e., determine the vector $\mathbf{v}'$, and also allocate the empty vehicles at the terminals, i.e., determine the vector $\mathbf{e}$.

Since both $g(v'_i)$ and $G(e_i)$ are functions of $H_0 Q_0(u_0)$ (which is no longer a constant to be ignored in the evaluation of the optimal), incremental analysis (which proved so useful in the previous two problems) is no longer valid. With the loss of the use of incremental analysis we also lose the simple structure of the problem and find ourselves forced to resort to more general programming approaches.

In particular, the mixed problem can be given a dynamic programming formulation. Unfortunately, this formulation requires extensive calculations which may seriously detract from its practical applicability.

It is evident that since $V_0 < D_0$, all available vehicles at the hub will be loaded (see Rule 1, p. 199). Consequently, all feasible solutions with which we are concerned must have $V_0 = \Sigma_{i \epsilon m} v'_i$. Let the starting feasible schedule be given by $e_i = e_i^0 = \max(0, V_i - D_i)$, and $v'_i = v_i^{0'}$ for all $i \epsilon m$. Without loss of generality we can take the cost of this starting feasible schedule to be zero. Let $f(\mathbf{e}; \mathbf{v})$ be the maximum incremental gain (i.e., reduction in cost) over the cost of the starting feasible schedule, when the new schedule is $(\mathbf{e}; \mathbf{v}')$. Then we have the functional equation

$$f(\mathbf{e}; \mathbf{v}') = \max \begin{cases} G(e_i + 1) + f(e_i + 1; \mathbf{v}') \text{ for all } i \epsilon m \\ g(v'_i - 1) - g(v'_j + 1) \end{cases} \tag{3-60}$$

$$+ f(\mathbf{e}; v'_i - 1, v'_j + 1) \text{ for all pairs } i, j \epsilon m$$

The functions on the right hand side of Eq. (3-60) are written in abbreviated form to indicate one less e_i at node i or an exchange of loaded vehicles between nodes i and j ($v_i' - 1$ increased to v_i and $v_j' + 1$ decreased to v_j'), with all other variables remaining at their previous values.

Note that in each iteration the vector $\mathbf{e}$ is reduced by one. Consequently, there are exactly $\Sigma_{i \in \mathbf{m}} e_i^0$ iterations of Eq. (3-60). Each iteration involves the evaluation of $m(m - 1)$ pairs of nodes and m nodes, i.e., m^2 values. The optimal schedule is the schedule corresponding to the maximum $f(\mathbf{e}, \mathbf{v}')$.

Although the functional equation approach of dynamic programming presents a "straightforward" formulation of the mixed problem, it is, in fact, computationally unwieldly because it involves a search in $2m$-dimensional space.

As a *heuristic* approach to the mixed problem, we propose the following iterative procedure which should converge on the optimal or near-optimal allocation in a reasonable number of iterations.

First, solve the Load Allocation problem assuming all $e_i = 0$. Then solve the Empty Vehicle problem. If, as a result, any e_i is different from 0, return to the Load Allocation problem assuming the allocation of empty vehicles just obtained. Repeat this process until the allocation of empty vehicles does not change from the beginning to the end of the iteration.

A numerical example of the mixed problem is given in the exercises at the end of this chapter.

COMMENTS AND BIBLIOGRAPHY

§**2.** The "Caterer" problem was first proposed by:

JACOBS, W. "The Caterer Problem," *Naval Research Logistics Quarterly*, Vol. 1, 1954, pp. 154–165.

The dynamic programming approach to the problem was first proposed by:

BELLMAN, R. "On a Dynamic Programming Approach to the Caterer Problem," *Management Science*, Vol. 3, 1957, pp. 270–278.

See also

ELMAGHRABY, S. E. "On The Dynamic Programming Approach to the Caterer Problem," *Journal of Mathematical Analysis and Applications*, Vol. 8, No. 2, April 1964, pp. 202–217.

§**3.** The quantitative study of inventory systems for purposes of minimizing operating costs has been traced back to:

HARRIS, F. "Operations And Cost," *Factory Management Series*, Chicago, A. W. Shaw Co., 1915, pp. 48–52.

The first book completely devoted to inventory systems is:

WHITIN, T. M. *The Theory of Inventory Management*, Princeton, N.J., Princeton University Press, 1953.

The following recent text is more analytical and also provides an excellent coverage of constrained inventory systems:

HADLEY, G., and T. M. WHITIN *Analysis of Inventory Systems*, Englewood-Cliffs, N.J., Prentice-Hall, 1963.

The material in this section also draws upon:

STARR, M. K. and D. W. MILLER *Inventory Control: Theory and Practice*, Englewood Cliffs, N.J., Prentice-Hall, 1962, §31.

CHURCHMAN, C. W., R. L. ACKOFF and E. L. ARNOFF *Introduction to Operations Research*, New York, Wiley, 1957, Chapter 10, by B. E. Rifas.

§4. Discussions of production-inventory systems are numerous:

HANSSMANN, F. *Operations Research in Production and Inventory Control*, New York, Wiley, 1962.

The model based on quadratic cost functions was first proposed by:

HOLT, C. C., F. MODIGLIANI and J. F. MUTH "Derivation of a Linear Decision Rule for Production and Employment Scheduling," *Management Science*, Vol. 2, No. 2, Jan. 1956, pp. 159–177.

HOLT, C. C., F. MODIGLIANI and H. A. SIMON "Linear Decision Rule for Production and Employment Scheduling," *Ibid.*, Vol. 2, No. 1, Oct. 1955, pp. 1–30.

The mathematical proof of the optimality of the linear decision rule under a quadratic criterion function is given in:

SIMON, H. A. "Dynamic Programming Under Uncertainty With a Quadratic Criterion Function," *Econometrica*, Vol. 24, No. 1, Jan. 1956, pp. 74–81.

The Linear Programming model is from:

ELMAGHRABY, S. E. "Smoothed Production Patterns: A Linear Programming Formulation," (talk to the Regional Conference of A.P.I.C.S.), Bridgeport, Conn., April 1963.

For a different approach to production smoothing using a quadratic criterion function see:

JOHNSON, S. M. "Sequential Production Planning Over Time at Minimum Cost," *Management Science*, Vol. 3, No. 4, July 1957, pp. 435–437 (and the list of references cited therein).

§5. The following references can be read in conjunction with §5:

SALVESON, M. "A Problem in Optimal Machine Loading," *Management Science*, Vol. 2, No. 3, April 1956, pp. 232–260.

MANNE, A. S. "Programming of Economic Lot Sizes," *Management Science*, Vol. 4, No. 2, Jan. 1958, pp. 115–135.

DZIELINSKI, B. P., C. T. BAKER, and A. S. MANNE "Simulation Tests for Lot Size Programming," *Management Science*, Vol. 9, No. 2, Jan. 1963, pp. 229–258.

GILMORE, P. C. and R. E. GOMORY "A Linear Programming Approach to the Cutting Stock Problem," *Operations Research*, Vol. 9, No. 6, Nov. Dec. 1961, pp. 849–859.

GILMORE, P. C. and R. E. GOMORY "A Linear Programming Approach to the Cutting Stock Problem—Part II." *Operations Research*, Vol. 11, No. 6, 1963, pp. 863–888.

§6. An excellent discussion of feedback and adaptive systems in which the notion of dynamic interaction plays an important role can be found in:

BELLMAN, R. E. and S. E. DREYFUS *Applied Dynamic Programming*, Princeton, N.J., Princeton University Press, 1962, Chapters 6–8.

§7. This discussion is based on:

    ELMAGHRABY, S. E. and A. S. GINSBERG   "The Optimal Loading of Linear Multi-Operation Shops," *Management Technology*, Vol. 4, No. 1, June 1964, pp. 47–58.

§8. This dynamic model is based on:

    MINAS, J. G. and L. G. MITTEN   "The Hub Operation Scheduling Problem," *Operations Research*, Vol. 6, No. 3, 1958, pp. 329–345.

EXERCISES

1. Consider the Caterer problem with the following data: Demand for 7 days: 150, 120, 50, 150, 60, 70, 90. Purchase price of new napkins: $1.50 per napkin. Cost of fast laundry: ($q = 2$ days); 30¢ per napkin. Cost of slow laundry: ($p = 3$ days); 10¢ per napkin.

   (a) Solve for the optimal policy by linear programming and dynamic programming approaches.

   (b) Suppose now that demand is known probabilistically to possess a uniform distribution with the mean demand on any day given by the figure above and a range equal to 20% of the mean demand.

   If the Caterer wishes to minimize his *expected* cost, is the policy obtained in (a) still optimal? Comment briefly.

2. Formulate the dynamic programming model of the caterer problem along the lines suggested in §2.2. In particular, show that if $f_i(x_i) = \max_{R_i} \Sigma_{k=i}^{n-1} v_k$, where R_i is the region defined by the inequalities $v_i \le x_i$; $v_k + v_{k+1} \le S - r_{i+2}$ for $k = 1, \ldots, n - 2$, and $v_k \le r_k$ for $i = 1, \ldots, n - 1$ and $x_i = S - r_{i+1} - v_{i-1}$, then a functional equation of the form

$$f_k(x_k) = \max_{v_k \le v_k^*} [v_k + f_{k+1}(S - r_{k+2} - v_k)]$$

   can be defined, where $v_k^* = \min (x_k; r_k; S - r_{k+2})$.[†]

3. In Problem 1, assume that the Caterer has a fourth alternative course of action: a special service laundry which cleans soiled napkins in one day but costs 50¢ per napkin.

   Solve for the optimal policy using the Transportation model of linear programming.

   Give the mathematical formulation of the dynamic programming approach and comment briefly.

4. Give examples of three operational systems in which feedback of "status" plays a central role in the decision-making process.

5. Give examples of three systems which can be treated from the "stationary interaction" point of view. Feel free to use systems treated in other chapters.

6. It is desired to produce an item to meet a given demand over a known planning horizon of N periods. The producing shop has limited machine capacity of H_t hours per period on regular time at a cost c per hour. No backorders and no overtime work are permitted. The cost of carrying inventory is given

[†]Elmaghraby, *Journal of Mathematical Analysis and Applications*; Vol. 8, No. 2, 1964.

as h/unit/period. Assume that a unit produced is available at the end of the period, and that a unit demanded is consumed at the end of the period.

(a) Construct a transportation model for the optimal scheduling of production.

(b) Show that if no capacity restrictions are present, the form of the optimal policy is independent of the values of the requirements. State this optimal policy.

(c) Assume that overtime is permitted at a premium cost b/hour, $b > c$. Is the transportation model still valid? Explain your answer.

7. Consider the LP model for smoothing production, inventory, and work force presented in §4.

Reformulate the model assuming that backorders are allowed at a cost of c/unit backordered per period. Assume that all other conditions and parameters are the same.

8. Consider the following production problem. The demand for an item for the next six months is as follows:

Demand Period	1	2	3	4	5	6
Demand	6	4	8	13	3	7

The initial inventory for the item is eight units. The required final inventory is 9 units. There is a lead time of one month between start of production and the availability of the finished product. If the storage cost is $0.2/unit/month, and the cost of *change* in production is $.07/unit, what is the optimal pattern of production and what is the corresponding minimum cost?

9. Three items are to be stored, A, B, and C. The relevant costs are as indicated in the following table.

Item	Purchase Price per Unit	Yearly Consumption	Cost of Ordering
A	2.50	100,000	$25
B	12.00	100,000	45
C	36.00	50,000	64

No backorders are allowed. The cost of investment is valued at 18% of average inventory.

(a) What is the EOQ for each item assuming independence? What is the total average investment? What is the TVC of inventory management per year?

(b) Assume that the available capital for average investment is limited to $I^* = \$19,550$. Re-evaluate, by the method of Lagrange multipliers, the EOQ's for the three items. What is the TVC under such conditions? Compare these results with the results above and comment briefly.

10. Consider the three items of the previous problem. The aggregate restriction on the capital investment yields a *linear* constraint in the various quantities.

Needless to say, the Lagrange-multiplier technique is equally applicable to the case of nonlinear aggregate constraints.

Suppose that it is desired to maintain the total setup time for all three items to within 160 hours each year. The setup time for each item is as follows:

> Items A and B: $\frac{1}{2}$ hour per setup
> Item   C   1 hour per setup

Then, since there are R_i/Q_i setups per year, we must have

$$\frac{100,000}{Q_A} \times \frac{1}{2} + \frac{100,000}{Q_B} \times \frac{1}{2} + \frac{50,000}{Q_C} \times 1 \leq 160,$$

which is nonlinear in the Q's. Although a simple change of variables reduces the above constraints to a *linear* constraint, it is required to determine the optimal Q^*'s with the above formulation. (In the next problem this approach will be useful.)

11. Suppose now that both constraints mentioned in Problems 9 and 10 above are imposed. Determine the optimal ordering quantities for all three products.

    Would the problem have a solution if the setup time allowance was restricted to 110 hours? Explain the reason.

12. Interpret the value of the Lagrange multiplier λ^* obtained in Problem 9. Contrast such interpretation with the value of the parameter α obtained in the following fashion:

> Let ΔC = TVC of constrained inventory minus the TVC of unconstrained inventory
> I_{opt} = total average investment of unconstrained inventory
> then $\alpha = \dfrac{\Delta C}{I_{opt} - I^*}$.

    Which of the two parameters, λ^* or α, would you consider as the true worth of the scarce resource (capital)? Explain your answer.

13. Consider the Machine Loading problem of §5. The following LP model has been suggested as a possible "simplification" over the LP of Egs. (3-35)–(3-36): Let X_i denote the number of units produced of product i; let b_j be the number of press-group hours available during the planning horizon; let β_{ij} denote the number of press-group j required to produce one unit of product i; and let p_i denote the profit measure per unit of i. Then

$$\text{Maximize} \sum_i p_i X_i$$

$$\text{subject to} \sum_i \beta_{ij} X_i \leq b_j \qquad j = 1, \ldots, n$$

$$X_i \geq 0$$

Discuss this model and show why it is a naive approach to the problem, and may lead to solutions which are "better" than what can in fact be obtained.

14. In the machine loading problem of §5, show that if π_1, π_2, ..., π_m are the Simplex multipliers of the m constraints, then either the slack variable y_i is eligible for introduction into the basis (because π_i is > 0), or else a *maximal* assignment A as determined by the *integer* LP:

$$\text{Minimize} \sum_i \pi_i a_i w_i$$

$$\text{subject to} \sum_i b_{ik} w_i \le n_k \qquad k = 1, \ldots, K$$

$$w_i = 0 \text{ or } 1, \pi_i \le 0$$

where b_{ik} is the number of machines in group k required by part i, and n_k is the total number of machines available in group k.

15. It is desired to produce five component parts 1 to 5, in such a manner that whenever a part is loaded on the shop for any period of time *all* the machines necessary for its production are available at the same time. The five parts go into three assemblies in the following quantities:

Part No.	Assembly	Quantity of Part per Assembly
1	A	2
2	A	1
3	B	4
4	B	2
5	C	1

Production must be in excess of 2,000 units of assembly A and in excess of 750 units of assembly B. There is no lower bound on the production of C. The profit gained from sale of products is:

$25.00 per unit of A
$17.00 per unit of B
$20.00 per unit of C.

There are five different machine classes in the shop, and the number of machines per class is as follows:

Machine Class	a	b	c	d	e
No. of Machines Available	2	4	1	3	2

The data on the manufacturing of the five component parts is as follows (this data is usually available on the "route sheets"):

Part No.	Operation No.	Class and No. of Machines	Rate of Production per hr.
1	1	ab–2	285
	2	c–1	213
	3	b–1	175
	4	de–2	150
2	1	a–1	150
	2	c–1	220
3	1	a–1	95
	2	cd–2	72
	3	bde–3	50
4	1	bd–2	100
	2	acd–2	320
	3	ce–1	215
5	1	c–1	472
	2	bd–2	200
	3	e–1	230

The contract specifies that the products must be delivered within a 4-week period. You may assume a 40-hour week. Any quantity produced beyond the minimum requirements will be accepted at the stated price.

Determine, through an LP formulation, the *optimal schedule* for maximum profit. Ignore, for the sake of ease of calculations, the possibility of loading two or more lots of any part.

Let X_j represent a maximal assignment, y_A production of A in excess of 2000 units, y_B production of B in excess of 750 units, and y_C production of C. Also, let y_i denote the *excess* in equation i, with y_6 denoting the slack in the total time constraint.

Start your iterations with the following basis:

$$B_0 = \begin{array}{|ccccccc|} X_1 & X_2 & y_A & X_3 & X_4 & y_6 \\ 150 & & -2 & & & \\ & 150 & -1 & & & \\ 50 & 50 & & 50 & 50 & \\ & & & 100 & & \\ & & & & 200 & \\ 1 & 1 & & 1 & 1 & 1 \end{array}$$

Notice that this basis is degenerate, with $X_4 = 0$.

16. Demand for three items over a 4-month planning horizon, as well as other production data, are indicated in the following table:

| Item | Month | | | | Setup Time, hr. | Production Time, hr. per Unit | Inventory Cost, $ per Unit Per Month |
	1	2	3	4			
1	5000	2000	3000	6000	15	0.02	0.01
2	230	190	150	250	7	0.18	0.04
3	875	1125	875	2000	10	0.10	0.02
Regular Time Production Capacity, hr.	290	250	300	275			
Overtime Production	70	60	70	70			

Cost of Regular Time: $4.0/hr.

Cost of Overtime: $6.50/hr.

It is desired to satisfy demand in any period with no backorders permitted, such that the total cost of production (both on regular time and overtime) and inventory (based on end-of-period inventory) is minimized.

Construct a linear programming model for the production-inventory system following similar (but not necessarily identical) reasoning to the model of economic lot size manufacturing of §5.

17. A machine for making paper produces reels of 100 in. width, and the following orders have been received:

> 150 rolls of width 11 in.
> 100 rolls of width 22 in.
> 80 rolls of width 32 in.
> 80 rolls of width 45 in.
> 50 rolls of width 54 in.
> 20 rolls of width 67 in.

It is required to satisfy these orders in such a way that the trim waste from reels is as small as possible. Obtain a starting basis of eight (8) legitimate maximal cutting patterns and proceed to determine the minimum-cost schedule, without completely enumerating all possible maximal cutting patterns.

18. In the Hub Scheduling problem of §8, solve for the "mixed problem" using the data of Tables 3-17 and 3-18 but substituting the following values for the available vehicles and the demand at the five cities.

		Terminals			
	Hub	1	2	3	4
Vehicles V_i	10	4	3	7	4
Outgoing Demand D_i	20	4	3	4	3
Incoming Demand D'	14	5	3	8	4
ℓ = 1		150	140	120	120
2		120	90	100	80
3		80	60	100	70
$\pi_{i\,\ell}$ 4		80		60	55
5		30		60	
6				60	
7				30	
8				30	

19. The cost of producing an item varies with the *square* of change in the level of production, and is given by:

$$\text{cost of production} = 80(P_t - P_{t-1})^2.$$

The cost of inventory is also proportional to the square of the difference between the actual inventory at the end of a period, I_t, and the desired level (of

12 units), and is given by:

$$\text{cost of inventory} = 20(I_t - 12)^2.$$

The forecast of sales for the next four months is given by:

$$S_1 = 30, S_2 = 15, S_3 = 45, S_4 = 20.$$

Initial levels of inventory and production are: $I_0 = 10$ and $P_0 = 15$, respectively. The desired terminal inventory is, naturally, 12 units. All demand must be satisfied.

(a) Solve the problem by the HMM model described in §4.1.

(b) Formulate a dynamic programming model of the problem and solve for the optimal production and inventory levels.

(c) Compare the two approaches from both the computational and other points of view.

20. Solve the above problem, assuming a set-up cost for production equal to $250. Notice the nonlinear character of this cost, which is incurred only when production is undertaken. Comment briefly on the approach used.

CHAPTER 4 / **Network Models**

§1. THEORY OF GRAPHS: INTRODUCTION

Although we have introduced some material from the theory of graphs in previous chapters (for example, Chapter 2), we did not explicitly recognize the discussion as such, nor did we spend any time analyzing the properties of graphs in general. Because of the importance of network models in the study of production processes, we devote this chapter to the discussion, in greater detail, of some of the fundamental notions of graph theory that are relevant to our subject matter and some of its applications.

Graph theory, which until very recently was regarded as an abstract mathematical subject, has been finding an increasing field of application in the various management, engineering, and physical sciences. Consequently, it is being recognized as one of the most important unifying concepts that underlie the several seemingly separate and independent applications. For example, a traffic network may represent in physical reality a radio communication, a railway transportation, a highway, or an airline network. All these different physical realities possess one feature in common: their elements can be represented by a network consisting of stations and links between stations. The topological structure of such networks can be represented by a graph with vertices and branches corresponding to the stations and links, respectively. The analysis of the graph determines the properties that are inherent in the topological structure of the graph and, therefore, common to all physical applications.

We will start the chapter by defining, in §2, some terms peculiar to graphs, and follow, in §3, with a discussion of the Shortest Route problem. Sections 4 and 5 present a rather fundamental technique, the so-called "labeling procedure," for determining the maximal flow in *undirected* networks, first in graphical format and then in tableau format, respectively. Section 6 discusses the important case of maximal flow in *directed* networks.

The following two sections apply the theory just developed to two well-known production problems: first to a special formulation of the

Transportation problem, presented in §7, and then to the Assignment problem, presented in §8. In this latter problem, there are, in fact, four different formulations, depending on the space of feasible solutions as well as on the objective function. In particular, there is the "Standard Assignment" problem, in which it is required to assign as many men as possible to available jobs subject to eligibility constraints. Then there is the "Bottleneck Assignment" problem, in which it is desired to assign machines to jobs (or conversely assign jobs to machines) so that the efficiency of the "bottleneck" operation, i.e., the operation with minimum efficiency, is maximized. Third, it may be desired to assign machines to jobs and maximize the total productivity from all machines. Finally, in the case of partially or totally ordered sets of tasks, assuming that all machines are equally efficient on all jobs, the problem is to assign the jobs to the minimum number of machines but still complete all the jobs on or before a specified time.

A topic strongly related to the Assignment problem is the Job Sequencing problem, which we will discuss in §9. We will present computationally efficient algorithms for the case of n jobs on 2 machines with, as well as without, start and stop lags. The case of more than 2 machines is more difficult, and a solution exists only for the special case in which the jobs have the same sequence on all machines. Due to the length of this procedure, we must forfeit its presentation and be content with citing it at the end of the chapter. However, we shall give the n-Jobs 3-Machines Sequencing problem which is due to Johnson. This is, in fact, a special case which is reducible to the n-Jobs 2-Machines problem.

For the general case in which no assumptions concerning job routes or processing times are made, we give a linear programming formulation due to Manne. As can easily be seen, the formulation is computationally unwieldy, giving rise to an excessive number of equations and variables.

Another closely related topic to the Assignment and Sequencing problems is the so-called "Line Balancing" problem. This is the classical problem faced in the design of progressive assembly lines. The discussion of this important problem will be given in §10.

§2. DEFINITIONS

Branch: This is a line segment with its distinct end points i and j (i.e., *nodes i* and *j*).

A branch will also be known as *element, link,* or *edge*. This definition is slightly restrictive: it specifies that end-points belong to the branch—which is a matter of convention rather than necessity—and that the end points are *distinct*. Naturally, we reserve the option to talk about a branch *without* its end points, which we will refer to as an *arc*. Also, the *nodes*, i.e., end points of the line segment, need not be distinct: a *self-loop* in which the two end points are the same is clearly a legitimate branch. *Nodes* are sometimes referred to as *vertices* or *junction points*. Now we are in a position to define a linear graph.

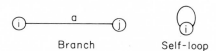

Linear Graph: This is a collection of branches that have no points in common other than nodes.

The definition is rather general. *Any* collection of branches constitutes a graph, usually denoted by

$$G = [N, A]$$

where N is the set of nodes and A is the set of arcs (see Fig. 4-1). In the engineering world, naturally, a graph has some physical significance. For example, if five cities can "reach" each other—by whatever means of communication: road, air, railroad, telephone, radio, etc.—a graph can be drawn to represent such communication. Such representation is given in Fig. 4-2; (a) shows that city *2* is connected directly with every other city. To bring such "hub" characteristics into evidence, (b) is drawn to repre-

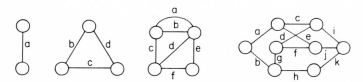

FIGURE 4-1   Examples of Linear Graphs

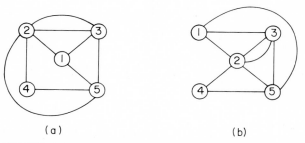

(a)   (b)

FIGURE 4-2   Communication among 5 Cities (a) and Isomorphic Graph (b)

sent the same linkage with city *2* in the center. Figure 4-2(b) is said to be *isomorphic* with 4-2(a) because there is a one-to-one correspondence between nodes and arcs joining nodes.

Branches are either *directed* or *undirected*. The resulting graph, or network, is consequently directed, undirected, or *mixed*, depending on whether *all* branches are directed or not or whether some are directed and others are undirected, respectively.

> *Connected Graph:* A graph in which it is possible to reach any node *j* from any other node *i* along branches in the graph is said to be *connected*.

Our discussions will be limited to connected graphs. A *chain* between nodes *i* and *j* is a connected sequence of branches that lead from *i* to *j* such that each node is encountered only once. Although the precise definition of a chain is cumbersome, the notion is simple. In the graph shown in Fig. 4-3, there are six chains between nodes *1* and *4*: (a, c); (b, d); (b, e, g);

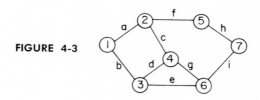

FIGURE 4-3

(a, f, h, i, g); (b, e, i, h, f, c); and (a, f, h, i, e, d). A *directed chain* has all branch orientations leading from *i* to *j*. On the other hand, a directed branch sequence from *i* to *j* in which some of the branches are traversed opposite to their orientation is called a *path*. Thus, a path may contain *forward* as well as *reverse* branches; a chain contains only forward branches.

A chain whose terminal nodes coincide is called a *loop* or *cycle*. Notice the difference between a cycle and a self-loop mentioned previously.

> *Spanning Tree:* A spanning tree is a connected subgraph of all nodes which contains no loops.

Obviously, every connected graph must have at least one tree. And conversely, a spanning tree could not exist unless the original graph were connected. It is equally evident that if G contains N nodes, the tree must contain exactly $N - 1$ branches. We shall presently see that this is a fundamental property that corresponds to a basis in linear programming. Corresponding to any tree T_j we shall give a special name to the arcs of G that are contained in the *complement* of T_j: we shall call them *chords* relative to T_j. Thus, in Fig. 4-4, arcs *b* and *d* are chords relative to T_1,

Graph G

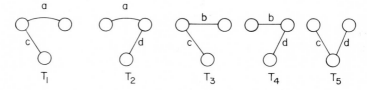

T_1 T_2 T_3 T_4 T_5

FIGURE 4-4   Graph G and Its Trees

b and c are chords relative to T_2, etc. In general, any connected graph with A arcs and N nodes contains $N - 1$ branches (of some tree) and $A - N + 1$ chords (corresponding to the chords of the tree).

> *Incidence:* An arc is incident on a node if the node constitutes one of its terminal points.

This definition gives us a measure of the *order of a node*: it is the number of arcs incident on it. Thus, a chain has all its nodes of order 2 except the start and terminal nodes which are of order 1. On the other hand, a cycle has all its nodes of order 2 (see Fig. 4-5).

As was stated before, throughout this chapter we shall deal only with *connected graphs*. We define the *rank R* of a graph G as equal to $N - 1$, which is the number of branches in a tree. The remaining $A - N + 1$ chords are called the *nullity* of G and are designated by η.

We can get a better sense of the reasoning behind these two definitions if we study graphs from the algebraic point of view. In particular, each graph has a number of matrices which describe the *incidence, circuit,* and *path* relationships. For example, consider the *directed* graph of Fig. 4-6. It has $N = 4$ nodes and $A = 6$ arcs.

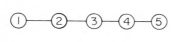

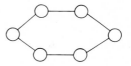

Chain : Nodes 2,3,4 of order 2
        Nodes 1,5 of order 1   Cycle: All nodes of order 2

FIGURE 4-5

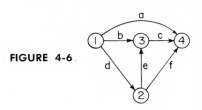

FIGURE 4-6

Incidence Matrix: We can construct the *incidence matrix* $V = [a_{ij}]$ as a matrix of N rows and A columns, with $a_{ij} = 1$ if edge j is incident *from* node i, $a_{ij} = -1$ if edge j is incident *on* node i, and $a_{ij} = 0$ otherwise.

		a	b	c	d	e	f	←Arcs
	1	1	1		1			
$V =$	2				-1	1	1	
	3		-1	1		-1		
	4	-1		-1			-1	

↑
Nodes

Note that each column contains exactly one $+1$ and one -1. Since the sum of the rows equals zero, the matrix is of order < 4. In fact, it is of order 3, since it can be shown that any three rows are independent. In general, V is of rank $N - 1$; i.e., there are exactly $N - 1$ independent rows (so that the value of the corresponding determinant $\neq 0$). This is precisely the rank of G given above, and is also equal to the number of branches in any tree of G.

Circuit Matrix: The circuit matrix $B = [b_{ij}]$ is a $k \times A$ matrix, where k is the number of circuits in G, and A is, as before, the number of arcs, and $b_{ij} = \pm 1$ if edge j is in circuit i and is of the same (opposite) orientation as the circuit and $b_{ij} = 0$ otherwise.

The orientation of a circuit is arbitrary, and an arc has the same orientation as a circuit if the nodes appear in the same sequence in both. In the graph of Fig. 4-7 there are 7 circuits, and B is given by

		a	b	c	d	e	f	←Arcs
	1	1	-1	-1				
	2		1		-1	-1		
	3			1		1	-1	
$B =$	4	1	-1			1	-1	
	5	1		-1	-1	-1		
	6		1	1	-1		-1	
	7	1			-1		-1	

↑
Circuits

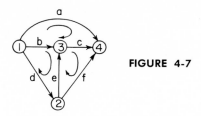

FIGURE 4-7

We show three circuits on the graph. The rank of B can easily be shown to be $A - N + 1$, which is the nullity of G as defined above.

Chain Matrix: The chain matrix $L = [\ell_{ij}]$ is constructed in a similar fashion to the circuit matrix: it is a $p \times A$ matrix, where p is the number of chains between the two designated nodes (one is usually labeled source s and the other terminal t), A is the number of arcs, and $\ell_{ij} = 1$ if edge j is in chain i and of the same orientation, $\ell_{ij} = -1$ if edge j is in chain i and of opposite orientation, and, $\ell_{ij} = 0$ otherwise. In Fig. 4-6, if we let the source be node 1 and the terminal be node 4, then,

$$
L =
\begin{array}{c}
 \\
1 \\
2 \\
3 \\
4 \\
5
\end{array}
\begin{array}{c}
\begin{array}{cccccc}
a & b & c & d & e & f
\end{array} \\
\left[
\begin{array}{cccccc}
1 &   &   &   &   &   \\
  & 1 & 1 &   &   &   \\
1 &   & 1 & 1 & 1 &   \\
  &   &   & 1 &   & 1 \\
  & 1 &   &   & -1 & 1
\end{array}
\right]
\end{array}
\leftarrow \text{Arcs}
$$

Chains

The rank of L is, in general, equal to p, the number of chains.

If the graph G is undirected, the matrices V, B and L would be similar to the above except that all entries are either 0 or 1.

§3. THE SHORTEST ROUTE PROBLEM

Suppose it is desired to find the shortest "distance" between some node s (start or source) and another node t (terminal) in a network. The "distance" d_{ij} between two nodes i and j need not be the physical length of the route between the two but may stand for any parameter of interest such as the cost of transfer or time of transfer, etc., from node i to j. It is assumed that the "lengths" of branches are known—the length of branch (i, j) in the direction $i \rightarrow j$ need not be the same as the length of the same branch traversed in the reverse direction $j \rightarrow i$; i.e., the matrix of "distances" need not be symmetrical. If node i does not connect with node j, the "distance" between the two is assumed infinite or, for the sake of digital computation, a very large number.

The shortest route problem can be formulated as a *linear programming* problem; it can also be given a *dynamic programming* formulation. We shall discuss both approaches in this section, but first we will exhibit a combinatorial method which bears a close resemblance to the "labeling technique" described in the following section.

3.1 Combinatorial Approach

Attach to the source s the number 0. Proceed in ascending node number from s (which is supposed to be node 1) attaching to each node j which connects with node i, written $i < j$, a number

$$k'_j = \min \{k_j; k_i + d_{ij}\}, k'_s = 0, j = s, 2, \ldots, N - 1, t$$

where k_j is assumed infinite if it has not been given a finite value before; otherwise it is equal to the value previously given. When t is reached, k'_t denotes the length of the minimum path. Trace the path backwards from t to s so that each node along the path has its k' equal to the k' of the succeeding node less the length of the branch connecting them.

Consider as an example the network of Fig. 4-8 with $a = 20$, $b = 16$, $c = 7$, $d = 6$, $e = 5$, and $f = 15$. The network and steps of analysis are

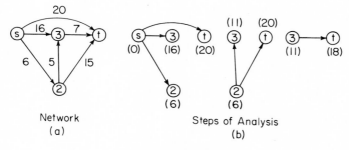

Network
(a)

Steps of Analysis
(b)

FIGURE 4-8

shown in Fig. 4-8(b). Thus $k'_t = 18$, which is the length of the shortest path. The path itself can be determined from: $k'_3 = k'_t - 7$; $k'_2 = k'_3 - 5$; $k'_s = k'_2 - 6$; hence, the shortest path is $(s; 2; 3; t)$.

3.2 Linear Programming Approach

The shortest route problem can also be formulated as a linear programming problem through the artifice of imposing an input flow of one unit into the source s and an output flow of one unit from the terminal t. Now, if the distances are interpreted as *costs* of transportation (per unit of flow) along the arcs, it is possible to write down a Transportation model of the problem in which it is desired to minimize the total cost of transporting the unit of input at s to the terminal t.

Such a Transportation model was discussed in §4.7 of Chapter 2, with the simple difference that there we were interested in *maximizing* the cost rather than minimizing it (this is because then we were interested in determining the *longest* route, which corresponded to the critical path in the network). We do not propose to repeat the discussion here, referring the reader to our previous exposition. But we wish to make four important remarks relative to the model. *First*, the matrix of Eq. (2-17) is the incidence matrix V defined above. Therefore, the L.P. formulation could be stated as:

Minimize $\mathbf{d}X$

subject to $VX = \mathbf{b}$,

where $\mathbf{b}$ is a vector of N entries, all of which are 0 except the first, which is equal to 1, and the last, which is equal to -1. *Second*, the optimum, when unique, corresponds to a spanning tree. *Third*, if the L-matrix (i.e., chain matrix) were known, the determination of the shortest route would be trivial indeed, since it reduces to $\min_i L_i\mathbf{d}$, where L_i is the ith row of L and $\mathbf{d}$ is a vector of the lengths of the arcs of the network.[†] And *fourth*, although the problem was stated as a Shortest Route problem, a reinterpretation in terms of network flows yields a Transshipment problem since, in effect, we do not necessarily choose to ship (the hypothetical unit commodity available at s) direct from s to t, but possibly prefer to "transship" it through some intermediate port (or ports).

3.3 Dynamic Programming Approach

We now present a dynamic programming formulation of the same problem and outline the algorithm of solution. This approach has the distinct advantage of straightforward generalization to the problem of finding the second best, third best, or in general the kth best route in a network.

Let d_{ij} be the "distance" between nodes i and j; $d_{jj} = 0$. Let u_i denote the shortest distance from node i to the terminal node N. Obviously, $u_N = 0$.

If the shortest route from i to N first passes through node j, then the path from j to N must be the shortest of all paths from j to N. That is,

$$u_i = \min_{j \neq i} (d_{ij} + u_j) \quad i = 1, \ldots, N - 1 \tag{4-1}$$

$$u_N = 0.$$

Equation (4-1) is a functional equation in which the optimal function u appears on both sides of the equal sign and cannot be solved in this form.

[†]Obviously, we must ignore any row i with some $a_{ij} < 0$.

To achieve the solution, define the sequence $\{u_i^{(k)}\}$ as follows: $u_i^{(k)}$ denotes the shortest path from i to N involving k links, $k \leq N - 1$. Therefore,

$$u_i^{(1)} = \min(d_{iN}) \quad i = 1, \cdots, N - 1 \tag{4-2}$$

with

$$u_N^{(1)} = 0.$$

Then,

$$u_i^{(2)} = \min_{j \neq i} (d_{ij} + u_j^{(1)}; u_i^{(1)}) \quad i = 1, \cdots, N - 1$$

with

$$u_N^{(2)} = 0;$$

and in general

$$u_i^{(k+1)} = \min_{j \neq i} (d_{ij} + u_j^{(k)}; u_i^{(k)}) \quad i = 1, \cdots, N - 1 \tag{4-3}$$

and

$$u_N^{(k+1)} = 0.$$

Iteration terminates either with the sequence $u_i^{(k+1)} = u_i^{(k)}$ for all i or when the new index $k + 1 = N - 1$, since in a network of N nodes it is not possible to have a route with more than $N - 1$ arcs and still be without loops. Finally, $u_i = \min_k \{u_i^{(k)}\}$.

For illustration, we shall again solve for the shortest route in the network of Fig. 4-8(a). Here, the maximum linkage is $k = 3$. Obviously,

$$u_s^{(1)} = 20; u_2^{(1)} = 15; u_3^{(1)} = 7.$$

Therefore,

$$u_s^{(2)} = \min[d_{s2} + u_2^{(1)}; d_{s3} + u_3^{(1)}; u_s^{(1)}]$$

$$= \min[21; 23; 20] = 20$$

$$u_2^{(2)} = \min[d_{23} + u_3^{(1)}; u_2^{(1)}]$$

$$= \min[12; 15] = 12$$

$$u_3^{(2)} = u_3^{(1)} = 7.$$

Finally,

$$u_s^{(3)} = \min[d_{s2} + u_2^{(2)}; d_{s3} + u_3^{(2)}; u_s^{(2)}]$$

$$= \min[18; 23; 20] = 18.$$

Therefore, the *length* of the shortest route is 18; the route itself is determined as before by moving backwards from the terminal node.

§4. MAXIMAL FLOW IN NETWORKS: THE LABELING PROCEDURE

A natural, though by no means elementary, question that comes to mind when studying networks is that of the maximal possible flow between two specified nodes of the network. The physical problem arises in almost every instance in which commodities—physical or otherwise—flow from a source s to a destination t. Thus, in communication networks we are interested in the maximal rate of *information* flow measured in bits per second; in a traffic network we are interested in the rate of traffic flow measured in number of cars per hour; etc. Interestingly enough, many physical nonflow problems can be *interpreted* in flow terms to great advantage with respect to insight into the behavior of the system and the ease of computation. We have just witnessed an example of such interpretation in the linear programming formulation of the Shortest Route problem, treated in §3.

Clearly, the problem of maximal flow is meaningful only if the branches of the network possess upper limits, called the *capacities* of the branches, denoted by $c(i, j)$, which no flow can exceed. Such a network is termed, naturally enough, a *capacitated* network. The capacity of a branch may be expressed in units or in units per unit time, according to the application.

Consider a network that possesses one source s and one terminal t; this is no restriction on the generality of the approach since we can always add a "master source" and a "master terminal" to any network of multiple sources and destinations. Such a network is shown in Fig. 4-9. For the

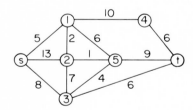

FIGURE 4-9 Undirected Capacitated Network

sake of concreteness of exposition, let the capacities of the various branches be as shown: e.g., $c(s, 1) = 5$; $c(1, 5) = 6$, etc. Notice that the network is undirected. The problem is to determine the maximal flow between s and t, assuming infinite availability at s.

We shall determine the maximal flow between s and t by the *labeling procedure* due to Ford and Fulkerson.[†] In spite of the extreme simplicity

[†]L. R. Ford and D. R. Fulkerson, *Flows in Networks*, Princeton University Press, Princeton, New Jersey, 1962.

of the procedure, its verbal description is rather awkward and, unfortunately, lengthy.

To start the procedure, assume any reasonable flow $\{f(i, j)\} \geq 0$. There is no question of feasibility, since $f(i, j) = 0$ for all (i, j) is certainly feasible. But one can usually do better than that. In this example, we start with the flow shown in Fig. 4-10. Each branch carries two numbers (f, r), where f is the flow through the branch, $f(i, j) \leq c(i, j)$, and r is the *residual capacity* $r(i, j) = c(i, j) - f(i, j) \geq 0$. Notice that branches $(s, 1)$, $(s, 3)$, $(2, 5)$, and $(3, t)$ are *saturated*, since $r = 0$ in all of them.

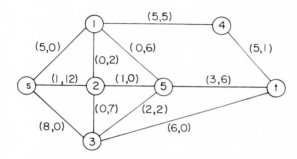

FIGURE 4-10   Feasible Flow

Inspection of Fig. 4-10 reveals that 12 more units *can* be transferred from s (which is assumed of infinite availability) to 2 because of the available residual capacity in arc $(s, 2)$. This fact is recorded by *labeling* node 2 with $(12; s)$: the first entry gives the quantity that *can* be transmitted and the second entry the origin of such flow.

When 12 units are available at node 2 it is obvious that two units and no more, due to the capacity of branch $(2, 1)$, can be transmitted to node 1, and seven units to node 3. Thus, nodes 1 and 3 can be labeled with $(2; 2)$ and $(7; 2)$ respectively. Thus, in labeling node j from node 2, $j = 1$ or 3, the flow is the minimum of two numbers: q_2, the quantity made available at node 2 by previously determined flow, and $r(2, j)$, the residual capacity in branch $(2, j)$. In general, if node j connects with node i, then node j can be labeled as (q_j, i), where

$$q_j = \min [q_i; r(i,j)] \text{ if } r(i,j) > 0. \tag{4-4}$$

Naturally, if $r(i,j) = 0$, node j *cannot* be labeled from node i. Proceeding in this fashion, the complete labeling of Fig. 4-10 is accomplished, as shown in Fig. 4-11. It is advisable to proceed in a systematic way such as: at stage k always start with the node bearing the smallest (or largest) number, label all nodes that connect with it which can be labeled and

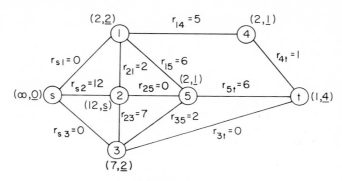

FIGURE 4-11

have not been labeled before (following the rule of Eq. 4-4), then proceed to the next higher (or lower) numbered node and repeat the process until:

1. All labeled nodes in stage k are exhausted. Then move to stage $k + 1$, i.e., to the nodes that have just been labeled from stage k.
2. The terminal t is labeled.

Once a node is labeled, it is not considered again for labeling.

When the terminal node t is labeled, which is termed a *"breakthrough,"* the cycle terminates and the flow can be increased by the amount q_t. Tracing backwards from t we can determine the chain that leads to such extra flow. The flow and residual capacities are then adjusted to reflect the increased flow, q_t, along all the branches of the chain.

The cycle of labeling and increasing the flow continues until no breakthrough is possible, i.e., until t cannot be labeled. This stage is reached in Fig. 4-12(c): nodes 2 and 3 are labeled but no other node can be labeled. The maximum flow has been achieved and is equal to the sum of the flow in all branches incident on either s or t; it is equal to 18 units.

The reader should consider Fig. 4-12(c) for a minute. Node t cannot be labeled in spite of the availability of an infinite supply at s, of 8 units at node 2 and 5 units at node 3, because, in a manner of speaking, all "roads are blocked" thereafter. That is, the residual capacities are all equal to zero for all arcs leading from these three nodes. It is an interesting observation that the *capacities* of these "blocked" branches add up to exactly 18 units.

This brings to the fore the notion of a *cut set*: it is a set of branches which, if "blocked," would prevent access from one node to another. In particular, since we are interested in flow between s and t, we focus our attention on cut sets that disconnect s and t and limit our discussion to them.

It is intuitively clear that if we enumerate all such cut sets (in Fig. 4-12(d) we illustrate with three other cut sets that separate s and t) and

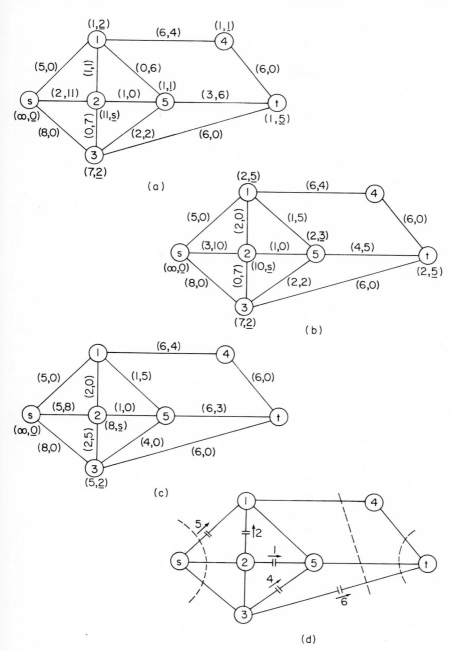

FIGURE 4-12 Steps of Iteration

calculate the sum of capacities of the branches comprising each cut set, $\Sigma_{(i,j)\in\mathcal{C}}\, c(i, j)$, we can determine the cut set $\mathcal{C}_{min}$ with the *minimal capacity*, denoted by C_{min} (there may be more than one such minimal cut-set). Since the minimal cut set $\mathcal{C}_{min}$, like any other cut set, would completely obstruct all flow from s to t if its branches were "blocked," it is impossible to transmit a flow from s to t larger than C_{min}, the capacity of $\mathcal{C}_{min}$.

We have just sketched a heuristic proof of the well-known *maximal-flow minimal-cut theorem* of networks: for any network, the value of the maximal flow from s to t is equal to the capacity of the minimal cut set of all cuts separating s and t.

Exhaustive enumeration of all cut sets is, of course, impractical for any large-size network. However, the minimal cut set can always be determined when *no breakthrough is possible* by restricting attention to those branches whose residual capacities equal zero. Conversely, if at any stage of the labeling process a cut set can be discerned whose capacity is equal to the flow into t, the optimum is achieved. This is a useful check when no breakthrough is possible.

In Fig. 4-12(c), such a minimal cut set can immediately be discerned: $\mathcal{C}_{min} = \{(3; t); (3; 5); (2; 5); (1; 2); (s; 1)\}$; and its capacity is 18 units. For illustration Fig. 4-12(c) has been redrawn in (d) with the branches of $\mathcal{C}_{min}$ actually cut to demonstrate the separation of s and t and the value of C_{min}.

§5. MAXIMAL FLOW IN NETWORKS: TABLEAU FORMAT

In §2 we defined three matrices that can be constructed from any network: V, B, and L. Conversely, given any one of these three matrices, a network can be drawn. Therefore, it must be apparent that all operations that can be performed on the diagrammatic representation of the network can also be performed in matrix format. This is sometimes advantageous especially for large networks where drawing the diagram is cumbersome. In this section we illustrate the labeling procedure in tableau format.

Again, we shall explain the theory relative to a numerical example. Consider again the network of Fig. 4-9. Since no flow occurs *into* s and no flow *out* of t, construct a tableau of 6 rows representing the six origins s to 5, and 6 columns representing the sinks 1 to t (see Fig. 4-13). Since the network is undirected, cells (i, j) and (j, i) will both have entries.

Each cell of the tableau contains three entries: the capacity of the branch, $c(i, j) = c(j, i)$, the flow in the branch, $f(i, j) = -f(j, i)$, and the residual capacity $r(i, j) = c(i, j) - f(i, j)$. Notice that if flow occurs from i to j then

$$r(j, i) = c(i, j) - f(j, i) = c(i, j) + f(i, j), \tag{4-5}$$

Stage	2	1	2	3	3	4
Label	(2,2)	(12,s)	(7,2)	(2,1)	(2,1)	(1,4)
Node	1	2	3	4	5	t
s	c=5, r=0, f=5	c=13, r=12, f=1	c=8, r=0, f=8			
1			c=2, r=2, f=0	c=10, r=5, f=5	c=6, r=6, f=0	
2	c=2, r=2, f=0		c=7, r=7, f=0		c=1, r=0, f=1	
3		c=7, r=7, f=0			c=4, r=2, f=2	c=6, r=0, f=6
4	c=10, r=15, f=−5					c=6, r=1, f=5
5	c=6, r=6, f=0	c=1, r=2, f=−1	c=4, r=6, f=−2			c=9, r=6, f=3

FIGURE 4-13   Tableau 1

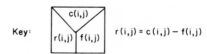

Key: $r(i,j) = c(i,j) - f(i,j)$

which corresponds to the intuitive notion of first "reversing" $f(i, j)$ and then consuming $c(j, i)$. In the tableau format, rows represent availabilities and columns destinations.

Figure 4-13 is constructed assuming the initial flow of the network in Fig. 4-10. The utility of the two topmost rows of the tableau will become clear presently. Since s is assumed of infinite availability, any cell along the s-row with $r(s, j) > 0$ defines a column j that can be labeled $(r(s, j); s)$. Such labeling is inserted in the appropriate cell along the row "Label." When all such columns have been labeled, the first *stage* is completed and the number 1 is inserted in the appropriate cells along the topmost row "Stage," and we proceed to the second stage of labeling.

For every labeled *column j* in stage 1, consider *row j* and label all *unlabeled* columns whose cells have residual capacities > 0 with the label $\{\min (q_j, r(j, k)); j\}$. When all such columns along row j are labeled, move to the next higher labeled *row*, i.e., a row corresponding to a labeled column in stage 1, and repeat the process. The cycle terminates when either a breakthrough is achieved, in which case column t is labeled, or no breakthrough is possible, in which case the optimal is achieved.

In Fig. 4-13, it is obvious that from s we can label only column 2 with $(12, s)$. This completes Stage 1.

Since *column 2* was labeled, we investigate *row 2*, bearing in mind that $q_2 = 12$. We can label column *1* with $\{\min (12, 2); 2\}$ and column *3* with $\{\min (12, 7); 2\}$. This completes Stage 2.

Stage	2	1	2	3	3	4
Label	(1,2)	(11,s)	(7,2)	(1,1)	(1,1)	(1,5)
Node	1	2	3	4	5	t
s	5; 0|5	13; 11|2	8; 0|8			
1			2; 3|-1	10; 4|6	6; 6|0	
2	2; 1|1		7; 7|0		1; 0|1	
3			7; 7|0		4; 2|2	6; 0|6
4	10; 16|-6					6; 0|6
5	6; 6|0	1; 2|-1	4; 6|-2			9; 6|3

FIGURE 4-14   Tableau 2

Stage	4	1	2		3	4
Label	(2,5)	(10,s)	(7,2)		(2,3)	(2,5)
Node	1	2	3	4	5	t
s	5; 0|5	13; 10|3	8; 0|8			
1			2; 4|-2	10; 4|6	6; 5|1	
2	2; 0|2		7; 7|0		1; 0|1	
3			7; 7|0		4; 2|2	6; 0|6
4	10; 16|-6					6; 0|6
5	6; 7|-1	1; 2|-1	4; 6|-2			9; 5|4

FIGURE 4-15   Tableau 3

Since *columns 1* and *3* were labeled in Stage 2, we start Stage 3 considering *row 1* first and then *row 3*. From row *1* we can label column 4 with {min (2, 5); *1*} and column 5 with {min (2, 6); *1*}; column 2 is already labeled. From row 3 no columns can be labeled either because they are already labeled or their $r(3, j) = 0$. This completes Stage 3.

Since *columns 4* and *5* were labeled in stage 3, we start stage 4 considering *row 4*. Remembering that $q_4 = 2$, it is immediately evident that column *t* can be labeled with {min (2, 1); *4*} = (1, 4). A *breakthrough* has occurred, and the flow in the various branches must be modified to reflect an increase of flow of $q_t = 1$ unit.

This has been done in Fig. 4-14. The cycle is repeated until the opti-

Stage		1	2			
Label		(8,s)	(5,2)			
Node	1	2	3	4	5	t
s	5; 0|5	13; 8|5	8; 0|8			
1			2; 4|-2	10; 4|6	6; 5|1	
2	2; 0|2		7; 5|2		1; 0|1	
3			7; 9|-2		4; 0|4	6; 0|6
4	10; 16|-6					6; 0|6
5	6; 7|-1	1; 2|-1	4; 8|-4			9; 3|6

Optimal

FIGURE 4-16   Tableau 4   Optimal

mum is achieved. The calculations are detailed in Figs. 4-14 to 4-16. Notice that in increasing $f(i, j)$, *the values of* $f(j, i)$ *are* decreased and $r(j, i)$ adjusted according to Eq. (4-5). Finally, the sum of flow in the *s-row* is equal to the sum of flow in the *t-column*.

§6. MAXIMAL FLOW IN DIRECTED NETWORKS

In the previous two sections we discussed the problem of maximal flow in undirected networks. This is the case in two-directional highways, two-way communication systems, pipelines, etc. However, in many instances flow can be accomodated only in one direction in all or some of the branches of the network. Examples of directed networks are: one-way communication channels (e.g., T.V. pictures can be sent from camera to receiver and not the opposite), power transmission systems (from high to low voltage), hydraulic systems (from pump to faucet), etc. In this section we will discuss briefly the problem of determining the maximal flow and minimal cut sets under such conditions.

The main difference between directed and undirected networks lies in the fact that for directed networks the capacity of a branch is defined > 0 in one direction only; the capacity in the reverse direction is $= 0$. Except for this difference, the treatment presented in the above two sections, §4 and §5, applies *in toto* to the case of directed networks.

To illustrate the procedure, we shall utilize again the same network of Fig. 4-9, but impose direction on the branches as shown in Fig. 4-17. The

FIGURE 4-17   Directed Network

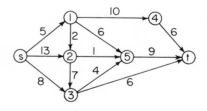

direction of flow is seen to be from a small numbered node to a larger one. Figure 4-18 presents the two steps of iteration required to determine the maximal flow. The latter is seen to be only 16 units; the reason for the reduction of flow from the undirected network is left as an exercise to the reader.

We remark that although the capacity of a branch (j, i) is $= 0$ in the direction $j \to i$, while $c(i, j) > 0$ in the direction $i \to j$, the *residual capacity* $r(j, i)$ may be different from zero at the various steps of iteration depending on the amount of flow, $f(i, j)$, from $i \to j$ since, by Eq. (4-5),

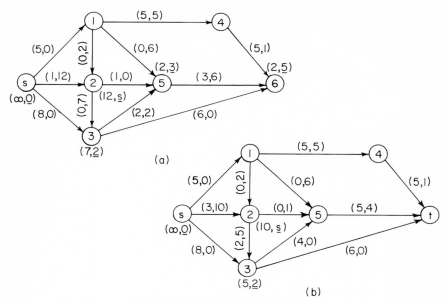

(a)

(b)

FIGURE 4-18   Steps of Iteration

$r(j, i) = 0 - (-f(i, j)) = f(i, j)$.   The labeling procedure is applied to such a branch as usual, i.e., with $r(i, j) = c(i, j) - f(i, j)$ and $r(j, i) = f(i, j)$.   Flow in the direction $j \rightarrow i$ corresponds to "reversing," either partially or totally, the existing flow.

As an illustration of such reversal of flow, consider again the network of Fig. 4-17 but with initial flow as shown in Fig. 4-19.   Since the flow $f(1, 2) = 1$, then $r(2, 1) = 1$.   Node 2 can be labeled from s.   Since $r(2, 1) > 0$, node 1 can be labeled from node 2.   Subsequently, nodes 4

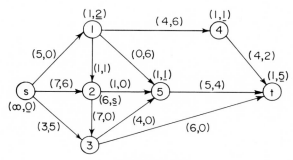

FIGURE 4-19

and then t can be labeled. Such flow would, in effect, reverse the unit flow from 1 to 2 and the *net flow* in branch $(1, 2)$ would be reduced to zero.

It is instructive to determine the minimal cut set of Fig. 4-18(b). Obviously, it is still $\mathcal{C}_{min} = \{(s, 1); (1, 2); (2, 5); (3, 5); (3, t)\}$. But now the capacity of branch $(1, 2)$ must bear a special interpretation if we are to obtain $C_{min} = 16$ units.

The cut set $\mathcal{C}_{min}$ separates the nodes of the network into two disjoint sets of nodes X and $\overline{X}$ which have no points in common and $\overline{X} = N - X$. Both X and $\overline{X}$ are connected subgraphs; X contains s and $\overline{X}$ contains t (see Fig. 4-20). Since the flow is from s to t, it is from X to $\overline{X}$; thus the

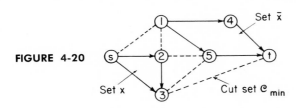

FIGURE 4-20

capacity of each branch of $\mathcal{C}_{min}$ is the capacity of flow *from X to $\overline{X}$*. Consequently, since $C(2, 1) = 0$ due to the imposed direction of flow, $C_{min} = 16$ units, and not 18 which would be obtained if the interpretation of flow from X to $\overline{X}$ is ignored.

§7. A TRANSPORTATION PROBLEM: NETWORK REPRESENTATION

Suppose it is required to transport a commodity from a number of sources $S_1, S_2, \ldots, S_m$ to a number of destinations $D_1, D_2, \ldots, D_n$. The commodity may be a produce, such as wheat, or machines such as new motors. Suppose that the total availabilities (where the availability at S_i will be denoted by a_i) are equal to or greater than the total demands, (where demand at destination D_j will be denoted by d_j); but transportation can take place along specified routes or channels of known capacities. Suppose for the time being that the problem is feasible—i.e., the capacity limitations are not such that it is impossible to satisfy the demand. What is the scheme of transportation that satisfies the demand at all destinations? Notice that in this formulation there is no question of minimizing the *cost* of such transportation.[†]

Represent the sources by nodes S_1 to S_m, destinations by nodes D_1 to D_n, and *permissible* routes by branches (S_i, D_j) with their respective

---

[†]Compare this formulation with the standard formulation of the Transportation problem of linear programming, where it is usually desired to satisfy demand *and* minimize cost.

capacities, $c(i, j)$, $i = 1, \ldots, m$; $j = 1, \ldots, n$; the result would be a *directed* network. If we still add a "master source" S, impose a capacity limit of a_i on branch (S, S_i), add a "master sink" D, and impose a capacity limit of d_j on branch (D_j, D), the problem can be *reinterpreted as a maximal flow* problem from S to D. The approach to the solution of this problem was given in §6 above.

To illustrate, consider the following Transportation problem. A commodity is available at three sources with $a_1 = 15$, $a_2 = 6$ and $a_3 = 3$ and is needed at four destinations with demands $d_1 = 2$, $d_2 = 7$, $d_3 = 9$, and $d_4 = 1$; permissible routes and capacities are as shown in the following tableau (see Fig. 4-21) with empty cells denoting unpermissible routes.

	D_1	D_2	D_3	D_4	a_i
S_1	$c(1,1)=3$	$c(1,2)=4$	$c(1,3)=10$		15
S_2		$c(2,2)=4$		$c(2,4)=1$	6
S_3	$c(3,1)=1$		$c(3,3)=2$		3
b_j	2	7	9	1	

FIGURE 4-21

The graphic representation is shown in Fig. 4-22(a); the fictitious master source S and master sink D are also added, and the fictitious routes between S, D, and the original nodes are shown dotted. The labeling technique can be applied to the network to yield the results shown in Fig. 4-22(b).

This type of Transportation problem can be given a linear programming

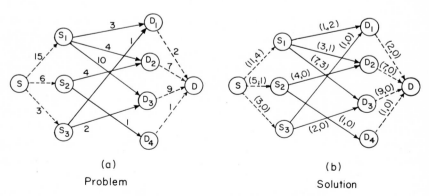

(a)
Problem

(b)
Solution

FIGURE 4-22   Transportation Problem I

formulation. Let X_{ij} denote the quantity shipped from source S_i to destination D_j. Then, we wish to

$$\text{Maximize} \sum_i \sum_j X_{ij} \qquad (4\text{-}6)$$

subject to:

capacity restrictions:	$X_{ij} \le c(i,j)$	all (i,j)
availability restrictions:	$\sum_j X_{ij} \le a_i,$	$i = 1, \dots m$
demand restrictions:	$\sum_{\substack{i \\ (i,j)\epsilon A}} X_{ij} = d_j.$	$j = 1, \dots n$

(4-7)

Except for the first set of capacity constraints, this would have been a straightforward standard Transportation problem with unit cost of transportation in all permissible cells and infinite cost in unpermissible cells. The capacity constraints complicate the problem to a considerable degree, and standard transportation algorithms such as Charnes' Stepping Stone method or the uv-method are no more applicable.

Of course, one can always fall back on general LP techniques such as the Simplex algorithm. The capacity constraints are "upper bounds" on the variables, and a method (due to Dantzig[†]) permits carrying out the Simplex calculations without explicit statement of such constraints. The network approach, however, is simpler, faster, and more transparent.

§8. THE MACHINE ASSIGNMENT PROBLEMS

There are several formulations of the Machine Assignment problem. Usually, the problem is presented in one of the following terms: there are n jobs (or tasks) to be performed and there are m machines (or individuals) available, with $n \ge m$.

1. If each machine can operate in a satisfactory manner only on a subset of the required jobs, what is the optimal assignment of jobs to machines *to complete as many jobs as possible*? Typical applications of this formulation are: assigning individuals to tasks, assigning berths to ships, assigning messages to communication channels, etc.

2. If each machine can operate on all the jobs but *with varying degrees of efficiency*—as measured, for example, by the machine's productivity per unit time—what is the assignment that *maximizes the minimum efficiency achieved*? This is a typical problem in assembly line production where semiskilled labor can be utilized on almost all the operations with varying levels of performance. The productivity of the whole line is the

[†] cf. footnote p. 170.

productivity of its weakest link or "bottleneck" operation. Hence, the interest in maximizing the minimum-productivity operation.

3. If each machine can operate on all jobs but with varying degrees of efficiency (or productivity), what is the assignment that *maximizes the total productivity of the machines available?* This problem arises in the context of machine shop loading, in the allocation of loads to carriers (airplanes, buses, trains, etc.), in assigning programs to computers, etc.

4. If a certain *order sequence of tasks is to be preserved* and all the machines can perform all the jobs *equally well*, determine the assignment that requires the minimum number of machines but still completes all jobs on or before a specified time *T*. (The set-up time and processing time for each job are known.) This formulation is typical of any "weakly ordered" set of jobs[†] in which, because of technological and other reasons, a known sequence is imposed on the manner in which jobs are to be performed. Such is the case, for example, in the majority of metal-working operations where it is not possible to tap a thread before the hole is drilled, in hospitals and clinical laboratories where analysis must precede diagnosis which, in turn, precedes operation, in the processing of films to produce prints, in road construction, etc.

Although it may be possible to formulate a generalized mathematical model that encompasses the above formulations as special cases, a great deal of insight into the nature of the problem would be lost, in addition to a possible loss in the computational aspects of arriving at a numerical answer. Therefore, we shall treat each of these four formulations individually.

8.1   m-Machines, n-Jobs, to Maximize the Number of Assignments Filled, $n \geq m$

Let i be the index of the machine number, $i = 1, \ldots, m$, and let j be the index of the job number, $j = 1, \ldots, n$. Let $a_{ij} = 0$ if machine i is "unfit" to work on the job j, and $a_{ij} = 1$ if it is fit. Let x_{ij} denote the assignment of machine i to job j. Clearly, x_{ij} is either 0 or 1. We wish to

$$\text{Maximize} \sum_{ij} a_{ij} \cdot x_{ij} \qquad (4\text{-}8)$$

subject to the restrictions that

$$\sum_{j} x_{ij} \leq 1 \quad \text{(one machine to no more than one job)}$$

and   (4-9)

$$\sum_{i} x_{ij} \leq 1 \quad \text{(one job to no more than one machine)}.$$

[†]A weakly ordered (or partially ordered) set is a set with a binary relation $\leq$, which satisfies the reflexive, antisymmetric, and transitive laws.

Obviously, since $n \geq m$, the maximum of Eq. (4-8) is m. The formulation in Eq. (4-8) and Eq. (4-9) is a special case of the Transportation model of linear programming. In fact, it is, in a manner of speaking, the most degenerate type since the assignment of any $x_{ij} = 1$ will always eliminate one row and one column.

Because of the special form of these restrictions, the question arises as to whether it is possible to reinterpret the problem and cast it in some other formulation that may lead to computationally efficient algorithms. Fortunately, the answer is yes. A network interpretation of this problem proves to be illuminating. To explain it, we consider the numerical example given in tableau form (Table 4-1). The 0 in any square denotes that

TABLE 4-1

Machines \ Jobs	1	2	3	4	5	6
1			0	0	0	
2		0			0	
3	0	0		0		0
4		0	0	0		0
5			0	0	0	0
6	0	0		0	0	0

$a_{ij} = 0$; for instance, machine 1 is "unfit" for jobs 3, 4, and 5, etc. It is immediately obvious that if we interpret the machines as sources and jobs as destinations, the "feasible" assignments can be represented by branches and the assignment of a machine to a job by "flow" along these branches. If we introduce a master source s and a master destination t and limit the capacities of branches $(s, 1), \ldots, (s, 6)$ as well as $(1, t), \ldots, (6, t)$ to unity, we achieve a representation of the problem in *directed network flow* terms (see Fig. 4-23). It is evident now that maximizing Eq. (4-8) is equivalent

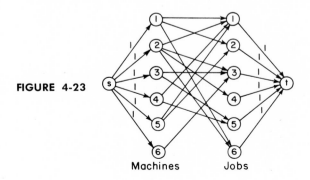

FIGURE 4-23

Machines   Jobs

to maximizing the flow from s to t. By applying the labeling procedure to either the tabular or graphical forms, the optimal can be determined. We chose to illustrate the procedure in tabular forms, starting with a feasible flow in Fig. 4-24(a) and reaching the optimal in (c). The circled 1's denote the assignments; the objective is to have a circled 1 in every column. An arrow at the bottom of any tableau indicates a column with no 1 in it (i.e., no assignment); the + along a row indicates the availability of a machine. Since the quantity involved is always unity the labeling notation is simplified by dropping the quantity and only indicating the source. In labeling

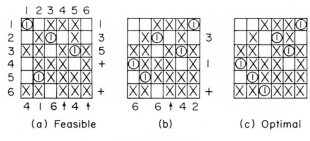

(a) Feasible   (b)   (c) Optimal

FIGURE 4-24

the tableaux above we proceeded from a small number line (row or column) to a high number line. The optimal is achieved when either all columns are "full" or breakthrough to an empty column is not possible.

The combinatorial character of this rather simple Assignment problem is interesting in its own right. Consider any job j: a number of machines are "candidates" to operate on it; the remaining machines are not "eligible." Suppose that we construct *for each job* the set of machines that are "eligible":

Job # j	1	2	3	4	5	6
Set of "fit" machines S_j	1, 2, 4, 5	1, 5	2, 3, 6	2	3, 4	1, 2

We can interpret the condition that every machine is assigned to, at most, one job as the condition to choose from each set S_j of "eligible" machines one machine to "represent" job j, i.e., to operate on it, so that the same machine does not "represent" any other job. This is known as the construction of a "Set of Distinct Representation," SDR for short. The question of whether every job *can* be represented in this SDR is answered by a theorem due to Hall:[†] *An SDR exists if and only if every union of k*

[†]P. Hall, "On Representatives of Subsets," *Journal of the London Mathematical Society*, Vol. 10, 1935, pp. 26–30.

jobs contains at least k distinct elements (machines). This theorem is intuitively obvious: if we had two jobs, j_1 and j_2, and both could be worked on only by *one* machine, it would be impossible to assign a *different* machine to each job. Two or more distinct machines must be eligible for such an assignment.

Hall's theorem gives the necessary and sufficient conditions for the *existence* of a solution; it does not tell us *how* to get it. But our discussion above indicates that the labeling technique is such an algorithm. In the simple numerical example we are dealing with, the SDR can be obtained by inspection:

Job # j	1	2	3	4	5	6
S_j	1, 2, 4, 5	1, 5	2, 3, 6	2	3, 4	1, 2
Representative Machine	4	5	6	2	3	1

Compare this SDR with the optimal solution obtained in the tableau above.

8.2 *n*-Machines, *n*-Jobs, to Maximize the Efficiency of the "Bottleneck" Operation

Let a_{ij} measure the "efficiency" (or productivity, or utility, etc.) of machine i on job j. For any given assignment A_k of machines to jobs, denote the minimum efficiency by $\min_{i,j \epsilon A_k} (a_{ij} \mid A_k)$. Our objective is to find the optimal assignment A^* in which

$$\min_{i,j \epsilon A^*} (a_{ij} \mid A^*) = \max_k \min_{i,j \epsilon A_k} (a_{ij} \mid A_k).$$

To fix ideas, suppose we are given 6 jobs and 6 machines and the "efficiency" table shown (Table 4-2). Consider the assignment A_1 given

TABLE 4-2

Machines	Jobs					
	1	2	3	4	5	6
1	1	3	2	⑥	1	1
2	④	2	0	8	3	1
3	8	1	1	2	0	⑨
4	0	5	4	⑧	8	2
5	2	6	⑨	0	2	4
6	3	②	1	6	7	1

by the circled cells which were arrived at by assigning machine 1 to the job with the highest "efficiency," assigning machine 2 to an *unassigned job* with the highest efficiency, and so on. One can see that

$$\min_{i,j \in A_1} (a_{ij} \mid A_1) = 2,$$

which is the "efficiency" of machine 6 on job 2.

The problem of shifting the assignments around in order to improve the objective is clearly a combinatorial problem. However, it can be cast in a network flow interpretation as shown in Fig. 4-25. Consider all *uncircled* cells whose "efficiency" is *greater than* $\min_{i,j \in A_1} (a_{ij} \mid A_1)$; these are isolated in Table 4-3. They represent the possible "routes" from the

TABLE 4-3

3		6		
4		8	3	
8				9
	5	4	8	8
	6	9		4
3			6	7

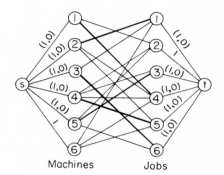

FIGURE 4-25

"sources" (machines) to "destinations" (jobs). The efficiency of any of these routes is > 2, by construction. Hence, if we eliminate the bottleneck assignment, i.e., drop branch (6, 2) from the network and try to achieve the same flow (of 6 "units") from s to t, we would arrive at a different assignment, say A_2, whose minimum "efficiency" is strictly greater than 2. This is an improvement. Repeating the process, we proceed from $A_1 \to A_2 \to \ldots \to A^*$.

In order to be able to achieve the same flow (6 units) from s to t it is clear that one must be able to label t from s with the branches of Fig. 4-25. It turns out that this is equivalent to demanding that the *uncircled* entries in the table of Fig. 4-25 admit exactly n (= 6) *independent cells*, i.e., cells such that no two lie along the same line (row or column). This is another interesting combinatorial problem which we do not propose to pursue any further; the interested reader is referred to specialized books on the subject and in particular to discussions of the König-Ergervary and Meyer theorems.

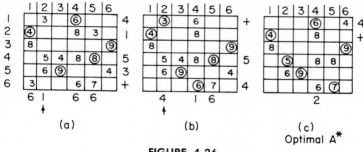

FIGURE 4-26

We proceed with the labeling procedure, starting with the above tableau to arrive at the optimal assignment shown in Fig. 4-26(c). Note that the "bottleneck" operation had "efficiency" 2 in the starting assignment A_1, and "efficiency" 4 in the final assignment A^*.

Finally, we remark that if the "efficiency" a_{ij} is equal to either 0 or 1, the problem, when feasible, reduces to the previous problem (§8.1).

8.3 *m*-Machine Categories, *n*-Job Types, to Maximize the Total Productivity

Let c_{ij} measure the productivity of machine category i when assigned to job type j. Let $x_{ij} \geq 0$ denote the number of machines of category i assigned to job type j. Suppose that machine category i contains a_i machines, and job type j contains b_j jobs. Then, it is required to

$$\text{Maximize} \sum_{ij} c_{ij} x_{ij} \tag{4-10}$$

subject to the restrictions that

$$\sum_j x_{ij} \leq a_i \qquad \text{(must not exceed availability of machine(s) category } i\text{)}$$

$$\sum_i x_{ij} \leq b_j \qquad \text{(must not assign more than what is needed for type } j\text{)}$$

This is a straightforward Transportation problem, which can be solved following the general algorithms for transportation-type problems.

Transportation problems bear the following network-flow interpretation, depicted in Fig. 4-27. The sources $S_1, S_2, \ldots, S_m$ have quantities $a_1, a_2, \ldots, a_m$ available. Each S_i is connected by a directed arc to all destinations $\{D_j\}$. The capacity of this connected branch is unlimited— the destinations $D_1, \ldots, D_n$ present demands $b_1, \ldots, b_n$. Introduce a master source s and a master destination t, and limit the capacity of branch (s, S_i) to a_i units and branch (D_j, t) to b_j units. Then the solution

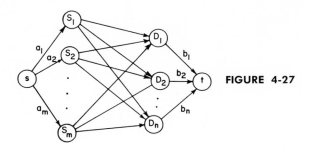

FIGURE 4-27

of the Assignment problem is equivalent to *maximizing the value of the flow* from s to t.[†] This is a *capacitated* network flow problem.

The steps of iteration are equivalent to the solution of a sequence of restricted network maximum flow problems in which the restricted network corresponds to the restricted primal problem of the primal-dual algorithm of linear programming. Unfortunately, space does not permit the detailed explanation of this technique. The interested reader is referred to chapter 3 of the book by Ford and Fulkerson, cited at the end of the chapter.

8.4 The Minimum Number of Machines to Accomplish a Set of Tasks

The formulation of the fourth type of Assignment problem as stated in the preamble to this section is rather general, and we specialize it to the following situation in this discussion. Suppose there are n jobs, each having the following pertinent data: the processing time, t_j; the set-up time, s_{jk}, between jobs j and k for all j and k; and the desired completion time, b_j. What is the minimum number of machines necessary to complete all jobs on time?

Knowledge of the completion time of job k, b_k, and the processing time, t_k, permits us to calculate the *starting* time, a_k. Now, any job j may fall in one of two categories: either its completion time falls prior to $a_k - s_{jk}$, or it falls after it. The two situations are represented diagrammatically by jobs j_1 and j_2, respectively, in Fig. 4-28. In the former case we state that task j_1 is a *permissible* precedent to task k, denoted by $j_1 < k$; in the latter case, task j_2 is *not* a permissible precedent. In general, we can *partially order* the jobs so that

$$j < k \quad \text{if and only if } b_j \le a_k - s_{jk} \tag{4-12}$$

assuming that $s_{jk} \le s_{ji} + s_{ik}$, which is a mild restriction.

[†]Compare this formulation with that of §7 in which it was desired to maximize the flow from s to t.

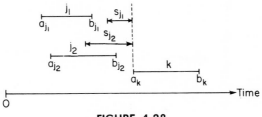

FIGURE 4-28

Obviously, the precedence relationship $<$ is transitive, i.e., if $i < j$ and $j < k$, then $i < k$. Moreover, we can represent the set of tasks by *nodes* and represent the $<$ relationship by a directed branch joining the two tasks. Therefore, a sequence of jobs $1, 2, \ldots, m$ can be performed by the same machine if and only if the following relationship holds among them:

$$1 < 2 < \cdots < m;$$

that is, if a *chain* exists between 1 and m in the resulting graph. The problem of finding the *minimum number of machines* is thus seen to be equivalent to *finding the minimum number of independent chains* in the directed networks. This, in turn, must be equal to the *maximum number of tasks, no two of which can be performed by the same machine.*

We have just stated a well-known theorem (due to Dilworth[†]) concerning the decomposition of graphs into independent chains. In effect, the theorem states that the minimum number of independent chains is equal to the maximum number of unrelated nodes (i.e., nodes i and j such that neither $i < j$ nor $j < i$). The problem of finding such *minimal decomposition* is our next order of business.

Consider the set of ten jobs given in Table 4-4. From the Gantt chart representation (Fig. 4-29), we can deduce the precedence relationships (ignoring transitive relations) shown below the figure. These relations are depicted in the graphs of Fig. 4-30. The graph in Fig. 4-30(a) can be

TABLE 4-4

Job Number	1	2	3	4	5	6	7	8	9	10
b_j	3	4	7	8	10	11	12	13	15	16
t_j	2.5	3.0	3.0	3.5	5.5	1.5	3.0	6.0	4.0	2.0
$a_j = b_j - t_j$	0.5	1.0	4.0	4.5	4.5	9.5	9.0	7.0	11	14

$$s_{ij} = 1.0 \text{ for } i,j < 5; \quad s_{ij} = 1.5 \text{ for } i,j > 5; \quad s_{ij} = 1.5 \text{ for } i \leq 5, j > 5$$

[†]R. P. Dilworth, "A Decomposition Theorem for Partially Ordered Sets," *Annals of Mathematics*, Vol. 51, No. 1, Jan. 1950, pp. 161–166.

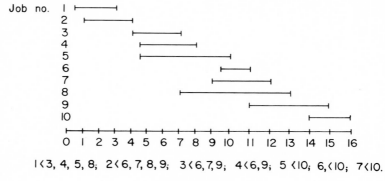

1 < 3, 4, 5, 8; 2 < 6, 7, 8, 9; 3 < 6, 7, 9; 4 < 6, 9; 5 < 10; 6, < 10; 7 < 10.

FIGURE 4-29

represented by the *bipartite* graph in Fig. 4-30(b), as well as by the table in Fig. 4-30(c). The graph in (b) is called "bipartite" because its nodes are divided into two subsets with arcs leading from nodes in one subset to nodes in the other. We can construct it from (a) by simply repeating the nodes *1* to *10* and designating one set of nodes, the sources, by $S = (x_1, \ldots, x_{10})$ and the other set, the terminals, by $T = (y_1, \ldots, y_{10})$. Each arc in (b) represents a precedence relationship *including transitive* precedence. For example, node x_1 connects with $y_3, y_4, \ldots, y_{10}$ since *1 < 3, 4, 5* and *8*, but *3 < 6, 7* and *9*, and *5 < 10*.

  The precedence relationships in (a) can be equally represented in tabular form, as shown in (c). The nodes are again represented vertically and horizontally along the margins, and a cell (x_i, y_j) is "permissible" if $i < j$. The permissible cells are indicated with heavy lines in the table. The bipartite graph of (b) gives only a few of the relations for the sake of avoiding cluttering of the diagram. The reader should satisfy himself that the bipartite graph in (b), when completed, as well as the table in (c), are two representations of (a).

  Suppose now that we wish to find a set of *independent branches* in the bipartite graph (b), i.e., a set of branches that do not have any common nodes. Such a set is given by the five heavy branches (x_1, y_3), (x_2, y_6), (x_3, y_7), (x_4, y_9) and (x_5, y_{10}). In the table they are represented by a set of independent cells, no two of which occupy the same line (row or column). Notice that in (a) two of these branches form a chain, *(1, 3, 7)*, of three nodes. The other branches form chains of two nodes each: *(2, 6)*, *(4, 9)* and *(5, 10)*. If we generalize the notion of a chain to include *one node chains*, we can say that the graph in (a) has been decomposed into *five* independent chains:

  [(*1, 3, 7*); (*2, 6*); (*4, 9*); (*5, 10*); *8*]

The node *8*, representing task *8*, is a one-node chain.

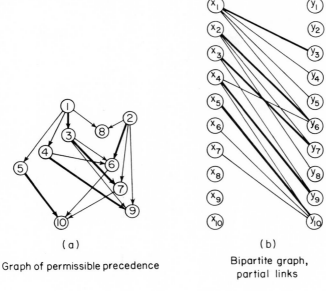

(a)

Graph of permissible precedence

(b)

Bipartite graph,
partial links

x_i \ y_j	1	2	3	4	5	6	7	8	9	10	
1			1								
2						1					
3							1				
4								1			
5									1	10
6										+
7										+
8											
9											
10											

6

(c)

Tabular form

FIGURE 4-30

Let ℓ_i be the number of links (i.e., arcs) in the ith chain, and let d be the number of chains into which the graph has been decomposed. In our example, $\ell_1 = 2$, $\ell_2 = \ell_3 = \ell_4 = 1$, $\ell_5 = 0$, and $d = 5$. Since each chain of r nodes contains exactly $r - 1$ links, we have, necessarily,

$$\sum_i \ell_i + d = n \tag{4-13}$$

where n is the number of nodes of the graph.

Of course, we are still interested in the *minimal decomposition* of the graph, because that determines the number of machines to be used. This is our original problem which started all this analysis. Have we obtained a minimal decomposition of the graph of (a)?

Before answering this question we make one further remark that has some theoretical significance. Suppose that instead of constructing an independent set of *branches* in (b), we set out to determine a *covering set of nodes*, i.e., a set of nodes whose removal would eliminate all arcs of (b). We could choose the set $(x_1, x_2, x_3, x_4, y_{10})$ or the set $(x_1, x_2, x_3, y_6, y_9, y_{10})$, etc. In the tabular form, a *cover* corresponds to a set of lines that "cover" every admissable cell—that is the origin of the word "cover." For example, the first covering set $(x_1, x_2, x_3, x_4, y_{10})$ corresponds to the first four rows and the last column. Notice that since a covering set C eliminates all arcs of the bipartite graph, any remaining nodes must be *unrelated*. This is evident from the two examples of covering sets considered. The cover $C_1 = (x_1, x_2, x_3, x_4, y_{10})$ leaves nodes 5, 6, 7, 8, and 9 "uncovered;" and these five nodes are certainly unrelated. The second cover $C_2 = (x_1, x_2, x_3, y_6, y_9, y_{10})$ leaves nodes 4, 5, 7, and 8 "uncovered," and these nodes are also unrelated. Let us denote the set of "uncovered" nodes by U. Then, obviously, the sum of the (number of nodes in C) + (the number of nodes in U) = (the total number of nodes). This verbal equation is usually written as

$$| C | + | U | = n. \tag{4-14}$$

We now come to the central result of this discussion. As a consequence of König's theorem, referred to previously, the maximum number of independent sets of branches is equal to the minimal number of covering nodes, i.e., $\Sigma_i \ell_i = | C |$. Consequently, by Eqs. (4-13) and (4-14), $d = | U |$; i.e., the minimum number of chain decompositions of a graph (which is what we are after, since it is equal to the minimum number of machines required) is equal to the maximum number of unrelated nodes.

The maximum number of independent branches is obtained when we have the maximum number of 1's in the table of Fig. 4-30(c). We treated this problem before and found that it could be solved in a straightforward manner by the labeling technique. It can be easily verified that the table given in Fig. 4-30(c) is the optimum since rows 5, 6, and 7, and column 10 can be labeled, but no breakthrough to any unlabeled column is possible.

Therefore, the minimal number of machines to perform the given ten tasks is *five*. In this optimal solution, the number of independent branches (in the bipartite graph) is 5; therefore, $d = 5$; hence the number of unrelated tasks $| U | = 5$. This is obvious since the cover corresponding to the optimal solution is rows 1, 2, 3, 4 (the unlabeled rows), and column 10 (the labeled column), leaving tasks 5, 6, 7, 8, and 9 "uncovered." These are all unrelated tasks, and five is the maximum number of unrelated tasks in the given set.

§9. THE JOB SEQUENCING PROBLEM

The assignment of machines to jobs can be viewed as the assignment of jobs to machines or, alternatively, the sequencing of jobs on the various machines. Slight reflection on our treatment in the previous section reveals that in the process of determining the minimal number of machines required we also assigned the machines to the jobs (and conversely) as well as *sequenced* the jobs on the various machines.

In this section we treat the special problem of *sequencing* jobs on machines, i.e., determining the order of processing of n jobs on each machine. The number of machines is assumed given, m. The following information is known relative to each job: its *processing time* on the various machines and its *start-lag* time and its *stop-lag* time between any two sequential operations. The nature of the jobs is such that they can be processed on any machine in any desired sequence, i.e., there are no technological or other relationships that determine a precedence relationship between any two distinct jobs. However, there are the usual restrictions on the processing of the same job on two sequential operations. For example, the job cannot complete the second operation before it has completed the first operation, etc. The objective of the analysis is to determine the optimal sequence where optimality is measured relative to the *completion time of all jobs*. That is, we wish to determine the sequence that minimizes the time of completion of all jobs, which is the completion time of the last job in the sequence.

The problem as formulated is rather restricted from a practical point of view. It overlooks several important features that are encountered in any real-life situation. For example, the number of jobs is assumed known and fixed. This is a *static* picture that rarely occurs. Also, there is an implicit assumption that all the jobs are *equally important* and we are required by the customer only to "finish as early as possible." This is also rarely the case; jobs, in practice, have various degrees of importance if not definite "due dates" at which time they must be completed, etc.

The fact is that the assumptions, implicit or explicit, are not half as restrictive as the available algorithms for solution. In particular, we know how to solve the above problem in the following case: if we have *only two machines*, call them A and B, and every job is processed on both machines in the same order; i.e., either all jobs start at A and finish at B, or the other way around. There are no algorithms for processing on three[†] or more machines except under the restrictive assumption of identical sequence on all machines, nor are there algorithms for even two *types* of machines with more than one machine per type. It seems that the combinatorial nature

---

[†]We shall presently see that, under certain conditions, the Three-Machine problem can be reduced to the Two-Machine problem and solved by the same algorithm.

of the problem has posed an insurmountable barrier, at least thus far, to analytical solution. At the end of this section we give a linear programming formulation of the n-Jobs, m-Machines problem, $m > 2$. The discussion of that model will reveal the computational difficulties involved.

9.1 The Two-Machine Sequencing Problem

It is assumed that there are only two machines, A and B, and that work flows through them in that order. Each job i has a vector (A_i, B_i), $i = 1, \ldots, n$, denoting the time on machines A and B, respectively. No set-up time between the various jobs is involved, or if a set-up time exists it is the same for job i irrespective of the preceding job and therefore can be lumped with the processing time and included in the estimates A_i and B_i. A job must be *completed* on machine A before it can be started on machine B. However, it may have to *wait* before being processed on B because of the occupancy of B with some other job.

Although the confinement of the model to only two machines is admittedly restrictive, it is by no means unrealistic. Several processing operations in the chemical, metal, and food industries can be considered as two-phase operations with storage facilities between the operations. Or, in a shop containing several operations, one may wish to concentrate on two "bottleneck" operations whose productivity controls the productivity of the whole shop, etc. In such applications, the model is of great assistance to the designer of the productive system.

The problem, then, is to determine a sequence $(i_1, \ldots, i_n)$ which will minimize the total elapsed time T. There are $n! = n(n - 1)(n - 2) \times \ldots \times 2 \times 1$ possible sequences, and exhaustive enumeration is out of all practical considerations for any real-life problem.

The algorithm proposed by Johnson[†] for the solution of this problem is extremely simple and can be summarized in the following four steps:

1. Find, for all jobs, the $\min_i (A_i, B_i)$.
2. If the minimum is A_k, i.e., the processing time of job k on machine A, schedule job k first.
3. If the minimum is B_k, schedule job k last.
4. Remove job k from the list of n jobs and repeat Steps (1) to (4).

The following numerical example should illustrate the procedure. Assume we have five jobs and their processing times are as given in Table (4-5). Applying Step (1), we find that the $\min_i (A_i, B_i) = B_2$; hence, according to Step (3), we schedule job 2 *last* i.e., it is sequence number 5, as shown. Job 2 is now deleted from the list of jobs and we are left with four jobs; to which we apply the Steps (1) to (4) to end up with the following optimal

---

[†] S. Johnson, "Optimal Two and Three-Stage Production Schedules With Set-up times Included," *Naval Research Logistics Quarterly*, Vol. 1, No. 1, 1954, pp. 61–68.

TABLE 4-5

Job	A_i	B_i	Sequence
1	8	7	3
2	4	①	5
3	9	5	4
4	6	10	2
5	2	3	1

sequence: 5-4-1-3-2. The total processing time of this optimal sequence is 31. For the sake of comparison, we plotted in Fig. 4-31 a Gantt chart with two sequences: the topmost is 1-2-3-4-5, i.e., the jobs are sequenced "as given," and the lower is the optimal sequence. The optimum saved 9 time units over the "as given" sequence.

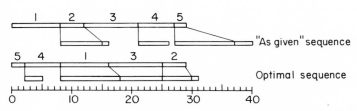

FIGURE 4-31 Gantt Chart of Two Sequences

It is interesting to note the following. *First*, there is *no idle time* on machine A in either sequence; in fact, machine A will be busy all the time under any sequence. This is an obvious consequence of the assumption that all jobs start at machine A. *Second*, machine B experiences some idle time which varies with the sequence adopted. It can easily be seen that the "goodness" of any sequence is measured directly by the *idle time on the second machine*. Therefore, the criterion for optimality could be equally stated in terms of the idle time on the second machine. *Third*, since in some actual life situations the second machine is not to be left idle, the duration of idle time on the Gantt chart can be taken as a measure of the in-waiting inventory that would be necessary to keep machine B busy all the time. Therefore, the optimal sequence scores on two accounts—it completes all the tasks as early as possible, and it reduces the required in-waiting inventory necessary to occupy machine B all the time. *Fourth*, the optimal sequence need not be unique; ties in step (1) of the algorithm will result in alternate optima. *Fifth*, it can easily be shown that jobs must be processed in the same sequence on both machines for minimum completion time.

Proof of Optimality of the Algorithm

We now show that the algorithm outlined in (1) to (4) above does indeed yield the optimal sequence. The proof is based on a simple but rather important property which we first describe verbally. Consider any sequence S_1 and suppose that we interchange the position of two jobs according to some specified rule to yield a different sequence S_2. If S_2 is "better" than S_1, then repetition of such interchanges must yield the optimum in a finite number of steps. This statement can be proved rigorously, but we take it as self-evident (or at least intuitively obvious). The proof of the optimality of the algorithm utilizes this property. First, we shall take any sequence, then exchange two jobs according to the rules of the algorithm (1) to (4) above and show that such exchange yields a better sequence.

Consider the Gantt chart shown in Fig. 4-32. Let A_i and B_i be defined as before; let X_j be the idle time on machine B between the $(j - 1)$st job

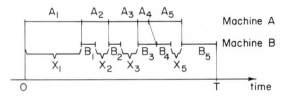

FIGURE 4-32

and the jth job in the sequence. For the rest of this discussion, j will denote the sequence number. Finally, let T be the total elapsed time. Consider machine B; obviously,

$$T = \sum_i B_i + \sum_i X_i.$$

Since ΣB_i is a constant, minimization of T is equivalent to the minimization of ΣX_i, a result which we already deduced. Also,

$$X_1 = A_1 \tag{4-15a}$$

while

$$X_2 = \max(A_1 + A_2 - B_1 - X_1; 0) = \max\left(\sum_i^2 A_i - B_1 - X_1; 0\right). \tag{4-15b}$$

The second equation stems from the fact that either the first job takes longer to process on the second machine than the second job on the first machine, as shown in Fig. 4-33, and then X_2 would be $= 0$ because there

FIGURE 4-33

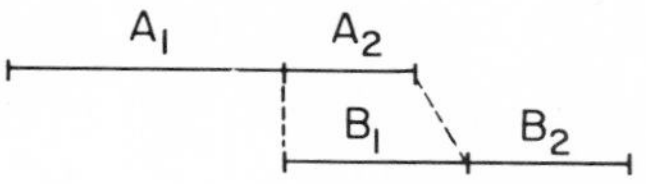

is no waiting involved, or B_1 is $< A_2$ and hence $X_2 > 0$ and is equal to $A_1 + A_2 - (X_1 + B_1)$.

Similarly,

$$X_3 = \max\left(\sum_1^3 A_i - \sum_1^2 B_i - \sum_1^2 X_i; 0\right), \tag{4-15c}$$

and so on to X_n. Now, adding the first two equations, then the first three equations, etc., we obtain the sums

$$X_1 = A_1 \tag{4-16a}$$

$$X_1 + X_2 = A_1 + \max\left(\sum_1^2 A_i - B_1 - X_1; 0\right)$$

$$= \max\left(\sum_1^2 A_i - B_1; A_1\right) \tag{4-16b}$$

$$X_1 + X_2 + X_3 = \max\left(\sum_1^3 A_i - \sum_1^2 B_i - \sum_1^2 X_i; 0\right) + \sum_1^2 X_i$$

$$= \max\left(\sum_1^3 A_i - \sum_1^2 B_i; \sum_1^2 A_i - B_1; A_1\right), \text{ etc.} \tag{4-16c}$$

In general,

$$\sum_1^n X_i = \max\left(\sum_1^n A_i - \sum_1^{n-1} B_i; \sum_1^{n-1} A_i - \sum_1^{n-2} B_i; \ldots; A_1\right)$$

$$= \max_{1 \le u \le n}\left[\sum_1^u A_i - \sum_1^{u-1} B_i\right] = D_n(S) \tag{4-16d}$$

where S is a given sequence. It is required to find the optimal sequence S^* such that

$$D_n(S^*) \le D_n(S) \quad \text{for all } S. \tag{4-17}$$

The four steps of the algorithm can be translated into the following rule: task i precedes task k if

$$\min (A_i, B_k) < \min (A_k, B_i), \tag{4-18}$$

and we are indifferent to sequence if equality holds. We now proceed to show that following this rule yields a "better" sequence.

Denote a sequence by "positions" numbered $1, 2, \ldots, j - 1, j, j + 1, \ldots, n$, and let S_1 be the sequence which has task k preceding task i in the jth position as shown schematically in Fig. 4-34. Let S_2 be the sequence

Positions	1	2	$\cdots$	j-1	j	j+1	j+2 $\cdots$	n
Tasks in S_1	1	2	$\cdots$	j-1	k	i	j+2 $\cdots$	n
Tasks in S_2	1	2	$\cdots$	j-1	i	k	j+2 $\cdots$	n

FIGURE 4-34

with i and k interchanged because the relationship of Eq. (4-18) holds for these two jobs. We wish to show that $D_n(S_2)$ is $< D_n(S_1)$. Let $K_u = \Sigma_1^u A_i - \Sigma_1^{u-1} B_i$; u denotes the position number. Let $K_u^{(1)}$ be evaluated for sequence S_1, and $K_u^{(2)}$ be evaluated for sequence S_2. From Eq. (4-16d)

$$D_n(S) = \max_{1 \le u \le n} \left(\sum_1^u A_i - \sum_1^{u-1} B_i \right) = \max_{1 \le u \le n} (K_u).$$

Notice that $K_u^{(1)} = K_u^{(2)}$ for $u = 1, 2, \ldots, j - 1, j + 2, \ldots, n$, but need not be equal for $u = j$ and $u = j + 1$. This may cause $D_n(S_1)$ to be different from $D_n(S_2)$. Clearly, if $\max (K_j^{(1)}, K_{j+1}^{(1)}) = \max (K_j^{(2)}, K_{j+1}^{(2)})$, then $D_n(S_1) = D_n(S_2)$, and it does not make any difference which sequence we adopt. However, if

$$\max (K_j^{(2)}; K_{j+1}^{(2)}) < \max (K_j^{(1)}; K_{j+1}^{(1)}), \tag{4-19}$$

then S_2 is preferred to S_1. But

$$K_j^{(2)} = \sum_1^j A_r - \sum_1^{j-1} B_r = K_{j-1} + A_i - B_{j-1}$$

since

$$K_{j-1}^{(1)} = K_{j-1}^{(2)} = \sum_1^{j-1} A_r - \sum_1^{j-2} B_r.$$

Also,

$$K_{j+1}^{(2)} = \sum_1^{j+1} A_r - \sum_1^j B_r = K_{j-1} + A_i + A_k - B_{j-1} - B_i$$

$$K_j^{(1)} = \sum_1^j A_r - \sum_1^{j-1} B_r = K_{j-1} + A_k - B_{j-1}$$

and

$$K_{j+1}^{(1)} = \sum_1^{j+1} A_r - \sum_1^j B_r = K_{j-1} + A_k + A_i - B_{j-1} - B_k.$$

Therefore, substituting in Eq. (4-19) we obtain: S_2 is preferred to S_1 if

$$\max (K_{j-1} + A_i - B_{j-1}; K_{j-1} + A_i + A_k - B_{j-1} - B_i)$$
$$< \max (K_{j-1} + A_k - B_{j-1}; K_{j-1} + A_k + A_i - B_{j-1} - B_k).$$

Subtracting $K_{j-1} - B_{j-1}$ from both sides of the inequality reduces it to:

$$\max (A_i; A_i + A_k - B_i) < \max (A_k; A_k + A_i - B_k).$$

Again, subtracting $A_i + A_k$ from both sides of the inequality reduces it to:

$$\max (-A_k; -B_i) < \max (-A_i, -B_k)$$

i.e.,

$$\min (A_i; B_k) < \min (A_k; B_i)$$

which is precisely the rule we adopted in selecting i to precede k. Hence, by consecutive application of the rule and the transitivity relationship mentioned above, we move, in a stepwise fashion, from S_1 to S^*, the desired optimum.

9.2 The Three-Machine Sequencing Problem

The statement of the problem is similar to the Two-Machine Sequencing problem above, except we have three processing times: A_i, B_i, and C_i for each job i, $i = 1, \ldots, n$, where C_i represents the processing time on the third machine.

This problem can be reduced to the Two-Machine Sequencing problem if one of the following two conditions holds:

$$\min \{A_i\} \geq \max \{B_i\} \text{ or}$$
$$\min \{C_i\} \geq \max \{B_i\},$$

TABLE 4-6

i	$A_i + B_i$	$B_i + C_i$
1	$A_1 + B_1$	$B_1 + C_1$
2	.	.
.	.	.
.	.	.
.	.	.
n	$A_n + B_n$	$B_n + C_n$

i.e., if processing time on the second machine is less than the processing time on either of the other two machines. In such a case, construct a table, such as Table 4-6, in which the time on the second machine is "lumped" with both times A_i and C_i. The algorithm for the Two-Machine problem is now applied to the time estimates in the two columns.

9.3 The Two-Machine Sequencing Problem with Arbitrary Start and Stop Lags

First we define explicitly what we mean by a "start lag" and a "stop lag." In certain instances, sequential operations can be overlapped so that the same job may be worked on in both operations at the same time. For example, in building a house, painting can start after some interior woodwork has been completed but before *all* the interior woodwork is finished. Or, if a "job" consists of several units, the second machine can start working on the job as soon as a few units are available, the minimum being one unit, etc. The *start lag*, a_i, measures the minimum time that must elapse between the *start* of the job on machine A and its *start* on machine B.

The *stop lag*, b_i, on the other hand, measures the minimum time that must elapse between the *completion* of the job on the first machine and its *completion* on the second machine. Considering the example of house building again, the frame construction cannot be completed before several days have elapsed after finishing the pouring of concrete.

In the problems of two-machine and three-machine sequencing discussed in §9.1 and §9.2 above, $a_i = A_i$ for all i, and $b_i = B_i$ for all i.

Let A_i, B_i, and X_i denote, as before, the time of processing job i on the first and second machines and the idle time between job i and the preceding job on the second machine, respectively. Let a_i and b_i be the start and stop lags for job i. Then we wish, by an argument similar to that given in §9.1 above, to

$$\text{minimize } C = \sum_{1}^{n} X_i.$$

The procedure to determine the optimal sequence is as follows:

a. Evaluate $(a_i - A_i)$ and $(b_i - B_i)$ for all i.

b. Determine $g_i = \max (a_i - A_i; b_i - B_i)$.

c. Form the set $M = (i \mid A_i < B_i)$; i.e., the set of jobs for which A_i is *strictly less than* B_i. For these, calculate $A_i + g_i$. Rank in order of *increasing* magnitude, $(1, 2, \ldots, k)$.

d. Form the set $N = (i \mid A_i \geq B_i)$. For these calculate $B_i + g_i$. Rank in order of *decreasing* magnitude; $(k + 1, \ldots, n)$.

e. The sequence $(1, 2, \ldots, k, k + 1, \ldots, n)$ is optimal.

The following numerical example illustrates the application of the procedure. Table 4-7 is divided into two parts by two closely spaced lines. The left part of the table is the data provided on the five jobs; the right part contains the computations following Steps (a) to (e) above. The representation of the optimal sequence in a Gantt chart form is shown in Fig. 4-35. Again we see that the jobs follow the same sequence on both machines. This is a restriction inherent in the present as well as in the previous formulation. The "independent sequence" Two-Machine Sequencing problem appears to be quite complex and has not been resolved to date.

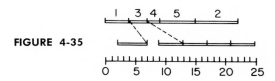

FIGURE 4-35

Proof of Optimality of the Algorithm

The proof that the above algorithm yields the optimal sequence is based on the same notion discussed in §9.1, namely, that if two jobs possessing the property outlined by the algorithm are switched around, a new sequence is obtained which is better. Invoking the transitivity property, the procedure must lead to the optimum in a finite number of steps. Because of its length, the proof shall be omitted.

9.4 The General Sequencing Problem: n-Jobs, m-Machines

The General Sequencing problem was given several linear programming formulations of which we present one. All formulations are *mixed linear programs*, i.e., linear programs in which some of the variables are constrained to be integers, for which an efficient computer program is still lacking. Hence, interest in these mathematical models is from a theoretical point of view, at least for the time being.

TABLE 4-7

					(a)		(b)	(c)			(d)			(e)
i	a_i	A_i	b_i	B_i	$a_i - A_i$	$b_i - B_i$	g_i	M	$A_i + g_i$	Rank	N	$B_i + g_i$	Rank	Sequence
1	1	4	3	5	−3	−2	−2	✓	2	1				1
2	4	7	1	4	−3	−3	−3				✓	1	5	5
3	4	3	6	4	1	2	2	✓	5	2				2
4	6	2	4	4	4	0	4	✓	6	3				3
5	4	6	3	4	−2	−1	−1				✓	3	4	4

Let x_{ij} denote the start time of job i on machine j; let t_{ij} be the processing time and α_{ir} be the fraction of job i completed on machine j before another job r is placed on the machine. Clearly, all above variables must be ≥ 0, but α_{ir} is distinguished by an added restriction: α_{ir} must be an *integer*. This stems from the desire to complete processing a job once it is assigned to a machine. Hence, α_{ir} is restricted to either 0 or 1. Finally, let z be the total manufacturing time, defined as the time of completion of the last job on the last machine (assuming start time $= 0$).

There are three types of linear constraints.

Technological Constraints. These take into account any precedence relationship due to technolognial or other reasons. For example, work on machine k for job i cannot start except after work on machine j has been completed:

$$x_{ik} \geq x_{ij} + t_{ij}. \tag{4-20}$$

Such constraints must be written for all jobs and all machines (taken in pairs) which occur along the job's route.

Noninterference Constraints. These constraints are to ensure that all of job i is completed on machine j before work on job r is started. $r \neq i$. Pick an appropriate large number, T, e.g.,

$$T = \sum_{i,j} t_{ij} \text{ ; clearly,}$$

$$|x_{ij} - x_{rj}| < T.$$

Also,

$$\left.\begin{aligned}
(x_{ij} - x_{rj}) + \alpha_{ir}(T + t_{rj}) &\geq t_{rj} \\
(x_{rj} - x_{ij}) + (1 - \alpha_{ir})(T + t_{ij}) &\geq t_{ij}.
\end{aligned}\right\} \tag{4-21}$$

Equations (4-21) are central to the model and their thorough understanding is essential. *Together*, they ensure the noninterference requirement. Consider machine j: either job i precedes job r, or vice versa. If job i precedes r, then $x_{ij} < x_{rj}$; in particular we want it to be at least t_{ij} units *before* x_{rj} (Fig. 4-36) and thus allow enough time to process all of job i. In effect, this is what the second inequality of Eq. (4-21) says: $\alpha_{ir} = 1$ and x_{rj} must be $\geq x_{ij} + t_{ij}$. Under these conditions, the first inequality is automatically satisfied. However, if *job r precedes i* on machine j, $\alpha_{ir} = 0$, and x_{ij} must be $\geq x_{rj} + t_{rj}$ in order to allow job r to be processed in its entirety. This is what the first restriction of Eqs. (4-21) now imposes; the second restriction is satisfied automatically.

FIGURE 4-36

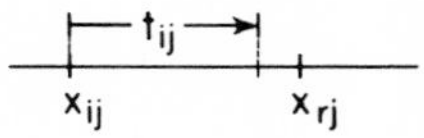

Thus, whether job i precedes job r, or r precedes i, on machine j, the two restrictions of Eqs. (4-21) cannot be *simultaneously* satisfied unless the first job is run complete. Of course the decision on whether i precedes r or vice versa is determined by the linear programming optimizing procedure. Equations such as Eqs. (4-21) must be written for each machine and for each pair of jobs.

Completion Time Constraint. The time of completion must be at least equal to the start time of the last job on the last machine plus its processing time,

$$z \geq x_{ij} + t_{ij} \tag{4-22}$$

for all i and all j.

The objective function is, as before,

$$\text{minimize } z. \tag{4-23}$$

A few remarks on this formulation: for n jobs on m machines we require $n(m-1)$ equations like Eq. (4-19), $n(n-1)m/2$ equations like Eqs. (4-21) and mn equations like Eq. (4-22); a total of $n(nm + m - 1)$ equations in $2mn + 1$ unknowns (excluding slack variables). This is a formidable computational problem, the magnitude of which can be gleaned from the following example. If $n = 100$, and $m = 10$, we have a *mixed* linear program of 100,900 equations in 2,000 unknowns, and shops giving rise to such values of n and m are considered small shops!

The objective function of Eq. (4-23) is to minimize the total manufacturing interval. None of the usual and important costs of manufacturing are explicitly recognized, nor are the due dates on the individual jobs. These latter can be taken into account, however, at the expense of further increasing the size of the program. The set-up time, and the costs involved therein, are excluded from the treatment, or else the set-up time of each job is assumed fixed and independent of the preceding jobs. The jobs are assumed to be independent of each other, i.e., each job is an entity in itself, and therefore the jobs need not be processed in the same order on the m machines. Finally, the formulation considers each job as an entity which *cannot be split* among two or more machines of the same kind, nor can it be overlapped on two sequential operations. Both considerations are practical everyday occurrences, and dismissing them detracts from the practicality of the model.

§10. THE LINE BALANCING PROBLEM

Henry Ford is usually credited with the assembly line, a feat of engineering of a type rarely attained, in that it has had enormous impact on production as well as on the society in which the production has taken place.

The assembly line is based on the following, rather simple, idea. The end product can always be decomposed into assemblies, subassemblies, sub-subassemblies, and so on down the line until the level of commodities is reached. Now, if this backward subdivision is reversed, we can define the operations, henceforth referred to as "*tasks*," which are necessary to group the commodities into components, the components into subassemblies, etc., until the finished product is reached. From now on we shall focus our attention on these tasks, always assuming that all other necessary factors of production (such as material, machines, and men) are available.

Let us assume that each task is well defined, and that its duration is a given number which is independent of other tasks and of the person (or machine) performing the task. Assume that task i has duration t_i.

It is clear that while some of the tasks can be performed at almost any point of the production line (e.g., fitting the name plate on the cover of a motor), the majority of the tasks must be performed in a specific sequence relative to some other task (for example, a hole has to be drilled before it is tapped). This gives rise to technological precedence relationships similar to those previously encountered in PERT-CPM,[†] the Materials Planning Problem,[‡] and the Assignment problem in §8.4 of this chapter. Such precedence relationships can be expressed as a matrix M in which an entry $m_{ij} = 1$ indicates that task i precedes task j, and $m_{ij} = 0$ indicates the absence of such precedence relationship. Obviously, the "precede" relationship is transitive; namely, if i precedes j and j precedes k, then i precedes k. This can be written: if $i < j$ and $j < k \rightarrow i < k$. As usual, the matrix can be translated into a network representation. Since it is impossible to find a task i which precedes itself, the network contains no cycles and no self-loops.

Since every product passes through the same sequence of production, a product is completed only when it leaves the last operation. Consequently, if q is the rate of production in units of product per unit of time, and c denotes the *cycle time*, i.e., the time between units completed, in units of time per unit of output, then, clearly,

$$c = 1/q.$$

For example, if the production of toasters is at the rate of $q = 8$ toasters per hour, clearly, $c = 60/8 = 7.5$ minutes per toaster.

For the time being, we shall assume that the assembly line is designed to produce *one* product. Later on we shall investigate the effects of waiving this and other assumptions.

[†]See §4 of Chapter 2.
[‡]See Problem 13 in Chapter 2.

A possible formulation of the Line Balancing problem is the following. Given a cycle time c in units of time per unit of output, a set of tasks $I = \{1, \ldots, i, \ldots, n\}$ to be performed according to specified precedence relationships (the latter are given by a precedence matrix M) and given the processing time t_i of task i, it is desired to find the minimum number of groupings of these tasks into stations so that: (1) each station consumes no more time than the cycle time c, and (2) the precedence relationships are respected.

This is not the only possible formulation of the Line Balancing problem. Here is another formulation: given the above information, minimize the cycle time c for a given number of stations J subject to the precedence requirements and to the condition that the total time at any station does not exceed c.

We shall concern ourselves with the first formulation of the problem.

10.1 A Network Model

A more formal statement of this formulation of the Line Balancing problem may be as follows. Given a finite set I, a partial order $<$ defined on I, a positive real-valued function t defined on I, and a number c, find a collection of subsets of I, $(S_1, \ldots, S_J)$, satisfying the following five conditions.

1. $\bigcup_{j \in J} S_j = I$ (the set of stations accounts for all the tasks).
2. $S_i \cap S_j = \phi$ (the empty set), $i \neq j$ (any task is in one and only one station).
3. $t(S_j) = \Sigma_{x \in S_j} t_x \leq c, j = 1, \ldots, J$ (station time $\leq$ cycle time).
4. if $x < y$ and $x \epsilon S_i$ and $y \epsilon S_j$, then $i \leq j$ (maintain precedence relationship).
5. $\Sigma_{j=1}^{J} [c - t(S_j)]$ is minimized. (Minimize total idle time.)

Several formulations, and particularly integer linear programming models, have been advanced for the solution of this problem. Unfortunately, they suffer from severe computational limitations and are considered, at least for the time being, interesting theoretical, rather than practical, formulations. This state of affairs naturally led to the prolification of *heuristic* approaches to the problem. These are "common sense" approaches which do not guarantee optimality of the answer obtained but, hopefully, improve on current answers. Later on we shall briefly describe one such heuristic approach, but first, we discuss a network formulation of the problem.

The mathematical model we are about to discuss transforms the objective function stated in (5) above to a *Shortest Route* problem in a network. This network is constructed in a very special way. In fact, it will turn out that we need not even evaluate the "length" of the various arcs in the network since it is sufficient to determine the route with the smallest *number* of arcs. This is an immediate consequence of the fact that minimizing the total idle time is equivalent to minimizing the *number* of stations. For,

$$\sum_{j=1}^{J} [c - t(S_j)] = \sum_{j=1}^{J} c - \sum_{j=1}^{J} t(S_j)$$

$$= Jc - \sum_{i\epsilon I} t_i$$

$$= Jc - \text{a constant.}$$

As we shall presently see, each arc through the network represents a station. The "length" of the arc represents the idle time in that station. Hence minimizing the "length" of a path is equivalent to minimizing the number of arcs along that path.

Now, to the construction of the network. Let A (for assignment) be a collection of tasks that can be processed without prior completion of any other tasks and in any order that satisfies the precedence relation *without regard to the cycle time c*. Let A_i, $i = 0, 1, \ldots, r$ be the entire collection of assignments with $A_0 = \phi$, the empty set, and $A_r = I$. Let the processing time of each assignment be the sum of the processing times of the tasks in the assignment,

$$t(A_0) = 0$$

and

$$t(A_i) = \sum_{x \epsilon A_i} t_x \qquad i = 1, \ldots, r.$$

Let assignment A_i be represented by node i. An arc (i, j) is directed from node i to node j if and only if

$$A_i \subset A_j \ (A_i \text{ is a proper subset of } A_j)$$

and   (4-24)

$$t(A_j) - t(A_i) \leq c \ (\text{the added tasks in } A_j \text{ constitute a feasible station}).$$

Obviously the difference $c - [t(A_j) - t(A_i)]$ measures the idle time in a station comprising the tasks that are in A_j but not in A_i. Note that the existence of an arc (i, j) therefore means the existence of a feasible station; the idle time in that station is given by

$$\ell(i, j) = c - [t(A_j) - t(A_i)] \geq 0. \qquad (4-25)$$

No arc enters node 0, the node corresponding to the empty assignment A_0, and no arc leaves node r, the node corresponding to the set of all tasks.

Then the resulting network is a finite directed network containing no loops from node 0 to node r on the set of all assignments.

Let us now interpret a path from 0 to r. Each arc represents a feasible station, and the sequence of these feasible stations starts with the empty set and terminates at the set I of all tasks. Consequently, a path of J arcs represents the allocation of the tasks to J feasible stations. According to our discussion above, the optimal allocation minimizes the length of the path, or equivalently, minimizes the number of arcs in the path.

Consider for a moment this latter objective. In any finite directed network with no loops such as we have here, if there are $r + 1$ nodes, then there is a maximum of r arcs from 0 to r (because any connected graph of N nodes contains at least one tree of $N - 1$ arcs). This may be taken as an upper bound on the number of stations. In practice, r may be quite large, and a much smaller upper bound is already available, viz., the number of tasks n. Consequently $J \leq n$.

A lower bound on the number of stations is equally available,

$$J \geq \left[\sum_{i \in I} t_i / c \right]$$

where the square brackets indicate the smallest integer larger than or equal to the quantity between brackets.

Consequently, we have

$$\left[\sum_{i \in I} t_i / c \right] \leq J \leq n.$$

A slight reflection reveals that the problem of finding the path with the smallest number of arcs between nodes 0 and r can be accomplished simultaneously while constructing the network itself. This path can be found as follows:

1. Start at node 0 and construct all arcs from it. There will be an arc $(0, i)$ joining nodes 0 and i if $t(A_i) \leq c$. The nodes reached are called first stage nodes.
2. Suppose the sth stage nodes are reached for the first time. For every node j among the sth stage, construct an arc to node k if the conditions of Eq. (4-24) are satisfied, namely, if $A_j \subset A_k$ and $\ell(j, k) = c - [t(A_k) - t(A_j)] \geq 0$.

The nodes reached from stage s for the first time are called the $(s + 1)$th stage nodes. Repeat Step 2 with $s = s + 1$ until node r is reached for the first time.

If the network is constructed in this manner, it is obvious that a path from node 0 to any other node will have the least number of arcs possible. Therefore, when node r is reached for the first time, any path traced from node 0 to node r represents an optimal solution.

To complete the description of the algorithm, it is necessary to devise an efficient method for generating the assignments. Undoubtedly several approaches can be, and have been, suggested. The following seems to be an efficient procedure which has the properties that:

1. No assignments are duplicated in the generation process.
2. Only assignments are generated.
3. Every assignment is generated.

The empty assignment, A_0, is considered as the first assignment. The tasks without any predecessors, as given by the precedence relationships, are placed in Stage 1. Call this set of elements D. Each subset of D is an assignment. At the end of Stage 1, the elements of D are deleted from the list of tasks.

We now define the terms "immediate following" of assignment A as a task which is an immediate successor of at least one task in A and is not preceded by any task not in A. For example, suppose that the tasks are constrained by the following precedence relationships:

Task:	1	2	3	4	5	6	7	8	9	10	11
Immediate Successors:	2, 7	3, 4	5	6	—	9	8	6	10	—	7, 10

Consider the assignment $A \equiv \{1, 2, 3\}$. Tasks 4 and 5 are "immediate followers" of A but task 7 is not because while it is true that 7 is the immediate successor of task 1 which is in A, task 7 must be preceded by 11 which is *not* in A.

In general, for any assignment A in Stage s, the undeleted immediate followers of A are placed in a list called $F(A)$. For *each subset* $f \subseteq F(A)$, $f \cup A$ is an assignment placed in stage $s + 1$. When all assignments in stage s have been considered, each element in $F(A)$, for all A in Stage s, is deleted and the process is repeated for stage $s + 1$. When all tasks are deleted the construction is complete.

As an illustration of the above algorithm, consider the nine tasks given in Table 4-8.

TABLE 4-8 Data For The Illustrative Problem

Task	Processing Time	Immediate Successors
1	5	2, 3
2	3	4, 6
3	4	7, 5
4	6	8
5	5	9
6	3	8, 9
7	4	9
8	5	—
9	3	—

The assignment generation process is shown in Table 4-9. For example, at Stage 2, one of the assignments generated contains the tasks (1, 2). Its undeleted immediate followers are tasks 4 and 6. So, in Stage 3, from the assignment elements (1, 2) the assignments generated are {1, 2, 4}, {1, 2, 6} and {1, 2, 4, 6}. The complete network of assignments is given in Fig. 4-37.

TABLE 4-9 Assignment Generation

Stage	Deleted Elements	Assignment Number	Assignment Elements	Assignment Time	Undeleted Immediate Followers
0		0	Empty set	0	1
1	1	1	1	5	2, 3
2	2, 3	2	1, 2	8	4, 6
		3	1, 3	9	5, 7
		4	1, 2, 3	12	4, 5, 6, 7
3	4, 5, 6, 7	5	1, 2, 4	14	
		6	1, 2, 6	11	
		7	1, 2, 4, 6	17	8
		8	1, 3, 5	14	
		9	1, 3, 7	13	
		10	1, 3, 5, 7	18	
		11	1, 2, 3, 4	18	
		12	1, 2, 3, 5	17	
		13	1, 2, 3, 6	15	
		14	1, 2, 3, 7	16	
		15	1, 2, 3, 4, 5	23	
		16	1, 2, 3, 4, 6	21	8
		17	1, 2, 3, 4, 7	22	
		18	1, 2, 3, 5, 6	20	
		19	1, 2, 3, 5, 7	21	
		20	1, 2, 3, 6, 7	19	
		21	1, 2, 3, 4, 5, 6	26	8
		22	1, 2, 3, 4, 5, 7	27	
		23	1, 2, 3, 4, 6, 7	25	8
		24	1, 2, 3, 5, 6, 7	24	9
		25	1, 2, 3, 4, 5, 6, 7	30	8, 9
4	8, 9	26	1, 2, 4, 6, 8	22	
		27	1, 2, 3, 4, 6, 8	26	
		28	1, 2, 3, 4, 5, 6, 8	31	
		29	1, 2, 3, 4, 6, 7, 8	30	
		30	1, 2, 3, 5, 6, 7, 9	27	
		31	1, 2, 3, 4, 5, 6, 7, 8	35	
		32	1, 2, 3, 4, 5, 6, 7, 9	33	
		33 = r	1, 2, 3, 4, 5, 6, 7, 8, 9	38	

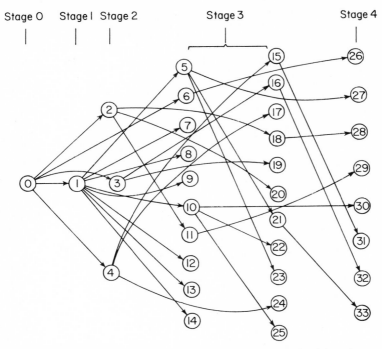

Stage 0   Stage 1 Stage 2   Stage 3   Stage 4

FIGURE 4-37   The Network of Assignments, A_i, of Table 4-9

Given a cycle time $c = 12$, the calculations needed to find the shortest route, or equivalently, a route containing a minimal number of arcs are shown in Table 4-10.

Starting at node 0, there are arcs to Assignments 1, 2, 3, 4, and 6. Hence, nodes 1, 2, 3, 4, and 6 can be reached with one arc. Then from node 1, there are arcs to Assignments 5, 7, 8, 9, 12, 13, and 14. So these nodes can be reached with two arcs. The procedure is carried out until Assignment 33($= r$) is reached for the first time. It is reached for the first time from node 21 with a path containing four arcs. These four arcs represent the four stations into which the nine tasks are to be grouped:

Station 1: $A_1 = \{1\}$

Station 2: $A_5 - A_1 = \{2, 4\}$

Station 3: $A_{21} - A_5 = \{3, 5, 6\}$

Station 4: $A_{33} - A_{21} = \{7, 8, 9\}$.

At this juncture, the reader may wonder, and rightly so, about the computational efficiency of this algorithm. Table 4-11 summarizes the

TABLE 4-10   **Shortest Route Calculations**

Minimum Total Number of Arcs to the Nodes	Node Number	Arcs to Nodes
0	0	1, 2, 3, 4, 6
1	1	5, 7, 8, 9, 12, 13, 14
1	2	11, 18, 20
1	3	16, 19
1	4	15, 17, 24
1	6	26
2	5	21, 23, 27
2	7	
2	8	10
2	9	
2	12	
2	13	
2	14	
2	11	22, 25, 29
2	18	28
2	20	
2	16	32
2	19	
2	15	31
2	17	
2	24	
2	26	
3	10	30
3	21	33
3	23	
3	27	
3	22	
3	25	
3	30	
3	29	
3	28	
3	32	
3	31	
4	33	

TABLE 4-11

Number of Tasks	Number of Assignments	Time in Seconds
9	33	<1
14	710	3
17	6320	360

computational experience of Gutjahr and Nemhauser.[†] They used the IBM 7090 which was programmed in FAP, but no attempt was made to optimize the computer program. It is easily seen that computing time and capacity requirements increase at a very rapid rate. Products with such small number of tasks are small assemblies which, in all probability, would show a small economic advantage of the *optimal* solution over any *good* allocation of tasks to stations. On the other hand, assemblies which involve tens or even hundreds of tasks, and which would greatly benefit from such analysis, are evidently well beyond the scope of computing feasibility.

The picture is even more discouraging than the above computing difficulties indicate. Task times are almost always assumed to be deterministic whereas in reality they are probabilistic with an unknown distribution function. Using time distributions, the line balancing procedure should establish a cycle time which balances the costs of finishing a percent of the finished parts in repair stations at the end of the line against the costs of idleness due to long cycle time.

In practice, it is often true that additional constraints are imposed on the problem. Examples are:

1. Some tasks must be performed in the *same* work station for reasons of quality control, special job classifications, time getting into and out of work positions, or the availability of special tools.

2. Some tasks require team work (two or more operators).

3. The requirement that the cycle time c must be $\geq \max_{i \in I} \{t_i\}$ can sometimes be overcome by permitting more than one operator to perform those tasks where $t_i > c$.

4. The dynamic nature of the product causes the design, as well as production methods, to change. These, in turn, may change the task times and upset any "balance" previously determined.

As a matter of fact, the design of a production line involves several factors; only one of these is line balancing. Other relevant factors not considered in line balancing, but which impinge on the design problem, are: in-waiting inventories between operations, down time, scrap, learning, employee absenteeism and turnover, etc.

Finally, we assumed always that the product is unique. In many applications, however, the same line is used for a number of different styles or product designs, which are introduced in batches or even perhaps in apparently random mixed sequence. The line balancing procedure is thus greatly complicated by the requirement that model-mix sequences be accommodated efficiently. While a number of different approaches have

---

[†]A. L. Gutjahr and G. L. Nemhauser, "Algorithm for the Line Balancing Problem," *Management Science*, Vol. 11, No. 2, November 1964, pp. 308–315.

been proposed and applied it should be observed that the problem has barely been examined and much work remains. In particular, the problem of optimizing the product sequences to an assembly line is in practice a source of continuing grievance.

10.2 A Heuristic Approach

We now describe a heuristic approach to the solution of the same Line Balancing problem treated above.

Consider the immediate-precede matrix M, and from it construct a complete precedence matrix M' which has an entry 1 in position ij if task i occurs prior to task j.

Calculate "positional weights" which are the sum of the time values for each specific task and all tasks which must follow. Let w_i be the positional weight of task i, and the vector $W = <w_1, w_2, \ldots, w_n>$ the vector of such positional weights. Obviously, W is easily obtained from

$$W = (I_n + M') \cdot <t_1, t_2, \ldots, t_n>$$

where I_n is the identity matrix of rank n.

Sort the task weights $\{w_i\}$ in a list of decreasing weights $w_{[1]} \geq w_{[2]} \geq \ldots \geq w_{[n]}$ where the subscript now indicates the ranked task. Assign tasks to stations in the following fashion.

1. Assign the task corresponding to $w_{[1]}$ to first station S_j, starting with $j = 1$.

2. Calculate $\ell = c - t_{[1]}$.

3. Assign the task corresponding to $w_{[2]}$ to S_j if the following two conditions are satisfied:

(a) The immediate predecessor of the task is in S_j;

(b) $t_{[2]} \leq \ell$.

Otherwise go to $w_{[3]}, w_{[4]}, \ldots, w_{[n]}$, repeating with each task the same test.

4. When the task corresponding to $w_{[n]}$ has been analyzed following Step (3), return to Step (1) but with a new station S_{j+1}. Continue Steps (1) to (4) until all tasks are assigned to stations.

To illustrate the procedure, we apply it to the nine tasks given in Table 4-8. The complete matrix $(I_n + M')$, as well as the vector $<t_i>$ are given in Fig. 4-38. It is easy to deduce the vector of positional weights W, also shown in Fig. 4-23. Consequently, the ranked positional weights are as given in Table 4-12.

TABLE 4-12

Task	1	2	3	4	6	5	7	8	9
Positional Weight	38	20	16	11	11	8	7	5	3
Immediate Predecessor	—	1	1	2	2	3	3	4, 6	5, 6, 7

```
     1  2  3  4  5  6  7  8  9
 1 [ I  I  I  I  I  I  I  I  I ]  [5]   [38]
 2 [    I  I  I     I        I  I]  [3]   [20]
 3 [       I     I     I        I]  [4]   [16]
 4 [          I              I   ]  [6]   [11]
 5 [             I                 I] [5]   [8]
 6 [                I        I  I ]  [3]   [11]
 7 [                   I        I ]  [4]   [7]
 8 [                      I      ]  [5]   [5]
 9 [                            I ]  [3]   [3]

     The matrix (I_n + M')        Vector  Vector
                                   <t_i>   <w_i>
```

$$\text{FIGURE } 4\text{-}38$$

The execution of the four steps of the procedure, assuming $c = 12$, is given in Table 4-13. Consequently,

$$S_1 = \{1, 2, 3\}$$
$$S_2 = \{4, 6\}$$
$$S_3 = \{5, 7, 9\}$$
$$S_4 = \{8\}.$$

If the reader compares this result with that previously obtained with the network model above, it becomes immediately obvious that the same optimum was reached. This is, however, fortuitous and cannot be guaranteed with such a heuristic approach.

TABLE 4-13

Station	Task i	Positional Weight	Immediate Predecessor	Task Time t_i	Cum Station Time $\Sigma_{S_i} t_i$	Unassigned Time $\ell = 12 - \Sigma_{S_i} t_i$
1	1	38	—	5	5	7
	2	20	1	3	8	4
	3	16	1	4	12	0
2	4	11	2	6	6	6
	6	11	3	3	9	3
3	5	8	3	5	5	7
	7	7	3	4	9	3
	9	3	5, 6, 7	3	12	0
4	8	5	4, 6	5	5	7

COMMENTS AND BIBLIOGRAPHY

§1. Several excellent books on the theory of Graphs and on Networks have recently appeared. We cite in particular:

BERGE, C.   *The theory of Graphs and Its Applications*, New York, Wiley, 1962.

ORE, O.   *Theory of Graphs*, Providence, R. I., American Mathematical Society, Colloquium Publications, Vol. 38, 1962.

§2. Several of our definitions and representation of graphs by matrices follow:

SESHU, S. and M. B. REED   *Linear Graphs and Electrical Networks*, Reading, Mass., Addison-Wesley, 1961.

Another early work on the connection between linear programming and the theory of electrical networks is:

DENNIS, J. B.   *Mathematical Programming and Electrical Networks*, The Technology Press, Cambridge, Mass., Massachusetts Institute of Technology, 1959.

§3. The combinatorial approach to the Shortest Route problem is due to:

VAJDA, S.   *Mathematical Programming*, Reading, Mass., Addison-Wesley.

The Linear Programming approach with imposed flow is due to:

CHARNES, A. and W. W. COOPER   "A Network Interpretation and a Directed Subdual Algorithm for Critical Path Scheduling," *Journal of the American Institute of Industrial Engineers*, Vol. 13, No. 4, pp. 213–218.

For a primal-dual linear programming approach to the same problem see:

DANTZIG, G. B.   *Linear Programming and Extensions*, Princeton, N. J., Princeton University Press, 1963.

The Dynamic Programming approach is based on a paper by:

BELLMAN, R. and R. KALABA   "On the kth Best Policies," *Journal of the Society of Industrial and Applied Mathematics*, Vol. 8, No. 4, 1960.

§4. The Labeling Procedure and the theorem of maximal flow-minimal cut are due to Ford and Fulkerson. An excellent reference to their work on which we drew heavily in this and subsequent sections, is their book:

FORD, L. R. and D. R. FULKERSON   *Flows in Networks*, Princeton, N. J., Princeton University Press, 1962.

§8. The four formulations of the Machine Assignment problem are due to Ford and Fulkerson; see reference cited above. It is interesting to compare their approach to the solution of the Assignment problem by the "Hungarian method" due to Kuhn:

KUHN, H. W.   "The Hungarian Method for Assignment Problem," *Naval Research Logistics Quarterly*, Vol. 2, 1955, pp. 83–97.

Systems of Distinct Representation have been studied by P. Hall, and others. The interested reader may consult:

HALL, P.   "On Representatives of Subsets," *Journal of the London Mathematics Society*, Vol. 10, 1935, pp. 26–30.

HOFFMAN, A. J. AND H. W. KUHN.   "On Systems of Distinct Representatives, in Linear Inequalities and Related Systems," *Annals of Mathematics Study*, Vol. 38, Princeton, N. J., Princeton University Press, 1956, pp. 199–206.

and references cited therein.

The solution of the Bottleneck Assignment problem is due to:

GROSS, O. "The Bottleneck Assignment Problem," Santa Monica, Calif., The RAND Corporation, Paper P-1630, March 6, 1959.

The Transportation Problem of Linear Programming, or the Hitchcock-Koopmans problem, has been extensively studied and programmed for digital computation. A complete discussion is included in:

HADLEY, G. "Linear Programming," Reading, Mass., Addison-Wesley, 1962.

The Chain Decomposition principle is due to Dilworth:

DILWORTH, R. P. "A Decomposition Theorem for Partially Ordered Sets," *Annals of Mathematics*, Vol. 51, 1950, pp. 161–166.

Also see other references to the subject in Ford and Fulkerson's book.

§9. The algorithm for the Two-Machine Sequencing problem is due to:

JOHNSON, S. "Optimal Two- and Three-Stage Production Schedules with Set-Up Times Included," *Naval Research Logistics Quarterly*, Vol. 1, 1954, pp. 61–68.

The algorithm for the Two-Machine Sequencing problem with start and stop lags is due to:

MITTEN, L. G. "A Scheduling Problem," *Journal of the American Institute of Industrial Engineers*, Vol. 10, No. 2, 1959, pp. 131–135.

An algorithm for the solution of the case of n-jobs on $m \geq 3$-machines assuming no passing (i.e., jobs are processed in the same sequence on all m-machines) is given in:

DUDEK, R. A. AND O. F. TENTON, JR. "Development of M-stage Decision Rule for Scheduling n-Jobs through m-Machines," *Operations Research*, Vol. 12, No. 3, May–June, 1964.

The more general Integer Linear Programming formulation is based on:

MANNE, A. S. "On the Job Shop Scheduling Problem," *Operations Research*, Vol. 8, No. 2, 1960, pp. 219–223.

Two other Integer LP formulations of the same problem are due to:

BOWMAN, E. H. "The Schedule-Sequencing Problem," *Operations Research*, Vol. 7, No. 5, 1959, pp. 621–624.

WAGNER, H. "An Integer Linear Programming Model for Machine Scheduling," *Naval Research Logistics Quarterly*, Vol. 6, No. 2, 1959, pp. 131–140.

§10. The following four references give different mathematical programming formulations, e.g., integer Linear programming and dynamic programming formulations, for the Line Balancing problem.

BOWMAN, E. H. "Assembly Line Balancing by Linear Programming," *Operations Research*, Vol. 8, No. 3, May–June 1960, pp. 385–389.

HELD, M. AND R. M. KARP. "A Dynamic Programming Approach to Sequencing Problems," *Journal of the Society of Industrial and Applied Mathematics*, Vol. 10, No. 1, March 1962, pp. 196–210.

HU, T. C. "Parallel Sequencing and Assembly Line Problems," *Operations Research*, Vol. 9, No. 6, November–December 1961, pp. 841–848.

WHITE, W. W. "Comments on a Paper by Bowman," *Operations Research*, Vol. 9, No. 2, March–April, 1961, pp. 274–276.

The particular network model presented in this section is due to:

GUTJAHR, A. L. and NEMHAUSER, G. L.   "An Algorithm for the Line Balancing Problem," *Management Science*, Vol. 11, No. 2, November 1964, pp. 308–315.

The heuristic approach discussed is due to:

HEGELSON, W. B. and D. P. BIRNIE   "Assembly Line Balancing Using the Ranked Positional Weight Technique," *Journal of Industrial Engineering*, Vol. 13, No. 6, November–December 1961, pp. 394–398.

Also see:

MANSOOR, E. M.   "Assembly Line Balancing—An Improvement on the Ranked Positional Weight Technique," *Journal of Industrial Engineering*, Vol. 15, No. 2, March–April 1964, p. 73.

For other heuristic approaches to the Line Balancing Problem, see:

HOFFMAN, T. R.   "Optimization Criteria and Assembly Line Balancing by Digital Computer," paper presented at the 7th Annual Meeting of the Institute of Management Science, October 1960.

A recent review of analytical as well as heuristic approaches to the Line Balancing problem is given in:

KILBRIDGE, M. D. and L. WESTER   "A Review of Analytical Systems of Line Balancing," *Operations Research*, Vol. 10, No. 5, September–October 1962, pp. 626–638.

EXERCISES

1. Determine the maximal flow between nodes 1 and 13 of the following network, interpreting the number on each arc as the arc's capacity in the direction shown. Indicate the minimal cut-set.

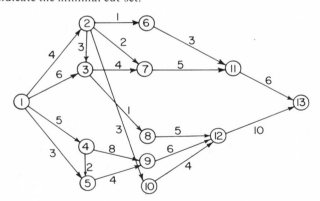

2. Determine the maximal flow in the network of Problem 1 assuming the arcs to be undirected and the arc capacities as shown. Comment briefly. Indicate the minimal cut-set.
3. If the numbers on the arcs of the network of Problem 1 are interpreted as lengths of the arcs rather than capacities, determine the shortest route between nodes 1 and 13.

4. We have always assumed that only the arcs of a network are capacitated. In practice, of course, the *nodes* may also be capacitated. If d_i is the maximum allowable flow in node i, this means that the total flow *into i* must not exceed d_i. Show how to reduce the problem to one in which only arcs are capacitated. (Hint: Replace each capacitated node by two uncapacitated nodes joined by a single capacitated arc.)

5. Consider the following network.

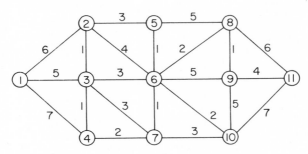

(a) Interpreting the number on each arc as the capacity of the arc, determine the maximal flow between nodes 1 and 11.

(b) Construct the dual graph of the network assuming nodes 1 and 11 as the source and terminal, respectively.

Verify that the shortest distance between the dual source and terminal is equal to the capacity of the minimal cut-set in the solution of Part (a).

6. Show how to reduce a Flow problem involving a number of sources and terminals to one in which there is only one source and one terminal.

7. Multiterminal networks are defined as networks in which any two nodes among a given set of nodes may serve as source and terminal. An example would be a telephone network in which messages may originate at any node (city) and terminate at any other node (city).

For any given pair of nodes, i_0, j_0, a straightforward application of the labeling procedure yields the desired maximal flow between these two nodes. Consequently, show that one must solve $\binom{n}{2}$ Maximal Flow Problems in the case of undirected networks, and $n(n - 1)$ Maximal Flow problems in the case of directed networks.

8. Consider the following "goose neck" network with the capacities shown on the arcs. Determine the maximal flow between any two nodes i and j, $i, j = 1$, ..., 8. Then construct a *tree* connecting the 8 nodes in which the arcs have

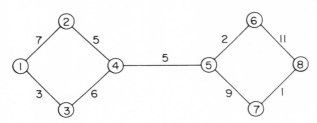

capacities equal to the maximal flows obtained and such that the maximal flow between any two nodes is given by the capacity of one arc of the tree.

9. Solve the Maximal Flow problem of Exercise 5 by constructing the matrix of arc capacities and following the matrix method.

10. Solve for the maximal flow of Exercise 8 by the matrix method.

11. Find all cuts between nodes 1 and 8 of the network of Exercise 8 and verify that the maximal flow between nodes 1 and 8 is equal to the capacity of the minimal cut.

12. Consider a Personnel Assignment problem in which six individuals are to be assigned to six jobs in such a way as to maximize the minimum productivity. Assume that the individual productivities on the various jobs are given by the following matrix. What is the optimal assignment?

Men \ Jobs	1	2	3	4	5	6
1	16	25	15	13	11	7
2	11	8	8	41	30	29
3	19	12	18	16	8	9
4	14	12	13	23	16	17
5	16	16	5	30	12	20
6	18	15	25	11	15	0

13. It is desired to award government contracts to the maximum number of contractors such that no contractor is awarded more than one contract. Unfortunately, some contractors are unqualified to handle certain jobs. Different contractors are qualified for different sets of jobs. In the following matrix, an 0 indicates unfitness for the job and the absence of an 0 indicates that the contractor is qualified for this particular job. Determine the maximum number of contracts that can be awarded.

Contracts \ Jobs	1	2	3	4	5	6	7	8	9	10
1	0		0	0		0		0	0	0
2	0	0		0		0	0			0
3		0	0		0		0		0	
4	0				0			0		
5		0				0				
6	0				0					
7				0		0			0	0
8		0						0	0	
9			0		0		0	0	0	
10	0			0				0	0	0

14. Construct the optimal sequence and draw the corresponding Gantt chart for the following set of jobs to be worked on two machines.

Job		1	2	3	4	5	6
Time on Machine A	A_i	6	5	10	6	1	4
Time on Machine B	B_i	6	1	4	10	2	5

What is the minimum time required for completing all jobs?

15. Consider the set of jobs of the previous problem and assume the following start lags (a_i) and stop lags (b_i)

Job	1	2	3	4	5	6
Start Lag a_i	2	1	3	5	0	2
Stop Lag b_i	2	2	1	5	1	3

Determine the optimal sequence. Draw a Gantt chart of the optimal sequence and compare it with the total completion time of the "as given" sequence.

16. Consider the set of jobs in Problem 14. There are 6! = 720 different sequences, but only 5! = 120 sequences starting with job 5. Enumerate these 120 sequences and draw a histogram of their durations. Could you make any generalization concerning the number of *different durations* as opposed to the number of different *sequences?*

17. The Sequencing problem is usually formulated with the objective of minimizing the total elapsed time. Suggest at least two other criteria and suggest, if you can, approaches to the solution of the Sequencing problem under these new criteria.

18. If the set-up time of a job is dependent on its position in the sequence, the problem of finding the optimal sequence changes its character in a radical fashion: The total elapsed time is now the sum of idle time, processing time *and* set-up time. Both idle time and set-up time are functions of the sequence.

Show that the One-Machine Sequencing problem can be cast as a "traveling salesman's" problem, and formulate a linear programming model for it.

19. Suggest a heuristic approach to the solution of the Sequencing problem in which we do not make the "no passing" assumption and in which the set-up time of any job is a function of its position in the sequence.

20. It is desired to find the minimum number of work stations on a production line to perform the following set of tasks and maintain the precedence relationships shown.

Task	1	2	3	4	5	6	7	8	9	10	11
Duration	2	4	3	5	6	4	2	5	3	3	6
Immediate Precedor	—	—	—	1, 2	3, 4	3	5	4, 7	6, 7	7, 8	10, 9

(a) Construct the immediate-precede matrix M
(b) Draw a directed network to represent the precedence relationships

   (c) Construct the complete precedence matrix M'
   (d) Solve for the optimal (i.e., minimum) number of stations assuming a
       cycle time $c = 10$.
   (e) Use a heuristic approach (either the one described in the text or one of
       your own) to reach an allocation.
   Comment briefly.

21. Suggest a heuristic approach for the solution of the Assembly Line problem
    when more than one product will be processed on the line in an unpredictable
    fashion.

22. It is desired to maximize the number of assignments of personnel to jobs
    given the following matrix of "unsuitability," where a 0 denotes that the
    individual concerned is unsuitable for the designated job. What is the maxi-
    mum number of such assignments?

Men \ Jobs	1	2	3	4	5	6
1	0		0		0	
2		0	0		0	
3			0		0	0
4	0	0		0		0
5	0			0	0	
6		0	0		0	0
7	0		0	0		0

23. Consider the Assignment problem of 22, and suppose now that it is known
    that the men can work on the various jobs with varying efficiencies as shown
    in the following matrix. Determine the assignment which maximizes the *total*
    efficiency.

Men \ Jobs	1	2	3	4	5	6
1	2	12	4	5	10	3
2	3	10	8	9	4	7
3	5	3	6	20	14	8
4	9	6	11	7	8	8
5	1	4	9	11	6	15
6	16	11	3	3	10	12
7	18	6	14	8	7	5

24. Determine the optimal sequence of performing the following six jobs on three
    machines, where optimality is relative to the minimum total duration criterion.

Job Number	1	2	3	4	5	6
Time on Machine A	8	11	7	13	12	5
Time on Machine B	4	5	2	4	4	5
Time on Machine C	14	9	9	6	6	10

25. The simplest sequencing problem is perhaps that of sequencing n jobs on one facility (e.g., a computer, a heat-treating oven, a single transportation facility such as a truck, etc.). In order to render the problem nontrivial, assume that job i has due date d_i and processing time a_i, $i = 1, \ldots, n$. A penalty cost, p_i, is incurred per unit time of delay beyond the due date d_i; no cost is incurred if job i is completed on or before d_i.

Show that for an optimal sequence job i precedes job j if and only if $p_i/a_i > p_j/a_j$, assuming all $d_i = 0$ (the present).

Then show that even when job splitting is permitted (into two or more parts to be processed separately by some facility) there exists an optimal schedule in which no job is split.[†]

26. Consider the problem of sequencing n tasks on a single facility in which task i consumes a_i time units for processing, and in which penalty is *continuously* accumulated at a rate p_i per unit time from the present and is *discounted* at a rate α from the present, such that the present value of a unit penalty at time t in the future is given by $e^{-\alpha t}$.

If the jobs are numbered in the order of their service, show that the present value of the total penalty costs is given by

$$ C = \sum_{i=1}^{n} p_i \left[1 - \exp \left(-\alpha \sum_{j=1}^{i} a_j \right) \right] / \alpha. $$

Then deduce that two consecutive jobs i and $i + 1$ should be switched around if

$$ p_{i+1} e^{-\alpha a_{i+1}} / [1 - e^{-\alpha a_{i+1}}] < p_i e^{-\alpha a_i} / [1 - e^{-\alpha a_i}]. $$

Finally, show that as $\alpha \to 0$ this condition reduces to the undiscounted condition for optimality in the previous problem.[‡]

27. A more general sequencing problem than those posed in the above two exercises considers $m \geq 2$ processing facilities. The cost structure is as follows. If job i is processed on facility j a set-up cost b_{ij} is incurred. Moreover, there is a penalty for late completion: if job i is completed at time t_{ij} on facility j, then a penalty cost $p_i(t_{ij})$ is incurred; $i = 1, \ldots, n; j = 1, \ldots, m$.

We shall make the important assumption that the *order* in which the different jobs are *selected for sequencing is fixed*. This leaves the choice of the facility on which the job is to be performed as the only decision. This, in turn, determines the sequence of performing the n jobs on the m facilities. Under this assumption, it is always possible to number the jobs such that when job i is considered for sequencing on the facilities, jobs 1 through $i - 1$ have already been sequenced (or, alternatively, jobs $i + 1$ through n have been sequenced).

Give a dynamic programming formulation of this Sequencing problem.

Apply the above dynamic programming theory to determine the optimal

[†]McNaughton, *Management Science*, October 1959.
[‡]Rothkopf, *Management Science*, January 1966.

sequence of $n = 5$ jobs on $m = 2$ identical machines. The pertinent data is as follows:

$b_{ij} = b$, a constant for all i, j.
$p_i(t_{ij}) = p_i t_{ij}$, linear in completion time t_{ij}
$a_{ij} = a_i$, since both machines are identical.
Order of selection: The numerical order given

Job Number	1	2	3	4	5
a_i		1	2	3	2	4
p_i		5	7	6	3	4

[Hint: Let $f_i(t_1, t_2, \ldots, t_m)$ be the minimum cost of completing jobs 1 through i such that facility j is free at time $t_j, j = 1, \ldots, m.$][†]

28. Consider the general problem of sequencing n jobs on m machines, in which each job i accumulates a penalty p_i per unit time from the present to the time of its completion. Assume that the route as well as the processing times of each job are known.

Formulate an L.P. model to minimize the total penalty incurred.

[†]Rothkopf, *Management Science*, January 1966.

CHAPTER 5 / Networks of Queues

§1. INTRODUCTION

Networks are encountered in a context different from that discussed in the previous chapter; namely, we encounter them as networks of queues or waiting lines.

Waiting lines arise either when stochastic demand is imposed on a facility for its "services," or when the behavior of the facility itself is probabilistic in nature, or both. Queues of people are encountered forming in front of cafeteria-type restaurants, queues of automobiles at turnpike toll booths, queues of airplanes at landing runways especially during foul weather when schedules are not adhered to, queues of jobs in front of a machine tool, queues of stocks of unsold new automobiles in the dealers' inventory, queues of messages at the central telephone exchange, and so forth. In almost every walk of life there are queues in the form of raw material, semiprocessed, or finished goods' inventories.

Queues are almost always viewed with concern. The cry is to reduce queues or to eliminate them. In many instances this is a legitimate objective. In others, it is foolish. It is inconceivable to dispatch a jet to Europe as soon as an overseas letter is received; the letter must *wait* until there are enough other letters to make the trip economically feasible. Fortunately, a regular service once every few hours is sufficient to provide the economic feasibility.

The concern, therefore, should not be to *eliminate* queues, but to *control* them to achieve specified economic or other objectives.

In the context of production and inventory systems, the impetus to the study of networks of queues has recently emanated from studies in job–shop operations. Such shops are characterized by customer-originating demand (rather than manufacturing to stock of standard items) for a variable product mix. Each job, or class of jobs, requires a different sequence of operations as well as different processing times in any individual operation due to differences in its engineering aspects. Thus, from the point of view of any individual operation or machine center, the demand for its "services" is a random variable which may or may not be stationary in time. The time it takes to render the "service" is another random variable.

Thus, all the prerequisites for the formation of a waiting line at the machine center are satisfied. And, to be sure, queues of jobs waiting to be processed are a common sight in such shops, to the discomfort of production managers and the delight of researchers. Literally hundreds of papers in technical and other journals as well as several score books and pamphlets, some of highly doubtful practical or theoretical value, have been written on the subject, and the end of the flood does not seem to be in view.

Queues are usually studied with the objective of improving the behavior of the system as a whole. Either objectively or subjectively, managers assign a certain loss to *waiting* and a loss to providing the facilities of service which are not demanded, i.e., *idle* facilities. The "break-even" point is the solution sought. It is the point of equilibrium between demand and service. Or, expressed differently, it is the point at which the marginal cost of providing additional service facilities is equal to the marginal cost of discomfort or economic loss to the customers.

§2. THE "IN-WAITING" OR "BUFFER" INVENTORY PROBLEM

The simplest nontrivial network is that composed of just one element: a branch joining two nodes s and t with flow from s to t. The source may be a single machine or a complex of machines, the branch may be a physical connection between the two nodes (such as a pipeline) or it may be a conceptual representation; the sink t may be another machine or complex of operations. Intermediate operations may exist between s and t, such as in Fig. 5-1(b); but if attention is focused on s and t alone (b) can be considered as essentially (a).

Material *between* s and t is "in-waiting"; material *at* s or t is "in-

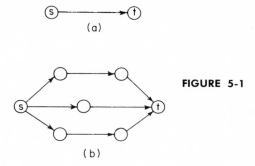

(a)

FIGURE 5-1

(b)

process." The total material in the system is equal to the sum of the two components:

Total material in system = ["In-waiting" inventory + "In-process" inventory].

Consider now the following problem. The average output of machine s is (necessarily) equal to the average consumption of machine t and is equal to r units/unit time. Machine s is subject to random failures of duration τ; the density function of τ is known, $g(\tau)$. The mean time between breakdowns of s is μ. If machine t is to operate continuously without interruption as much as possible, a hand-to-mouth policy between s and t would not be satisfactory since any stoppage of s would cause cessation of work at t. We require in-waiting inventory or buffer stocks between the two operations that "takes up the slack" in the system. (In essence, we are "decoupling" the two operations by introducing such in-waiting inventory, which is a common practice, the degree of decoupling being a function of the in-waiting inventory.) As the buffer inventory is increased from 0 to ∞, the dependence of t on s decreases from complete dependence to independence. The question is: *what is the optimal level of the buffer inventory?*

Optimality is to be measured relative to an economic criterion that takes into account the costs of inventory and the costs of idle time on machine t. Let

B = level of buffer inventory; B^* the optimal level.
h = cost per unit time of carrying one unit of buffer inventory.
c = cost per unit time of idle time on machine t.
μ = average time between breakdowns of machine s.

Assume, for the sake of simplicity, that the maximum duration of breakdowns of s is small relative to μ, as sketched in Fig. 5-2. Then for all practical purposes the average buffer inventory is equal to B. The cost of carrying such inventory per unit time is hB. On the other hand, machine t will be idle if the duration of the breakdown, τ, is long enough for the buffer stocks to be depleted, i.e., if $\tau > B/r$. The expected cost of idle

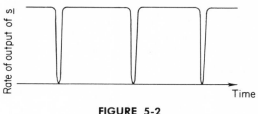

FIGURE 5-2

time is then

$$c \int_{B/r}^{\infty} (\tau - B/r)\, g(\tau)\, d\tau.$$

Since breakdowns occur, on the average, once every μ time units, there will be $1/\mu$ breakdowns per time unit. Hence, the total cost is

$$C = hB + (c/\mu) \int_{B/r}^{\infty} \left(\tau - \frac{B}{r}\right) g(\tau)\, d\tau.$$

Differentiating C with respect to B and equating to zero we obtain

$$\frac{dC}{dB} = 0 = h + \frac{c}{\mu} \left(\frac{-1}{r}\right) \int_{B/r}^{\infty} g(\tau)\, d\tau = h - \frac{c}{r\mu}[1 - G(B^*/r)]$$

where $G(\tau)$ is the cumulative distribution function of τ. Therefore,

$$B^* = r \cdot G^{-1}[1 - r\mu h/c].$$

Naturally, $r\mu h/c$ must be < 1; otherwise G^{-1} is not defined and $B^* = 0$. The interpretation of the case $r\mu h/c > 1$, rewritten as $c/\mu < rh$, is that the cost of one unit of idle time at each breakdown (which occurs $1/\mu$ times per unit time) is less than the cost of storing r units.

As a numerical illustration, let $g(\tau) = 2e^{-2\tau}$, an exponential function with mean $\bar{\tau} = 0.5$ days (see Fig. 5-3). $G(\tau) = \int_0^{\tau} 2e^{-2\tau} d\tau = 1 - e^{-2\tau}$;

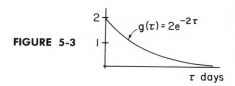

FIGURE 5-3

τ days

therefore $G^{-1}(u) = 0.5 \log 1/(1 - u)$. Let $\mu = 24$ days, $h = \$0.005$, $c = \$12$ and $r = 40$ units/day. Then

$$B^* = 40 \times G^{-1}\left[1 - \frac{40 \times 24 \times 0.005}{12}\right] = 73 \text{ units.}$$

It is interesting to note that the parameters of the problem imply a *level of confidence of continuous operation of machine t*, and vice versa. In particular, with 73 units in the buffer inventory, τ will have to be greater than $73/40 = 1.825$ days for the buffer inventory to be consumed. This occurs with probability less than $1 - G(1.825) = 0.026$. In other words, the probability that the buffer inventories will be consumed during a single breakdown is less than 2.6%.

Thus, an equivalent formulation of the problem is as follows. Given that r = 40 units/day and $g(\tau) = 2e^{-2\tau}$, what is the necessary buffer stock level to guarantee that it will be exceeded during any single breakdown interval less than 2.6% of the time, i.e., operating at confidence level of continuous operation of 97.4%? This second formulation is naturally *more general* than the first since different values of the parameters μ, h, and c would still yield the same B^*. The reader can verify for himself that values of μ = 50, h = \$0.002 and c = \$10 would still result in B^* = 73. In fact, any values of the three parameters satisfying 100 μh = c will yield the same B^* and the same confidence level.

§3. ELEMENTS OF QUEUEING SYSTEMS

In this section we introduce some of the terminology of queueing systems. We shall also discuss very briefly some of their outstanding features.

A queueing system is completely described by specifying its three basic elements:

1. The pattern of arrivals.
2. The service mechanism.
3. The queue discipline.

Since, as was mentioned above, problems of congestion arise due to the nondeterministic character of either arrivals or service, or both, and since probability is the calculus of random events, it is only natural that any intelligent discussion of these problems must be heavily weighted towards probability theory.

3.1 The Pattern of Arrivals

For the sake of uniformity with the general literature on queueing theory, we shall refer to the elements generating the demand on the service facility as *customers*, it being understood that this is a generic term that may refer to people, jobs, etc.

Customers can arrive equally spaced in time. This is the case of scheduled patients in a hospital who adhere to their schedule. It is also exemplified by finished items on a conveyor belt before the final packing operation.

Perhaps the most interesting, and certainly the most widely studied pattern of arrival is the *completely random* pattern. The terms "completely random" have a precise mathematical meaning which is not to be confused with a "haphazard" manner of arrival. We proceed now to give the exact mathematical definition of these terms.

Let the probability that one arrival will take place in a very short interval of time Δt be given by the rather innocent-looking but extremely consequential expression

$$\lambda \cdot \Delta t + o(\Delta t) \tag{5-1}$$

where λ is the average rate of arrival per unit time (one hour, say), and $o(\Delta t)$ indicates a term which is of a much smaller order of magnitude than $\lambda \cdot \Delta t$ especially as $\Delta t \rightarrow 0$, and therefore can be neglected when we approach the limit. Equation (5-1) says, in effect, that the probability of one arrival is approximately *proportional* to Δt. Suppose that the probability that no customers will arrive during Δt is $1 - \lambda \cdot \Delta t - o(\Delta t)$. This, together with Eq. (5-1) implies that the probability of *two or more* arrivals during Δt is $o(\Delta t)$, which can be ignored as $\Delta t \rightarrow 0$.

Note that the probability of one arrival as given by Eq. (5-1) is independent of where Δt lies. To put it more vividly, consider the diagrammatic representation of completely random arrivals shown in Fig. 5-4,

FIGURE 5-4 Completely Random Arrivals

where the dots represent customers and the distance between any two dots represents the interval of time between their arrivals. We have chosen two short intervals A and B of duration Δt each. Interval A occurs after a string of arrivals has taken place; B occurs after a long gap between arrivals. Still, by Eq. (5-1) the probability of an arrival in interval A is *equal* to the probability of an arrival in interval B. Complete randomness, as defined by Eq. (5-1), implies *complete independence of past history*. This is a very unique property indeed.

At this point, it may be of interest to pursue the matter just a little further. For example, one may ask: what is the probability of exactly r arrivals in a time interval of length h? To obtain this, suppose we divide the interval h into m short intervals of duration Δt each; i.e., $h = m \cdot \Delta t$. Then each infinitesimal interval represents an experiment with two outcomes: success (i.e., one arrival) or failure (i.e., no arrival), having ruled out the possibility of more than one arrival. This is a binomial experiment with probability of success $p = \lambda \cdot \Delta t$ and probability of failure $q = 1 - \lambda \cdot \Delta t$. The (fictitious) experiment is conducted m times. The probability of r successes is given by the well-known formula

$$p_r = \lim_{\Delta t \to 0} \frac{m!}{r!\,(m - r)!}(\lambda \cdot \Delta t)^r (1 - \lambda \cdot \Delta t)^{m-r}$$

$$= \lim_{m \to \infty} \frac{m!}{r!\,(m - r)!}\frac{\lambda^r h^r}{m^r}(1 - \lambda h/m)^{m-r} \text{ since } h = m \cdot \Delta t$$

$$= \frac{(\lambda h)^r}{r!} \lim_{m \to \infty} \frac{m!}{m^r (m - r)!}(1 - \lambda h/m)^{m-r}$$

But

$$\lim_{m \to \infty} \frac{m!}{m^r(m - r)!} = \lim_{m \to \infty} \frac{m(m - 1)(m - 2) \cdots (m - r + 1)}{m^r}$$

$$= \lim_{m \to \infty} \left(1 - \frac{1}{m}\right)\left(1 - \frac{2}{m}\right) \cdots \left(1 - \frac{r - 1}{m}\right) = 1.$$

Also, $\displaystyle\lim_{x \to \infty} \left(1 + \frac{1}{x}\right)^x$ is easily obtained by binomial expansion as $1 + 1 +$

$\dfrac{1}{2!} + \dfrac{1}{3!} + \ldots = e$. Hence,

$$p_r = \frac{(\lambda h)^r}{r!} e^{-\lambda h} \tag{5-2}$$

which is the well-known Poisson distribution with mean λh. Figure 5-5 sketches the shape of the distribution for three values of λh. If we substi-

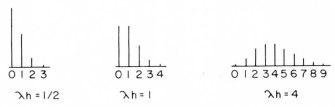

$\lambda h = 1/2$ $\lambda h = 1$ $\lambda h = 4$

FIGURE 5-5

tute for $r = 0$ in Eq. (5-2), we get $p_0 = e^{-\lambda h}$, an exponential function. That is, the probability of *no arrival* in a period of duration h is $e^{-\lambda h}$. One can easily deduce that the probability *density* function of the *length of interval t_0 between arrivals* is given by $p(t_0) = \lambda e^{-\lambda t_0}$, the exponential distribution function.

These are very interesting results. And they are a direct consequence of the definition of *completely random* arrivals given in Eq. (5-1).

Another pattern of arrival is the *distributed arrivals*, which is a direct generalization of the completely random pattern discussed above. Under this mode of arrival the length of the interval between arrivals follows a known probability distribution other than the exponential.

Of course, one can enumerate many more arrival patterns. For example, *batch arrivals* in which case demand for service does not occur individually but in groups. This is the case of people waiting for buses, or of college cafeterias which receive fractions of whole classes that happen to terminate at the same hour, etc. However, the above should be sufficient to clarify our meaning concerning different patterns of arrival. We turn next to the discussion of service mechanisms.

3.2 The Service Mechanism

We wish to distinguish among three facets of the service mechanism: its *availability*, its *capacity*, and the *duration of service*. These are three independent variables; any one of them may be deterministically or probabilistically known. All three must be specified if we are to achieve a complete definition of the service mechanism.

The service mechanism may be *available* at certain times but not available at others. Such is the case, for example, in large computer installations where routine maintenance is scheduled the first hour of each morning, during which time the computer is not available for use. Of course, failure of the computer system would result in the same condition except that this is a random, i.e., probabilistic, occurrence. Absence of employees at lunch hours, closure of certain routes during military maneuvers, etc., are examples of unavailable service mechanisms. Such availability or unavailability must be specified for a meaningful study of the system.

Next is the question of *capacity*; i.e., if the service is available, how many customers can be served simultaneously? The capacity of the service mechanism may be fixed, e.g., the number of machines available in a shop, or the capacity may be varying over time, e.g., the number of toll booths along turnpikes.

Finally, we must specify the characteristics of the *service time*. An argument similar to that developed above concerning the arrival distribution can be made, but we will not repeat it here. The service time can be a constant for all customers or possess the exponential distribution $\mu e^{-\mu h}$, which *implies complete randomness* with parameter μ, or any other distribution. We can also add the complication of different *types of customers*, each type possessing its own distribution, or we may stipulate that the time of service is a function of the queue length: the longer the queue the faster the service, etc.

3.3 The Queue Discipline

This is the final element in the complete specification of a queueing system. By "discipline" is meant the manner in which customers are to be selected for service *once they are in the queue.*

Here we must distinguish between two cases: the *single-server system* and the *multiple-server system.*

In the *single-server system* (unit capacity) the customers are assigned *priorities* and they are serviced in the order of their *priorities.* There are several *priority rules* whose variety, needless to say, is bounded only by the imagination and ingenuity of the analyst. The simplest rule is, of course, a *random* assignment. Here "random" means simply "equally probable" and the assignment of a priority to any specific customer is accomplished by a random choice among the set of possible priorities. Although many managers of queueing systems would shudder at the notion of such a haphazard way of assigning priorities to waiting customers, it turns out that they, in effect, adopt such a rule when they follow the rule "first-come first-served," or any variations thereof, whenever the pattern of arrival is random.

A peculiar type of priority assignment gives rise to the so-called *preemptive* priorities. Under such a rule, the service mechanism, upon the appearance of a job with a higher priority, would cease working on the customer it had been servicing (if it were busy with another customer) and service the newly-arrived customer (possibly to the chagrin of everyone else in the queue). Such preemptive priority systems are by no means uncommon: a millwright gang would stop working on lighting fixtures if it were notified of a major breakdown in the shop.

The *multiserver system* (multiunit capacity) gives rise to somewhat different problems. Some units of the facility may specialize in certain services and customers requiring that service are forced to go there. If more than one server is capable of performing the required service, *jockeying*, i.e., moving from a long queue to a shorter one, becomes a factor to be considered. Such jockeying may be intentional and worked into the queue discipline, or it may be random.

The general mathematical study of queueing systems, which is beyond the scope of this book, is rendered the more fascinating and concomitantly the more difficult by considering such real-life problems as *balking*, *reneging*, varying the rate of service, etc. Balking occurs when a customer decides not to join a queue longer than a certain length, a common behavior which for many businesses, such as cafeterias, may mean a loss of income. Reneging is leaving the queue *after having joined it* and having *waited* for a certain length of time. Finally, the rate of service may change as a function of the length of the queue: sometimes servers work faster when they see a long queue waiting, and sometimes the opposite effect takes place; resignation sets in because it seems that the job will *never* get done.

§4. A SIMPLE QUEUE: THE ONE-SERVER STATION

We now discuss the simplest type of queue: that containing one station with one server. However, this simple case contains all the elements of the most general formulation. The system is represented graphically as shown in Fig. 5-6. The "outside world" acts as a source of completely random

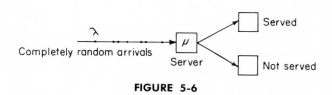

FIGURE 5-6

arrivals. The service mechanism has space for *only one* customer in the queue. If another customer arrives and finds the position occupied, he leaves unserved and never returns again. Thus, the system can be in one of two possible states: busy with one customer, which we denote by state B, or idle, state I. This is, for example, an approximate representation of a telephone booth in a railway station if we assume that the customers are in a rush, or of a gasoline-filling pump on a highway in which there are numerous such stations of equivalent grade.

We suppose that arrivals are completely random with mean rate of arrival λ. Suppose also that service is completely random with average service rate μ, i.e., the distribution of service time is exponential with mean $1/\mu$. Then, based on the definition of completely random events, the probability of an arrival in the interval between time t and time $t + \Delta t$ is $\lambda \cdot \Delta t$, to a first order of approximation. The probability of no arrivals during that period is $1 - \lambda \cdot \Delta t$. It is similar for departures or service: the probability of service being completed in the small interval Δt is $\mu \cdot \Delta t$, and the probability that it will not be completed is $1 - \mu \cdot \Delta t$, all to the first order of approximation.

Now, for the system to be in state I, i.e., idle, at time $t + \Delta t$, there are only two possibilities:

1. The system was in state I at time t, i.e., it was idle, and no customers arrived in the small time interval Δt.
2. The system was in state B, i.e., busy, at time t and service was completed during the small interval Δt, leaving the system empty and idle at time $t + \Delta t$.

The third possibility of more than one occurrence during Δt, (e.g., an arrival and departure) has been already ruled out as being of a much smaller order of magnitude than the two possibilities (1) and (2), and tends toward zero as $\Delta t \to 0$.

Now, let $p_X(t)$ denote the probability of being in state X at time t. Then the probability of being in state I at time $t + \Delta t$ is given by

$$p_I(t + \Delta t) = p_I(t)(1 - \lambda \cdot \Delta t) + p_B(t)(\mu \cdot \Delta t) \tag{5-3}$$

where the first term after the equality sign is the probability of Case (1), and the second term is the probability of Case (2). The two probabilities are added because the two cases are mutually exclusive.

A similar argument can be presented for the probability that the system will be in state B, i.e., busy, at time $t + \Delta t$. Here, the two possibilities are:

3. It was in state B at time t, and service was not completed during Δt.

4. It was in state I at time t and one arrival took place during Δt.

We immediately deduce that

$$p_B(t + \Delta t) = p_B(t)(1 - \mu \cdot \Delta t) + p_I(t)(\lambda \cdot \Delta t). \tag{5-4}$$

We can rewrite Eqs. (5-3) and (5-4) in the following form:

$$p_I(t + \Delta t) - p_I(t) = -\lambda \cdot \Delta t \cdot p_I(t) + \mu \cdot \Delta t \cdot p_B(t)$$

$$p_B(t + \Delta t) - p_B(t) = -\mu \cdot \Delta t \cdot p_B(t) + \lambda \cdot \Delta t \cdot p_I(t).$$

Dividing both equations by Δt, we obtain:

$$\frac{p_I(t + \Delta t) - p_I(t)}{\Delta t} = -\lambda \cdot p_I(t) + \mu \cdot p_B(t)$$

$$\frac{p_B(t + \Delta t) - p_B(t)}{\Delta t} = -\mu \cdot p_B(t) + \lambda \cdot p_I(t).$$

Now letting $\Delta t \to 0$, the left hand side of both equations becomes the differential of the function,

$$\frac{d}{dt}[p_I(t)] = -\lambda \cdot p_I(t) + \mu \cdot p_B(t)$$

$$\frac{d}{dt}[p_B(t)] = -\mu \cdot p_B(t) + \lambda \cdot p_I(t). \tag{5-5}$$

Equation (5-5) is a system of ordinary differential equations which can be solved explicitly if we recognize that there is one more condition that we know exists and therefore must bring to bear. Namely, at any time t the system must be either in state B or state I. Hence,

$$p_B(t) + p_I(t) = 1. \tag{5-6}$$

If we so desire, we can now obtain an explicit expression for $p_B(t)$ and $p_I(t)$. However, rather than do this, we shall use a heuristic argument to give us a short cut to some of the results we want.

To this end we introduce the notion of a "*steady-state*" probability distribution. It seems intuitively appealing that after a long interval of time the system will "settle down" to occupy either state B or state I a certain proportion of the time, irrespective of the starting position of the system. This is so because after several transitions the effect of the original position diminishes to zero. When this steady state is reached, the *rate of change* of $p_I(t)$ or $p_B(t)$ with time will also approach zero (the rate of change of a constant is zero). Of course, all of this verbal argument can be stated and verified rigorously, and conditions for the *existence* of such steady-state probabilities derived. However, for our purposes, we shall forfeit such mathematical rigor and assume that the steady-state probability distribution function exists. Then, since $d/dt\,[p_X(t)] = 0$, we have from Eqs. (5-5) and (5-6),

$$0 = -\lambda \cdot p_I(t) + \mu \cdot p_B(t)$$

$$0 = -\mu \cdot p_B(t) + \lambda \cdot p_I(t)$$

and

$$1 = p_B(t) + p_I(t).$$

The first two equations are identical, but either of them together with the third equation yields

$$p_B(\infty) = \frac{\lambda}{\lambda + \mu} \text{ and } p_I(\infty) = \frac{\mu}{\lambda + \mu}. \tag{5-7a}$$

A discussion of the result in Eq. (5-7a) should prove illuminating. If the system *starts* with the probability of being in either state the same as the probability given by Eq. (5-7a), then the probability of being in either state *never changes*. It is therefore called *stationary probability distribution*.

Notice that the probability p_I also measures the probability of a customer arriving to find the system *free*.

The ratio $\rho = \lambda/\mu$, the ratio of rate of arrival to rate of departure, claims a prominent position in queueing problems. This can be seen from Eq. (5-7a) which can be expressed in terms of ρ as

$$p_B = \frac{1}{1 + 1/\rho} \text{ and } p_I = \frac{1}{1 + \rho}. \tag{5-7b}$$

It is evident that as $\rho \to 0$, $p_B \to 0$, and $p_I \to 1$, which is obvious since the server will be idle most of the time if his rate of output far exceeds the input rate of demand for his services. Conversely, as $\rho \rightarrow \infty$, $p_B \rightarrow 1$, and $p_I \rightarrow 0$.

§5. A SLIGHT GENERALIZATION: UNLIMITED QUEUE LENGTH

Suppose that the length of the queue, which *includes the customer being served*, is not restricted as in the above situation but can be any integer $n \geq 0$ (see Fig. 5-7). Suppose also that the customers can, or must, wait to be served either because they do not mind waiting or, which is the more common cause, there is nowhere else to obtain the same service. These are the conditions encountered at railway ticket offices, bank tellers, or the local post office in a small town.

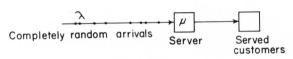

Completely random arrivals · Server · Served customers

FIGURE 5-7

Now that the size of the queue, n, is not limited to 0 or 1, but can range over all positive integers (at least theoretically), the system can be in *state n* (i.e., the length of the queue is equal to n) at time $t + \Delta t$ if one of the *three* following possibilities takes place:

1. The system was in state n at time t and no arrivals or departures took place during Δt. The probability of this occurring, according to our assumptions, is $(1 - \lambda \cdot \Delta t - \mu \cdot \Delta t) \cdot p_n(t)$.
2. The system was in state $(n - 1)$ at time t, i.e., the queue was shorter, and one arrival took place. This occurs with probability $\lambda \cdot \Delta t \cdot p_{n-1}(t)$.
3. The system was in state $(n + 1)$ at time t, i.e., the queue was longer, and one departure took place. This occurs with probability $\mu \cdot \Delta t \cdot p_{n+1}(t)$.

Since these states are mutually exclusive the probabilities add and we obtain

$$p_n(t + \Delta t) = p_n(t)(1 - \lambda \cdot \Delta t - \mu \cdot \Delta t) + p_{n-1}(t) \cdot \lambda \cdot \Delta t$$
$$+ p_{n+1}(t) \cdot \mu \cdot \Delta t. \tag{5-8}$$

This equation is reminiscent of Eqs. (5-3) and (5-4) of the previous section, and indeed it is the generalization of either of the equations to the present case.

Skipping over the formal mathematical arguments since, in essence, they are similar to the above except that they are slightly more complicated, we arrive at the steady-state probabilities

$$p_n = (1 - \rho)\rho^n \tag{5-9}$$

where ρ is, as before, that important ratio λ/μ.

Equation (5-9) has some interesting consequences. For one thing, it has no meaning for $\rho > 1$ since probabilities can never be negative. The probability distribution function of Eq. (5-9) has the following general shape shown in Fig. 5-8. It is a well-known distribution function in statistical

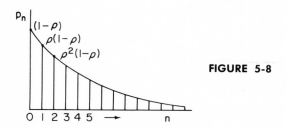

FIGURE 5-8

theory and is called the *geometric distribution* because of the manner in which probability decreases (geometrically). Its mean is given by:

$$m = \sum_0^\infty n \cdot p_n = \rho/(1 - \rho)$$

and its variance is

$$\sigma^2 = \sum_0^\infty n^2 \cdot p_n - m^2 = \rho/(1 - \rho)^2.$$

More interestingly, the probability of a queue of length greater than N is $\sum_N^\infty p_n = (1 - \rho) \sum_N^\infty \rho^n = \rho^N$, a negligible fraction for large N. For example, if $\rho = 0.9$, then the average size of the queue is 9 customers, one of whom is being served and 8 of whom are waiting. This, incidentally, does *not* mean that after some time we expect to find 9 customers in the queue. In fact, the probability of that event is given by Eq. (5-9) to be $(0.1)(0.9)^9 = 0.0387$, or less than 4%. It simply means that the size of the queue will fluctuate from 0 to very large numbers; if we observe and record the queue size for a very long period of time and divide the sum of the observed lengths by the number of observations taken, we would obtain a number very close to 9. This is a very loosely worded interpretation of the well-known "law of large numbers" in probability theory.

The probability that the length of this queue will be larger than 20 customers is $(0.9)^{20} = 0.119$. That is, in approximately 7 out of 8 observations the queue will be shorter than 20, and only 1/8th of the time will it be longer. Note that with $\rho = 0.9$ we are pretty close to "saturating" the capability of the service mechanism, and yet the probability of a queue of more than 30 customers is less than 5%.

Looking at the same problem from the other point of view, the server will be idle if the length of the queue is zero, and the probability of that event is $p_0 = (1 - \rho) = 0.1$. Thus, the server will be idle 10% of his time *in the long run*. Again, this does not mean that we will find the server idle six minutes out of every hour, or that he might as well go home (if the server is human) or shut down (if it is a machine) at 2:42 P.M., since the last forty-eight minutes (10% of 8 hours) are idle. Great care must be taken in interpreting these and other probability statements.

To illustrate the type of economic evaluation undertaken in studies of queueing systems, let the cost of service be $25/hour and the cost of waiting $2.50/hour of waiting. This approximates the case of workers waiting to have their tools repaired in a factory. Assuming that the above mathematical model applies, i.e., assuming that arrivals are random, service time is exponentially distributed, and a queue discipline of first-come, first-served, the average waiting time per customer must be evaluated. The derivation of this parameter is beyond the scope of our discussion but the final formula is strikingly simple:

$$\text{Average waiting time per customer in queue } w = \frac{1}{\lambda} \frac{\rho}{1 - \rho}.$$

Since the average size of the queue is $(\rho/(1 - \rho))$, the average total waiting time is $(\rho/(1 - \rho))^2/\lambda$, a function of ρ for any given λ. The marginal value of decreasing ρ (i.e., increasing the service rate μ and therefore reducing the waiting in the queue) is given by the derivative

$$\frac{d}{d\rho}\left[\frac{2.5}{\lambda}\left(\frac{\rho}{1 - \rho}\right)^2\right] = \frac{2.5}{\lambda} \frac{2\rho}{(1 - \rho)^3}.$$

But the cost of customers waiting is balanced by the cost of idle service, whose marginal value is $25. Consequently, the optimal ρ^* is determined from the equation

$$\frac{2.5}{\lambda} \frac{2\rho}{(1 - \rho)^3} = 25,$$

a cubic in ρ for any given λ. For example, if $\lambda = 10$ customers per hour, the optimal ρ^* is approximately 0.755; i.e., the service rate must be set at approximately 13.24 customers per hour.

§6. QUEUES IN PARALLEL

The situation here is slightly different and is depicted in Fig. 5-9. There are m service facilities which need not be busy all the time. In fact, if one customer arrives he will occupy one server and the rest remain idle; two customers occupy two servers, etc., until m customers or more are in the system when all m servers are busy. If n is $> m$, exactly m customers will be served and the $n - m$ will be waiting for service.

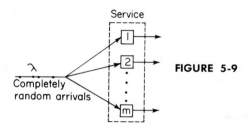

FIGURE 5-9

To represent the situation in mathematical terms, it is obvious that arrivals are unaffected by the number of servers available. We shall assume, as before, completely random arrivals with mean arrival rate λ. On the service side, however, the situation is more complicated. Assuming exponentially distributed service time of mean $1/\mu$, the rate of service *varies with the number of customers* in the system:

$$
\begin{aligned}
\mu_1 &= \mu & \text{if } n &= 1 \\
\mu_2 &= 2\mu & n &= 2 \\
&\ \ \vdots & &\ \ \vdots \\
\mu_{m-1} &= (m-1)\mu & n &= m-1 \\
\mu_n &= m\mu & n &\geq m.
\end{aligned}
\tag{5-10}
$$

Suppose that we specify, as before, the state of the system by the number of customers in the system, both being served and waiting. Then the system can transfer from state $(n-1)$ to state n with a probability differential $\lambda \cdot \Delta t$, and undertake the transition from state n to state $n-1$ with probability differential $\mu_n \cdot \Delta t$, where μ_n is as defined by Eq. (5-10). A system of differential equations similar to Eq. (5-5) can be written, from which the steady-state probability distribution of the queue size can be deduced to yield:

$$
p_1 = \frac{\lambda}{\mu} \cdot p_0; \ p_2 = \frac{\lambda^2}{2!\mu^2} \cdot p_0; \ p_3 = \frac{\lambda^3}{3!\mu^3} \cdot p_0; \cdots; p_{m-1} = \frac{\lambda^{m-1}}{(m-1)!\mu^{m-1}} \cdot p_0
$$

$$p_n = \frac{\lambda^n}{m^{n-m} \cdot m! \mu^n} \cdot p_0 \quad \text{for } n \geq m.$$

Since the state probabilities must add up to unity,

$$p_0 \left[1 + \frac{\lambda}{\mu} + \frac{\lambda^2}{2! \mu^2} + \cdots + \frac{\lambda^{m-1}}{(m-1)! \mu^{m-1}} + \frac{m^{m-1}}{(m-1)!} \sum_{n=m}^{\infty} \left(\frac{\lambda}{m\mu} \right)^n \right] = 1$$

Let S denote the quantity between square brackets, and let $\rho = \lambda/m\mu$. Then,

$$S = \left[1 + m\rho + \frac{(m\rho)^2}{2!} + \cdots + \frac{(m\rho)^{m-1}}{(m-1)!} + \frac{(m\rho)^m}{m!(1-\rho)} \right] < \infty$$

Therefore,

$$
\begin{aligned}
p_0 &= 1/S \\
p_n &= (m\rho)^n/n!S \quad \text{for } n = 1, \ldots, m-1 \\
p_n &= m^m \rho^n / m!S \quad \text{for } n \geq m.
\end{aligned}
\tag{5-11}
$$

Since a compact formula is not possible, a numerical example should help drive the results home. Let $m = 3$; i.e., there are three servers in the system. Then

$$S = 1 + 3\rho + \frac{9\rho^2}{2} + \frac{9\rho^3}{2(1-\rho)} = \frac{2 + 4\rho + 3\rho^2}{2(1-\rho)}.$$

Hence,

$$p_0 = \frac{2(1-\rho)}{2 + 4\rho + 3\rho^2}; \quad p_1 = \frac{6\rho(1-\rho)}{2 + 4\rho + 3\rho^2}; \quad p_2 = \frac{18\rho^2(1-\rho)}{2 + 4\rho + 3\rho^2}$$

and

$$p_n = \frac{27\rho^n(1-\rho)}{2 + 4\rho + 3\rho^2} \quad \text{for } n \geq 3.$$

Specifically, if $\rho = 0.9$, all three servers will be idle with probability $p_0 = 0.025$, two servers will be idle with probability $p_1 = 0.067$, and one server will be idle with $p_2 = 0.182$. That is, the equivalent of one server idle $3(0.025) + 2(0.067) + 1(0.182) = 0.391$ of his time. Compare this result with the average waiting time in the single-server queue with the *same ratio* ρ: the three servers in parallel would wait approximately four times as long as the single server, although the system is empty only 2.5% of the time. This is an interesting result. Expressed in a different way, m servers can handle traffic *density* more than m times the individual server, which is a common observation.

§7. QUEUES IN SERIES

The simplest case, of which many variants exist, is the case of sequential service centers with one server per center, in which the customer immediately joins the queue at station i upon completing service in station $i - 1$, and leaves the system upon completion of service at station N, the last in line. In practice, this is exemplified by any straight line production system, Fig. 5-10.

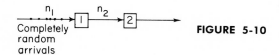

FIGURE 5-10

For the sake of clarity, consider only two stations in sequence. Assume, as before, that customers arrive in a completely random fashion with average arrival rate λ; assume also that the duration of service in both stations is exponentially distributed with means $1/\mu_1$ and $1/\mu_2$, respectively. Let $p(n_1, n_2, t)$ denote the probability that at time t a queue of length n_1 is at station 1 and a queue of length n_2 is at station 2; both queues include the customers being served. Let $p(n_1, n_2, t + \Delta t)$ be defined similarly at time $t + \Delta t$. Finally, we make the usual assumption that the probability of two or more events in the infinitesimal time interval Δt is of a small order and approaches 0 as $\Delta t \to 0$. The following reasoning results in the system of Eqs. (5-12) below:

1. $n_1 = 0$ and $n_2 = 0$ at time $t + \Delta t$ if either (a) the system was empty at time t and no arrival took place, or (b) $n_1 = 0$ and $n_2 = 1$ at time t, and one departure occurred leaving the system empty.

2. $n_1 = 0$, $n_2 = n_2^0 > 0$ at time $t + \Delta t$ if at time t either (a) $n_1 = 0$, $n_2 = n_2^0$ and no arrivals or departures took place during Δt, or (b) $n_1 = 0, n_2 = n_2^0 + 1$ and one departure took place during Δt, or (c) $n_1 = 1, n_2 = n_2^0 - 1$ and service was completed on one customer in the first station during Δt.

3. $n_1 = n_1^0 > 0$; $n_2 = 0$ at time $t + \Delta t$; similar alternatives to Case 2 above.

4. $n_1 = n_1^0 \geq 0$; $n_2 = n_2^0 > 0$ at time $t + \Delta t$ if at time t either: (a) $n_1 = n_1^0$ and $n_2 = n_2^0$ and no change occurred, or (b) $n_1 = n_1^0 + 1$, $n_2 = n_2^0 - 1$ and service was completed in the first station; or (c) $n_1 = n_1^0$, $n_2 = n_2^0 + 1$ and service was completed in the second station, or, finally, (d) $n_1 = n_1^0 - 1$, $n_2 = n_2^0$ and one arrival took place during Δt:

$$\frac{d}{dt} [p(0, 0, t)] = -\lambda \cdot p(0, 0, t) + \mu_2 \cdot p(0, 1, t) \quad \text{for } n_1 = n_2 = 0$$

$$\frac{d}{dt}[p(0, n_2, t)] = -(\lambda + \mu_2)p(0, n_2, t) + \mu_1 \cdot p(1, n_2 - 1, t)$$
$$+ \mu_2 \cdot p(0, n_2 + 1, t) \qquad n_1 = 0, n_2 > 0$$

(5-12)

$$\frac{d}{dt}[p(n_1, 0, t)] = -(\lambda + \mu_1)p(n_1, 0, t) + \mu_2 \cdot p(n_1, 1, t)$$
$$+ \lambda \cdot p(n_1 - 1, 0, t) \qquad n_1 > 0, n_2 = 0$$

$$\frac{d}{dt}[p(n_1, n_2, t)] = -(\lambda + \mu_1 + \mu_2)p(n_1, n_2, t) + \mu_1 \cdot p(n_1 + 1, n_2 - 1, t)$$
$$+ \mu_2 \cdot p(n_1, n_2 + 1, t) + \lambda \cdot p(n_1 - 1, n_2, t) \qquad n_1, n_2 > 0.$$

The steady-state equations have the solution

$$p(n_1, n_2) = \rho_1^{n_1} \cdot \rho_2^{n_2} \cdot p(0, 0)$$

(5-13)

where $\rho_1 = \lambda/\mu_1$, $\rho_2 = \lambda/\mu_2$ and $p(0, 0)$ is evaluated from the condition that the sum of probabilities add up to unity; i.e.,

$$\sum_{n_1, n_2} \rho_1^{n_1} \cdot \rho_2^{n_2} \cdot p(0, 0) = \frac{p(0, 0)}{(1 - \rho_1)(1 - \rho_2)} = 1$$

i.e.,

$$p(0, 0) = (1 - \rho_1)(1 - \rho_2).$$

The probability of n_1 units in the first queue is obtained by summing over all n_2,

$$p(n_1) = \rho_1^{n_1}(1 - \rho_1)$$

and similarly for the second queue,

$$p(n_2) = \rho_2^{n_2}(1 - \rho_2).$$

The interpretation of these equations is interesting and may come as a surprise. Substituting for the last three equations into Eq. (5-13), we see that

$$p(n_1, n_2) = p(n_1)p(n_2).$$

Therefore, the two queues *act independently*, each with a completely random arrival of mean λ, the mean rate of arrival to the system. Therefore, the two queues can be treated separately and the results of the study of the single server with random arrivals and exponential service time of §5 can be applied here to each station.

Naturally, this rather startling result is crucially dependent on our assumptions concerning arrivals and service in station 1. Independence will not hold if, for example, arrivals to the first queue are equally spaced or if there is a limitation on the length of the queue in front of either station.

The above results can be generalized in a straightforward manner to more than two service stations. In particular, the analogues to the above relations for a chain of N service stations are:

$$p(n_1, n_2, \ldots, n_N) = \prod_{i=1}^{N} \rho_i^{n_i}(1 - \rho_i)$$

and

$$p(n_i) = \rho_i^{n_i}(1 - \rho_i) \qquad i = 1, \ldots, N.$$

§8. AN APPLICATION: THE DESIGN OF IN-WAITING (OR IN-TRANSIT) STORAGE FACILITIES

One of the most difficult of plant layout and design problems is the design of in-waiting facilities. We have touched on this problem in §2 in the context of the optimal amount of buffer inventory between two operations. Optimality was then measured relative to an economic criterion that comprised the costs of carrying inventory and of idle time on the second machine. The assumption was made that the first machine always had work ahead of it, i.e., conceptually an infinite queue.

In this section we discuss a related, but slightly different problem. The factors to be considered here are not the costs mentioned above but rather the cost of space allocated to such inventory as well as the cost of increased service capacity. In particular, the question is how much space and storage equipment should be allocated at all the between-operation phases of a manufacturing process.

The usual approach to this problem calls for the consideration of storage areas preceding the operations, in terms of providing space for the necessary quantity of material or parts to supply the following operation for a specific period of time. In the case of raw materials stores area preceding the first operation, such factors as the desired rate of production, the available rate of supply, the projected production forecast, and the estimated reliability of supply would be considered. For between-operations stores, usually called "banks," "buffers," or "floats," some of the above factors would be considered, and in addition, emphasis would be placed on the likelihood of a work stoppage at the preceding operation and on the estimate of the average delay time. The actual buffer inventory is then determined by consideration of all these factors. We shall consider a simple model of such a problem.

Assume a straight line production where machines and equipment have been chosen in order to achieve balance, and the production of each operation feeds directly into the next one along prescribed transfer lines. This directly relates to between-operations materials handling since in straight line production, storage between operations is often storage in transit, i.e., storage and handling are performed simultaneously as in the case of conveyors between operations.

In any mechanized production line, such as chemical or food processing, the output of operation 1 should, theoretically at least, feed directly into operation 2, and so on, so that virtually no space is needed between operations. The output of the whole line should be the specified output, which is determined by the speed of the motors or the nominal output of the first machine.

In practice, however, this seldom happens. Temporary adjustments of the machines are usually required. A certain "dropout" occurs at each station causing its input to "shrink" in processing. Our problem is to evaluate the proper lengths of the conveyor between operations or stations, taking into account the probable fluctuations of output at the different operations.

In the simplest case, we can assume that each station "delivers" the product either to the subsequent station or to a fictitious station which we designate by D. Good product flows from phase j to phase $j + 1$; defective product flows from j to D. The schematic representation of the flow in the system is shown in Fig. 5-11 which is drawn for five operations.

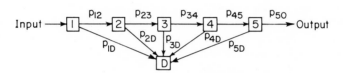

FIGURE 5-11 Schematic Flow with Dropout

Suppose the percent defective in each station is known and given by $p_{i,D}$; then $p_{i,i+1}$ represents the probability of flow from station i to station $i + 1$ and $p_{i,D} + p_{i,i+1} = 1$. Let the flow *into* station 1 be completely random, and assume the service time at each station to be exponentially distributed with parameter μ_i. Then, based on our discussion in the previous section,

$$\lambda_i = \lambda_{i-1} \cdot p_{i-1,i} \quad \text{with } \lambda_1 = \lambda \text{ and } p_{0,1} = 1,$$

and the probability of a queue of size n_i at station i is given by

$$p(n_i) = \rho_i^{n_i} (1 - \rho_i)$$

where

$$\rho_i = \lambda_i / \mu_i.$$

For example, if $\lambda_1 = 15$ units/unit time, $\mu_i = 16$ units/unit time for all i and $p_{iD} = 0.05$ for all i (i.e., 5% defective at each station), then

$$\rho_i = \frac{15}{16}(0.95)^{i-1} = 0.9375 (0.95)^{i-1}.$$

If we desire that the conveyor system accommodate the queue in front of each operation 98% of the time, the length of the conveyor must be capable of accommodating

$$n_i = \frac{\log 0.02}{\log \rho_i} - 1$$

i.e., $n_1 \cong 60$; $n_2 \cong 33$; $n_3 \cong 23$; $n_4 \cong 17$; $n_5 \cong 14$. The successive decrease in the required length of the conveyor is a direct consequence of the assumed "shrinkage" in the quantity of the product together with the assumed equal capability of the stations in the production line. Alternatively, we could have fixed the length of the conveyor between two successive operations and derived the permissible *decrease in capacity* for the same level of confidence.

§9. QUEUES IN SERIES WITH LIMITED STORAGE

Our treatment of the series of N sequential stations is open to the objection that we permitted unlimited lengths of queues at the various stations. In many instances this is a good approximation to practice, since if the limit is high relative to the average length of the queue, the error committed in assuming it infinite is negligible.

There are instances, however, in which the size of the queue at any station is restricted—sometimes restricted to 1, which means that no waiting is tolerated at all between stations and the unit in the queue is the unit being served. This situation is exemplified by steel rolling mills in which one ingot at a time is released from the reheating ovens, it being essential for one roll to feed directly into the next operation so that no cooling of the reduced billets takes place.

Different sequential operations impose different restrictions on the between-operations queues. Thus, a unit whose service is completed at station m may

1. Emerge from station m and join the queue (if any) at station $m + 1$, provided that the length of that queue is less than $(q_{m+1} - 1)$.
2. Emerge from station m only if station $m + 1$ is free; otherwise it "blocks" station m. This would also occur if the size of the queue in (1) is equal to q_{m+1}. Station m can still accept arrivals in *its* queue provided that the size of its queue does not exceed q_m.
3. Emerge from station m only if station $m + 1$ is free; otherwise it *blocks* station m *and all previous stations*. Therefore, all units move together. This type of movement is sometimes called "unpaced belt production lines."

The objective of this section is to indicate how the study of the behavior of such queueing systems can be carried out. We are particularly interested in the added phenomenon of *blocking*. It has the serious consequence of reducing the utilization of the blocked stations. It is intuitively clear that while the last station, station N, is never blocked, the effect of blocking is increasingly felt as we proceed toward the first station which suffers the most. The utilization of the facility can, in fact, be measured by the utilization of its first station.

As a prelude to the case of N sequential stations, consider a single station whose queue size is limited to q. That is, customers are permitted to wait until q customers are in the queue *including the customer being served*. Thereafter, arrivals are not permitted to line up in the queue. Translating this verbal description into mathematical terms, we say that the rate of arrival is equal to λ until $n = q$ when the rate is equal to 0,

$$\lambda_n = \begin{cases} \lambda & n = 0, 1, \ldots, q. \\ 0 & n > q \end{cases} \tag{5-14}$$

This exemplifies a rate of *arrival* which is a *function of the size of the queue* (compare with Eq. (5-10) in which the rate of *service* was a function of the size of the queue). It is easy to write down the steady-state equations:

$$-\lambda \cdot p_0 + \mu \cdot p_1 \qquad\qquad = 0$$
$$-(\lambda + \mu) \cdot p_n + \lambda \cdot p_{n-1} + \mu \cdot p_{n+1} = 0 \quad \text{for } 1 \le n \le q$$
$$-\mu \cdot p_q + \lambda \cdot p_{q-1} \qquad\qquad = 0.$$

Utilizing the usual condition that $\Sigma_{n=0}^q \, p_n = 1$, the solution of the above system of difference equations is given by:

$$p_n = \rho^n \cdot \frac{1 - \rho}{1 - \rho^{q+1}} \quad n \le q. \tag{5-15}$$

The average size of the queue, which includes the customer being served, is given by:

$$\mathcal{E}(n) = \sum_{n=0}^{q} n \cdot p_n = \rho \cdot \frac{1 - \rho^q(q + 1) + \rho^{q+1} \, q}{(1 - \rho)(1 - \rho^{q+1})} \tag{5-16}$$

and the average waiting time for a customer is $\mathcal{E}(w) = 1/\lambda \cdot \mathcal{E}(n)$.

Returning now to our original problem of stations in series, we consider the case of *two sequential stations* in which the size of each queue is *limited to one unit*, as depicted in Fig. 5-12. For the first station we distinguish three states: empty (0), busy (1), and blocked (b). For the second station we distinguish two states: empty (0) and busy (1). The important point to remember in this model is the special interpretation of state (b) in station 1. Upon completion of service at station 2 *two events occur simultaneously*: the release of the customer from 2 and the immediate accept-

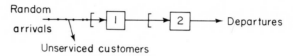

FIGURE 5-12

ance of the blocked customer in 1. This represents no violation of our basic assumption concerning completely random variables in that the only occurrence during the infinitesimal time interval Δt is still the completion of the service in the second station.

Let $p(n_1, n_2)$ be the steady-state probability that station 1 is in state n_1, and station 2 in state n_2. We can easily write down the system of equations:

$$-\lambda \cdot p(0, 0) + \mu_2 \cdot p(0, 1) = 0 \qquad \text{(in state } (0, 0) \text{ at } t + \Delta t)$$

$$-(\lambda + \mu_2) \cdot p(0, 1) + \mu_1 \cdot p(1, 0) + \mu_2 \cdot p(b, 1) = 0$$
$$\text{(in state } (0, 1) \text{ at } t + \Delta t)$$

$$-\mu_1 \cdot p(1, 0) + \lambda \cdot p(0, 0) + \mu_2 \cdot p(1, 1) = 0 \qquad \text{(in state } (1, 0) \text{ at } t + \Delta t)$$

$$-\mu_2 \cdot p(b, 1) + \mu_1 \cdot p(1, 1) = 0 \qquad \text{(in state } (b, 1) \text{ at } t + \Delta t)$$

$$-(\mu_1 + \mu_2) \cdot p(1, 1) + \lambda \cdot p(0, 1) = 0 \qquad \text{(in state } (1, 1) \text{ at } t + \Delta t)$$

where λ is the rate of arrival at station 1, and μ_1 and μ_2 are the rates of service at stations 1 and 2, respectively. The solution of this system of equations, given in terms of $p(0, 0)$, is

$$p(0, 1) = \rho_2 \cdot p(0, 0)$$

$$p(1, 1) = \{\lambda \rho_2 / (\mu_1 + \mu_2)\} p(0, 0)$$

$$p(b, 1) = \{\mu_1 \rho_2^2 / (\mu_1 + \mu_2)\} p(0, 0) \qquad (5\text{-}17)$$

$$p(1, 0) = \rho_1 \{1 + \lambda / (\mu_1 + \mu_2)\} p(0, 0).$$

Imposing the condition $\Sigma\, p(n_1, n_2) = 1$, we deduce

$$p(0, 0) = S^{-1} = [1 + \rho_1 + \rho_2 + \rho_1 \rho_2 + \mu_1 \rho_2^2 / (\mu_1 + \mu_2)]^{-1} \qquad (5\text{-}18)$$

In the special case where $\mu_1 = \mu_2$, S of Eq. (5-18) reduces to

$$S = (3\rho^2 + 4\rho + 2)/2$$

and from Eq. (5-17) we obtain

$$p(0, 1) = \rho S^{-1}, p(1, 1) = \rho^2 S^{-1}/2 = p(b, 1)$$

$$p(1, 0) = (\rho + \rho^2/2) S^{-1}.$$

The probability of blocking, $p(b, 1)$ is of special interest since it indicates the maximum possible utilization of the system,

$$p(b, 1) = \rho^2 / (3\rho^2 + 4\rho + 2)$$

which approaches $\frac{1}{3}$ as $\rho \rightarrow \infty$. That is, even if we assume that the first station can be kept busy all the time, the utilization of the system is less than $\frac{2}{3}$ in the case where $\mu_1 = \mu_2$. This points to the need for μ_2 to be $> \mu_1$ under such operating conditions for better utilization of the system (see Problem 9).

Our treatment thus far can be generalized in two directions: (1) we can permit a finite queue of length q to develop at station 2 and place no bounds on the size of the queue at station 1; and (2) we can treat three or more sequential stations. For Case (1), Hunt[†] obtained the following bound on the possible utilization, u_{max}, of the system

$$u_{max} = \mu_2(\mu_1^{q+1} - \mu_2^{q+1})/(\mu_1^{q+2} - \mu_2^{q+2})$$

which reduces to

$$u_{max} = (q + 1)/(q + 2)$$

for the same rate of service in both stations.

The second mode of generalization will not be treated here since it involves no new principles while the size of the system of steady-state equations grows large.

§10. JOB-SHOP OPERATION: QUEUES IN SERIES AND IN PARALLEL

The most general type of queue networks is the case of queues in parallel which are also *randomly* in series, i.e., the order in which the (multiple server) stations are organized in series formation is random. This is exemplified by the flow of material in job-shops.

Suppose we have M machine centers (or departments or, in general, service facilities). Each center contains one or more machines—hence the "parallel" characterization of service—with the service characteristics of each center not necessarily similar to the others. Center m, $m = 1, 2...$, M, is assumed to contain r_m machines of identical service characteristics.

Let us designate the totality of service facilities as the "System." Jobs arrive at center m from two sources: (1) from outside the System, e.g., new jobs for which the first operation is performed at center m; and (2) from inside the system, i.e., from other centers (see Fig. 5-13). This is a generalization of the concept introduced in a previous section and was represented schematically in Fig. 5-11. Suppose that jobs arrive at center m from *outside* the System in a Poisson-type time series with mean λ_m which may be different for different centers. In any center m service can be assumed to be on a first-come, first-served basis or any other queue discipline that does *not* depend on the routing of the job or its service times.

[†]Gordon C. Hunt, "Sequential Arrays of Waiting Lines," *Operations Research*, Vol. 4, No. 6, December 1956, pp.674–683.

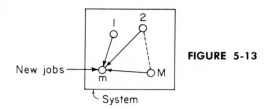

FIGURE 5-13

We also assume that service time is exponentially distributed with mean $1/\mu_m$ which need not be the same for all centers.

Upon completion of service in center m, the job is transferred instantaneously to another center k, $k \neq m$, with probability p_{mk}. Naturally, there is a positive probability that service on any job is completed, so that a job will leave the system with certainty.

Let g_m be the average arrival rate for jobs at center m from both sources: inside and outside the System. Under steady-state conditions we must have

$$g_m = \lambda_m + \sum_k g_k \cdot p_{km} \quad m = 1, 2, \ldots, M. \tag{5-19}$$

To put it in words: the rate of arrival at center m is equal to the sum of two components: (1) arrivals from outside the System, at rate λ_m; and (2) arrivals from inside the system, i.e., from other centers. This latter is given by the fraction of arrivals at these other centers which are destined to go to center m next.

Let n_m denote the number of jobs in the queue at center m; i.e., r_m jobs are in-process and $n_m - r_m$ jobs are in-waiting in front of center m. Finally, let $P_n^m(t)$ denote the probability that at time t exactly n_m jobs are at center m.

Since there are M centers we say that the system is *in state N* when there are exactly n_1 jobs at center 1, n_2 jobs at center 2, etc., i.e., the vector $N \equiv (n_1, n_2, \ldots, n_M)$. For ease of notation we shall denote the state of the system which differs from N by one job in center i by N_{-1} or N_{+1} depending on whether there is one job less or one job more at center i. The state where there is one job less at center i and one job more at some other center j will be denoted by N_2. It is natural then to speak of $P_N(t)$ as the probability that the system is in state N at time t.

The assumptions of exponential arrival and service times are equivalent to assuming that in a very short interval of time h, the probability of an arrival to center m is $g_m \cdot h$ and the probability of a departure is $\mu_m \cdot h$; the probability of one or more occurrences during h is of an order higher than h and approaches 0 as h approaches 0.

Enumerating all the possible ways in which the System can be in state N at time $t + h$, we obtain (see the derivation of Eqs. (5-3), (5-4), and (5-8)):

$$P_N(t + h) = \{1 - h\Sigma\lambda_i - [\Sigma\ \alpha_i(n_i) \cdot \mu_i]h\}P_N(t)$$
$$+ \ \Sigma\ \alpha_i(n_i + 1) \cdot \mu_i \cdot p_i^* \cdot h \cdot P_{N_{+1}}(t)$$
$$+ \ \Sigma\ \lambda_i \cdot \delta_i \cdot h \cdot P_{N_{-1}}(t)$$
$$+ \ \Sigma\Sigma\ \alpha_j(n_j + 1) \cdot \mu_j \cdot p_{ji} \cdot h \cdot P_{N_2}(t) + o(h) \qquad (5\text{-}20)$$

where

$$p_i^* = 1 - \sum_k p_{ki}$$

$$\alpha_i(n_i) = \min(n_i; r_i) \quad \text{and} \quad \delta_i = \min(n_i; 1).$$

Subtracting $P_N(t)$ from both sides of Eq. (5-20), dividing by h, and letting $h \to 0$ yields the system of differential equations (similar to Eq. (5-5) above):

$$\frac{d}{dt}[P_N(t)] = -\{\Sigma\lambda_i + \Sigma\ \alpha_i(n_i)\mu_i\}P_N(t)$$
$$+ \ \Sigma\ \alpha_i(n_i + 1) \cdot \mu_i \cdot p_i^* \cdot P_{N+1}(t) + \Sigma\ \lambda_i \cdot \delta_i \cdot P_{N-1}(t)$$
$$+ \ \Sigma\ \Sigma\ \alpha_j(n_j + 1) \cdot \mu_j \cdot p_{ji} \cdot P_{N_2}(t).$$

Under steady-state conditions $d/dt[P_N(t)] = 0$. This yields a set of *difference equations* in P_N, $P_{N_{-1}}$, $P_{N_{+1}}$ and P_{N_2} which can be solved to yield (dropping the t)

$$P_N = P_{n_1}^1 \cdot P_{n_2}^2 \cdots P_{n_M}^M \qquad (5\text{-}21)$$

where,

$$P_k^m = \begin{cases} P_0^m(g_m/\mu_m)^k/k! & k = 0, 1, \ldots, r_m \\ & m = 1, 2, \ldots, M \\ P_0^m(g_m/\mu_m)^k/r_m!(r_m)^{k-r_m} & k = r_m, r_{m+1}, \ldots, \\ & \text{and } g_m < \mu_m \cdot r_m. \end{cases} \qquad (5\text{-}22)$$

The proof that Eqs. (5-21) and (5-22) are the solution to Eq. (5-20) can be seen by substitution and the following two relationships which are the result of the definitions of p_{ij}, p_i^*, $\alpha_i(n_i)$, δ_i and Eq. (5-19),

$$\sum_i p_i^* \cdot g_i = \sum_i \left(1 - \sum_k p_{ki}\right)g_i = \sum_i \lambda_i$$

and

$$\sum_i \sum_j [\mu_i \cdot \alpha_i(n_i)/g_i] p_{ij} \cdot g_j = \sum_i [\mu_i \cdot \alpha_i(n_i)/g_i] \sum_j p_{ij} \cdot g_j \qquad (5\text{-}23)$$

$$= \sum_i [\mu_i \cdot \alpha_i(n_i)/g_i](g_i - \lambda_i)$$

$$= \sum_i \mu_i \cdot \alpha_i(n_i)$$

$$- \sum_i \lambda_i \cdot \mu_i \cdot \alpha_i(n_i)/g_i.$$

P_0^m of Eq. (5-22) is uniquely determined from the condition

$$\sum_n P_n^m = 1.$$

The interpretation of the above results is illuminating. Since the joint probability P_N is the product of the individual probabilities (see Eq. (5-21)) the centers behave *independently*. This may seem a startling result, especially in view of everyday experience. However, attention is drawn to the assumptions of the model. The results rest squarely on the assumption that the arrival and service rates at each center are independent of arrivals and service rates at other centers. This, together with the assumption of Poisson input and output, leads to the results shown.[†]

Admittedly, very few shops, if any, behave according to this model. Its value lies in providing a datum against which other models of behavior are compared and from which extensions are studied. We proceed now to discuss a few such extensions.

(a) In the above model the rate of service at center m increased linearly up to r_m customers in the queue and then remained constant for $n_m \geq r_m$. Also, arrival from outside the system was assumed at a constant rate λ_m.

Now suppose that we introduce the following two modifications:

(1) Let the rate of service be an arbitrary function of the length of the queue at center m, and denote it by μ_n^m. This means that while the duration of service is still assumed exponentially distributed, the instantaneous value of the parameter of the exponential distribution is some function of the size of the queue. This is a long stride towards the closer representation of systems in which the work force is varied according to the amount of work, or systems in which overtime work is permitted to alleviate congestion. It also covers the following interesting situation. Work at any center is allowed to accumulate up to a limit $\bar{n}_m$ after which work is diverted to identical facilities with large capacities. This is ef-

[†]Implicit in the above model is the existence of "loops," i.e., a job with the route $i \to j \to \cdots \to m \to i$.

fected by subcontracting the additional work or by "opening up" reserve service facilities.

(2) Allow the input to each center m from *outside* the system to follow some known stationary probability distribution function where the subscript 0 designates the "outside world" (see Fig. 5-14). (Thus p_{0m} is the probability that center m is the *first* operation on the job, while p_{m0} designates the probability of transfer from center m to the "outside world," i.e., completion of the job.) Jobs *arrive* in a Poisson fashion with

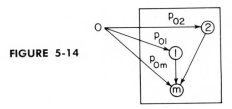

FIGURE 5-14

mean λ and join the queues according to the probability distribution function $\{p_{om}\}$. Hence, Eq. (5-19) changes to

$$g_m = \lambda \cdot p_{0m} + \sum_{k=1}^{M} g_k \cdot p_{km}. \qquad (5\text{-}24)$$

Let us define P_n^m and P_N as before to denote the probability of n units in the queue at station m and $N \equiv (n_1, n_2, \ldots, n_M)$ units at stations 1, 2, ..., M, respectively. Then the following result due to Jackson,[†] holds: *The steady state probability of the system being in state N is given by the product of individual probabilities.* Thus the M centers behave independently. Specificially,

$$P_N = P_{n_1}^1 \cdot P_{n_2}^2 \cdots P_{n_M}^M$$

where

$$P_n^m = u_n^m / S_m,$$

$$u_0^m = 1; u_n^m = \prod_{i=1}^{n} (g_m/\mu_i^m); S_m = \sum_0^\infty u_n^m, \qquad (5\text{-}25)$$

and g_m is given by Eq. (5-24). The derivation of Eqs. (5-25) follows identical steps to the derivation of Eq. (5-22). Again, it is remarkable that the centers behave in a seemingly independent fashion.

[†]James R. Jackson, "Networks of Queues with Controlled Service Rates," Western Management Science Institute, Working Paper No. 10, August 28, 1962.

(b) Other extensions of the basic model were also made by Jackson.[†] Significant among them is the generalization of the rate of *input* to any arbitrary function of the size of the queue. The interpretation of this generalization is as follows. Jobs are *received* in a completely random fashion; i.e., the receipt of orders is a Poisson time series. However, the *release* of jobs to the shop is a function of the size of the queue at the various work centers. The generalization in (a) is still retained in that the rate of service at each station is assumed to be an arbitrary function of the size of the queue at that center.

Two particular modes of behavior are of special interest. The first is the immediate injection of a job in the shop as soon as the total number of jobs in the system falls below some specified number. This practice, or variations thereof, is not uncommon. The second is the immediate rejection of jobs if the size of the queue at any station grows beyond a specified limit. The job simply by-passes the station to the next in its route, perhaps to come back later.

§11. NON-POISSON INPUTS AND OUTPUTS

In the previous ten sections we discussed simple networks of queues with completely random arrivals and departures—i.e., with Poisson input and output time series. The reader may begin to wonder if other modes of behavior exist and question the status of their development.

That other patterns of arrival and service exist has already been indicated in §2 in the discussion of the various input and output patterns; there can be no question concerning their *existence*. However, the *solution* of such queueing systems, in the sense of complete characterization of the transient and steady-state behavior of the queues, poses a difficult question. The mathematical tools of analysis are often sophisticated, but the majority of the results pertain to the steady-state behavior of the system. Little is known concerning transient behavior.

In this section we discuss a technique due to Erlang—a pioneer in the study of problems of telephone congestion—called the "method of stages," which is an ingenious way of synthesizing non-Poisson input and service distribution functions from the exponential distribution function.

The advantages of such an approach are obvious. We have seen in the previous sections that queues characterized by Poisson inputs and outputs are relatively easy to analyse. The ease of their analysis stems from the fact that a system of linear differential-difference equations, such as Eqs. (5-5) and (5-12), can be written almost routinely, and their solution

[†]See bibliography at the end of the chapter.

is relatively straightforward. Therefore, the approach offers to reduce almost intractable problems to the domain of numerical solution if not complete analytical solution.

Consider the distribution (i.e., density) function of the duration of service. In some sense the following two distributions shown in Fig. 5-15 represent two extremes: the constant service time distribution is equivalent to *certainty* while the exponential distribution represents *complete*

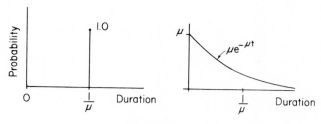

FIGURE 5-15

randomness. The mean service time in both cases is $1/\mu$, but the variance of the first is 0 while the variance of the second is $1/\mu^2$. Therefore, the coefficient of variation v (= standard deviation/mean) is 0 and 100%, respectively. Obviously there are instances of service distributions with coefficients of variation between these two extremes.

The Erlang distribution (*E*-distribution)

$$f(x) = \frac{(k\mu)^k}{\Gamma(k)} (x)^{k-1} e^{-k\mu x}, \Gamma(k) = (k-1)! \tag{5-26}$$

is such a distribution since its mean is $1/\mu$ and its variance is $1/k\mu^2$. Hence, its coefficient of variation is $1/\sqrt{k}$ which varies from 1 to 0 as k increases from 1 to ∞. It is instructive to study the relationship between the *E*-distribution of Eq. (5-26) and another well-known distribution function, the χ^2-distribution. In Eq. (5-26), make the change of variable $k\mu x = y/2$; then $dx = dy/2k\mu$, and we have

$$f(y) = \frac{1}{2^k \Gamma(k)} y^{k-1} e^{-y/2}$$

which is the χ^2-distribution with $n = 2k$ degrees of freedom.

The power and utility of the *E*-distribution of Eq. (5-26) stems from the fact that *it is also the distribution of the sum of k independent identically distributed random variables with density function $k\mu \cdot e^{-k\mu t}$,* the exponential distribution function.

Therefore we can look upon an E_k-service distribution function with coefficient of variation $\nu < 1$ as though it were generated by a customer passing through k *sequential* stations (with $k = 1/\nu^2$) each one of which would possess an exponential service function. Therefore, instead of analyzing *one* service facility with the given E_k-distribution, we now analyze a *series of k* service facilities. The price we have to pay for synthesizing the actual distribution in terms of the sum of k exponentially-distributed variables is to enlarge the size of the system of linear differential-difference equations to be solved. Fortunately, for moderate values of k, and thanks to large scale digital computers, the price is still well worth paying.

To illustrate the analysis, consider the case of one service facility. Suppose that study of service data reveals that it is Erlangian with $k = 3$ (i.e., coefficient of variation $\nu \simeq 0.57$) and average service rate μ. Assume arrivals to be completely random with mean rate λ. Then an *equivalent* system is as shown in Fig. 5-16. We shall denote the three fictitious sta-

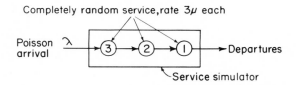

FIGURE 5-16 Equivalent Representation of Erlangian Service

tions as "internal stations." Note that the rate of service in each internal station is necessarily k times the overall rate of service. Let n denote, as before, the number of customers in the queue including the customer being served.

At any instant of time the service facility is either empty—i.e., $n = 0$—or there are n units in the system: $n - 1$ customers in the queue and one customer being serviced. This latter can be in any one of the k internal stations, which we have numbered in Fig. 5-16 to indicate the number of stations "to go." The customer enters at station k, moves to $k - 1$, and so on until he reaches station 1. As long as he is being serviced in *any* internal station, the service facility is "occupied" and no other customer may enter the system (hence, the duration of "occupancy" of the service facility is the sum of k random variables, each representing the time of service at the internal station). Since the rate of service of any internal station is $k\mu$, the rate of service of the facility is only μ customers per unit time.

The steady-state probability equations can be written in a straight-forward manner. They are, for the case $k = 3$,

$$-\lambda \cdot p_0 + \mu' \cdot p_1 = 0 \quad \text{for } r = 0 \quad (\mu' = 3\mu)$$
$$-(\lambda + \mu')p_1 + \mu' \cdot p_2 = 0 \quad r = 1$$
$$-(\lambda + \mu')p_2 + \mu' \cdot p_3 = 0 \quad r = 2$$
$$-(\lambda + \mu') \cdot p_r + \lambda \cdot p_{r-3} + \mu' \cdot p_{r+1} = 0 \quad r = 3, 4, \ldots$$

(5-27)

The subscript of p in Eq. (5-27) is the "number of stations to go." If there are n customers in the system, $n - 1$ of them will be in the queue and they have $k(n - 1)$ internal stations "to go." The one customer being serviced can be in any one of the k internal stations, say in station i. Therefore he has i internal stations "to go." Therefore, the total is $r = nk - k + i$. Obviously, transition of the system is from $r + 1$ to r when service is completed in any internal station, and from $r - k$ to r when an arrival takes place since an arrival increases the number of stations "to go" by k. The first three equations of Eq. (5-27) are the boundary conditions; the last equation gives the general equilibrium probability of transition.

Let $P(z) = \Sigma \ p_r \cdot z^r$; i.e., $P(z)$ is the z-transform of $\{p_r\}$, (see §9 of Chapter 6). Then, multiplying each equation in Eq. (5-27) by z^r where r is as given in Eqs. (5-27) and adding over all r, we get:

$$-\lambda \left[p_0 + p_1 z + p_2 z^2 + \sum_3^\infty p_r z^r \right] - \mu' \left[p_1 z + p_2 z^2 + \sum_3^\infty p_r z^r \right]$$

$$+ \mu' \left[p_1 + p_2 z + p_3 z^2 + \sum_3^\infty p_{r+1} z^r \right] + \lambda \sum_3^\infty p_{r-3} z^r = 0 \quad (\mu' = 3\mu).$$

That is,

$$P(z) = \frac{\mu' p_0 (1 - z)}{\mu' + \lambda z^4 - (\lambda + \mu')z} = \frac{p_0}{1 + \rho' z[(1 - z^3)/(1 - z)]}$$

$$= p_0 \sum_0^\infty (\rho' z)^j \left(\frac{1 - z^3}{1 - z} \right)^j = p_0 \sum_0^\infty \rho'^j (z + z^2 + z^3)^j \quad (5\text{-}28)$$

where $\rho' = \lambda/\mu' = \lambda/3\mu$. From the definition of $P(z)$ it is obvious that $P(1) = \Sigma_0^\infty \ p_r = 1$. Substituting for $z = 1$ in Eq. (5-28), we immediately obtain:

$$p_0 = 1 - 3\rho' = (1 - \rho) \qquad \rho = 3\rho' = \lambda/\mu.$$

Interestingly enough, the proportion of idle time is independent of the form of the distribution in this case. To obtain the steady-state probability p_r, we notice that it is the coefficient of z^r in the expansion of Eq. (5-28). It can be shown that if $r = j + 3i + m$,

$$p_r = (1 - \rho) \sum_m \sum_j \sum_i \rho'^m (-1)^i \binom{m}{i}\binom{m + j - 1}{j}$$

where the summation is taken over all the partitions of r as indicated. For the lower values of r, which are usually of the greatest interest, p_r, is easily obtained by direct substitution in Eq. (5-27). For example,

$$p_1 = \rho'(1 - \rho)$$

$$p_2 = \rho'(1 + \rho')(1 - \rho)$$

$$p_3 = \rho'(1 + \rho')^2(1 - \rho), \text{etc.}$$

The average number of "stations to go" is given by $\Sigma_0^\infty r \cdot p_r = \dfrac{d}{dz} P(z) \Big|_{z=1}$. Thus, differentiating Eq. (5-28) we obtain:

$$\mathcal{E}(r) = p_0 \sum_0^\infty \rho'^j \cdot j(z + z^2 + z^3)^{j-1}(1 + 2z + 3z^2) \Big|_{z=1}$$

$$= 2\rho/(1 - \rho) \qquad \rho = 3\rho'.$$

The average waiting time is $\mathcal{E}(w) = \mathcal{E}(r)/\mu' = 2\rho/\mu'(1 - \rho)$. Suppose that the average number of customers in the system is $\bar{n}$; their average "number of stations to go" is $3(\bar{n} - 1) + 3/2$, since $\bar{n} - 1$ customers are in the queue and one customer is "halfway." This must be equal to $\mathcal{E}(r)$; hence,

$$\bar{n} = \mathcal{E}(n) = \frac{2\rho}{3(1 - \rho)} + \tfrac{1}{2}.$$

The average time in the queue at any internal station is simply $\mathcal{E}(w)/3$.

Clearly, a similar analysis can be undertaken for E-distribution of *arrivals*. In this case the E-distribution is synthesized by k internal stations in series prior to the service facility which is assumed Poissonian, as shown in Fig. 5-17. Notice that the simulator is preceded by an infinite

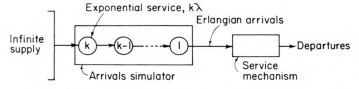

FIGURE 5-17   The Case of E_k Arrivals and Random Service

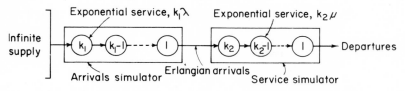

FIGURE 5-18   The Case of Erlangian Arrival and Service

supply source; hence, the simulator is never empty. Finally, the treatment can be generalized to *Erlangian arrival and service* distribution functions as shown in Fig. 5-18. In both cases, the equilibrium equations can be written in a straightforward manner. Except for modest values of k_1 and k_2 (the number of internal stations in the arrival and service simulators, respectively), the system of equations tends to be large and intractable.

The E-distribution of Eq. (5-26) has another interesting and useful interpretation. Consider the simple case of a single server with exponential service time and random arrivals. What is the distribution function of the time between, say, the nth arrival and the $(n + k)$th arrival? Since the time between two *consecutive* arrivals has the exponential distribution $\lambda e^{-\lambda t}$, the elapsed time for k arrivals, call it t_k, is the sum of k independent and identically distributed random variables, each possessing the exponential distribution function $\lambda e^{-\lambda t}$. We already know that t_k has the Erlang distribution

$$f(t_k) = \frac{\lambda^k}{\Gamma(k)} (t_k)^{k-1} e^{-\lambda t_k}. \tag{5-29}$$

The mean of this distribution is k/λ and its variance is k/λ^2.

Next, consider a single facility with k channels of service in parallel, as depicted in Fig. 5-19. Assume random arrivals with mean rate λ.

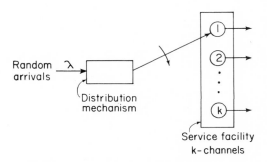

FIGURE 5-19   Rotational Allocation of Arrivals

Finally, suppose that a mechanism distributes arrivals over the k channels in the following fashion: the first arrival is assigned to channel 1, the second to channel 2, and so on; the $(k + 1)$st arrival is assigned to channel 1, etc. Clearly, the distribution of time between assignments to any channel is given by Eq. (5-29).

One useful application of this concept is to the analysis of orderly division of arrivals over k service stations in parallel. Such rotational assignments are common in restaurants (first party to waitress 1, second party to waitress 2, . . .), real estate offices, etc. The case of $k = 2$ was treated by Morse who gave the following results (see Fig. 5-20):

$$p_0 = 1 - \rho \qquad\qquad\qquad \rho = \lambda/\mu$$

$$p_n = \rho\left[\tfrac{1}{2} - 2\rho + \sqrt{\tfrac{1}{4} + 2\rho}\right]\left[\tfrac{1}{2} + 2\rho - \sqrt{\tfrac{1}{4} + 2\rho}\right]^{n-1}$$

and

$$\mathcal{E}(n) = \left[2\rho + \sqrt{\tfrac{1}{4} + 2\rho} - \tfrac{1}{2}\right]/4(1 - \rho).$$

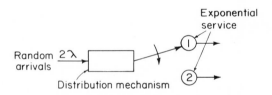

FIGURE 5-20   Rotational Allocation of Arrivals

Notice that rotational assignment results in Erlangian distribution of time between arrivals to both stations 1 and 2, which is given by

$$f(t) = (2\lambda)^2 t \, e^{-2\lambda t}.$$

On the other hand, if the splitting of arrivals is conducted in a *random* fashion so that an arrival is assigned to station 1 with probability α and to station 2 with probability $(1 - \alpha)$, as depicted in Fig. 5-21, the resulting distribution of time between arrivals to both stations is still *Poissonian* with mean $\alpha(2\lambda)$ and $(1 - \alpha)(2\lambda)$, respectively. Such randomized allocation of arrivals occurs in shops due to defective production, or it may represent the division of traffic at a road junction, etc.

This discussion suggests the possible simulation of non-Poisson arrival or service distributions by *internal stations in parallel*. We are led to suspect that such an arrangement would lead to coefficients of variation $v \geq 1$, since simulation by internal stations in series resulted in $v \leq 1$. In fact, this is the case. We illustrate the approach by a simple example.

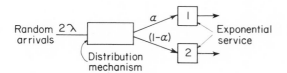

FIGURE 5-21 Randomized Allocation of Arrivals

Suppose that we have a system with random arrivals, and a distribution mechanism that assigns an arrival to internal stations 1 and 2 with probabilities α and $(1 - \alpha)$, respectively (see Fig. 5-22). Once a customer is assigned to an internal station, the whole service facility is considered occupied until his service is completed. Arrivals during such a period in which the facility is occupied join the waiting queue.

Let s denote the duration of service in the facility. Clearly, the function $f(s)$ given by

$$f(s) = \alpha \cdot \mu_1 \cdot e^{-\mu_1 s} + (1 - \alpha) \cdot \mu_2 \cdot e^{-\mu_2 s}$$

is the probability distribution function of the duration of service. It is easy to determine that

$$\bar{s} = \mathcal{E}(s) = \alpha/\mu_1 + (1 - \alpha)/\mu_2$$

and

$$\sigma_s^2 = \text{Var}(s) = \alpha(2 - \alpha)/\mu_1^2 - 2\alpha(1 - \alpha)/\mu_1\mu_2 - (1 - \alpha^2)/\mu_2^2$$

and therefore the coefficient of variation is

$$\nu = [\mu_2^2 \cdot \alpha(2 - \alpha) - 2\mu_1\mu_2 \cdot \alpha(1 - \alpha)$$
$$+ \mu_1^2(1 - \alpha^2)]^{1/2}/[\alpha\mu_2 + (1 - \alpha)\mu_1]$$

It is easy to see that $\nu \geq 1$. In particular, if $\mu_1 = \mu_2 = \mu$, $\nu = 1$. If $\mu_1 = m\mu_2$; i.e., the rate of service in internal station 1 is m times the rate

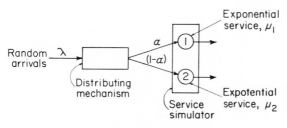

FIGURE 5-22

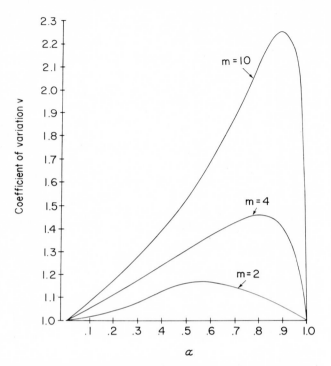

FIGURE 5-23 **Coefficient of Variation v as a Function of α for Three Values of m**

of service in station 2, $m \geq 1$, then

$$\overline{s} = [m - \alpha(m - 1)]/m\mu_2$$

$$\sigma_s^2 = [m^2 - 2\alpha(m - 1) - \alpha^2(m - 1)^2]/m^2\mu_2^2$$

and

$$\nu = [m^2 - 2\alpha(m - 1) - \alpha^2(m - 1)^2]^{1/2}/[m - \alpha(m - 1)].$$

Figure 5-23 gives the coefficient of variation ν as a function of α for $m = 2, 4,$ and 10.

§12. MORE COMPLICATED SYSTEMS: SIMULATION OF NETWORKS OF QUEUES

At this point the reader must be convinced of two things. First, that the network models we have treated thus far are drastic simplifications of real life problems. And second, in spite of their simplicity, we still needed rather powerful mathematical tools for their analysis.

Many an engineer designing a conveyor system or analyzing flow in a job shop, a highway traffic system, or a communication network has found himself with little, if any, guidance from theory. This brings to the fore two important characteristics of queueing theory:

1. It is a descriptive theory, not a normative one. It is a tool of analysis, not of synthesis. If optimization of an objective function is introduced in the analysis, it is usually done obliquely and in very special cases.
2. Complicated networks usually lead to intractable mathematical formulations.

In an attempt to answer the persisting design problems, the engineer resorts to the technique of simulation. Some significant results have been achieved in the fields of communication engineering. Very few results of any import were achieved in the areas of industrial and civil engineering. It is hoped that with the more powerful simulation languages available today the analyst will be spared the drudgery of developing the simulator and can devote his time and effort to his primary objective which is developing the queue network system itself.

For a more detailed discussion of the technique of simulation see Chapter 7, §3.4.

COMMENTS AND BIBLIOGRAPHY

§2.   The discussion in this section is based on a model by

HANSSMANN, F.   *Operations Research in Production and Inventory Control*, New York, Wiley, 1962.

Several books and papers were consulted in the preparation of the material in Sections 3 through 11.

SAATY, T. L.   *Elements of Queueing Theory with Applications*, New York, McGraw-Hill, 1961.

This book contains a comprehensive bibliography on the theory of queues and related topics.

The following monograph is a delightful introduction to the subject of queueing.

COX, D. R. and W. L. SMITH   *Queues*, New York, Wiley, 1961.

We also drew upon the following book:

MORSE, P. M.   *Queues, Inventories and Maintenance*, New York, Wiley, 1958.

An exposition of the mathematical foundation of queueing theory can be found in Saaty's book, mentioned above, or in

FELLER, W.   *Introduction to Probability Theory and Its Application*, New York, Wiley, 1957.

§8.   The material of this section is based on

ELMAGHRABY, S. and E. RICHMAN   "Design of In-Process Storage Facilities," *Journal of Industrial Engineering*, Vol. 8, 1, January–February, 1957.

§9.   The first analysis of this problem appeared in

HUNT, C.   "Sequential Arrays of Waiting Lines," *Operations Research*, Vol. 4, No. 6, December 1956, pp. 674–683.

§10.   Analytical work on network models of job shops is due to Jackson and his co-workers.

JACKSON, J. R.   "Networks of Waiting Lines," *Operations Research*, Vol. 5, No. 4, August 1957, pp. 518–521.

JACKSON, J. R.   "Networks of Queues with Controlled Service Rates," Western Management Science Institute, Working paper No. 10, August 28, 1962.

JACKSON, J. R.   "Job Shop-like Queueing Systems," Western Management Science Institute, Working paper No. 27, January 1963.

JACKSON, J. R., R. T. NELSON, and A. A. GRINDLEY   "Research on Job Shop-like Models: A Progress Report," Western Management Science Institute, Working paper No. 12, July 18, 1962.

§12.   For references on the application of simulation techniques to the studies of networks of queues, see the references cited in the report by Jackson, Nelson, and Grindley mentioned above.

EXERCISES

1.   Determine the necessary buffer inventory between two sequential processes if the first is subject to random breakdowns whose duration is approximately normally distributed with mean $\bar{\tau} = 1.5$ hours and standard deviation $\sigma = 25$ minutes. A study of the pattern of failure of the first machine revealed that failures occur randomly at the rate of once every 40 hours. It is required to operate at a confidence level of 98% concerning the operation of the second machine.

2.   The operation of the blast furnaces is continuous all year round. Tapping the furnace, i.e., extracting the molten pig iron, can be considered a random event, since it is a function of several factors. For simplicity, we shall assume it is completely random, and that is not too bad an assumption in the case of more than one furnace.

   Pig iron is usually further refined to yield the various kinds of steel for construction, machinery, railroads, etc. The molten iron is kept in large containers which are lined with refractory material and heated to keep the iron molten. The demand of the open hearth furnaces and Bessemer converters for the molten pig iron is random in nature, especially if there is a battery of such furnaces, which is usually the case. We assume that it is Poisson with mean μ.

   If the average rate of production of pig iron is 14 tons per hour per blast furnace, and a plant has three such furnaces, while the average demand for the open hearth furnace is 60 tons per 8 hours, and there are 6 such furnaces, determine the required capacity of the container to guarantee with a probability of 98% that both types of furnaces will be satisfied.

3.   Workers in a machine shop complain of the unavailability of an overhead crane. Investigation reveals that demand for the crane occurs with a mean

of 15 calls per hour. The duration of occupancy of the crane is not uniform; some jobs require simple and fast transportation while others require positioning of heavy equipment on machines. The probability distribution function of the duration of service is $f(x) = 0.04 \, e^{-0.04x}$.

  a. Are the complaints justified? Give a quantitative answer.

  b. If an identical crane is installed, would the situation be improved? State your answers in probabilistic terms.

4. Consider a single-server facility in which the server regulates his rate of output according to the size of the queue: $\mu_n = n^c \cdot \mu$ where c and μ are constants greater than 0. The rate of arrival is λ. Assume no limitation on the size of the queue ahead of the station. Show that the steady-state probabilities are given by the solution to the system of difference equations

$$\rho \cdot p_0 = p_1 \qquad\qquad \rho = \lambda/\mu$$
$$(\rho + n^c)p_n = \rho \cdot p_{n-1} + (n + 1)^c \cdot p_{n+1} \qquad n > 0,$$

and hence deduce that

$$p_0 = 1/S$$
$$p_n = \rho^n/(n!)^c \, S,$$

where $S = \Sigma_0^\infty \rho^n/(n!)^c$.[†]

5. In the model of Problem 4, suppose that the rate of arrival is also a function of the size of the queue: $\lambda_n = (n + 1)^a \lambda$. Usually a is < 0, which implies a slow-down of arrivals as the size of the queue increases; λ is > 0. Show that the system of steady-state equations is given by

$$\rho \, p_0 = p_1 \qquad\qquad \rho = \lambda/\mu$$
$$[(n + 1)^a \rho + n^c] \, p_n = n^a \rho \, p_{n-1} + (n + 1)^c \, p_{n+1} \qquad n > 0,$$

and hence deduce that if $S = \Sigma_0^\infty \rho^n (n!)^{a-c}$,

$$p_n = (n!)^{a-c} \cdot \rho^n \, S^{-1}.$$

6. A dispatcher of a fleet of 8 taxicabs receives calls at the rate of 40 calls per hour. The average length of a trip is 8 minutes, which includes waiting, loading, etc.

  a. Calculate the total expected idle time of the fleet.

  b. If the revenue from a trip can be roughly estimated at $0.15 per minute and the expenses estimated at $4.00 per hour for the driver and $0.80 per hour for the taxicab, would he be justified in retiring one or more taxicabs if customer dissatisfaction is estimated at $0.08 per minute of waiting?

7. A suggestion was made to pool 3 fork trucks available in the storeroom with 5 fork trucks in the shop in a general service department under a single management. The analyst tried to substantiate his proposal with quantitative

[†]Conway and Maxwell, *Journal of Industrial Engineering*, Vol. 12, No. 2, 1961.

measures of idle time, average number of waiting customers, and average waiting time. The following are his basic data:

	Storeroom	Shop
Rate of demand	20	30
Rate of service	22	38

Present the analyst's argument.

8. A communications engineer wishes to determine the number of service channels he should provide for a certain level of service. Assuming input calls arrive at an average rate of 60 calls per minute, and each channel can handle an average of 15 calls per minute, what is the minimum number of channels required for a probability of congestion (i.e., all channels busy) of less than 1%?

9. Consider the case of two operations in sequence. Let $\lambda = 40$ units per hour and $\mu_1 = 45$ units per hour. Determine μ_2, the rate of service in the second operation, if it is desired to achieve a utilization factor of at least 80% for the whole system. The maximum size of queue permitted is 1 in both operations.

10. For the two-stage sequential queues with no limitation on the length of the queues, show that the probability of having n units in the system is given by

$$p_n = (n + 1)\rho^n (1 - \rho)^2 \qquad \rho = \lambda/\mu, \mu_1 = \mu_2 = \mu,$$

and that the mean number of units in the system is

$$\bar{n} = 2\rho/(1 - \rho).$$

What is the average waiting time? What is the average total service time (= processing and waiting)? Finally, show that for a general N-stage process,

$$p_n = \prod_{k=1}^{n} (N + k - 1)\rho^n (1 - \rho)^N/n!$$

(Hint: use the z-transform of the single stage and the fact that p_n is the convolution of N functions.)

11. Let the behavior of two sequential stations be described by the model of Problem 5. That is, assume the rate of arrival to be a function of the size of the queue at station 1,

$$\lambda_{n_1} = (n_1 + 1)^a \lambda$$

and that the rate of service at each station is a function of the size of the queue at that station (simulating speed-up in the case of congestion),

$$\mu_{n_1} = n_1^b \cdot \mu \qquad b > 0$$

$$\mu_{n_2} = n_2^c \cdot \mu \qquad c > 0.$$

Determine the equilibrium probability equations assuming no limitation on the size of the queue at either station. Then show that the probability of having n_1 units in the first queue and n_2 units in the second is given by

$$p(n_1, n_2) = [(n_1 + n_2)!]^{-a}(n_1!)^{-b}(n_2!)^{-c} S^{-1},$$

where S is to be determined so that the sum of all probabilities is equal to 1.

12. Generalize the truncated queueing model of §9 to M queues in parallel, $M < q$. In particular, show that p_n is given by

$$p_n = \begin{cases} (M\rho)^n p_0/n! & 0 \le n < M, \rho = \lambda/\mu \\ (M)^M \rho^n p_0/M! & M \le n \le q. \end{cases}$$

13. The plant engineer who designed the following assembly line assumed he will obtain a "balanced" line since the service rates are increased and decreased in proportion to the split in the total flow between the two branches. If $\lambda = 40, \mu_1 = 45$, study the behavior of the system from the point of view of congestion and idle time at the various operations. (See Fig. 5-24.)

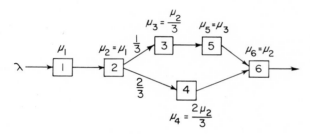

FIGURE 5-24

14. A refinery receives crude oil in tank A in a Poissonian fashion with mean λ. The crude oil is pumped randomly from A at an average rate μ_1 into the cracking process B. (See Fig. 5-25.) Assume, for simplicity, that only two

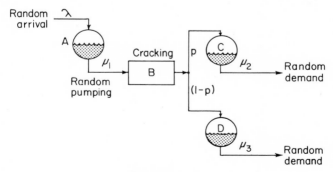

FIGURE 5-25

products result from the cracking operation in proportions p and $(1 - p)$. The first product is stored in tank C and the second in tank D. Demand on the finished products is assumed random with means μ_2 and μ_3, respectively.

If the capacities of the three tanks are K_A, K_C, and K_D, respectively, and $\mu_1 > \lambda, \mu_2 + \mu_3 = \mu_1$, determine the probability of:

   a. Demand on first product not satisfied.

   b. Demand on second product not satisfied.

   c. Tank A empty—system inoperative.

CHAPTER 6 / FEEDBACK CONTROL SYSTEMS

§1. INTRODUCTION

Although the term feedback has a simple and intuitive meaning, an attempt to state an explicit definition meets with difficulties. However, when feedback is for control purposes we can easily ascertain its existence and nature. In essence, whenever control is effected through the comparison of the *actual* output of a system with its *desired* output, feedback control is present. Therefore, the essence of feedback is such a comparison. Since the comparison involves the evaluation of the *difference* between the two quantities, it is usually referred to as "negative feedback."

The theory of feedback started in the field of electronics in conjunction with improving the performance of certain amplifiers used in telephony, but was, in fact, traced by Norbert Wiener to James Clarke Maxwell's 1868 treatise on governors of steam engines. Bellman and Dreyfus claim, however, that the theory's date is even earlier since "a governor invented by Huygens for the regulation of clocks was used for windmills and water wheels before the advent of the steam engine."[†]

Whatever its origin, feedback control plays an important role in our life—Wiener has pronounced it the foundation of every self-regulating element in the world, whether living or inanimate. The simple process of reaching for a pencil involves complicated feedback phenomena—as complicated, perhaps, as that involved in guiding a missile to a predetermined target several thousand miles away.

In 1948 the important paper by Shannon and Weaver[‡] on the mathematical theory of information appeared, and for the first time a measure of "information" was available. This prompted investigators in the field of control to modify their concepts to include the "flow of information"—

[†] R. Bellman and S. Dreyfus, *Applied Dynamic Programming*, Princeton University Press, Princeton, 1962, p. 246.

[‡] C. E. Shannon and W. Weaver, *The Mathematical Theory of Communication*, University of Illinois Press, Urbana, Ill., 1949.

which, in reality, is not *physical* flow—and attempt to treat it similarly to the flow of current through wires or the flow of liquid through pipes. Inevitably, *conceptual* systems, rather than hardware systems, became associated with feedback control. In this book, our concern is with such conceptual systems as production, inventory, and distribution, whether or not they involve hardware.

We point out that the study of the theory is of great importance to Industrial Engineers, Management Scientists, Operations Researchers, or any other discipline engaged in the design and implementation of control systems. This is so for two reasons. First, several problems of such systems can be successfully treated from the point of view of feedback control theory. In the following sections we will give several illustrations to substantiate this contention. Second, even if no direct utility of the theory is encountered by the practicing engineer in the analysis or synthesis of decision and control systems within his immediate sphere of endeavor, the conceptual framework of analysis gained through the study of feedback control theory is of great use.

For example, the mere awareness of the concepts of transfer function, the transient and steady-state performances, the measurement of error, and the varying of input depending on the magnitude of such error, conditions the design of the system to a great extent.

A feedback control system can be represented by the following basic diagram (Fig. 6-1). The lower loop is the feedback loop; its absence would

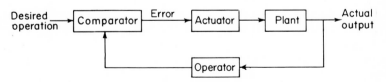

FIGURE 6-1   Basic Feedback Loop

render the system "open." (Strangely enough, such an open system is sometimes referred to as "open loop" in spite of the absence of any "loop.") Without feedback there is no interaction between the actual output and the desired output.

Several systems are designed "open," either because the error involved is infinitesimal and can be ignored, or because it is uneconomical to construct the feedback loop.

For example, several voltmeters are built as an open system. The deflection of the indicator is not fed back to be compared with the desired deflection, as in Fig. 6-2(a). That such a feedback is possible is shown in Fig. 6-2(b), in which a potentiometer is provided to give rise to a voltage

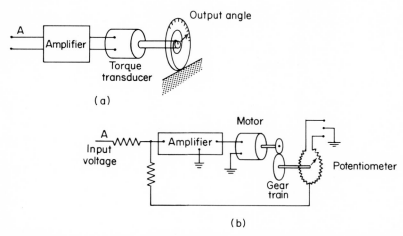

FIGURE 6-2 (a) Open Measurement of Voltage at A, and (b) Feedback Measurement of Voltage at A

which is proportional to the output. The torque transducer is actuated by the difference between this voltage and the input voltage.

On the other hand, consider the traffic lights at a busy intersection. The purpose of installing such lights is to ensure a smooth flow of traffic in *all* directions (although sometimes this is not apparent). Therefore, one would expect that the duration of the lights, whether red or green, in any direction, would be a function of the intensity of traffic in all directions. In other words, the behavior of the lights should be controlled by the lack of smooth flow in any direction. This would necessitate a feedback system. In reality, a very small minority of traffic lights at intersections are designed to operate in such a fashion. The majority of them are open systems, in which the duration of the green (or red) light is predetermined independently of the intensity of traffic in any direction. When such open-system behavior threatens to produce chaos, the whole system is shut off, and a policeman, with his built-in feedback systems, takes over!

As with other fields of engineering, feedback control draws upon certain mathematical and physical sciences which then become an integral part of its language and operational tools of design. Among the most important tools are: differential and integral calculus, the operational calculus based on the one-sided and two-sided Laplace transform in the case of continuous time functions, and the z-transform in the case of sampled data or discrete time functions.

In the following section, and in Sections 7 and 8, we will present a brief outline of the most salient results in these areas, which will be drawn

upon in the subsequent sections. We emphasize that the treatment is, by
necessity, rather sketchy, and the reader is urged to complement his
knowledge by referring to some of the literature listed at the end of the
chapter.

§2. THE OPERATIONAL CALCULUS BASED ON THE LAPLACE TRANSFORM

2.1 The One-Sided Laplace Transform

The study of systems in the time domain—i.e., when inputs, outputs,
and the behavior of the components are expressed as functions of time—
is oftentimes rather cumbersome and sometimes almost impossible.
Engineers, in their search for operational methods of analysis and synthesis, utilized several transforms which are known by different names but
are essentially based on the same principle. Thus, the Heaviside calculus,
the Laplace transform, and the Fourier transform represent three attempts
at devising an operational calculus which is based on the transformation
from the time domain to the complex-plane domain. In this section, we
will treat the one-sided Laplace transform, hereafter referred to as
$\mathcal{L}$-transform.

As will be seen shortly, there are some definite advantages to the use of
the $\mathcal{L}$-transform. Most important among them is the replacement of the
operations of differentiation and integration in the time domain by simple
algebraic operations such as multiplication and division, in the "complex"
or "frequency" domain. Consequently, both analysis and synthesis are
carried out in the frequency domain, and, when the design is complete, the
final results are reinterpreted in the time domain. The resulting conceptual clarity and manipulative ease cannot be overlooked.

Definition. Let $f(t)$ be any function of time and let s be the complex
variable $s = \sigma + j\omega$, where $j = \sqrt{-1}$. Let $\mathcal{L}$ be the operational symbol
indicating that the quantity it prefixes is to be transformed. Then we
define

$$F(s) = \mathcal{L}\,[f(t)] = \int_0^\infty f(t)\,e^{-st}\,dt \qquad (6\text{-}1)$$

as the $\mathcal{L}$-transform of $f(t)$. Hereafter, we will assume that the conditions
for the existence of $F(s)$, which are rather general in nature, are always
satisfied.

Of course we can obtain the $\mathcal{L}$-transform of a function of any argument
other than time. The variable t is used here because it is the most common
variable in systems design.

2.2 Examples

1. Let $f(t) = c$, a constant (Fig. 6-3). Then $\mathcal{L}[f(t)] = \int_0^\infty c\,e^{-st}\,dt = c/s$. A function closely related to the above is the step function shown in Fig. 6-4. Its $\mathcal{L}$-transform is also c/s. The reason is obvious: the transform ignores all information about $f(t)$ for $t < 0$ (hence the name "one-sided"

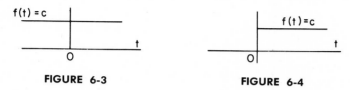

FIGURE 6-3   FIGURE 6-4

Laplace transform). This is important when we are seeking the *inverse transformation*, i.e., when we wish to obtain the time function $f(t)$ from knowledge of $F(s)$, as we shall see below.

If $c = 1$, the *unit step function* defined by

$$u(t) = \begin{cases} 0 & t < 0 \\ 1 & t \ge 1 \end{cases} \tag{6-2}$$

has the transform $1/s$. The designation $u(t)$ is usually reserved for this function.

It would be of interest to plot the transform $\mathcal{L}[u(t)]$ in the complex plane. Since $F(s) = 1/s$, put $s = j\omega$ to obtain

$$F(j\omega) = -j/\omega$$

which plots along the imaginary axis as shown in Fig. 6-5. Presently we shall give the rationale behind substituting $j\omega$ for s in $F(s)$.

2. Let $f(t) = c\,e^{-\alpha t}$; then

$$\mathcal{L}[f(t)] = \int_0^\infty c\,e^{-\alpha t}e^{-st}\,dt = c/(\alpha + s).$$

In general, $\mathcal{L}[cf(t)] = c\mathcal{L}[f(t)]$ when c is a constant.

The plot of $F(j\omega)$ in the complex plane is obtained from

$$F(j\omega) = \frac{c}{\alpha + j\omega} = \frac{c(\alpha - j\omega)}{\alpha^2 + \omega^2} = \frac{c\alpha}{\alpha^2 + \omega^2} - j\frac{c\omega}{\alpha^2 + \omega^2}.$$

Let Re[$\cdot$] denote the real part of a complex variable, and Im[$\cdot$] denote the imaginary part. Then

$$\text{Re}[F(j\omega)] = \frac{c\alpha}{\alpha^2 + \omega^2} \quad \text{and} \quad \text{Im}[F(j\omega)] = \frac{-c\omega}{\alpha^2 + \omega^2}$$

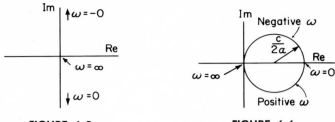

FIGURE 6-5   **FIGURE 6-6**

which yields a circle with center at the point $c/2\alpha$ on the real axis (Fig. 6-6).

3. Let $f(t) = ct$, the "ramp" function; then

$$\mathcal{L}[f(t)] = \int_0^\infty ct\, e^{-st}\, dt.$$

The integration can be done by parts as follows. Let $u = t$ and $dv = e^{-st}\, dt$; then $du = dt$ and $v = -e^{-st}/s$. Therefore,

$$\mathcal{L}[t] = uv\,\Big|_{t=0}^{\infty} - \int_0^\infty -\frac{1}{s}e^{-st}dt = 1/s^2.$$

Hence,

$$\mathcal{L}[f(t)] = c/s^2.$$

In general, it can easily be shown through successive integration by parts that

$$\mathcal{L}[(t^n)] = n!/s^{n+1}.$$

4. Let $f(t) = \sin \beta t$; then

$$\mathcal{L}[(\sin \beta t)] = \int_0^\infty \sin \beta t \cdot e^{-st}\, dt.$$

But $\sin \beta t = (e^{j\beta t} - e^{-j\beta t})/2j$; therefore,

$$\mathcal{L}[\sin \beta t] = \frac{1}{2j} \int_0^\infty (e^{j\beta t} - e^{-j\beta t})\, e^{-st}\, dt$$

$$= \frac{1}{2j}\left[\frac{1}{(s - j\beta)} - \frac{1}{(s + j\beta)}\right] = \frac{\beta}{s^2 + \beta^2}.$$

Similarly, it can easily be shown that

$$\mathcal{L}[\cos \beta t] = \frac{s}{s^2 + \beta^2}.$$

2.3 Properties of the $\mathcal{L}$-transform

The following are among the most useful properties of the Laplace transform for our purposes.

Linearity.   The transform of a linear combination of time functions is the linear combination of their transforms.

$$\mathcal{L}[af(t) + bg(t)] = a\mathcal{L}[f(t)] + b\mathcal{L}[g(t)] \tag{6-3}$$

Real Differentiation Theorem.   The transform of the derivative of a function is given by

$$\mathcal{L}\left[\frac{d}{dt}f(t)\right] = sF(s) - f(0^+) \tag{6-4}$$

where $f(0^+)$ is the initial value of $f(t)$ evaluated as $t \to 0$ from the *positive* side of the real axis.

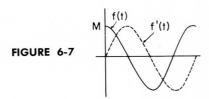

FIGURE 6-7

For example, consider the cosine function with amplitude M shown in Fig. 6-7; its derivative is a sine wave with amplitude $M\beta$. Application of the theorem gives

$$\mathcal{L}\left[\frac{d}{dt} M\cos\beta t\right] = M \cdot s \frac{s}{s^2 + \beta^2} - f(0^+)$$

$$= M \frac{s^2}{s^2 + \beta^2} - M = M \frac{-\beta^2}{s^2 + \beta^2}.$$

But

$$\mathcal{L}[-M\beta\sin\beta t] = -M\beta \frac{\beta}{s^2 + \beta^2} = M \frac{-\beta^2}{s^2 + \beta^2},$$

as before.

Real Integration Theorem.   The transform of the integral of a function is given by

$$\mathcal{L}\left[\int f(t)dt\right] = \frac{F(s)}{s} + \frac{\int_{0^+} f(t)\,dt}{s} \tag{6-5}$$

Where $\int_{0^+} f(t)\, dt$ is evaluated as $t \to 0$ from the positive side. We also have

$$\mathcal{L}\left[\int_0^t f(t)\, dt\right] = \frac{1}{s} F(s)$$

and

$$\mathcal{L}\left[\int_a^t f(t)\, dt\right] = \frac{1}{s} F(s) + \frac{1}{s} \int_0^a f(t)\, dt.$$

Translation Properties. The following two properties exhibit the symmetry relationship between the time function and its $\mathcal{L}$-transform. Let

$$f(t) = \begin{cases} 0 & t < a \\ g(t - a) & t \geq a; \end{cases}$$

then,

$$F(s) = e^{-as} G(s) \tag{6-6}$$

where $G(s)$ is the $\mathcal{L}$-transform of $g(t)$. Conversely, let

$$g(t) = e^{at} f(t).$$

then

$$\mathcal{L}[g(t)] = \mathcal{L}[e^{at} f(t)] = F(s - a). \tag{6-7}$$

The proof of this and the previous two theorems is straightforward and is accomplished by direct substitution in the definition of the transform.

The Convolution Integral. The following integral plays an important role in servomechanism theory:

$$y(t) = \int_0^t f(t - \tau)\, g(\tau)\, d\tau \quad t \geq 0 \tag{6-8}$$

and is sometimes written as

$$y(t) = f(t) * g(t). \tag{6-9}$$

Its $\mathcal{L}$-transform is given by

$$\mathcal{L}[y(t)] = Y(s) = F(s)G(s) \tag{6-10}$$

where $F(s)$ and $G(s)$ are the $\mathcal{L}$-transforms of $f(t)$ and $g(t)$, respectively. It is seen that convolution in the time domain is equivalent to *multiplication* in the complex plane.

The importance of the convolution integral of Eq. (6-8) lies in the fact that it represents the output of a system whose *impulse response* (explained in the next paragraph) is $g(t)$ when the system is acted upon by input $f(t)$.

The impulse response of a system can be considered as a *weighing function*: the output $y(t)$ at any instant of time depends on the input at the same time and at all *earlier* times; the degree of dependence on the past is determined by the weighing function $g(t)$.

$$f(t) \longrightarrow \boxed{g(t)} \longrightarrow y(t)$$

This is apparent from Eq. (6-8), which can be made even clearer if we consider its discrete analogue,

$$y(N\Delta) = \sum_{k=0}^{N} g(k\Delta)f(N\Delta - k\Delta)$$

$$= g(0)f(N\Delta) + g(\Delta)f(N\Delta - \Delta) + \ldots + g(N\Delta)f(0).$$

The Transform of Product. The "dual" of the above relationship is also true: the $\mathcal{L}$-transform of the *product* of two time functions is the convolution of their individual $\mathcal{L}$-transforms. Thus,

$$\mathcal{L}[f_1(t)f_2(t)] = F_1(s) * F_2(s)$$

$$= \int_{-\infty}^{\infty} F(s_1)F_2(s - s_1)ds_1. \tag{6-11}$$

The Initial Value Theorem. Since analysis is usually conducted in the frequency domain while interpretation of the results is sometimes required in the time domain, the following two theorems establish the corresponding values of the function at $t \to 0$ and $t \to \infty$.

$$\lim_{t \to 0} f(t) = \lim_{|s| \to \infty} sF(s). \tag{6-12}$$

This relationship is valid if both $f(t)$ and its time derivative $f'(t)$ have $\mathcal{L}$-transforms and the limit $\lim_{|s| \to \infty} sF(s)$ exists.

The Final Value Theorem. It can also be stated that if $f(t)$ and $f'(t)$ have $\mathcal{L}$-transforms, and if $sF(s)$ is analytic on the imaginary axis and the positive half of the complex plane (i.e., possesses no singularities in these regions), then,

$$\lim_{t \to \infty} f(t) = \lim_{|s| \to 0} sF(s). \tag{6-13}$$

As an illustration of these two theorems, consider the time function,

$$f(t) = e^{-at} \cos bt;$$

its $\mathcal{L}$-transform is given by (applying the translation property):

$$F(s) = \frac{s + a}{(s + a)^2 + b^2}.$$

Then,

$$\lim_{t \to 0} f(t) = \lim_{|s| \to \infty} s F(s) = \lim_{|s| \to \infty} \frac{1 + a/s}{(s + a)^2/s^2 + b^2/s^2} = 1.0$$

which is in consonance with our knowledge that $f(0) = 1.0$. Also,

$$\lim_{t \to \infty} f(t) = \lim_{|s| \to 0} s F(s) = \frac{s^2 + sa}{(s + a)^2 + b^2} = 0,$$

again a result in agreement with the known fact that the amplitude is exponentially decaying to zero.

Conjugate Transforms.   Let $F(s)$ be the $\mathcal{L}$-transform of $f(t)$, then,

$$\mathcal{L}\,[f(-t)] = F(-s) = \overline{F}(s). \tag{6-14}$$

To put it in words: the $\mathcal{L}$-transform of the image of the time function about the vertical axis is the complex conjugate[†] of the original transform.

2.4 The Inverse $\mathcal{L}$-Transform

Thus far we have been dealing with *direct transformation*, i.e., we have obtained the $\mathcal{L}$-transform from knowledge of the time function. Once analysis is conducted in the complex plane, the final results may be adequately represented in the complex plane. However, oftentimes it is desirable to translate such results back into the time domain. This process is called the *inverse transformation* and is denoted by $\mathcal{L}^{-1}$.

If $F(s)$ is given, then the corresponding $f(t)$ is defined as the solution to the integral equation.

$$\int_0^\infty e^{-st} f(t)\,dt = F(s).$$

In the advanced works on complex variables it is proved that if this equation has a solution then the solution is unique (Lerch's Theorem).[‡] Thus, the relationship between a function and its transform is similar to the relationship between a function and its integral. However, in Laplace transformation a uniqueness property is present; viz., for any function $f(t)$, if an $\mathcal{L}$-transform exists, it is unique within the range of definition of $f(t)$, and vice versa.

[†] A complex number is given by $a + jb$; its complex conjugate is given by $a - jb$. Note that the product of a complex number and its conjugate is a real positive number $a^2 + b^2$.

[‡] F. B. Hildebrand, *Advanced Calculus for Engineers*, Prentice Hall, 1949, p. 62.

Hence, tables of inverse transforms can be constructed similar to the more familiar tables of integrals. For instance, we already know that

$$\mathcal{L}^{-1}\left[\frac{1}{s}\right] = u(t), \tag{6-15a}$$

$$\mathcal{L}^{-1}\left[\frac{c}{\alpha + s}\right] = ce^{-\alpha t} \tag{6-15b}$$

$$\mathcal{L}^{-1}\left[\frac{c}{s^2}\right] = ct \tag{6-15c}$$

$$\mathcal{L}^{-1}\left[\frac{\beta}{s^2 + \beta^2}\right] = \sin \beta t \tag{6-15d}$$

and

$$\mathcal{L}^{-1}\left[\frac{s}{s^2 + \beta^2}\right] = \cos \beta t. \tag{6-15e}$$

Extensive tables of $\mathcal{L}$-transforms are published; tables of the most important and frequently used transforms can be found in any book on servomechanism theory.

Should the inverse transform not be readily available, it can be obtained by first decomposing $F(s)$ into elementary functions:

$$F(s) = F_1(s) + F_2(s) + \ldots + F_n(s).$$

Such decomposition can be obtained by partial fraction expansion. Now, if the $F_i(s)$'s are simple functions whose transforms are known, then,

$$\mathcal{L}^{-1}[F(s)] = \mathcal{L}^{-1}[F_1(s)] + \ldots + \mathcal{L}^{-1}[F_n(s)].$$

For example, let $F(s) = (5s + 13)/(s^2 + 6s + 5)$, and it is desired to obtain the inverse transformation $f(t)$. The denominator can be written as $(s + 5)(s + 1)$, which immediately suggests:

$$F(s) = \frac{5s + 13}{s^2 + 6s + 5} = \frac{k_1}{s + 5} + \frac{k_2}{s + 1}$$

where k_1 and k_2 are constants to be evaluated by any one of several techniques. Obviously, if both sides of the above equality are multiplied by $(s + 5)$ we obtain

$$\frac{5s + 13}{(s + 1)} = k_1 + k_2 \frac{s + 5}{s + 1}.$$

Now putting $s = -5$ immediately yields $k_1 = 3$. Similarly, if we multiply both sides of the equality by $(s + 1)$ and put $s = -1$ we obtain $k_2 = $

$(5s + 13)/(s + 5)\big|_{s=-1} = 2$. Hence, the partial fraction expansion is

$$F(s) = \frac{3}{s + 5} + \frac{2}{s + 1}.$$

Consequently,

$$\mathcal{L}^{-1}[F(s)] = f(t) = \mathcal{L}^{-1}\left[\frac{3}{s + 5}\right] + \mathcal{L}^{-1}\left[\frac{2}{s + 1}\right].$$

$$= 3e^{-5t} + 2e^{-t}.$$

Finally, since we are dealing exclusively with linear systems, the *principle of superposition* applies: if $f_1(t)$ is an input to a system of impulse response $g(t)$ and results in output $y_1(t)$, and if $f_2(t)$ is another input causing output $y_2(t)$, then an input $af_1(t) + bf_2(t)$ composed of a linear combination of the two individual inputs gives rise to the same linear combination of outputs, $ay_1(t) + by_2(t)$.

§3. THE STABILITY OF SYSTEMS

3.1 Differential Equation Representation

The analysis of feedback control systems revolves around the study of the response of the system to various inputs. The response $y(t)$ to some forcing function $f(t)$ is usually described by a linear differential equation of the nth order of the form

$$a_0(t)\frac{d^n y}{dt^n} + a_1(t)\frac{d^{n-1}y}{dt^{n-1}} + \ldots + a_{n-1}(t)\frac{dy}{dt} + a_n(t)y = f(t) \qquad (6\text{-}16)$$

where $a_0(t), \ldots, a_n(t)$ may be arbitrarily specified functions of t. A "solution" of Eq. (6-16) means determining the most general expression of the response $y(t)$ which if substituted into the left-hand side of Eq. (6-16) gives the prescribed right hand side $f(t)$.

We shall be interested in linear differential equations with constant coefficients such as:

$$a_0\frac{d^n y}{dt^n} + a_1\frac{d^{n-1}y}{dt^{n-1}} + \ldots + a_{n-1}\frac{dy}{dt} + a_n y = f(t). \qquad (6\text{-}17)$$

To be sure, if $a_1, \ldots, a_n$ are identically equal to 0, the solution of Eq. (6-17) would be accomplished by n successive integrations of the relationship $d^n y/dt^n = f(t)/a_0$, with each integration introducing an independent constant of integration. Thus, it might be expected that the general solution of Eq. (6-17) would also contain n independent arbitrary constants. In fact, when $f(t)$ is a definite function of time a general solution to Eq. (6-17) can usually be written as the sum of $n + 1$ functions:

$$y = y_0(t) + c_1 e^{\alpha_1 t} + c_2 e^{\alpha_2 t} + \ldots + c_n e^{\alpha_n t}. \tag{6-18}$$

The first term $y_0(t)$ is called the *particular solution*; the rest of the terms on the right-hand side are collectively the general solution to the *homogeneous differential equation*:

$$a_0 \frac{d^n y}{dt^n} + a_1 \frac{d^{n-1} y}{dt^{n-1}} + \ldots + a_{n-1} \frac{dy}{dt} + a_n y = 0 \tag{6-19}$$

and are called the *complementary function*. That this latter function is the solution to Eq. (6-19) can easily be seen from the substitution $y(t) = e^{\alpha t}$, which yields $d^m y/dt^m = \alpha^m e^{\alpha t}$; hence,

$$(a_0 \alpha^n + a_1 \alpha^{n-1} + \ldots + a_{n-1} \alpha + a_n) e^{\alpha t} = 0.$$

Therefore, $\alpha_1, \alpha_2, \ldots, \alpha_n$ of Eq. (6-18) are the roots of the *characteristic equation*:

$$a_0 \alpha^n + a_1 \alpha^{n-1} + \ldots + a_{n-1} \alpha + a_n = 0. \tag{6-20}$$

The c's in Eq. (6-18) are n constants to be evaluated from the initial conditions.

If all the roots of Eq. (6-20) are different, Eq. (6-18) is the correct form of the solution. However, if two or more roots are equal, the form of the solution must be modified. In this case, terms of the form $t\, e^{\alpha_m t}$, $t^2\, e^{\alpha_m t}$, etc. are found in the solution. Let ℓ be the linear operation defined by

$$\ell = a_0 \frac{d^n}{dt^n} + a_1 \frac{d^{n-1}}{dt^{n-1}} + \ldots + a_{n-1} \frac{d}{dt} + a_n,$$

and suppose that the two roots α_1 and α_2 are equal. Then we must have

$$\ell\, [e^{\alpha t}] = (\alpha - \alpha_1)^2 (\alpha - \alpha_3) \ldots (\alpha - \alpha_n) e^{\alpha t}.$$

It follows that not only the right-hand side itself but also its partial derivative with respect to α must vanish when $\alpha = \alpha_1$. The same must be true of the left-hand side. Thus we must have

$$\ell [e^{\alpha t}]_{\alpha = \alpha_1} = \ell [e^{\alpha_1 t}] = 0$$

and

$$\ell \left[\frac{\partial}{\partial \alpha} (e^{\alpha t}) \right]_{\alpha = \alpha_1} = \ell\, [t\, e^{\alpha_1 t}] = 0,$$

so that the part of the homogeneous solution corresponding to the double root α_1 can be written in the form

$$c_1 e^{\alpha_1 t} + c_2 t\, e^{\alpha_1 t}$$

as was to be shown.

In general, counting multiple roots according to their multiplicity permits the convention that there are n roots of the homogeneous Eq. (6-19). The α_i's are either real or complex numbers; in the latter case they must occur in conjugate pairs (for otherwise some of the final coefficients will be imaginary, which is an impossible characterization of the behavior of a physical system).

In theoretical discussions it is convenient to use the form of Eq. (6-18) to represent the behavior of the system even when complex roots exist. However, from a practical point of view, some insight can be gained in combining such terms and representing the real nature of the functions. Let α_1 and α_2 be a conjugate pair of complex roots. Then,

$$
\begin{aligned}
c_1 e^{\alpha_1 t} + c_2 e^{\alpha_2 t} &= c_1 e^{(\sigma + j\omega)t} + c_2 e^{(\sigma - j\omega)t} \\
&= e^{\sigma t}(c_1 e^{j\omega t} + c_2 e^{-j\omega t}) \\
&= e^{\sigma t}(d_1 \cos \omega t + d_2 \sin \omega t)
\end{aligned}
$$

if $d_1 = c_1 + c_2$ and $d_2 = j(c_1 - c_2)$. Naturally, for d_1 and d_2 to be real, c_1 and c_2 must be complex conjugates.

We have thus reached the conclusion that if all terms with complex roots in Eq. (6-18) are combined, the *entire complementary function will be made up of real exponentials and sine and cosine functions multiplied by real exponentials*. Hence, if some exponent α_m is positive, it will give rise to an exponentially increasing value of $y(t)$ as $t \rightarrow \infty$. On the other hand, a positive σ_k will give rise to undamped sinusoidals, i.e., sinusoidals whose envelope increases exponentially as $t \rightarrow \infty$. In either case, any input function $f(t)$ will eventually lead to an "exploding" system; e.g., see Fig. 6-8. The system is said to be "unstable."

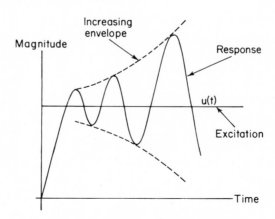

FIGURE 6-8   Example of Unstable System

Thus, the study of stability of systems revolves around the determination of the existence or nonexistence of positive real roots of the homogeneous differential Eq. (6-19). We now proceed to translate these conclusions into the language of the operational calculus based on the Laplace transform, and to this end we need the notion of "transfer function."

3.2 The Transfer Function

The relationship between a dependent variable y (output) to another variable x (input) can, in general, be written in the form of a linear differential equation:

$$a_0 \frac{d^n y}{dt^n} + a_1 \frac{d^{n-1} y}{dt^{n-1}} + \ldots + a_n y = b_0 \frac{d^m x}{dt^m} + b_1 \frac{d^{m-1} x}{dt^{m-1}} + \ldots + b_m x$$

$$(6\text{-}21)$$

i.e., a relationship involving a linear combination of the functions $y(t)$ and $x(t)$ and their derivatives. If we assume for the moment that y is dependent only on x, Eq. (6-21) completely describes the behavior of the component under study. Upon taking the $\mathcal{L}$-transform of both sides of Eq. (6-21), and assuming zero initial conditions, we obtain

$$(a_0 s^n + a_1 s^{n-1} + \ldots + a_n) Y(s) = (b_0 s^m + b_1 s^{m-1} +$$

$$\ldots + b_m) X(s)$$

by the real differentiation theorem discussed above. The dependence of $Y(s)$ on $X(s)$ can be better written as

$$Y(s) = \frac{b_0 s^m + b_1 s^{m-1} + \cdots + b_m}{a_0 s^n + a_1 s^{n-1} + \cdots + a_n} \cdot X(s).$$

The function

$$G(s) = \frac{b_0 s^m + b_1 s^{m-1} + \cdots + b_m}{a_0 s^n + a_1 s^{n-1} + \cdots + a_n} \qquad (6\text{-}22)$$

may be regarded as the ratio, $Y(s)/X(s)$, of the $\mathcal{L}$-transform of the output to the input, or merely as a shorthand notation for the differential Eq. (6-21). In any event, $G(s)$ is called the *transfer function* of the component and plays a dominant role in the analysis and synthesis of feedback control systems, as will be seen shortly.

A few properties of the transfer function $G(s)$ are worth noting even at this early stage. *First*, $G(s)$ is, in general, a rational function of the complex variable s, i.e., it is a ratio of two polynomials in s. *Second*, the transfer function permits algebraic manipulation which otherwise would

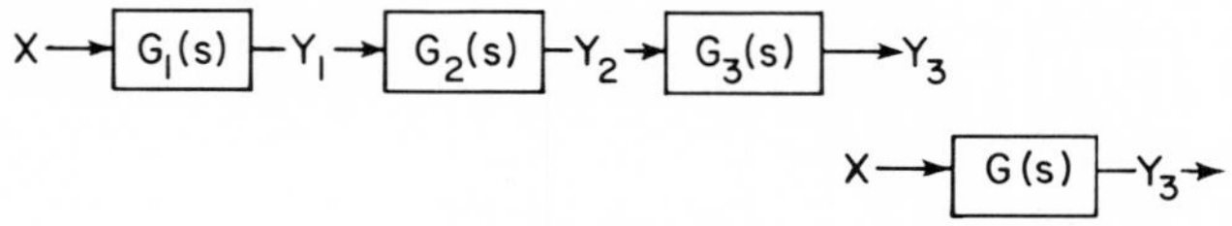

FIGURE 6-9

have necessitated the solution of complicated differential equations. For example, suppose that several components are connected in tandem as in Fig. 6-9 so that the output $Y_1(s)$ of the first component is related to the input $X(s)$ by

$$Y_1(s) = G_1(s) \cdot X(s),$$

and the output of the second component is related to $Y_1(s)$ by

$$Y_2(s) = G_2(s) \cdot Y_1(s),$$

and so forth; finally:

$$Y_n(s) = G_n(s) \cdot Y_{n-1}(s).$$

Then clearly the relationship between the final output $Y_n(s)$ and the input $X(s)$ can be obtained by eliminating the intermediate variables Y_1, $Y_2, \ldots, Y_{n-1}$. In particular,

$$Y_n(s) = G_1 \cdot G_2 \ldots G_n \cdot X(s)$$

$$= G(s) \cdot X(s).$$

Here $G = G_1 G_2 \ldots G_n$ is the transfer function of the cascaded system.

Third, $G(s)$ can be written as

$$G(s) = \frac{(s - s_1)(s - s_2) \cdots (s - s_m)}{(s - s_a)(s - s_b) \cdots (s - s_n)} \tag{6-23}$$

where $s_1, \ldots, s_m$ are the *m*-roots of the numerator, called *zeros*, and s_a, $\ldots, s_n$ are the *n*-roots of the denominator, called the *poles*. Obviously, $G(s)$ can be specified as in Eq. (6-22) or, alternatively, by giving the location in the complex plane of the zeros and poles of the function and the ratio of the leading terms b_0/a_0.

3.3 The Block Diagram[†]

In our discussion above we made use of an important device: the *block diagram*. For purposes of *analysis* all the necessary information about a component is conveniently and succinctly summarized in its transfer function. The physical reality of the component is, in this respect, im-

[†]See also §2 of Chapter 2.

material. It does not matter whether the original component giving rise to a particular $G(s)$ is a valve, an electrical network, or a chemical reactor. Hence, any diagrammatic representation of the component need not contain such information. It is sufficient for the complete symbolic representation to give the two variables involved—input and output—and the transfer function. The result is a block diagram.

$$X(s) \longrightarrow \boxed{G(s)} \longmapsto Y(s) \longrightarrow$$

3.4 Frequency Response

Thus far our discussion has been concerned with the complementary function $\sum_i c_i \cdot e^{\alpha_i t}$. We now discuss briefly the particular solution $y_0(t)$ in Eq. (6-18).

We have just seen that if the behavior of the component is stable, then the complementary function must "die out" after a period of time; hence, it is a *transient solution*, and the behavior of the component is given by $y_0(t)$, the *"steady-state"* solution.

Traditionally, steady-state analysis has concerned itself with the study of the frequency response of the component, i.e., the output $y_0(t)$ which will be observed when the system is subjected to a sustained input driving function of constant amplitude and frequency such as a sinusoidal. There are several good reasons for such concentration of effort; we mention only the following two. *First*, several inputs do exhibit such characteristics or can be represented (through Fourier analysis, for example) to a fairly reasonable degree of accuracy with a sinusoidal or a linear combination of sinusoidals of varying frequencies and phase angles. *Second*, a very simple relationship exists between the frequency response and the transfer function of the system. In fact, if the input is a sinusoidal

$$f(t) = A \sin \omega t,$$

its Laplace transform is given by

$$F(s) = \frac{A\omega}{s^2 + \omega^2}.$$

Let the response of a system, $R(s)$, to a sinusoidal forcing function be given by

$$R(s) = G(s)F(s)$$

$$= G(s)\frac{A\omega}{s^2 + \omega^2}. \tag{6-24}$$

Normally, $G(s)$ is a rational function of the form $N(s)/D(s)$, and the characteristic equation $D(s)(s^2 + \omega^2) = 0$ has the roots $s_1, s_2, \ldots, s_n$,

$j\omega$, and $-j\omega$; therefore,

$$(s - s_1)(s - s_2)\ldots(s - s_n)(s + j\omega)(s - j\omega) = 0. \tag{6-25}$$

The general solution of Eq. (6-24) is of the form

$$R(t) = K_1 e^{s_1 t} + K_2 e^{s_2 t} + \ldots + K_n e^{s_n t}$$
$$+ K_{j\omega} e^{j\omega t} + K_{-j\omega} e^{-j\omega t}.$$

If the system is stable the first n terms must $\rightarrow 0$ as $t \rightarrow \infty$, and we are left with the steady-state solution:

$$R_{ss}(t) = K_{j\omega} e^{j\omega t} + K_{-j\omega} e^{-j\omega t} \tag{6-26}$$

where

$$K_{j\omega} = (s - j\omega) \frac{N(s)}{D(s)} \frac{A\omega}{s^2 + \omega^2} \bigg|_{s=j\omega} = \frac{A G(j\omega)}{2j}$$

and

$$K_{-j\omega} = (s + j\omega) \frac{N(s)}{D(s)} \frac{A\omega}{s^2 + \omega^2} \bigg|_{s=-j\omega} = \frac{A G(-j\omega)}{-2j}.$$

Consequently,

$$R_{ss}(t) = \frac{A}{2j} [G(j\omega) e^{j\omega t} - G(-j\omega) e^{-j\omega t}].$$

Putting $G(j\omega) = |G(j\omega)| e^{j\psi}$ and $G(-j\omega) = |G(j\omega)| e^{-j\psi}$ for some ψ, we finally obtain

$$R_{ss}(t) = A |G(j\omega)| \left[\frac{e^{j(\omega t + \psi)} - e^{-j(\omega t + \psi)}}{2j} \right]$$

$$= A |G(j\omega)| \sin(\omega t + \psi). \tag{6-27}$$

Therefore, any system of transfer function $G(s)$, when excited by a sinusoidal time-varying forcing function, yields a steady-state behavior which is expressed by the complex quantity $R(t)$ whose amplitude is $A |G(j\omega)|$ and phase $\psi(j\omega)$. If $A = 1$, the steady-state response is given directly by $G(j\omega)$. In other words, a sinusoidal input of amplitude unity gives rise to a sinusoidal output of magnitude equal to the magnitude of the transfer function, $|G(j\omega)|$, evaluated at frequency ω, and phase angle between output and input equal to the phase angle of the transfer function, $\arg[G(j\omega)]$.[†] In general, both of these numbers are functions of the input frequency ω, and the frequency dependence of these numbers is called the *frequency response* of the system.

[†]$G(j\omega)$ is a complex quantity which can always be reduced to $a + jb$. The phase angle θ of such a quantity is given by $\theta = \tan^{-1} b/a$. The angle θ is referred to as $\arg[G(j\omega)]$.

3.5 Stability of Systems

Now we are in a better position to discuss more fully the question of stability which was touched upon before.

Problems of stability arise in the context of any system or organization whether it be inanimate or human. Examples of instability can be drawn from the field of servomechanism (e.g., the "hunting" of motors), from the field of physiology (e.g., ataxia, or the continuous oscillation of the hand when reaching for an object without ever grasping it), from social organization theory (e.g., the "vicious cycle" of individual repression in highly regimented organizations, which leads to rebellion which, in turn, leads to more strict regimentation, and so on to the point of explosion), and from almost every field of human endeavor.

For any system, stability must ultimately be defined in terms of the response of the output of the system to any *bounded* input. We know from Eq. (6-18) and the subsequent discussion that if any of the exponents $\{\alpha_i\}$ have positive real parts, then the corresponding terms exhibit an amplitude which grows without bound as $t \rightarrow \infty$. For most bounded inputs the transient response is unbounded, and consequently, the whole system is unstable.

Hence, *absolute stability* for a linear system is defined in terms of bounded outputs for all possible bounded inputs. A system in which a disturbance is not eventually damped out is called "absolutely unstable." Naturally, absolute stability, though an important criterion for a system, is sometimes not enough for a satisfactory performance, especially when the damping effect occurs after a long period of time.

In the following, we will translate the conditions for absolute stability into the necessary conditions on the transfer function $G(s)$. Consider the feedback system shown in Fig. 6-10. The following algebriac equations relate the inputs and outputs of the two transfer functions:

$$E(s) = X(s) - H(s) \cdot Y(s),$$

$$Y(s) = G(s) \cdot E(s).$$

Hence,

$$Y(s) = \frac{G(s)}{1 + G(s) \cdot H(s)} \cdot X(s).$$

The frequency response of the system is given by

$$\frac{Y}{X}(j\omega) = \frac{G(j\omega)}{1 + G(j\omega) H(j\omega)}.$$

If the system is absolutely unstable and is linear, then $Y/X (j\omega) \rightarrow \infty$ at some value of $j\omega$. This can happen only if the denominator is zero, i.e., only if

$$1 + G(j\omega) H(j\omega) = 0. \tag{6-28}$$

Equation (6-28) is of fundamental importance in the study of feedback systems, and to emphasize its importance it is often called the *characteristic equation* of the system. In general, the left-hand side of Eq. (6-28) is a rational function of s, similar to Eq. (6-22) and may be written as

$$1 + GH(s) = \frac{(s - s_1)(s - s_2)\cdots(s - s_m)}{(s - s_a)(s - s_b)\cdots(s - s_n)} = 0. \tag{6-29}$$

Obviously, for stability the only significant values are the zeros of Eq. (6-29), $s_1, s_2, \ldots, s_m$, since only these can make the frequency response become infinite. In particular, since only zeros with positive real parts are important, it is logical to confine the investigation of stability to the right-hand half of the s-plane, which includes the imaginary axis, $\sigma = 0$.

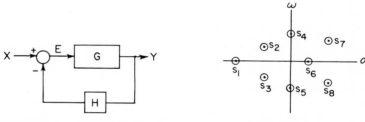

FIGURE 6-10 Feedback Loop   **FIGURE 6-11**

For example, in Fig. 6-11 we drew some zeros: s_1 gives rise to a negative exponential; s_2 and s_3 are conjugate roots and give rise to damped oscillations. All other zeros shown give rise to either sustained oscillation (s_4 and s_5), or increasing exponential (s_6), or increasing sinusoidal (s_7 and s_8). The condition for absolute stability is now the condition that the zeros of the characteristic Eq. (6-29) do not lie in the right-hand half of the s-plane.

To determine whether or not any roots of the characteristic Eq. (6-29) fall into the right half plane, analytical as well as graphical techniques are available. Of the analytical methods, we mention the Routh-Horwitz criterion, which can be found in any text on calculus or servomechanisms. Several graphical techniques—the Nyquist diagram, the root-locus diagram, etc.—are available whenever the transfer function is easier to obtain experimentally. Space does not permit us to enter into greater detail in these subjects; the interested reader can consult any of the specialized books on servomechanism theory.

§4. A SIMPLE R-C NETWORK

In this and the following section we illustrate the theory presented above by application to simple physical systems.

Consider an R-C network as shown in Fig. 6-12, with input voltage $e_i(t)$ which induces an output voltage $e_0(t)$. It is desired to find $e_0(t)$ for any given $e_i(t)$.

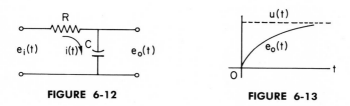

FIGURE 6-12   FIGURE 6-13

In the time domain one can immediately write the following equations:

$$e_i(t) = R \cdot i(t) + \frac{1}{C} \int i(t)\, dt$$

and   (6-30)

$$e_0(t) = \frac{1}{C} \int i(t)\, dt.$$

Taking the $\mathcal{L}$-transform of Eq. (6-30), and assuming zero initial conditions, we get

$$E_i(s) = R \cdot I(s) + \frac{1}{Cs} I(s)$$

and

$$E_0(s) = \frac{1}{Cs} I(s),$$

which combine to yield

$$\frac{E_0(s)}{E_i(s)} = \frac{1}{RCs + 1},$$

which implies that the transfer function

$$G(s) = \frac{1}{\tau s + 1}, \tau = RC, \text{ the time constant}^\dagger \text{ of the network.}$$

$$E_i \longrightarrow \boxed{\frac{1}{RCs + 1}} \longrightarrow E_0$$

[†]The time constant of a system is defined as the time required for the error in a step input to be reduced to $1/e$ of its original value.

Response to Unit Step Function u(t)

It is instructive to study the behavior of the system under a unit step function as shown dotted in Fig. 6-13. That is, we consider the initial conditions as our datum, hence they are equated to zero, and assume a unit change in e_i, i.e., $u(t) = 1.0$. The power of the operational calculus and the concepts of transfer function are now evident. Since

$$E_i(s) = \frac{1}{s} \text{ (See Example 1, §2)}$$

then,

$$E_0(s) = \frac{1}{\tau s + 1} \cdot \frac{1}{s} = \frac{k_1}{\tau s + 1} + \frac{k_2}{s}$$

where k_1 and k_2 are constants of the partial fraction expansion, to be evaluated from $k_1 s + k_2(\tau s + 1) = 1$, i.e.,

$$k_1 + k_2\tau = 0 \quad \text{or } k_1 = -k_2\tau$$

and

$$k_2 = 1.$$

Therefore,

$$E_0(s) = \frac{1}{s} - \frac{\tau}{\tau s + 1}.$$

The inverse transform of $E_0(s)$ is immediately available as

$$e_0(t) = u(t) - e^{-t/\tau}.$$

Notice that the exponential term tends to 0 as $t \rightarrow \infty$, and the output voltage eventually reaches the same level as the input, as indicated by the solid curve in Fig. 6-13.

Response to a Pulse Input

We pursue the matter one step further. Consider a change in $e_i(t)$ for a duration α as in Fig. 6-14. Then, again taking the initial conditions as our datum, we have

$$f_i(t) = \begin{cases} 0 & t < 0 \\ 1 & 0 \le t \le \alpha \\ 0 & t > \alpha \end{cases}$$

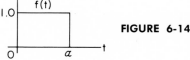

FIGURE 6-14

Now,

$$\mathcal{L}[f(t)] = \int_0^\infty f(t)e^{-st}\,dt = \int_0^\alpha e^{-st}\,dt = \frac{1}{s}[1 - e^{-\alpha s}],$$

a result which could be arrived at with equal ease by considering the pulse as the sum of two unit step functions, one positive at time 0 and the other negative at time α, (see Fig. 6-15). The $\mathcal{L}$-transform of the first is $1/s$, and of the second (utilizing the translation property of Eq. (6-7)) is $e^{-\alpha s}/s$.

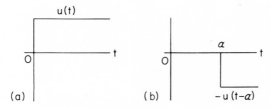

FIGURE 6-15

Therefore,

$$E_0(s) = \frac{1}{(\tau s + 1)} \cdot \frac{1}{s}(1 - e^{-\alpha s}).$$

$$= \left[\frac{k_1}{s} + \frac{k_2}{\tau s + 1}\right](1 - e^{-\alpha s}).$$

Solving for k_1 and k_2 as before we obtain

$$E_0(s) = \left[\frac{1}{s} - \frac{\tau}{\tau s + 1}\right](1 - e^{-\alpha s})$$

$$= \left[\frac{1}{s} - \frac{\tau}{\tau s + 1}\right] - e^{-\alpha s}\left[\frac{1}{s} - \frac{\tau}{\tau s + 1}\right]. \qquad (6\text{-}31)$$

Again utilizing the translation properties of Eq. (6-6), the inverse transform of Eq. (6-31) is

$$e_0(t) = \begin{cases} 1 - e^{-t/\tau} & 0 \le t \le \alpha \\ 1 - e^{-t/\tau} - \{1 - e^{-(t-\alpha)/\tau}\} & \\ \quad = e^{-(t-\alpha)/\tau} - e^{-t/\tau} & t > \alpha, \end{cases}$$

which is shown in the solid curves of Fig. 6-16. Obviously, the maximum deviation from the datum level ($e_0 = 0$) occurs at $t = \alpha$, at which point

$$e_0(t) = 1 - e^{-\alpha/\tau}.$$

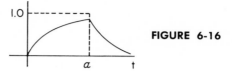

FIGURE 6-16

If the duration of the pulse, α, is small compared to τ, the time constant of the network, we can approximate e_0 by

$$e_0(\text{max}) = 1 - \left(1 - \frac{\alpha}{\tau}\right) = \frac{\alpha}{\tau} = \frac{\alpha}{RC}.$$

Interpreted, the normalized peak response of the system is equal to the quotient of the duration of pulse, α, and the network time constant RC.

§5. A SIMPLE INVENTORY CONTROL SYSTEM

Suppose we are concerned with maintaining the inventory $I(t)$ at a specified level I_0. Any discrepancy between the two quantities is recognized as an error, $E(t)$, which can be positive or negative denoting understorage or overstorage, respectively. A decision to increase or decrease production $P(t)$ is made based on the magnitude of the error $E(t)$. We shall assume that no lag exists between giving the instruction to manufacture and the execution of the command; i.e., we assume the transfer function of the production department to be unity. Accumulation of inventory is through production, and depletion is through sales, or load, S. The control system can be depicted as a feedback loop as shown in Fig. 6-17.

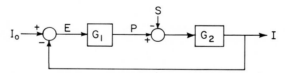

FIGURE 6-17   Simple Inventory Control System

Here, G_1 is the decision operator acting on the error E and G_2 is the operator acting upon the net difference $(P - S)$. In particular, since we are assuming continuous operation the inventory $I(t)$ is the accumulation, i.e., *integration*, of this net quantity,

$$I(t) = \int_0^t [P(t) - S(t)]\,dt. \tag{6-32a}$$

$$E(t) = I_0 - I(t) \tag{6-32b}$$

and from the definition of the problem

$$P(t) = g_1[E(t)] = g_1[I_0 - I(t)], \tag{6-32c}$$

where g_1 is an operator to be defined presently. The $\mathcal{L}$-transform of Eqs. (6-32) is

$$I(s) = \frac{1}{s}[P(s) - S(s)]; \text{ i.e., } G_2(s) = 1/s,$$

and

$$P(s) = G_1(s)[I_0(s) - I(s)],$$

again assuming zero initial conditions. With no loss of generality we can assume $I_0 = 0$ and obtain

$$I(s) = \frac{-1}{s + G_1(s)} \cdot S(s). \tag{6-33}$$

The system transfer function is seen to be equal to

$$G(s) = \frac{-1}{s + G_1(s)},$$

relating the time varying output $I(t)$ to the time varying input $S(t)$. Of course, $G_1(s)$ is not known and is to be determined to achieve certain objectives. We discuss three possible forms of $S(t)$.

First Form of S(t)

Let $S(t)$ be the unit step function $u(t)$; then $S(s) = 1/s$ and Eq. (6-33) becomes:

$$I(s) = \frac{-1}{s[s + G_1(s)]}.$$

For stability, we must have no roots of the characteristic function

$$s[s + G_1(s)] = 0 \tag{6-34}$$

in the right-hand side of the s-plane. Obviously $s = 0$ is one root of Eq. (6-34). In order to evaluate the other roots we must specify $G_1(s)$. Consider the following four possible forms of $G_1(s)$:

1. Let $G_1(s) = a/s$, where a is a real constant > 0, then

$$s + G_1(s) = 0 = s + a/s$$

i.e.,

$$s^2 + a = 0,$$

which yields $s = \pm j\sqrt{a}$, which are two imaginary roots lying on the imaginary axis $\sigma = 0$. Therefore, the system is *unstable*. In fact, the pair of complex conjugate roots gives rise to undamped sinusoidal output.

2. Let $G_1(s) = a/s + b$ where a and b are real constants > 0. Then, $s + G_1(s) = 0 = s + a/s + b$. That is, $s^2 + bs + a = 0$, or

$$s = \frac{-b \pm j\sqrt{4a - b^2}}{2}.$$

The system is absolutely stable since the real part is always < 0 (see Fig. 6-18). If $4a = b^2$ the two roots are equal and the system is said to be

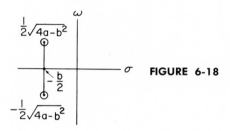

FIGURE 6-18

critically damped. If $4a > b^2$, the system oscillates with a decreasing envelope (see Fig. 6-19).

3. Let $G_1(s) = a/s + b + cs$, a, b, and c are real constants. Then, $s + G_1(s) = 0 = s + a/s + b + cs$, i.e., $(c + 1)s^2 + bs + a = 0$, and

$$s = \frac{-b \pm j\sqrt{4a(c + 1) - b^2}}{2(c + 1)}.$$

Obviously, the system is absolutely stable if a, b, and $(c + 1)$ all have the same sign.

4. Let $G_1(s) = (1/s^k)(a + bs)$, $k \geq 1$, a and $b > 0$. It can easily be shown that the system is still absolutely stable.

The transfer function $G_1(s)$ represents a rule of decision. Since $P(s) = G_1(s)E(s)$, this rule determines, on the basis of information concerning the current deficit or excess of inventory, the rate $P(t)$ at which manu-

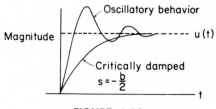

FIGURE 6-19

facturing should be conducted. Interpretation of the above transfer functions should prove illuminating.

In (1) we have seen that $G_1(s) = a/s$ leads to an unstable system. With this operator, Eq. (6-32c) becomes

$$\frac{d}{dt} P(t) = a \cdot E(t),$$

which means that the rate of production should be increased or decreased by an amount proportional to the error. That such a correction is not sufficient can be seen from the operator in (2), $G_1(s) = a/s + b$, which yields

$$\frac{d}{dt} P(t) = a \cdot E(t) + b \cdot \frac{d}{dt} E(t). \tag{6-35}$$

That is, the rate of production is proportional to the error as well as to the *rate of change* of the error. Prima facie, it is not intuitively obvious that the final term of Eq. (6-35) is essential to stability. Similar reasoning applies to the transfer functions in (3) and (4).

Second Form of S(t)

Suppose next that demand exhibits some linear trend and is given by the ramp function

$$S(t) = \alpha t \quad \text{for } t \geq 0, \alpha > 0.$$

Then $\mathcal{L}[\alpha t] = \alpha/s^2$ which, upon substitution in Eq. (6-33) yields

$$I(s) = \frac{-\alpha}{s^2[s + G_1(s)]}.$$

Reasoning similar to that above shows that for the system to be stable $G_1(s)$ must be of the form

$$G_1(s) = \frac{1}{s^{k+1}} (a + bs) \quad \text{with} \quad k \geq 1.$$

Third Form of S(t)

Finally, suppose that $S(t)$ is sinusoidal

$$S(t) = A \cos \omega t \quad \text{for} \quad t \geq 0.$$

Then if the system is stable, the steady-state output is also sinusoidal with different amplitude and phase angle.

If, for example, $G_1(s) = a/s + b$, the system transfer function

$$G(s) = \frac{-1}{s + G_1(s)} = \frac{-s}{s^2 + bs + a} = \frac{-s}{(s - s_1)(s - s_2)},$$

where s_1 and s_2 are the roots of the characteristic equation, $s^2 + bs + a = 0$. Therefore, the magnitude of the output $|I(t)|$ is given by

$$|G(j\omega)| = \sqrt{G(j\omega)\,G(-j\omega)}$$

$$= \frac{\omega}{\sqrt{(\omega^2 + s_1{}^2)(\omega^2 + s_2{}^2)}}$$

For any given roots s_1 and s_2 the magnitude $|I(t)| \to 0$ as $\omega \to 0$, a not unexpected result since *at* $\omega = 0$, the sinusoidal reduces to a unit *impulse* at $t = 0$ which, for a stable system, is damped; and $|I(t)| \to A/\omega$ as ω grows large.

The phase angle between the output $I(t)$ and the input $S(t)$ in the case of a sinusoidal input is again given by

$$\beta = \arg[G(j\omega)] = \tan^{-1} - \frac{s_1 s_2 - \omega^2}{\omega(s_1 + s_2)}.$$

It is interesting to note the *attenuating* and *filtering* effects of the system on any sinusoidal input. For small ω the output follows the input rather closely, but as $\omega \to \infty$, the amplitude of the output $\to 0$ and the phase angle $\to -90°$. In essence, the system cannot respond to highly oscillatory input due to its "inertia" and will stay at rest.

To sum up, it is evident that we must be careful in choosing the decision operator $G_1(s)$ since instability can easily be induced into the system. We have seen an example of such induced instability when the correction to the error in the level of inventory was made proportional to the magnitude of the error itself, but that instability was removed when the correction was made also to depend on the rate of change of the error. Moreover, the operation $G_2(s)$ is, in fact, the accumulation of the net input (= production minus demand) into the storeroom, $G_2(s) = 1/s$. A storeroom, then, can be mathematically represented by the operation $1/s$ in a feedback loop.

§6. A PRODUCTION-INVENTORY SYSTEM WITH DETERMINISTIC DEMAND

A more relastic extension to the analysis of the previous section is to permit inventory to fluctuate about its desired value in order to be able to reduce the fluctuations in the rate of production to satisfy demand. This is so because it is reasonable to assume that manufacturing cost is minimized when manufacturing is stabilized while inventory cost is minimized when inventory is minimized. However, the optimal strategy to minimize the *sum* of the two costs lies somewhere between these two extremes.

Consider a system as represented by Fig. 6-20. It differs from the system shown in Fig. 6-17 in the presence of the variable D and the transfer functions G_2 and G_4. D represents the *decision* made based on the error *and the pattern of demand*; G_2 is included to permit explicit recognition of any difference between the actual production $P(t)$ and the decision $D(t)$

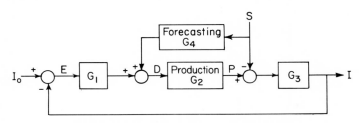

FIGURE 6-20 **A Production Inventory System**

due to, for example, production lag. In effect, $G_2(s)$ is the transfer function of the production subsystem. The transfer function G_4 represents any operator on the demand that assists in the determination of the decision D; for example, statistical forecasting. Clearly, G_3 represents the accumulation of inventory in the storeroom.

Suppose the load $S(t)$ is sinusoidal,

$$S(t) = a \cos \omega t$$

then in the steady state both production and inventory will be sinusoidals,

$$P(t) = b \cos \omega t + \beta \sin \omega t$$

$$I(t) = c \cos \omega t + \gamma \sin \omega t$$

where a, b, β, γ are real constants. But we know from Eq. (6-32a) that $I(t)$ is related to both $P(t)$ and $S(t)$ by

$$\frac{d\,I(t)}{dt} = P(t) - S(t). \tag{6-36}$$

Substituting from the above sinusoidal expressions we get

$$-c\omega \sin \omega t + \gamma\omega \cos \omega t = b \cos \omega t + \beta \sin \omega t - a \cos \omega t,$$

whence,

$$\gamma\omega = b - a \quad \text{and} \quad -c\omega = \beta. \tag{6-37}$$

Our objective is to minimize the *total* cost of production and inventory. We shall assume that the cost associated with $P(t)$ is proportional to the square of the amplitude of its oscillation, i.e., that it is of the form $\rho |B|^2$, where $|B|$ is the amplitude of $P(t)$. Similarly, we assume that the cost of holding inventories is $\delta |C|^2$ where $|C|$ is the amplitude of $I(t)$. Hence, we wish to minimize

$$\xi = \rho |B|^2 + \delta |C|^2$$
$$= \rho (b^2 + \beta^2) + \delta (c^2 + \gamma^2) \tag{6-38}$$

subject to the conditions of Eq. (6-36). Substituting for c and γ from Eq. (6-37) into Eq. (6-38), taking partial derivatives of ξ with respect to b and β, and setting these equal to zero we find:

$$b = \frac{a\delta}{\rho\omega^2 + \delta}, \beta = 0$$

$$c = 0, \gamma = \frac{-a\rho\omega}{\rho\omega^2 + \delta},$$

whence,

$$P(t) = \frac{a\delta}{\rho\omega^2 + \delta} \cos \omega t$$

and

$$I(t) = \frac{-a\rho\omega}{\rho\omega^2 + \delta} \sin \omega t.$$

As $\omega \to 0$, $P(t) \to a$, a constant rate of production, while $I(t) \to 0$, i.e., small fluctuation in inventory. On the other hand as $\omega \to \infty$, $P(t) \to 0$, i.e., small change in production, while $I(t) \to 0$, i.e., small fluctuation in inventory, but $\gamma\omega \to -a$; i.e., $\omega I(t) \to -a \sin \omega t$.

Now we return to the specification of the transfer functions of the various components of the system to yield the desired minimum. For brevity we write, $I(s)/S(s) = G(s)$, and let $P(s)/S(s) = H(s)$. Then from Eq. (6-32a),

$$s I(s) = P(s) - S(s),$$

or, dividing by $S(s)$,

$$H(s) = 1 + s G(s). \tag{6-39}$$

The transfer function $H(s)$ corresponding to the optimal solution is found readily as follows. From the definition of the impulse response and the convolution integral, Eq. (6-8), we have

$$P(t) = \int_0^t H(\tau) \cdot S(t - \tau) d\tau.$$

For a sinusoidal load $S(t) = \cos\omega t = [e^{j\omega t} + e^{-j\omega t}]/2 = Re[e^{j\omega t}]$ where $Re[\cdot]$ means the real part of the quantity between brackets,

$$P(t) = \int_0^t H(\tau) \cdot \frac{1}{2} [e^{j\omega(t-\tau)} + e^{-j\omega(t-\tau)}]d\tau$$

$$= \frac{1}{2} e^{j\omega t} \int_0^t H(\tau) e^{-j\omega\tau} d\tau + \frac{1}{2} e^{-j\omega t} \int_0^t H(\tau) e^{j\omega\tau} d\tau$$

$$= \frac{1}{2} [e^{j\omega t} H(j\omega) + e^{-j\omega t} H(-j\omega)] = Re[e^{j\omega t} \cdot H(j\omega)].$$

Since $P(t)$ is a real function, we must have

$$P(t) = Re[e^{j\omega t}] \cdot Re[H(j\omega)]$$

$$= S(t) \cdot Re[H(j\omega)].$$

We immediately deduce that

$$Re[H(j\omega)] = \frac{P(t)}{S(t)} = \frac{b}{a} = \frac{\delta}{\rho\omega^2 + \delta}.$$

Hence,

$$H(s) = \frac{\delta}{-\rho s^2 + \delta}$$

and

$$G(s) = \frac{1}{s}[H(s) - 1] = \frac{\rho s}{-\rho s^2 + \delta}.$$

Unfortunately, the characteristic equation of both $H(s)$ and $G(s)$ contains one positive root $s = \sqrt{\delta/\rho}$. Hence *a system with these transforms would be unstable.* This undesirable result stems from the fact that we designed the transforms to minimize costs for *steady-state operation.* This will not, in general, automatically satisfy conditions on the *transient* behavior of the system. This, in turn, points out the fallacies and possible pitfalls perpetrated in the evaluation of the parameters of complicated systems with several interacting components and demonstrates, to a degree, the power of analysis followed here.

To remedy the situation we approximate the optimal solution by replacing the denominator of $G(s)$ by $(s\sqrt{\rho} + \sqrt{\delta})^2$, a critically damped system $(s = -\sqrt{\delta/\rho})$. The system now is absolutely stable with the transient term in $P(t)$ of the form

$$A t e^{-\sqrt{\delta/\rho}\,t}$$

because of the double root, $s = -\sqrt{\delta/\rho}.$

We now return to the specification of the linear operators G_1 and G_2 of Fig. 6-19. (G_3 is given; see Eq. (6-36)).

Assume for the moment that production is instantaneous, i.e., $G_2 = 1$, then,

$$\frac{I}{S}(s) = G(s) = \frac{G_4 - 1}{s + G_1}, \text{ assuming } I_0 = 0.$$

In order to obtain the transfer $G(s) = (-\rho s)/(s\sqrt{\rho} + \sqrt{\delta})^2$ (obtained as a correction to $G(s) = (-\rho s)/(\rho s^2 - \delta)$) let

$$G_4(s) = 1 - \rho s \quad \text{and } G_1(s) = \rho s^2 + s[2\sqrt{\delta\rho} - 1] + \delta. \tag{6-40}$$

Moreover, we have from Eq. (6-39),

$$H(s) = 1 + s\,G(s)$$

$$= \frac{2s\sqrt{\rho\delta} + \delta}{(s\sqrt{\rho} + \sqrt{\delta})^2} = \frac{P}{S}(s).$$

In the case of instantaneous production response $P = D$, we have

$$(\rho s^2 + 2\sqrt{\rho\delta}\,s + \delta)\,D(s) = (2\sqrt{\rho\delta}\,s + \delta)S(s),$$

which yields in the time domain,

$$\rho\frac{d^2 D(t)}{dt^2} + 2\sqrt{\rho\delta}\frac{dD(t)}{dt} + \delta D(t) = 2\sqrt{\rho\delta}\frac{dS(t)}{dt} + \delta S(t).$$

In the case where there is a fixed production lag of τ units,

$$G_2(s) = e^{-\tau s},$$

and we have

$$G(s) = \frac{e^{-\tau s}G_4 - 1}{s + G_1 e^{-\tau s}}; H(s) = \frac{e^{-\tau s}(G_1 + s\,G_4)}{s + G_1 e^{-\tau s}}.$$

Since $H(s) = P(s)/S(s)$ and $P(s)/D(s) = G_2(s) = e^{-\tau s}$, we obtain

$$\frac{D}{S}(s) = \frac{G_1 + s\,G_4}{s + G_1 e^{\tau s}}.$$

Substituting for any values of G_1 and G_4, such as the values given in Eq. (6-40), we can obtain the decision $D(t)$ as a function of the sales $S(t)$.

§7. AUTOCOVARIANCE AND POWER SPECTRA

In the previous sections we studied a few production systems from the point of view of feedback control theory. Throughout our analysis we assumed that we are dealing with *deterministic* systems. Even the disturbances to the systems were supposed to be some known functions such as the unit step function, $u(t)$, or a sinusoidal, cos $(\omega t + \phi)$, or a ramp function, bt, etc. The disturbances are permitted to be any assortment of these functions, but it is assumed that it is a *known* assortment. And since we are dealing with *linear* systems, the principle of superposition applies and the output of the system is the *sum* of the individual outputs.

In practice, we would not be introducing gross errors if we assume that the *response* of the system is deterministic and time invariant. However, in many instances we simply cannot treat the input disturbances as deterministic time functions. Consider, for example, the following systems.

1. A radar antenna is subject to gusts of wind of unknown magnitude and duration except in a statistical sense. The servocontrol system which maintains the antenna in rotation should be designed from this point of view.

2. A production-inventory system is subject to customer demand. The latter is stochastic in nature, possibly with known or unknown cyclical and trend patterns. The random disturbances to sales cause random disturbances in both production and inventory. In fact, the disturbances have random repercussions in every facet of behavior of the total system. Clearly, the design of the system must take cognizance of this fact.

3. A process-control system depends on the quantitative measurement of certain parameters—temperature, pressure, rate of flow, etc. Here, randomness can be introduced into the system in two ways. First, the measured parameters may exhibit random variation if they are functions of some (external) random variable—weather, outside demand, etc. Second, the measuring instruments themselves are not perfect but introduce errors which are random and stationary (over a reasonable period of time).

The list of practical examples in which randomness exists can be extended. In fact, there is no need to convince anybody about the existence of unpredictable (i.e., random) disturbances to any system—people who deal with real-life situations know too well of their existence. However, it is only fairly recently that a methodology of attacking the problem of systems design *taking randomness explicitly into account* has been developed.

The theory is based on the following important assumption: *we wish to optimize the performance of the system relative to the mean-squared-error criterion*. If any other criterion is adopted (such as the minimization of the *absolute error* between desired and actual performance, the minimization of the cumulative errors over a finite period of time, or the minimizations of the terminal-point error, etc.), the theory presented below is inapplicable. Moreover, we remind the reader that we are still dealing with *linear* feedback control systems. Nonlinear systems, even of the simplest type, are beyond the scope of this treatise.

Although most of the information with which we shall be concerned is in the form of *time series*, it is conceptually helpful to assume the existence of a *continuous signal* which is sampled at regular intervals of time to yield the given time series (see Fig. 6-21). Clearly, if sampling is frequent enough, the time series will closely resemble the hypothetical (or actual) signal, while infrequent sampling may yield the wrong interpretation as shown in Fig. 6-21.

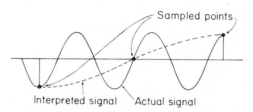

FIGURE 6-21 Sampling of a Continuous Signal

Let $x(t)$ be any continuous time-varying function referred to as the *signal*. Whenever the information on $x(t)$ is available only at discrete points of time Δt apart, we obtain the *time series $x(t)$*

7.1 The Autocovariance Function

The autocovariance function $\phi(\tau)$ of a signal $x(t)$ whose average is assumed, for convenience, to be zero is defined by the equation:

$$\phi(\tau) = \lim_{T\to\infty} \frac{1}{2T} \int_{-T}^{T} x(t+\tau) \cdot x(t)\, dt. \tag{6-41}$$

If the signal $x(t)$ is a random signal from an ensemble whose statistical characteristics are time invariant, i.e., if $x(t)$ is a sample from a stationary random process, then the time average given in Eq. (6-41) is equal to the ensemble average (the ergodic property). Hence, an equivalent definition of $\phi(\tau)$ is:

$$\phi(\tau) = \mathcal{E}\,[x(t) \cdot x(t+\tau)] \tag{6-42}$$

where $\mathcal{E}$ represents the mathematical expectation (average) over the ensemble. Naturally, if the mean $\mathcal{E}\,[x(t)] = \mu \neq 0$ then a term μ^2 must be subtracted from the definitions in Eqs. (6-41) and (6-42).

The autocovariance function $\phi(\tau)$ plays an important role in variance-minimization problems such as we are dealing with here, since it can be proved that it contains all the pertinent information on $x(t)$ required for such minimization. It is well to note that

$$\phi(0) = \mathcal{E}[x^2(t)] = \text{Var}[x(t)]$$

since we assumed $\mu = 0$; hence $\phi(\tau) \leq \phi(0)$ for all τ.

The reader should get the "feel" of the definition of $\phi(\tau)$ before proceeding any further. Since the value of the function at t is multiplied by the value of the function at $t + \tau$, the autocovariance function is a function only of the "spacing" τ between the two readings. This follows immediately from the assumption of stationarity. If whenever $x(t)$ is large, $x(t + \tau)$ is also large in magnitude, then $\phi(\tau)$ will be large (either positive or negative, depending on the signs of $x(t)$ and $x(t + \tau)$) indicating a strong "tie" or "correlation" between the two values. On the other hand, if $x(t + \tau)$ does not consistently bear any relationship to $x(t)$, the product will tend to "average out" to zero, and $\phi(\tau)$ will be small.

Thus, the magnitude of $\phi(\tau)$ measures, in some sense, the strength of the relationship between the value of the function at times t and $t + \tau$, while the sign of $\phi(\tau)$ measures the direction of the relationship. Note that if $\phi(\tau)$ is normalized through division by $\text{Var}[x(t)] = \phi(0)$, the result would be the *autocorrelation* function.

As an illustration of the concept of the autocovariance function and the manner in which it is calculated, we consider two simple examples.

Example. Random Telegraph Wave

Suppose we have the following time function (Fig. 6-22): at any instant of time the value of the function is a random variable X which is either 0 or 1 with equal probabilities; traversals between these two values occur at discrete instants of time. The number of traversals in a period of length T is Poisson distributed with mean λ, i.e., the probability of k traversals in period T is given by

$$P(k, T) = \frac{(\lambda T)^k e^{-\lambda T}}{k!}$$

where λ is the average number of traversals per unit time. Utilizing the ensemble definition of autocovariance, we obtain

$$\phi(\tau) = \sum_{x_1} \sum_{x_2} x_1 x_2 \cdot p(x_1, x_2)$$

where $p(x_1, x_2)$ is the probability of the time function having the value x_1 at time t and x_2 at time $t + \tau$. Since $X(t)$ is equal to 0 or 1, it is obvious that the only term contributing to the summation is that in which both $x_1 = 1$ and $x_2 = 1$. The probability of this event happening is equal to the probability that an *even* number of traversals has occurred between

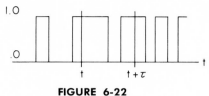

FIGURE 6-22

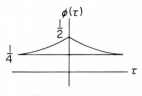

FIGURE 6-23

t and $t + \tau$, i.e.,

$$p(x_1, x_2) = p(x_1 = 1; k \text{ even}) = p(x_1) \cdot P(k \text{ even}) = \frac{1}{2} P(k \text{ even})$$

since X can assume 0 or 1 with equal probabilities. But the probability that k is even in the interval τ (which may be positive or negative) is given by

$$\sum_{k \text{ even}} \frac{(\lambda |\tau|)^k}{k!} e^{-\lambda |\tau|} = \frac{e^{-\lambda |\tau|}}{2} \left[\sum_{k=0}^{\infty} \frac{(\lambda |\tau|)^k}{k!} + \sum_{k=0}^{\infty} \frac{(-\lambda |\tau|)^k}{k!} \right]$$

$$= \frac{e^{-\lambda |\tau|}}{2} [e^{\lambda |\tau|} + e^{-\lambda |\tau|}]$$

$$= \frac{1}{2} [1 + e^{-2\lambda |\tau|}].$$

Hence,

$$\phi(\tau) = \frac{1}{4} [1 + e^{-2\lambda |\tau|}] = \frac{1}{4} + \frac{1}{4} e^{-2\lambda |\tau|}$$

and is shown in Fig. 6-23. Notice that for large $|\tau|$, $\phi(\tau) \simeq 1/4$ which is equal to the square of the average $\mu_x = 1/2$. Intuitively, this result is appealing since for large τ one expects little dependence between the two magnitudes of X, and the product $x_1 x_2$ is equal to the product of their "most likely" values, viz., the average values.

Had we assumed the wave to be centered about zero, as in Fig. 6-24, i.e., $X = \pm 1$ with probability $1/2$, the constant term in ϕ would vanish.

Example. A Poisson Signal

As a second example consider a signal which is constant for an interval and jumps discontinuously from one value to another at each interval; Fig. 6-25. The magnitudes in successive intervals are independent and Poisson distributed with mean λ,

$$P[X(t) = k] = \frac{\lambda^k}{k!} e^{-\lambda}.$$

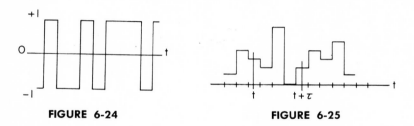

FIGURE 6-24   FIGURE 6-25

Such a signal may be an approximation to the demand rate during one period (week, month, etc.). Since we know the probability distribution function, we again use the definition of Eq. (6-42):

$$\phi(\tau) = \sum_{k_1} \sum_{k_2} k_1 k_2 \cdot p(k_1, k_2);$$

here $p(k_1, k_2)$ is the probability that $X = k_1$ at time t and $X = k_2$ at time $t + \tau$.

If the time points t and $t + \tau$ fall within the same interval, the two values of X are equal and the value of the product is equal to k_1^2, say. The probability of this event is identical to the probability that the two time points t and $t + \tau$ lie in the same interval, which is evidently equal to $1 - |\tau|$ if $|\tau| \leq 1$ and is 0 if $|\tau| > 1$.

If t and $t + \tau$ do not fall within the same interval, the two values k_1 and k_2 are *independent*, hence the joint probability $p(k_1, k_2) = p(k_1) \cdot p(k_2)$. The double summation can now be decomposed into the product:

$$\sum_{k_1} \sum_{k_2} k_1 k_2 \cdot p(k_1, k_2) = \sum_{k_1} k_1 \cdot p(k_1) \sum_{k_2} k_2 \cdot p(k_2) = \lambda^2.$$

Hence, the autocovariance function:

$$\phi(\tau) = \begin{cases} \sum_0^\infty k_1^2 \cdot p(k_1)(1 - |\tau|) + \lambda^2 & |\tau| \leq 1 \\ \lambda^2 & |\tau| > 1. \end{cases}$$

But $\sum_0^\infty k_1^2 \cdot p(k_1) =$ second moment of X about the origin $= \mathrm{Var}[X] + \lambda^2 = \lambda + \lambda^2$. Therefore, $\sum_0^\infty k_1^2 \cdot p(k_1)(1 - |\tau|) + \lambda^2 = (\lambda + \lambda^2) \cdot (1 - |\tau|) + \lambda^2 = \lambda(1 - |\tau|) + \lambda^2(2 - |\tau|)$, and

$$\phi(\tau) = \begin{cases} \lambda(1 - |\tau|) + \lambda^2(2 - |\tau|) & \text{if } |\tau| \leq 1; \\ \lambda^2 & \text{if } |\tau| > 1. \end{cases}$$

$\phi(\tau)$ is shown in Fig. 6-26. We remark that the autocovariance function is, in fact, independent of the probability distribution of the signal since it is of the form (average)^2 + (2nd moment) $(1 - |\tau|)$. Also, since the average of the signal is $\neq 0$, a "d-c component," to borrow from electrical engineering terminology, is present in $\phi(\tau)$.

7.2 The Power Spectrum

The two-sided Laplace transform of the autocovariance function is given by

$$\Phi(s) = \int_{-\infty}^{\infty} \phi(\tau) e^{-s\tau} d\tau. \tag{6-43}$$

Notice that the definition in Eq. (6-43) differs from our previous definition of the one-sided Laplace transform in that the limits of integration now extend from $-\infty$ to $+\infty$. This is necessitated by the fact that $\phi(\tau)$ is defined for both positive and negative τ. It was not required in the dynamic analysis of systems since then one could always assume that the disturbance started at $t = 0$.

The inverse transform of Eq. (6-43) is given by

$$\phi(\tau) = \frac{1}{2\pi j} \int_{c-j\infty}^{c+j\infty} \Phi(s) e^{s\tau} ds \tag{6-44}$$

when c is chosen so that the integral is analytic for $\sigma \geq c$.

Some important properties of $\Phi(s)$ are of interest to us. Since $\phi(\tau)$ is a real function, Φ is symmetrical about the vertical axis. Also, $\phi(0) = \int_{-\infty}^{\infty} \Phi(j\omega) d\omega/2\pi = \sigma^2$, the variance of the random process.

As an illustration, consider the autocovariance function of the random telegraph wave obtained in the first example above,

$$\phi(\tau) = \frac{1}{4} \left[1 + e^{-2\lambda|\tau|} \right]$$

we have

$$\Phi(s) = \frac{1}{4} \int_{-\infty}^{\infty} \left[1 + e^{-2\lambda|\tau|} \right] e^{-s\tau} d\tau$$

$$= \frac{1}{4} \cdot \delta(j\omega) + \frac{1}{4} \int_{-\infty}^{0} e^{2\lambda\tau - s\tau} d\tau + \frac{1}{4} \int_{0}^{\infty} e^{-2\lambda\tau - s\tau} d\tau$$

$$= \frac{1}{4} \delta(j\omega) + \frac{\lambda}{4\lambda^2 + \omega^2}, \qquad s = j\omega.$$

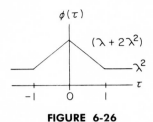

FIGURE 6-26

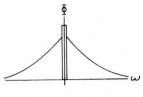

FIGURE 6-27

$\Phi(\omega)$ is shown in Fig. 6-27. The impulse function, $\delta(j\omega)$, which gives Φ a spike at zero frequency, reflects the presence of a mean $\neq 0$ of the random process.

The function $\Phi(j\omega)$ is termed the "power density spectrum" or, for short, the "power spectrum" and measures the distribution in frequency of the power of a signal or a noise. It is easy to show that $\Phi(j\omega)$ as defined in Eq. (6-43), and after substitution for $s = j\omega$, is equivalent to

$$\Phi(j\omega) = X(j\omega)X(-j\omega) = |X(j\omega)|^2. \tag{6-45}$$

when $\phi(\tau)$ is defined by Eq. (6-41).

$$x(t) \longrightarrow \boxed{g(t)} \longrightarrow y(t)$$

If $x(t)$ is the input signal to a system whose impulse response is $g(t)$, the output $y(t)$ is obtained from the convolution integral repeated here:

$$y(t) = \int_{-\infty}^{t} g(t_1)x(t - t_1)\,dt_1.$$

Similarly,

$$y(t + \tau) = \int_{-\infty}^{t+\tau} g(t_2)\,x(t + \tau - t_2)\,dt_2.$$

Substituting in Eq. (6-43) for the autocovariance of the output

$$\Phi_y(s) = \int_{-\infty}^{\infty} \phi_y(\tau)\,e^{-s\tau}\,d\tau$$

we obtain, after some algebraic manipulation,

$$\Phi_y(s) = G(s)\cdot G(-s)\cdot\Phi_x(s). \tag{6-46}$$

Equation (6-46) gives the power spectrum of the output in terms of the power spectrum of the input and the transfer function of the system.

§8. SAMPLED DATA SYSTEMS

When information on the "signal" is available in the form of time series $x(t)$, the Laplace transform $\mathcal{L}[x(t)]$ will be a function of $e^{-s\cdot\Delta t}$ where Δt is the spacing between observations. Now define

$$z = e^{s\cdot\Delta t}; \tag{6-47}$$

then $\mathcal{L}[x(t)]$ can be written as a function of z^{-1}, denoted by $\mathcal{L}_z[x(t)]$. The resulting transform is called the z-transform, $X(z)$.

The list of properties of the $\mathcal{L}$-transform given in §2.3 for continuous signals is applicable to the discrete case with some obvious modifications. The following is a partial list of these properties.

1. If $y(t) = \Sigma_{r=0}^{t} g(r) \cdot x(t - r)$, then $Y(z) = G(z) \cdot X(z)$, where $Y(z)$, $G(z)$ and $X(z)$ are the $\mathcal{L}_z$-transforms of the respective time functions.

2. $\mathcal{L}_z[x_1(t) \cdot x_2(t)] = X_1(z) * X_2(z)$; i.e., the $\mathcal{L}_z$-transform of the product of two time functions is the convolution of their respective z-transforms.

3. If $X(z) = \mathcal{L}_z[x(t)]$, then $\mathcal{L}_z[x(-t)] = X(z^{-1}) = \overline{X}(z)$.

4. $$\mathcal{L}_z[x(t + \theta)] = z^\theta \left\{ \mathcal{L}_z[x(t)] - \sum_{t=0}^{\theta-1} x(t) z^{-t} \right\}$$

and

$$\mathcal{L}_z[x(t - \theta)] = z^{-\theta} \left\{ \mathcal{L}_z[x(t)] + \sum_{t=1}^{\theta} x(-t) z^{t} \right\}.$$

These relationships are valid only if θ is a multiple of Δt.

5. $\lim\limits_{t \to 0} g(t) = \lim\limits_{z \to \infty} G(z)$ (initial value theorem)

$\lim\limits_{t \to \infty} g(t) = \lim\limits_{z \to 1} (1 - z^{-1}) G(z)$ (final value theorem).

6. For absolute stability, the transfer function of the system, $G(z)$, must have all its poles inside the unit circle. Poles lying *on* the unit circle give rise to undamped sinusoidals.

7. $\phi(\tau)$ is defined as

$$\phi(\tau) = \lim_{n \to \infty} \frac{1}{2n - h} \sum_{q=-n}^{n} x(q \cdot \Delta t) \cdot x(q \cdot \Delta t + \tau)$$

where $\tau = h \cdot \Delta t$ and h is integer, or equivalently,

$$\phi(\tau) = \mathcal{E}[x(q \cdot \Delta t) \cdot x(q \cdot \Delta t + \tau)]$$

for any integer q.

8. The $\mathcal{L}_z$-transform of $\phi(\tau)$ is given by

$$\Phi(z) = \sum_{\tau=-\infty}^{\infty} \phi(\tau) z^{-\tau}.$$

Notice that $\Phi(z)$ is a series in negative and positive powers of z, the constant term being $\phi(0)$.

If $\Phi(|1|) < \infty$, we have, by Cauchy's Theorem,

$$\phi(0) = \frac{1}{2\pi j} \oint_{|z|=1} \Phi(z) \frac{dz}{z}. \tag{6-48}$$

9. Finally, we have

$$\Phi_x(z) = X(z) \cdot X(z^{-1}),$$

and the power spectrum of the output y is related to the power spectrum of the input x by

$$\Phi_y(z) = G(z) \cdot G(z^{-1}) \cdot \Phi_x(z). \tag{6-49}$$

Tables of z-transforms (and their inverses) are available; once the reader has familiarized himself with the calculation of the z-transforms of a few simple functions and grasped the fundamental significance of the transform, he should more profitably concern himself with the application of these concepts to operational systems.

The next two sections are devoted to such applications. In §9 we will study the behavior of an automatic quality control system—automatic in the sense that the necessary corrections to errors are "built-in" the system and are automatically evaluated and executed. In §10 we will study a hypothetical production-inventory system which differs from that studied in §6 in that demand is assumed stochastic and data on the parameters of performance (e.g., output) are available only at discrete points of time.

§9. AN AUTOMATIC QUALITY CONTROL SYSTEM

Production systems which are monitored either continuously or periodically to ascertain the quality of their outputs are finding increasing applications in the chemical, steel, food, electronic, and other industries. In this section we will study the behavior of a simplified automatic control system.

We remark that a fundamental difference exists between *automated* systems and *mechanized* ones. In the former, the corrective decisions for every possible eventuality are automatic, i.e., they require no human intervention except in emergencies. The incorporation of an automatic decision-making "black-box" as an integral component of the system is of fundamental importance since any decision made at time t, say, will affect the output of the process during the interval $(t, t + 1)$ (assuming no delay in execution), as well as *all future decisions* (i.e., decisions at $t + 1$, $t + 2, \ldots$).

Let μ_0 be the desired value of the output of some process; say, μ_0 is the nominal diameter of a shaft in a turning process. Let $m(t)$ be the deviation of the actual mean μ from μ_0; i.e.,

$$m(t) = \mu(t) - \mu_0.$$

Let $e(t)$ be the *measured* deviation (from the nominal μ_0) at sampling period t; $e(t)$ is assumed to be composed of $m(t)$ plus some *random* error $x(t)$. The latter is assumed normally distributed about $m(t)$ with mean 0 and variance σ^2. Let $s(t)$ be the definite (but unknown) shift in the mean of the process that occurred between the $(t - 1)$th and the tth observation. Finally, let α be the proportion of the measured error $e(t)$ corrected after each sample; i.e., let the decision to correct be according to the following:

> *Rule:* For any $e(t)$ introduce a correction in the mean of the process equal to $-\alpha \cdot e(t)$.

For simplicity, assume that there is no delay between the decision and the correction made, i.e., assume the transfer function of the controlled machine to be unity. Then we have,

$$m(t) = m(t - 1) + s(t) - \alpha \cdot e(t - 1)$$
$$e(t) = m(t) + x(t)$$

(6-50)

where $s(0) = m(0) = e(0) = 0$, (i.e., the process starts at its desired mean).

Clearly, the actual deviation from the mean at time t is the accumulation of all previous shifts and corrections, as can be seen from Eq. (6-50). Thus, recursively,

$$m(1) = s(1)$$
$$e(1) = s(1) + x(1)$$
$$m(2) = s(1) + s(2) - \alpha\{s(1) + x(1)\}$$
$$= (1 - \alpha) \cdot s(1) + s(2) - \alpha \cdot x(1)$$
$$e(2) = (1 - \alpha) \cdot s(1) + s(2) - \alpha \cdot x(1) + x(2)$$

etc., and in general:

$$m(t) = \sum_{j=0}^{t} (1 - \alpha)^j \cdot s(t - j) - \alpha \sum_{j=1}^{t-1} (1 - \alpha)^{t-j-1} \cdot x(j)$$

(6-51)

and

$$e(t) = m(t) + x(t).$$

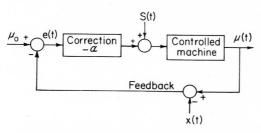

FIGURE 6-28 Feedback Control Loop

Figure 6-28 represents the feedback loop of control; and Fig. 6-29 gives the variation in $m(t)$ due to the shifts $s(t)$ as well as the corrections $-\alpha \cdot e(t)$ in two consecutive time periods $t - 1$ and t.

We are primarily interested in three aspects of the behavior of the system. These are:

1. The random variability of the output induced by the random variability in the input.
2. The transient behavior of the system, especially its response to step and ramp functions.
3. The steady-state behavior of the system, including questions of stability.

Conceptually, we can consider $s(t)$ as the signal component of the input, and $x(t)$ as the noise component (note that $x(t)$ may contain the random part of $s(t)$). The two components of the input are assumed to be independent, which greatly facilitates the analysis. In particular, since the system under study is assumed to be linear, we can, by the principle of superposition, study the effect of each of the two components of the input separately, assuming the other component to be equal to zero. The behavior of the system is then the sum of the two independent effects.

First we carry out the analysis without utilizing the z-transform theory. This will assist in introducing the subject and in indicating the power of the transform when it is used later.

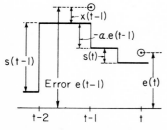

FIGURE 6-29 Variation in m(t)

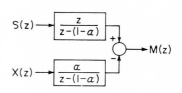

FIGURE 6-30

From Eq. (6-51) we have that

$$\text{Var}\,[m(t)] = \alpha^2 \sum_{j=1}^{t-1} (1 - \alpha)^{2(t-j-1)}\,\sigma^2$$

and

$$\text{Var}[e(t)] = \text{Var}\,[m(t) + \sigma^2.$$

But

$$\lim_{t\to\infty} \text{Var}\,[m(t)] = \alpha^2 \sigma^2 \lim_{t\to\infty} \sum_{j=1}^{t-1} (1 - \alpha)^{2(t-j-1)}$$

$$= \sigma^2 \frac{\alpha}{2 - \alpha} \lim_{t\to\infty} [1 - (1 - \alpha)^{2t}],$$

which is finite if $0 < \alpha < 2$. In this range of stability,

$$\text{Var}\,[m(t)] = \frac{\alpha}{2 - \alpha}\,\sigma^2$$

and
$$0 < \alpha < 2$$

$$\text{Var}[e(t)] = \frac{2}{2 - \alpha}\,\sigma^2.$$

Notice that the correction must be in the opposite direction to the error $e(t)$; hence, the substraction of the term $\alpha e(t - 1)$ in Eq. (6-50). Moreover, at no time should the correction be greater than twice the measured error, $\alpha < 2$, which stands to reason.

Since the magnitude of α determines the *speed of response* of the system, i.e., the speed with which any definite shift in the mean is corrected, the

TABLE 6-1

α	Fraction of s_0 remaining after				Time Constant	Var $[e(t)]$ $\times \sigma^2$
	1st adj.	2nd adj.	3rd adj.	4th adj.		
0	1.0	1.0	1.0	1.0	∞	1.0
.2	0.8	0.64	0.512	0.41	5	1.11
.5	0.5	0.25	0.125	0.06	2	1.33
.8	0.2	0.04	0.008	0.001	1	1.66
1.0	0	0	0	0	1	2.0
1.2	-0.2	0.04	-0.008	0.001	1	2.5
1.5	-0.5	0.25	-0.125	0.06	2	4.0
1.8	-0.8	0.64	-0.512	0.41	5	10.0
2.0	-1.0	1.0	-1.0	1.0	∞	∞

determination of the *optimal* value of α must take into account both factors: the variability in $m(t)$ and the speed of response of the system. Table 6-1 gives the values of these two measures of performance as functions of α, when a unit shift in the mean occurs at $t = 0$.

Naturally, no value of α larger than $+1$ will be chosen since no improvement in the speed of response accrues while the variability of the process increases.

Next, we carry out the analysis utilizing the z-transform of Eq. (6-50). Let $S(z) = \Sigma_{t=0}^{\infty} s(t) z^{-t}$; and let $X(z)$, $M(z)$ and $E(z)$ be defined similarly. Then we have

$$M(z)(1 - z^{-1}) = S(z) - \alpha z^{-1} E(z)$$

$$E(z) = M(z) + X(z),$$

hence,

$$M(z) = \frac{z}{z - (1 - \alpha)} \cdot S(z) - \frac{\alpha}{z - (1 - \alpha)} \cdot X(z). \tag{6-52}$$

$S(z)$ can be interpreted as the z-transform of the signal, i.e., the definite, though unknown, shifts in the mean of the process, while $X(z)$ is interpreted as the z-transform of the accompanying noise. Figure 6-30 depicts the relation between $M(z)$ and both $S(z)$ and $X(z)$.

For *stability* we must have, by Property (6) of §8:

$$|z| = |(1 - \alpha)| < 1, \text{i.e.}, 0 < \alpha < 2.$$

To study the variation in the output due to the random component of the input, $x(t)$, assume $s(t) = 0$ for all t. Then, by Eq. (6-49) we have

$$\Phi_m(z) = G(z) \cdot G(z^{-1}) \cdot \Phi_x(z)$$

$$= \frac{\alpha}{[z - (1 - \alpha)]} \cdot \frac{\alpha}{[z^{-1} - (1 - \alpha)]} \cdot \Phi_x(z)$$

where $\Phi_m(z)$ and $\Phi_x(z)$ are the power spectra of $m(t)$ and $x(t)$, respectively. Since $x(t)$ is assumed independent of all previous values of x, then obviously the autocovariance function $\phi_x(\tau) = 0$ for all $\tau \neq 0$, and $\phi_x(\tau) = \sigma^2$ for $\tau = 0$. Hence, $\Phi_x(z) = \sigma^2$, a constant independent of z. Then, by the Cauchy equation, Eq. (6-48), the inverse transform

$$\phi_m(0) = \text{Var}[m(t)] = \frac{1}{2\pi j} \oint_{|z|=1} \frac{\alpha^2 z \sigma^2}{[z - (1 - \alpha)][1 - (1 - \alpha)z]} \cdot \frac{dz}{z}$$

$$= \frac{\alpha}{2 - \alpha} \cdot \sigma^2, 0 < \alpha < 2, \tag{6-53}^\dagger$$

†For details of contour integration see Appendix 1.

and consequently the variance of the observed error $e(t)$ is given by

$$\text{Var}[e(t)] = \phi_m(0) + \sigma^2 = \frac{2}{2 - \alpha} \cdot \sigma^2. \tag{6-54}$$

Thus, if no shift in the mean takes place, i.e., $s(t) = 0$ for all t, the random component of the error, $x(t)$, would induce variability in the mean of the process about the nominal value μ_0. The expected value $\mathcal{E}[m(t)]$ is obviously equal to zero—i.e., the process is *unbiased*. However, $\text{Var}[m(t)]$ is given by Eq. (6-53) and is seen to increase with increasing α.

The error in the output, as measured by $e(t)$, experiences increased variability as can be seen from Eq. (6-54). Therefore, even under the condition $s(t) = 0$ for all t, *the percent defective will increase* because of the corrective action taken ($\alpha \neq 0$). It is important to note that under the condition $s(t) = 0$, $\text{Var}[e(t)]$ will be equal to its lower bound, σ^2, if and only if $\alpha = 0$, i.e., when *no correction* is made.

In order to study the *transient response* of the system to various signals $s(t)$, ignore for the moment the random component $x(t)$. Then,

$$M(z) = \frac{z}{z - (1 - \alpha)} \cdot S(z), 0 < \alpha < 2,$$

and we have, for example:

1. If $s(t) = s_0$ for $t = 1$ and $s(t) = 0$ for $t > 1$, i.e., if only one shift in the mean occurred during the first period, then,

$$S(z) = s_0 z^{-1}$$

whence,

$$M(z) = \frac{1}{z - (1 - \alpha)} \cdot s_0$$
$$= s_0 z^{-1}[1 + (1 - \alpha)z^{-1} + (1 - \alpha)^2 z^{-2} + \cdots].$$

By definition of $M(z)$, therefore, $m(1) = s_0$, $m(2) = (1 - \alpha)s_0$, $m(3) = (1 - \alpha)^2 s_0$, etc., an exponentially decreasing series. Eventually $m(\infty) \cong 0$, and the step input s_0 would have been completely corrected for.

2. If $s(t) = s_0$ for $t \geq 1$, i.e., if a shift of constant magnitude recurred in every period, then,

$$S(z) = \frac{s_0 z^{-1}}{1 - z^{-1}},$$

whence,

$$M(z) = \frac{1}{z - (1 - \alpha)} \cdot \frac{s_0}{1 - z^{-1}}$$

$$= \frac{s_0}{\alpha[1 - z^{-1}]} - \frac{s_0}{\alpha[1 - z^{-1}(1 - \alpha)]}$$

$$= \frac{s_0}{\alpha} \{[1 - (1 - \alpha)]z^{-1} + [1 - (1 - \alpha)^2]z^{-2} + \cdots\}$$

Therefore,

$$m(1) = s_0, m(2) = \frac{s_0}{\alpha} [1 - (1 - \alpha)^2], m(3) = \frac{s_0}{\alpha}[1 - (1 - \alpha)^3], \text{etc.,}$$

a series which yields an $m(t) \geq s_0$ for $0 < \alpha \leq 1$ and an $m(t) \leq s_0$ for $1 \leq \alpha < 2$. This is a rather interesting result whose interpretation is illuminating. In essence, it states that if we have, for example, a continuously deteriorating cutting tool which introduces an error s_0 in each interval, the error in the mean of the process will be equal to s_0/α. This value then measures the lag in the correction behind the cumulative error due to correcting only a fraction of the error at each sampling point.

Clearly, the transient behavior of the system to other types of input signals can be analyzed in a similar fashion. Figures 6-31(a) and 6-31(b) give $m(t)$ for the two types of signals discussed in (a) and (b) for $\alpha = 0.5$.

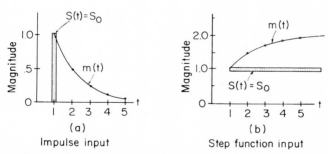

(a)   (b)
Impulse input   Step function input

FIGURE 6-31   Response of System to Two Signals; $\alpha = 0.50$

Discussion

We presented above the analysis of the behavior of the proposed quality control system under the conditions of (1) purely random input and (2) two completely known time functions. The results of this analysis are given in Eqs. (6-52) through (6-54) and in Fig. 6-31, all of which contain the information concerning the three aspects of the behavior of the system mentioned on p. 375.

We note that for all $\alpha > 0$, the variance of $e(t)$ is strictly greater than σ^2, which is the variance of the random component $x(t)$. Clearly, this is the price paid for the possibility of correcting any real shift, $s(t)$, should such a shift occur. Putting $\alpha = 0$ would mean that *no correction* is made at all. This would reduce $\text{Var}[e(t)]$ to its lower bound σ^2 but, on the other hand, a permanent shift in the mean of the process would never be corrected.

If the minimization of the variance of the error, $\text{Var}[e(t)]$, which, by definition, is induced by the *random* component of the input, were our only objective, there would be no problem in determining the value of α: we would put $\alpha = 0$. However, the minimization of $V[e(t)]$ is *not* the only objective of the proposed automatic system. We also wish to correct any permanent shift in the mean of the process. This introduces the necessity of determining a value of α other than zero, depending largely on the type of shifts to be expected as well as the specifications of the performance of the system (e.g., a specified maximum time constant, a maximum overshoot, etc.).

The transient behavior of the system is crucially dependent on the value of α. Small values of α give rise to a "sluggish" system, while large values of α (within the limits of stability) yield fast responsive systems with or without overshoots depending on the characteristics of the signal.

On the other hand, the steady-state behavior of the system is also a function of α as well as of the input signal. For purely *random* inputs it is easy to see from Eq. (6-50) that the system is *unbiased* for all values of α. However, Fig. 6-31 indicates that while a step input is eventually corrected, a ramp input gives rise to a steady-state error, $m(\infty) > 0$. The magnitude of this error is greater than s_0 for $\alpha < 1$ and is smaller than s_0 for $\alpha > 1$.

Again, we emphasize that we are faced, in deciding upon a value of α, with *two conflicting criteria*: the speed of response of the system to real shifts in the mean, which demands a large α, and the minimization of $\text{Var}[e(t)]$ which requires as small an α as possible. The optimal value of α is, by necessity, the result of optimizing an objective (or subjective) function that combines both these requirements in one overall criterion.

Although our analysis was conducted separately for the two components of the input, the "signal" and the "noise," we recognize that in all probability the actual input to the system will be a combination of these two "pure" types. The output of the system will then be the *sum* of its responses to the two independent components of the input.

Finally, a brief historical note. The "proportional control" rule discussed above exhibits a rather special feature in its treatment of past data: it discounts past information in such a manner that observations far removed from the present have an almost negligible effect on the decision made at the present time. This is evident, for example, in our analysis of a step input $s(1) = s_0$, which makes a small contribution indeed (exactly

$(1 - \alpha)^{t-1}s_0)$ to the error and, consequently, to the correction made at time t, provided t is large enough.

This type of discounting past information has been termed "exponential smoothing" by Brown,[†] and it was used by him to forecast future demand in an inventory control problem. He empirically investigated the value of α and suggested 0.10 as a "good" value to adopt in inventory problems. Winters[‡] extended the exponential smoothing approach to take into account cyclical and trend effects using more than one smoothing parameter. Our analysis above reveals that the smoothing parameter α can be established based on a rational choice between the desired speed of response of the system and the maximum variance of the error that can be tolerated.

Roberts,[††] on the other hand, termed the same type of smoothing of past information "geometric moving average" and used it to construct process control charts which have the advantage of being more sensitive to a "true" shift in the mean of the process than the regular type of control charts.

It seems that the first treatment of the subject from the point of view of feedback control theory is due to Bishop.[*] He derived some of our results by statistical arguments.

Perhaps the main reason behind the rather wide adoption of this rule, under whichever name it is disguised, is the fact that it is the simplest possible rule to adopt. It contains exactly one parameter, α, and it represents a linear interpolation between the last observation and the previous linear interpolation.

§10. A DISCRETE PRODUCTION-INVENTORY SYSTEM WITH STOCHASTIC DEMAND

In §6 we discussed a production-inventory system in which demand was assumed continuous and deterministic. In this section we treat a similar system when the inputs and outputs are discrete and random.

Although inventory systems may exist independently of production systems, as in department stores, we shall discuss production and inven-

---

[†]R. E. Brown, *Statistical Forecasting For Inventory Control*, McGraw-Hill, 1959. Input data is said to be "smoothed" by a system whose weighting function is $g(t)$ if $\int_0^\infty g(t)dt = 1$. See the references cited at the end of the chapter; also see Appendix 2 for a discussion of exponential smoothing.

[‡]P. R. Winters, "Forecasting Sales By The Exponentially Weighted Moving Averages," *Management Science*, Vol. 6, No. 3, April 1960, pp. 324–342.

[††]S. W. Roberts, "Control Chart Tests Based On Geometric Moving Averages," *Technometrics*, Vol. 1, No. 3, 1959, pp. 239–250.

[*]A. B. Bishop, "A Model of Optimum Control Of Stochastic Sampled Data Systems," *Operations Research*, Vol. 5, No. 4, Aug. 1957, pp. 546–550.

tory systems in which customers' demand is satisfied from stock which, in turn, is replenished from the production facilities. A large number of manufacturing concerns fit into this pattern of activities. Under these conditions it is clear that control of production and inventory can be accomplished through one of two extreme modes of behavior:

1. The two subsystems can be virtually isolated from each other through the accumulation of large inventories, and then each subsystem controlled individually.

2. The inventory system can be reduced in size almost to the point of vanishing through immediate production to satisfy customer demand and thus be left with just the production subsystem to control.

The first course of action entails large outlays of capital investment in inventories, while the second course entails continuous disruption of manufacturing processes, which is equally expensive. Clearly, the ground between these two extremes holds the greatest promise for economical operation. This necessitates the study of the whole production-inventory system since the study of any subsystem independently of the other necessarily ignores the *interaction* between the two and fails to achieve the desired economic objectives.

If we assume that customer demand is satisfied from inventory—in order to reduce delivery intervals to a minimum—production will serve to replenish stock either in compensation for past withdrawals or in anticipation of future demand. In other words, the production subsystem is manipulated to behave in a reactive or predictive mode, whichever action is deemed necessary.

On the other hand, it is recognized that "cushion" inventories (or "safety stocks") are carried as a protective measure against *random* variation in demand. We can ensure that such variability is minimal by correctly forecasting future demand. However, since the forecast of demand is but one of several inputs to the production-inventory system, it cannot be considered an end in itself.

In this section we shall deal with reactive control; the study of predictive control is beyond the scope of this book.

10.1 A Linearly Compensated System

Assume that it is desired to maintain the safety stock at some fixed level I_0 and to react to demand fluctuations through changing the production level $p(t)$. The inventory level I_0 is a function of demand variability and the desired level of service and is determined in an optimal fashion through balancing the costs of carrying inventory which may not be needed for some time and the loss due to unfulfilled demand because of lack of sufficient inventories. The determination of the optimal level of

I_0 subject to stochastically varying demand is treated elsewhere in this book — see Chapter 1 and the references therein.

We shall start by discussing a decision rule which, prima facie, appears to be "logical." However, closer scrutiny will reveal that it results in an *unstable* system, i.e., a system in which an error in the level of safety stock is either never corrected or increases without bound.

Let $i(t)$ = level of inventory at the *end* of period t.

$\quad p(t)$ = actual production in period t.

$\quad d(t)$ = decision made at the beginning of period t concerning the correction in the production level.

$\quad s(t)$ = actual demand during period t, known only at the end of the period.

$\quad x(t)$ = random component of demand about the average, assumed normally distributed with mean 0 and variance σ_x^2.

$\quad e(t)$ = error in the level of inventory at the end of period t.

Assume that when the production department is subjected to a sudden demand for increased production it exhibits a lag of η time units before achieving the new objective. Finally, assume the corrective action is according to:

$\quad$*Rule:* For any $e(t)$, introduce a correction in the level of production equal to $\alpha \cdot e(t)$.

Then,

$$d(t) = \alpha \cdot e(t - 1)$$

so that

$$p(t) = p(t - 1) + d(t - \eta)$$

$$= p(t - 1) + \alpha \cdot e(t - \eta - 1). \qquad (6\text{-}55)$$

We also have

$$i(t) = i(t - 1) + p(t) - s(t),$$

$$e(t) = I_0 - i(t),$$

hence,

$$e(t) = e(t - 1) - p(t) + s(t). \qquad (6\text{-}56)$$

The z-transforms of Eqs. (6-55) and (6-56) yield, after some algebraic manipulation,

$$P(z) = \frac{\alpha z^{-\eta-1}}{(1 - z^{-1})^2 + \alpha \cdot z^{-\eta-1}} \cdot S(z)$$

and

$$E(z) = \frac{1 - z^{-1}}{(1 - z^{-1})^2 + \alpha \cdot z^{-\eta-1}} \cdot S(z).$$

The condition for absolute stability of the system is that

$$|z_1| < 1, \; |z_2| < 1, \ldots, \; |z_{\eta+1}| < 1$$

where $z_1, z_2, \ldots, z_{\eta+1}$ are the $(\eta + 1)$ roots of the characteristic equation $z^{\eta+1} - 2z^\eta + z^{\eta-1} + \alpha = 0$. It can easily be shown that *no value of α* satisfies the stability conditions, i.e., the system is inherently *unstable* (compare with §6).

The reason for this instability becomes apparent if we notice that Eq. (6-55) relates the new level of production, $p(t)$, to the previous level, $p(t - 1)$, rather than to a fixed reference production level (as in Eq. (6-57) below). Clearly, the decision rule adopted must be changed if a stable system is to be achieved. Figure 6-32 illustrates the fluctuation of $e(t)$ when the system is subjected to a *unit impulse* at $t = 0$, with $\alpha = 0.5$ and $\eta = 0$.

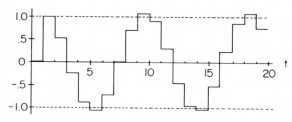

FIGURE 6-32   Error in Inventory, $\alpha = 0.50, \eta = 0$

10.2   A Stabilized System

In order to remedy the situation let the correction be according to:
Rule: For any $e(t)$, increase the average production level by $\alpha \cdot e(t)$.
Therefore,

$$d(t) = \alpha \cdot e(t - 1) \text{ as before}$$

so that

$$p(t) = p_0(t) + d(t - \eta)$$
$$= p_0(t) + \alpha \cdot e(t - \eta - 1) \tag{6-57}$$

where $p_0(t)$ is equal to the average demand.[†] As was noted before, this formulation causes $p(t)$ to be related to a fixed level of production, $p_0(t)$. The z-transforms of Eqs. (6-56) and (6-57) combine to yield

$$P(z) = \frac{1 - z^{-1}}{1 - z^{-1} + \alpha z^{-\eta-1}} P_0(z) + \frac{\alpha z^{-\eta-1}}{1 - z^{-1} + \alpha z^{-\eta-1}} S(z) \tag{6-58}$$

[†]In order to maintain the linearity of the system, we assume that $i(t)$ and $p(t) \geq 0$ for all t.

and

$$E(z) = \frac{-1}{1 - z^{-1} + \alpha z^{-\eta-1}} P_0(z) + \frac{1}{1 - z^{-1} + \alpha z^{-\eta-1}} S(z). \qquad (6\text{-}59)$$

Fig. 6-33 depicts the feedback system under this decision rule. Now the condition for absolute stability of the system is that

$$|z_1| < 1, \ |z_2| < 1, \ldots, \ |z_{\eta+1}| < 1$$

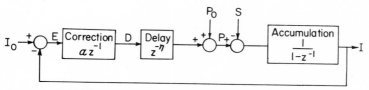

FIGURE 6-33   Feedback Loop in Reactive Control

where $z_1, \ldots, z_{\eta+1}$ are the $\eta + 1$ roots of the characteristic equation $z^{\eta+1} - z^{\eta} + \alpha = 0$.   Table 6-2 is easily constructed (by applying the Routh-Hurwicz criterion to the transformed characteristic equation in λ when z is put equal to $(\lambda + 1)/(\lambda - 1)$) and gives the bounds on α for roots falling within the unit circle in the z-plane.

TABLE 6-2.   Stability Limits on α

Delay	Char. eqn.	Limits on α
0	$z - 1 + \alpha$	$0 < \alpha < 2.00$
1	$z^2 - z + \alpha$	$0 < \alpha < 1.00$
2	$z^3 - z^2 + \alpha$	$0 < \alpha < 0.618$
3	$z^4 - z^3 + \alpha$	$0 < \alpha < 0.446$

The response of the system to random demand is manifested in the variability of both the production level, $p(t)$, and the error in the inventory level, $e(t)$. From Eqs. (6-58) and (6-59) we have

$$P(z) = \frac{\alpha}{z^{\eta+1} - z^{\eta} + \alpha} \cdot S(z)$$

and

$$E(z) = \frac{z^{\eta+1}}{z^{\eta+1} - z^{\eta} + \alpha} \cdot S(z).$$

Hence, utilizing Cauchy's integral equation, Eq. (6-48),

$$\phi_p(0) = \frac{1}{2\pi j} \oint_{|z|=1} \frac{\alpha^2}{(z^{\eta+1} - z^{\eta} + \alpha)(z^{-\eta-1} - z^{-\eta} + \alpha)} \cdot \Phi_s(z) \cdot \frac{dz}{z}$$

and

$$\phi_e(0) = \frac{1}{2\pi j} \oint_{|z|=1} \frac{1}{(z^{\eta+1} - z^\eta + \alpha)(z^{-\eta-1} - z^{-\eta} + \alpha)} \cdot \Phi_s(z) \cdot \frac{dz}{z}$$

Assuming as before that $\Phi_s(z) = \Phi_x(z) = \sigma_x^2$, a constant independent of z, and represents the variance of the random component of $s(t)$, we have, for example, for $\eta = 0$,

$$\text{Var}[p(t)] = \frac{\alpha}{2 - \alpha} \cdot \sigma_x^2$$

and   (6-60)[†]

$$\text{Var}[e(t)] = \frac{1}{\alpha(2 - \alpha)} \cdot \sigma_x^2,$$

while for $\eta = 1$,

$$\text{Var}[p(t)] = \frac{\alpha(1 + \alpha)}{(1 - \alpha)(2 + \alpha)} \cdot \sigma_x^2$$

and   (6-61)[†]

$$\text{Var}[e(t)] = \frac{(1 + \alpha)}{\alpha(1 - \alpha)(2 + \alpha)} \cdot \sigma_x^2.$$

By substituting for various values of α in Eqs. (6-60) and (6-61), Fig. 6-34 is easily plotted giving the standardized variance of both $p(t)$ and $e(t)$ as a function of α.

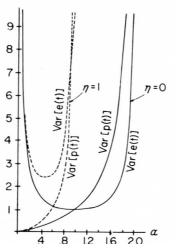

FIGURE 6-34

[†]For details of contour integration see Appendix 1.

It is immediately evident that an increase in η increases the variability of both $p(t)$ and $e(t)$ rather appreciably, especially for $\alpha \geq 0.20$. For example, if $\alpha = 0.50$, purely random variation in demand would cause the production and the error in inventory to fluctuate approximately 34% *more* with an increase in η from 0 to 1.

The response of the system to an impulse or step variation in demand is easily obtained from Eqs. (6-58) and (6-59). We first note that *for the case $\eta = 0$*, if $s(t) = p_0(t)$ for all t, i.e., if demand is perfectly forecasted, $S(z) = P_0(z)$ and Eq. (6-58) reduces to $P(z) = P_0(z)$ while Eq. (6-59) gives $E(z) = 0$, as is to be expected.

If $p_0(t) = p_0$ for $t \geq 0$, assume $s(0) = p_0 + 1$ and $s(t) = p_0$ for $t > 0$, i.e., assume a *unit impulse* in demand occuring at $t = 0$. Then,

$$P(z) = \frac{\alpha z^{-\eta-1}}{1 - z^{-1} + \alpha z^{-\eta-1}} + \frac{p_0}{1 - z^{-1}},$$

which gives, for $\eta = 0$,

$$P(z) = p_0 + (p_0 + \alpha)z^{-1} + [p_0 + \alpha(1 - \alpha)]z^{-2}$$
$$+ [p_0 + \alpha(1 - \alpha)^2]z^{-3} + \cdots.$$

By definition, therefore,

$$p(0) = p_0$$
$$p(1) = p_0 + \alpha$$
$$p(2) = p_0 + \alpha(1 - \alpha)$$
$$p(3) = p_0 + \alpha(1 - \alpha)^2$$
$$p(n) = p_0 \text{ for large } n.$$

A *unit step* function input is given by: $p_0(t) = p_0$ for $t \geq 0$; $s(t) = p_0 + 1$ for $t \geq 0$. Then, for $\eta = 0$, Eq. (6-58) reduces to

$$P(z) = \frac{\alpha z^{-1}}{1 - z^{-1} + \alpha z^{-1}} \cdot \frac{1}{1 - z^{-1}} + \frac{p_0}{1 - z^{-1}}$$

$$= \frac{p_0 + 1}{1 - z^{-1}} - \frac{1}{1 - z^{-1} + \alpha z^{-1}}$$

$$= p_0 + (p_0 + \alpha)z^{-1} + (p_0 + 2\alpha - \alpha^2)z^{-2}$$
$$+ (p_0 + 3\alpha - 3\alpha^2 + \alpha^3)z^{-3} + \cdots.$$

Therefore,

$$p(0) = p_0$$
$$p(1) = p_0 + \alpha$$
$$p(2) = p_0 + 2\alpha - \alpha^2$$

$$p(3) = p_0 + 3\alpha - 3\alpha^2 + \alpha^3$$

$$p(n) = p_0 + 1 \text{ for large } n.$$

Figure 6-35 depicts the response of production to a unit impulse and unit step function in demand, assuming $\eta = 0$ and $\alpha = 0.5$. Similar analysis can be conducted to reveal the response for other values of η as well as the transient and steady-state responses of $e(t)$.

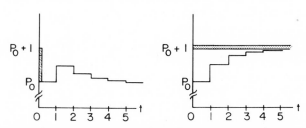

FIGURE 6-35   Response of Production to Impulse and Step Inputs

Concerning the question of *system stability*, Table 6-2 shows that increasingly longer delays in the response of the production department to a decision to increase or decrease the rate of production in order to maintain stability imposes stricter limitations on the freedom of choice of α.

Thus, it is evident that as η, the production facilities delay time, increases, the *speed of response* of the system deteriorates due to two effects. First, it is due to the very fact that η increased, which, by definition, means a slower system. Second, it is due to the increased restriction on the permissible values of α. For example, an increase of η from 2 to 3 increases the minimal time constant of the system (i.e., the time constant corresponding to the largest permissible α) from 3 to 5 time units. In general, the minimal time constant is approximately equal to

$$\eta + [\log 0.37/\log(1 - \alpha_{max})]$$

where α_{max} is the maximum permissible α for absolute stability.[†]

Perhaps the major criticism to reactive control systems is the absence of any "learning" from past experience and capitalizing on this knowledge to minimize future errors. The discussion of *predictive* control is beyond the scope of this book.

[†]Since the proportion of the error corrected is α, we wish to find the exponent n such that the total amount corrected is equal to 0.67. That is, $\alpha + \alpha(1 - \alpha) + \ldots + \alpha(1 - \alpha)^n = 0.63$. Upon summing the geometric series and taking logarithms, the above expression follows.

§11. INDUSTRIAL DYNAMICS

The concepts of feedback control discussed above are concepts of systems, since attention is always focused on the quantitative description of the behavior of individual components and the interaction of each component with the other components of the system. The totality of the system and its unity, are best expressed in the input-output analysis which is carried out, and which was exemplified in the previous sections.

It is not difficult to see that these concepts are general in character. They are applicable equally well to the analysis and synthesis of total production systems or even total enterprises. Such extension into the domain of business undertakings has been termed "Industrial Dynamics" by Forrester.[†] The objective here is to integrate the several functional areas of an organization into a conceptual and manageable whole and to provide an organized and quantitative basis for designing more effective organization policy.

Industrial Dynamics has been received with some enthusiasm on the part of enlightened management which has been attempting to discover optimal or near-optimal approaches to integrating the diverse activities under their control. There is little doubt that a great deal more has to be learned about the modeling of enterprises and the analysis of large scale feedback systems which are subject to stochastic inputs before the approach bears any fruitful results.

COMMENTS AND BIBLIOGRAPHY

§1. The field of feedback control is rich with excellent books on both theory and application. The following books were consulted:

THALER, GEORGE J. and ROBERT G. BROWN *Servomechanism Analysis*, New York, McGraw-Hill, 1953.

TRUXAL, JOHN G. *Control System Synthesis*, New York, McGraw-Hill, 1955.

WILTS, CHARLES H. *Principles of Feedback Control*, Reading, Mass., Addison-Wesley, 1960.

§2. The mathematical theory of differential equations and the Laplace transform are found in any major book on modern mathematics. The following two books were found to be particularly helpful and easy to follow:

HILDEBRAND, F. B. *Advanced Calculus for Engineers*, Englewood Cliffs, N. J., Prentice-Hall, 1961.

VAN DER POL, B. and H. BREMMER *Operational Calculus Based on the Two-Sided Laplace Integral*, Cambridge, England, Cambridge University Press, 1955.

§4. This example is based on the excellent book by Campbell, who was one of the pioneers in the field of applying feedback control theory to Process Control:

[†]Jay W. Forrester, "Industrial Dynamics," The M. I. T. Press, 1961.

CAMPBELL, DONALD, P.   *Process Dynamics, Dynamic Behavior of the Production Process*, New York, Wiley, 1958.
Also, we refer to his early article: "Dynamic Behavior of Linear Production Systems," *Mechanical Engineering*, Vol. 75, 1953, pp. 279–283.

§5, §6. The material in these two sections is based on the pioneering work of:
SIMON, HERBERT A.   "On the Application of Servomechanism Theory in the Study of Production Control," *Econometrica*, Vol. 20, 1952, pp. 247–268.

§7. The study of control systems from the statistical point of view was originated by:
WIENER, NORBERT   *Extrapolation, Interpolation and Smoothing of Time Series*, New York, Wiley, 1950.
The following two texts give a fairly clear development of the subject:
DAVENPORT, JR., W. B. and W. L. ROOT   *Introduction to the Theory of Random Signals and Noise*, New York, McGraw-Hill, 1958.
LANING, J. H. and R. H. BATTIN   *Random Processes in Automatic Control.* New York, McGraw-Hill, 1956.

§8. The theory of sampled-data systems and the z-transform can be found in several of the above-mentioned references, for example, in Truxal's book. The following two references were also consulted:
HELM, H. A.   "The z-transformation," *The Bell System Technical Journal*, Vol. 38, No. 1, 1959, pp. 177–196.
RAGAZZINI, J. R. and G. F. FRANKLIN   *Sampled-Data Control Systems*, New York, McGraw-Hill, 1958.

§9, §10. The linearly compensated system of §9 has been treated by several authors at different points in time:
BISHOP, ALBERT B.   "A Model of Optimum Control of Stochastic Sampled Data Systems," *Operations Research*, Vol. 5, No. 4, August 1957, pp. 546–550.
BROWN, ROBERT E.   "Exponential Smoothing for Predicting Demand," presented at the 10th National Meeting of the Operations Research Society of America, San Francisco, November 16, 1956.
ROBERTS, S. W.   "Control Chart Tests Based on Geometric Moving Averages," *Technometrics*, Vol. 1, No. 3, 1959, pp. 239–250.
Brown's exponential smoothing approach received extensive treatment in his book:
BROWN, ROBERT E.   *Smoothing, Forecasting, and Prediction of Discrete Time Series*, Englewood Cliffs, N.J., Prentice-Hall, 1963.
For further discussion of exponential smoothing in forecasting see the Appendix to this book as well as the following paper:
WINTERS, R. P.   "Forecasting Sales by the Exponentially Weighted Moving Averages," *Management Science*, Vol. 6, No. 3, April 1960, pp. 324–342.
The remainder of the material of these two sections is based on the following paper:
ELMAGHRABY, SALAH E.   "On the Feedback Approach to Industrial Systems Design," *Management Science, Models and Techniques*, Vol. 1, New York, Pergamon Press, 1960.

EXERCISES

1. Give an example for each of the following cases and explain briefly its operation.
   (a) A household appliance with an "open loop" control and another appliance with a "closed loop" control.
   (b) —ditto—but in the context of managerial budgetary controls.
   (c) —ditto—but in the context of traffic on the turnpike.
2. In the economics literature it is common to view the economy as a loop of flow of goods and services among consumers, government, producers, etc. Draw a schematic of such flow and specify its inputs, outputs, feedback loops, etc.
3. In the simple R-C network shown obtain the output, $e_0(t)$, under the following two conditions: (a) $e_i(t) = a \cos \omega t$; (b) $e_i(t) = bt$. In both cases sketch the input and output functions.

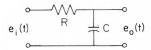

4. Consider a mechanical system composed of a mass M suspended from a spring of stiffness K as shown in Fig. 6-36. (This may be considered as a crude representation of the suspension of an automobile wheel.) The electrical analogue of such a system is also shown in Fig. 6-36.

Mechanical system   Electrical analogue

FIGURE 6-36

Suppose that the point of suspension of the spring is subjected to a forcing function $f_i(t)$; determine the movement of the mass M assuming that: (a) $f_i(t) = u(t)$; (b) $f_i(t) = a \cos \omega t$. (Note: if a current $i(t)$ passes through an inductance L the voltage at the terminals of the inductance is given by $L \, di/dt$.)

5. (a) Consider the Simple inventory model of §5 and assume demand to be a step input $S(t) = u(t)$. Plot the magnitude of the output assuming a correction in the rate of production equal to three-fourths the error in inventory.
   (b) Assume now that $S(t) = a \cos \omega_0 t$, representing a seasonally fluctuating demand with no trend. Obtain the expression for $I(s)$ and write the general expression for $I(t)$.

(c) Suggest a reasonable criterion for estimating the coefficients of any decision function $G_1(s)$.

6. Suppose that it is known that the demand $S(t)$ on a product, though random from period to period, possesses a linear trend upwards in its mean value. It is desired to incorporate such knowledge in an adaptive system of control.

   Suggest a means of changing the objective level of inventory, I_0, in the model of §5 to reflect such adaptive control. Draw the block diagram for the new system.

7. Consider the proportional control discrete loop shown in Figure 6-37, in which $x(t)$ is the random noise (assumed normally distributed with mean 0 and variance σ^2) and $S(t)$ is the signal. Let $\hat{I}(t) = I_0 - I(t)$, and let $P(t)$ denote the deviation from the desired level required to maintain I_0.

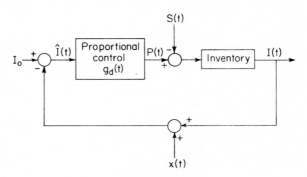

FIGURE 6-37

   (a) Determine the transfer functions (in the z-transform domain) of the proportional controller, G_d, and of the inventory accumulation.
   (b) Show that the condition for stability is still $0 < \alpha < 2$, where α is the constant of proportionality.
   (c) Ignoring $x(t)$ (or equivalently, putting $x(t) = 0$), show that if $S(t)$ can be represented by a ramp function, $S(t) = bt$ (e.g., linear trend in sales), then the difference $\hat{I}(t)$ is given by $\hat{I}(t) = (b/a)[t - \{(1 - \alpha)/\alpha\}\{1 - (1 - \alpha)^t\}]$.

   The following four problems refer to the quality control model of §9.

8. In the proportional control system of §9, assume that $s(t)$ is also a random signal, normally distributed with mean 0 and variance σ_s^2. Show that Var $[m(t)] = (\alpha^2 \sigma_x^2 + \sigma_s^2)/\alpha(2 - \alpha)$.

9. Let $x(t)$ be normally distributed with mean 0 and variance $\sigma_x^2 = 0.36$. Determine the optimal α if it is desired to maintain the output within the limits $\mu_0 \pm 0.10$ not less than 95% of the time.

10. Suppose that the input in the proportional quality control model of §9 is all noise; and is composed of two components: $x(t)$ which is $N(0, \sigma_x^2)$ and $s(t)$ which is $N(0, \sigma_s^2)$; corresponding to a random error in the measuring device and a random signal, respectively.

(a) Draw the feedback control diagram.

(b) Determine the input-output transfer function.

(c) Determine the bounds on α for a given maximum variance of $m(t)$.

11. Assume $s(t)$ to be the ramp function $s(t) = kt$; and the only noise in the system is $x(t)$ which is $N(0, \sigma_x^2)$.

(a) Determine the input-output transfer function .

(b) Reinterpret $m(t)$ in the time domain; and plot the function $m(t)$ against t.

Computers in the Design and Operation of Production Systems

CHAPTER 7

§1. INTRODUCTION

Although the life history of electronic computers as we know them today is less than twenty years old, computers are already in their third generation and are playing an increasingly important role in our daily life. In many instances, we are not even conscious of their tremendous impact. In fact, they have ushered in the "second industrial revolution" which, although still in the making, promises to be of as great, if not greater, influence on our social behavior, our patterns of thought, and our scientific and engineering outlook and endeavors as the first industrial revolution.

One travels on a turnpike and receives a punched card as his "ticket," which is clearly marked: "do not mutilate," because it is to be processed by a computer system at a later date. The monthly bills for electricity, telephone, gas, etc., arrive on punched cards. One listens to the radio or watches TV at election time and is told that the analysis of the votes is carried out on a computer, and the large networks vie with each other for the early and accurate prediction of the outcome. Space flight and the air defense of many countries are today computer-based activities. Although the reader may abhor the idea, our very safety—little as it is in this age of atomic bombs and ballistic missiles—is dependent on the proper functioning of computers.

It is not difficult to extend the list of computer applications in every walk of life—even the entertainment and leisure fields did not escape the computer. If one lacks a partner, there are computers programmed to play checkers, tic-tac-toe, black jack, and Monopoly!

The "revolution" that is taking place stems from the following important fact. The computer is a new tool which, by its unique characteristics, enables us not only to perform old and familiar tasks more efficiently and expeditiously, but also to attempt new and unheard of tasks in

394

novel environments. It is this second aspect of the impact of computer technology that holds the greatest promise—as well as the greatest threat —to a new way of social life.

An analogy should clarify the point. The discovery of radio waves and the theory and technology of short-wave transmission replaced, in many applications, the transmission of messages by the pigeon, the pony express, the smoke signal, the sound of drums, etc. The transmission of messages through radio waves—no minor feat in itself—is an example of the application of a new tool to old and familiar needs. But this is not the case in radio astronomy or the electronic microscope. Here, the new science and technology of electromagnetic waves opened completely new vistas of endeavor which were nonexistent and would have continued to be nonexistent if it were not for the discovery of such waves.

Computers can be used to perform old functions in a new and "better" way. Or, they can be used in completely new and unheard of applications. For example, one can use the computer to add a large set of numbers. In such a case, the computer is replacing the abacus and the desk calculator, and all their varieties. The computer can add more quickly and more accurately. This would be using the computer to do the same old job, but in a new way. It is an "appliqué" approach.

On the other hand, the computer can be used as an on-line component of real-time operation for the control of a complex activity such as petroleum refining or air traffic control. Here, the function is a new one— it has never been performed before, and, in fact, it never before existed as a function.

We will devote this chapter to a review and analysis of the impact of computers on production systems. Our discussion is divided into three major parts, depending on whether the computer is used as:

1. A data processor, presented in §2
2. An aid to design functions, presented in §3
3. An integral component of the control system, presented in §4.

As will be seen, each usage raises its own individual problems, although some problems are common to all three areas of application.

The use of the computer as a data processor basically provides a service more expeditiously and economically. The other two usages of the computer, as an aid to design and as an integral part of the control system, open new horizons to the engineers and management scientists. Our discussion of these two usages will take us into a closer and more detailed look at the technique of simulation and heuristic decision making. The chapter concludes with a note of urgency since it discusses the problem of design of computer-based control systems and points out current deficiencies in our knowledge.

§2. COMPUTERS IN DATA PROCESSING SYSTEMS

2.1 Definition

It is difficult to give a formal and precise definition of the terms "data processing" since they convey different meanings to different people and have actually been used to denote widely varying undertakings. For example, Martin,[†] in his book *Electronic Data Processing*, defines the terms as the "... gathering, recording and manipulation of numbers and alphabetical symbols that are necessary for the proper functioning of a modern business organization." Needless to say, the "gathering" and "recording" functions are intuitively obvious, but the "manipulation" term is rather vague and all-emcompassing since almost every activity concerning symbols is "manipulation" of these symbols.

On the other hand, Ledley,[†] in his book *Programming and Utilizing Digital Computers*, devotes Part 3 of the book to "Data Processing." The titles of the chapters in this part of the book indicate *his* interpretation of data processing: Chapter 9, Fundamentals of Numerical Analysis; Chapter 10, Boolean Algebra; and Chapter 11, Searching, Sorting, Ordering and Codifying.

In this chapter, we adopt the more restrictive definition of data processing, namely, the recording, sorting, ordering, analysis, summarization, and reporting of information. In this vein, analysis involves mathematical manipulation of data in order to bring out its characteristics for purposes of reporting. The definition excludes mathematical manipulation for the purposes of tactical or strategic *decision making*, such as optimizing, solving for the value of parameters, evaluating functions, or the determination of the criteria of decision.

2.2 Reasons for Data Processing

Why is the processing of data necessary? A great deal has been written about the growing importance of "white collar" activities in modern productive systems. The growth and complexity of today's enterprises necessitate the diffusion of responsibility and authority, and consequently, the dissemination of data, in raw or transformed form, to a large number of people.

Managerial decision making, even when concentrated in a handful of people, is dependent on the feedback of a large amount of data. If management is not to be overwhelmed with unnecessary and trivial details, the essential character of the data relevant to the decision to be made must be presented. This necessitates the processing of data.

[†] See the references at the end of this chapter.

Data processing is important in a completely different context, that is, the context of thought, design, and innovation. As will be explained in greater detail in the section on computers as an aid to design, it can be easily established that even in that never-never land of creative thought a large percentage of the "thought" involves the processing of data, i.e., the storage and retrieval of previous information, the summarization of such data, its transformation, and so forth.

The processing of data is sometimes dictated by the world outside the production system itself. For example, the government regulations concerning cost accounting, employment records for tax purposes, labor practices, etc., necessitate the processing of certain data in a specified fashion.

The Original Occurrences

Two fallacies have permeated computer applications in the area of data processing in the world of business and caused the disenchantment of management with such applications.

The first is the belief that the computer will eliminate reports and thus save clerical expenses. If anything, the converse is closer to the truth. Since it is so easy to generate reports from data in machine form (printers are up to 1000 lines per minute) *more* and not less reports usually end up being generated.

The second fallacy is the belief that the greatest contribution of an electronic data processing system lies in the fact that prior to its installation a study is usually conducted (by the "Methods and Procedures" department) in which the existing paper "system" is thoroughly scrutinized in order to improve it. The contention is that it is the computer that provided the impetus for such study (even if no computer is installed after all).

It is not difficult to see through such an argument. For one thing, if the original paper "system" needed overhaul, that should have been done independently of the question of computer acquisition. In addition, such an attitude biases the decision for a computerized data processing system since it will be credited with all the benefits, some of which cannot be rightfully claimed by the computer. The inflated picture may lead to the wrong decision and to bitter recriminations afterward. In this context, one is reminded of a similar argument which was advanced some years ago (and is still used occasionally) for installing wage incentive plans, the contention there being that a comprehensive "methods study" is undertaken before the installation of the plan.

It is well to keep in mind that scientific and engineering innovations are created in response to the needs for solving certain pressing problems.

However, the new tools which are the fruits of such innovations, while they partially or totally solve the old problems, give rise to *new* problems of their own. The cycle of challenge and response is then repeated with the newly created problems.

Thus, the electronic computer may indeed have solved the problem of speed: the current generation of computers carries out addition in nano-seconds (i.e., milli-microseconds). But, this very high capability of modern computers creates the need for a different design of the data processing system in order to utilize such capabilities.

In essence, the challenge boils down to the following. Electronic data processing must be designed afresh from the point of view of information needs and information utility. It is not merely a substitute for clerical efforts.

An example should help drive the point home. The payroll department in any large company is one of the oldest and most venerated of all administrative departments. (After all, it is the one handing out the paychecks!) Therefore, it may come as a surprise to many managers that the department may be eliminated completely in the process of designing and installing an integrated data processing system. To be sure, the *functions* of the department need not, and certainly are not, eliminated. But the existence of a separate link in a long chain (or, perhaps, loops) of information transmission may not be needed any more.

After all, the payroll department assembles all the information concerning working hours, absenteeism, overtime, rate of pay, deductions, etc., and carries out rather lengthy but straightforward arithmetical calculations which yield the desired paychecks. Since each item of data necessary for these calculations is available—or can be made available—in the data processing system, it is necessary only to combine these seemingly separate entities into a total integrated system.

This brings to the forefront the following important concept which, though not new, is worthy of restatement. If one studies carefully the amazing number of reports that are presented daily, weekly, monthly, or even yearly to both management and operating personnel, one finds that they have been generated by the occurrence of certain events which we shall term *original occurrences*. These have been added, subtracted, grouped, or reclassified in various forms to result in the multitude of reports encountered in modern productive systems.

If such *original occurrences* are captured early in the game, say *at their source*, an integrated data processing and control system can be developed which relates all the activities of the firm to these occurrences, with the resultant reduction in both cost and time of operation.

The design of data processing systems—or for that matter, control systems in general—from this point of view offers the following advantages:

1. *Fewer basic inputs to the system.* The original occurrences are the only outside inputs to the system. In many instances, these original occurrences are already in machine language form or can be appropriately translated. For example, employee clocking cards, inventory withdrawals, payment receipts, scrap tickets, position of a moving object, etc. are all available or can be made available at their source in machine language.

Any reduction in input necessarily leads to a more efficient system because it results in (a) *fewer errors*, since the number of errors is a function of the number of entries made; (b) *savings in time* in the preparation and actual input of the data; (c) *fewer reference files*, since the original occurrences can serve more than one purpose (for example, the act of withdrawing material may be utilized in updating the on-hand inventory, in inventory valuation, in crediting the consuming department, in calculating the efficiency of material utilization, in triggering a new order on the suppliers, etc.); (d) *better insurance against catastrophic events*, since all results of previous computations can be reconstructed from previously available results and the new original occurrences.

2. The possibility of achieving *true integration* of the various functional activities. For example, the production and inventory functions, long at odds with each other, can be integrated in a total control system in which both functions serve the primary purpose of the enterprise, rather than serve their independent masters.

3. *Increased flexibility.* The design and implementation of a data processing system is in response to current and expected needs. But no matter how diligently the designer tries to approach perfection, he is constrained by an environment that includes the people receiving the outputs of the data processing system. Their whims and wishes cannot be totally ignored and, for better or worse, eventually will be reflected in the final system implemented.

But the environment changes, and a piece of information demanded by a manager in the past may not be so important to him after a while, or perhaps not important at all to his successor. It is so much easier to discard a report and generate a new report to meet the needs of the new environment when the system is structured to accept the original occurrences than when any other summarization or modification of such occurrences is used.

2.3 Some Design Considerations

While it is not our ambition to give a comprehensive treatment of the design of data processing systems (whole books are written on the subject; see, e.g., Gotlieb and Hume's book cited at the end of the chapter), we feel obliged to give emphasis to some of the most important considerations in such design. Our discussion is to be taken in context with the above argument concerning integrated data processing systems.

One can view a data processing system as a set of (a) *programs* (i.e., instructions to perform the functions outlined in the definition of data processing) which act on (b) *inputs* and already existing (c) *files* to result in (d) *outputs* in the form of displays (visual or audio). Superimposed on these four elements are questions of (e) *reliability*, (f) *selection* of equipment, and finally (g) the *coordinating plan* of operation. In the following paragraphs we discuss, in some detail, each one of these seven aspects of the design problem.

(a) *Programs.* Basically, there are two problems attached to programs. First, there is the question of efficiency versus adaptability to changes, and second, the question of the manner of construction of the whole programming subsystem.

Beginning with the first question, there is a tendency on the part of some programmers and coders to "squeeze the last drop" out of a program, i.e., construct it in such a way that it is as efficient as possible relative to loops, storage, fixed data, etc. Some may go even further and code in basic machine language rather than use some compiler with its macroinstructions. A great deal of personal pride and sense of achievement account for such behavior. Moreover, certain advantages accrue, such as saving in time and memory utilization. But the price paid may be very high indeed in terms of adaptability to future changes.

Like any other system in the world, whether animate or inanimate, its extreme specialization—and hence its outstanding success in a specific activity—may doom it to failure should the environment change in some appreciable measure. In computer programs, the problem becomes one of understanding the special tricks of the original programmer, and of the capability to modify the program without destroying the delicate balance already in existance.

The second problem is related to the first, but is of a more general nature. It is concerned with the interaction among the various components of the program or among different programs.

While it is always possible to construct one large program which is an entity that cannot be divided into smaller units, this is not a recommended procedure. In the long run, it is much better to subdivide the overall problem into smaller problems and construct a programming system which is *modular* in character, with clearly defined points of contact of one module with other modules. The seemingly unwarranted loss in computing efficiency is more than compensated for by the ease in debugging, maintenance, and the incorporation of future changes.

(b) *Inputs.* There are two aspects to input: the determination of the content of inputs and the origination of data. The former is unquestionably the most difficult to determine and is arrived at only after a thorough investigation of the needs of the system.

There are several means of entering data into the computer system, depending on the design of the hardware itself. Input can be through punched cards, punched paper tape, magnetic tape, console switches, console typewriter, or any other external input device which is electrically connected to the computer. The input data may originate in any one of several forms, including the written and spoken word.

Perhaps the most important consideration in the study of inputs is concerned with errors. There are two kinds of input errors: errors of *omission* and errors of *commission*. The designer of the data processing system need not resign himself to the presence of large numbers of errors, but he must come to grips with the fact that some errors of both kinds will, sooner or later, be introduced into the system. In (e), we will discuss in greater detail questions of reliability and checking of input as well as output data.

(c) *Files.* A data processing system is, to a large degree, a data storage and retrieval system. Hence, the files of the system play an important role in the mode of operation of the system.

Careful consideration should be given to the number, type and size of the files. For example, in an inventory control system, one may construct one master file which contains *all* the data on each item in inventory including both fixed data (e.g., denomination, cost per unit, suppliers, storage location, etc.) and variable data (e.g., quantity on order, amount in inventory, current investment, recent purchases, current transactions, etc.). Also, one may divide the data into two or more files. The decision affects the size of the computing system (e.g., the need for input–output buffering; the number of magnetic tapes, etc.), the speed of operation, (e.g., read-in time versus computing time), the interaction with other programs (e.g., cost accounting), and finally, the construction of the program concerned with the function itself (e.g., the calculation of economic ordering quantities).

Another important consideration in the design of the filing system is the question of availability of information. Modern computing equipment offers an amazingly wide variety of storage media. The proper selection of the particular medium for a particular piece of data is consequently made that much more difficult. The criteria of choice among them are, obviously, of an economic nature. The objective is to minimize the overall operating cost. A piece of data may be stored in random access memory, which renders it immediately available for retrieval. But this advantage is obtained at a premium price. Data also can be placed in pseudorandom storage such as discs and drums. A third alternative is tape, either magnetic or punched paper tape. Finally, there are always the punched cards. The cost of *storage* (per bit or character) decreases as we move down the list from random access memory to punched cards. But the cost of *retrieval* increases along the same path.

Little attention has been given to the construction of the file itself: (1) the encoding of information to serve many purposes (e.g., the identification number of a record may serve as identification of its memory location as well as for sorting purposes according to one or more characteristics); (2) the arrangement of data within the file itself for easy reference and retrieval as a function of usage relative to other pieces of data; (3) the size of the individual records; etc.

Finally, the function of *file maintenance* should be contemplated and specified at the time of specifying the other aspects of the filing system. Needless to say, no information is permanent in the long run, and provisions for the proper maintenance of each file, either individually or in consortium with other files, need no emphasizing.

(d) *Output.* Traditionally, data processing outputs have been in the form of printed documents. Needless to say, such is a self-imposed restriction that need not, and certainly does not, exist in all cases.

From both theoretical and practical points of view, the designer of data processing systems can, and certainly should, choose from an almost unlimited variety of visual and audio displays. A selection of a particular output form should be governed by its frequency of generation, frequency of usage, the need for permanence of the output, the information content of the displayed message, and its relation to other components of the system. For example, the proportion of defective output in a process may be displayed on a television screen, punched on a card, typed on a sheet of paper, or broadcast over an intercom system. Which one of these (or other) displays is finally chosen is an economic decision to be based on the above mentioned factors.

One final comment should be made. The output of a data processing system may not be external to the computer at all, in fact, as we shall see below when we discuss computer applications to engineering design and computers as an integral component of the final control system, a large proportion of such output may be internal to a communication system. The output of the data processing system is, then, the input to some other system which utilizes the same hardware.

(e) *Reliability.* We have encountered the question of system reliability in other parts of the book, cf. Problem 20 in Chapter 1 and Problem 3 in Chapter 2. We now discuss the question of reliability in the context of data processing systems, and we accomplish such an objective by looking at the various sources of error and the steps taken for their detection and correction.

Essentially, there are three sources of error: *errors in the input*, *machine malfunctions*, and *program errors*.

As was briefly mentioned in (b) above, there are two types of input errors: errors of *omission* and errors of *commission*. Errors of omission are caused by several reasons, such as: (1) lack of proper motivation of the personnel charged with transmitting the data, (2) inconvenient location of input facility, which encourages delay and subsequent forgetfulness, (3) deficient prior training and indoctrination, (4) lack of time to perform the transmission, (5) lack of concrete definition of the procedure of transmission, etc.

A great deal is still to be learned about this area, which is only a subclass of the general problem of human behavior in the modern industrial complex of man–machine systems.

Relative to errors of commission, we are interested in *logical* errors, i.e., errors in the informational context of the data rather than in its format.

Not all logical errors can be detected, and only a few among those detected can be corrected. Consider, for example, a transmission from operation k to the effect that q units have been completed. There is the possibility of *two* errors in this simple transmission, and both are logical errors. First, the quantity q must be checked against any previously reported quantity, say q_{k-1}. Clearly, q must be $\leq q_{k-1}$ if no material is added in the intervening processes; a transmission of $q > q_{k-1}$ would indicate an error in either q or q_{k-1}. In such a case, it would not be possible to correct the error without consultation with the shop. This is an example of a logical error that is detected but not corrected. Note that if $q < q_{k-1}$, an error still may exist, due to the transmission of the wrong q. This would be an example of an error that is neither detectable nor correctable.

Second, the operation number, k, must be checked for correctness by referring to the predetermined route of this particular job. In case of error, the correct operation number can be inserted. This exemplifies a logical error that is both detected and corrected.

Note that both checks discussed above require access to large data files and involve rather complicated programming logic.

Needless to say, the correct design of input and output media entails careful studies of the quantities of data handled, the frequency of their transmission, and the training of personnel transmitting them. The haphazard accumulation of various hardware components and computer programs is both costly and ineffectual.

Machine malfunction can be minimized by carrying out a well-conceived maintenance and checking procedure. Most large scale computer establishments devote the first hour of each working day to routine maintenance and checking. This latter may be either a standard testing program, which tests each component of the computer hardware, or a marginal test in which different sections of the computer system are run under conditions which are more extreme than those tolerated during normal operations.

Of course, in order to safeguard against machine malfunctions, one can always insist on the complete duplication of certain components of the computer such as the arithmetic unit. This idea has been incorporated, for example, in the UNIVAC computer. Whenever the outputs of the duplicated units vary from each other, this is taken as a signal of a malfunction *in either or both of them.*

Various techniques have been adopted in the design of the computer to further safeguard against machine malfunction or errors in calculations. Although we cannot attempt a detailed description of error detection and correction techniques, a few examples should prove illuminating.

A *parity bit* is added to the representation of each character to make the number of ones in a character always odd (or even). For example, on a machine with the 8421 system (commonly referred to as the Binary Coded Decimal system, BCD), i.e., in which any number between 0 and 15 is represented as the sum of 1, 2, 4, and 8 bits, the number 3 is represented by 3 bits, the first two add up to 3, and the third is the parity bit (see Fig. 7-1).

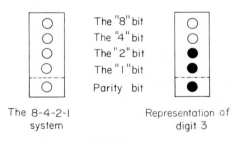

The "8" bit	
The "4" bit	
The "2" bit	
The "1" bit	
Parity bit	

The 8-4-2-1   Representation of
system   digit 3

FIGURE 7-1

Moreover, redundancy can be used not only on digits, but on larger units of information such as words or blocks of words as well. A good example is the method of "casting out nines" to check arithmetic operations such as addition, multiplication, subtraction, and division.[†] For example, to multiply 35 × 12, the first number is 8 (mod 9) and the second

[†]Two number a and b are said to be equal modulo 9 if the remainder of division by 9 is equal for both. Thus, 16 and 322 are equal (modulo 9).

is 3 (mod 9); the product should be 6 (mod 9) since $35 \times 12 = 420 = 46 \times 9 + 6 = 6 \,(\text{mod } 9)$.

The idea of parity check can be carried further to the checking of individual digits as well as words in serial-parallel machines. For example, the number 549631 can be represented in the 8421 system as follows:

TABLE 7-1

	8	4	2	1	Parity
5		1		1	1
4		1			0
9	1			1	1
6		1	1		1
3			1	1	1
1				1	0
Parity	0	0	1	1	1

Notice that we have a row parity as well as a column parity. The parity-parity bit checks the array. The detection of the position of error is extremely simple under this scheme, and this method is extensively used in checking data on magnetic tapes.

Finally, the reliability of the data processing system can be enhanced through *programming checks*. These range over a wide variety of techniques, depending on the logical structure of the application. For example, calculations can be repeated *in toto*, or data can be checked for rationality and consistency whenever that is possible, etc.

(f) *Selection of Equipment.* An electronic data processing system can be viewed as an undertaking which should be subjected to the same type of engineering economical analysis that one usually carries out before the acquisition of a new truck or a new warehouse, or before indulging in a new investment project. However, there are certain considerations which are peculiar to data processing systems. We briefly mention a few.

It seems superfluous to state that the selection of equipment is dependent on the functional specifications of the system and *vica versa*. While it is theoretically advisable to determine what is *needed* first and then select the equipment that best accomplishes the objective, it is practical to keep in mind also what is *possible* from both technological and economic points of view when deciding upon what is needed. The design of a data processing system, or of any system for that matter, does not proceed in an orderly sequence of steps but rather in concentric cycles.

An important point to bear in mind in the selection of equipment for data processing is the rate of technological change. Significant advances in one or more components of the system have been realized on the average of once every three years over the past fifteen years. This should affect not only the selection of the hardware but also the decisions concerning buying, leasing or renting time, and the degree of finality and permanence of the programs.

In §4 we will discuss the philosophy of selection of equipment in control systems. Since the same arguments apply to the selection of equipment for data processing, we refer the reader to that section for the continuation of this discussion.

(g) *Monitor Programs.* Large scale electronic data processing systems are expensive to acquire and expensive to run. Consequently, a great amount of thought should be given to the full utilization of the available time and equipment. This thought is usually referred to as "software."

In the more advanced applications of large scale computer systems, whether for data processing or for scientific calculations, it has been found that designing a master program—called the Monitor Program—which coordinates the various components of the system (see items (a) to (d)) in an automatic or semiautomatic fashion is essential for achieving such utilization.

The Monitor is an expensive investment; estimates run between 3 to 5 man-years of programming effort alone. The Monitor controls other programs; it does not possess its own inputs and outputs. In a sense, the Monitor is similar to a stage manager who does not do any acting himself, but who controls and directs the movement of actors, prompters, lights and curtains, etc. Should an actor be late, or for some reason be unable to perform, a substitute actor is found, or perhaps a replacement act. If the wrong cue is given, an error is committed and subsequent action is taken.

The automatic functioning of the Monitor is almost a must for its correct functioning and contribution to the overall performance of the system. Semiautomatic performance is necessitated whenever the hardware is insufficient to handle all the data at the same time. This is the case, for example, with limited numbers of magnetic tapes or output equipment.

A great deal more can be said about data processing systems. Suffice it to say here that the demand for information is like the demand for goods; utility depends on time, place, and form. Data processing is basically the function of providing the desired data to satisfy all these objectives. The above discussion was intended as a guide in the design of such systems. We now turn to the discussion of computers as aid to design.

§3. COMPUTERS IN ENGINEERING DESIGN

3.1 What Is Design?

To *design* is to plan, to sketch a preliminary pattern or outline, to form in the mind, or to contrive. While we do not attempt to give any formal definition of engineering design, we take it to mean *the creative application of engineering science to the evolution of useful end products.* Thus, an architect designs a house, the civil engineer a bridge or dam, the mechanical engineer a steam turbine, the industrial engineer a machine scheduling system, and so forth. The essence of engineering design rests with its ability to be *creative* and *applied.*

The definitions are necessarily vague because we are trying to characterize simultaneously the function of design and the individual who performs the function, the designer. We think of the designer as being creative, highly motivated, in possession of great strength in technical proficiency and perseverance, and flexible of mind. He is aware of the economic factors surrounding his endeavors. Moreover, he is a creative social force, possessing communicative as well as organizational abilities.

Nevertheless, systematic studies of the process of thought and innovation are beginning to lift the cloak of mystery in which the subjects of design and creativity have been shrouded. And, it is becoming more and more evident that much of the process of design is composed of very mundane things, such as data processing, information storage and retrieval, trial and error procedures, and experimentation, as well as simple old fashioned common sense. There is even conjecture that the moment of revelation, the "Aha," is in fact the result of a long and serious search —one not very dissimilar in nature from the search of a computer for a specific piece of data placed on magnetic tape.

Be that as it may, it is still true that psychologists have not yet discovered why an idea is created by one man and not by another who is faced with the same problem, nor have they succeeded in programming a computer to perform such creative feats. Consequently, we are forced to retain the old ideas and to accept the presence of a role for "intuition," "insight," and "the creative self" in the process of design. But we also know enough about the process of innovation and creativity to offer, or rather insist upon providing, assistance to the designer in performing his creative work. The computer forms the core of this assistance.

Structured and Unstructured Design Problems

Problems of engineering design can be classified into two main categories:

(a) *Structured problems*, in which the variables are known, the functional relationships among these variables are well-defined, and complete rigor (in a mathematical sense) is possible. Such problems lend themselves to formal statements of problem, model, and solution, and, when solvable, are usually amenable to precise algorithmic procedures.

(b) *Unstructured problems*, which are characterized by poor definition of the functional relationship among the variables as well as uncertainty in the behavior of any individual variable.

Naturally, there are engineering design problems which possess a bit of both; they are partly structured and partly unstructured. Nevertheless, the above categorization is a convenient vehicle for our discussion.

One encounters structured problems in the classical studies of the various branches of engineering. The design of an AM receiver for a given bandwidth is a good example in electrical engineering. The design of a gear train to reduce speed from the turbine speed to the generator speed is an example in the field of mechanical engineering. The design of an N-type truss to carry a specified load over a given span is a standard example in civil engineering, and so forth.

Unstructured problems lie predominantly in the domain of systems engineering. While it is true that some entire systems are structured, it is equally true that as the size of the system increases so does its complexity, and structure suffers as a consequence.

The field of industrial engineering is replete with excellent examples of unstructured problems. This is certainly due to the relative novelty of a field in which many of the problems are treated by rough and ready techniques without real understanding of the factors at play or their interaction. But it is also due to the type of problems treated. These are, by their very nature, large-scale systems with perhaps hundreds of interacting factors, some of which are human, both personal and social. The electrical engineer's systems of capacitors and resistors are relatively simple compared with such real-life systems encompassing men, machines, and institutions. The industrial engineer's goal is to move the system under his study toward the structured end of the scale as far as is economically and technically feasible.

The Role of the Computer

Where in this conglomeration of structured, semistructured, and unstructured problems of design does the computer fit? There are, in fact, three levels of computer participation in the design function.

(a) There is the outright take over by the computer of the whole design function. This is *automated design* and takes place in highly structured design problems.

(b) In the second level, the designer retains the power of decision and exercises the right of choice, with the computer as his helper and silent slave. It performs faithfully, expeditiously, and with unbelievable precision whatever functions he assigns to it. This is *computer-aided* design.

(c) In the third level, the designer builds into the computer the rules of decision and choice that are thought to yield a good (though not necessarily optimal) result and permits the computer to carry out the design to termination. He still exercises his prerogative of choice by passing final judgement on the end product. If dissatisfied, he modifies the rules which he introduces into the computer in the first place. At this level, the computer designs the product, whereas man designs the system (including the computer) which designs the product. This is *heuristic design* and takes place in poorly structured problems.

In the following sections we will illustrate each function and give the theoretical foundation for its accomplishment.

3.2 Computers in Highly Structured Design Problems: Automated Design

Design has always seemed to be a personal activity. The suggestion that it can be automated at all often sounds almost sacrilegious and is usually received with utter disbelief.

Yet, it is a fact that the design process in well-structured engineering problems is composed of a sequence of calculations (possibly of a lengthy nature), together, perhaps, with some data processing in the form of table lookup or file search and the final summarization and editing of results. But all these are functions to which the computer is uniquely suited. The "take over" by the computer of such design problems can be complete, and it certainly is.

In these circumstances, the computer is a "formula applicator," a large calculator, and a data processor. Even the choice of a "safety factor," which cannot be claimed to be a masterful example of engineering genius, can be made by the computer.

For example, the depth of a cantilever beam can be calculated from knowledge of its length, width, and load. The correct diameter and thickness of a pipe can be determined from its length and pressure drop. The thickness of an insulating wall can be evaluated by numerical techniques from data giving the desired temperature drop and the characteristics of the refractory material. The list of such examples is quite impressive.

Automated design goes beyond this stage of merely specifying the end product. For several years there has been tangible evidence that the computer's contribution can extend to the specification of the necessary parameters for the production function and, better still, to the control of production itself. Consider, for example, the design of mechanical cams. The form is well defined mathematically by the functions they are to perform. The complete design of a cam also calls for specified rules for the choice of raw material and cam dimensions. Naturally, the input or output information is not in the form of drawings. Rather, it is given as numerical tables and text. It is a simple step to place such output on magnetic tapes or punched paper tapes which are then used on numerically controlled machine tools to control the production of the cams. The computer has thus carried the design to the very beginning of the production cycle.

Small electric motors are more complicated examples of products which are designed today in a completely automatic manner. For a given specification, the computer chooses standardized iron cores for stator and rotor design as well as rotor axles and casings. It also makes some engineering computations for the wire dimensions and the windings. The input to such an automatic design procedure is simply a table form in which the desired performance data are filled in by the engineer. The computer output need only be a list of standard parts and data on wire, the configuration of the windings, and the turns to be wound.

Automated design may be of a still more sophisticated nature. Consider, for example, the design of electronic circuits. Entered are the design parameters of a specified function (bandwidth, *db* loss, etc.). The output is a circuit diagram with component values *plus* a production wiring diagram for the *optimal* wiring of the circuit. Alternatively, the output may be in the form of tape for the control of numerical machines that perform the wiring operation (rather than in the form of a diagram).

The list of examples can be extended indefinitely because the number of applications of this type is growing every year. However, the above should be sufficient to illustrate the scope and power of automated design. Since engineering and scientific research is directed toward the solution of new and outstanding problems, one can expect that more and more currently unstructured design problems will become structured as knowledge is gained. Consequently, one may anticipate that the role of the computer will grow and the design of an increasing number of products or systems will become automated.

3.3 Computers in Poorly Structured Design Problems: Computer-Aided Design

Most design problems are dependent upon so many design parameters in such an *implicit* way that no precise mathematical formula can be derived. Consequently, the designer resorts to cut and try methods, and the process of design may be represented schematically as shown in Fig. 7-2. The process of design is then considered creative and highly original, but much of this process really consists of establishing procedures which will solve part of the design problem using information available to the designer from his memory, handbooks, files of his company, etc. Much of this information can be stored and specified in computer programs.

In this new role, computers provide quantitative data on the basis of which the engineer can make qualitative decisions. Computers assist in two ways: (a) they allow the designer to handle larger and more representative design situations, and (b) they speed up the analysis.

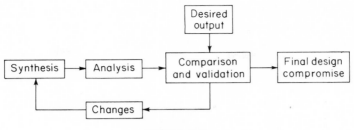

FIGURE 7-2

Apart from using the computer as a large desk calculator, which requires no elaboration here, the designer may use the computer in one of three capacities: (a) as a display mechanism (graphical or numerical), (b) as a simulator, and (c) as a heuristic problem solver.

In this section we will discuss briefly the use of the computer as a display mechanism and leave the use of the computer as a simulator or as a heuristic problem solver to the following sections. However, since a great deal of that discussion depends on a complete understanding of the technique of simulation, we shall first present a more thorough analysis of this concept, after which we return to the main stream of our discussion.

The Computer as a Display Mechanism

Perhaps the most creative of all engineering problems are those in which the structure and shape of the object are not known (e.g., the design of a moon landing craft, etc.). However, even these totally creative examples of design have a large element of synthesis of ideas already exhibited in earlier works. Starting a design problem with a "clean slate" is usually not truly the case, since some degree of carry over from previous experience is present.

In these design problems there are usually two problems: (a) how to communicate ideas and information to the computer in graphical as well as numerical or symbolic data and (b) how to make the computer assist the designer once it understands this information. The first problem stems from the fact that in the early stages of the game the designer is thinking in terms of only rough sketches and "doodling pads." The second problem is just a follow up of the first; in particular, having fed the desired information into the computer in the desired form, to what use can the computer put it?

It is clear that the overall character of an object is given by its *form* and its *structure*. The first specifies its shape, and the second specifies how the components fit together. Form can be described by a sketch, by specifying a large number of points, or by specifying a finite set of component curves from which the desired shape is synthesized. The first approach is purely graphical, and the last two are combined numerical-graphical methods.

All three approaches are utilized in modern design techniques to communicate form to the computer and make the computer communicate shape to the designer.

In a pioneering experiment at MIT, a computer is connected to a cathode ray tube; the designer "draws" on the surface of the tube with a "light pen," and the sketch is read by the computer. The latter is programmed so that when given the proper instruction it projects on the surface of the cathode ray tube the isometric projection of the object together with its projections on all three reference planes. The object can be rotated, enlarged or reduced, and have any particular member of it manipulated in any manner desired (elongated, curved, straightened out, etc.). The designer can "erase" or add new components at will and can always see the results of his trials on the cathode ray surface. In this manner, the computer assists the designer in visualizing shape and acts as his "sketch pad." (See Fig. 7-3.)

In Sweden, it is reported that development runs along the last two approaches, viz., towards the development of a descriptive language which

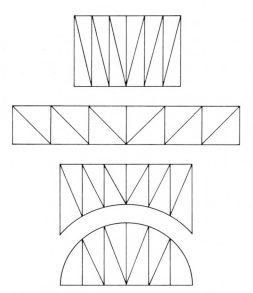

FIGURE 7-3 Manipulation of Truss to Check Stress and Strain in Linkages under Specified Loads.

gives form, structure and content (e.g., elastic content). For example, consider the cantilever truss shown in Fig. 7-4. It is composed of four members a, b, c, d, and has four joints. The structure formed by these beams can be described by the *incidence matrix* shown to the right (sometimes called *coincidence matrix*). We have discussed incidence matrices in Chapter 4, Section 2, and the reader should satisfy himself that such a concise representation gives the structure of any truss or network.

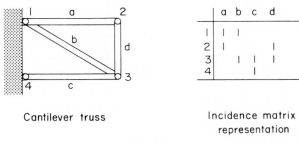

Cantilever truss

Incidence matrix representation

FIGURE 7-4

Representation can also be accomplished using an "alphabet" composed of a few basic geometric figures such as a straight line, semicircle, curve, etc. The coincidence matrix then specifies the type of curve connecting any two points. For example, the odd-shaped body shown on the left of Fig. 7-5 can be represented by the coincidence matrix on the right, where the entry in the matrix denotes the type of curve joining the two coordinate points.

Although computer-aided engineering design is still in its infancy, its

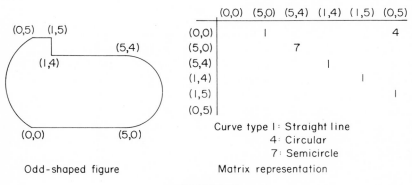

Odd-shaped figure

Matrix representation

FIGURE 7-5

achievements are sufficiently outstanding to dispel any skepticism concerning its practical utility.

For example, consider the design of the 120 ft. diameter radar antenna
called Haystack, built for the USAF and Lincoln Laboratory. In its
design, the reflector had to meet tolerances of ± 0.075 in. maximum total
deviation at any point on the quarter acre structure.

> "The reflector support consists of 1300 members which form five concentric
> and trussed rings interconnected by tension rods and strategically placed
> compression members. In effect, these are used to preload the structure to
> minimize deflection. The stiffness and deflection analysis of this complex
> structure was performed by manipulating large matrices that take into ac-
> count the contribution of each number. All the design analyst had to furnish
> as input were the x, y and z coordinates of joint locations, section properties,
> and end restraints of the individual members, plus boundary or support con-
> ditions for the total structure and applied loading conditions.

> One might think of linkages as pin-connected trusses (as in Fig. 7-6). It is
> possible to sketch such linkages on the screen as a computer input and then
> to move a dividing link—by turning a knob on the scope control—so that
> the designer can observe the complex motions that are generated even by the
> simplest of linkages.

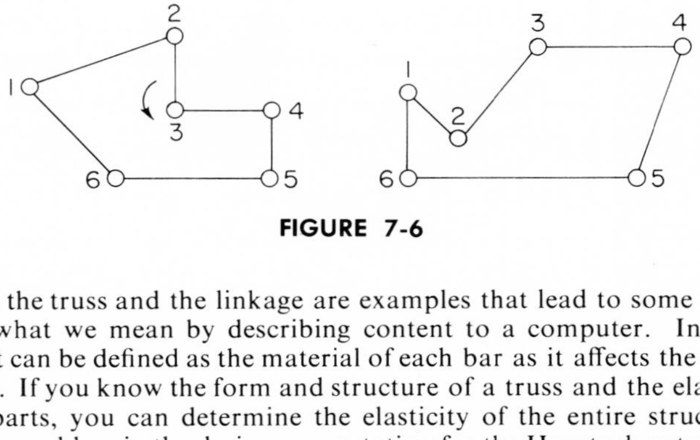

FIGURE 7-6

> Both the truss and the linkage are examples that lead to some understand-
> ing of what we mean by describing content to a computer. In these cases
> content can be defined as the material of each bar as it affects the elasticity of
> the bar. If you know the form and structure of a truss and the elastic content
> of its parts, you can determine the elasticity of the entire structure, which
> was one problem in the design computation for the Haystack antenna."[†]

Another significant contribution of the computer in this capacity is the
assistance it renders in visualizing complex geometric figures. For example, engineering a highway system, say an interchange, involves the
visualization of the road profile as seen by drivers from different seat
heights and different locations. The computer provides such perspective.
The input is composed of three previously calculated tables: the road pro-
files (by height and radius) of a set of road sections, the contour of the
road in plan view, and the terrain cross section at different locations. The

---

[†]B. Langefors "Automated Design," *International Science and Technology*, February,
1964, pp. 96.

computer produces successive sketches on a scope screen that show road slopes and curves as they would appear to a driver in a car seat.

Continuing research in this area promises a revolution in engineering design techniques, because it places at the disposal of the designer a very powerful tool of analysis and display.

3.4 Simulation

Introduction

In the past few years, simulation has come to occupy a prominent position as a tool of design and problem solving.

To *simulate*, according to Webster's Collegiate Dictionary, is "to feign, to attain the essence of without the reality." In substance, therefore, every representation is a form of simulation and must involve some reduction or change from reality. The degree of difference between the simulation and the real system (real in the sense of capability of construction, not present existence) depends, of necessity, on the objective of simulation. In particular, the differences lie in those aspects of the real system which cause it to be real and which are irrelevant to the study.

An example should clarify this rather lengthy definition. To the supplier of army uniforms, the sizes of uniforms that he makes should conform to some statistical distribution, which is the same distribution of the sizes of men recruited in the army. Now, if we need to conduct some simulation studies on these uniforms, say an inventory study, the system that we would be investigating would be composed of, among other things, random numbers that conform to the specific statistical distribution. This is the *essence* of the real-life situation of interest to us, and it is naturally the feature that we must retain in the simulation model. The other features that make real life situations "real" are irrelevant to our study. Thus, the names of the army personnel requisitioning the uniforms from the storeroom, their religion or political affiliation, their disposition towards army life, or their ideas on current social problems are completely irrelevant facts. Some of these facts may be relevant to other studies.

Simulation usually involves a great number of calculations, hence the common phenomenon of using computers in simulation. However, it is important to bear in mind that large scale digital (or analog) computers are not *necessary* to conduct simulation studies—a great deal can be done and has been done with pencil and paper and with the possible aid of a desk calculator.

Having stated the above, we recall that this chapter is devoted to the use of computers as aids to design. Consequently, we shall confine our discussion to computer simulation. In this context, to "construct a simulation" means to program one for digital computation. Needless to say, all previously stated desiderata in good programs discussed under "Computers in Data Processing Systems" apply to simulators.

Simulation may or may not involve *Monte Carlo* experimentation. In other words, the functional relationships among the various components of the model may or may not involve a random element which is subject to some known probability law. For example, one can simulate the flow of jobs in a manufacturing shop assuming a completely deterministic system, with the object being the experimental determination of the distribution of completion time as a function of the job sequence. Whenever Monte Carlo simulation is adopted, sampling from the populations of the random variables is necessarily used. Population sampling also extends to sampling attributes and events whenever complete enumeration is not feasible or not possible, such as in the simulation of the behavior of a job shop mentioned above. But population sampling may also be used as a problem-solving technique of its own right. Consider, for example, the following problem. Suppose it is desired to determine the surface area of a lake which is of irregular shape and contains several islands, as shown in Fig. 7-7. Instead of engaging in a frontal attack on the problem, let

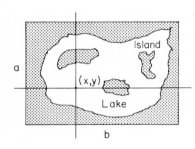

FIGURE 7-7 The Problem of Finding the Area of an Odd-Shaped Lake

us reconstruct it in the following manner. Enclose the lake in a rectangle of sides a and b. Now, any point (x, y) chosen at random is either on land or in the water. The proportion of points falling in the water approaches the relative water area to the area of the rectangle as the number of such sample points grows large.

In summary, then, simulation is a problem-solving technique, the success of which relies on the representation of the essence of the real-life problem, and which may or may not involve Monte Carlo experimentation. In the following sections we will take a closer look at the technique itself.

Why Simulate?

All of the above discussion leads to the conclusion that simulation is a *technique*. It is not a theory; rather, it is a problem-solving methodology.

In fact, it is one of many problem-solving techniques available to the systems engineer. It need not be the best technique for *all* problems. In fact, oftentimes it is a very poor technique indeed.

This naturally brings up the question: when is simulation useful as a problem-solving technique? We mention the most prominent among the reasons for simulation, which may also serve as a list of the *uses of simulation*.

1. There is an absence of any compressed and complete mathematical formulation of the problem, or great difficulty is encountered in *solving* such formulation if one exists. The complexity of the system may be the reason for either of these eventualities. For example, to date it has not been possible to reduce the operation of a large business firm to a neat set of mathematical equations.

2. Scientific investigation proceeds from observation to hypothesis to experimentation and finally, to validation. Simulation may be the *only possible way* of experimentation because of the impossibility of conducting the experiments and observing the phenomena in the actual environment. This is true, for example, of studies of the thrust of rocket motors for use in interplanetary space. Alternatively, simulation may be the *cheapest* way of conducting such experiments when compared with experimentation with the real system, a pilot plant, or even in the laboratory. This is the case in the determination of a new warehouse location, for example.

Simulation can be considered the ultimate in controlled experimentation since even random or chance variability can be replicated with the greatest of ease. The statement "with all other factors remaining constant" can be made literally true. This absolute control of the experiment may be a very desired feature, but it does raise some problems of comparative validity which we shall discuss below under problems of simulation.

3. A simulation is a very powerful *educational* device. The very act of constructing a simulation is instructive to all participants, since complete familiarity with the simulated system is a prerequisite. It is a very good *training* device, especially if combined with some physical representation of the system. To be able to "see" and "play with" the system, that is to say, with its simulation, is of tremendous value in (a) gaining insight into the relative importance of the various factors, (b) perceiving the system as a whole with all its interacting elements, (c) selling new ideas and gaining enthusiasm for proposed changes.

4. Simulation may actually assist the process of innovation and discovery by imparting such "feel" for the problem as mentioned in (3). The output of simulation is data, and data, whether real or artificial, may suggest new questions or avenues of research not envisaged at the start of simulation. More than one instance is on the record of an investigation

which started by asking certain questions only to be diverted more than once to more interesting, and oftentimes more fundamental, questions.

The power of simulation in this respect is apparent in the study of new policies or in acquiring new equipment. *Before* the new policy is instigated or the equipment installed, the simulation can answer many questions, point out unforeseen problems, and indicate the relative merits and demerits of alternatives. This may avoid a great deal of expense and disillusionment later on.

5. Besides the complete control of the experimental environment mentioned above (2), simulation affords complete control over *time*. This immediately yields two results: (a) a sort of "slow motion" study of fast-acting events can be made (as well as a "speed up" of slow-moving events), and (b) one can handle several projects moving at different rates, such as in attack-defense maneuvers.

6. Finally, simulation can be used as a check on analytical solutions. To quote from Morgenthaler[†] "In a recent missile study, the author arrived at a closed-form expression for the approximate expected damage to a circular target area due to an impacting circular cluster of warheads whose mass center was normally distributed about the target center. There were no tabled values against which to check the accuracy of the approximation. It seemed desirable to "check" the formula against some known cases before employing it widely in the Operations Research study. Using cut-out paper damage circles, a circular target, and a table of random normal deviates, it was possible to obtain 'experimental' data which checked out the analytic result."

Having discussed at some length the reasons why simulation is "good," it would seem only fair to give the reader the other side of the coin and draw up a list of why simulation is "bad." A brief list of the limitations of simulation is given on page 440. In order to grasp the full significance of these limitations, we will take a slight detour in the next two sections to discuss the construction of a simulation and the importance of simulation languages in facilitating such construction, respectively. Then we shall return to the subject of problems in simulation and the limitations of the technique.

On the Construction of a Simulation

How does one obtain a simulation of a complex system? There is no uniform step by step method recommended for the construction of a simulation, but since a simulation is a *model* of the system, it must follow that the approach to the construction of a simulation is identical to the

---

[†]G. W. Morgenthaler, "The Use and Application of Simulation in O. R.," *Progress in O. R.*, R. L. Ackoff, ed., Wiley, 1961, Chapter 9, p. 374.

construction of a model; see §2 of Chapter 1. In particular, each component of the system is represented by a mathematical model, and the interactions among the components are specified. A computer program is then written to perform in concordance with the mathematical model. When a simulation is "run," the program proceeds step by step through short intervals of time, pausing at the end of each interval to perform the indicated functional response of the components and to evaluate the status of the system. In the process of so doing, various statistics and measures of performance are calculated. Thus, it is possible to obtain the history of the performance of the system under any given conditions. By repeating the experiment under different conditions—different either in a deterministic or probabilistic fashion—it is possible to compare results and decide upon a "better" set of decision rules.

The following are a few remarks on the methodology of constructing a simulation.

First, it is important to *possess detailed acquaintance* with each component of the system and its manner of interaction with other system components. If the smallest elements into which we can divide a system are themselves of unknown behavior, either deterministically or probabilistically, simulation is not feasible.

Second, detailed and precise *definition of the nature and scope of simulation* must be made as early as possible. There are strategic as well as tactical considerations in this respect: (a) the objective of the simulation, (b) the sources of input data, their form and content, (c) the financial, computer, and manpower support available or necessary; (d) the duration and extent of the simulation, and (e) the experimental design that will yield the desired information, and the manner in which each "test run" is to be executed.

Third, it must be evident that one advantage of simulation is that it *requires no simplifying assumptions*; the model can be made as complicated as desired. This advantage can be easily turned into a disadvantage by the "dressing up" of the simulator to give it the "appearance of reality." This may prove, in the end, to be the death trap of the simulation and is too often the case to be dismissed lightly.

The reason for such an unpleasant ending is simply the following. A simulation is a model that is "run" rather than "solved" in order to obtain results. Consequently, by its very nature, simulation is incapable of generating its own solutions, and is, therefore, confined to the analysis of the behavior of the system under any specified conditions. In short, simulation is an "if-then" tool of analysis. It immediately follows that simulation, when not used as a mere descriptive tool, is best suited for *comparing alternatives*. If the number of factors affecting the result under any given alternative is large, a valid comparison among alternatives can be made only after each alternative has been tested under *all possible combinations* of the interacting factors. This can be a very large number indeed, and oftentimes it is of such astronomical magnitude that complete factorial experimentation is ruled out from the start. Of course, design models other than complete factorials exist and do permit valid comparison among alternatives. However, the number of necessary experiments under such designs may still be inordinately large if the number of variables becomes excessive. In stochastic processes, the problem is further complicated by the necessity of taking representative random samples of the different measurements.

The price of encompassing *all* factors affecting the real life system, and therefore being "realistic," is an unwieldy simulator and a mass of data that does not mean a thing. On the other hand, a simulation which ignores many factors may lead to erroneous conclusions. The art of simulation lies in balancing these two extremes and in coming up with meaningful results.

Apart from the question of factorial interaction, which is a question of size of experimentation, there is the question of *abstraction* and *reduction*; is the simulation going to be the same *size* as the real system? This is a question of *content* of the simulation proper. For example, suppose it is desired to simulate a shop containing 400 machine tools of different capabilities. Should the simulation contain exactly 400 machine tools, or would a smaller number suffice? What is the "essence" of the problem here? In particular, would fifty machine tools do? How about *three* machine tools?

Almost every analyst who is concerned with simulation will, sooner or later, be faced with the question of the extent and validity of abstraction and reduction. It is not possible to give a hard and fast rule in this respect, since the question of validity of representation depends on the real system being represented. Limiting cases may or may not contain the essence of the complete system, and if they do not, it would be a mistake to generalize from the limiting case to the parent system.

For example, a point is a circle of radius zero; it is a limiting case. And yet, no amount of study of the properties of the point will reveal anything concerning the properties of a circle of radius greater than zero. Or, consider the following example from economic theory. The so-called "Robinson Crusoe Economics" is the economics of one man, assumed to be a "rational economic man," against "nature." The entrepreneur, which is the usual decent name given to such man, is out to maximize *his* utility. The "Robinson Crusoe Economics," which dominated economic thought for over two centuries, is the limiting case of real life economics and is a valid model of monopolistic economy. But it is *not* a valid representation in the case of duopoly (or two giant firms controlling the market). There is a fundamental element which is present in duopolistic markets which is completely absent in the Robinson Crusoe theory. That element is *competition*, and it took the genius of von Neumann to develop the mathematical theory of two-person games to represent such a system.

But even the two-person game theory falls short of representing the market under oligopoly (or a few firms controlling the market). There is an added element which is present in oligopoly but is completely absent in both the Robinson Crusoe theory or the 2-person game theory. That element is *collusion*. Again, it took the genius of von Neumann to develop the *n*-person game theory. It is instructive to note that the 3-person game theory contains *all* the elements of the *n*-person situation, and it is amusing to remark that as *n* grows large, the theory reverts to the Robinson Crusoe economic theory!

Thus, we see that no amount of study on the one-machine shop will reveal anything concerning the many-machine shop, except perhaps the negative result that one cannot generalize from the one-machine study to the many-machine case.

In general, as was stated before, the level of abstraction and the degree of reduction are functions of the real system under study. Achieving the *essence* of the real problem must not be confused with achieving the *like* of the real problem.

One final remark concerning the construction of a simulation: in many instances it may not be feasible to carry out a frontal attack on a problem, or it may be preferable (from time, effort, or other points of view) not to carry out such an attack. Rather, it may be possible to solve easily *another problem* whose solution gives the result sought in the first place. This is a standard "trick," and a rather clever one, in mathematical and engineering analysis in general. We encountered an example of such a "trick" in the discussion of the shortest route problem, §3.2 of Chapter 4. There, instead of solving the Shortest Route problem we solved a minimal cost-of-flow problem by a straightforward Linear Programming approach. The solution to the latter problem yielded the answer to the former.

We encountered the same "trick" in the previous section when we wanted to calculate the surface area of an odd-shaped lake. There, we solved a probabilistic problem (which was, in effect, the determination of the binomial parameter p denoting the probability of the sample point falling in the water area) whose solution also yielded the surface area of the lake.

In many simulation experiments, the well-known ergodic principle is invoked: instead of determining the desired statistical characteristics from the study of a very large number of events occurring at the *same time*, we observe the behavior of a few events *over a very long period* of time. Sometimes this is much easier to do, and the results are equivalent.

Simulation Languages

Introduction.   Readers of cartoons and science fiction are familiar with computers that allow their employers to write their problem in vague terms on a slip of paper and drop it into a slot.   The computer then proceeds to instruct everybody around on what *they* should do.   Unfortunately, or perhaps fortunately, this blissful state of affairs has not been reached yet, and it is most likely, at least for some time to come, that man will be instructing the computer on what *it* should do.   In fact, these instructions must be sufficiently complete and precise so that they leave absolutely nothing to the "discretion" of the computer.

The communication between man and machine, just as the communication between one man and another, is effected through the medium of a *language*. It is the purpose of this section to discuss computer languages, particularly as they relate to the technique of simulation.

To this end, we need to review a few concepts widely used in the field of computer data processing. *Programming* encompasses three main activities. They are: block diagramming, coding, and "debugging." A *block diagram* is a model of the behavior of the system and expresses, in graphical form, the logic of the system. A block diagram thus serves the dual purpose of representing the system and specifying the desired logic of operation according to which the computer should conform.   A block diagram is usually developed in several stages, beginning with a gross overall view of the behavior of the system and ending with a detailed specification of the logic of operation.

The second function, *coding*, entails the detailed specification of the location and form of input and output in memory, the allocation of memory among the various portions of the program (input-output, reference tables, working storage, and the program itself), and the detailed translation of the block diagram logic into machine understandable language.

Finally, *"debugging"* is the common term given to discovering and correcting the errors, logical and otherwise, in the previous two functions.

Our main concern here is with the second function, coding, or, in general, the problem of preparing a machine understandable program.

It became evident in the very early stages of computer development that the chore of coding in basic machine language weighs heavily on those who wish to utilize computers, and that the work involved in coding acts as a serious inhibitor to the wide usage of computers in the various fields of science, engineering, and business.   In particular, the user usually thinks in a language which is very different from the basic machine language. For example, a mathematician thinks in terms of mathematical symbols and notation, while a businessman thinks in terms of common

English language. The basic machine language (where a 1 may stand for "addition" and an asterisk for a drum location) is really a nonsense symbol language from the user's point of view. Effort for the past two decades has been directed towards the elimination of this barrier by devising "higher languages" which more and more approximate the language in which the user usually thinks. The fruits of such efforts show in *assembly* programs, *interpretive* routines, and *compilers*. All three are symbolic programming systems which can be classified as attempts towards *automatic* programming.

An *Assembly Program* (or Symbolic Program) permits the user to write his commands in pseudoinstructions, where a pseudoinstruction is usually mnemonic for the function to be performed. For example, in the IBM 1401 computer system, A stands for "add," and ZA stands for "zero and add," and so forth. The assembly program then proceeds to translate from these pseudoinstructions to machine language instructions. It also assigns actual machine memory addresses for "names" of data or instructions and translates from decimal to binary notation. Coding in pseudoinstructions for use on assembly programs represents the first level of departure from direct machine language coding.

The second level of development is, naturally enough, to make one pseudoinstruction represent several machine language instructions. For example, instead of programming the various operations performed in taking the square root of a number, which may result in 10 separate instructions, it is sufficient to indicate in one instruction that one wishes to evaluate the square root. The assembly program would then analyze the pseudoinstruction, construct the necessary machine instructions by reference to standard subroutines and end up with the desired machine language instructions. In this fashion, the programmer is asked to write in *macroinstructions*; the assembly program translates into *microinstructions*.

There are two modes of operation at this level of abstraction. In the first mode, *interpretive routines* act upon the macroinstructions as they appear in the program. A supervisory program calls in the proper subroutines *each time* the pseudoinstruction is executed. This is wasteful in operating time and in machine memory capacity because all the subroutines as well as the supervisory program must be in the computer all the time. However, the necessary coding instructions are extremely easy to learn, and computer operation is very elementary indeed. This mode of operation was utilized extensively in simple engineering and scientific work, where individuals were permitted direct access to the computer to evaluate simple problems, but is now almost obsolete.

The second mode of operation is through a *compiler*. The action of a compiler is similar to interpretive routines except that the pseudoinstructions are "compiled" into a machine language program once and for all in a separate machine run. In performing the act of translation, the compiler also allocates machine memory to the various components of the program.

Compilers have distinct advantages over other modes of operation. Among these are the following: (1) Since the whole computer memory and logic is available to the compiler during the translation run, a more sophisticated language may be used which more closely approximates the language in which the user thinks. (2) Compilers have built-in error-detection subroutines which, together with the resemblance of the programming language to the user's own thinking language, render correction and "debugging" a much easier task indeed.[†] (3) Compilers provide a common language to the users of various computing equipment.

The major disadvantages of compilers are the following: (1) The possible inefficiency in their inability to capitalize on individual machine characteristics. This manifests itself in longer processing time compared with a well-written symbolic assembly program. (2) Loss of access to certain logic features of the equipment; e.g., examination of the bit structure of a character. (3) Less efficient use of memory because of various reasons such as use of memory for program linkages, absence of tight packing of words, etc.

The most widely used compilers are FORTRAN (Formula Translator), basically a language for scientific and engineering systems, and COBOL (Common Business Oriented Language), which is, as the name indicates, primarily for business activities.

It is not difficult to project into the future of computer languages. The trend is toward higher and higher levels of abstraction, so that the movement is from macro- to macro-macroinstructions. This is especially successful if the language is restricted to a specified field, such as structural engineering design or manufacturing processes. In the following, we will study the development of such specialized languages in a very particular field, the field of system simulation.

Advantages of Simulation Languages. The problem of preparing a simulation falls into two tasks. The first is to construct a model of the system, and the second is to program such model for computer input and manipulation. Simulation languages are intended to facilitate the second task by reducing by a considerable measure the amount of effort expended between the construction of the model and the availability of a computer program for simulation. This is accomplished through a language which is a *description of the model* independent of the particular computer being used. The analyst is required to be familiar only with the system and

[†]Advantages 1 and 2 of compilers are also shared by Assembly or Symbolic programs.

the descriptive language of the model, leaving the question of detailed conversion into a computer program to a compiler program which is responsible, later on, for such conversion into detailed computer instructions. Needless to say, such a simulation language relieves the analyst of the major burden of familiarity with the simulated system *and* with the computer which is used for running the simulation.

The major difference between simulation languages and the general purpose scientific or business languages mentioned above lies in the specialization of the former, which permits them to be more powerful though of a much more limited "vocabulary." Thus, power and subsequent saving in programming time and effort are bought at the expense of flexibility and adaptability to a variety of problems.

Currently, there are two simulation languages which are predominantly in use: GPSS (General Purpose Systems Simulation) and SIMSCRIPT. The two languages are very different in structure, and the reader whose duties necessitate the simulation of systems is urged to familiarize himself with the power and limitations of *both* languages.

Other simulation languages have been developed,[†] and undoubtedly many more will be forthcoming. It is highly improbable, however, that there will be any radical departure from the concepts of these two languages unless a new generation of computers is developed with radically different logical structures.

We illustrate the concept of simulation languages with an example of a simple manufacturing process using GPSS.

GPSS (General Purpose Systems Simulation). This language was developed by Geoffrey Gordon[‡] of IBM, on whose various writings we shall rely in this brief resumé. The utility of GPSS has been largely in simulating traffic systems, such as communications, manufacturing, and air terminal control systems. In such systems the basic unit of interest, called *transaction*, is followed through the system and its movement studied with respect to path, congestion and occupancy problems. The physical components which operate on the transactions are called *items of equipment*. An item of equipment is either of unit capacity, such as a machine, which can accomodate only one transaction at any time, and will be called a *facility*. Or, the item of equipment is of multiple capacity, such as a multi-channel switching system, and will be called a *store* whether or not it is in fact used for storing.

Similar to any other language, GPSS has a fixed set of symbols together

---

[†]For example: "The Job Shop Simulation," IBM Corporation, Data Systems Division, New York, revised ed., 1960, "TABSOL, The Language of Decision Making," T. F. Kavanaugh, *Computers and Automation*, Sept., 1961, pp. 15–22.

[‡]G. Gordon, "A General Purpose Systems Simulator," *IBM Systems Journal*, Sept. 1962.

with a "dictionary" giving the meaning of each symbol, and a "grammar" specifying the usage of each symbol. The symbols are geometric shapes: circles, rectangles, trapezoids, etc., and there are 35 such symbols. Five examples of such symbols are shown in Fig. 7-8.

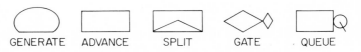

GENERATE   ADVANCE   SPLIT   GATE   QUEUE

FIGURE 7-8   Examples of GPSS Symbols

The simulation program specified by the analyst is a *block diagram* constructed in a specific fashion. Each block of the diagram represents a step in the action of the system, and lines joining the blocks indicate the sequence of events. To represent the alternative courses of action that may be followed by the system, more than one line may leave a block. Correspondingly, one block may be entered by way of more than one line to indicate that the step represented by that block occurs in more than one sequence of events.

The block diagram is distinguished by two aspects. First, each block is given a number which serves as its "name." Second, each block representing an action which consumes time is given a *block time* which may be a fixed integer, a random variable, or a function of either.

All block types except terminal points of the system may have two exits. The exits are distinguished by referring to them as exits *A* and *B* and they are defined by giving the number of the block to which the exit leads; these latter are called *next blocks A* and *B*. The routing of the transaction may be specified in either conditional or unconditional forms. For example, a *conditional* mode of selection would be to attempt exit *A* first, and if the transaction is refused entry to next block *A*, it will attempt to exit via next block *B*. If neither exit is free, the transaction will be delayed and will leave by the exit which becomes free first. If both become available simultaneously, exit *A* is chosen. This pattern may simulate preference in actual behavior between the two exits. On the other hand, an *unconditional* selection may behave in the following fashion. A random selection with equal probability is made among all next blocks whose numbers fall between next block *A* and next block *B*, inclusive. If exit is not permitted because of occupancy of that particular block, the transaction waits until the block is free. For example, if next block *A* is number 20 and next block *B* is number 29, the simulator will choose with probability 1/10 among the blocks number 20, 21, 22, ..., 29. The block selected is the one to which the transaction is routed. Such a model may be a representation of the random selection by arriving customers from among a given set of service facilities.

The movement of a transaction from block to block constitutes an *event*, which occurs at some point of time. The simulation program maintains a record of the times at which these events are due to occur, and proceeds by executing the events in their correct time sequence. In case any transactions cannot move because of some obstruction in their paths, the program moves them as soon as these obstructing conditions are removed (which movements themselves would constitute events.) *Time* is measured on a *master clock* which is internal to the simulation. The unit of the *clock time* is specified by the programmer and constitutes the basic unit in which all system time measurements are taken.

The program proceeds from the time of occurrence of one event (or events, if all occur at the same clock time) to the time of occurrence of the next event(s). The clock time is thus advanced by the elapsed time between the two occurrences.

In a simulation, *structure* is obtained by specifying the logical relationships among the variables. GPSS provides the symbolism required for the specification of such decisions. For example, HOLD, SEIZE, RELEASE, INTERRUPT, RETURN specify a variety of such decisions either on the item of equipment or on the transaction.

Moreover, simulation is conducted to accumulate some statistics on the various conditions of the system. For example, we may be interested in the proportion of time a facility is utilized, or perhaps in the degree of its utilization, or in the amount of congestion at a given facility, etc. Again, a number of blocks give such information directly: QUEUE, MARK, TABULATE, etc.

Finally, the GPSS language provides for the use of *functions* in the various aspects of simulation. For example, it was mentioned before that the *block time* may be a function of a constant or a function of a random variable. Or, the selection of the next block may be a function of some condition of the system, and so on. In GPSS, a function is a numerical value computed from a table of numbers defined by the user, and there are two types of functions: step functions and linear-interpolation functions, Fig. 7-9. The first type, as in (a), is given by

$$f(x) = y_k \text{ for } x_{k-1} < x \le x_k, \quad k = 0,1,\ldots,n$$

The second type, as in (b), is given by

$$f(x) = y_{k-1} + \frac{y_k - y_{k-1}}{x_k - x_{k-1}}(x - x_{k-1}) \text{ for } x_{k-1} < x \le x_k, \quad k = 0, 1, \ldots, n.$$

The function is indicated to the program by designating its kind and specifying the coordinate points (x_k, y_k).

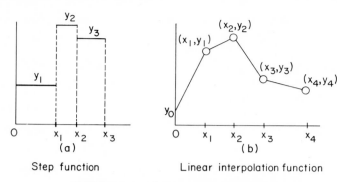

(a) Step function   (b) Linear interpolation function

FIGURE 7-9 The Two Types of Functions

The reader may wonder how the block diagram logic is communicated to the computer. This is accomplished through punched cards of fixed format depending on the block or the function being represented.

To summarize, GPSS views the real system as composed of *facilities* and *stores* through which *transactions* pass following some logical decisions. The behavior of these transactions as they filter through the various components of the system is the subject of the simulation. Representation of the system and the interaction among its components are accomplished by *block diagramming* the system according to a well-specified language.

Instead of proceeding with the detailed description of GPSS language, giving its dictionary and grammar, we will illustrate its usage by a simple manufacturing problem.[†] This should give the reader an idea about the language and its utility. But, like any other language, mastery can be gained only through practice. The reader who wishes to pursue the subject further may refer to the complete manual on GPSS written by G. Gordon and listed at the end of the chapter. Other examples of the use of GPSS can be found in Smith's article, also listed at the end of the chapter.

The example shown in Fig. 7-10 represents a simple manufacturing process in which one job at a time is processed. The job requires that three parts be made and these are made concurrently. When all parts are ready, they are assembled and the next job is started.

In order to understand the complete block diagram, we first define the blocks used in it and indicate their usage.

GENERATE

The GENERATE block creates transactions. The rate of flow is specified in terms of an interarrival time between successive transactions. The X value specifies the entry time of the first transaction; the Y value specifies the time between the creation of transactions;

†G. Gordon, *op. cit*, p. 31.

and the Z value specifies the priority of the transaction (any number between 0 and 7, inclusive).

The execution of the GENERATE command is in the following fashion. When the program encounters the GENERATE block it immediately creates a transaction. The transaction is scheduled to enter the block after an interval that is computed from the X and Y values. For example, if X = 1000, and Y = 10, the first transaction is created and is scheduled to enter the GENERATE block at clock time 1000. At that time, the transaction will be placed at the GENERATE block. The next block is then selected for the transaction, according to the

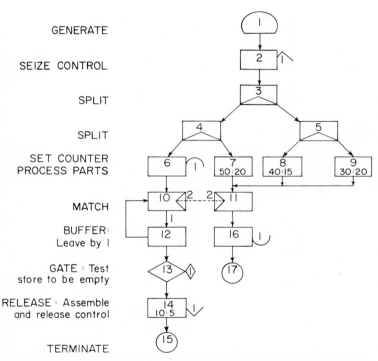

GENERATE

SEIZE CONTROL

SPLIT

SPLIT

SET COUNTER
PROCESS PARTS

MATCH

BUFFER:
Leave by I

GATE : Test
store to be empty

RELEASE : Assemble
and release control

TERMINATE

FIGURE 7-10   Block Diagram of Simple Manufacturing Problem

selection mode at the GENERATE block. If successful, it enters, and the GENERATE block becomes empty. If unsuccessful, it *stays* in the GENERATE block. If this latter case happens, at time $X + Y$ = 1010 a new transaction will *not* be created. At time 1020, a new transaction will be created only if the delayed transaction in the GENERATE block has succeeded in exiting in the interval 1010–1020, inclusive. Thus, delays at the exits of a GENERATE block reduce the rate at which transactions enter the block diagram. The queue in the GENERATE block will never exceed 1, even though the specified interarrival time (10 units in our example) may be less than the service time on the exit facility.

SEIZE

The SEIZE block records the usage of a facility, whose block number is given by X, by a transaction that enters the block. The facility will not be returned to available status except when the transaction enters, later on, a RELEASE block. When a facility is seized, any other transaction will be refused entry to the SEIZE block. The fate of that rejected transaction is not specified at the SEIZE block, however, but at the block from which the transaction is attempting to exit (a GENERATE block in our example). An action time at the SEIZE block is computed in the usual fashion. If no action time is given, it is interpreted as being zero. The advantage of this SEIZE-RELEASE setup is the ability to evaluate the time a transaction consumed seizing a facility.

RELEASE

The RELEASE block performs the operation required to place the facility indicated by the value of X, in the "available" status. It counteracts the action of the SEIZE block. In fact, a transaction may not release a facility unless the facility has already been seized by the *same transaction*. A host of system statistics is updated at the RELEASE block, such as duration of seizure, cumulative seizure of facility, average occupancy, etc.

SPLIT

The SPLIT block creates a duplicate of each transaction that enters the block. The SPLIT block never refuses entry to a transaction. An action time is computed for the transaction. The new transaction receives the same parameter values, priority and transit time as the original transaction. In addition, both transactions receive an identifying code which will permit the program to search for other members of the same set of transactions. The next block is selected for each of the transactions in the following manner: the original transaction is sent to next block A of the split block, and the duplicate is sent to next block B.

ADVANCE

The ADVANCE block performs two actions: (1) computation of the number of clock units which a transaction is to spend at the block, and (2) selection of a block to which that transaction will be sent after the computed interval has elapsed. The principal use of the ADVANCE block is to represent an event in a system that requires a period of time or choice of paths but does not alter the status of an item of equipment. The duration of processing is usually given by the mean and the spread, which are written inside the block thus, $m{:}s$. As indicated before, there are alternate methods for specifying the duration of processing, but we need not go into them here.

ENTER
(STORE)

The ENTER block is one in a family of three, which are: STORE, ENTER and LEAVE. The STORE block allows a transaction to occupy space in the store specified by the value of X for as long as the transaction is in the block. The ENTER block allows a transaction to take up space in the store but the space is not given back until a transaction (not necessarily the same one) enters a LEAVE block.

The Y field of the ENTER block (as well as of a STORE block) specifies the number of spaces needed for the transaction in the storage. Needless to say, this number need not be unity. The program compares the requested number of units of space with the unused space. If the number of units requested is not greater than the number currently available, the following steps are executed. Otherwise, the transaction will either be delayed or diverted, according to the selection mode and exits at the block from which the transaction is attempting to exit. Incidentally, when the space requested is a parameter, and therefore each transaction may call for a different number of units of storage, it is possible for a later transaction requesting fewer units to pass a delayed transaction which requested more units than were currently available in storage. When the transaction is admitted in the store, the program updates the storage content, computes time of occupancy, and selects a next block in the usual fashion. If the transaction cannot leave the selected exit or exits, no storage units are released.

The LEAVE block is used to make available some previously occupied space in an ENTER block. The action of a LEAVE block is the reverse of the ENTER block; X specifies the store, and Y specifies the units of space relinquished. Certain statistics of interest to the

LEAVE

simulation are computed such as: length of time for which the storage has remained at its current contents, a count of the total number of units that have passed through the storage, etc.

The MATCH block serves to synchronize the progress of two transactions of an assembly set. Instead of joining the pair of transactions, the MATCH block permits them both to continue advancing independently through the block diagrams, but the realization

MATCH

of a match permits other events to occur. The operation of a MATCH block is as follows: The transaction that is attempting to enter a MATCH block is removed from its previous block and a next block is selected for the transaction. The X field of the MATCH block specifies the number of another MATCH block, termed "the conjugate MATCH block." If the matching of the two events is accomplished, the first member of the pair, which was placed in an indefinitely delayed state, is made ready to advance. If its action time is zero, the transaction is placed in the current event list. It should be noted that in either case the program continues processing the transaction that has just entered the conjugate MATCH block.

The GATE block is used to test the status of a simulated logical condition or an item of equipment. It is similar to the IF statement in FORTRAN. The GATE block operates by refusing entry to transactions unless the specified test is passed. It is possible to test twelve

GATE
(Facility)

conditions by a GATE block, such as facility in use (U), facility not in use (NU), facility interrupted (I), facility not interrupted (NI), etc.

The TERMINATE block removes transactions from the system. Upon arrival of a transaction, the count of the total number of transactions that have entered the TERMINATE block is incremented by 1. The TERMINATE block is also useful in terminating a

TERMINATE

run, and there are two ways to do this, involving the use of TERMINATE blocks and START cards. (a) The run may be ended on a count of a specific number of terminations, coded in the X field of the START card. All TERMINATE blocks having an R coded in their X field will contribute towards the end count; which is kept in common. (b) The run may be ended on a predetermined value of the relative clock time, coded in the Z field of the start card. If this method is used, no TERMINATE/R blocks should be in the model. Both methods of ending a run can be used simultaneously by coding both the X and Z fields of a START card and using at least one TERMINATE/R block. The run will then end on whichever end condition is met first.

With this background we are now in a position to draw the block diagram of the manufacturing problem. Referring to Fig. 7-10, notice that facility #1 is seized at the beginning and is released only upon completion of all three units of the assembly at block 14. The cascade of SPLIT blocks generate four identical transactions, three of which represent the parts to be manufactured, and they go to ADVANCE blocks simulating the manufacturing processes. The fourth transaction occupies three units in store #1.

The matching operation is simply a device to guarantee seizure of the facility #1 until all three parts are completed. Upon entering store #1 (block 6), the transaction immediately advances to the MATCH block 10 where it waits. As soon as the first part is finished, it enters the conjugate MATCH block 11, and a match is realized. As a consequence, the conjugate transaction in block 11 proceeds to LEAVE block 16, where it reduces the number of units in store #1 by unity. At the same time, the original transaction in block 10 proceeds to ADVANCE block 12. As it attempts to exit from ADVANCE block 12, it enters a GATE block 13 which tests for "store empty" condition. Since only one part of the assembly has been completed, store #1 still has two units in "storage," and the GATE condition is not satisfied. The program is then returned to MATCH block 10 where the cycle is repeated. When all three parts are completed, the store will become empty and the GATE condition satisfied. The assembly operation is simulated by RELEASE block 14, wherefrom the job is removed from the system. In this particular example, simulation can be set up to terminate after 100 such assemblies.

The preceding discussion of GPSS should serve to illustrate the structure and use of simulation languages.

At the time of this writing, active research is being undertaken at several places for the construction of even simpler languages which require the minimum familiarity with the computer or its language. Notable among these endeavors is an attempt to obtain structure through questionnaire.[†]

[†]H. Markowitz, A. S. Ginsberg, and P. M. Oldfather, "Programming by Questionnaire," RAND Memorandum RM-4460-PR, April, 1965.

Specifically, the engineer or researcher is given a set of, say, 120 questions, the answers to which are fed into the computer and serve to trigger off a compiler, resulting in a simulation program.

While these attempts are still in the embryo stage, they undoubtedly give a glimpse into the future of languages for communication with computers.

We now turn to a brief discussion of the problems of simulation.

Some Problems in Simulation

The idea of simulation is so patently simple that it is not easy to restrain oneself from adopting the simulation approach in almost every problem one encounters. True, it *is* a brute force approach, a fact which may be repulsive to the aesthetic nature of a few systems engineers. But they are a minority—the overwhelming majority are interested in getting an answer to their immediate problems, and the end justifies the means!

However, it is precisely these desired ends that should be uppermost in one's mind; are they really achieved by simulation? The disenchantment with the technique may be summarized in the words of Conway[†] who has had "eight years of more or less continuous use of simulation on a variety of problems and frequent discussions with other practitioners: I believe that, in general, simulation models take longer to construct, require much more computer time to execute, and yield much less information than their authors expected."

But *why* is this the case? The answer lies in the fact that while the *idea* of simulation is very simple, the actual execution of the idea poses many questions of a delicate and subtle nature. While the complete understanding of these problems can be acquired only after intimate and prolonged exposure to simulation studies, a fairly good idea may be gained from a brief exposition of their nature. Unfortunately, simulation theory still lacks the definitive answers to these questions. It is hoped that as more research is done on the technique of simulation, independent of the real system being simulated, the answers will be forthcoming.

The Steady-State Problem. In many system simulations, it is meaningful to study only the behavior of the system under "normal" operating conditions. Translated, this implies that all "pipelines" are filled and that the statistical distribution of measured entities have reached their "steady-state" distributions.

There are two ways to achieve these conditions. The first is to start the simulation with the system "empty" and allow a long enough time of operation for all pipelines to fill and such steady state to be reached. The

[†]R. W. Conway, "Some Tactical Problems in Digital Simulation," *Management Science*, Vol. 10, No. 1, Oct., 1963, pp. 47–61.

second is to start the system at some partially or totally filled stage and
allow a shorter time of operation to arrive at the steady state.

The difficulty with both approaches is that "steady state" is not as well-
defined a "state" as the name may suggest. It is not a characteristic of a
condition of the system as indicated by the various measured parameters,
but rather it is a property of the *long run averages* of these parameters and
their statistical distributions. The only way to determine whether the
steady-state has been reached or not is to allow a long enough time of
operation, compute some statistics, and compare these with the steady-
state statistics. But how long is "enough time?" And what about systems
whose steady state statistics are not known *a priori*, such as in simulation
of nonexisting systems?

Some of the presteady-state statistics may be useful in the study of tran-
sients in the system, but otherwise they are of little use. In effect, they
represent lost time and expense. If this is combined with the uncertainty
concerning being in the steady state, the analyst is justified in feeling un-
easy about his conclusions. This may account for the fact that almost all
reports on simulation studies preface their conclusions with the admoni-
tion that they are "tentative and are based on a limited amount of observations," no matter how long the simulation has actually been run!

The Time Synchronization Problem.   Simulation can be conducted in real
time. However, this is rarely done. Usually simulation is run in pseudo-
time, *i.e.*, *machine time* which is either faster or slower than real time
operation. Thus, we can imagine an internal *master clock* which is set at
time zero when simulation starts and is stopped only at the end of the run.
This master clock measures the internal time of the simulation. Incidentally, the ratio of real time to its representative simulation time is
called the *simulation ratio*.

For example, the inventory operations of the firm over several years can
be simulated in *one hour* of computer time. The master clock would
simulate the passage of days, months and years, and the advance of one
time-unit on the master clock may represent the passage of one day in real
time. This is an example of simulation which is faster than the real system.
On the other hand, the movement of a neutron through a gaseous
chamber may consume, in reality, one millionth of a second but may be
simulated in a few minutes of computer time. This would be an example
of simulation slower than real life.

In large system simulations there are usually a large number of events
that occur over time. Whenever an event occurs, the system is "updated,"
which implies that the occurrence is recorded in the appropriate files, and
all the necessary calculations based on it are executed. For example, in an
inventory simulation, an event may be the occurrence of a withdrawal.

This affects the "on-hand" inventory file, the withdrawals statistics, and the cost statistics, as well as the ordering and replenishment procedures. In this instance, updating the system means the complete evaluation of the effects of such an event on the components of the system.

One way to keep track, *i.e.*, synchronize, the occurrence of such events is to advance the master clock by one time-unit at a time and scan all entities and their measurable attributes (to use the parlance of SIM-SCRIPT) for the occurrence of an event. If an event occurs, the system is updated; otherwise the master clock is advanced one more time-unit and the process repeated. It is easy to see that if there are k such attributes to be checked, and if the total running time is T, there will be Tk scannings in the course of the simulation. If the average elapsed (simulation) time between the occurrence of events is m, there will be, on the average, Tk/m such updatings. If m is large, many of the scannings will be fruitless in the sense that they will result in no events.

Another way to achieve synchronization is to attach to each attribute a small "clock," henceforth referred to as the *attribute clock*. At the occurrence of an event the attribute clock is advanced to the time of the next occurrence. Now, if the attribute clocks are ranked in order of magnitude, the smallest among them denotes the (simulation) time of the next occurrence. The master clock is then advanced *directly* to that time, the event is noted, and the system updated. The process is then repeated with the newly-advanced attribute clock. It is easy to see that if k is large and m small, the frequency of occurrence of events would be so high that there is a good probability that the minimum attribute clock will cause the master clock to advance only one time-unit after all, which reduces the present approach to the previous one!

In general, if we assume the same average number of occurrences as before, Tk/m, and we know that it takes $(k - 1)$ comparisons to find the minimum attribute clock, the choice between the two approaches reduces to picking the minimum of Tk and $Tk(k - 1)/m$ comparisons.

Of course, better search and comparison schemes than the above can be devised. For example, suppose that the set of attribute clocks is divided into two equal subsets, I and II, and that the minimum of I is smaller than the minimum of II. Then clearly, if the system is updated and the minimum attribute clock of I advanced to the time of the next occurrence, the ranking of the attribute clocks in II will not be disturbed. Consequently, we rank only *half* the attribute clocks, namely those in subset I. We have thus reduced the chore of ranking to $(k/2 - 1)$ comparisons instead of $k - 1$. Now, the choice is between Tk and (Tk/m). $\{(k/2 - 1) + 1\} = Tk^2/2m$.

Needless to say, the process of subdividing the original set of attribute clocks into smaller subsets can be carried to r subsets, $r = 3, 4, \ldots$, with the choice being between Tk and $Tk\{(k/r - 1) + (r - 1)\}/m = Tk(k/r + r - 2)/m$. However, the programming and record-keeping effort may outweigh the advantages obtained for large r.

One final remark before proceeding to a different problem in Simulation Theory. In the above discussion it was not our intention to instruct the reader on how synchronization is accomplished, since the above approaches are almost self-evident. It *is* our intention, however, to indicate a *type* of problem encountered in the construction of the simulation itself and point out the need for its consideration. Computer time wasted in search may be greatly reduced by the judicious choice of the technique used for effecting such search.

A Measurement Problem. In general, there are two kinds of entities: *permanent* and *temporary*. A permanent entity exists for the duration of the simulation; a temporary entity exists only for part of the simulation. For example, in air traffic simulation the runway is a permanent entity, while an airplane is a temporary entity. Entities have attributes which are measurable—for example, the runway is either occupied or vacant—and it is the changes in these attributes that constitute "events."

Temporary entities give rise to a peculiar type of problem in some simulation studies, in particular those involving stochastic variation. To wit, temporary entities may be created in a sequence different from that of their retirement. For instance, airplanes may "arrive" in one pattern but may "land" in a completely different pattern due to differences in fuel supply, mechanical condition, weather conditions, etc. The question is *which* temporary entity should be included in the simulation run?

The answer to this question clearly depends on the real system being simulated. Consider the following two alternatives: (1) Fix the duration of the run and include entities whose *complete life span* falls within the duration. (2) Fix the starting time and the number of entities to be studied and run the simulation until all these entities are created and retired.

The first procedure leaves the *sample size* as a random variable. Some entities may be created during the period of simulation but are not yet retired when simulation is stopped, and conversely, some of the "pipeline" entities may retire during the period of simulation but their starting time may be earlier than that of the simulation. Consequently, the sample size on which deductions are to be made may be very small indeed (unless the simulation time is long).

The second procedure leaves the *duration* of simulation as a random variable. This might be undesirable, especially if a great number of runs are to be conducted, which usually is the case.

If T, the duration of simulation decided upon *a priori* in the first procedure, is large enough, the first procedure will be indistinguishable from the second as far as the sample size is concerned, though it may differ in other respects (such as initial conditions, the achievement of steady state, etc.).

Clearly, in a system where the duration is limited, such as in air attack, the first procedure is more representative of the real system. On the other hand, the inventory of a firm which does not plan to go out of business in the foreseeable future is better represented by the second procedure.

Again, it is important to realize that the decision concerning the manner in which temporary entities are included in the sample affects the very results obtained from subsequent analysis. It is possible that a comparative advantage of one policy over another is obscured or even reversed simply by a change in the method of determining which temporary entities are to be included in the sample.

The Question of Validity. For the purposes of our present discussion, validity is to mean correct representation. But representation is mostly a subjective feeling, because "likeness" is hard to assess. One can, of course, demand as a minimum prerequisite for validity that for at least one set of conditions the simulation should produce results consistent with the performance of the real system. Yet this is no *guarantee* that the simulation is a valid representation, since it may fail the test under a different set of conditions. Such a test is essentially a null test of hypothesis; if the test fails, the simulation is firmly declared *invalid*, but if it succeeds no such firm assertion can be made concerning its *validity*. On the other hand, one cannot demand that the simulation yields consistent results under *all* conditions, for then there would be no need for simulation in the first place!

The result of simulation is a measurement on an attribute of a permanent or temporary entity. In Monte Carlo simulation, this measurement is subject to error. The validity of the measurement is then dependent on the magnitude of the variability of the measurement, that is, its *precision*. The question of validity therefore resolves into the question of precision in the statistical sense.

Randomness is inherent in physical experimentation, even in completely deterministic systems, due to the random error in the measuring devices. The magnitude of such error is known in digital simulation since it is the error in the rightmost digit of the measurement, and this can be made as small as desired. The second and most important source of randomness in simulation is the variation in the exogenous input data. This, in turn, can be controlled in two ways. First, a fixed set of real-life input data is used on each alternative policy under investigation and the different responses to this one set compared. For example, if a new rule for inventory replenishment is suggested, it can be tried on actual demand over the past five years. The result of the simulation is compared with the performance of the real system under the existing rules, and the better rule is chosen. The major argument against such a procedure is that the performance of the new rule has been tested under *one* set of conditions which may be, by chance, particularly favorable or unfavorable to it.

The second approach is to generate a set of random demand drawn from a distribution possessing the same statistical characteristics as actual demand. Although a certain appearance of impartiality has been achieved, the same objection still holds.

We seem to have reached an impasse. It is generally acknowledged that the best way to compare two alternatives is "under identical conditions." But whenever that is achieved, the result is open to dismissal as being not necessarily representative!

All arguments seem to indicate that "identical conditions" should be taken in a statistical sense, and that alternatives must be compared by repeated experimentation under a stationary *causation system*. Replication through choice of different sets of random numbers guarantees independence of measurements but requires a prodigious number of experiments. Moreover, whenever possible, some "scaling" of the simulation results should be made in relation to the real system.

Precision can be measured by the *variance* of the experimental results, and the variance can be minimized by averaging over a large sample size. Let x_i denote one such average; for example, x_i may be the average inventory on hand over the simulated period. The variability of X_i (capital letters denote the random variable and small letters the value they assume *after* the experiment) can be determined through replication, say n times. Each replication requires a "warm up period" to achieve steady-state conditions, which is wasteful in time and effort. It easily can be shown that a long run of size $2n + 1$ experiments (the one experiment is discarded for "warming up") yields a global average which is "better," that is, more precise, than the average $\overline{X}$ of the separate n experiments. Variability of this global average, denoted by $\overline{Z}$ can be obtained by "chopping up" the long run into $2n$ sets: the X_i's and the Y_i's, which are alternately located, as shown in Fig. 7-11. For let $\overline{X}$ and $\overline{Y}$ denote the averages of the

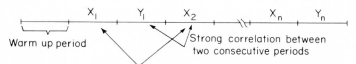

FIGURE 7-11

two subsets, respectively, then

$$\overline{Z} = \frac{\overline{X} + \overline{Y}}{2}$$

whose expected value is equal to the expected value of $\overline{X}$ on the n experiments. But comparing the variances, we have

$$\text{Var}(\overline{X}) = \frac{\sigma^2}{n} = \text{Var}(\overline{Y})$$

while

$$\text{Var}(\overline{Z}) = \text{Var}\left[\frac{1}{2n}\sum_1^{2n} X_i\right] = \frac{1}{4n^2}[2n\sigma^2 + 2(2n - 1)\text{Cov}(X_i, X_j)]$$

where $\text{Cov}(X_i, X_j)$ is the covariance of two separate X_i's. Since the determinant of the covariance matrix is always nonnegative, and in this case the covariance of all nonadjacent variables is assumed to be zero, it follows that $\text{Cov}(X_i, X_j) \le \sigma^2/2$. Consequently,

$$\text{Var}(\overline{Z}) = \frac{1}{4n^2}[2n\sigma^2 + 2(2n - 1)\text{Cov}(X_i, X_j)]$$

$$\le \frac{\sigma^2}{2n}\left(1 + \frac{2n - 1}{2n}\right) < \frac{\sigma^2}{n} = \text{Var}(\overline{X})$$

When the correlation of nonadjacent values are significant, the variance of $\overline{Z}$ is given by

$$\text{Var}(\overline{Z}) = \frac{\sigma^2}{4n^2}\left[2n + 2\sum_{s=1}^{2n-1}(2n - s)\rho_s\right]$$

where s is the spacing between two X_i's and ρ measures the correlation between X_i and X_{i+s}. This correlation is usually significant and should be estimated from pilot runs to determine how measurements are to be taken. Moreover, they should be checked again during the actual experimentation.

Unfortunately, the problem of validity is complicated by the fact that more than one statistic is usually derived from the same set of data. These statistics are then utilized in several calculations, and because of the strong correlation among these statistics, it is extremely difficult to assess the variability of the results.

In view of the above discussion, the reader may wonder how *any* conclusions can be drawn from simulation. Fortunately, simulation is used most often to compare alternatives, and *absolute* measurements are not important. What is important is the *relative* preference of one alternative over another. Even under highly imprecise measurements, some idea can be gained about such relative advantages.

A final question connected with the study of validity is the question of *initial* or *starting conditions*. We have seen above how the starting conditions may affect the time of reaching the steady state. Here, we wish to discuss the effect of the starting conditions on the measured result itself.

Suppose that simulation is used to compare two alternatives, *A* and *B*, and suppose that enough is known about each alternative to realize that there is an appreciable difference between them under steady-state operation. Each alternative possesses, however, its own "reasonable" starting conditions. The question is to determine the magnitude of that difference. Is it justifiable to start each alternative under its own advantageous starting conditions, or should a common starting condition be set for both alternatives?

The answer to this question is not easily determined. It seems "unfair" to suspect that project *A* is better than project *B*, to start both projects under their most suitable conditions, obtain a result which confirms the suspicion, and then use this result as a "proof" of the superiority of *A* over *B*! And yet it is equally "unfair" to handicap *A* by any adverse starting conditions if, in fact, it can be started in real life under favorable conditions and continue to operate under equally favorable conditions!

Perhaps a possible way out of this dilemma is to measure the performance of both projects under identical starting conditions which are a compromise between the two conditions favorable to either project individually *as well as* measure the performance of both projects under their respective most favorable conditions. The cost of added experimentation may be amply justified by the insight gained concerning the relative performance of the two projects.

Simulation As A General Problem Solving Technique.   Several other problems of simulation exist, the majority of which are peculiar to the simulated system and therefore vary from problem to problem. For example, in systems of several concurrent inputs and events the problem of synchronization takes on more serious dimensions. In systems possessing variable environments, the problem of adaptability of the simulation to change in its very structure becomes important, and so on.

Simulation as a problem-solving tool is still a novel development. The above brief list of problems should caution the analyst against setting high hopes and glossing over important details. In particular, the following are some of the reasons given *against* simulation:

(a) It is a slow and expensive undertaking. In the majority of cases it requires large-scale computing facilities which may not be available. A simulation may take several man-years to construct and several more to run and analyse the results, with no guarantee of optimality.

(b) It is imprecise, and there is no known measure of the degree of its imprecision.

(c) It is almost always a specific tool for a specific application, in spite of the large expenditures in effort, time, and money that usually go into it. One rarely encounters a simulation which has been used in more than one study.

(d) Because the output is in numerical terms, a certain degree of definitiveness is accorded to the results and more is read into them than is really justified. In many cases, the underlying imprecision renders the whole mass of data meaningless.

(e) Simulations have a tendency to grow large in spite of the analyst's conscientious effort to keep their size to a minimum. In fact, a simulation is never complete; there are always a few more experiments that should be conducted to render the picture clearer.

Examples of the Use of Simulation As an Aid to Design

It is safe to state that the past few years have witnessed the use of simulation as a design tool in an ever-increasing variety of undertakings in widely varied fields. This is attested to by the number of symposia that have been held (and the number of books and articles that have been published) concerning the extent to which the technique of simulation has permeated the various fields of science and engineering as a basic tool of design. It is not our intention (nor is this the place) to present another survey of the same area. Suffice it here to mention that, apart from classical Monte Carlo applications to engineering and mathematical problems, simulation has been extensively used in both the military and civilian systems to the point where, today, it is almost impossible to find a problem in either field which has not been treated in one formulation or another by the technique of simulation. Morgenthaler[†] gives a fairly complete survey of the various problems attacked by this approach, and lists 93 references on the subject of applications of simulation and gaming. In this section, to illustrate the use of simulation as a tool of design, we pick up the thread of discussion of two problems for which analytical models have been proposed in previous chapters and pursue the matter further. In this fashion, we are, hopefully, able to impress upon the reader that simulation is *another approach* to the same problem. Moreover, we shall be in a position to contrast the models proposed in both problems with the previously-discussed analytical models.

Example: The Warehouse Location–Allocation Problem

The general problem of warehouse location–allocation can be stated as follows: given a set of factories and customers, and given all relevant

[†] Morgenthaler, *op. cit*, pp. 392–405.

information about them, it is required to determine:

> how many warehouses
> where are the warehouses to be located $\Big\}$ Location problem
>
> which customers to be served by which
> warehouse
> what volume should each warehouse handle $\Bigg\}$ Allocation problem
> what modes of distribution should be used

and minimize some overall cost function.

The problem in its general form has defied complete analytical solution because of its complexity. Various factors contribute to such complexity:

1. Variation in *customer characteristics* relative to: size of order, frequency of ordering, mode of transportation (rail, ship, truck, air) and product mix.

2. Variation in *factory characteristics* relative to: product mix, capacity of each product line, and the cost of changing this capacity.

3. Variation in *warehouse characteristics* relative to: the service policy as indicated by the desired reliability of satisfying demand and by the acceptable delay in delivery, together with the functional relationship between such delay and customer demand.

4. *Nonlinearities* in the overall cost function: the transportation costs are, in reality, nonlinear from factory to warehouse and from warehouse to customer. The cost of transportation varies with the size of the order shipped, the distance it travels, the geographic location of roads, and the means of transportation. Moreover, warehousing costs are nonlinear, the overhead costs are of the 0, 1 type, since they are incurred if the warehouse exists and they are not if the warehouse does not exist. The variable costs are nonlinear functions of the size of the throughput and the required safety stock (usually taken as proportional to the square root of the throughput).

Several approaches have been proposed for the solution of the problem. They can be classified under two categories: mathematical approaches and trial and error approaches. The first category depends on constructing a mathematical model, which embodies many simplifying assumptions, and attempts to arrive at an "optimal" solution. At the end of this chapter, we will give two references which utilize the mathematical approach to solve similar (but otherwise differently restricted) warehouse location–allocation problems.

The second category tries several "reasonable" solutions and picks the best from among them, but it makes no claim to optimality. In this section, we discuss a *simulation* approach, while in a subsequent section we will discuss a *heuristic* approach.

A study of both categories, mathematical as well as trial and error, reveals that none of the attacks on the problem necessarily achieved optimality, and that each investigation attempted to break up the large problem into two smaller ones. The consensus seems to be to determine the *location* of the warehouses in some heuristic fashion and then solve the allocation problem optimally.[†] The rationale behind such an approach is that the choice of location is usually constrained by many external factors which drastically reduce the theoretically possible alternatives to a relative few. The determination of the optimal allocation for each alternative location pattern is then a much easier task.

The Approach Using Simulation. Rather than talk in generalities, we consider a concrete case. This is an application which was conducted by Shycon and Maffei[††] for the H. J. Heinz Company, a large food products manufacturer, in which the simulation approach was used.

Typically, production is performed at a few factories in different locations (and of different capacities and products) and the product is shipped to a number of warehouses strategically located throughout the continental United States. Certain factors forced the company to take a fresh look at its distribution system. These were primarily related to shifts in population centers and principal markets, the emergence of brand identification as a prime marketing factor, technological changes in distribution methods, the growth of a large retail operations, and the changes in marketing techniques. Added to these, of course, is the fact that the cost of the physical distribution of products to markets has been rapidly increasing.

A little thought reveals that if all customers were large consumers, if all of them gave the factories sufficient advance notice (i.e., lead time) of their requirements, and if all factories produced the full line of products, there would really be no need for warehousing. Warehouses exist because the three "ifs" listed above are not realized. The problem confronting the company then is the following: how to design its distribution system with *production* carried out at the factory, *mixing* (of different products to satisfy a given customer's demand) carried out at "mixing points" which sometimes coincided with the factories and sometimes with the warehouses, and *storing* carried out at the warehouses.

The characteristics of each component of the system were considered in great detail. A partial list of these characteristics has been presented above (p. 442). A simulation was constructed which permitted the study of a large number of warehouses and thousands of demand centers in different geographic locations. Any alternative configuration was represented by a particular location of the warehouses and a particular allocation of distribution. Simulation by Monte Carlo methods under any given

[†] Compare with the Factory Location–Allocation problem of §4.3 of Chapter 1.
[††] H. N. Shycon and R. B. Maffei, "Simulation—Tool in Better Distribution," *Harvard Business Review*, Nov.–Dec. 1960, pp. 65–75.

configuration resulted in a vector of values of certain measures of performance which are of primary interest to management, such as the cost of transportation, cost of warehouse operation, delay in delivery, level of customer service, etc. By varying the configuration, a new vector of values was obtained, and repeated experimentation led to the decision on the "best" configuration among those considered.

As was pointed out above, the basic impetus to such simulation was to evaluate alternative policies of distribution. But once the simulation was constructed, it became obvious that it could be used with equal facility to evaluate policies concerning other aspects of the company's operation. This is typical of the simulation approach; the very act of constructing a simulation uncovers underlying assumptions, previously determined practices, and alternative ways of performing old or contemplated functions, which lead to new avenues of research not contemplated at the beginning of constructing the simulation. In the words of Shycon and Maffei[†]:

> "The method for performing the Heinz study has provided great facility for studying other aspects of the business which are at least as important as the development of an optimal distribution system. When the simulation was developed, it was thought important to build a general-purpose tool, one which management could use at any time, future as well as present, to study questions of major concern. It was not, however, until the simulation was designed that it was fully realized that the tool provided such facility for studying a wide range of perplexing management problems. Specifically:

> "*Distribution cost studies*—Customers can be separated by areas, types, shipment sizes, salesmen, type of carrier, channels of distribution. We could get estimates of distribution costs on the basis of each or any combination thereof.

> "*Locational studies*—The number and location of factories could be changed, for example, rather than altering the warehouse configuration. Then, too, the effect on the company's operations of a sudden shift in customer type or location could be studied.

> "*Studies related to products*—The product mix at each factory can be changed arbitrarily to observe whether adding product capacity would change distribution costs appreciably. Similarly, customer consumption patterns can be altered to see what effect such changes will have on distribution costs.

> "*Studies related to time*—Customer data can be altered in order to reflect gross annual volume changes by product line. These data would then be used to determine distribution costs. Thus, it can be seen what effect proposed changes in sales policy, prices, or new products would have on customer purchasing frequency, order size or volume. The possible effect on distribution costs and on profitability can be estimated experimentally."

As a footnote to the various policies considered, any customer who can be satisfied from any factory was so designated, and that portion of de-

[†]Shycon and Maffei, *op. cit*, p. 74.

mand was subtracted from the total. This was easily accomplished by designating a demand level at which it is economical to ship directly to the customer. The remainder of the demand was the subject of investigation through simulation.

What are the advantages of such an extensive and expensive undertaking? First, the achievement of a degree of realism not achieved by any other approach. Second, the availability of a tool of analysis for distribution *as well as* manufacturing and marketing policies. If the tool is utilized as extensively as its capabilities indicate, there is little doubt that it more than pays for itself.

Example: The Sequencing Problem and Population Sampling

The *Sequencing* problem is the problem of determining the order of processing N jobs on M machines and achieving a specified objective such as: minimizing the total elapsed time, minimizing in-waiting inventory, minimizing total order delay, etc.

We have treated the Sequencing problem in a previous chapter (see §9 of Chapter 4). There, our treatment was analytical in character. We discussed the N-Jobs 2-Machine Sequencing problem with and without stop and start lags. Under the stipulation of processing the jobs in the same sequence on both machines, optimal algorithms were given. Under the same stipulation, an optimal solution of the N-Jobs, M-Machine problem was also cited. Finally, we presented an L.P. model for the general case which did not stipulate the same sequence on all machines but accepted any given job "routes" and manufacturing precedence relationships.

As we pointed out at the time, the optimal algorithms are valid under very restrictive assumptions. In the absence of these assumptions, we were led to an L.P. model which is computationally infeasible. We also remarked that all these solutions and mathematical models were optimal relative to the "elapsed time criterion."

A few other studies were concerned with optimal sequences under different criteria—see the references at the end of this chapter as well as of Chapter 4—and research is continuing in this fertile and largely unexplored area. But, at least for the moment, in the absence of computationally feasible analytical solutions of a general nature, it is only natural to think of simulation as a possible approach to the study of the sequencing problem. We will discuss such an approach now. The procedure is rather simple and straightforward and certainly has applications to other problems. To be specific, the approach is applicable to problems involving functions defined on discrete and *finite*, but very large, sets.

The following observation is rather central to the understanding of the simulation approach in the sequencing problem. In spite of the existence of a very large number of *different sequences* (in fact, amounting to no less than $N!$ sequences), there is a much smaller number of *different durations*. This is equally true in many other cases. In general, one can make the statement that, in these cases, while the space of individual occurrences may contain a very large number of points, a function defined over these points assumes a much smaller number of different values. Needless to say, this is not true of *all* functions. For example, if the space of points x contains all integers from 1 to $N!$, and the function is defined as $f(x) = x^2$, there will be exactly $N!$ different values of the function.

To illustrate this observation in the context of sequencing, consider the problem of sequencing the following $N = 4$ jobs on $M = 2$ machines with no stop or start lags and with the same sequence on both machines:

Job Number	1	2	3	4
Processing Time on First Machine	3	6	7	2
Processing Time on Second Machine	5	1	4	9

There are $4! = 24$ different sequences, whose durations can be easily evaluated (possibly with the assistance of a Gantt chart). These are given in the following Table 7-2:

TABLE 7-2

Sequence	Duration	Sequence	Duration	Sequence	Duration
1, 2, 3, 4	29	2, 3, 1, 4	31	3, 4, 1, 2	26
1, 2, 4, 3	24	2, 3, 4, 1	31	3, 4, 2, 1	26
1, 3, 2, 4	27	2, 4, 1, 3	26	4, 1, 2, 3	22
1, 3, 4, 2	24	2, 4, 3, 1	26	4, 1, 3, 2	21
1, 4, 2, 3	22	3, 1, 2, 4	27	4, 2, 1, 3	22
1, 4, 3, 2	22	3, 1, 4, 2	22	4, 2, 3, 1	24
2, 1, 3, 4	29	3, 2, 1, 4	30	4, 3, 1, 2	21
2, 1, 4, 3	27	3, 2, 4, 1	30	4, 3, 2, 1	23

There are only 9 different durations with the following frequency curve (Fig. 7-12).

This observation leads immediately to the following conclusion. For large N and a given product mix, one expects that the frequency function illustrated below can be approximated by some theoretical probability distribution function, say $\gamma(d)$, where d is the duration of any sequence. Consequently, one can *estimate* the theoretical distributions $\gamma(d)$ by Monte Carlo sampling. This, in fact, is what the simulation approach purports to do.

For example, consider the following sequencing problem. There are

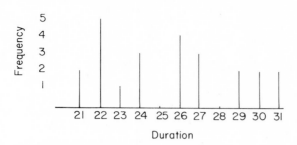

FIGURE 7-12 Frequency of Occurance of Total Duration.

$N = 100$ jobs and $M = 10$ machines, and the processing time of a job on any machine is an integer between 0 and 9. What is the optimal sequence?

There are actually $(N!)^{10}$ different sequences, if one allows the possibility of a different sequence on each machine. Naturally, complete enumeration of the sequences is not at all practical, and, faced with the above problem, Monte Carlo Sampling is the logical approach. Such simulation was actually constructed in the following fashion.[†] One hundred random numbers between 0 and 1 were selected, and the jobs 1 to 100 were ranked according to the values of the corresponding random numbers. This yielded the sequence of jobs on the first machine. The process was repeated for each of the 10 machines, which finally resulted in one overall sequence and one total duration d. The experiment was repeated 3,000 times, and the empirical frequency distribution was fitted with a normal distribution function of mean μ equal to the sample mean ($\mu = 656.81$) and standard deviation σ equal to the sample standard deviation ($\sigma = 20.8$), see Fig. 7-13. The experimentally determined duration times ranged

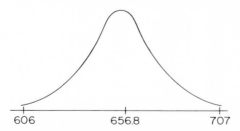

FIGURE 7-13 Fitted Normal Distribution to Empirical Data.

[†]J. Heller, "Some Numerical Experiments for $M \times J$ Flow Shop and its Decision—Theoretical Aspects," *Operations Research*, Vol. 8, No. 2, March–April 1960, pp. 178–184.

from a minimum of 606 to a maximum of 707 time units. Duration times were obtained at all intermediate integer values, and it was only near the tails of the distribution that the sampling failed to find schedule times.

The above information can be put to practical use in the following fashion. Consider the problem of sequencing jobs (of the same product mix) on an operational basis, i.e., as an everyday (or every period) activity. Suppose that the above information is known to the scheduler and, in the absence of a better technique, he resorts to sampling through simulation. Suppose, further, that after n trials the minimum sequence he obtains is of duration d_n^* time units. Should he continue sampling with the hope of obtaining a better sequence, or should he quit sampling and be content with his trial results?

Obviously, this is a decision-theoretic problem which depends on two things: the minimum duration d_n^* actually obtained after the n trials, and the chances of obtaining, through random sampling, a better sequence. The dependence on both variables is best expressed in the *loss function*, which the scheduler must construct to arrive at the optimal "stopping rule." This is the rule which tells the scheduler when to stop sampling; that is, when it is "no longer worth his while" to continue sampling. The loss function quantifies this "worth," and the decision rule optimizes such worth.

Let the cost of experimentation be a per experiment. If the simulation is conducted in a computer, a would be the cost of the computer time to sample, to calculate the duration, to compare with the previously obtained minimum, and finally, to print out the results. Let b be the measure of utility of a unit of time saved in the duration of the sequences. The measurement of b is admittedly more difficult than of a because there is no *à priori* knowledge of where the saving in time is going to occur. Consequently, an average figure over all the machines must be taken. Alternatively, one may consider that the M machines are devoted to the production of these N products (and a time unit saved affects all machines), and again an average figure is taken. Let $\phi(x)\,dx$ denote the normal probability density function with the estimated mean μ and standard deviation σ i.e.,

$$\phi(x)\,dx = \frac{1}{\sqrt{2\pi}\sigma}\ \exp\left[\frac{-(x-\mu)^2}{2\sigma^2}\right]\,dx.$$

If an extra experiment is conducted (the $(n+1)$th experiment), it may yield a sequence of duration $d \geq d_n^*$, which represents no improvement at all, and the experiment would be discarded. On the other hand, it may yield a sequence of duration $d < d_n^*$, which represents an improvement and therefore will be retained. The expected saving in time from the

$(n + 1)$th experiment is given by

$$b \int_{-\infty}^{d_n^*} (d_n^* - x) \phi(x) \, dx = b d_n^* \, \Phi \left(\frac{d_n^* - \mu}{\sigma} \right) - b \int_{-\infty}^{d_n^*} x \, \phi(x) \, dx$$

where $\Phi(z)$ is the cumulative standard normal probability function.

Naturally, an experiment will be conducted when the expected marginal gain is greater than the marginal cost, i.e., the extra sample will be taken if

$$b \left[d_n^* \, \Phi \left(\frac{d_n^* - \mu}{\sigma} \right) - \int_{-\infty}^{d_n^*} x \phi(x) \, dx \right] > a.$$

Otherwise, experimentation halts, and the best sequence thus far obtained is implemented.

Needless to say, in practice some further steps may be taken toward the improvement of the best sampled sequence. For example, if the same order of jobs is used on all machines, the sequence on the first two machines can always be subjected to the algorithmic analysis discussed in §9.1 of Chapter 4. (Such a step could have also been taken at the start of the analysis.)

To sum up, the simulation approach to the Sequencing problem is simple and easy to apply. If offers a practical solution to a problem which defies analytical methods. Notice that the simulation can be used as a tool for design of the production system itself, as well as an operational tool for everyday decision making.

The approach is not without its drawbacks, however. For one thing, a change in the product mix (relative to the processing times) requires a revision of the underlying probability distribution. And for another, the case of a true "job shop" in which the different jobs have different routes (i.e., order of processing on the M machines) is still unsolvable by this approach.

3.5 Heuristic Design

Heuristic reasoning has been defined as "reasoning not regarded as final and strict, but as provisional and plausible only, whose purpose is to discover the solution of the present problem."[†] Heuristic reasoning is pragmatic and opportunistic. It claims no "best properties" for a solution (for example, optimality), but evaluates a solution on its operational utility as an improvement over previously-available solutions. A specific heuristic is justified because it is plausible, because it narrows the domain of search

[†]Gyorgy Polya, *How to Solve It*, Doubleday Anchor Books, New York, 1957, p. 113.

for optimal solutions, and because experimentation proves that it "works," that is, it improves on previous solutions.

The heuristic approach stands in sharp contrast to the analytical or algorithmic approaches. While the former is inductive, pragmatic, open-ended, and with no claim to optimality or even attainment of a desired degree of accuracy, the latter are deductive and inalterable, and they achieve optimality (or approach it with a known degree of accuracy).

An excellent example of analytical algorithmic approaches is linear programming (L.P.). The preceding chapters are replete with operational problems which were formulated as L.P. models, and whose optimal solutions were subsequently determined.

We have also had a chance to deal with the heuristic approach to problem solving in previous chapters. For example, a heuristic approach was introduced when discussing project activity networks (such as CPM) subject to resource availability constraints (see §4.10 of Chapter 2). In another context, we again resorted to heuristic methods when we discussed the Assembly Line Balancing problem of §10, Chapter 4. In both these instances, the formal analytical approaches proved inadequate to yield a solution.

In this section we give a third example of the heuristic approach, in which we pursue the problem of location–allocation discussed in the previous section. But before we do that, we will spend a few moments on the place of computers in the heuristic approach and the central role which computers will play in the success of the approach.

The following Fig. 7-14 is a simplified schematic diagram of the process of design. When the designer utilizes the computer as a large desk calculator, the contribution of the computer is restricted to the inner loop. What we would like to suggest here is that when computers are used for heuristic design, the designer relegates to the computer the technical and tactical decisions in design; that is, the computer will be programmed to make decisions for the functions of the two *inner* loops of Fig. 7-14, with the designer retaining control only on strategic decisions of the two outermost loops.[†]

If and when "learning" is incorporated into the computers of the future, the designer may relegate to the computer the third inner loop too. His final control will be exercised through establishing the criterion.

The fundamental changes that the above prospects introduce into the notions of design, and especially systems design, need no elaboration. Heuristic design emerges as one step in a logical sequence of steps in which the computer absorbs an increasing *proportion of* what is currently known as design.

[†]For a discussion of the various levels of decision, see §5 of Chapter 1.

Finally, while it is easy to see the distinction between the algorithmic (or analytical) approach and the heuristic approach, it is not equally easy to grasp the difference between the heuristic approach and the simulation approach. On the surface, the two appear to be the same since both approaches involve trial and repeated experimentation, and both may use the Monte Carlo technique in the conducting of individual experiments.

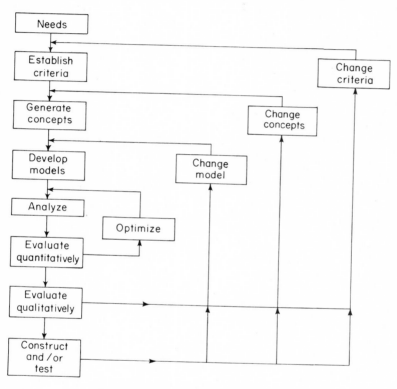

FIGURE 7-14 The Process of Design

Briefly, the difference lies in the absence of *internal* decision rules which are capable of modifying the answer (or some other decision rule) in the case of simulation, and the presence of such rules in heuristic problem solving. Stated differently, in simulation alternatives must be supplied "from the outside," but in heuristic problem solving, the alternatives are generated *internally* following a set of rules called *the heuristics*.

We proceed now with the illustration of heuristic design as applied to the Location–Allocation problem.

Example: Heuristic Design; The Warehouse Location–Allocation Problem

The statement of the warehouse location–allocation problem was given in §3.4, where a simulation approach to the problem also was discussed. The heuristic approach discussed below is due to Kuehn and Hamburger,[†] on whose writings we heavily rely.

The heuristic program consists of two parts: (1) the *main* program, which locates warehouses one at a time until no additional warehouses can be added to the distribution network without increasing total costs, and (2) the "*Bump and Shift*" (B and S) routine, begun after processing in the main program is complete, which attempts to modify solutions arrived at in the main program by evaluating the profit implications of dropping individual warehouses (bumping) or of shifting them from one location to another.

The answer arrived at in the main program (i.e., a specific location–allocation of warehouses) is based on three principal heuristics. They are:

1. *Most geographic locations are not promising sites for a regional warehouse; locations with promise will be at or near concentrations of demand.* The use of this heuristic in searching for and screening of potential warehouse locations permits the investigator to concentrate upon substantially less than 0.01% of the United States territory, and thereby eliminates mountains, marshes, deserts, and other desolate areas from consideration. For example, starting with 20,000 potential sites, this heuristic helps reduce the number of candidates to be seriously investigated to a mere 100 or 150 sites. To be sure, the program may as a result miss a good location, but this is highly improbable. And in any case, if management or the program operator is interested in evaluating any specific locations of this type, these can be entered as alternatives.

2. *Near optimal warehousing systems can be developed by locating warehouses one at a time, adding at each stage of the analysis that warehouse which produces the greatest cost savings for the entire system.* The use of this heuristic reduces the time and effort expended in evaluating patterns of warehouse sites. Thus, if there are M possible warehouse locations, of which M' have already been assigned, the heuristic requires investigating no more than $(M - M')$ alternatives instead of 2^M alternatives which a frontal attack on the problem would have demanded. To be sure, one can think of several classes of examples in which this heuristic would not work very well. However, the heuristic is acceptable if only as a first approximation which can later be modified to investigating two or three locations at a time.

[†]A. A. Kuehn and M. J. Hamburger, "A Heuristic Program For Locating Warehouses," *Management Science*, Vol. 9, No. 4, July 1963, pp. 645–657.

The following heuristic further reduces the number of sites investigated at any stage.

3. *Only a subset of the (remaining) potential locations need be evaluated in detail at each stage of the analysis. This subset is composed of those N(≪ M) locations which, considering only* local *demand, would result in the greatest cost savings if the demand is serviced by a* local *warehouse rather than by the system existing in the previous stage.* This heuristic states that at any stage of iteration we can do reasonably well by locating the next warehouse in one of the *N* areas chosen on the basis of *local* demand and related warehousing and transportation costs (see Step 3, Fig. 7-15, Flow Diagram). The degree of reduction in computing attributed to the use of this heuristic can be gleaned from the estimate that if *M* is of the order of 150 potential sites, *N* is only of the order of 10.

In the detailed evaluation of each of these *N* locations (called buffer locations) at each stage, the program either (1) eliminates the site from further consideration if it is uneconomical considering the *total* system, (2) assigns a warehouse to that location, or (3) returns the location to the list of potential warehouse sites for reconsideration at later stages of the program (Steps 4, 6, and 7, respectively, in Fig. 7-15).

Any site whose addition would not reduce *total* distribution costs is eliminated from further analysis in the main program. (This may happen even though the site was chosen as a buffer location based on local considerations.) Incidentally, it it possible to maximize such reduction in cost by formulating the problem as a *Transhipment* problem. Of those sites which reduce total costs, that location which affords the greatest savings is assigned a warehouse; all others are returned to the list of potential warehouse sites. When the list of potential warehouses is depleted, all sites have either been eliminated or assigned a warehouse, and the program enters the B and S routine (Fig. 7-15).

The B and S routine is designed to modify solutions reached in the main program in two ways. It first eliminates (bumps) any warehouse which is no longer economical because some of the customers originally assigned to it are now serviced by warehouses subsequently located. Again, some optimizing technique, such as the transhipment model of linear programming, may be utilized in this respect.

Then, to insure the servicing of each of the territories previously established from a single warehouse within each territory in the most economical manner, the program considers shifting each warehouse from its currently assigned location to the other potential sites (original list) within its territory. It should be noted that this routine does not guarantee that each territory will in fact be serviced in the most economical manner.

The basic steps of the heuristic program are summarized in the Flow

1. Read in:
   a) The factory locations.
   b) The M potential warehouse sites.
   c) The number of warehouse sites (N) evaluated in detail on each cycle, i.e., the size of the buffer.
   d) Shipping costs between factories, potential warehouses and customers.
   e) Expected sales volume for each customer.
   f) Cost functions associated with the operation of each warehouse.
   g) Opportunity costs associated with shipping delays, or alternatively, the effect of such delays on demand.

2. Determine and place in the buffer the N potential warehouse sites which, considering only their local demand, would produce the greatest cost savings if supplied by local warehouses rather than by the warehouses currently servicing them.

3. Evaluate the cost savings that would result for the total system for each of the distribution patterns resulting from the addition of the next warehouse at each of the N locations in the buffer.

4. Eliminate from further consideration any of the N sites which do not offer cost savings in excess of fixed costs.

5. Do any of the N sites offer cost savings in excess of fixed costs?

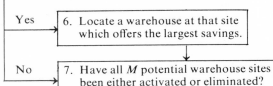

Yes

6. Locate a warehouse at that site which offers the largest savings.

No

7. Have all M potential warehouse sites been either activated or eliminated?

No

Yes

8. *Bump-Shift Routine*
   a) Eliminate those warehouses which have become uneconomical as a result of the placement of subsequent warehouses. Each customer formerly serviced by such a warehouse will now be supplied by that remaining warehouse which can perform the service at the lowest cost.
   b) Evaluate the economics of shifting each warehouse located above to other potential sites whose local concentrations of demand are now serviced by that warehouse.

9. Stop

FIGURE 7-15

Diagram, Fig. 7-15. It is well to note that in any practical application, several factors enter to limit the number of alternatives investigated. For example, in many cases *à priori* judgments can be made which state that customers in certain geographic regions will not be serviced from potential warehouses in other regions (e.g., no shipping from the East Coast to California if the factory is located in the Midwest). In addition, customers can frequently be aggregated into concentrations of demand because of close geographic proximity, thus reducing the number of demand centers.

Moreover, the program automatically eliminates from the search list potential warehouse sites and warehouse–customer combinations that no longer offer promise of cost reduction. As a result, by the time the program has located two or three warehouses, the list being searched is frequently reduced by 90%. The reduction in list size continues as more warehouses are added, speeding up the analysis on each cycle.

Experience with this heuristic program is limited, but is certainly encouraging. For example, the program was tried on 12 sample problems. The problems represented all combinations of three sets of factory locations: (1) Indianapolis, (2) Jacksonville, Florida, and (3) Indianapolis and Baltimore, and four levels of fixed warehouse costs ranging from $7,500 to $25,000 for each warehouse in the system. Each sample problem considered only a single product. Transportation costs and costs associated with shipping delays were assumed to be proportional to the railroad distance between shipping points. As a further simplification, the variable costs of operating the warehouses were assumed to be linear with respect to the volume of goods processed. Consequently, these costs did not affect the optimal warehouse system and were not considered any further. The size of the buffer (N) was set equal to 5 in each of the twelve sample problems. It was assumed that there were 50 concentrations of demand scattered throughout the U.S. Twenty-four of these centers of demand were treated as potential warehouse sites. The metropolitan population of each of these areas was used to represent sales potential, a population of 1,000 representing one unit of demand.

The results obtained from these 12 cases (three factory locations and four different warehouse fixed costs) show that improvement was possible over the final results of the B and S routine in only four cases. In each of these four cases, the improvement consisted of replacing a warehouse at Houston with a warehouse at Dallas. This improvement was not found by the shift portion of the B and S routine since Dallas was not being serviced from the Houston warehouse. In any case, the improvement ranged between 0.13% and 0.20% of the initial (no warehouse) cost, which is rather insignificant. The complete pattern of improvement as exhibited by the various stages of the heuristic program is summarized in Table 7-3. It easily can be seen that the major reduction in cost occured in the main

TABLE 7-3

Factory Location	Item	Warehouse Initial Cost				
		$7,500	$12,500	$17,500	$25,000	
Indianapolis	No Warehouses	$1,248,688	$1,248,688	$1,248,688	$1,248,688	
	Cost Reduction after Main Routine	446,843	389,924	348,835	319,759	
	Cost Reduction after B&S Routine	97	2,507	2,989	0	
	Improvement Not Found by Heuristic Program	1,585	1,585	0	0	
Jacksonville	No Warehouses	$1,832,861	$1,832,861	$1,832,861	$1,832,861	
	Cost Reduction after Main Routine	741,487	688,912	646,622	587,137	
	Cost reduction after B&S Routine	0	0	0	0	
	Improvement Not Found by Heuristic Program	0	0	0	0	
Baltimore and Indianapolis	No Warehouses	$899,770	$899,770	$899,770	$899,770	
	Cost Reduction after Main Routine	282,433	237,917	237,917	174,604	
	Cost Reduction after B&S Routine	0	0	0	0	
	Improvement Not Found by Heuristic Program	1,806	1,585	0	0	

routine, with the B and S routine accounting for less than 1% of improvement in cost.

The time required to reach a solution for the 12 sample problems in the main program totaled 72 minutes on an IBM-650 with RAMAC disc storage. The individual problems required an average of 2 minutes set-up time and 30 seconds per warehouse located. Experimentation with, and analysis of, the heuristic program indicates that computation time increases at a much slower rate with increases in problem size than is the case with linear programming algorithms designed to handle fixed cost elements. It appears that the problem set-up time increases linearly with the product of the number of warehouses, the number of products, and the number of concentrations of demand. The time required for locating warehouses increases (approximately) linearly with the size of the buffer (N), the number of products, and the number of customers, but almost negligibly with the number of potential warehouse sites. The effect of multiple factories on set-up time is at most linear; if capacity constraints are not operative the effect is substantially less than linear. Surprisingly, increasing the number of factories actually tends to decrease the total warehouse location time, since there is no effect on the time required to locate individual warehouses, and the total number of warehouses located will generally be reduced.

The heuristic program was limited in several respects. For instance, it dealt with only one product or a fixed product mix; extension to different products is yet to be accomplished. The time required for the solution of large scale distribution problems is still excessive, unless the problems are simplified beyond the level now thought to be desirable. Finally, the program does not take into consideration the fact that customers need not necessarily receive all of their shipments from a single warehouse if all factories do not produce all products. It is meaningful and, in fact, more representative of current practice to satisfy a customer order from several warehouses, or from one warehouse at one time and from another warehouse at a different time, depending on the product mix in the order.

§4. THE COMPUTER AS AN INTEGRAL COMPONENT OF THE CONTROL SYSTEM

In Sections 2 and 3, it was legitimate to view the computer as a helpful but nevertheless curious and slightly esoteric *aid* to whatever we wished to accomplish. We could still entertain the idea of a strange new device— so strange, in fact, that it had to be separated from everything else (and everybody else) in a remote air-conditioned, humidity-controlled, glass-lined room. One could peer at the monster, or rather glance at it respectfully from a distance, never actually touching it, and he would rarely be honored by admittance to its inner sanctum.

In this section, this can be tolerated no longer. Sanctum or no sanctum, the computer must now be regarded as a component of the system to be designed. The computer may be a very important component indeed, but it is no more to be regarded as an entity unto itself, independent, aloof, and almost dictatorial in its demands. As a component of the very operating system it may be assisting to design, it is subject to the demands of the overall system and is controlled by its performance.

Yet, it is important to realize that a computerized production control system is a radically different system from a noncomputerized one. The difference rests with the presence of the computer.

Because of the presence of this one new element in the system, it will soon be evident that new problems arise which require, for their successful resolution, new ideas, new approaches, new techniques and methodologies, and new structures, organizationally and otherwise.

In the remainder of this section we shall concern ourselves with some of these problems. We shall use as our vehicle for illustration the activity of manufacturing. Our hope, of course, is that by discussing the problems of computerized control systems in the context of manufacturing we are also delineating the factors to be considered in general and emphasizing the difference that a computerized system presents.

In particular, we shall discuss the following five areas: (a) the structure of the control system: independent, time-shared, and central-and-satellite systems, (b) the adaptive nature of control systems, (c) error detection and error correction in computerized system, (d) the degree of control in the system, and (e) organizational aspects of control systems.

The reader must realize that this is a partial list of problem areas. He is urged to contemplate any control system he is particularly familiar with, delineate its deficiencies and strengths, and relate them to these and other areas of control.

4.1 The Problem of Structure

Production control, even when defined in its wider sense, does not encompass *all* the activities of the firm. Consider a manufacturing concern. It is evident that such important activities as payroll and its associated functions, market analysis, sales reports, the compiling of financial statements, personnel records, purchasing functions, and so forth cannot be legitimately included under the title "production control." It is equally evident that production control *interacts* with each one of the former activities. The mode as well as the strength of the interaction varies with the activities concerned, but none can be termed "remote" or "weak." In fact, the interaction strongly affects the participating components to a marked degree either in the short or long run.

The final design of the control system is dependent on the strategy of approach (related to the structure of the system), and there are at least three such strategies. The *first* calls for the fragmentization of the factory or industrial complex into smaller units, such as individual shops or activities, and for designing control systems for each fragment as an independent entity. The *second* considers such subsystems as components of one integrated overall system which is to be controlled on one large computing facility. The *third* takes a middle of the road attitude, in that it recognizes the unity of the components in a system while granting semi-autonomy and special-purpose status to some components. We have termed the first strategy "the independent approach;" the second strategy is called "central control," and the third strategy "central and satellite control." Each strategy has things to recommend it, and each has its drawbacks.

Consider the *first*, the *independent approach*. Under this approach, subsystems are designed and implemented to function independently of other subsystems, except perhaps for the transfer of certain data from one subsystem to another.

The approach will have the following consequences, which must be recognized and consciously taken into account at the time of design:

1. The computing and associated service facilities will tend to be: (a) small, and (b) tailor-fitted to the individual subsystems in order to result in the optimal utilization of these facilities.
2. The required data files and information systems will be independently constructed to suit the specific requirements of each subsystem, with possible duplication or extensive translation from one language to another (say from punched paper tape to cards).
3. The design of the system will be restricted to small economic scales. This is a direct result of the division of the firm into smaller *independent* systems.

It is an open question as to whether or not the above three consequences are desirable. But the following four points can certainly be listed among the positive advantages of such an approach.

1. The possibility of *on-line real-time* control, that is, the possibility of almost instantaneous response to occurrences within any one system. It is true that such control can be achieved in other designs—such as time-shared computer systems—but it would certainly require larger and more complicated equipment and involve far more sophisticated programs.
2. It is possible to place each control system in the hands of the people responsible for such control. This may have certain repercussions on

reinforcing the organizational boundaries among the various functions in the firm. On the other hand, it has the distinct advantage of
"winning over" the personnel to the new tool placed at their
disposal.

3. The reduction of data flow over communication circuits, and the
   better utilization of information storage and processing equipment.

4. Less vulnerability to equipment breakdowns.

In order to visualize what the independent approach really entails, consider a hypothetical firm which is composed of four "shops." In each shop
one encounters the multitude of accounting and control functions with
which we are all familiar. In the following Fig. 7-16 we have depicted the

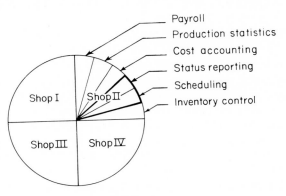

FIGURE 7-16

firm as a circle whose four quarters represent the four shops. For Shop II
we have listed six of these functions: inventory control, shop scheduling,
status reporting, cost accounting, quality control, and payroll. As an
example of the independent approach we have indicated by heavy lines
that the two functions "status reporting" and "shop scheduling" are to
be performed on an independent control system for Shop II. Other functions in Shop II may be grouped in a similar fashion, and similar functions
in other shops may be controlled independently from Shop II. Consequently, there may in fact be *four independent* subsystems for the control
of the two functions, "status reporting" and "shop scheduling," in the
four shops.

Now one easily can visualize the total picture under such an approach:
there will be a number of subsystems, which may not be of uniform design
either conceptually or in their computing facilities. These subsystems act
independently of each other with each under the direction and control of
the personnel responsible for controlling each subsystem. For example,

each shop supervisor controls his production scheduling subsystem, the accounting department controls payroll and cost accounting, the storeroom of each shop controls its inventory, and so forth.

Let us now consider the *second* approach, *central control*. As the name implies, the strategy here is to centralize the gathering of information, computing, and the making of decisions. This strategy has equally far reaching consequences. For example, it may offer the following advantages:

1. The possibility of achieving true integration of the various functions and activities. This is based on the premise that once the *original occurrences* (see §2.2 above) are in the system, all decisions can be made, concerning all facets of the system, with considerable ease and saving in cost.
2. It would be possible to capitalize on the economies of size that are usually inherent in larger systems.
3. The larger computing facilities may permit more sophisticated approaches to the same decision problem and, consequently, better decisions.

If we refer to our hypothetical firm again, we can represent the central control system schematically as shown in Fig. 7-17.

Here, the same functions as shown in Fig. 7-16 are involved. Complete integration and centralized control are depicted by concentric circles which cross functional and shop boundaries.

Central control is not without its serious drawbacks. We mention just three of them:

1. By virtue of dealing with larger systems, central control involves more effort, takes longer to complete, and requires commitment to larger sums of money. Consequently, it is more difficult to justify, and the failure of the system may prove disastrous.

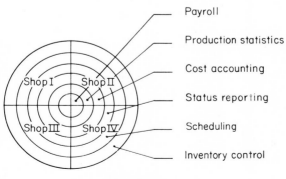

Payroll

Production statistics

Cost accounting

Status reporting

Scheduling

Inventory control

FIGURE 7-17

2. There is the problem of scheduling the computing facilities to serve all "masters" equally well.

3. Information wields power, a fact which has been recognized over the centuries by every dictator or aspiring dictator. A central computing system is, by its very nature, the ultimate in concentrated information. The problem that naturally arises is who is to exercise the final control over the functions of the firm, the line executives who are responsible (at least theoretically) for the conduct of the activities or the information "tzar." There is more than one instance on record where those who possessed information and the tool for the correct decision extended their influence over the domain of the *source* of such information. We shall have more to say about this general point of organization later on in our discussion of the organizational aspects of computerized systems.

Finally, there is the *third strategy* of *central and satellite systems*. This approach, while novel and largely experimental, may succeed in avoiding the pitfalls and drawbacks of either extremes represented by the previous two approaches, retaining the good features of both.

The "satellites" can be tailored to individual jobs, thus capitalizing on some special features of computing or input-output devices. For example, a satellite can be a special-purpose computer for the solution of linear programs. Linear programming problems in the areas of shop scheduling, inventory control, and production smoothing, to name just a few, can be placed on the satellite computer by the central computer, while the latter continues with other functions. When the satellite has completed the solution of a problem, the central processor accepts the solution in its priority sequence and incorporates it in its master operations.

As another example, the satellite system may be a production control subsystem whose output is communicated to the central processor upon request or in a preassigned priority sequence. In this case the satellite is a general purpose computer, but of a smaller capability than the central processor.

The concept that emerges from such an approach is that of a *hierarchy of decision* as well as a *hierarchy of communication–computation hardware*. Needless to say, any configuration may evolve in actual practice, with some satellites communicating directly with other satellites, and all subsystems communicating (one way or both ways) with the central system.

Let us pursue a little further our example of the four shops. A possible configuration would be as shown in Fig. 7-18.

Here, the scheduling and status reporting functions are assumed different for the four shops, and hence, are implemented on four satellite subsystems, with the central system coordinating the reporting from all four

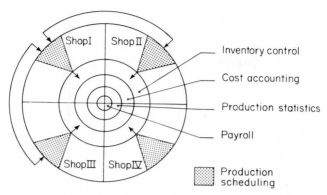

Inventory control

Cost accounting

Production statistics

Payroll

Production scheduling

FIGURE 7-18

subsystems plus executing the other functions of payroll, cost accounting, inventory control, and production statistics. Note the direct lines of communication between the production scheduling subsystems for Shops I, II, and III.

Now, the question is which of the above three strategies is optimal. Unfortunately, the answer is not known. Worse still, the *determinants* of the answer are not known. A great deal of research is needed to provide the basic knowledge necessary for arriving at intelligent answers to this question.

In our opinion, research in the area of *structure* of computerized control systems is best conducted in the field, that is, on actual operating systems. Only through the slow and painstaking process of accumulating the results of such research can the designer of new control systems, in about ten or fifteen years hence, possess the know-how required.

4.2 Adaptive Control Systems

The development of a control system requires highly skilled personnel and represents a considerable investment in "software" development. Normally, the special talents required for the development of the system are not available for "running" it when it is completed, nor is it desirable that these talents be available for such an activity.

Since we all recognize that assumptions of "stationarity" (i.e., of projecting the past into the future) may be correct for the short run but certainly do not hold in the long run, it is essential that the system be designed to be *adaptive* in its control. That is to say, the system must be capable of changing its mode of operation as well as the decision rules themselves, according to an ever-changing environment. This poses two important problems:

First: to design the system so that it is dependent on a small number of parameters, and

Second: to incorporate the adaptive character of these parameters in the system *at the time of design* of the system.

The success or failure of the *continuing* performance of the system is dependent upon making the correct decisions concerning these two points.

To illustrate, consider the design of a control system in which forecasting is done by the method of exponential smoothing.[†] It is recognized that α, the parameter of exponential smoothing, is a function of the variability of the *trend* in demand. In particular, large alphas are used if the average level of demand changes appreciably from period to period, while small alphas are used in the absence of increasing or decreasing long-range trends. Thus, the choice of α is really a statistical decision problem.

In order that the system operates under all market conditions, the value of α must be adapted dynamically to the changing environment. This constitutes an adaptive system in which the value of the parameter α is determined by a procedure which is built into the system. In essence, therefore, the system does not contain the value of α, but the process by which the correct value of α under all circumstances is determined.

Notice that the statistical estimation of α may be dependent on information outside the sphere of control of the system, such as when trends are based on the Gross National Product or the Index of Industrial Activity. At the time of design of the system, such a fact must be recognized and provisions made to ensure the availability of such information to the system on a continuing basis.

Moreover, the optimal value of α may be affected by factors external to the statistical estimating procedure but internal to the system as a whole. We have seen an example of such factors in the existence of a time lag in some of the components of the system. In our analysis of feedback control systems (§10 of Chapter 6) we discovered that the time lag in production severely limits the maximum value of α if the forecast of future activities also includes some correction of current status.

Needless to say, the control system would have contained different information and different mathematical models if forecasting were done by the method of autocorrelation analysis, or multiple regression, or moving averages. The important concept to remember is that each approach necessitates a special design of the system to maintain it on a functional basis under changing environment.

Concepts of adaptive control systems are novel, and most applica-

---

[†] See Appendix 2 for a discussion of exponential smoothing, and see §9 of Chapter 6 for the relationship with feedback control.

tions have been limited to hardware design, particularly in the military field. This is unfortunate, since current advances in the theory will not be made public except after a number of years. Past experience indicates the direct applicability of such theories to peaceful usages, such as to production–inventory systems.

Adaptive control systems should be designed to take advantage of optimizing procedures such as Box's "Evolutionary Operation" approach.[†] This is particularly possible in computerized systems since the basic data as well as the decisions based on them are all available in the computing system.

4.3 Error Detection and Correction

The question of error detection and correction in computer systems has been discussed at length previously; see §2.3 and the discussion of reliability therein.

There is little to be added which is peculiar to systems in which the computer is an integral part of the system itself, except perhaps to point out that under such circumstances the designer of the control system has the freedom of choice of the point at which detection and correction of an input error are performed. In particular, an error in the input can be detected upon its transmission at any one of the following points: (1) the input device, (2) the central data collection system, (3) the computer system, and (4) the output.

Each one of these alternatives implies a different concept in the design of the control system, as well as a different cost of implementation.

For example, in order to detect a logical error at the *input* and request the correct input we may need an "on line" computer which is capable of receiving the input data, analyzing it, and *feeding back* any discernible errors. Incidentally, in this case, we must also have output displays at the input.

Clearly, there is an optimal distribution of error detection among these four points, which has to be determined for each control system as it is designed. Research in this area should concern itself with the study of the criteria as well as the measures of effectiveness which are to be utilized in arriving at such an optimal solution, and the economies of achieving a certain level of reliability.

4.4 The Problem of the Degree of Detail in Control

It is self-evident that a functional relationship exists between the complexity of the mathematical models developed and the complexity (as well

[†]G.E.P. Box, "Evolutionary Operation: A Method For Increasing Industrial Productivity," *Applied Statistics*, Vol. 6, No. 2, 1957, pp. 3–23.

as the cost) of the computing system that implements such control. The more detailed is the mathematical treatment, the more *time consuming* it is to arrive at an answer, and the more *expensive* is the *equipment* necessary to arrive at such an answer.

The problem of concern to us here is not merely whether one should use, say, a dynamic programming model or a less complicated theory, which in itself is a very important question. Rather, it is the question of the *complete system design* and whether it should be oriented toward the control, at a high level of mathematical sophistication, of almost *all* the activities or just toward the major functions of the system. True, in many cases it is extremely difficult to subdivide activities into "major" and "minor," and even if such a division were possible it would still be difficult to determine where the control of some of the minor activities does not seriously affect the performance of the major ones. Still, the question is too basic to be lost in a battle of semantics or circular definitions. Research effort should be directed to the study of this problem with the view of arriving at satisfactory answers.

As an example, consider the following problem. A job shop consisted of a large number of machines of various kinds, makes, and capacities. The labor grades in the shop varied from the highly skilled automatic machine setter to the unskilled operator. The machines were of different "ages," which implies that two identically-looking machines do not give the same performance because of differences in their accuracies due to the wear and tear on the older machine. The question that confronted the management of that shop was the following: how finely should the loading, scheduling and status reporting functions on these machines be conducted? If the machines were grouped in gross units, say by type or class (lathes, mills, grinders, etc.), the resulting shop load, schedule, and status reports would be susceptible to gross errors and could fall short of providing management with the information it needed. On the other hand, if each machine were considered by itself, the control system would have several hundred machines to load and schedule in smooth production patterns, which is no minor task.

In fact, this seemingly innocent question of machine grouping affects not only the mathematical model of smoothing production, but also the construction of the whole system (which includes the data-transmission and computation system) in both size and cost. It is intimately related to the following questions:

1. The philosophy of operation, and whether control will be atomistic, reaching down to the individual worker and machine, or general in character, dealing only with larger groupings.
2. The efficiency in manpower utilization and the accuracy of load forecasting. (Clearly, the freedom of the first line supervision in assign-

ing men to machines will be dependent upon the classification of both men and machines.)

3. The possibility of alternate routings in the shop and the size of the necessary master files that must be maintained to keep accurate status reports.

4. The treatment of multiple lots of the same product and the accounting of lots that "split" from "parent" lots.

There are two other problems which are closely related to the problem of degree of detail in control. These are: the problem of the *optimal periodicity of control* and the problem of the *optimal range of the planning horizon.*

We have stated in the preface to this section that the existence of the computer has radically changed the concepts relating to the control of production. Perhaps the most outstanding example of such change is the question of the periodicity of control.

It is clear that manual control procedures are limited in three respects:

1. Their breadth of coverage is limited because of the insurmountable problem of communication among a large number of activities.

2. Their degree of refinement is limited by the computational difficulties in carrying out error-free extensive hand calculations.

3. Their cycle of control is necessarily long because of the time required to manually compile and present the necessary information. Management, sometimes, becomes cognizant of deviations from the planned course weeks after the deviations have taken place when action is futile anyway.

Computerized production control systems can, and do, eliminate all three restrictions. Consequently, the designer of the system possesses, for the first time, almost unlimited range in the choice of either the scope of the control system or the periodicity of effecting such control.

Preliminary research in this area indicates that shortening the sampling period, and consequently shortening the control cycle, entails more extensive revision of the operation of the system than has been hitherto suspected. For example, if the loading of a shop is to be accomplished daily, rather than weekly or monthly, one must have accurate daily status as well as large random access files. If the interval is further shortened to hourly control rather than daily, the mathematical model as well as the computer configuration will again be different.

The *range of the planning horizon* may also undergo radical revisions under the concepts of computerized production control. The new element introduced here is the possibility of fast reaction taking into account information which is very recent. In some instances, the horizon can be extended to encompass activities in the far future. This is mainly due to the possibility of projecting *several interacting activities* into the future.

In either case, the effect of such decisions on the overall performance of the system is in need of critical analysis and evaluation.

If we carry the argument for a shorter cycle of control to its logical conclusion, we find ourselves faced with one of the most fundamental questions of current production control theory, namely the question of the advisability of "real time" control. By this is meant adaptive control systems which respond to the original occurrences *immediately* after they are transmitted to the system. We would like to emphasize the difference between real time *status reporting* and real time *control*. In the former, the occurrence of an event is known immediately after it has taken place, while in the latter, *action* is taken based on that occurrence.

It is important to realize that computerized control systems are, in general, man-machine systems in which men and machines are linked by moderately complex lines of communication. Programmable decisions[†] are executed by the computer, and the decision time usually ranges from a few minutes to a few hours. In contrast, unprogrammable decisions are made by humans whose decision time may be several hours or even days. Under emergency conditions, such as in national defense, the time required for human reaction to a decision-demanding situation may be reduced to a few seconds. This is usually achieved through elaborate systems design and extensive and continuous training. Under normal industrial conditions, however, it is highly doubtful that we can expect such high speed in decision making on a day to day basis. In many instances, such a rate is not even possible due to the inadequacy of information. Since the time of reaction of the total control system is the sum of the times of reaction of its longest path, the question arises as to the optimal manner in which such time of reaction can be reduced. Currently, the tendency seems to "purge" the control system as much as possible of the human element. This, however, need not be feasible or even desirable.

The question of "real time" control is thus seen to be a question involving the very structure of the control system, the degree of "automation" achieved, and the selection and training of the human elements in the system.

We can see that a discussion of the degree of refinement in control has led us to a discussion concerning questions of whom to control, how frequently to control, and how much control is required.

4.5 The Organizational Aspects of Computerized Control Systems

In our discussion of independent and time-shared facilities, we touched lightly on the subject of the organizational aspects of computerized con-

[†] See §1 of Chapter 1.

trol systems. Now, we would like to devote more time to a brief discussion of this subject.

The field of organization of production systems is in a highly unsatisfactory shape indeed. The scarcity of theoretical foundations for its precepts or analytical expositions of its phenomena points out the need for a more solid foundation than has been hitherto available. The need could have been ignored or glossed over in the past when decisions were the result of some cooperative sort of judgment which was neither precise nor dependent upon fast response for its correct execution.

Under the conditions of computerized production control systems, however, such a state of affairs cannot be tolerated. There are several reasons for this, among which we would like to single out the following:

1. Errors in the various components of the systems are brought to the forefront in a forceful manner. These same errors would have passed completely unnoticed under the previous modes of operation.

2. Information on the performance of the various components of the system, which was not previously available is now available at regular and relatively short intervals. This renders control possible where it used to be impossible.

3. The capability of fast reaction by the system demands that decisions be made expeditiously, and consequently, requires the exact definition of the authority to make the decision.

4. The required information for integrated control systems emanates from various sources which cut across traditional organizational boundaries. The same can be said about the outputs of the system.

5. Integrated control systems attempt to avoid local suboptimization, which can be achieved only at the expense of some other components of the system. Optimization of the performance of the total system usually deprives each subdivision of some of its previously-established prerogatives. A new definition of the lines of authority and communication is required to enforce the new decisions.

   The classical example in this context is the traditional conflict between the inventory subsystem and the manufacturing subsystem. The inventory manager tries to maintain minimum inventory by varying the load on the shop, while the shop attempts to maintain a steady work force by absorbing demand fluctuations in the inventory. An integrated system would, in all probability, result in higher inventories than the storeroom manager would like to see and more fluctuation in the shop load than the shop supervisor wishes to entertain.

All these reasons combine to highlight the problem of organization in computerized control systems. We may ask: what structure is best for time-shared facilities or for central-and-satellite systems? When should the newly called-for decisions be made, and by whom? What are the responsibilities and authorities of the staff personnel who develop and monitor the system? What pattern of growth should the system take?

These are important questions on which the success or failure of extremely well-designed systems—from the analytical point of view—may depend. A control system will "fail" if the personnel controlled by it work against the system rather than with it.

4.6 The Synthesis of Total Production Systems

We conclude this section with a plea for what is coming to be known as *the synthesis of total production systems.*

Until now, we have always assumed that the technology of production is known and fixed, and that the control system, whether computerized or not, is superimposed on such technology.

Now we wish to challenge such an assumption in order to expand the scope of the design of the control system to include the design of the technology that permits production. This implies that: (a) the design of the product, (b) the design of the process by which the product is going to be realized, and (c) the design of the control system that monitors and adjusts such production to achieve explicitly stated objectives are three facets of one and the same problem, namely, the design of production systems. It also implies that consideration of one aspect of this three-faceted problem in exclusion of the other two leads to suboptimal systems and would impose undue restrictions upon the forgotten two other facets of the problem.

Needless to say, such complete integration of synthesis of production systems has not been realized except in a few cases. These latter have proven to be outstanding examples of what can be accomplished if such an approach were adopted. Perhaps the main reason for the rarity of applications of this approach is that it represents the most radical departure from conventional and well-established techniques. The untrodden path seems uninviting to many, though over the centuries it has proven to delight its travellers far beyond their wildest expectations.

The essence of this approach lies in the asking of the following question: what are the stated criteria for production, and what are the best technology and control system to satisfy these criteria? This is a very different question from the one usually heard: those few machines are idle—what can we manufacture with them?

In this approach the control of production is not a separate activity but rather an integral part of the design of the technology or process of production. Because of the novelty of the approach, many questions still remain unresolved. The solution of these problems requires the combined efforts of mathematicians, electrical and electronic engineers, industrial engineers, physicists, and psychologists. This attests to the complexity of computerized control systems and to the extent of the area of their impact.

The electronic computer is one of the most complex pieces of equipment ever built. The problem of the design of computerized production systems is not to build a computer, or to repair one if it breaks down. On the other hand, the function is just as complex and difficult.

We repeat, at the expense of being redundant, that truly fruitful results from the application of computers and computer technology to production control systems require a fundamental change in approach—an understanding involving much more than that of mechanization or streamlining of existing procedures. What is needed is a willingness to rethink the problems of the production systems, from the vantage point of available modern technologies.

The years to come are still to witness the realization of the full potential of these new tools.

COMMENTS AND BIBLIOGRAPHY

§2. Several good books exist on the design and operation of data processing systems. We cite the following three:

GOTLIEB, C. C. and J. N. P. HUME *High Speed Data Processing*, New York, McGraw-Hill, 1958.

LEDLEY, R. S. *Programming and Utilizing Digital Computers*, New York, McGraw-Hill, 1962.

MARTIN, E. W. JR. *Electronic Data Processing, An Introduction*, Homewood, Ill., Irwin, 1965.

§3. The use of computers in engineering design is relatively novel, hence, original material can be found in scattered papers and company reports. A good place to start is:

LANGEFORS, B. "Automated Design," *International Science and Technology*, February, 1964, pp. 90–97.

Also, the references cited at the end of this rather easy to read article should be consulted if any closer look at some of these applications is desired.

A more recent use of computers in design applications can be found in issue 7 of *Search*, "DAC-I System, Design Augmented by Computers," published by the Technical Information Department of the General Motors Research Laboratories.

The simulation technique is the subject of several books and articles; in particular see:

CONWAY, R. W. "Some Tactical Problems in Digital Simulation," *Management Science*, Vol. 10, No. 1, October 1964, pp. 47–61.

GORDON, G. "General Purpose System Simulator," *International Business Machines, Data Processing Division*, R. 20-4025-0, 1964.

HOUSEHOLDER, A. S. et. al. (eds.) "Monte Carlo Method," *NBS Applied Mathematics Series*, No. 12, Washington, D. C., U. S. Government Printing Office, 1951.

MARKOWITZ, H. M., A. S. GINSBERG and P. M. OLDFATHER "Programming by Questionnaire," Rand Memorandum RM-4460-PR, April 1965.

MARKOWITZ, H. M., B. HAUSNER and H. KARR *SIMSCRIPT. A Simulation Programming Language*, Englewood Cliffs, N. J., Prentice-Hall, 1963.

MORGENTHALER, G. W. "The Use and Application of Simulation in O. R.," *Progress in Operations Research*, R. L. ACKOFF (ed.), New York, Wiley, 1961, Vol. I, Chapter 9.

SMITH, E. C. JR. "Simulation in Systems Engineering," *IBM Systems Journal*, September 1962.

The Warehouse Location–Allocation problem was approached by the method of simulation by:

SHYCON, H. N. and R. B. MAFFEI "Simulation—Tool for Better Distribution," *Harvard Business Review*, November–December 1960, pp. 65–75.

The approach to the Sequencing problem by population sampling is from:

HELLER, J. "Some Numerical Experiments for M × J Flow Shop and its Decision-Theoretical Aspects," *Operations Research*, Vol. 8, No. 2, March–April 1960, pp. 178–184.

This paper is based on the more extensive report:

HELLER, J. "Combinatorial, Probabilistic and Statistical Aspects of an M × J Scheduling Problem," AEC Computing and Applied Mathematics Center, Institute of Mathematical Sciences, N. Y. U., 1959.

The definition of heuristic design is from:

POLYA, G. *How to Solve It*, New York, Doubleday Anchor, 1957, p. 113.

The Schematics of the process of design is from:

BAUMANN, D. M., S. J. FENVES and L. A. SCHMIT, JR. "The Impact of Computer Concepts on Engineering Design," National Science Foundation, Committee on the Use of Computers and Mathematical Techniques in Engineering Design, 1965.

The heuristic approach for locating warehouses is given in:

KUEHN, A. A. and M. J. HAMBURGER "A Heuristic Program for Locating Warehouses," *Management Science*, Vol. 9, No. 4, July 1963, pp. 643–666.

The following references treated the Location–Allocation Problem from the analytical point of view.

BALINSKI, M. L. and H. MILLS "A Warehouse Problem," report prepared for Veterans Administration by *Mathematica*, Princeton, N. J., April 1960.

For a general discussion see:

EDDISON, R. T. "Warehousing, Distribution and Finished Goods Management," *Progress in Operations Research*, D. B. HERTZ and R. T. EDDISON, (eds.), New York, Wiley, 1964, Vol. II, Chapter 4.

§**4.** The discussion in this section is largely based on the paper:

ELMAGHRABY, S. E. "Research in Computerized Production Control Systems," presented to the 13th Annual Conference of the Institute of Industrial Engineers, May 1962, and appearing in the Proceedings, pp. 269–280.

EXERCISES

1. Construct a block diagram depicting in a functional manner the performance of an inventory control system in a plant having 5,000 employees, $40 million annual sales, approximately 250 different major products, and approximately 20,000 items in inventory worth a total of $8 million.

   Include as many functions as you consider necessary for insuring effective cost control, such as status reporting, ordering, physical count, customer order information, etc.

   Describe, in flow diagram form, the logic behind the operation of such a system. Make a list of the necessary files and classify each with respect to its degree of permanency and the frequency of its maintenance requirements.

   Finally, give an estimate of the computer system requirements (computing speed, input-output facilities, type and size of memory, etc.).

2. Suppose that the technical design of a control system has been accomplished and that management is at the stage of deciding on the computing facility to be purchased, leased, or rented.

   State as precisely as possible the determinants of such a decision. In particular, what cost factors, reliability indices, service requirements, anticipated future technological improvements, "software" resources, etc., influence such a decision.

   Could you construct a mathematical model for determining the optimal alternative?

3. Suppose that errors are introduced in a data transmission and control system at the rate of 2% of the characters entered, (i.e., reliability of 98%). The system can be designed to check for errors and correct them at any one of three points: the input source, the buffer magnetic tape storage, and the buffer output tape, or any combination of these three points. Assume all errors are equally detectable and correctable, with the following costs and probabilities:

Point of Detection	Input Device	Input Buffer Tape	Output Buffer Tape
Cost/1000 Char.	$7	$17	$28
Probability of Detection	0.50	0.75	0.90
Cost of Error in Final Output Per 10 Errors		$35	

   What is the optimal (i.e., minimum cost) checking pattern in this system?

4. Give an example of a product whose design may be accomplished by the computer. State the different parameters of the design and the functional relationships among these parameters.

5. The text gave examples of the use of the computer as a display mechanism in some structural problems and in other applications. Give at least one example of a design problem in the field of industrial engineering in which the computer

can also be utilized as a display device and a fast data processing tool (hint: for example, consider some of the network models discussed in Chapters 4 and 5).

6. What are the most important factors in favor of simulation as a problem-solving technique?   Mention at least three such factors in order of their importance.

7. A producer of chemical material is confronted with the following problem. The demand for a product by a particular customer is known probabilistically over the finite planning horizon. Let the subscript i denote any particular customer product. Different customers require different products, which can be classified by a common characteristic, namely color. Such classification is important from the manufacturing point of view because the sequence of processing the different customer products is dependent upon the color of the products (due to differences in clean up time). Under such circumstances, it is meaningful to talk about a *group* of color products. Let r denote a group, and let it range from 1 to R. In any color group r, let the index for customer products, i, range from 1 to m_r. In other words, group r contains m_r customer products.

The production facilities are composed of N different types of machines. In any type n, $n = 1, \ldots, N$, there is more than one machine, say u_n machines. Any customer product may be processed only on a subset of the available machine types. Such feasibility or infeasibility of assigning customer product i to machine type n is given by a matrix T whose entry t_{in} is either 1 or 0 according to whether processing is feasible or not, respectively.

The problem of scheduling production is further complicated by the fact that actual production—in terms of quantity produced, set-up and processing times, and the cost of production—is dependent upon the particular assignment of customer products to processors. This is because production on any processor type is in economic manufacturing quantities (EMQ's) of all customer products in the same color group which have been assigned to that particular processor. Since the EMQ of the combination of two or more customer products is, in general, different from the sum of the individual EMQ's for each customer product, it is obvious that the combined EMQ will depend on the particular customer products assigned to the same processor. Equally obvious, the EMQ of any subset of customer products (in the same group) assigned to one processor is a function of the sum of the rates of demand, $\Sigma_{i \in n} d_i$, of all customer products in the subset and is different for different subsets as well as for different types $n \in N$.

It is required to determine the *quantities* and *sequence* in which the customer products in all color groups are to be produced on the N different machine types such that (a) the capacity of each machine type is not exceeded during the scheduling period (taken as 4 weeks) and (b) the total manufacturing cost (which includes set up cost, processing cost, inventory cost, and back-schedule cost) is minimized.

Make any necessary assumptions necessary to construct a mathematical model of this problem, and construct a simulation to try out different scheduling and sequencing decision rules. State such rules and explain the reasons for adopting them.

APPENDIX 1

Contour Integration In The Complex Plane

A function $F(s)$ of the complex variable $s = \sigma + j\omega$ is said to be *analytic* in a region if the function and all its derivatives exist in the region. The points at which the function (or any of its derivatives) does not exist are called *singularities*. We are interested in functions of complex variables with only finitely many isolated singularities in the finite part of the s-plane. In particular we limit our attention to functions with finitely many *poles* (which are only one of several possible kinds of singularities) in the finite s-plane.

For example, the function

$$F(s) = \frac{s + 5}{(s - 1)^2(s + 2)}$$

has a double pole at $s = 1$ and a single pole at $s = 2$, since, at these two points, $F(s) = \infty$.

By the definition of analyticity, we can always draw a circle centered about the pole in which it is the only singularity as in Fig. A-1, and the function $F(s)$ is analytic at all points except at the pole itself.

If the pole is of order n at $s = s_1$, then within a small circle around s_1 the function $(s - s_1)^n F(s)$ must be analytic and can be expanded in a Taylor series about s_1,

$$(s - s_1)^n F(s) = A_n + A_{n-1}(s - s_1) + A_{n-2}(s - s_1)^2 + \cdots$$
$$+ A_2(s - s_1)^{n-2} + A_1(s - s_1)^{n-1} + B_0(s - s_1)^n$$
$$+ B_1(s - s_1)^{n+1} + B_2(s - s_2)^{n+2} + \cdots. \quad (A-1)$$

At any point *except* s_1 within the small circle, $F(s)$ is given by

$$F(s) = \underbrace{\frac{A_n}{(s - s_1)^n} + \frac{A_{n-1}}{(s - s_1)^{n-1}} + \cdots + \frac{A_2}{(s - s_1)^2} + \frac{R_{s_1}}{(s - s_1)}}_{H_1(s)}$$

$$+ \underbrace{\overbrace{B_0 + B_1(s - s_1) + \cdots}^{Q_1(s)}} \quad (A-2)$$

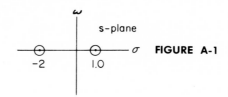

FIGURE A-1

This is the Laurent series for $F(s)$ valid in the vicinity of the pole at s_1 (in fact, in a region extending to the nearest pole). Notice that the series of Eq. (A-2) is composed of two parts: *the principal part*, $H_1(s)$, in which $(s - s_1)$ appears with a negative exponent, and a part, $Q_1(s)$, in which $(s - s_1)$ has a positive exponent. Also, the coefficient A_1 of Eq. (A-1) has been rewritten R_{s_1} in Eq. (A-2). The coefficient R_{s_1} is called the *residue* of the function $F(s)$ at the pole s_1. The residue bears highlighting because of its unique importance, easily gleaned from the following theorem:

Theorem 1: If $F(s)$ has a pole of order n at $s = a$, then

$$\oint_{C_a} F(s)\, ds = 2\pi j\, R_a \tag{A-3}$$

$$\text{where } R_a = \frac{1}{(n-1)!} \left[\frac{d^{n-1}}{ds^{n-1}} \{(s-a)^n F(s)\} \right]_{s=a}$$

and C_a is a closed contour enclosing the pole $s = a$ but excluding all other poles of $F(s)$.

In the case of a *simple pole* ($n = 1$) it can be easily shown that if $F(s) = N(s)/D(s)$, a rational function of s, then

$$R_a = \frac{N(a)}{D'(a)}$$

where $D'(a)$ is the derivative of $D(s)$ with respect to s evaluated at the pole $s = a$.

For example, consider again the function $F(s) = (s + 5)/(s - 1)^2(s + 2)$; we have a simple pole at $s = -2$. Here $D(s) = (s - 1)^2(s + 2)$; so that $D'(-2) = [(s - 1)^2 + 2(s - 1)(s + 2)]_{s=-2} = 9$, and $R_{-2} = 1/3$.

In general, if $F(s)$ is a *rational* function $N(s)/D(s)$ of the complex variable s (and this is the type of function we have been dealing with hitherto), it can be expanded into partial fractions of the form

$$F(s) = H_1(s) + H_2(s) + \ldots + H_m(s) + a_0 + a_1 s + \ldots + a_p s^p$$

where H_1, H_2, etc., are the *principal parts* of the Laurent expansion about the various poles, and the polynomial is of degree p, where p is the difference between the degrees of $N(s)$ and $D(s)$.

The residue at pole s_k is denoted by R_{s_k} and is given by the coefficient of $1/(s - s_k)$ in the expansion $H_k(s)$. Thus, if

$$F(s) = \frac{s + 5}{(s - 1)^2(s + 2)}, \text{ we must have}$$

$$F(s) = \frac{A_2}{(s - 1)^2} + \frac{R_1}{(s - 1)} + \frac{R_{-2}}{(s + 2)} \tag{A-4}$$

where A_2, R_1 and R_{-2} are evaluated by either of two methods:

1. Equating Coefficients: since

$$\frac{s + 5}{(s - 1)^2(s + 2)} = \frac{A_2}{(s - 1)^2} + \frac{R_1}{(s - 1)} + \frac{R_{-2}}{(s + 2)}$$

then we must have

$$s + 5 = A_2(s + 2) + R_1(s - 1)(s + 2) + R_{-2}(s - 1)^2$$

i.e.,

$$R_1 + R_{-2} = 0$$
$$A_2 + R_1 - 2R_{-2} = 1$$
$$2A_2 - 2R_1 + R_{-2} = 5.$$

These three equations in three unknowns yield $A_2 = 2$, $R_1 = -1/3$ and $R_{-2} = 1/3$ (as before).

2. Utilizing Eq. A-3: multiplying both sides of Eq. (A-4) by $(s - 1)^2$ we obtain

$$\frac{s + 5}{s + 2} = A_2 + R_1(s - 1) + (s - 1)^2 \frac{R_{-2}}{(s + 2)}$$

If s is now put equal to 1, A_2 is determined

$$A_2 = 2.$$

Next,

$$R_1 = \frac{1}{(2 - 1)!} \left[\frac{d}{ds} \{(s - 1)^2 F(s)\} \right]_{s=1}$$

$$= \frac{d}{ds} \left[\frac{s + 5}{s + 2} \right]_{s=1} = -1/3$$

Finally, multiplying Eq. (A-4) by $(s + 2)$ leaves

$$\frac{s + 5}{(s - 1)^2} = \frac{A_2}{(s - 1)^2}(s + 2) + \frac{R_1}{(s - 1)}(s + 2) + R_{-2};$$

now let $s = -2$ and R_{-2} is determined

$\quad R_{-2} = 1/3$.

The following theorem, known as Cauchy's residue theorem, gives the value of the contour integral of a complex function in terms of its residues.

Theorem 2: $\oint_C F(s)\, ds = 2\pi j\, \Sigma_{k=1}^{n}\, R_{s_k}$.

That is, if C is the boundary of a region in which $F(s)$ is analytic except at a finite number of poles, then $\oint_C F(s)\, ds$ is given by $2\pi j$ times the sum of the residues of $F(s)$ in the region.

If this theorem is combined with Cauchy's integral of Eq. (6-48), we immediately obtain

$$\phi(0) = \frac{1}{2\pi j} \oint_{|z|=1} \Phi(z) \cdot \Phi(z^{-1}) \frac{dz}{z} = \sum_{k=1}^{n} R_{s_k}$$

where the summation extends over all poles of $F(z) = \Phi(z)\Phi(z^{-1})/z$ in the unit circle $|z| = 1$.

APPENDIX 2 / Forecasting by the Method of Exponential Smoothing

Assume that information on a specific characteristic of a system (say information on production, total sales, the temperature of a reactor, the number of participants in an activity, etc.) is available at regular intervals of time (a day, a month, etc.). At any time t it is assumed that the past history of the process is known. This constitutes the available knowledge. It is desired to estimate the mean value of the process at some future time τ periods ahead.

Let $y(t)$ be the observation in period t and let α be a constant, henceforth referred to as the "smoothing constant." Normally α is a fraction between 0 and 1. An intuitively meaningful approach to estimating the current mean of the process is to correct totally or partially for the discrepancy (i.e., error) between the previously estimated mean and the current reading. Let $\bar{y}(t-1)$ denote the previously estimated mean, and $\bar{y}(t)$ denote the new estimate of the mean of the process (see Fig. 2A-1). Then it is "reasonable" to put

$$\bar{y}(t) = \bar{y}(t-1) + \alpha[y(t) - \bar{y}(t-1)]$$

or equivalently,

$$\bar{y}(t) = \alpha y(t) + (1 - \alpha)\bar{y}(t-1). \tag{2A-1}$$

By recursive substitution for $\bar{y}(t-1), \bar{y}(t-2)$, etc., we obtain

$$\bar{y}(t) = \alpha \sum_{n=0}^{t} (1 - \alpha)^n y(t-n), \tag{2A-2}$$

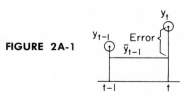

FIGURE 2A-1

an equation which exhibits the estimate $\bar{y}(t)$ in terms of all available knowledge.[†] The advantage of Eq. (2A-1) over Eq. (2A-2) is the fact that we need only have $\bar{y}(t - 1)$ available rather than all previous information $y(0), y(1), \ldots, y(t - 1)$, with the subsequent simplification in data processing.

Notice that if t is large, i.e., if the process has been in existence for a long period of time, then

$$\bar{y}(t) \simeq \alpha \sum_{n=0}^{\infty} (1 - \alpha)^n y(t - n). \tag{2A-3}$$

Let $Y(t)$ be a random variable whose probability distribution function is stationary in time, with a finite mean μ and variance σ^2. The estimate $\bar{Y}(t)$ is consequently a random variable whose expectation, from Eq. (2A-2), is given by

$$\mathcal{E}\bar{Y}(t) \simeq \alpha \sum_{0}^{\infty} (1 - \alpha)^n \, \mathcal{E} \, Y(t - n)$$

$$\simeq \alpha \sum_{0}^{\infty} (1 - \alpha)^n \mu, \quad \text{by assumption of stationarity}$$

$$= \mu$$

Hence, in the case of *pure random* fluctuations, the estimate $\bar{Y}$ is asymptotically *unbiased* in the mean μ. However, the variability of $\bar{Y}(t)$ is less than the variability of the individual values of $Y(t)$ because

$$\text{Var}\,[\bar{Y}(t)] = \text{Var} \left[\alpha \sum_{0}^{\infty} (1 - \alpha)^n \, Y(t - n) \right]$$

$$\simeq \alpha^2 \sum_{0}^{\infty} (1 - \alpha)^{2n} \sigma^2 = \frac{\alpha}{2 - \alpha} \sigma^2 \tag{2A-4}$$

We immediately deduce that for a finite value of Var $[\bar{Y}(t)]$—i.e., for a stable estimate $\bar{y}(t)$, the correction α must be

$$0 \leq \alpha < 2. \tag{2A-5}$$

As was pointed out before, α is usually between 0 and 1. Moreover, Var $\bar{Y}(t)$ is always $\leq \sigma^2$ when $\alpha < 1$.

[†]Notice how the dependence of $\bar{y}(t)$ on previous history, $\{y(t - n)\}$, decays exponentially; hence the name "exponential smoothing."

The above discussion refers to purely random fluctuations, i.e., it assumes no trend in the mean of the process. Now introduce a linear trend

$$y(t) = a + bt + \epsilon \tag{2A-6}$$

where ϵ is the random variable with mean 0 and variance σ^2. The model of Eq. (2A-6) assumes that the "true" mean of the process is given by $a + bt$, on which is superimposed a random error ϵ.

It can be shown that under the exponential smoothing scheme the new estimate of the slope, $\overline{b}(t)$ is related to the previous estimate of the slope, $\overline{b}(t - 1)$ by the following relationship:

$$\overline{b}(t) = \alpha\,[\overline{y}(t) - \overline{y}(t - 1)] + (1 - \alpha)\,\overline{b}(t - 1), \tag{2A-7}$$

i.e., the estimate of the slope itself is exponentially smoothed because $\overline{y}(t) - \overline{y}(t - 1)$ measures the change in the mean in one period.

Substituting for $y(t)$ in $\overline{y}(t)$ we obtain

$$\overline{y}(t) = \alpha \sum_{0}^{t} (1 - \alpha)^n [a + b(t - n) + \epsilon(t - n)].$$

As $t \to \infty$, the expected value

$$\mathcal{E}\,\overline{Y}(t) = a + bt - b\left(\frac{1 - \alpha}{\alpha}\right). \tag{2A-8}$$

Let $\hat{Y}(t + \tau)$ be the forecast of the mean of the process at time $t + \tau$, i.e., τ time intervals after time t. From Eq. (2A-6) we have

$$\mathcal{E}\,Y(t) = a + bt \tag{2A-9}$$

Comparing Eq. (2A-9) with Eq. (2A-8) we immediately see that $\overline{Y}(t)$ is *biased* in estimating the mean of the process at time t. The amount of bias is exactly $-b(1 - \alpha)/\alpha$. Therefore, if we subtract this bias from $\overline{y}(t)$ as defined in Eq. (2A-1), we get an *unbiased* estimate of the mean of the process at time t. This is, in a manner of speaking, our "forecast" for period t although it is nonsense to talk about a "forecast" after the fact. However,

$$\hat{y}(t) = \overline{y}(t) + b\left(\frac{1 - \alpha}{\alpha}\right)$$

represents the unbiased estimate of the mean of the process at time t. Clearly, the forecast τ periods ahead is given by

$$\hat{y}(t + \tau) = \hat{y}(t) + b \cdot \tau = \overline{y}(t) + b\left(\frac{1}{\alpha} + \tau - 1\right) \tag{2A-10}$$

where b is estimated by exponentially smoothing $\overline{y}(t)$ and $\overline{y}(t - 1)$ as given by Eq. (2A-7).

INDEXES

Author Index

Subject Index